T0144104

Blockchain in Healthcare

Innovations that Empower Patients, Connect Professionals and Improve Care

David Metcalf, PhD
John Bass
Max Hooper, PhD
Alex Cahana, MD
Vikram Dhillon

CRC Press
Taylor & Francis Group
Boca Raton London New York

CRC Press is an imprint of the
Taylor & Francis Group, an **informa** business

A PRODUCTIVITY PRESS BOOK

CRC Press
Taylor & Francis Group
6000 Broken Sound Parkway NW, Suite 300
Boca Raton, FL 33487-2742

© 2019 by David Metcalf, John Bass, Max Hooper, Alex Cahana, and Vikram Dhillon
CRC Press is an imprint of Taylor & Francis Group, an Informa business

No claim to original U.S. Government works

Printed on acid-free paper

International Standard Book Number-13: 978-0-367-03108-4 (Hardback)

This book contains information obtained from authentic and highly regarded sources. Reasonable efforts have been made to publish reliable data and information, but the author and publisher cannot assume responsibility for the validity of all materials or the consequences of their use. The authors and publishers have attempted to trace the copyright holders of all material reproduced in this publication and apologize to copyright holders if permission to publish in this form has not been obtained. If any copyright material has not been acknowledged please write and let us know so we may rectify in any future reprint.

Except as permitted under U.S. Copyright Law, no part of this book may be reprinted, reproduced, transmitted, or utilized in any form by any electronic, mechanical, or other means, now known or hereafter invented, including photocopying, microfilming, and recording, or in any information storage or retrieval system, without written permission from the publishers.

For permission to photocopy or use material electronically from this work, please access www.copyright.com (http://www.copyright.com/) or contact the Copyright Clearance Center, Inc. (CCC), 222 Rosewood Drive, Danvers, MA 01923, 978-750-8400. CCC is a not-for-profit organization that provides licenses and registration for a variety of users. For organizations that have been granted a photocopy license by the CCC, a separate system of payment has been arranged.

Trademark Notice: Product or corporate names may be trademarks or registered trademarks, and are used only for identification and explanation without intent to infringe.

Visit the Taylor & Francis Web site at
http://www.taylorandfrancis.com

and the CRC Press Web site at
http://www.crcpress.com

This book is dedicated to all the fine men and women whose voices are represented in this book who will shape Blockchain in Healthcare now and in the future.

Table of Contents

About the Authors

David Metcalf has more than 20 years of experience in the design and research of Web-based and mobile technologies converging to enable learning and health care. Dr. Metcalf is Director of the Mixed Emerging Technology Integration Lab (METIL) at UCF's Institute for Simulation and Training. The team has built mHealth solutions, simulations, games, eLearning, mobile and enterprise IT systems for Google, J&J, the Veterans Administration, U.S. military, and the UCF College of Medicine among others. Recent projects include Lake Nona's Intelligent Home prototype and SignificantTechnology, a mobile-enabled online degree and eResource kit. Dr. Metcalf encourages spin-offs from the lab as part of the innovation process and has launched Moving Knowledge and several other for-profit and nonprofit ventures as examples. In addition to research and commercial investments, he supports social entrepreneurship in education and health. Dr. Metcalf continues to bridge the gap between corporate learning and simulation techniques and nonprofit and social entrepreneurship. Simulation, mobilization, mobile patient records and medical decision support systems, visualization systems, scalability models, secure mobile data communications, gaming, innovation management, and operational excellence are his current research topics. Dr. Metcalf frequently presents at industry and research events shaping business strategy and use of technology to improve learning, health, and human performance. He is the coeditor and author of Blockchain Enabled Applications (2017) (With Dhillon and Hooper), Connected Health (2017), HIMSS mHealth Innovation (2014) and the HIMSS Books bestseller mHealth: From Smartphones to Smart Systems (2012).

John Bass is the Founder and CEO of Hashed Health, a healthcare innovation firm focused on accelerating the design, development and meaningful utilization of blockchain technologies and networks. John has over 20 years of experience in healthcare technology with expertise in collaborative health platforms, patient engagement, systems integration, supply chain, clinical performance and value-based payments. At Hashed Health, John's team partners with public and private sector clients to develop distributed and decentralized solutions that solve health delivery challenges. John is an internationally recognized speaker on blockchain and decentralized healthcare technology. Prior to Hashed Health, John was CEO at InVivoLink, a surgical patient registry and care management start-up which sold to HCA in 2015. John's experience also includes healthcare B2B startup empactHealth. com which was acquired by Medibuy / Global Healthcare Exchange. John is a native of Nashville and has a Chemistry degree from the University of North Carolina, Chapel Hill.

Max Hooper is the chief executive officer of Merging Traffic. He is responsible for the company's management and growth strategy, serving as the corporate liaison to the financial services industry and various capital formation groups. Prior to starting the company, he was cofounder of Equity Broadcasting Corporation (EBC), a media company that owned and operated more than 100 television stations across the United States. He was responsible for activities in the cable, satellite, investment banking, and technology industries and during his tenure it grew to become one of the top 10 largest broadcasting companies in the country. A lifelong learner, Hooper has earned five doctorate degrees: PhD, DMin, PhD, ThD, and DMin from a variety of institutions. Hooper studied financial technology with cohorts at MIT, and cryptocurrency and business disruption with corhorts at the London School of Economics. As an avid runner, he has completed more than 100 marathons and an additional 20 ultra-marathons, which are 50- or 100-mile runs. He has completed the Grand Slam of Ultra Running. Hooper is committed to his family and is a husband, father to five children, and grandfather to seven grandsons. He is active in many organizations and serves on various boards of directors. He works globally with several ministries and nonprofit aid groups, and was honored to speak at the United Nations in New York in 2015.

Dr. Alex Cahana is a Venture Partner and HealthCare, MedTech Advisor at CryptoOracle. With over 25 years of experience in clinical medicine Dr. Cahana consults multiple national and international private and public companies, start-ups and healthcare organizations on blockchain technology, digiceutical integration and healthcare redesign.

He works with State and Federal agencies on healthcare policies and is a Subject Matter Expert for the Department of Defense, the Veterans Health Administration, the NFL Players Association, the Institute for First Responder Wellness and Bastyr University.

After serving as Professor and Chief of the Division of Pain Medicine at the University of Washington, Dr. Cahana is an Affiliate Professor in Science, Technology and Health Studies, and has published over one hundred articles.

He is a decorated Officer of the Israeli Defense Forces and received multiple awards, among them -- the American Pain Society Center of Excellence; Joint Commission on Accreditation of Healthcare Organizations (JCAHO) Best Practice; the Association of American Medical Colleges (AAMC) Innovation Health Care award; and the University of Washington President's medal for remarkable leadership, social impact and public service.

Vikram Dhillon is a research fellow in the Institute of Simulation and Training at the University of Central Florida where he studies the integration of emerging technologies into existing infrastructure. The focus of his recent work has been on decentralized ledger technologies. He holds a Bachelor of Science degree in Molecular Biology from the University of Central Florida, where his focus was bioinformatics. Currently, he is a DO-MBA candidate at the College of Medicine, Nova Southeastern University. He is the author of several scientific papers in computational genomics and two books, the most recent one on blockchain enabled applications. He has also written in-depth articles for the Bitcoin Magazine and letters for the New York Times. He was previously funded by the National Science Foundation through the Innovation Corps program to study customer discovery and apply it to commercialize high-risk startup ideas. He is a member of the Linux Foundation and has been active in open source projects and initiatives for the past several years. He often speaks at local conferences and meetups about programming, design, security, and entrepreneurship. He currently lives in Fort Lauderdale, Florida, and writes a technology-focused blog at opsbug.com.

About the Technical Contributors

Art Director/ Production Editor:

Michael Eakins is the Creative Lead of the Mixed Emerging Technology Integration Lab (METIL) at the Institute for Simulation & Training and has 9+ years of production experience for simulation, training, and gaming. He received his M.F.A. in Digital Media at the University of Central Florida in 2017. Michael has produced a wide variety digital / print publications across multiple industries such as education, industry, and academia.

Technical Editor:

Katherine Shaw is a graduate student persuing a Master of Arts degree in Technical Communication at the University of Central Florida. She has been producing technical documentation for the U.S. Navy as a Department of Defense contractor for four years.

About the Contributing Authors

For bios and information on our 50+ contributors please visit:
https://hashedhealth.com/blockchain-for-healthcare-book/

Acknowledgements

The authors of this book would like to acknowledge the following individuals for their assistance with the development of this publication:

David Metcalf would like to thank Katy, Adam and Andrew for their patience during the extended hours and effort while putting the book together and colleagues and students at UCF and through the NSF I-Corps program that identified the power of Bitcoin and Blockchain technology years ago and shared their knowledge and future strategies that inspired us to pursue this area of research early. Thank you to my coauthors and our outside collaborators and contributors, and of course to God for the wisdom, ability and grit to bring this effort to life.

John Bass: I am gratefully aware that my work in the blockchain space has been made possible by a lot of people who are part of my life today and who have helped me in the past. These people, in various ways, have given me a safe space to learn, think, try, fail and improve. They include my incredible family (Fe, Gidgie, Sadie Mae, Mattie James), my incredible co-workers at Hashed, all the incredible people who have invested in and supported Hashed Health and the Nashville Blockchain Meetup, Charlie and Devin from Martin Ventures, the team at Fenbushi, David and the team at BTC, the writings of Andreas Antonopoulos, the research of Michael Porter, blockchain innovators before me including Vitalek and whoever Satoshi Nakamoto is, Dr. John Morris, Eddie Pearson and the startup team at empactHealth.com, my friends at GHX, the startup team at InVivoLink, all the incredible customers who took an early chance on working with Hashed Health, and everyone who has contributed so much energy to Procredex, Signal Stream, Bramble, and the queue of products to come from Hashed Health... thank you all for being a part of my life and a part of this book.

Dr. Max Hooper would like to thank his co-authors and colleagues at UCF/ METIL Lab, along with a special thanks to Mindy Hooper for her help and support. Additionally, he would like to thank God's inspiration, guidance, direction, and wisdom. He would like to acknowledge his leadership.

Alex Cahana would like to dedicate this book to his wife Professor Ruthi Landau, always the reasoning voice behind his decade-long disruptive work, to his daughter Mya, the youngest and earnest blockchain enthusiast he knows, and to the everlasting memory of his parents, Professors Shai and Lydia Cahana (TNZBH).

Vikram Dhillon would like to dedicate this work to Aaron Hillel Swartz and his legacy.

About this Book

Since our earliest days of working on ways that blockchain may change the world of healthcare our team of authors has repeatedly connected and surveyed the landscape to assess what is real and postulate on what may come next. Our 2013 / 2014 NSF I-Corps HealthShares project taught us many dos and don'ts using the early protocols around electronic health records to fitness and wellness data. Throughout the years we have had the privilege of meeting incredible thought leaders and practitioners who have shaped the early days of blockchain in healthcare and whom we expect to be driving forces in building the future. We have attempted to distill and crystalize those voices throughout the text.

The book is divided into three major sections that describe the foundations and background of blockchain in healthcare, the realization of where the current state of the art is at this moment in time, and with examples of credible use cases currently underway, and a view of the future that is as diverse as the intersections of blockchain and artificial intelligence, genomics, medical tourism, or smart cities. Our team believes that the true power of blockchain will be unleashed when you consider blockchain and [insert a compelling technology, process, business, or discipline]. This blank represents not only health or healthcare, but also the important sub-disciplines that blockchain technology can help unlock the potential for automation of complex processes through smart contracts or linking to digital currencies or providing a trusted transaction record for a variety of healthcare operations and functions that can be improved through trust and transparency. Throughout the book we have attempted to provide case studies to add realism and practicality to an otherwise technical and philosophically driven topic. You will also see areas with timely information from leaders in healthcare and blockchain in the form of transcripts. These transcripts are important placeholders for ideas and concepts that link sections of the book together and have a companion landing page for the print version of the book and direct media integrated or links from the eBook versions. Hearing the voice of leaders and their distinct style and passion coming through on the page or in media is an important component of expressing the personality and humanity of what could be seen as a dry and technical topic area. The editor's notes at the beginning of each chapter provide further context for why a particular topic is important and how it links to other parts and the whole of blockchain in healthcare.

We hope you enjoy the myriad views of blockchain and how it will continue to influence and shape healthcare, among many vertical industries. We are only just beginning the journey of the fundamental shifts and disruptions underway in our society.

- David Metcalf, Ph. D., December 2018

Introduction to Blockchain: Impact Across Industries

Blockchain technology is nothing short of a technological revolution that mimics the magnitude of the World Wide Web. In simple terms, blockchain is a digital version of a ledger book that once served as a tamper-proof record for financial institutions. However, from a technology standpoint, blockchain emerged as a solution to a famous cryptographic challenge called the Byzantine Generals Problem. To that end, the first implementation of a blockchain was seen in Satoshi Nakamoto's paper "Bitcoin: A Peer-to-Peer Electronic Cash System" which introduced the world to Bitcoin. In this brief chapter, we will go over selected readings that share recent developments in blockchain and what industries are prone to be disrupted by blockchain. Over time, new technological advances have completely dissociated blockchain from just being the foundations of Bitcoin. It has a new life beyond a ledger book for a currency. Presently, the major innovations are happening in the deployment of blockchain and services being built on top of it. Fred Wilson explains this better, in terms of phases of a technological revolution such as the blockchain in a blog post. He is referring to Carlota Perez's book on Technological Revolutions and Financial Capital:

For those that are not familiar with Carlota's work, she studied all of the major technological revolutions since the industrial revolution and how they were impacted by and how they impacted the capital markets. What she found was that there are two phases of every technological revolution, the installation phase when the technology comes into the market and the infrastructure is built (rails for the railroads, assembly lines for the cars, server and network infrastructure for the internet) and the deployment phase when the technology is broadly adopted by society (the development of the western part of the US in the railroad era, the creation of suburbs, shopping malls, and fast food in the auto era, and the adoption of iPhones, Facebook, and ridesharing in the internet/mobile era).

Let's begin our discussion with what kind of a problem blockchain solved. Alex Moskov writes in a post on CoinCentral about this unique solution:

You've come at just the right time – we've got this city surrounded but have an unfortunately complicated logistics issue here. We have two armies, one on each side of the enemy city, and we need to attack at the same exact time. The city is strong enough to defend itself against one of our armies, but not strong enough to defend against two at the same time. If we don't attack at the same time, we lose. And losing sucks.

So, the generals of each army need to agree on the exact moment of when to attack. They communicate by sending a messenger back and forth through the enemy city. There's no other way to communicate – cell phone service wasn't the best around 600 AD.

For example, General A will send the message "Hey General B, we're going to attack on Thursday. Can we count on you to attack with us?" The messenger then runs through the city and delivers the message to General B, who in turn responds, "We can't do Thursday, group pilates. How about Friday? If we attack on Friday, will you attack with us?" And then the messenger runs through the city to deliver the message to General A, and so forth.

However, here's the kicker: the messenger could potentially get caught in the city and replaced by a #fakenews messenger, who will intentionally try to deceive the other general to attack the city at the wrong time, dooming our army to a loss.

There is no way to check if the message is authentic, so how do we, as the finest military strategists in the land, create a "trustless" system that ensures victory in attacking the city?

And that's the Byzantine Generals Problem.

The above dilemma isn't necessarily limited to just two generals. In a distributed network such as that of Bitcoin's, all participants and nodes are essentially of equally hierarchy. So, now instead of needing to reach verification and agreement between two parties, we need all participants to approve, while neutralizing corrupt or misleading players.

The agreement between all of these nodes is called, you guessed it, consensus.

The solution to the Byzantine Generals Problem isn't simple by any means. It involves some hashing, heavy computing work, and communication between all of the nodes (generals) to verify the message.

Even though the Byzantine Generals Problem was more of an academic concept, the solution that Nakamoto proposed introduced us to one of the most important concepts in all distributed ledger technologies: Consensus. The idea that every member on the node can agree on a canonical global state of the blockchain without needing to trust each other. This removal of trust from the network has allowed transactions to propagate the network, get mined and verified by parties that all get rewarded for their contribution to the network. The reward structures have changed over time as new ideas on how to use blockchain emerge. wrote an article in HBR discussing five major innovations in the blockchain world:

Five major innovations in the blockchain world:

The first major blockchain innovation was bitcoin, a digital currency experiment. The market cap of bitcoin now hovers between $10–$20 billion dollars, and is used by millions of people for payments, including a large and growing remittances market.

The second innovation was called blockchain, which was essentially the realization that the underlying technology that operated bitcoin could be separated from the currency and used for all kinds of other interorganizational cooperation. Almost every major financial institution in the world is doing blockchain research at the moment, and 15% of banks are expected to be using blockchain in 2017.

The third innovation was called the "smart contract," embodied in a second-generation blockchain system called ethereum, which built little computer programs directly into blockchain that allowed financial instruments, like loans or bonds, to be represented, rather than only the cash-like tokens of the bitcoin. The ethereum smart contract platform now has a market cap of around a billion dollars, with hundreds of projects headed toward the market.

The fourth major innovation, the current cutting edge of blockchain thinking, is called "proof of stake." Current generation blockchains are secured by "proof of work," in which the group with the largest total computing power makes the decisions. These groups are called "miners" and operate vast data centers to provide this security, in exchange for cryptocurrency payments. The new systems do away with these data centers, replacing them with complex financial instruments, for a similar or even higher degree of security. Proof-of-stake systems are expected to go live later this year.

The fifth major innovation on the horizon is called blockchain scaling. Right now, in the blockchain world, every computer in the network processes every transaction. This is slow. A scaled blockchain accelerates the process, without sacrificing security, by figuring out how many computers are necessary to validate each transaction and dividing up the work efficiently. To manage this without compromising the legendary security and robustness of blockchain is a difficult problem, but not an intractable one. A scaled blockchain is expected to be fast enough to power the internet of things and go head-to-head with the major payment middlemen (VISA and SWIFT) of the banking world.

The use of blockchain technology to simplify business processes and overhaul revenue structures for major industries is already underway. Microtransactions without high processing fees and automated contracts for services make blockchains very attractive to certain industries that rely heavily on digital assets. Nicolas Cole from Digital Press shares his thoughts on Hackernoon on the five industries that are in the process of being transformed by blockchain:

Here are 5 industries that are about to be heavily disrupted by blockchain:

1. Gaming

Cryptocurrencies might seem new, but in reality, they've been around for nearly a decade (if not longer).

My first introduction to cryptocurrencies was nearly 10 years ago, when I sold some of the gold I'd earned in the World of Warcraft for USD. At 17 years old, I had successfully accumulated a digital asset, and then sold that digital asset for fiat—something that, today, seems entirely novel.

The gaming industry has been pioneering the digital landscape since the moment it was born. But the next step for gamers is to be able to buy, sell, track, and trade their digital assets in a way that has otherwise been done across forums and sites like eBay. For example, by leveraging blockchain technology, gamers will soon be able to trade the ownership of in-game items through smart contracts, or buy and sell assets using cryptocurrencies.

In addition, one of the biggest issues independent game developers face is monetizing their games and entering markets across the world. One project I'm advising, called MagnaChain, is the world's first public blockchain for game developers, by game developers, allowing devs to bring previous games or build new games directly onto the blockchain.

When you consider how quickly the gaming industry has grown into the mainstream, it's not difficult to imagine the scalability that will come with a more connected and integrated global economy within the gaming sphere.

2. Music

If there's one industry that needs a massive digital overhaul, it's entertainment—specifically music.

One of the biggest issues that musical acts and artists face is getting paid appropriately. There are countless stories of remarkably successful bands going broke because of poorly structured label deals, or labels that don't pay effectively, period. In addition, although streaming sites like Spotify and Apple Music are working hard to make streaming a viable revenue stream for artists, the payouts are still pennies on the dollar compared to what artists made for CD sales just ten years prior.

As blockchain projects begin to appear in this space, one of the biggest pain points the technology is looking to solve is giving artists the ability to "sell" ownership portions of their music—think crowdfunding, but exponentially better. In the same way a company can hold an Initial Coin Offering to raise capital and allow users to share in the upside of the company, musicians will soon be able to tokenize or sell portions of their music, and give users the ability to collect royalties on the % of the ownership they hold.

3. Biotech

Over the past few years, digital health has been one of the hottest industries to invest in. But combine healthcare with blockchain, and the sky is the limit.

One niche within healthcare that has shown a significant amount of promise is biomedical technology—an umbrella term encompassing the development and engineering of technological solutions, specifically related to the treatment and diagnosis of disease.

In order for these kinds of innovations to manifest, certain materials are necessary to have an industry-wide impact. Graphene, a semi-metal composed from a single layer of carbon atoms and arranged in a hexagonal lattice, is one of them. For context: the atomic arrangement of graphene makes it one million times thinner than paper. In fact, graphene is so thin that it's considered 2-dimensional. Graphene is also the strongest known material in the world.

Cool stuff, right?

One of the first blockchain-based graphene companies playing in this space is called GraphenTech, and is developing proprietary technology that will enable the manufacturing of graphene on an industrial scale, at a fraction of the cost. This is just one example of how biomedical technologies will begin leveraging blockchain to gain a competitive edge, and a nod toward the vast realm of possibilities for blockchain to be integrated into all aspects of healthcare and biotech—from the manufacturing side, to the way consumers interact with their everyday health providers.

4. News

If blockchain enthusiasts are driven by a more transparent and trustworthy future, then few industries are as ripe for disruption as the news landscape.

As a digital writer, I am all too familiar with the never-ending list of issues the Internet faces when it comes to content prioritization. When a news story breaks, or a major event happens in the world (politically, socially, etc.), how we come across that information, where, and through whom, drastically informs our opinion of it. For proof, look no further than the stark differences between experiencing the news through, say, Fox News, CNN, and Twitter.

One of the projects I was brought on to advise about a year ago in this space is called RedPen, with the mission of the company to better understand what the entire Internet is thinking and feeling about a given topic. I was fascinated by the aim of the company because, as someone who makes a living by writing things online people pay attention to, even I'm aware that the publishing landscape is inherently flawed. RedPen's goal is to give users insight into more than just what one columnist, at one publication, thinks about a given event—but what the entire Internet's sentiments add up to, and what the general consensus is for each and every narrative.

This is just one approach to solving the issues that plague the news and digital content industries, but rest assured the amount of opportunity in this space for disruption will be abundant for a good while.

5. Finance

And finally, if there's one industry that is about to be overhauled from top to bottom by leveraging blockchain technology, it's finance.

This is one of those topics that has already been beaten into the ground by cryptocurrency enthusiasts shouting its potential from the rooftops. But the truth is, the finance world is very aware of the impact cryptocurrencies will have on the old world's way of exchanging value. For proof, look no further than J.P. Morgan's recent patent filing to tokenize securities.

While the idea of "everyone paying with Bitcoin" might seem like the next step for our economy to go digital, I don't believe this is the end goal—or even the biggest shift we're about to experience as a society. The real financial shift is going to come with passive actions, or value being exchanged without two people needing to interact directly. A few examples here would be: your electric car automatically charging itself at a light (and the money being extracted from your digital wallet), or funds being automatically withdrawn from your account when you exit a grocery store.

The financial shift we are going to observe over the next decade is going to encompass so much more than simply "using crypto more than fiat." Blockchain is going to make it possible to automate so many different areas of our lives that require payments, that it won't even be a conscious decision to use crypto over, say, USD. It will simply be part of the way the product or service operates, intentionally constructed to be as seamless as possible for the consumer.

Beyond that, expect to see global economies go through a huge adjustment as money starts pouring in and out of countries that have otherwise been entirely disconnected from the rest of the world.

Summary

In this chapter, we're beginning to introduce the concepts that we will cover throughout the book. We gave a very brief introduction to the history of blockchain, but our main focus was on the deployment and applications built on top of blockchain. The major industries disrupted by blockchain all have a separate chapter with more in-depth discussion. Finally, the chapter provides some outlook into the future of blockchain integrating more and more into the fabric of our society.

References

1. Carlota Perez's work was taken from Fred Wilson's post at his blog AVC, linked here: https://avc.com/2015/02/the-carlota-perez-framework/

2. The CoinCentral blog post is available here: https://coincentral.com/byzantine-generals-problem/

3. Vinay Gupta's post on the HBR can be found here: https://hbr.org/2017/02/a-brief-history-of-blockchain

4. Finally, Nicolas Cole's article on blockchain disrupting industries can be found here: https://hackernoon.com/5-industries-about-to-be-disrupted-by-blockchain-technology-d963c3988b91

FOUNDATIONS OF BLOCKCHAIN IN HEALTHCARE

Chapter 1: Introduction

John Bass

https://hashedhealth.com/blockchain-for-healthcare-book/

Editor's Note:

To kick us off, John Bass, one of our lead authors and head of Hashed Health will link and distill our excitement across multiple industries and hone this down to both an introduction and overview of critical points related to blockchain and healthcare. John has been working on ideas for blockchain and healthcare for over 3 years, making him one of the earliest pioneers and thought leaders. His understanding of the space reflects not only the early history, but an ongoing concern for the transformation currently underway and over the horizon in our future. He further outlines the sections of the book and the importance of the people who have so graciously contributed to the book.

"Change is possible, change is necessary, and change is coming."

- Alex Azar, Secretary of Health & Human Services, 2018 [1]

What makes us believe we can change healthcare? Of all industries, healthcare is the most in need of change and the most resistant to it.

For years we've been aware of outrageous costs, uneven quality, and variations in access. For years we have been debating, reforming and innovating. Evidence shows that costs will continue to rise, leaving consumers and employers to pay the tab. [2] Yet our core healthcare payment and care delivery systems remain roughly unchanged.

We seem destined to repeat the same conversation. Healthcare is too expensive. Costs are highly variable and have no relationship with quality. The system encourages overconsumption, but consumers, burdened with ever-increasing pressure, have no way to shop for what is often their largest annual expense. We are no longer surprised when every new report says that Medicare will be insolvent sooner than we had previously thought. [3]

And so, as healthcare costs move beyond 20% of GDP in the United States ($11,000 per capita), we accelerate towards a national crisis. By 2026, health spending is projected to approach $5.7 trillion. [4]

With aging populations and expensive new devices and therapies, the problem only gets more acute. Patients, employers, and governments are balking as benefit costs erode profits and salaries. At the same time, many healthcare enterprises are doing well, with pharmaceutical companies and insurance companies raking in the highest profits. [5]

It's not that these companies are doing anything wrong. They are excellent operators of their business models. We have designed a system that feeds on consolidation, silo'd data lakes, and a fee-for-service buffet. It's an "every CFO for himself" focus rather than a patient value focus. And the CFOs who win at this game tend to be the best fee-for-service billers, rather than the best at delivering high quality, low cost care.

The United States is a wealthy country but it's unclear how long that can continue. Currently, we operate in a low-trust, high cost environment where consumers are increasingly and justifiably dissatisfied with the value we receive for our healthcare dollars.

It is perhaps predictable under these circumstances, that as costs rise, consumer trust decreases. According to Edelman's Trust Barometer, trust in our healthcare enterprises is down across the board, with the largest declines aimed at pharmaceutical and insurance companies. [6]

At some point over the next ten years, either suddenly or gradually, either through crisis or through planning, we as a community will be forced to change.

The escalating crisis of confidence provides an opportunity to take a new look at what our optimal healthcare system might look like. What do we want to design for?

First off, let's make it much, much less expensive. Any ideal system must begin by addressing the real problem: cost.

The cost problem is all about prices and administrative burden.

Prices are a problem because we have a marketplace that is structurally flawed. It does not allow for the rational buying and selling of products and services. There is no competition, little information on value (cost and quality), and little choice for consumers.

The administrative burden is largely due to the fundamental lack of transparency, trust and alignment between key stakeholders in care delivery.

Solving the cost problem effectively means transitioning from a volume-based system to one centered on value for the patient, where patients can rationally shop for products and services.

Stakeholders such as providers, insurance companies, pharma companies, and device manufacturers should prosper if they improve the health of their customers. Competition in the market should be on value. Individuals should be equipped with the requisite information that allows them to make rational choices resulting in transparency to both the cost and the outcomes data for services, drugs and other products. By resetting the market can we fully realize the promise of patient-centered care or the potential of precision medicine.

Additionally, our ideal future will also reset the use and sharing of patient data. In this future state, we would have a patient-centered system with the user experience and an architecture purpose-built for secure data sharing. Such a system would empower patients and providers to team up on health and wellness concerns while allowing patients to use their data as they wish. The patient would decide whether or not to sell her data to a pharma company or donate her data to a clinical trial. A high quality, patient-centered longitudinal health record is a necessary part of our future in healthcare.

Our current healthcare system works exactly as it was designed. Much of what we do today looks like miracles compared to just ten years ago. But these miracles are slow and we often don't have a way to pay for them. The current system is not sustainable. A common refrain over the last few years is that healthcare needs a mulligan. We don't need a mulligan… we need to play a new, less expensive game with a new set of rules governing the complex relationship between commerce and care.

Blockchain and distributed ledger technologies are an important enabler for re-thinking the commerce-care relationship. This family of technologies allow us to re-consider how we deliver and pay for healthcare products and services. Blockchain is not the silver bullet that will fix all of our healthcare problems. But blockchain plays an important role as an enabler of the answers we seek.

The purpose of this book is to provide a window in to a convergence of technical and social forces that provide evidence that we are, at last, entering a period of change.

The answers we seek come through the convergence of many things technical, financial, and social. Blockchain brings these forces together in a meaningful, scalable way.

The answers come through a convergence of powerful new technologies including the Internet of Things, Machine Learning, and Artificial Intelligence… technologies that need a secure, trusted, decentralized source of truth in order to scale. Blockchain provides us with new ways of developing products using a collaborative market level data structure instead of a silo'd enterprise focus. We can leverage the concept of digital assets to record the fingerprint of a claim, a product, a service, a purchase order, or a device and re-think how it moves through a frictionless value chain.

The answers we seek come through our ability to embed monetary policies, behavioral economics, and the belief systems of communities in to open source software. Over tie, token economies will create the potential for amazing network effects where the users of a system share incentives to see the value of the token increase.

The answers come through new precision payments solutions that support the precision medicine approaches key to treating patients in the future.

The answers come through brand new business models and marketplaces that represent new ways of solving old, expensive problems.

Blockchain brings these answers together in a secure, scalable way. These new economic systems and business models are unlike anything healthcare has ever seen.

Over time we can trade the traditional proprietary systems in for more efficient, effective, collaborative structures that solve market-level challenges rather than focusing on solving silo'd challenges that bloat the collective whole.

Unfortunately, we can't jump to the end. We have to build a bridge from where we are to where society wants to be in terms of preventing and treating disease and paying for services. Blockchain represents a great socio-economic experiment that has just begun.

Results from our experiment will be realized when innovators with a fundamental understanding of complex healthcare issues can match up a use case with a technical and non-technical solution to the problem at hand. That is harder than it sounds.

First, innovators must have a deep understanding of the use case. It helps to have experience in healthcare because the devil is always in the healthcare-specific, "why does it work that way" details.

Second, innovators must have an understanding of the technical options. Protocol and language matter. There are a growing number of choices in terms of technical solutions. The wrong choice leads to a dead end. The most common way to waste time and money is to only approach a use case from a technical perspective, or to assume that one protocol is appropriate for any use case.

Third, innovators must realize that by solving the problem from a technical perspective, she has to be unlocking a new business model that is at least twenty times better than what exists today. She would be wise to stay away from use cases with regulatory concerns. Otherwise the cost and effort could result in disappointment.

Finally, she must bring together at least a viable network around the product she builds in order to make the product come to life. Without the network and a successful governance structure, any solution is just an expensive academic exercise. Network orchestration and governance is the last mile and it is often a long one.

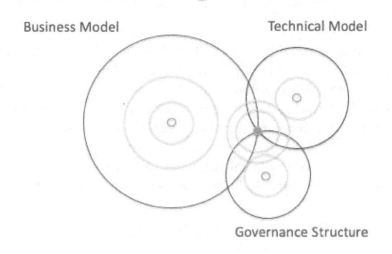

Image 1: For Blockchain Use Cases, the Relationship Between the Technical Model, Business Model, and Governance Structure is the key to success.

It is not easy to find that sweet spot between the technical solution for a business problem, the business model enabled by that technical solution, and a governance structure that makes the solution come alive. In these early days, most good use cases fail when put to that test today.

Much of the hype we read in the news focuses on solutions where there is immaturity in one or more areas of the model. Over time, as the technology matures, as new business models come alive, and as healthcare constituents become more comfortable with concepts of decentralization, we will open up new use cases that currently sit out of reach.

While frustrating, these constraints represent the current field of play. Finding the sweet spot is challenging but very rewarding. There are no shortage of innovators, enterprises, and venture capitalists ready to try.

The purpose of this book is to provide a window in to a convergence of technical and social forces that provide evidence that we are, at last, entering a period of change. A variety of contributors in the book explore how the conversation amongst enterprises and innovators is unfolding. Our contributors describe emerging concepts in blockchain and distributed ledger technology that can help address some of the fundamental issues that have brought us to this unsustainable place in healthcare and society.

In the first section, we describe the technology in an accessible way. In the second section, we describe use cases and design models that are surfacing as near-term solutions. Finally, we explore how blockchain and related technologies may evolve over time.

The contributors to this book include a wide spectrum of healthcare veterans and blockchain thought-leaders. It is important to note that the contributors in this book use the term "blockchain" in different ways. Satoshi and Bitcoin maximalists believe in a very strict, libertarian definition of blockchain. If you read the Satoshi Whitepaper, you will read about a blockchain which is open, public, and decentralized. Using a slow, ultra-secure, energy-intensive Proof of Work algorithm, it is purpose-built to move trust to the software and solve for issues of immutability, censorship resistance, and decentralized trust specific to cryptocurrency transactions. [7]

Over time, the wave of blockchain-inspired innovation has swelled beyond Bitcoin. Well-intentioned mavens like those in this book have used Satoshi's original vision for Bitcoin to solve for new problems that require a more broad definition of what a digital asset can be. They use the blockchain-inspired ledgers as a source of truth for market-level operating systems and development platforms. They use the ledger to record the fingerprint of digital assets and move these new assets in ways that are less expensive, result in less friction, and are more in line with a sustainable vision of patient-centered, community-enabled care.

Many of these innovators have continued to use the word "Blockchain" to represent a spectrum of trust-based operating systems and trust-based transactional platforms. At one end of this spectrum sits Bitcoin's open, decentralized system. At the other end of the spectrum are distributed ledger technologies (DLT). Distributed ledgers are like the blockchain's younger, less disruptive little sister. Distributed ledgers represent newer, less decentralized protocols tweak the protocol with trade-offs that favor other properties such as privacy, confidentiality, permissioning, speed, and throughput. Along the spectrum from distributed to decentralized, we find a growing list of tools and protocols can be used to solve business problems.

There are important differences between the two ends of the spectrum. The choice of a technical protocol has everything to do with the business problem, the new business model, and the governance structure necessary to make the network viable.

The "blockchain" is not one thing. It's a growing and rich ecosystem of protocols and belief systems that will stitch together over time. The use of the term "blockchain" to represent this full spectrum from open and decentralized to private and permissioned is hotly debated, especially by Bitcoin maximalists and those with a longer term vision of how the Internet should operate. In this book we do not attempt to engage in this specific debate, but we do attempt to represent ideas across the spectrum.

It is clear that most of the products that will be used in a meaningful way in the short term are business-to-business (B2B) distributed ledger solutions, rather than consumer-focused, decentralized solutions. Most of these B2B distributed ledger solutions typically take on a corporate-focused belief system, rather than a decentralized blockchain approach designed to empower the patient. Over time, we predict that we will move down the spectrum to realize the vision of consumer-focused, decentralized systems. We are not sure how long that will take, but we believe that true change will be driven by the consumer and leverage the network effects promised by decentralized blockchain protocols. B2B solutions on distributed ledgers will be a change agent. Consumer-focused solutions on open, community owned and operated blockchain protocols are likely to be the true disruptor. As open and decentralized blockchain protocols mature, we will no longer need to sacrifice speed for security, trade confidentiality for openness, or create friction as a result of tokenization.

We believe in decentralization, but we also believe we need to employ a practical approach that meets the healthcare world where it is now, in 2019. In the short term, our job is to build a bridge to a decentralized, self-sovereign world that, as of now, remains future state. We have to get from here to there. For now, decentralization is a beautiful dream. It will take time for it our models to mature and for decentralization in healthcare to become real.

The reader will also notice that we talk relatively little about cryptocurrencies in the first two sections of the book. It is likely that cryptocurrencies play a role in the next ten years by assisting with more intelligent value-transfer and, perhaps most importantly, consumer network effects. But for now, forcing a cryptocurrency on the actors in healthcare adds friction instead of removing it. That may change over time as cryptocurrencies and the technologies that allow consumers to use them improve. The opportunity for powerful new crypto economics in healthcare could take time, but that opportunity has remarkable potential for network effects unlike anything the health and wellness market has ever seen before.

Some readers may also be disappointed that we save the world's favorite use case, Medical Records on the Blockchain, for the future section. There are companies building these solutions now, but the current immaturity of the technical, business, and governance structures related to the medical records use case will limit its large-scale adoption in the near term. Self-sovereign medical records are attractive, but will take time to realize at scale. Any project dealing with medical records is using the ledger to track hashes, distributed identifiers, and pointers to external data sources. Even so, there remains regulatory uncertainty around protected information that is sure to be a limiting factor for longitudinal health records and self-sovereign medical identity, especially in the U.S. This is a use case that is likely to mature more quickly in emerging markets. The medical records-related use cases that are possible in the short term look more like access controls and policy sharing tools.

We believe in decentralization, but we also believe we need to employ a practical approach that meets the healthcare world where it is now, in 2019. We are building a bridge to a decentralized, self-sovereign world that, as of now, remains a beautiful dream. We have to get from here to there.

Also, it's important to realize that the innovators in this book are experimenting. This book contains ideas and thoughts about a range of distributed and decentralized topics. As of the writing of this book, the first of these (Jose Arrieta's HHS Procurement project, Procredex, the Synaptic Alliance, and Signal Stream) are going to market. Few are proven and most early attempts will fail for a variety of technical and non-technical reasons.

Many will argue that some of the use cases described in this book could be adequately resolved using a more traditional centralized database. For some use cases, this perspective is accurate. Some of the use cases in this book only need a blockchain when you consider how that database would be managed and by whom.

It's a matter of who or what we trust today, and who or what we want to trust in the future. It may be that, for certain use cases, we are comfortable with enterprise belief systems governing an enterprise business-to-business network. It may be that not everything needs to be decentralized. Not every business model is fifty times better on the blockchain or on a distributed ledger. Perhaps not all our value chains are low trust. But many are, and this new technology will prove in time to be an important and evolving change agent for those areas of healthcare where trust, transparency, and incentive alignment are in short supply.

Transformation won't be easy and won't happen overnight. It will require us to shift our paradigm from a model that rewards the centralized business models that underpin many of the largest healthcare companies today. It will require us to double-down on the shift from volume to value. It will ask us to trust software protocols where we formerly trusted intermediaries. After all, the waste in healthcare is some company's profit.

We can think of the early days of the Internet as an analogue. In the late 90's and early 00's we introduced a new technology that ushered in the concept of a shared operating system. At that time, companies like empactHealth.com and The Global Healthcare Exchange were born out of an effort to bring together the networks of healthcare companies to work together in a new way. At first, companies were nervous that the new way of working would disrupt their interests. The hard part was not the technology… it was convincing companies to think and work differently.

In return for learning to work together in new ways, we can expect to see new ecosystems in healthcare arise that are in line with the needs of patients, employers and other communities. These ecosystems will center around new types of market structures that provide more efficient access to health resources. New marketplace models hold the promise of rationality and transparency. Consumers can make choices based on information, cost, and a seller's reputation for delivering value. Innovative offerings can be listed on new exchanges by innovative sellers that reflect the needs of innovative buyer groups like Amazon, JP Morgan Chase, CMS and the VA. The winning innovators will differentiate themselves based on trust and value.

To succeed, we will plan to use a variety of new distributed and decentralized protocols that embody the belief systems of their creators who come together around solving industry-level problems of centralization. These parties (new and old) have already begun to come together to collaborate and offer an alternative to healthcare's current value chains that keep us locked in 1990's era pipelined processes where rent-seeking rules the day. We are starting down the path of building ground-up economies that use programmable value transfer to automatically respond to behavior, quality and outcomes. We will no longer need to depend on infrastructure that is not designed to support value.

We will get there network-by-network. It will take time, but the decentralizing forces that have been unleashed cannot be put back. Hiding from these realities is akin to hiding from the Internet in 1999. But in 2019 we are talking about an Internet of value. That's potentially a much bigger story that will shift the landscape in dramatic ways over the next 10 years. It just might be the United States only viable alternative to the next financial crisis.

No matter how you feel about the ideas coming to life within this book, perhaps the greatest opportunity is in the conversation itself. We are exploring new ways of solving old problems in the world's largest market. It's a market that has everything to do with our most important asset... our health.

References

1. https://www.forbes.com/sites/leahbinder/2018/03/08/surprisingly-bold-policy-speech-from-trumps-new-hhs-secretary/#bfb4fde1b6af

2. https://www.modernhealthcare.com/article/20180613/NEWS/180619961

3. https://www.healthleadersmedia.com/finance/medicare-faces-insolvency-2026-three-years-earlier-last-years-projection

4. https://www.reuters.com/article/us-usa-healthcare-spending/us-healthcare-spending-to-climb-53-percent-in-2018-agency-idUSKCN1FY2ZD

5. https://www.axios.com/health-care-industry-on-track-massive-q2-profits-1533226387-dacec8f8-c9f5-406c-a49e-1103e3316c64.html; https://www.cnbc.com/2018/04/17/unitedhealth-earnings-up-more-than-30-percent.html

6. https://www.edelman.com/post/trust-in-healthcare-2018

7. https://bitcoin.org/bitcoin.pdf

Chapter 2:
Precision Payments & Precision Contracts

John Bass

https://hashedhealth.com/blockchain-for-healthcare-book/

Editor's Note:

In this chapter, John takes a deeper dive into the opportunities and challenges currently faced in the healthcare system with particular emphasis on value-based medicine followed by a pragmatic look at Hashed Health's Signal Stream to give an initial glimpse of how new modeling languages like DAML for digital assets may provide a strong vision for the future of data handling across the industry in a more fully transparent way.

The efficient and effective delivery of healthcare services remains one of the world's great financial and social challenges. The United States feels these problems most because we spend close to 20% of our gross domestic product on healthcare, yet we still suffer from high variability in quality and patient experience.

For years, there have been well-intended but ineffective efforts to manipulate the current system to make it more sustainable. Entrepreneurs continue to build applications and implement process improvements that aim to resolve our cost and quality issues. We may make progress in specific areas, yet we seem to only add to the cost and infrastructure bloat at the system level. Costs around the world continue to rise because we fail to address the underlying structural issues that get in the way of value for the patient.

Over the last ten years there's been a shift in thinking about how to resolve these issues. That shift falls under the banner of value-based healthcare delivery. The basis of this shift is in the realization that the goal of care delivery is not one of cost, it's one of the relationship between cost and outcomes (aka value).

It is worth noting that this discussion around a shift from volume to value tells you a lot about how irrational our healthcare system is currently. In other industries the price of a product or service is an agreement on the value of that product or service. In our current healthcare system, our designers have removed degrees of rationality, competition and choice from the market. Without rationality borne of information, transparency, and trust, we are left with conversations that focus on how to introduce value. Our true goal is to change the conversation to something more productive and sustainable.

Michael Porter's "Fundamentally New Strategy"

"The history of health care has been littered with 'silver bullets' that didn't make an impact." —Michael Porter [1]

Harvard Business School professor Michael Porter has done extensive research in the healthcare field and has pioneered the value-based healthcare delivery framework. This framework focuses on the idea that healthcare systems should strive to deliver maximum value for patients.

Instead of approaching care as an individual site, specialty or intervention, Porter espouses an approach that considers the patient's medical condition over the full episode of care. "What people like me are used to doing is stepping back and looking at the system as a whole– this complexity of how you integrate all these interventions that ultimately indicates success." [2]

From both a clinical and a financial perspective, the focus is on addressing the full set of results that matter to the patient, instead of the narrow interests of each participating entity. In this model, outcomes become the driver of reducing costs.

In 2015, Porter introduced his value-based strategic agenda, which includes a detailed analysis of the following framework:

1. Re-organize Care Around Patient Conditions Using the Concept of Integrated Practice Units
2. Measure Outcomes and Costs for Every Patient
3. Move to Bundled Payments for Care Cycles
4. Integrate Multi-Site Care Delivery Systems
5. Expand Geographic Reach To Drive Excellence
6. Build an Enabling Information Technology Platform [3]

In earlier research, Porter offered the concept of In fact, according to Porter, zero-sum competition between healthcare system participants actually "divides value instead of increasing it."

Healthcare enterprises often compete in "zero-sum" ways that are not aligned with the interests of consumers and the desired outcome of the job at hand. [4] In many ways, today's healthcare enterprises compete with the very patients they serve. Instead of focusing on patient outcomes, the traditional system focuses more on billing, narrowing choice, shifting costs, creating leverage, maximizing reimbursement, and retaining patients. Benefiting at the expense of the patient is no path to value.

Definition of Value-Based Care

A scalable, sustainable healthcare system must focus on value for the patient. That may sound simple and obvious, but in reality, the shift to value-based systems requires some fundamental changes in how we think about the organizing health care value chains that are responsible for the delivery and payment for products and services. It requires a shift away from disparate activities and systems towards a tightly integrated and collaborative approach.

Value is defined as the relationship between cost and quality. In a value-based healthcare delivery model, providers are paid based on the outcomes achieved. Under value-based programs providers are incented to help patients improve the individual's health and continue living in an evidence-based way. Providers are exploring how these incentive structures can affect the care for chronic diseases, surgeries, drugs, medical devices, and other products and services. This differs from the traditional fee-for-service approach which pays based on the amount of healthcare services delivered.

Value-based arrangements are all about risk. Fee-for-service arrangements do not carry risk, which is essentially an agreement to assume responsibility for care at a pre-agreed rate. The amount of risk assumed by the provider goes up as you move from fee-for-service to global capitation models where a doctor or group is paid a pre-determined amount for all the care related to a patient or population of patients.

History of Value-Based Care

Quality improvement in healthcare is almost as old as healthcare itself. Our efforts to systematically improve quality has been developing formally over the last century and has steadily evolved towards more mature systems of quantifying, measuring and, finally, incentivizing quality.

The use of financial incentives as a strategy to drive improvements in care dates back even further among private payers and Medicaid programs, with limited experimentation occurring in the early 1990s; more widespread use of pay for performance began to pick up steam in the late 1990s and early 2000s. Published evidence from pay for performance programs implemented by private-sector payers between 2000 and 2010 showed mostly modest results in improving performance. Public and private payers have continued to experiment with the use of financial incentives as a lever to drive improvements in care ever since.

More recently CMS, as part of the Affordable Care Act (ACA) of 2010, initiated The Hospital Value-Based Purchasing (VBP) Program which began making incentive payments to providers based on that provider's performance against specific quality baseline measures. This was an effort to achieve the IHI's 2007 vision of the Triple Aim, which is the simultaneous improvement of the patient care experience, improve the health of a population, and reduce per capita health care costs. [5] The VBP Program has proven to be one of the most important parts of the ACA in terms of setting the stage for more efficient delivery of care.

With the ACA in place, providers began testing variations of a few types VBP models (with varying levels of assumed risk), including:

- Shared savings models- Shared savings models are fee-for-service models where annual spend is measured against a baseline; if spend is below the baseline then the provider receives a bonus payment. This is a one-sided risk model.

- Bundled payment models- Bundled payments models pay for the services under a certain condition over a period of time (for example a knee replacement episode of care); organizations are allowed profit through reduced spending on care inside the bundle.

- Shared risk models- Under shared risk models, hospitals and providers receive performance-based incentives to share cost savings and also have penalties for excess costs of the delivery of care.

- Global capitation models- Global capitation is a high-risk arrangement where a provider (or group of enterprises) collaborate for a fixed payment for all of the services related to a patient or a population of patients, regardless of what services are consumed.

These early pay for performance programs have matured over time to include more broad measures and a wider range of incentives.

More recent alternative payment models include accountable care organizations (ACOs), new bundled payment models with new quality and cost design features, the Patient Centered Medical Home (PCMI) and the Physician Value-Based Modifier Program. The move from fee for service to value is still fairly new to care delivery, and these programs are clearly a work in progress in terms of how to optimally design programs that achieve lower cost, higher quality, and a good patient experience. With each new model we continue to test counterparty response to different incentive models and slowly phase in more risk for the counterparties in these contracts. Institutions who learn how to best manage risk are at an advantage in terms of the rewards under value based models.

VBP models are still evolving today and we are learning about the optimal conditions for executing on these strategies. The US government in particular now seems primarily interested in simplifying value-based models that have shown signs of lowering spending on care delivery. [6] The administrative burden and the complexity of these initiatives has been a limiting factor in realizing gains from these models. [7]

Examples of Value-Based Agreements

In the pharma space, many insurance companies are employing value-based agreements with pharma companies around the performance of drugs. Drug companies and payers are employing product-specific agreements that result in a rebate should the product not perform according to an agreed-upon clinical endpoint. The basic mechanics for these contracts assume the patient's compliance to a protocol will result in an outcome claimed by the manufacturer. This type of agreement is used in around the world to hold pharmaceutical companies accountable for the results they claim. Value-based agreements in the pharmaceutical space are especially popular in Europe.

These value-based agreements are especially important with new high value specialty pharmacy areas where treatments, when used appropriately, can save lives, but can cost hundreds of thousands of dollars. One example is a gene therapy drug called Luxturna, which has shown evidence that it will restore sight to children with a certain rare disease, at a rate of $425,000 per eye. [8] More of these ultra-expensive drugs, gene therapies and "precision medicines" are coming. One potential new drug from Novartis that treats spinal muscular atrophy could cost $4 million to $5 million.

These and other gene therapies are often being made available under "outcomes-based rebate arrangements." The manufacturer of Luxturna, Spark Therapeutics, gives payers a refund if the patient's vision doesn't improve in a specific amount of time. [9] Other companies are exploring payment plans that spread these costs out over the life of the patient, similar to a value-based mortgage. In fact, it is difficult to understand how these drugs could ever go to market without a value-based system. For certain product lines, specialty pharma and orphan drug manufacturers are now more concerned with reimbursement than they are with FDA approval.

In a 2018 Wall Street Journal article, University of Pennsylvania's Ezekiel Emanuel commented, "When I was training as an oncologist nearly three decades ago, we dreamed of curing cancer. Today, advances in cellular immunotherapy make it no longer a dream: A cure for cancer has become possible, even probable. But tragically, the costs of these drug therapies are so high that the American health care system can't afford them. A potential revolution in cancer care may be stymied by the high price of drugs, which suggests that we need to reconsider how we price them." [10]

The pressure to prove the value of expensive products is taking hold in the medical devices space as well. Medtronic PLC CEO Omar Ishrak seems to embrace that his company must take on more risk in future payment models. [11]

"In a value-based world, payment will be intricately tied to demonstrated value. This heightens the importance of innovating to deliver value and of measuring value creation. Medtronic is focused on going beyond the current structure for clinical trials to measure broader value for patients" Ishrak said.

Even so, medical device companies like Medtronic may find the change difficult. According to Ishrak, "We've got to break down barriers and build long-term, focused, collaborative relationships where our incentives are aligned, so if you win, we win; if you lose, we lose." [12] That's no easy feat for a healthcare incumbent.

For healthcare services, there are many forms of value-based care. One popular model is bundled payments. A bundled payment is a way to set cost and quality benchmarks for a procedure (ex. total knee replacement), measure performance against that benchmark, and reimburse actors based on their aggregate performance. It requires associating cost and performance (ex. outcomes measures) across a diverse set of clinical and financial information from independent businesses (ex. surgeon, clinic, hospital, implant manufacturer, rehabilitation, etc) who are all informally organized around the patient's episode. The purpose is to incentivize high quality, low cost behaviors across an uncoordinated group of corporate actors who have traditionally sought to maximize their own transactions and revenue without fiscal regard for outcomes or patient experience.

These and other value-based and performance-based payment systems are powerful tools in re-aligning our payment models in healthcare with quality and value. However, the design of these models is limited in terms of the actors involved, the source systems used to adjudicate the contract, and the value transfer characteristics. Counterparties are limited. Source systems today are primarily claims. And the exchange of money is generally retrospective in the form of a rebate or a retrospective reconciliation. When the reimbursement occurs a year after the knee replacement, the design is clearly sub-optimal, especially in driving incentives for high quality, low cost behaviors.

In many ways, it's the employers who are in position to capitalize on the opportunities in new value-based reimbursement models. A recent report by Duke-Margolis Center for Health Policy and the Robert Wood Johnson Foundation stated that "Employer-sponsored plans are well-positioned to innovate because they are not constrained by some of the same limitations as other market segments. For example, traditional Medicare has taken the lead in advancing value-based payment reform, but it has little ability to innovate in its network and benefit design." Employers can be faster and more flexible in changing networks, experimenting with network design, updating benefits and implementing new payment models. [13]

A 2018 survey from the National Business Group on Health found proof that employers are increasingly interested in innovating on how health care is delivered and paid for. "40% of employers have incorporated some type of value-based benefit design in which employers receive reduced cost sharing or premium reductions when they take steps to manage chronic conditions or obtain higher-quality or more efficient care." The survey also found that 21% of employers plan to promote ACOs in 2018 but that number could double by 2020 as another 26% are considering offering them." [14]

State plans are showing similar interests. For example, the Washington State Health Care Authority plans to transition 80% of the care they purchase to value-based. Knowing that they are left with the bill if nothing changes, governments and employers are not waiting around any more. According to Marcia Peterson and Sarah Rolph of the Washington State Health Care Authority, these programs are "a step toward making health care as simple, cost effective, and transparent as possible." [15]

New value-based insurance design efforts are also showing promise. The University of Michigan's Center for Value-Based Insurance Design (V-BID) program has established itself as a leader in this new field which attempts to align a consumer's out-of-pocket costs with the value of services while recognizing that value depends heavily on the site of care and the specific patient's characteristics. The basic principle is one that aims to remove the financial barriers to essential, high value products and services. [16]

In the non-profit space there are concepts around social impact bonds and outcomes-based finance that also share characteristics with the models described here.

Opportunities & Challenges

Value-based agreements still represent a fairly small but rapidly growing part of the healthcare system. According to an Optum sponsored survey by NEJM Catalyst, 42% of respondents (clinical leaders, clinicians, and executives at US-based organizations that deliver health care) say that value-based reimbursement models will become the primary revenue model in the U.S. [17]

There are signals that value-based payments work. For example, a JAMA study in 2017 showed that bundled payments for knee replacements saved U.S. taxpayers $5577 or 20.8% per joint replacement across 3942 patients. [18]

Though encouraging, these successes have proven hard to sustain and scale. They result in tremendous administrative burden due to systemic failures of trust, transparency, and incentive-alignment. Silo'd relational databases passing transaction-focused claims data have been tremendously successful at facilitating strict, standardized fee-for-service transactions, but are too rigid and inflexible for value-based transactions at scale. Contractual systems and processes that only care about transactions are a limiting factor in our transition from volume to value. This additional contract administrative complexity currently results in higher billing costs for providers and payers. [19] In order to scale value-based systems, we need to incorporate new design patterns, new source systems, new counterparty options, new value exchange capabilities, and a real-time view in to the relationship between cost and quality.

Today, the fundamental health infrastructure we have in the United States is designed around a transaction-focused, corporate-focused delivery model. So the primary focus is volume for the corporation, or more specifically the financial transaction for each corporate entity. Our delivery system and its current foundational infrastructure are designed for billing. Electronic Medical Records systems are primarily billings systems designed to maximize claims, which are medical bills submitted to insurance carriers for products and services provided to a patient. Fee for service creates an atmosphere where the best providers are the best billers and collectors of what is owed by consumers who, as costs rise, are less and less likely to be able to pay.

We are realizing that trying to bolt value-based solutions to these underlying systems may address silos of opportunity, but serve to add to the overall infrastructure bloat. In order to address the market-level issues we face, we must reconsider the wisdom of building applications atop a foundation designed for volume and silo'd interests.

The "bolt on" approach exacerbates our market-level problems. In most cases one of the counterparties in the agreement runs a calculator and says "trust me… I'll show you the answer when we are done." In a low-trust environment this doesn't work well. An alternative in these scenarios is for each enterprise to do its own math and then at some point, perhaps one month, six months or a year later when we have finished cobbling together all the cost and quality information, the enterprises come to find out we have different numbers on their calculators. Then the reconciliation battle begins.

Providers and other enterprises are scrambling to understand how to take on risk in an environment still bound by zero-sum competitive forces. The ability to assume risk is largely driven by transparency and trust in data and "trust but verify" collaboration. Without a change, healthcare providers and payers will opt for the status quo and we will continue to live in an unsustainable volume-focused world. This is not how you scale a program, especially one that centers on risk. Many of today's value-based systems have no visibility to the process whatsoever. As a result, it's asking a lot for enterprises to embrace risk-based models on expensive procedures.

If we want to realize the potential for precision medicine, we need to introduce precision payments and precision contracting tools. With precision payments comes new, right-sized, simplified, fair insurance and risk models. With these new models comes the opportunity for optimizing risk, coverage, meaningful incentives, and innovative value transfer.

Today, the fundamental health infrastructure we have in the United States is designed around a transaction-focused, corporate-focused delivery model. So the primary focus is volume for the corporation, or more specifically the financial transaction for each corporate entity. Our delivery system and its current foundational infrastructure are designed for billing. Electronic Medical Records systems are primarily billings systems designed to maximize claims, which are medical bills submitted to insurance carriers for products and services provided to a patient. Fee for service creates an atmosphere where the best providers are the best billers and collectors of what is owed by consumers who, as costs rise, are less and less likely to be able to pay.

Without a transformation to a value-focused system, we are faced with a future that focuses on more aggressive cost management. This cost-cutting will likely come in the form of less choice, less competition, haphazard reimbursement cuts, and other unproductive financially-focused measures. That's not the future we want to see.

Blockchain Solutions

If value is all about the relationship between cost and quality, then the very concept of value-based care suggests a need to reconsider our existing fee-for-service technical infrastructure. The merging of clinical and financial paradigms is challenging, especially to traditional for-profit health system CFOs who have built careers around the concept of "heads in beds" and systemic business incentives that pay more when more care is delivered.

To make the shift from volume to value, we must consider the basic infrastructure that we are dealing with. We need an enabling information technology platform that fits Michael Porter's Value Agenda. [20]

Blockchains are purpose-built to solve issues of trust, transparency and incentive alignment across multiple counterparties. One of a blockchain's core concepts is that of programmable value exchange. Using the blockchain, we can design and embed economic systems in the patient's full cycle of care. This will allow us to use a shared source of truth upon which we can program value exchange based on behaviors, compliance to protocols and attestations from source systems.

We now have the opportunity to design new infrastructure that inherently respects the relationship between cost and outcomes. We can design for value. We can design for the relationship between what you pay and what you do. We can design for the relationship between what you pay for a drug or service and it's value for you as the patient with a specific indication. We can more closely connect value transfer to the activities we want to incentivize. We are free to choose to incorporate traditional infrastructure or not. We are no longer bound by the traditional constructs and design patterns for value-based agreements.

Signal Stream

The first example of such a platform is Signal Stream, a Hashed Health product. Signal Stream is designed to solve the administrative burdens related to contract adjudication and, in doing so, also allows counterparties to innovate on contract design.

Signal Stream uses a distributed ledger that acts as a source of truth between counterparties and value-chains who want pay or incentivize behaviors based on a shared definition of value. Trusted source systems record clinical, financial, and patient experience information to the ledger. Atop the ledger runs software that automates business processes and moves value based on ledger activities. In this way, the value chain shares an operating system designed for value. It operates as a shared, trusted calculator that drives transparency, trust, and incentive alignment for legal contracts, payment contracts, risk-based agreements, value-based insurance models, dynamic pricing systems, public health contracts, social impact bonds, outcomes-based finance and other types of innovative contracts. It allows all parties to view the status of the agreement in real-time, based upon pre-agreed-upon data feeds and a pre-agreed-upon contract agreement structure.

This type of distributed ledger system requires a specific set of tools. For example, Signal Stream runs on a distributed ledger from Digital Assets called DAML. DAML is not a blockchain. It is not open, public or decentralized. DAML is a modeling language built specifically for contracts. This domain-specific language is used by Signal Stream to model transaction templates which define the rights and obligations of multiple counterparties. By design, it provides transaction-level confidentiality and a high throughput rate required for this set of contracting use cases. It is designed to perform in a way that the open public blockchains and other distributed ledgers are not capable of performing today.

Reducing costs by reducing administrative burden is a good start. It allows for products such as Signal Stream to solve real problems for real companies in today's world. But real improvements will require more than just removing the administrative burden specific to value-based initiatives. As we transition from no-risk arrangements to full-risk arrangements we need to get move innovative with the design of care management and value-transfer systems.

Therein lies perhaps the most interesting opportunity for Signal Stream and products like it. These systems promise to move beyond the current flawed design of these contracts. Counterparties looking to share such an operating system can move beyond the rigid traditional definitions of claims, static source systems, and retrospective value transfer. These systems allow us to innovate in terms of who the counterparties are, what the source systems are, and how the money flows between counterparties. Counterparties could include the physician or the patient, which could be helpful in high value specialty pharma episodes or bundled payment scenarios. It is important that we have visibility to what is happening outside the care setting, so source systems for the ledger could include wearables, home monitoring equipment, or other non-traditional IoT actors. Signal Stream's shared calculator can include a banking and settlement layer that moves value in real time, dramatically improving incentives and cash flow between organizations.

The success of these systems will serve to reinforce the drivers of value-based care delivery in the US and around the world. Transparency to outcomes measurement, which is one of Michael Porter's central drivers, and the ability to embed the transparency of outcomes in to the care management and payment process will create a force multiplier for value-based healthcare.

These innovations are exciting because they change the conversation around next-generation concepts including value-based insurance design, right-sized benefits products, dynamic pricing for drugs, risk models, social impact bonds, supply chain contracting, and even outcomes-based finance in developing countries. Using this type of distributed ledger solution begins us on the path towards a more decentralized model for payments and incentive structures. Our ability to scale these kinds of programmable value transfer solutions has the potential to fundamentally change the dysfunctional relationship between commerce and care.

References

1. https://www.medtronic.com/content/dam/medtronic-com/global/Corporate/Documents/value-based-healthcare-event-summary.pdf

2. https://hbr.org/2013/10/the-strategy-that-will-fix-health-care

3. http://www.healthforum-edu.com/summit/PDF/2015/SUM15michaelporter.pdf

4. https://hbr.org/2004/06/redefining-competition-in-health-care).

5. http://www.ihi.org/resources/Pages/Publications/TripleAimCareHealthandCost.aspx

6. https://www.hhs.gov/about/leadership/secretary/speeches/2018-speeches/remarks-on-value-based-healthcare.html

7. https://www.beckershospitalreview.com/hospital-physician-relationships/complexity-of-new-payment-models-thwarts-progress-in-physician-practices-4-findings.html?origin=cioe&utm_source=cioe

8. https://www.cnn.com/2018/01/03/health/luxturna-price-blindness-drug-bn/index.html

9. https://www.npr.org/sections/health-shots/2018/11/14/665782026/a-search-for-new-ways-to-pay-for-drugs-that-cost-a-mint

10. https://www.wsj.com/articles/we-cant-afford-the-drugs-that-could-cure-cancer-1537457740

11. https://www.wsj.com/articles/medtronic-moves-to-a-new-health-care-model-pay-only-if-it-works-1519096141

12. https://www.medtronic.com/content/dam/medtronic-com/global/Corporate/Documents/value-based-healthcare-event-summary.pdf

13. https://healthpolicy.duke.edu/sites/default/files/atoms/files/value_innovations_by_employers_examples_beyond_cost_sharing.pdf

14. https://www.businessgrouphealth.org/news/nbgh-news/press-releases/press-release-details/?ID=334

15. https://catalyst.nejm.org/center-of-excellence-redesigning-payment/

16. http://vbidcenter.org

17. https://catalyst.nejm.org/transitioning-fee-for-service-value-based-care/?utm_campaign=Connect%20Weekly&utm_source=hs_email&utm_medium=email&utm_content=67862611&_hsenc=p2ANqtz-9ZryNTF6GzBLnX8rhquvqWb5C0qig_g1g7KbFUygtEGNRDH_wiT_3WBzox2n2I61lD-BPDUbQiAWMj0PTp1GRL5M48CA&_hsmi=67862611

18. https://catalyst.nejm.org/what-are-bundled-payments/

19. https://www.healthaffairs.org/do/10.1377/hblog20161003.056892/full/

20. https://hbr.org/2013/10/the-strategy-that-will-fix-health-care .

Chapter 3:
Protocols & Business Patterns

John Bass

https://hashedhealth.com/blockchain-for-healthcare-book/

Editor's Note:

In this chapter, John reviews the various early protocols and their potential influence and impact from the earliest Bitcoin and Ethereum to new business patterns like non-fungible tokens and their very own Bramble as an example of a decentralized transactional platform. Providing practical examples throughout the text for cases – Usecases or case studies helps bring blockchain and healthcare to a reality whether through community datasets, market models, medical records, self-sovereign identity or privacy cases like the GDPR case-study example. Multiple models for how protocols will impact blockchain and healthcare are presented.

In 2015, "Mastering Bitcoin: Programming the Open Blockchain" was the bible for blockchain developers. Andreas Antonopoulos turned the light on for entrepreneurs around the world who were looking to understand how the cryptocurrency really worked. It remains mandatory reading at Hashed Health and many other blockchain companies, even today when the innovations taking place exist on other protocols. Antonopoulos provided an on-ramp for the those interested in the technology, and it inspired many of the early leaders in the space by helping them understand the realities of the technology and the social forces behind the bitcoin movement and everything that has happened since..

Bitcoin

Bitcoin is "A network that allows you to replace trust in institutions, trust in hierarchies, with trust on the network. The network acting as a massively diffuse arbiter of truth, resolving any disagreements about transactions and security in a way where no one has control."

"At the end of the day, bitcoin is programmable money. When you have programmable money, the possibilities are truly endless."

— Andreas M. Antonopoulos, The Internet of Money

Throughout history, banks and third-party institutions have existed to provide trust between multiple parties of a transaction. Bitcoin radically challenged this construct, allowing transactions to take place within a protocol, without the need to depend on third-party entities. By moving trust from the intermediary to the protocol, Bitcoin changed the way money flows and set the stage for the Internet of Money. All the Blockchain initiatives we talk about today are a result of Bitcoin.

The earliest ideas of blockchain in healthcare considered anchoring to the Bitcoin blockchain. In early 2015, as the healthcare-focused Nashville Blockchain Meetup was forming, we studied how we might anchor to Bitcoin. For example, Colored Coins were, at the time, one of the more innovative ways of associating the fingerprint of a real-world asset to the Bitcoin blockchain. Outside of healthcare there were experiments to use Colored Coins for stocks, bonds, futures and real estate. [1]

At the time, companies like Coinprism, a wallet service for colored coins, were the thought leaders. What Coinprism's Flavien Charlon was doing was way ahead of its time.

"While we have been one of the first in the area of blockchain tokens, long before ethereum was even released, the ecosystem has since shifted towards ERC-20, which is more flexible and more powerful than bitcoin-based systems," said Charlon in 2018, when Coinprism announced it was shutting down. "The unpredictability of transactions fees and confirmation times in the past couple of years have also made it hard to argue bitcoin is a good platform for this."[2]

While most projects in healthcare thus far have chosen to anchor to Ethereum and newer protocols described later in this chapter, some initiatives still post-hole to the Bitcoin blockchain, primarily because of the proven stability of the Bitcoin protocol. It is, by far, the most battle-tested and secure of all the protocols. The Bitcoin blockchain has never been breached.

Factom, for example, was an early builder of private networks, posting transactions to the Bitcoin network as a way for private ledgers to have high trust in their shared record keeping. By anchoring to the Bitcoin blockchain, participants in the network share a high-confidence, albeit expensive, source of truth.

However, Bitcoin is not designed as a development platform. It is very slow, has very low throughput rates, 10-minute block times, and a very narrow definition of its digital asset. As the cost of Bitcoin skyrocketed in 2016 and 2017, anchoring to Bitcoin became more and more expensive. As a result, entities are forced to minimize ledger events.

Over time it has become more clear that, in many use cases today, public blockchains may not be the best protocol choice. As he wound down Coinprism, Flavien Charlon commented "In 99% of use cases we're seeing, blockchain is unfortunately a sub-optimal choice as a technology. Blockchains have many disadvantages in terms of speed, scalability, costs and user experience. Unless censorship resistance is a critical requirement (which it rarely is, especially in the enterprise blockchain space where participants all know each other), blockchain is rarely the right technological choice." He went on to say, "In the end it was about intellectual honesty. I didn't like having to support projects that were trying to use blockchain for the sake of using blockchain, when I knew a centralized, more boring architecture would actually do a better job." [3]

Ethereum

Whereas Satoshi Nakamoto's Bitcoin Whitepaper [4] is often credited as a catalyst to the current blockchain revolution, the Ethereum Whitepaper was a dramatic breakthrough in unlocking the power of decentralized and distributed technologies.[5]

As world-changing as Bitcoin is, it is not easily repurposed for alternative blockchain applications. Developers were faced with a tough choice – go through the labor-intensive process of creating a completely new blockchain, or attempt to expand past the limitations of the current protocol.

Whereas Bitcoin was specifically constructed to administer a specific use of blockchain technology, Ethereum was created to provide a framework to run all decentralized applications. Ethereum includes a Turing-complete programming language for users to create "smart contracts", or arbitrary rules that dictate the execution of actions. The breakthrough lies in the inclusion of a complete programming language, empowering complete freedom for developers to build any application they wish.

Now, Ethereum is the second largest blockchain protocol in the world, behind only Bitcoin. Any person attempting to understand how future applications will sit atop blockchain protocols should start with understanding Ethereum.

Below is a brief, simplistic, high-level outline explaining how the Ethereum blockchain works: A new transaction is sent to the nodes (computers) on the network.

1. The nodes aggregate and store these transactions within a block in chronological order.

2. The nodes each work to solve an energy and computationally intensive Proof-of-Work (PoW) algorithm puzzle.

3. The first node on the network to solve the puzzle then broadcasts to the rest of the network.

4. Other nodes accept the solution if the answer is valid.

5. The nodes signal acceptance by beginning to work on the following block.

The process is similar to Bitcoin. Algorithms regulate the difficulty of the PoW puzzles to maintain a constant frequency of block creation (about every 12-15 seconds). The winning miner is rewarded with five ether. This process has two main functions – it allows new Ether to be circulated without a central authority and it validates transactions in a decentralized manner. The mining process makes hacking nearly impossible, due to the sheer computing power required to reverse prior transactions.

Ethereum is planning to transition to an alternative mining process, Proof-of-stake (PoS), which many believe will be more scalable and much more energy efficient. Instead of puzzles being solved through computational energy, PoS validates new blocks by having miners stake Eth. Validators collect Eth as a network reward when they validate a new block. The probability of validating a block is related to the validator's stake.

Although Bitcoin may be more well known, Bitcoin exists primarily as digital gold. Meanwhile, Ethereum has become a platform for distributed computing, distributed applications, and digital tokens. In the words of creator Vitalik Buterin, Ethereum is "a fundamentally new class of cryptoeconomic organisms—decentralized, jurisdiction-less entities that exist entirely in cyberspace, maintained by a combination of cryptography, economics and social consensus." [6] In other words, it represents a whole new way of thinking about and building systems.

Ethereum has largely been responsible for the proliferation of Initial Coin Offerings (ICOs), which took the world by storm in 2017. At the end of 2017, the market cap for the over 850 new cryptocurrencies was $800 billion. [7] Many believe the ICO tokens are Ethereum's 'killer app.' Using Ethereum, development teams around the world could create their own cryptographically secure financial systems using tokens to drive network effects, fractionalize support and make the movement of value more intelligent. These new economies are programmable. They can be programmed in ways the traditional economy and fiat currency cannot. But the real power of tokens is the ability to create network effects. The holder of the token has an incentive to see that token's value rise.

Though many questions remain surrounding both ICOs and tokens, what Ethereum accomplished is extremely exciting. The potential for using the token economics to drive network effects in healthcare is not likely to go away, although it likely will not look the same as it did in 2017.

Healthcare innovators are now using Ethereum and a new breed of related technologies to build out various use cases and concepts. Smart contracts are fairly immature but are showing tremendous promise in automating business processes and programming value exchange in healthcare use cases.

The Spectrum of Trust-Based Operating Systems

Now, in 2019, we have a spectrum of tools and technologies to solve more and more problems. This spectrum of trust-based operating systems runs from decentralized protocols (ex. Bitcoin, Ethereum) to Distributed Ledger Technologies "DLT" (ex. Fabric, DAML, Corda, Quorum). All along this spectrum we can select from a rapidly maturing list of software systems designed to solve technical, business, or governance challenges.

The technologies at the Blockchain end of the spectrum are extremely secure, slow, and generally expensive to run (because of the price of the cryptocurrencies that serve as the network's gas). The Blockchain end of the spectrum embraces decentralization, even though in most cases decentralization in 2019 is still a beautiful dream. Blockchains are more disruptive and aspirational in nature. The belief systems embedded in Blockchain applications are generally more consumer-focused or community-focused belief systems. Over time, this is likely where the more disruptive use cases will exist, but it will take us a while to get there.

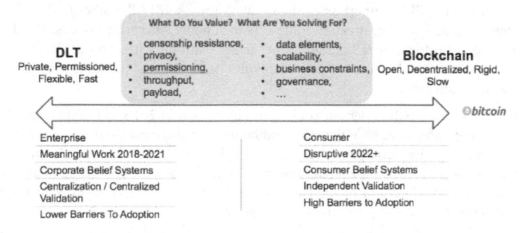

The Spectrum of Trust-Based Operating Systems, John Bass, Hashed Health 2018

The DLT end of the spectrum is where most of the meaningful use cases exist today. DLT is the world of the enterprise. As a result, DLT solutions tend to be business-to-business infrastructure projects that solve market-level business problems using the belief systems of the minimally viable network of businesses who step forward to help develop, pilot, and deploy them. These are not decentralized systems. These are shared ledgers with some elements of centralization. Many use cases in healthcare require privacy, confidentiality and high throughput, which currently means using DLT.

Protocols Used In Healthcare Today

Hyperledger Protocols

Hyperledger, part of the Linux Foundation, began shipping production code in 2017 with it's Fabric 1.0 release. It now has over eleven active projects in its ecosystems. Most are enterprise-focused DLT protocols.

Fabric, the most well known of the Hyperledger protocols, is perhaps the most widely used protocol with over 50 different networks in production, a few of which are healthcare or life sciences focused. Fabric is associated with IBM, but Hyperledger is working hard to encourage diversity in the core contributors for Fabric and the other protocols in the family. Fabric 1.4 is a recent release that attempts to introduce elements of confidentiality to the protocol, which was not originally designed for privacy.

One of Fabric's core principles is to allow a defined set of actors in a network to grow and shrink the network dynamically. The actors run nodes which allows them to both publish information to the network and read information from the network. It uses a modified Kafka commit log (an append-only data structure) as its consensus mechanism, and the core team is adding support for other, more robust consensus mechanisms that will be important as the network grows. [8] Like other DLT platforms, it makes decentralization trade-offs to support enterprise use cases. Fabric aims for a one-protocol fits all model, rather than positioning itself optimally for one category of use cases. Most cloud providers offer 'as-a-service' products for Fabric, which eases installation.

The first known, public demonstration on Fabric was in 2016. Hashed Health used Fabric .07 to demonstrate how Fabric could be used to share provider demographic data between insurance companies. It caused a splash at HIMSS 2017 as the first public demonstration of a blockchain use case in healthcare– the first time many in healthcare had even heard of blockchain. A year later, HIMSS designated a part of the showroom floor exclusively for blockchain innovation.

In 2018, the number of POCs built on Fabric flourished. Perhaps the most widely known healthcare use case on Hyperledger Fabric is Change Healthcare's use case for transparency in to Change Healthcare's high-volume claims infrastructure. According to a press release announcing the project in January of 2018, the network is processing up to 550 transactions per second and 50 million claim events every day. [9]

Hyperledger Sawtooth is another fairly mature protocol in the Hyperledger family. Sawtooth is now in its 1.1 release and is largely backed by Intel but is growing in its diversity of contributors. In 2017, Pokitdok, a respected healthcare integration innovator and early leader in the blockchain space, announced its Dokchain initiative on Sawtooth. With Dokchain, Pokitdok intends "to link systems, insurers, technology, supply chain companies and financial institutions. The goal is to record transactions that capture the history and process the administrative piece of an individual's care." Sawtooth and Intel's SGX chip allow Pokitdok "to protect select code and data from disclosure and modification." [10] Sawtooth went in to its 1.0 production status in January of 2018. [11]

Perhaps the most exciting and highest potential protocol in the Hyperledger family is the Indie project, backed by the Sovrin Foundation. Indie is a platform for digital identity known as self-sovereign identity. Its traction has been greatest with national ID systems in Sierra Leone and business identification in British Columbia. Indie is a fairly new protocol (not yet in 1.0 release) but has become an exciting leader in the decentralized identity area.

Finally, Hyperledger Burrow is an interesting implementation of an Ethereum virtual machine (EVM) designed for enterprise use. This project allows you to deploy Ethereum smart contracts on top of Fabric and Sawtooth. The convergence of Ethereum and Hyperledger opens some new doors and further proves that the blockchain is not just one thing. The enterprise DLT world is already mixing with the more decentralized world. Under Brian Behlendorf's leadership, Hyperledger is leading this open-source community in a thoughtful, pragmatic way.

DAML

Digital Assets' DAML platform takes a different approach. First off, it is not a blockchain and Digital Assets is quick to clarify that they do not even see it as a "protocol." DAML is not trying to be Fabric, an application-specific one-size fits all protocol. Digital Assets sees it as an "expressive language designed for financial institutions to model and execute agreements with certainty and finality." [12]

DAML is most well-known for its work with the Australian Stock Exchange, who expects to see savings of $23 Billion from the deployment of the more efficient market-level financial transaction platform. [13]

DAML combines a set of features that distinguish it from other DLT platforms. At the heart of the platform is DAML itself, a domain-specific modeling language used to create transactional templates that define counterparty and related third-party behavior. The majority of enterprise-focused DLT platforms offer the ability to create application logic that can operate on the ledger (so-called Smart Contracts). Developers usually employ a general-purpose programming language to develop smart contracts. By contrast, DAML is specifically designed to model business and commercial agreements. Business concepts drive core structures of the language itself. What makes DAML unique is that it is a domain-specific language, designed specifically for modeling business transactions and contracts.

Built on a functional programming foundation, DAML can feel a little restrictive at first, limiting the approaches a developer can take to define a transaction. Indeed, our developers initially found it off-putting. However, within a few short days, we understood that these seeming limitations actually deliver great advantages. DAML is designed for formal correctness. In other words, contracts and transactions written in DAML operate precisely as expected—essential for business trust and value. On other DLT platforms, we need to decide how best to approximate a business interaction and constantly test to assure that the approximation behaves as required. With DAML, there is no need to approximate.

One of the more difficult design problems with DLT is transparency of the ledger. Many DLT platforms bear a resemblance, or even a direct relationship, to the original cryptocurrency blockchain platforms. These early platforms were designed for radical transparency. This transparency is essential to both their operation in open, un-permissioned environments and their trustless, tamper resistant nature. For enterprises, this transparency at best complicates and at worst limits the benefits of DLT. DLT platforms such as Fabric, Quorum and Enterprise Ethereum have introduced confidentiality features like private channels, private data collections and hidden contracts, while still operating on transparent, yet permissioned, ledger networks. While important, these platform developments are secondary designs, often at odds with the original design intention of the platform itself.

By contrast, transactional confidentiality in DAML is a first-class feature. Transactions are only visible to direct counterparties and/or third parties who have been explicitly granted rights to view. Prior to DAML, Hashed Health's design work was constrained to either "data sharing" use cases in which confidentiality is not essential or to overly-complicated transactional data models which attempt to preserve confidentiality on an otherwise open ledger. Privacy is an essential regulatory requirement in the healthcare industry. DAML's focus on confidentiality as an essential business requirement has given us a powerful tool to extend our design and DLT product development.

In 2014, as the financial services and other industry began to consider DLT technology, the scale limitations of open and even permissioned DLT platforms quickly became apparent. Supporting scales of only a few dozen to at most a few thousand transactions (ledger updates) per second, many DLT platforms are incapable of supporting the throughput requirements of enterprise workflows.

In healthcare, the needs don't often approach those of financial markets. In fact, there's an old saying that in healthcare, any process taking less than 30 days is "real-time." But as DLT solution designs move from proof-of-concept to production, the problem of scalability is becoming acute. In 2018, Hashed Health has begun work on a number of solutions which require scales beyond the abilities of many DLT platforms. In DAML, we have found a reliable DLT platform that can accommodate the transactional scales exceeding 10,000 transactions per second. This radical scalability has allowed us to begin designs to address the core payment infrastructure in healthcare including fee-for-service claims processing, risk-based payment contracts, and other health plan and pharmaceutical financial workflows.

DAML has been the choice of a few healthcare contracting use cases in 2018.

In spring of 2018, Hashed Health participated in the developer preview program for the Digital Asset Modeling Language (DAML) SDK and the Digital Asset DLT platform. Soon after, DAML served as the foundation for Hashed Health's healthcare contracting platform, Signal Stream.

Signal Stream enables clients to automate multi-party agreements and create an outcomes-based contract adjudication and management platform. This shared performance view is real-time and synchronized through a distributed ledger contractual engine. Addressable areas of healthcare include value- or risk-based contracts, procurement contracting, pharmaceutical rebates and outcomes-based payments and health plan administration. For Hashed Health, DAML seemed like the right platform choice to help reduce the administrative burden related to value-based contract automation and begin to innovate in terms of contract, source systems and counterparty actor design.

Corda

Like DAML, R3's Corda platform pushes the boundary of what a blockchain or, more specifically, what a Distributed Ledger is. The structure for Corda correlates ledger entries without sharing a universal truth. The focus is to converge on a common system of record between companies who share a business or value exchange process.

The open-sourced "community" version of Corda is available for anyone to use or modify. In addition, Corda Enterprise is available through a licensing agreement with R3. Unlike DAML, Corda markets itself as a blockchain even though it does not seem to fit the fully decentralized definition we typically attach to open, public, decentralized protocols.

An example of a healthcare blockchain application on Corda is HSBlox, announced in summer 2018. HSBlox intends to use smart contracts for a wide variety of multi-party transactions, from patient referrals to bundled payment programs. Perhaps more importantly, the HSBlox announcement signals that R3, the first consortium in the financial services space, is entering the healthcare arena. They intend to begin recruiting healthcare payers, hospitals, physician providers, and patients to their Corda platform. [14]

Quorum

Quorum is an enterprise-focused fork of the Ethereum blockchain created at JP Morgan. The protocol has been tuned for high speed, high throughput transactions where transaction privacy is maintained amongst a permissioned network of actors. Like DAML and Corda, Qurorum was designed for the financial services industry and is now looking to expand in to healthcare. What primarily differentiates Quorum from Hyperledger, DAML and Corda is Quorum's close tie-ins to the Ethereum blockchain.

Quorum was chosen by the Synaptic Health Alliance as the protocol for is provider demographic data sharing use case, announced in 2018. The Synaptic project and their affinity for Quorum as a protocol for provider demographic data sharing is described elsewhere in this book.

Business Patterns

While the protocols covered in this section are among the most proven, there are other protocols becoming available that are purpose-built to solve specific technical, business, and governance problems. As protocols mature, we expect to move up the spectrum from distributed towards open and decentralized.

Meanwhile, exciting new business and technical patterns are emerging that help us imagine how we can solve old problems in new ways in the near future.

NFTs

Cryptokitties are breedable, collectible, unique digital cats. These crypto-collectibles were the first of the non-fungible token applications, made possible by a relatively new Ethereum token standard call ERC 721. ERC 721 represents unique digital assets. This standard defines how these digital assets interact with smart contracts. Ownership of these digital collectibles is tracked on the blockchain.

https://www.cryptokitties.co/

NFTs are different from your standard ERC20 cryptotoken, the standard for fungible tokens. Eth and every other commonly known token before Cryptokitties is fungible. With a fungible token like BTC or ETH, each digital asset is the same. Two people with two ETH can swap equal amounts without gain or loss. In addition, any amount is divisible into greater or lesser amounts. Non-fungible tokens, on the other hand, are non-divisible and unique.

An example of a healthcare use case that leverages NFTs is Hashed Health's Bramble project.

NFTs in Practice: Bramble

Hashed Health's Bramble seeks to introduce an innovative, rational market structure powered by a decentralized transactional platform for the buying and selling of healthcare services. Bramble's core belief system is in a market centered on competition, choice, and value. The platform's core element is the conversion of a unit of healthcare services into a unique, non-fungible, transferable digital healthcare asset which can be offered for sale on a prepaid or other basis through a decentralized marketplace. Consumers who purchase digital healthcare assets will redeem them at the point of service. This simple core transaction liberates healthcare providers from unnatural market frameworks and inefficient revenue cycle systems. Feedback loops from buyers and sellers reinforce reputation and enable smart shopping. For the first time, consumers can make purchasing decisions based on price, competition, choice, and value. Providers can sell products directly to consumers at prices based on value and reputation. The Bramble platform is specifically designed to solve the current global problem of flawed systems for buying and selling healthcare services.

Bramble represents discrete and combinable healthcare service offerings via a non-fungible token (NFT) created by healthcare delivery professionals or organizations and enabled to be offered directly to the buyer or the consumer.

By placing the ultimate settlement system outside of the control of any of the transacting parties, we can ensure an independence of the overall infrastructure to serve the needs of buying and selling communities.

The Bramble engineering team and others in the Ethereum community have been actively working to innovate around how NFTs operate. For this use case, we have adapted NFTs in several ways to meet the complexities of the healthcare environment and our belief in a rational market. NFTs can be time-bound. They can expire. They can have multiple owners. They can be rented. They can be time-sliced. They can be schedule-able. You can have rival tokens, meaning there can only be one at any given time owned by one person. Or multiple people can own one at a time. This allows Bramble to allow providers to create very flexible service offerings with a variety of descriptions, terms and conditions, and pricing characteristics. Not only do they meet the needs of today's world, but they also allow providers to innovate in terms of product, service, pricing characteristics and benefit design models. Services can be priced one way on Tuesday and another way on Saturday evening. Services and products can be sold individually or in bulk. Services can be standard shoppable healthcare services, like an MRI, or creative new services like six months of diabetes care. Services can be pre-paid or can adopt a programmable value transfer paradigm (aka Signal Stream). Bramble supports bids, asks, and bounties. Bramble allows buyers and sellers to organize, buy, and sell in brand new ways. In doing so, it enables a new kind of buyer and seller activism that is in line with where the market is headed.

It is the non-fungible token that allows for Hashed Health to innovate around the unique digital products and services of the future.

Token Curated Registries & Community Curated Datasets

Healthcare is full of lists. List of doctors, lists of patients, lists of implanted devices, lists of clinical trial participants, lists of orders, and many others. Hospitals and their business partners have buildings full of people who are using and curating lists. If you know these people, you know that the majority of them like to complain about their lists. They complain about their lists because the lists they use are inaccurate, out of date, or out of order. The errors in these lists plague our healthcare value chains and are a driver of significant costs.

Centralized lists suffer from many of the problems inherent to healthcare as a whole. These problems are the root of the administrative burdens that plague our industry. The problems include issues of trust, transparency, and alignment of incentives. Some actors use lists as a weapon to gain advantage over a trading partner. In the current world, you are forced to trust that the owner of the centralized list is acting in good faith.

By moving these resources out of the silo, you have the potential to move the cost of curation from the enterprise to the community while also potentially creating new value streams for curation. Early stakers on high quality data assets have the potential to do well financially while reducing the costs related to inaccurate, incomplete files.

Community Curated Datasets, also known as Token Curated Registries (TCRs), are a possible solution to the problem of centralized lists in healthcare.

By moving the curation of the dataset from a centralized operator to an incentivized community, we introduce a new technical and business solution to the old problem of managing lists.

In this model, community members hold token, and the value of that token is reflected in the quality of the list. Therefore, it can be assumed that community members are incentivized to maintain an accurate, high quality list while attracting new, high quality data providers and curators.

The basic mechanism is:

- Community participants make a list available to other community members along with a financial stake on the list.

- Community participants can challenge a list or items on the list by staking against that data and forcing a vote.

- Community participants can vote to add or remove data that has been challenged.

- If the challenge passes, the stake serves as a reward to the challengers and voters.

The thought-leaders in the TCR / TCM space include Mike Goldin, Simon de la Rouviere, Ryan Selkis, and Nick Dodson. The leading companies outside healthcare include AdChain (advertising), Delphi (arbitrators), Messari (ICOs), Ocean (AI) and DIRT Protocol (multi-purpose).

In the healthcare space, very few TCR strategies have been announced. One of the first was a small ICO startup in 2017 called MedCredits. MedCredits has announced they will use a TCR mechanism to curate physician lists as key infrastructure for their teledermatology market. This model assumes that physicians will want to "seek entry to the physician registry in order to be granted the privileges of being a physician in the ecosystem including access to patient data." To participate, physicians would purchase the MEDX token in order to stake their application, which would also include images of their licenses and other credentials. Community members would have an opportunity to challenge an applicant with successful challengers and voters receiving the stake of a failed application. Whether physicians will be comfortable with this model, especially after the 2018 token crash, is still to be determined. It will likely take quite some time for the market to adjust to this concept.

Hashed Health chose not to use a TCR in the current implementation of ProCredEx (provider credentialing) because of the belief that, in this use case, we need to meet the market where it is in terms of readiness to solve the credentialing problem. This effort to solve a real problem for real companies in today's world was a driver of a different technical and business model decisions for the team as the project began.

Instead, Hashed Health has chosen to explore TCR and TCR-related strategies in a few different use cases where the design pattern could provide a meaningful new solution to an old problem in master data management. Hashed Health and its partners are currently experimenting with TCRs in a variety of master data management initiatives that are scheduled to be announced in mid-2019. These projects generally explore taking silo'd, enterprise-curated datasets and transforming them in to community-curated datasets. The value of this community curation model is to reduce the cost and effort of managing this information enterprise-by-enterprise while enabling expert curators (individuals or groups) to receive value for market curation efforts.

In early 2019 it is clear that TCRs are not ready for prime-time, but are a design pattern worth watching because of its promise to move the curation of a silo'd data structure to a better, faster, and overall cheaper community utility.

Marketplace Models

Many of the early business models in healthcare adopt a marketplace construct. For example, both Procredex and Bramble, two of the early use cases in 2018, have a marketplace business model construct. In Procredex, the digital asset being traded on the exchange is a verified artifact proving a physician's identity. Enterprises (health systems, health plans, and others) who have this information can make those artifacts available through the data market to those who need it.

With Bramble, the digital asset traded on the exchange is a non-fungible token that represents a unique service or product being made available by a seller with pricing and all required terms and conditions for redemption. That digital asset can be used for traditional products and services (for example, shoppable health services) or entirely new services (for example, six months of diabetes care). The marketplace also allows for innovation in terms of how the buy side and the sell side of the market are organized. This model allows Bramble to create a competitive, rational market for the buying and selling of services without the need for any intermediaries.

Many see opportunity for a similar data market for medical records information or genomics data. A data market that allows patients to open and close the door to their medical record data could represent an incentive model that encourages adoption. Consumer adoption has always been one of the fatal shortcomings of consumer-focused health records initiatives of the past.

Medical Records Innovation

There have been many efforts to improve medical records interoperability, and some of these programs have demonstrated meaningful results. For example, recent studies indicate that Health Information Exchanges (HIE) improve the efficiency, cost-effectiveness, quality, and safety of health care delivery. [15]

The Health Insurance Portability and Accountability Act (HIPAA) makes it clear that patients have a right to their medical record data. Specifically, the Privacy Rule insists that covered entities provide access to data when requested.

Pre-blockchain initiatives such as OpenNotes have attempted to make the process of sharing information easier. The OpenNotes 2010 demonstration project included 105 physicians and 20,000 patients. A subsequent study of the initiative found that 99% of patients said they wanted to continue using the systems and not a single doctor turned off access. In addition, 75% reported improved retention of care plan information and improved control of their care, while two thirds of patients reported improved adherence to pharmaceutical protocols. [16]

In 2018, Apple introduced a series of initiatives to tackle medical record data sharing. First they released an update to their Health app that allows an individual to receive medical record information from participating providers. Later in the year, Apple announced the Apple Health Records API, which enables an ecosystem of application developers to use data in iOS products. This product "may put pressure on health care systems – in the form of 80 million US iPhone users – to increasingly allow patient access to data." [17] Apple has also signed an agreement to work with the Department of Veterans Affairs to give medical records access to veterans with iPhones.

Since then, you've seen other technology companies such as Google and Amazon getting into the medical records mix. At a White House event in August of 2018, Amazon, Google, IBM, Microsoft, Oracle, and Salesforce came together around a pledge to reduce barriers to interoperability. [18]

The standards community seems to also be positioned for a breakthrough as they advance the HL7 FHIR Argonaut Project, which maps data fields to a standard format. [19]

Meanwhile, EHR vendors see an opportunity to leverage their position to grow. Epic's release of Orchard and Cerner's release of the App Gallery both represent new marketplaces for applications similar to the App Store and the Play Store. According to a 2018 article in NEJM Catalyst by William Gordon, Aneesh Copra, and Adam Landman, "these new marketplaces will need close, multi-stakeholder input to ensure revenue incentives do not lead to stifled innovation and information blocking." [20]

Amazon became more active in late 2018 as well. In November 2018, Amazon announced plans to sell software that reads medical records and make suggestions for improving value. Also in November, Amazon announced their "serverless" Amazon Quantum Ledger Database, "a fully managed ledger database that provides a transparent, immutable, and cryptographically verifiable log owned by a trusted authority." [21] The strategic choice of Nashville, TN for it's new operations hub may also have to do with Nashville's reputation as a healthcare hub and Amazon's strategy in healthcare. [22]

Self-Sovereign Medical Identity

As Amazon and others innovate with distributed ledgers that have elements of centralization that seem well-suited for today's world a self-sovereign identity movement is.emerging that assumes a more decentralized stance.

Self-sovereign identity is the idea that an individual's identity should be fully controlled and maintained by that individual, instead of by the HIE or the enterprise. In today's world, companies store large amounts of identity information in centralized databases. These centralized data structures are used for commercial benefit of the companies that hold them and are prone to theft.

Rather than storing large honey-pots of identity information in centralized databases, promoters of self-sovereign identity concepts advocate for personally-controlled data that is more secure and can be controlled and, when appropriate, monetized by the individual. It is assumed that by empowering patients to control their own data, it would improve interoperability while improving the patient's experience across disparate providers.

It's no surprise that interest in self-sovereign identity has grown as trust in enterprises to appropriately use and protect this data has declined. Breaches of large data sets are common. In 2016 alone, over 450 data breaches affected over 27.3 million patient records. [23] The behaviors and data policies used by many of today's incumbents and startups have set the stage for these emerging self-sovereign medical identity initiatives.

If innovators could give the consumer the ability to open and close the door to their medical identity, then consumers could theoretically establish control over their information and use it as they wish. Patients could use a QR code, much like they do a Coinbase bitcoin wallet, to provide and stop access to medical professionals as needed. Physicians who are looking to be credentialed at a facility could release that information selectively as needed in order to more efficiently and effectively treat patients and be paid for treatment. Consumers, not companies, could choose to monetize their data on a data market or donate it to clinical trials as they wish. This will take years to come to fruition, but when it does it may be the incentive for consumers to adopt longitudinal health records in mass.

GDPR

The General Data Protection Regulation (GDPR) is a broad and strict legal framework in the European Union designed to protect personal data privacy. First proposed in 2012, it became effective on May 25, 2018 and transformed the business and technical models of many digital companies.

Key GDPR regulations include:[24]

- Individuals have "right of access" under which enterprises must explain what data is being used and how to request information related to use.

- Individuals have the "right to be forgotten" which forces enterprises to delete personal information upon request.

- Individuals have the "right to portability" so they may move data between companies upon request.

- Companies must implement data protection measures and perform "data protection impact assessments" that explain risks and describe how those risks are handled.

GDPR's reach extends beyond the EU. Anyone doing business with EU citizens are in range of GDPR's rules and penalties.

Blockchain and GDPR align from a "privacy by design" philosophical perspective. Both assume the rightful owner of personal data is the person, so both encourage the return of control of one's digital identity to the consumer.

However, once you move past philosophy, it is clear that GDPR and blockchain concepts of self-sovereign identity are currently at odds. For example, the "right to be forgotten" does not align with immutability. Decentralization challenges the concept of "data processors." And a wide distribution of nodes by definition means extending the network beyond European Union borders.

New innovations may bring blockchain and GDPR closer together, but much work remains and only time will tell if and how these two concepts will co-exist.

References

1. Bradbury, Danny (14 June 2013). "Colored coins paint sophisticated future for Bitcoin".

2. https://www.coindesk.com/blockchain-startup-coinprism-to-shut-down-in-2-days

3. https://www.coindesk.com/blockchain-startup-coinprism-to-shut-down-in-2-days

4. https://bitcoin.org/bitcoin.pdf

5. https://gavwood.com/paper.pdf

6. https://medium.com/@VitalikButerin/a-proof-of-stake-design-philosophy-506585978d51

7. https://cointelegraph.com/news/combined-crypto-market-capitalization-races-past-800-bln

8. https://epicenter.tv/episode/262/

9. https://www.changehealthcare.com/press-room/press-releases/detail/change-healthcare-announces-general-availability-of-first-enterprise-scale-blockchain-solution-for-healthcare

10. https://www.healthcareitnews.com/news/pokitdok-gains-healthcare-traction-hyperledger-sawtooth-intel-collaboration

11. https://www.hyperledger.org/announcements/2018/01/30/hyperledger-releases-hyperledger-sawtooth-1-0

12. https://hub.digitalasset.com/blog/introducing-the-digital-asset-modeling-language-a-powerful-alternative-to-smart-contracts-for-financial-institutions

13. https://www.forbes.com/sites/michaeldelcastillo/2018/08/15/asx-details-23b-opportunity-behind-upgrade-to-tech-inspired-by-bitcoin/#6868d46f7a37

14. https://www.r3.com/news/r3-teams-up-with-hsblox-to-launch-the-corda-healthcare-community/

15. https://medinform.jmir.org/2015/4/e39/

16. https://catalyst.nejm.org/opennotes-knowing-change-health-care/

17. https://catalyst.nejm.org/patient-led-health-data-paradigm/?utm_campaign=Connect%20Weekly&utm_source=hs_email&utm_medium=email&utm_content=67862611&_hsenc=p2ANqtz-9ZryNTF6GzBLnX8rhquvqWb5C0qig_g1g7KbFUygtEGNRDH_wiT_3WBzox2n2I61lD-BPDUbQiAWMj0PTp1GRL5M48CA&_hsmi=67862611

18. https://www.wsj.com/articles/amazon-starts-selling-software-to-mine-patient-health-records-1543352136

19. https://www.hl7.org/documentcenter/public_temp_9908C80A-1C23-BA17-0C44729319265E89/pressreleases/HL7_PRESS_20180227.pdf

20. https://catalyst.nejm.org/patient-led-health-data-paradigm/?utm_campaign=Connect%20Weekly&utm_source=hs_email&utm_medium=email&utm_content=67862611&_hsenc=p2ANqtz-9ZryNTF6GzBLnX8rhquvqWb5C0qig_g1g7KbFUygtEGNRDH_wiT_3WBzox2n2I61lD-BPDUbQiAWMj0PTp1GRL5M48CA&_hsmi=67862611

21. https://aws.amazon.com/qldb/

22. https://www.tennessean.com/story/news/2018/11/16/amazon-nashville-yards-gov-bill-haslam-mayor-david-briley/2006460002/

23. https://www.healthcare-informatics.com/news-item/cybersecurity/2017-breach-report-477-breaches-56m-patient-records-affected

24. https://cointelegraph.com/news/gdpr-and-blockchain-is-the-new-eu-data-protection-regulation-a-threat-or-an-incentive

Chapter 4:
Communities & Consortia

John Bass

Sofia Shirley

Editor's Note:

In this chapter, John and Sofia Shirley delve into some of the earliest communities and consortia beginning with R3, Hyperledger, Hashed Health, Enterprise Ethereum Alliance and discussion of where these early consortia may lead us in the future.

Why Is Community So Important in Blockchain?

These are still early days in the blockchain space. We are still very much in market-development mode, so one primary reason for community-building is to educate, ideate, and otherwise organize and support blockchain project development efforts from both a technical and a non-technical perspective.

Blockchain necessitates collaboration; without it, the technology doesn't add much value beyond a traditional database. Consortia and community-building have provided a way for interested contributors to join forces, set standards, align incentives, and establish required infrastructure for future use.

Consortia are generally groups of companies coming together around industry-specific business-to-business solutions. These players are often competitors in the traditional sense. Companies join blockchain consortia for a variety of reasons: they may want to remain up-to-date on the emerging technology, they may want to hear from industry peers, or they may just not want to be left behind. However, there is one reason that underpins the need for all blockchain consortia: ultimately, blockchain can only be as effective as the network of organizations or people behind it. Without the network, any blockchain effort is just an expensive academic exercise. Blockchain networks take on the belief systems of these members. The founders decide the rules that will dictate where value accrues on the network, what specific problems are solved, and how governance will work. By influencing these rules, companies put themselves in position to plan new services along the on and off ramps for these new market constructs.

Consumer-focused and decentralization-focused Initial Coin Offerings (ICOs) focus more specifically on community building efforts around token sales through the development of a community of network contributors. For these projects, community-building is a key activity because the community represents important financial, technical, and social contributors to the project. They are key to growth and the promise of network effects of the token economics model. In 2017, those companies who executed a token sale to consumers and investors realized that community-building was as important as the technical architecture and the go-to-market strategy. Without wide distribution of the token, it was hard for them to argue they were truly decentralized.

History of Consortia in Enterprise Blockchain

R3: A Financial Services Consortia Leader

Enterprise blockchain software firm R3 paved the way for industry-specific blockchain consortia. R3 began a blockchain consortium on September 15, 2015, led by its CEO David Rutter. The initial partnership included nine prominent banks such as Barclays and Goldman Sachs. [1] Rutter's insider connections with the leaders of these companies was a key driver of his success.

Once the initial group was publicly on board, the "fear of missing out" that was created by R3 and the important first few members in September 2015 is remarkable. After just two weeks, 13 more financial partners joined. By the end of the year, banking institutions from around the world were showing up at R3's headquarters wanting in.

"We have placed an emphasis on working with the market from day one, and our partners recognize that a collaborative model is the best way to quickly, efficiently and cost-effectively deliver these new technologies to global financial markets," Rutter said to Bitcoin Magazine at that time. [2]

The R3 Series A funding included over forty investors and raised $107M from investors such as HSBC, Temasek, Bank of America, Merill Lynch, Wells Fargo, UBS, Barclays, and others. [3] Despite a few high-profile exits in the years since, the R3 consortium now includes over 200 members.

"We recognize that a platform's strength comes from a flourishing ecosystem of partners: developers, support providers, application builders, systems integrators, independent software vendors and various other participants," R3 states on their website. [4]

It didn't take long for R3 to move from convener to protocol developer. By 2016, the company was hard at work on their Corda platform. The move from consortium to protocol provider and the expansion from financial services to insurance, healthcare, and other industries is still unfolding. Despite a few high-profile exits in the years since, the R3 consortium now includes over 200 members.

"We recognize that a platform's strength comes from a flourishing ecosystem of partners: developers, support providers, application builders, systems integrators, independent software vendors and various other participants," R3 states on their website.

Hyperledger: The Open Source Consortia Leader

About three months after the initial announcement of the R3 consortium, the Linux foundation established the Hyperledger consortium.

Hyperledger plays an important role in creating the open source infrastructure under which organizations can develop meaningful solutions. Through the consortium, companies can collaborate on common building blocks, pooling together their resources rather than wasting time all solving the same problems individually. Their primary audience are entities interested in contributing code to Hyperledger's growing family of open source protocols.

Digital Assets donated the Hyperledger brand and the initial code that kicked off the effort. Its thirty founding members have now grown into 259 from across the business space. JP Morgan, Intel, and AMEX are just three of Hyperledger's eighteen Premier members.

"The Linux Foundation has achieved an unbelievable feat in bringing together a community of traditionally competitive institutions. To facilitate such extensive collaboration between startups, financial and non financial corporations and technology giants is an enormous win for the whole distributed ledger industry as firms look to leverage mutually beneficial code for the common good," said Blythe Masters, CEO of Digital Asset, as quoted on the The Linux Foundation website. [5]

Membership in the Hyperledger consortium has also reached over 200, which a rapid growth rate that doubled membership over the past year. Members can be found across the globe in North America, Europe, the Middle East, and Asia Pacific, and concentrated in China, which contributes over 25% of the members.

"We grew pretty quickly in 2016-2017. We had 288 members at last count – most of these are companies, but a few include nonprofits, central banks, and government agencies, and we're really happy at the diversity of that crowd," said Brian Behlendorf, Executive Director of the Hyperledger Project, in a November 2018 Epicenter podcast. [6]

As it has grown, the number of open source projects under the Hyperledger flag has also grown. In 2016, Hyperledger was primarily a Fabric shop and, at the time, Fabric was very much aligned with IBM. Since then, Behendorf has worked hard to diversify the core contributors in Fabric and a number of new protocols including Sawtooth, Indy, Burrow, and others.

The Hyperledger Health Care Working Group was formed in 2016 after a conversation between Brian Behlendorf, Micah Winkelspecht of Gem, John Bass of Hashed Health, and David Bailey of BTC Media.

"It's always been a part of the vision of the Hyperledger project that we're building foundational technologies for blockchain that are never necessarily tied to financial use cases. This is as foundational as an operating system, a database, a programming language," Behlendorf said in regards to Hyperledger beginning this specifically healthcare-focused working group. [7]

Hyperledger's core purpose is open source contributions. Typically the companies participating in the consortium are there because the developers at that organization are interested in contributing to and building upon one or more of the Hyperledger protocols. That remains the core purpose, although Hyperledger has also seen a growing segment of its audience engaging in use case ideation and collaboration in its discussion forums.

Hashed Health- The Healthcare Blockchain Market Developer

Hashed Health is often recognized as the first "consortium" to form in the healthcare space, although the firm has never really been comfortable with being branded a "consortium." For Hashed Health, the community-building efforts were more about market development than open source code contributions.

Hashed Health was founded in 2016 with the intention of developing solutions to problems in the healthcare space using blockchain and distributed ledger technologies. However, at that time there was no market in healthcare for these products. The early team had a number of use cases in queue, but it was not clear which products, protocols, and networks would mature the fastest. So Hashed started by building communities around specific use cases and gaining insights in to who was ready to adopt, and which protocols were ready to solve real problems.

The process of healthcare blockchain community-building started informally with the Nashville Blockchain Meetup, which quickly grew from a few members to over 1000 people. What started as a meetup then turned in to the Distributed:Health Conference led by Nashville's BTC Media. The 2016 conference was the first healthcare blockchain conference in the world and drew over 300 attendees.

Distributed:Health became the launchpad for Hashed Health and has since become the premier event for many other companies and healthcare blockchain products announcements. It was at this conference that Kaiser Permanente, IBM, Accenture, Gem, and Hashed Health kicked off the Hyperledger Health Care Working Group. Since then, Change Healthcare and a variety of other healthcare and technology vendors have used the Distributed:Health stage to announce their initiatives. [7]

After its early successes in 2016, Hashed moved quickly to expand its community building efforts, dubbed "Collective," to focus on global community building. Within a year, Hashed Health was organizing and participating in community events across the United States as well as in London, Dubai, Shanghai, Tel Aviv, Toronto, Melbourne, and Tokyo. An online community of over 1000 people have come together on the company's online forum to discuss use cases, protocols, events, and other industry news.

In 2017, Hashed Health continued to mature its services and product development efforts which provided Hashed Health with the ability to build a number of Proof-of-Concepts while providing the firm with a front-row seat in understanding the emerging market and product-network fit. Instead of moving to the protocol as R3 had done, Hashed focused on launching a portfolio of healthcare-specific solutions with baked-in network partners on existing protocol platforms.

Over time, as the market matured, Hashed Health increasingly focused on organizing the market around specific product initiatives rather than one large "consortium" group. An example of a product-specific consortium is the Procredex initiative. This team of companies which includes large US-based health insurance companies and regional health systems announced they would organized around an industry utility model for solving issues related to the credentialing of physicians. [8]

Other Consortia

Over forty consortia have been launched to organize blockchain enterprises around a wide variety of use cases in financial services, insurance, healthcare, and many other areas. [9]

As the business-to-business market matured (and as the ICO market crashed), the market more openly embraced enterprise-focused activities. More consortia and organizations of businesses began to align, mostly outside of healthcare. Two well-known non-healthcare analogues include the Enterprise Ethereum Alliance and MOBI.

The Enterprise Ethereum Alliance, founded in 2017, began with 30 members and has grown to over 500 in the following 18 months. Its goal is to be the standards body that facilitates the adoption of Ethereum for enterprise use. In October 2018, EEA announced a collaboration with Hyperledger to further combine forces. The alliance allows developers on Hyperledger to comply with EEA certifications to ensure compatibility.

MOBI, on the other hand, is devoted specifically to the mobility industry. As such, it is significantly smaller than the EEA but has nonetheless managed to capture over 80% of global auto-manufacturing by volume through its members. Members range from key automakers such as Ford and BMV, key blockchain players such as IBM and ConsenSys, and academic institutions and NGOs as well.

"The future of blockchain innovation will be led by consortia and similar open-innovation working groups. This is a different model that is unnatural to many: Competitors, suppliers, regulators, government agencies, and other consortia themselves will all convene around the same table," wrote Ashley Lannquist, Co-Founder of MOBI, on the Blockchain Unleashed: IBM Blockchain blog. [11]

In the healthcare space, communities continue to align around project-specific and company-specific initiatives. For example, Lisa Maki and Ted Tanner at Pokitdok created the Dokchain Alliance, which included a variety of healthcare industry players who came together in 2017 to ideate around Pokitdok's existing API and thought-leading blockchain integration strategies.

Meanwhile, the Synpatic Alliance formed around the idea of esablishing a shared data structure for provider demographic data. These efforts were primarily led by Mike Jacobs at Optum and Kyle Culver at Humana.The Center for Supply Chain Studies is another loose consortium of healthcare companies who are focused on track and trace for pharmaceuticals use case.

In 2019, we expect to see new alliances between companies forming in supply chain, payments, and other areas of healthcare. The successful consortia seem to be those where there already exists a viable use case with a technical foundation, an innovative business model, and an open governance policy at the center. Those consortia who can prove they are successful at an initial effort should be able to grow their value and their constituency. Growing a consortia requires proof that there is real work going on with value being created for those involved. In 2019, companies are more interested in doing than talking.

2019 Will Be The Year of Governance

2016 and 2017 were all about community building and initial enterprise engagement in healthcare. 2018 saw the first true product efforts start to mature. As those products look to commercialize, 2019 looks to be the "year of governance."

Governance is the last mile in standing up meaningful solutions in the blockchain and distributed ledger space. As energy and investment continues to swing towards the near-term business-to-business infrastructure projects, broad and solutions-focused consortia will play an important role in organizing the leading adopters of distributed ledger solutions and doing the hard work of defining the governance structures that make projects come alive.

Interest in working groups and consortia will evolve as projects prove themselves and value is demonstrated. However, we also expect many well-intentioned and well-architected projects to experience non-technical failures as a result of the complexities of governance. Issues such as value-accrual will certainly be a challenge to many projects which have otherwise solid technical and business models. At the end of the day, good projects must act like good businesses. To be successful, all projects must bring together partners and competitors in shared-value networks. Collaborative models do not come naturally in healthcare. It requires leadership, industry know-how, and a new way of thinking. These collaborative business and governance models are the future, but getting there could take time and learning from failure. Participating with your peers in a workgroup offers an easy way to stay abreast of these activities and lessons learned.

References

1. https://www.reuters.com/article/us-banks-blockchain/nine-of-worlds-biggest-banks-join-to-form-blockchain-partnership-idUSKCN0RF24M20150915

2. https://bitcoinmagazine.com/articles/r-blockchain-development-initiative-grows-to-banks-worldwide-1443553081/:14

3. https://www.r3.com/news/r3-secures-largest-ever-investment-for-distributed-ledger-technology-with-usd-107-million-from-over-40-institutions/

4. https://www.r3.com/ecosystem/

5. https://www.linuxfoundation.org/projects/case-studies/hyperledger/

6. https://epicenter.tv/episode/262/

7. https://www.coindesk.com/hyperledger-launches-blockchain-working-group-for-healthcare

8. https://hashedhealth.com/procredex-dpp-announcement/.

9. https://www2.deloitte.com/insights/us/en/focus/signals-for-strategists/emergence-of-blockchain-consortia.html#endnote-sup-2

10. https://www.ibm.com/blogs/blockchain/2018/06/introducing-mobi-the-mobility-open-blockchain-initiative/

Chapter 5:
Developing a Professional Credentials Exchange Leveraging Distributed Ledger Technology

Anthony D. Begando

https://hashedhealth.com/blockchain-for-healthcare-book/

Editor's Note:

In this chapter, Anthony Begando describes the problems and challenges that blockchain may help solve in professional credentials related to medicine and healthcare. Specific practitioner data may be verified and validated across practitioner, payers and provider networks. And lead to multiple sources of trust and new distributed ledger technology like professional credential exchange that can meet current market challenges and provide technical expansion into the future. To add further realism and a concrete example, Anthony closes with a user-story, credentialing a fictitious doctor and walks through the stages of blockchain for healthcare credentials.

Overview

The Professional Credentials Exchange (ProCredEx) is being developed to create a disruptive and transformative solution addressing the historic challenges facing healthcare practitioner credentialing. Credentialing is a mandated process utilized throughout the industry to confirm a practitioner's identity and to ensure that person can competently deliver patient care within a specific clinical setting (e.g., hospital, outpatient clinic, telehealth provider) . Within the private sector, practitioners (e.g., MDs, PAs, advanced practice nurses) must also be credentialed by every payer contracted for reimbursement by that organization. Malpractice insurers, licensing and certification boards, volunteer organizations, the military, and CMS/Medicaid all require various forms credentialing as well. This often results in practitioners forming and maintaining redundant credentials datasets with 12 to 25+ independent entities.

The process for initially completing credentialing for a newly hired/contracted practitioner often takes four to six months from recruitment, appointment, and completion of payer enrollment. In many cases, the process can extend to over a year if a practitioner is moving across state lines and requires supplemental licensing. Practitioners cannot deliver or bill for services until this work is completed (with a few exceptions from CMS and State Medicaid organizations allowing for retroactive billing). Credentialing must be re-performed every two years for care delivery organizations and every three years for payers. In the interim, all expirable credentials (e.g., licenses, board certifications, DEA clearances) must be tracked and confirmed to be active and unlimited. Finally, healthcare organizations should be actively monitoring numerous sanctions issuing authorities (e.g., OIG, licensing boards, etc.) regularly to monitor compliance with all members of their clinical staff. Delays, inefficiencies, miscommunications, and errors in these processes directly impact recruitment, revenue cycle, cost, quality of care, and retention.

ProCredEx is addressing these challenges by creating a market for exchanging verified credentials data by and between market counterparties across all facets of the healthcare industry.

A Survey of Common Credentialing Practices

Healthcare Delivery Organizations

Healthcare organizations utilize similar practitioner data and artifacts to fulfill their specific internal credentialing requirements. In the case of healthcare delivery organizations (e.g., health systems, delivery networks, outpatient specialty clinics, telehealth providers, long term care facilities), credentialing normally begins within the recruitment activity following the determination by an organization that a specific practitioner meets their high-level clinical and professional criteria and is sought for appointment to the clinical staff. An organization typically will run queries from the National Practitioner Data Bank (NPDB), Drug Enforcement Agency (DEA), Office of Inspector General (OIG), and order a criminal background check to identify any anomalies or "red flags" that would immediately raise concerns regarding further engagement. Thereafter, practitioners are required to complete an Application for Appointment, Request for Privileges, and several other initial onboarding forms, their current curriculum vitae (CV), and all required credential artifacts. These artifacts often include:

- Personal Identification (NPIs, Driver's License, Passport, State Medical ID Cards)
- Current Photograph
- Educational Transcripts & Post-graduate Medical Education Program Certifications
- Board Certifications (Current & Expired)
- Professional Licenses (Current & Expired)
- DEA & CDS Licenses (Current & Expired)
- Foreign Medical Graduate Certification (ECFMG)
- Employment History
- Employment Gap Narratives
- Delineations of Privileges & Procedure Counts
- Scope of Practice (Non-Physician Providers)
- Affiliation History
- Professional References
- Clinical Certifications & CMEs
- Occupational Training Certificates
- Malpractice Insurance Coverage History
- Malpractice Settlement & Claims History
- Adverse Actions & Narratives
- Practice Information (Affiliations & Locations)
- Immunization History
- Personal Health History

Upon delivery, the practitioner will coordinate with the credentialing professionals working within the Medical Staff Services Office or Credentialing Department throughout their initial credentialing episode to respond to questions, clarify discrepancies, and provide supplemental information.

The credentialing professionals performing the credentialing work itself decompose the practitioner's submitted forms, CV, and provided artifacts to develop an initial worklist of tasks necessary to verify clinical competency in accordance with the policies, procedures, and bylaws for that specific organization. This initial assessment seeks to confirm alignment with the specific clinical privileges sought by the practitioner and the specific devices, techniques, procedures, and competency guidelines established for each location requested privileges will be awarded. Thereafter, credentialing professionals complete defining their initial worklist and begin the laborious process of verifying, synthesizing, and analyzing this data.

Regulators and accreditors mandate that individual practitioner credential artifacts be confirmed through obtaining primary source verification (PSV) of that credential to ensure its authenticity and reliability. Sources include educational institutions, employers, licensing boards, training programs, specialty boards, government agencies, and the like. The paradigms surrounding PSV requirements and methodologies originated decades ago to mitigate the risks stemming from nefarious individuals manipulating or falsifying paper documents (e.g., medical licenses, educational transcripts, board certifications) submitted for credentialing. While many primary sources have automated verification utilities, most market constituents still utilize a largely manual process for performing verifications. For example, a common verification technique involves credentialing staff members navigating to a primary source's website, looking up the sought-after practitioner and credential, and then taking a print screen of that information and using that image as proof of the PSV. This method is also commonly used by credentialing software vendors utilizing keystroke emulators and "screen scraping" technologies to obtain these images.

Several common credential elements are also notoriously difficult to obtain and verify. This includes medical malpractice insurance cover sheets, malpractice claim/settlement data, employment histories, prior privilege delineations and procedure counts, practitioner narratives regarding past claims and/or adverse events, and peer references. Obtaining this data is often done through letters, emails, or faxes requesting verification which, in turn, are received in many of the aforementioned mediums. These types of verifications regularly take weeks or months to obtain—often requiring multiple follow-ups by credentialing staff members. In many cases, the delays in obtaining and verifying these elements stem from the sources themselve being inundated with numerous, often redundant, independent requests for this information.

Collectively, credentialing professionals work for several weeks or months to finish the artifact collection and verification process for every credentialing or recredentialing episode queued for completion. Many are working on scores of episodes concurrently. This work continues until all remaining artifacts are obtained and verified for each active episode. Thereafter, the newly created practitioner credentials file (PCF) is submitted for review by a senior credentialing staff member or manager. These individuals assess credential elements singularly and collectively to determine, in the aggregate, if the information meets an organization's specific clinical guidelines, business rules, and validation checks. When discrepancies or areas of concern are found, practitioner engagement, research, and investigations are performed to attempt resolution. Credentialing staff members continue this work until the PCF reaches a point where an initial competency determination can be made and readied for the approval process.

Decisions regarding practitioner credentialing and staff appointment are nearly universally tied to a multi-step series of reviews of collected and verified credentials information. The analysis itself is often a complex process performed by senior medical staff members. For healthcare delivery organizations, upon completion of the initial credentialing compilation and assessment process, the PCF is typically forwarded through a series of reviews initiated by the cognizant department head or supervisor, a peer-based credentials committee, an executive-level medical committee, and finally approved by an organization's Board of Directors for staff appointment and awarding of clinical privileges. Many of these committee reviews are set on a fixed schedule, naturally limiting the pace by which a PCF can proceed through the final review process. Upon completion of the approvals process, practitioners are formally appointed to the clinical staff and awarded privileges.

Thereafter, the credentials for appointed practitioners must be maintained by verifying expirable artifact renewals (e.g., occupational licenses, board certifications, DEA licenses), adding updated training, education, and occupational artifacts, practice and affiliation data, and any other material information that may impact a practitioner's status or competency.

Finally, healthcare delivery organizations are mandated to reperform credentialing for all members of their clinical staff every two years. The intent of biennial recredentialing is to ensure that organizations are actively reviewing the entirety of a practitioner's credential dataset to reconfirm competency and awarded privileges. While the methods used to perform this work vary across the industry, most healthcare delivery organizations require practitioners to reapply for staff appointment and privileges following much of the same processes used in their initial appointment. Given the degree and sophistication of the credentialing technology deployed within a specific setting, this process can vary from a complete resubmission of all required credentials information to electronically providing updates to their existing data and active credential artifacts through a credentialing system user portal. This information is, once again, reviewed and assessed by the medical staff services or credentialing department staff and then forwarded through same hierarchical approval processes used for initial credentialing.

Payer Enrollment & Credentialing Practices

Prior to being eligible for reimbursement for patient care delivery from healthcare insurers, Practitioners must enroll in the insurance contracts aligned with organizations for which they are employed, contracted, or affiliated. According to a study published by CAQH (CAQH, 2016), the average healthcare delivery organization maintains 12 independent payer contracts. Metropolitan health systems and large physician groups often maintain in excess of 25 contracts.

The payer enrollment process requires healthcare delivery organizations maintaining these contracts to take the practitioner data and verified credentials information collected during the credentialing process and repurpose it to complete the various forms and artifact requirements for each contracted payer, CMS/Medicare, state Medicaid agencies, and any other affiliated third party requiring this data. While CAQH offers a state-specific standard Application for insurers, the credentialing requirements, forms, and data submission methods for enrollment vary widely between payer organizations.

Following the submission of the required practitioner data by a delivery organization, payers then consume this information and route it though their own independent credentials verification and approval processes—repeating much of the same work that was performed by the organization seeking a practitioner's enrollment in the first place. The time required for payers to complete their own credentialing, approval, and contract enrollment processes can range from three weeks to over five months. In the interim, practitioners cannot bill for services for patients covered under those contracts unless specific rules exist for retroactive billings.

Per various accreditation standards, payers must recredential enrolled practitioners every three years. In the interim, they must also track changes to practitioner data and expirable credentials. In their unique case, payers rely upon timely and accurate changes to demographic, practice, and affiliation data for maintenance of their practitioner directory data. In a recent study by CMS (Center for Medicare Services, 2017), 52.2% of payer directories were found to have inaccurate data. Both CMS/Medicare and state Medicaid agencies have begun levying significant fines on payers for these errors as patients rely significantly on the accuracy of this data in selecting health plans that cover the practitioners which they are currently—or plan to be—seeing for their own healthcare needs.

Current State

The current state of credentialing practices across the healthcare industry can be summarized as being inefficient, burdensome, and wholly redundant. For example, if a practitioner maintains privileges at three hospitals, an outpatient clinic, a telemedicine delivery platform, and is enrolled with 18 payers, they are separately and continuously maintaining this information with 23 separate business partners. In the example cited above, it is likely that this practitioner is in some form of recredentialing episode almost every 60 days. Further, every update to their demographic, practice, or credentials information must be independently communicated to each business partner according to their own rules, requirements, and methods of communication.

Financially, the completion of credentialing and payer enrollment is essentially the initiation of revenue cycle activities. Simply stated, one cannot bill for services until these activities are complete. According to the Merritt Hawkins 2016 Inpatient/Outpatient Revenue Survey (Merritt Hawkins, 2017), the average daily net revenue for a hospital-based physician was approximately $7,500.00. Therefore, assuming that a physician bills, on average, 20 days each month, hospitals and health systems are forfeiting $150,000.00 per month while credentialing and enrollment activities are underway.

The redundancy inherent within credentialing and payer enrollment activities stems from a lack of trusted information being available to market constituents to easily obtain and rely on. While several organizations (e.g., AMA, FSMB, CAQH) provide offerings that consolidate some verified credentials information, their cost, reliability, and accuracy are often at issue by recipients.

From a technical perspective, most commercial credentialing systems have enforced the paradigm of organizational singularity and, other than reaching out to common on-line source websites or databases, provide little automation supporting electronically sharing credentialing artifacts between organizations. Further, these systems assume that the data required to complete a credentialing episode will be created and maintained through data entry by both the practitioner (via an online "Application") and the credentialing staff using business rules and validation checks unique to that organization. Therefore, requests from external organizations for credentialing data verifications are often fulfilled through artifacts physically delivered via mail, fax, or email. In all cases, the redundant and repetitive collection and verification of this data creates a substantial, industry-wide burden that must be addressed.

Market Factors

The economics of healthcare are changing rapidly. The transition to value-based care, the growth in practitioner employment, population health initiatives, and general market consolidation are indicative of this change. In the past, delays in credentialing were often overlooked as routine administrative annoyances within the staff appointment process. In today's healthcare market, the inherent inefficiencies in credentialing directly impact financial performance, operational capabilities, and quality of care.

Substantial growth in rapidly emerging markets such as telemedicine, outpatient care, specialty clinics, and direct-to-patient care are moving the perception of care delivery from being hospital-centric to a more collaborative and patient-centric landscape. Organizations seeking to participate in these delivery channels are often substantially challenged by the impedances inherent in current credentialing practices.

For example, a large metropolitan teaching hospital seeks to extend its neurology department's reach by adding a tele-stroke program to its offerings. It identifies and contracts with 30 rural critical access hospitals within a 150-mile radius to establish this capability. In order to fully activate this offering, all 12 neurologists participating in the program must be credentialed and appointed to each of the participating rural hospital's clinical staff. Completing all 360 credentialing episodes may take months or over a year to initially conclude with on-going expirables management and recredentialing continuing perpetually. When this reality arises, the parties seeking to create this program may become apathetic or simply frustrated by the degree of administrative support required to initiate remote services. This is a common reason why healthcare organizations struggle to execute successfully on these initiatives.

Over 13 million individuals across thousands of organizations in the U.S. healthcare market must be credentialed in accordance with the collective requirements of all parties involved in care delivery or reimbursement-- creating complex, interrelated data demands. Hundreds of millions of credentialing transactions take place annually. Failing to maintain current and accurate credentials with each and every facility, payer, network, ACO, and the like creates major implications that can be further complicated by geography, practice diversity, and specialty type.

The Opportunity

The emergence of distributed ledger technology (DLT) creates a substantial opportunity for developing an industry-wide solution for gathering and distributing credentials data across all market constituents. Using this technology, in concert with advanced data science and machine learning, a credentials exchange can be created to facilitate significant components of the process-- dramatically reducing the cost, complexity, risks, and time related to the dated practices driving this work today.

DLT provides individuals and organizations with a highly secure, immutable, and verifiable ledger that can collect and deliver credentials data by and between individuals, organizations, and primary sources across a highly efficient, decentralized distributed network. Through the use of smart contracts, individual organizations can specify precisely what information, artifacts, business rules, and validation checks it desires to meet its own unique credentialing requirements—regardless of the systems they use today. Collectively, these requests can be presented to practitioners for authorization, fulfillment, and attestation in a unified manner. Updates to credentials or practitioner data (e.g., license renewal, change of address, OIG sanctions) can be distributed synchronously, in real time, to ensure all authorized parties engaged with that practitioner are using current and accurate data. Further, as verified credential elements are considered work products and assets by many organizations, an exchange creates a commercial platform for trading and monetizing those digital assets between network members.

Finally, through working with regulators and accreditors, the requirements surrounding PSV activities can be transformed to accept credential verifications performed by exchange members—ultimately enabling the exchange itself to be considered a primary source and begin the process of eliminating redundant collection and verification of this information across the market.

Forming the Exchange

The exchange must evolve as a collaborative solution defined and governed, initially, by a consortium of industry leaders and then ultimately deployed as an industry-focused utility. This consortium is known as the ProCredEx Design Partner Program. The exchange must be viewed as a value-added resource—and not a competitor—to many in the marketplace today. As with all innovations, the exchange may displace some inefficient or dated offerings. However, if developed collaboratively, credentialing software vendors, most primary sources, and key data aggregators should look to aligning with and ensuring the success of the exchange as a distinct competitive advantage.

Technical Considerations

Due to the nature of the exchange itself, its core architecture will require several major components to support its function. Intrinsically, the exchange's technical architecture must be massively scalable, 100% cloud-based, HIPAA/HI-TECH compliant, multi-lingual/international, and deeply secure.

As with all large-scale technology endeavors, the exchange presents a number of key technical attributes and challenges that must be addressed:

- Data Complexity. Credentials data is inherently unstructured and non-standardized. Further, anything can be defined as a "credential" and required as data and/or artifacts within a credentialing episode. Therefore, the exchange data layer must support the "typing", processing, and storage of distinct, unique credential artifacts comprised of standardized data elements. We have developed the exchange data model using a hybrid database engine comprised of MongoDB (credentials data, business rules, and other unstructured data), AzureSQL (transaction processing), and a high-performance cache to meet this core requirement.

- Analytical Complexity. The contextual assessment of credentials information can and will vary between every organization assessing it. Hence, the exchange must allow for every member of the exchange to define and assess that data within the rules, validation checks, and requirements that are specific to their needs.

Further, the exchange will use machine learning technologies to predict risks and anomalies in the data spanning the platform.

- Industrial-level DLT Performance. As mentioned earlier, within the US healthcare market hundreds of millions of credential artifact verification transactions are executed annually. In a model our team developed in late 2017, we predicted that over 200 million credential verification transactions alone occur annually between health systems and payers for physicians and non-physician practitioners. As such, the DLT protocol supporting the ledgering of owned data assets, counterparty transactions, queries, and analyses being run against the exchange ledgers must perform at scale. The evolution of third generation DLT protocols over the past three years has been directed at purpose-built protocols that support permissioned exchange-level performance requirements (i.e., 50,000-100,000 transactions per second) versus the single- or double-digit performance limitations that exist within second generation protocols engineered to largely support cryptocurrency-oriented use cases.

- User Experience. All user facing applications within the exchange's suite of applications are developed in HTML-5 utilizing responsive design techniques for use on most devices. Further, all applications execute entirely within the cloud and utilize strong encryption and identity management functions for security. The exchange will come to market with three user facing applications targeted at the primary constituencies working within the exchange: Participants (i.e., Practitioners), Credentialing Authorities, and Primary Sources/Data Aggregators.

- Third-party Integration. The exchange utilizes RESTful APIs to allow both technology vendors (and their clients), larger payers/health systems, data aggregators, and primary sources to interact electronically with the exchange. While a significant portion of the market still utilizes paper documents, desktop systems, and manual processes for credentialing, enabling technology vendors to utilize the exchange to simplify and greatly improve the efficiency of their client operations will create incentives for organizations to upgrade or acquire their modern, SaaS-based software products.

Design Partner Program

As mentioned earlier, the Design Partner Program is intended to aid the firm in collaboratively validating product designs, technical work flows, market economics, assisting with beta testing and operational pilots, and supporting the firm's early go-to-market activities. Thereafter our Partners will drive immediate scaling by building the go-to-market supply for the exchange by ledgering significant numbers of verified credential assets.

Our partners represent a diverse range of market disciplines, to include:

- Large, Integrated Health Systems
- National Payer Platforms
- National Outpatient Specialty Clinic Firms
- Leading Telemedicine Providers
- National Credentials Data Aggregators and Verification Firms
- National Locum Tenens / Contract Clinical Staffing Firms
- Global Professional Services Providers

Operationally, Design Partners meet monthly, either on-site or virtually, to discuss product strategy, review plans and progress, support pilot planning and deployment, and, where applicable, participate in pilot activities. Further, Design Partners are asked to provide periodic ad hoc support as subject matter experts regarding questions the product team may have.

In recognition of their support, Design Partners are given first mover opportunities to supply verified credential assets into the exchange infrastructure and enjoy discounted exchange transaction and subscription fees over a multi-year timeframe. Ultimately, the Design Partner Program will transform into the exchange Governance Committee—overseeing policy, economics, and development priorities.

User Story – Credentialing Dr. Smith at Mercy Hospital East.

Consider the following user story as a functional example of how the exchange will facilitate a common credentialing episode and transform that activity from a months-long to hours- or days-long event:

Mary, a member of the medical staff services office at Mercy Hospital East, creates a smart contract within the exchange's credentialing authority app defining the credentialing requirements for general surgeons seeking appointment at their facility. She builds the contract by first, selecting the existing template for medical doctors used by that facility, then adds the credentials specifically required for general surgeons. This includes confirmation that any member of the department has the training and images of the completed certificates for all surgical devices those practitioners seeking privileges to use. She also adds an exchange rule to the contract that confirms those specific training credentials were completed with the last 24 months.

The following week, Mary uses the credentialing authority app to request credentials from Dr. Smith, who is being recruited by Mercy to join their Medical/Surgical Department. Dr. Smith receives a message within the participant app on his smart phone notifying him that Mercy Hospital requests his credentialing information in order to present them to the chair of the Surgery Department for her review. He authorizes the transaction and Mary receives a message indicating his acceptance. The exchange then executes the General Surgery smart contract for Mercy which begins memorializing each transaction involved in the initial compilation activity. The exchange locates 124 of the 126 data elements required within the Application for Appointment and 34 of the requested 36 verified credential artifacts within Dr. Smith's current profile. The exchange, through data aggregation members, locates current licenses, board certifications, OIG reports, and DEA/CDS certificates. The rules engine executes the specified validation rules within the smart contract and locates one discrepancy related to an unexplained work history gap of 94 days in 1997-- greater than the maximum 30-day gap specified by the rule used by the hospital within their medical doctor contract. Mary is notified of the initial result of the smart contract execution and sees the tasks created to resolve the discrepancies. Dr. Smith also receives a message describing the missing items: (1) a da Vinci device training certificate, (2) three current letters of reference (including two from peers and at least one from a current/former supervisor) which cannot be more than 90-days old, and (3) the need to submit a written narrative describing the work gap in 1997.

Dr. Smith calls his office manager, Sheila, whom Dr. Smith has selected as an authorized delegate, and asks her to pull a copy of the da Vinci training certificate Dr. Smith completed last year and upload it to the exchange. She opens the participant app on her smart phone, selects the training certificate task, enters the data required for the credential (training organization, location, date, hours of training, and outcome) and, using her phone, takes a picture of the certificate, attaches it to the credential element, and saves it within Dr. Smith's profile.

After hanging up with Sheila, Dr. Smith, opens the participant app on his iPad and navigates to the Private Artifacts section within his profile (those which are not generally available to requestors to review). As he had recently completed a recredentialing episode at Northside Hospital, he located three references prepared by his colleagues and the Surgery Department chair. While Dr. Smith cannot view the content of the reference letters themselves, he can see that the transactions were completed by Dr. Jones, Dr. Kelly, and Dr. Patel at Northside in the last month. He selects those elements and authorizes the exchange to share them (including the content) with Mary at Mercy. He also selects a PDF document from his Private Artifacts describing the 1997 work gap he had submitted to Northside a few years earlier.

The narrative described that he and his wife had planned to move to Indiana to be closer to her family and that Dr. Smith had planned to resign from his practice, make the move, and join a new practice in Indianapolis. Shortly after resigning, Dr. Smith's wife was diagnosed with breast cancer and they chose to remain in Virginia where they could work with oncologists Dr. Smith was familiar with. Dr. Smith chose to remain out of work to support his wife during her surgery and initial chemotherapy. He returned to work several months later, taking a position at Memorial Hospital. He also marked the Document for sharing with Mary at Mercy Hospital.

Finally, the participant app asks him for the two missing data elements—his primary vehicle license plate number, and the payment method he would like to use for paying Mercy's $400 appointment fee. He completes both steps, the exchange smart contract directs the platform to rerun all rules on the now completed data set, and finds no further anomalies. The participant app then prompts Dr. Smith to answer 15 attestation questions, which he does, and then submits his completed package.

Mary receives a message that Dr. Smith's package is complete and ready for review. She navigates to the credentialing authority app, and selects Dr. Smith's credentialing package. She scans the cover page to confirm that the rules engine found no further anomalies, and all required items were completed. She opens the NPDB report provided by her credentialing system and notes that there are no reported adverse actions and one malpractice claim settled in 2001 for $10,000. She locates a narrative provided by Dr. Smith describing the claim and sees that it was likely frivolous and not concerning. She notes that the narrative was supplied by Dr. Smith several years ago, verified three times by separate independent exchange members, and submitted to 58 members since publication.

She navigates to the reference letters that were submitted, quickly reviews them for suitability, and clicks through the credential element's transaction history to confirm they, in fact, were supplied by Northside Hospital by Drs. Jones, Kelly, and Patel. She reads the narrative regarding the work gap in 1997 and confirms the originator was Dr. Smith and that Northside Hospital had also received a copy several years back. She also reviews the submitted da Vinci training certificate and sees that it was supplied by Shiela at Dr. Smith's office and that she is an authorized delegate. Mary calls the company who trained Dr. Smith (Intuitive Surgical)—who is not a member of the exchange— and primary source verifies the training and the data supplied with the credential. She then marks the training credential as "verified" through contacting the vendor directly and recording the name of the individual she spoke with to gain the verification. Mary then selects the verified credential and submits it to the exchange to both update Dr. Smith's profile and gain a credit for the submission within Mercy's exchange account.

Mary then messages, Dr. Liang, chair of the Medical/Surgical Department, that Dr. Smith's credentials package is complete, "clean," and ready for her review.

Conclusion

Many concepts have been theorized regarding the development of a solution to resolve the redundancy, cost, impedances, and inefficiencies involved in credentialing. DLT provides the impetus to solve the hardest problem in the solution set: How can one trust that the information is reliable? While no one can ensure 100% security or infallibility of any system, the intrinsic nature of DLT immutability and security can substantially answer that question and, in concert with the other components discussed herein, create the solution to this problem that the market is demanding.

References

1. Assurance, N. C. (2018, 25 18). Accreditation Report Cards. Retrieved from NCQA: National Council on Quality Assurance - https://reportcards.ncqa.org/#/other-health-care-organizations/list?p=19&program=Credentials%20Verification%20Organization&program=Credentialing

2. CAQH. (2016, 09 16). Defining the Provider Data Dilemma. Retrieved from www.caqh.org: https://www.caqh.org/sites/default/files/explorations/defining-provider-data-white-paper.pdf

3. Center for Medicare Services. (2017, 1 17). Online Provider Directory Review. Retrieved from www.cms.gov: https://www.cms.gov/Medicare/Health-Plans/ManagedCareMarketing/Downloads/Provider_Directory_Review_Industry_Report_Year2_Final_1-19-18.pdf

4. Merritt Hawkins. (2017, 1 1). 2016 Revenue Survey . Retrieved from www.merritthawkins.com: https://www.merritthawkins.com/uploadedFiles/MerrittHawkins/Content/Pdf/Merritt_Hawkins-2016_RevSurvey.pdf

Chapter 6:
An Entrepreneurs's Journey: The Early Days of Blockchain in Health

Diego Espinosa

Editor's Note:

This chapter is the first in a series of personal and humanizing stories of some of the early leaders in blockchain telling their story in their own words of how they became experts and early leaders in the emergence of blockchain and health. Diego Espinosa tells the powerful and personal story of his journey of using personal health records of his own statins to track, manage and "cure" is type-2 diabetes. His personal story as a leader punctuates his expertise in defining a distributed ledger that could scale his example based on the power of personal health records that goes beyond the traditional electronic health record system.

How did a former Wall St. money manager come to obsess over blockchain and healthcare data?

Like a lot of blockchain stories, mine had the quality of tumbling down a rabbit hole. Instead of fantasy, though, the experience was more about grasping reality: our healthcare system is itself sick. The root cause is not money or regulation; not a question of the latest sophisticated EKG apps or robotized OR's.

The root of the problem is data. It is actually a simple problem. The solution is also not that complex. It will take some doing. I have no doubt that we will get there, although it will take longer than many people hope. It will not cost that much money. It will instead tax our ability to cooperate, a capacity that is, fortunately, innately human.

Oh yes, and the solution, the Rx for healthcare, will doubtlessly involve blockchain. To understand why takes a little build-up. The reason is lots of things that are supposed to require a blockchain in fact do not. This is not one those. Understanding why requires us to understand the problem at its root, and why blockchain can help solve it.

To explain how blockchain comes into play, below I alternate between discussing my own experience as an early start-up founder and delving into healthcare technology itself. At the end, I lay out a process that suggests itself, and that healthcare enterprises can use to design their blockchain data projects.

My time in medicine was spent bedside, off and on, over a period of thirty years. Those of you who logged 100+ hours at the side of a hospitalized loved one know what I'm talking about: specialists doing their rounds, blood lab results, EKG's scrolling endlessly, hushed decisions on treatments. These all form part of an informal caregiver's education. The prospect of becoming a patient has a way of further focusing the mind.

So my informal education and instinct for self-preservation both gave me a lifetime's worth of interest in what causes disease, and how to best avoid it.

That is how I came to be a poster child for heart disease prevention. Doctors I've met universally complain about patient lifestyle choices. They feel like a mechanic at a demolition derby. Not so in my case. My low fat diet was impeccable. Colorful boxes and bags of baked chips, cereal and pasta lined my pantry. My fruit bowls overflowed with bananas and apples. Upright containers of OJ, Gatorade and low-fat yogurt crowded my fridge.

I saw my doctor regularly. With his help I became a pharmaceutical fan, taking my statins for years. Submerging my LDL below 90 was not enough. There were new treatments that might drop it further, so I perked up at the sound of drug commercials. Plus I ran and ran: thirty miles a week, including a weekly ten-miler with a running group that happened to include two doctors.

And yet, despite all that, it was not a surprise when I found myself knocking on the door of Type 2 diabetes (T2D).

We are in the middle of a diabetes epidemic, with 600m expected globally by 2040. In the U.S., toss a beach ball in a stadium and nearly one in two that touch it are likely to have T2D or its pre-cursor, pre-diabetes. One in two adults, to be sure, but the rate of adolescent T2D is also climbing.

We tend to think about T2D as a disease of aging. That view is increasingly wrong. Fifteen-year-olds are showing up in doctor's offices with non-alcoholic fatty liver disease, an associated malady. The rate of adolescent diabetes is rising along with its cousin, obesity. Metabolic syndrome is a pre-cursor to diabetes and coronary artery disease, and it develops over decades. So, load on to the T2D shopping cart of symptoms high blood pressure, low HDL (so called "good" cholesterol), high triglycerides and obesity. All of these can manifest well before receiving one's first AARP mailer.

When I received my T2D diagnosis, I dove into the cause of diabetes. The concept of metabolic syndrome caught my interest. Reading about its five markers surprised me. I fuzzily remembered mine going bad for a long time. I had a few blood labs handy, the most recent ones. The first order of business was to get the rest of them and see.

That was my first brush with the problem of health data.

My historical blood labs took months to collect. Multiple requests went unanswered. The doctors' offices were little help. My physicians were part of big healthcare networks. They didn't handle requests for historical data. The more they went unfilled, the more urgency and disappointment I felt. Clearly, it would be interesting to know what the progression of this disease had been like. Yet my current doctor seemed happy to be ignorant of it. My previous ones were okay contributing to that ignorance.

Finally, I was able to piece together enough records to confirm the pattern. Yes, in fact my numbers either fell and then remained stable for years (HDL) or went from the lower left of a chart to the upper right (blood pressure, weight, triglycerides, A1c). One down, four up, all wrong directions, all obvious trends.

I was sick, by the definition of medicine. Not only did I have T2D, but my chances of having heart disease were much higher than I had envisioned. Whose fault was it? That seemed a relevant question.

I thought about my doctors. They had kept my LDL low. This was what they were trained to do. I did my part too — the disease prevention poster child. My insurance companies all covered the relevant treatments. The pharma companies produced the drugs that the doctors endorsed. The food companies generated healthy alternatives. Many carried the American Heart Association's seal of approval. My wife and even kids all supported me in eating healthy and exercising. Everyone did what they were supposed to do. The ones in business got paid for it. The ones in my social circle received my appreciation.

The feedback signals were aligned. I had all the right stakeholders involved, and they were getting the message, "keep doing more of what you are doing." Based on my numbers, that was clearly not going to work.

When I thought this through, I came to a sudden realization. It may sound obvious now, but the idea flashed in my mind like an incandescent flare.

Multiply me by about 600m people, all with similar stories, and you start to get an idea of where the problem lay. A tiny few of us had access to all of our personal health data. None of our stakeholders did either, especially not the doctors. I was an engineer by education, and a stock analyst by training. A chart showing a strong trend is something that I could easily interpret. If it were a bridge deteriorating, one could point to a level on the chart and say, "shore it up so it never hits here". If it were a stock chart, we would say, "sell below this point".

In both cases, we would never just stand by as the chart deteriorated.

We would measure, probe, ask why, experiment, anything but just have it fail on our watch. I reasoned: doctors were not that different. Show them 600m charts deteriorating, and the group of them — all smart, capable professionals — will have the same instinct. All the people running insurance companies would find it hard to deny the cost savings, the pharma companies would jump at the chance to help arrest the fall.

Create 600m people's worth of personal health histories, and there is little chance that you get 600m people's worth of T2D.

That seemed like a worthy goal.

Blockchain is a shared ledger that we can use to record all those health histories.

"Can use" does not mean "have to use". A good place to start for any blockchain project is to think about solving the problem without a blockchain.

There are two reasons to start elsewhere. The first is simply that blockchain is about the worst tech you can use to record things digitally, except in special cases. Databases have been around for decades. They can scale into the billions of users (in the case of Facebook, for instance) at high transaction throughput. The fact that we can host them in the cloud is gravy.

The second is that only by process of elimination can we know if those special cases apply.

So, let's imagine the personal health record use case on a normal database. We set a back-end up on AWS and with a consumer-facing app. Consumers use the app to obtain and track their health information. We make their life easier by providing the app API's to dozens of partners: hospital EHR's, wearables, devices, etc. That is all doable today, and many such apps exist. The API's make it easy to import data into a user's personal data record. The technology works beautifully. The data base scales. It handles whatever throughput the app throws at it.

Those database-centered apps have been around. We refer to them as PHR's, or personal (sometimes patient) health records. Can you name one? Most people would not be able to. They have not exactly taken off.

That means one of two things: 1) I'm wrong about how beneficial health data is for patients, and how valuable it is for stakeholders; or 2) something is blocking database technology from solving the personal health record problem.

Some would say it's "1)". For instance, the CEO of a major EHR vendor is purported to have been asked by Vice President Joe Biden why he could not get access to his health data. The CEO apparently replied something like, "It is thousands of pages. What would you do with it?". The implication is that access is not the issue. It's the uselessness of data to the patient, and to anyone they might care to share it with.

I would say "1)" is not a widely held view. The vast majority of people I've encountered in the healthcare system agreed: patient data is a valuable asset. So put them, and myself, down for "2)": something is blocking data base technology from doing its job.

The most obvious reason is "interoperability". EHR's use different data standards. Downloading from multiple vendors leads to mis-labeling, and this, in turn, could have tragic consequences. The industry has hacked away at the interoperability problem for years. It has a ways to go.

Yes, it is difficult to pull data from multiple EHR's into a single PHR. However, it is not impossible if one uses it for more fault-tolerant purposes. For instance, metabolic syndrome has just five biomarkers, three from blood labs and two from devices. How much could be done to combat diabetes if everyone, from birth on, collected and/or tracked those, plus a dozen related blood lab results, one's genome, activity data from wearables, basic nutrition surveys, and medication prescriptions? This simple data set might encounter issues due to interoperability, but errors would not be that hard to spot. Any errors that got through may affect a person's prevention strategy. That's not the kind of thing that might land them in the ER.

Yes, interoperability is a major issue for the healthcare system. At the same time, it is not what is holding back the system from creating robust, valuable personal health records, ones that we can use to attack heart disease and diabetes, two of the "Big 5" chronic diseases.

Something else must be blocking that value creation. Something, perhaps, that could be fixed by using blockchain technology.

I am not a doctor. Yet I did reverse my own Type 2 diabetes.

I have the data to prove it.

The moment those numbers came in, I knew they had an outsized significance. I had done a fair amount of pharma investing. As a Portfolio Manager in charge of a $10b fund, I researched and traded hundreds of millions of dollars in pharma stocks like Roche and Novartis. No drug that I knew of, whether existing or in development, could move my numbers like that.

I had just run an "n-1" experiment, so called because there was one person in the trial.

The first phase of the experiment lasted decades. I followed my doctors' recommendation of a low fat diet and statins. The result: I was a T2 diabetic and had metabolic syndrome. Whatever the merits of the doctor's advice and prescriptions, the experiment did not work. I had the blood labs to prove it. My response was to look around for an alternative.

My research quickly uncovered a bunch of T2D success stories, people that trumpeted outright reversals. They didn't seem like crackpots. Many were doctors, some engineers. These people could interpret their own blood labs. They posted their results on Twitter, sometimes in graphs.

Those people had adopted a ketogenic diet, or keto for short. A diet also known as "LCHF", for low-carb/high-fat.

The group had a theory about why the reversal should happen, sometimes called the "insulin resistance" hypothesis. I won't go into its merits. It did, in fact, make sense to me, but that is not why I chose to go on keto. Instead, it was something far simpler. It was the notion of conducting a low-risk experiment.

Keto could affect metabolic syndrome data in as little as 10 weeks. Eating low carb and high fat went against my doctor's advice. It might even kill me. But in just 10 weeks? Probably not. If I ran an experiment, I could quickly see if the diet worked in my case, and without jeopardizing my long-term health. And anyway, could the result be worse than what my low-fat diet produced?

I decided to run a 10-week n=1 trial. I stuck to the diet fairly well. In that time, if anything, I exercised less. Nothing else changed in terms of my lifestyle. When the trial period was over, I took my blood labs.

I remember getting the call from my doctor. "Wow, what did you do?" he asked. I told him. His response was, "I can't condone eating that much fat. Eventually, it will kill you."

The data told a different story. My HDL had doubled after flat-lining for years. My triglycerides crashed to below my HDL (some believe this ratio should be less than three, and mine was now one-half). My A1c fell by 1.6 points. I had lost twenty pounds.

I was no longer diabetic, and my risk of heart disease had dropped.

I wondered, what if everyone that went on keto — hundreds of thousands of people, perhaps even millions — collected their metabolic syndrome biomarkers? What if they could prove to my doctor that they achieved dramatic reversals in diabetes and metabolic syndrome. Would he change his mind and encourage his other diabetics patients to try it? And if their numbers changed, would he then advocate to his profession to try these low-risk experiments with their patients and allow them to collect the data proving the results? If this happened on a small scale and then grew like a contagion, could this alter the course of the diabetes epidemic?

So was born the idea for Healthcoin, my healthcare blockchain venture.

PHR's had limited success. They just never seem to rack up users. Great in theory, stunted in concept. Something had blocked them. What was it?

One word: silo.

A ledger is a simple concept. It is a place to record what happens, and, better yet, the "truth" of what happens. Having recorded the truth, we can go back and refer to it, check and verify it, use it to incentivize, coordinate, resolve disputes, and more.

All databases are ledgers. The vast majority of databases are kept by a central authority. Usually, each institution — companies, governments, non-profits, schools — keeps its own ledger. We trust them to be the "source of truth" about what happens.

In the healthcare industry, insurance companies record their customers' coverage, premiums and claims. The government tracks our Medicare claims and payments as well as drug approvals. Hospitals and doctors use EHR ledgers to record vaccines, diagnoses, tests, treatments, billings and insurance claims. Pharmaceutical companies keep records of drug trials, including the results of individual participants. Publishing houses curate and archive academic research trial results. Devices like wearables and watches report the truth back to the app providers.

Imagine that the same person appears in all of those ledgers. Let's call that person Bob. "The truth about Bob," is kept by a bunch of central authorities. That creates a problem. What if Bob, or people helping Bob, want to access the whole truth about him?

That brings us back to the silo. The truth sits behind round concrete walls reaching up to blue skies. Bob could find a way in to each database, make a request to each central authority. But the silos tower over Bob. Large enterprises own them. Each pursues their own agenda. Responding to the request is costly and annoying at best. At worst, it surrenders data that they see as theirs to control and monetize.

Bob knocks on the walls of the silos. He walks their circumference, looking for an unlocked door. The truth about Bob, though, stays inside. There is no way of knowing how much of the truth each silo holds. There is not even a way of knowing whether that truth is, in fact, correct.

Now, let's say Bob manages to free a substantial portion of the truth about him. He uses a PHR app that peers into the silos. All Bob needs to do is put in the names of the hospitals and, presto, his data appears on the app. But even if the app can do this successfully, silos still block the truth. The reason is the PHR is itself a silo. It is a database that the PHR app company controls. What if Bob uses multiple PHR's throughout his lifetime? What if he switches from an Android PHR to an iOS one? He may find it difficult to get a hold of the truth about him from the app itself, just as it can be tough for us to move our music from one app to another? Also, the bigger that PHR gets, the more the hospitals and insurers will resist sharing Bob's truth with them, for fear of the PHR app's own agenda. Will they help the hospital's competitor in some way? Just what does it plan to do with all this data? The silos all have competing agendas beyond helping Bob. The PHR, if it is successful, erects yet another concrete tower.

If Bob had the truth about his health data, if he held It in a place that belonged to him and not in a silo, then Bob could use it to improve his health.

That would require that Bob have access to a ledger owned by Bob himself, because Bob is the only entity that has his interest at heart. In addition to owning his data, Bob could share it freely. He could send blood labs to his fellow keto enthusiasts to prove the results of his experiments and incentivize them to stick to the diet; he could show doctors how much he exercises and what foods he eats; he could share with pharma companies what happens to his health after a trial; he can show his insurer that he deserves a discount due to his proven biomarker improvements.

What could Bob use as such a ledger?

One simple answer is a spreadsheet. Let's say, miraculously, all blood labs arrive in the form of a .csv formatted file that Excel, can import. Now Bob can collect the truth about himself in the spreadsheet. He can self-store and share it. The problem is trust and privacy. First, Bob may not be a good keeper of the truth. He has an incentive to alter it, say, to get those insurance discounts. Nothing stops him from editing his ledger. Second, if he sends the information in his spreadsheet to someone via email, they automatically know it came from him. Sharing the data requires him to give up his privacy.

The blockchain is a special type of ledger, one that solves the problems of silo's, self-storage and privacy.

In its most democratic incarnation, a public chain, has three attributes that address each of those problems.

First, anyone can write to the ledger, and anyone can see what is there. No one decides on who can participate because no one owns it. A public chain is the antithesis of a silo. Picture it as "the single source of truth". It's like a scoreboard in a public park full of ongoing chess and pick-up soccer games. Who won what game? Let's agree and write the outcome to the board. We can check later when one or another player claims the victory. All of us can use the board. It records all the games. We don't have to worry about a board keeper being bribed, or selling us advertising, or charging us. Scoreboards are ledgers; blockchains are publicly operated scoreboards. Bob can use one to record and share a type of "game score": the outcome of his efforts to improve his health over his lifetime.

Second, there is a process for agreeing on the order of what is stored, and also for not changing it. That means we know what happened before and after, and we can trust that the chain of events has not been altered.

Third, we can use cryptography to store the information and protect privacy. Bob is not "Bob" on the blockchain. Instead he is known as an alphanumeric string, one that he generates. Encryption not only to hides his true identity. It can also obfuscate his data. People looking at his records on the chain would need his secret encryption key to turn the gobbledy gook into blood lab results.

To recap: Silos block us from freely collecting and sharing our health data. The only way to escape those silos is to keep the data ourselves. If we keep it on a personal database — like a spreadsheet or a PHR — then we create problems of trust, or we just generate a new silo. Shared ledgers get around the silo challenge. The blockchain is a type of shared ledger with three key attributes (public, ordered, private). These allow it to act like a public scoreboard, one that Bob can use, finally, to harness the power of his data.

The ketogenic discovery stayed with me.

I kept thinking of drug companies chasing after multi-billion dollar blockbuster drugs. What would they think of the ketogenic diet? What if they could mine the data from diabetes reversals and use it to target promising sources of research?

That also led me to think of insurers. Their customers, large enterprises, face escalating healthcare costs and need to cap them. Corporate wellness programs populate the landscape. They typically track some kind of health data and reward health improvements. As always, though, they operate in a silo. They take snapshots of an employee's health journey, not the full bio-pic.

And then think about what goes on outside the formal healthcare system. We see doctors for minutes at a time, a few days a year. They cannot monitor or advise on everything that happens outside their office. Our family and friends sway our lifestyle choices, as do therapists, health coaches and nutritionists. All of these could benefit from access to data about the progression of our health.

Continuous prevention buttressed by continuous data collection and sharing. It is radical, simple and could have a far-reaching impact on our health.

The radical part is not just the concept that we can optimize our health expression over a lifetime,. It's that so many stakeholders could benefit from helping us do so. The list above is long: individuals, their families and friends, pharma, insurance, employers, doctors.

Collecting and sharing personal health data is one of those rare win-wins from cooperation. All that is needed is a place to collect the data, and a way to drive initial adoption. Once there, the system itself would see the opportunity and align around it.

To most healthcare participants I spoke to, that sounded Pollyannaish. I did an early round of research, talking to as many of them as I could. They were friendly enough. Getting meetings was surprisingly easy. Later I realized they treated me like a clueless foreign tourist. "Look, that's a great idea, but you have to understand: healthcare is where great ideas come to die," one EHR executive helpfully volunteered.

Win-win cooperation blocked by inertia. A shared ledger solved the silo problem in theory. In practice, the silo owners needed some prodding. How to do that?

I quickly realized blockchain was a weird mix of cryptography and cooperation design. Magic happens on the chain through technology. It enables a shared ledger, a single source of truth we can live by.

But magic also needs to happen off the chain and in the sphere of human social energy. This is not unique to blockchain. It's true of so-called "platform apps" like uber or Airbnb. In the case of uber, that magic gets riders and drivers to cooperate with each other. Uber just provides some location and reputation data. The users do the rest. If ride-sharing were a hurricane, Uber's initial adopters would be its data-driven genesis, like a small but growing thundershower off the west coast of Africa.

Only in the case of healthcare, uber seems too simple. The ride-share app enables a "two-sided" market. Healthcare requires a dozen or so actors to cooperate. Plus, there is a paradox. Large enterprises carry weight. They get listened too. They are also threatening, and others resist their dominance. Their attempts at cooperation meet resistance. Start-ups, on the other hand, appear insignificant. They threaten no one. At the same time, no one takes them too seriously.

Early on in Healthcoin's evolution I came to the realization. Blockchain was about shared ledger technology. It was also equally about designing the kernel of a self-reinforcing dynamic. The more powerful that original design, the more chance that even large enterprises would be swept up by its swirling arms. Each one, by joining, would make the network more valuable, making it more attractive for others to join. This is the network dynamic characterized by "Metcalf's Law".

What kernel could we design for Healthcoin? What early users could we prod to start exchanging and deriving value from personal health data such that it would compel others to follow? This is the question that occupied my mind in the early months of the project.

Blockchains are ledgers that can be public, ordered and configured to maintain user privacy in both identity and data. Above I went over the technology that enabled those three key attributes. There are two additional attributes, though, that bear discussion. They are both key to driving the type of cooperation that Healthcoin sought to spark.

Because blockchain ledgers are ordered in time, we can know with certainty what happened when. This means that if I send you something, everyone with access to the ledger knows that in "time t0" I had it, and in "time t1" you now have it. This comes in handy for sending valuable items to each other, or, more specifically, digital representations of valuable items.

I'm referring to blockchain tokens. Their representation on the ledger is simple. A limited number of tokens are "minted" at the outset, in what is called a blockchain "wallet" belonging to an individual's "address". Once there, they can be transferred to other addresses. Each time a transfer is done, every user of the chain can see who owns the token and where it came from.

The most well-known blockchain token is bitcoin. The bitcoin blockchain is a shared ledger that exists to record bitcoin transfers. At any point in time, we can know whose alphanumeric pseudonym owns how many bitcoins. This comes in handy in "keeping score" of payments to each other. It is what makes bitcoin a viable digital currency, or cryptocurrency. If this sounds far-fetched, it is useful to think of hundred dollar bills. These are worthless pieces of paper. Their usefulness comes from the fact that they can be transferred from one person to another. There is no doubt about who holds it at any given moment. Hundred-dollar bills form a ledger that we use to "keep score", just like Bitcoin. One has no more intrinsic value than the other.

A "token" is just a digital entry, something that has a fixed quantity and can be sent back and forth. The important thing, for healthcare at least, is that a token can be used to incentivize cooperative behavior, both of patients and their stakeholders.

There is one remaining attribute of a blockchain to discuss.

In addition to hosting "tokens", a blockchain ledger can also contain code. That code is added to the ledger in an ordered list. That way we know when it was executed, and what its output was, with certainty. Imagine that we made a bet of $10 on the outcome of a pick-up soccer game. We know the scoreboard will reflect the final score. We can wait until the score gets posted, and then agree to meet and exchange the $10. The problem is one of us may not show. To eliminate this risk, the blockchain allows us to code a line into the ledger: "if the winner of game x is the Panthers, then I pay you 0.0015 bitcoin (the equivalent of $10)". Moreover, we each send that bitcoin amount to the address of the line of code, and it holds it for us until the bet is paid out and returns the unused stake.

That bet is just one example. We can code anything into the ledger. This converts it into more than a "source of truth" on what happens. It makes it into a "source of truth" about what will happen under certain conditions: "if this happens, then that will happen".

The code entries in the ledger are called "smart contracts". They are programmable agreements that exist in digital form rather than on paper. This is not a bad way to think about them. However, I prefer a different framing.

The ledger code acts as a time machine. The basic ledger itself describes the past, from just now all the way to the beginning of the ledger. The ledger code describes the future, from now until time immemorial.

Describing the future is really important. The reason lies in the nature of cooperation. Much of it revolves around doing things that cost us today in expectation of a future reward. This goes all the way back. As hunter gatherers, we shared our food today with others that might reciprocate tomorrow. Our expectation of the future relied on relationships and reputation. Both helped us to align along the same imagined result (i.e. they will share with me next time they bag a mastodon).

To recap: the blockchain is not only a shared ledger, our scoreboard in the public park. It also helps us transfer digital value to each other, and it allows us to agree on the future. Both of these attributes are key to human cooperation.

Including cooperation that produces a healthcare data win-win.

Early on, we decided to focus Healthcoin on using the blockchain to prove that someone had improved their health.

The reason was simple. Proven prevention could spawn a new dynamic between a key pair of actors: employees and employers.

Enterprise payers foot the bill for healthcare costs. An absence of preventive care hits them the hardest. They also have clout. Their influence begins at the firms they keep in business: insurers. Through insurers, their thread of influence extends to the pharmaceutical firms, device makers, hospitals and physicians that those insurers pay.

Change in healthcare is glacial. That's a fact. Another fact is that enterprises ax expenses quickly. They do it all the time. They depend on it to fuel profit growth.

If enterprises knew which prevention strategies cut costs, and which didn't, they could direct insurers to cover those that do. But they don't have the staff to hack through a forest of research papers. They rely on the medical system for that. Insurers are happy to go along with their conclusions and pass the cost along.

Employees proving health improvements to their employers circumvents the medical system, that part of the network most resistant to change. Imagine thousands of employees of a company demonstrating diabetes and heart disease prevention through lifestyle change. Rewarding that behavior leads to more of it, and to further cost cuts. Insurers then pressure healthcare networks to support that behavior. Pharma companies see the opportunity to develop drugs that amplify its effect.

The more proven instances of disease prevention, the more the network aligns along the behavior that produces it. The key was to get enterprises to start the thunderstorm that would lead to the hurricane.

The core idea behind Healthcoin was to report blood lab results directly to a patient's blockchain identity. An algorithm would read through the results and compute the improvement in health, generate a normalized improvement score, and grant Healthcoin tokens based on it. Those tokens, could, in turn, be purchased by employers at a pre-determined price. Privacy was an issue, but the pseudonymity of blockchain identifies offered protection. Employers would not see specific names, only their alphanumeric representations.

Putting this incentive system on the blockchain had a key advantage. Unlike similar incentive plans offered by single employers via well ness apps, the employee would control their healthcare data. They could share it with new employers and anyone else they chose. Moreover, employees could use the same identity to keep collecting healthcare data over their lifetime. In short, the blockchain gave employees "portability" of their data and incentive participation.

The use case for blockchain was solid. We had hit on a way to drive self-reinforcing behavior in the system. Just like uber did, but for a greater number of stakeholders. We settled on a short-term plan: bootstrap a crude version of the platform based on a fork of an existing chain. Our first tech build was on.

Why do you need a blockchain for that?

That question dogs the sector.

That seems unusual, even for infant technologies. IBM's CEO once wondered why anyone would need a personal computer. Microsoft's second CEO was famously skeptical about smart phones.

There seems to be something different about blockchain, though. Enterprises seem committed. Start-ups raise billions in capital. And yet, many continue to question the tech's very legitimacy.

The skeptics are not crazy. A current undermines blockchain, like a rip tide yanking at its legs. It pays to understand this current, and also how important it is to avoid it.

Improper use of blockchain threatens blockchain more than anything. It drives confusion and disbelief. I believe this technology has more improper use than most for a reason. It has to do with the nature of network behavior.

First, I'll dispense with the obvious misuses. First is using blockchain tokens principally as a means of raising capital through ICO's. Some were outright scams. This was unfortunate but also not unusual in technology bubbles. Most of the rest — the vast majority of ICO's — belonged to ill-designed projects. I've received dozens of such pitch decks. The common theme: their token would be used for little else but to pay doctors, or to offer the token holder a discount on medical services.

No one needs a healthcare blockchain token to pay their doctor. They can use U.S. dollars for that. Worse, paying a doctor in a healthcare token hands them a volatile currency. As we saw in 2018, the value of such tokens can plummet. Most doctors will want to trade out of the token and into U.S. dollars so they can be confident of paying their bills. This cuts demand for holding the token. In expectation of that, it is not surprising that many of them have gone to zero.

One also does not need a blockchain to offer discounts. Companies do it all the time using central databases.

A rule of thumb emerges. When a combo of databases and fiat currencies do a good job of performing a function, it's unclear why a project needs its own blockchain token.

What can't central databases do well?

Achieve cooperation through data sharing across silos. The first question to ask when evaluating a blockchain use case is, how does a shared ledger foster data sharing and other forms of cooperation? The second is, how does its blockchain token incentivize that cooperation?

Bitcoin is an example of decentralized cooperation. No one owns the bitcoin ledger. Everyone can use it to hold tokens and transfer them to others. It is a currency that no state issues. It acquires its value through our own shared belief in its future value. Bitcoin solves a problem of money issued by central authorities. That money tends to depreciate during inflation and financial crises. To avoid that kind of money, yes, we do need a blockchain.

Beyond simple, bitcoin-like cooperation, things get murky quick.

For instance, do we need a blockchain for enterprises to cooperate on tracking products through a supply chain? They could all get together and start an association to do that. Each firm could delegate staff, they could draw up governance documents, build a database, and use it to record transactions between them. They can even log the transactions in a way that is auditable, ensuring that no one tampers with the "source of truth". Why use a blockchain, which is much more inefficient than a database?

Every enterprise blockchain application involves central authorities. It has to, because that is what firms are.

The answer to why enterprises may want to use blockchains for cooperation has little to do with technology.

Instead, it has to do with governance. Blockchain is like a pre-commitment to cooperation, like a constitution. Cooperation is embedded in the design and architecture of the software. It is harder to ignore or override it. Committees appointed by consortiums don't exactly have a long track record of success. Soon, line managers start wanting to pursue self-serving agendas. Or the committee members become insular and unresponsive to their consortium's needs.

It is easy to say, "blockchains aren't needed because we can just agree to use a database," but it ignores the fact that we usually can't just agree to use a database.

In enterprise blockchain applications, we trust firms — central authorities — to perform certain functions, and we delegate others to hardwired, decentralized cooperation. We carefully pick and choose what and who we want to trust. This design process is challenging. It is safe to say that the whole blockchain community is still coming to terms with it. It is learning through constant ideation and trial and error. There is no other way to describe what blockchain project teams have to go through.

That is the undertow, the rip tide, the thing that makes blockchain different. The technology is immature, and so is our knowledge of how to use it to solve problems. When someone asks, do you need a blockchain for that, the best teams feel a twinge of doubt: do we, and how do we make sure? And then, it's back to thinking it through, for the nth iteration.

Healthcoin was no exception. Our early prototype was rife with centralization. For instance, we coded the normalization algorithms used to score health improvements and generate token rewards. Also, we developed the patient-facing app for on-boarding and data uploading.

What was the chain itself supposed to be for then? Two purposes: one was recording a user's health data and attaching it to their self-sovereign identity; and the second was recording and sending tokens that reflected health improvement. This enabled users to store and share their own data on the chain.

It was a prototype. As we quickly learned, the design posed challenges. Not fatal ones, but ones that limited its use. Fortunately, we had time to think through them. Our start-up had been accepted to a top digital health accelerator: TMCx, run by the innovation arm of the Texas Medical Center in Houston. TMCx's staff took a chance with us as blockchain-based healthcare applications were still in their infancy. Their staff was supportive and connected us to the Center's broader ecosystem. It was a perfect place to find sounding boards for new, innovative concepts.

On to the early challenges we discovered.

First, to run the algorithm on the data and calculate a reward, we needed to get the data onto a database. We did not need to keep it there. The code itself would delete it as soon as it ran the algorithm. Still, this meant that users needed to trust us to maintain their privacy, and firms that rewarded users needed to trust us to not edit the data.

We asked ourselves: since both users and employers/payers needed to trust Healthcoin, why not just run the whole thing on a central database?

There were positive answers. Keeping the data on the blockchain meant that the user would have it forever. They did not need to rely on Healthcoin to store it. That was a big plus. The same was true of issuing blockchain tokens as incentives. This gave the user's reward a certain universality. Healthcoins would be recognized by multiple firms. They could plug into the network and participate easily, compared to us running a silo'd "points" system like other reward programs.

Still, achieving on-chain privacy was a significant problem. On a public chain, a user's data was visible to the public. Sure, users were only identifiable by their on-chain address — the alphanumeric pseudonym. This gave a measure of protection, but it was not complete enough. What happened if their identity became known, or could be determined through the data itself? The MVP use case was tracking metabolic syndrome markers, a less-sensitive data set. We determined that some users would be comfortable taking that risk.

That helped, but clearly, we would have to ring-fence our early pilots to prevent data leaks. Fortunately, our potential partners expressed an interest in testing this "proof of concept". We had a tailwind of enterprise curiosity about how to use the technology, especially for sharing healthcare-related data. The point was to learn, and the only way to learn was to test in a way that virtually guaranteed user privacy.

Also, we knew our prototype was a stepping stone to a more intelligent chain, either Hyperledger or Ethereum, On those blockchains, we could use a combination of encryption and smart contracts to minimize our profile as a central authority. We were in discussions with both IBM's Watson division (on the Hyperledger side) and ConsenSys (on the Ethereum side). Each brought a potential solution to many of the challenges posed by the prototype.

The two opportunities could not be more different. IBM Watson was a gateway into the enterprise world. They offered incentives to put Healthcoin on their version of Hyperledger with their help as co-developers, and to connect us with their clients as potential partners.

ConsenSys was the opposite. The firm was a two-track experiment. First it supported multiple, early blockchain ventures to boot up an ecosystem of apps and helpful protocols for the Ethereum blockchain. Second, it operated along the lines of a holacracy. The firm had minimal hierarchy and avoided org charts. Distributed decision-making gave the firm an edge in exploring, as opposed to executing on a management's rigid plan.

As TMCx came to an end, Healthcoin decided to go with ConsenSys. The clincher came when I grasped what I thought was the main benefit of public blockchains: their ability to form highly connected networks of identities. More on this below.

I headed into the epicenter of decentralization, a place where I could solve Healthcoin's challenges by getting access to the leading edge of public blockchain technology.

Above I talked about how the "why blockchain" question was like an ever-present undertow. The answer really comes down to figuring out how to make decentralized cooperation create value.

Blockchain is a shared ledger that helps to break down silos and lets information flow freely. That enables cooperation across individuals and organizations. It allows us to coordinate our activity without an agenda-setting central authority. I wrote about how that can help people achieve better health by obtaining and sharing their own health data with the health ecosystem. Now I want to probe a little deeper into identity, data, and the nature of cooperation. My goal here is to show how and why cooperation creates value in a more abstract sense. This is really the crux of what Blockchain is all about. It requires a shift in mindset, especially since little of our formal education teaches us about cooperation.

At the basis of it is identity.

We think of our personal identity as being our own. It is natural to claim, "I am the one who is me". Who else would it be? In the current digital world, that self-identity concept is wrong. This is important. We spend hours each day in that world. It often shapes our relationships. It gives us valuable services and knowledge that are integral to our daily life. Who we are there is key to our identity overall.

In the digital world, in apps like Facebook for instance, we don't get to have our own identity. We have identities that digital firms grant to us, i.e. our logins. The login is like a name-badge. We have to wear it to access an app's walled garden. It is not technically our name, because when we leave the garden we have to relinquish the name tag. It is (except in some cases) of no use anywhere else.

There, we interact with other name-tag wearing visitors. That interaction is watched and recorded by the app. It attaches the data from that interaction to our login identity. To the app, we are our login combined with data about "that login person". For instance, Google, recently, has begun to log me into Chrome when I log into gmail. It also probably knows where I've been through Google maps. It knows

I am "that login person" when I search, browse, move and communicate. The data it has about "that login person" is growing like kudzu. Google crunches it and uses it to serve me up ads and search results. It's clients — advertisers — pay for those results. So, Google and Facebook's apps are, in some ways, just there to get us to produce that data.

The app is just the maze. We are the mice. Their firms are the clipboard-toting, white lab coat-wearing scientists. I lay that out not to criticize Google and Facebook, but to explain the meaning of digital identity. The form it takes is critical. It either allows or prevents our decentralized cooperation.

I'm not sure of the exact number. My educated guess is Google, Facebook, and a handful of other firms control 80% of our digital expression. Their data extends to health, even if (for the moment) they are not connected to EHR's. For instance, it's quite possible they know when I'm ill well before I visit a doctor. It's even possible they know, based on my eating, driving and habits and posts, whether I may get sick in the future.

Why is all that important?

Imagine if instead of "that login person", I was just, in fact, "me". I could collect all that data as I interacted with social, location, search, music, transportation, video and browsing apps. My new, digital "me" identity would get me into every digital app and record every digital experience. This is just not that hard. All I need is a universal, portable digital "me" identity, a place to store the data, and a way to share it with others. All without a central authority being in charge.

"Digital me" could do wonders with that data. I could share a much more extensive data set with my healthcare advisors. For instance, an AI could crunch through it and suggest what eating, driving and social habits would produce the best, longest-living, healthiest, happiest "me". The advice would be tailored. Not, "on average, based on a study population of n=1000". Not specific to the performance of one of my organs. Not in the service of a company set on its own agenda. Instead, based on the totality of my individual data and the whole of my biological system (including genome).

It doesn't stop there.

My independent storage, the place for the data, can also house software code. I can use that code to let others know my limits and preferences. I can let them know the extent to which I'll relax my privacy, for whom and in exchange for how much incentive. I can also lay down the limits of my choices. Low carb (<20%), but not very low carb (<10%). I will spike my blood glucose once a day, by eating some sugar after dinner, but otherwise I want to minimize insulin secretion. I want to have more real connections and spend less time on my phone. My preferences will set boundaries for the algorithms, make them more effective.

Now that "me", with its data and preferences, can freely interact with other identities that also have data and preferences. Buildings can get feedback on allergen data from a device, and my own allergy levels from blood labs. They can track how that affects productivity and set an ROI for better air filtering. Buses and subway cars can dispatch with near-full knowledge of rider commute patterns and preferences. These are all examples of cooperation enabled by technology.

I think of it as "scalable decentralized cooperation". Before, we could pull it off in groups of 150, the so-called Dunbar's number. This is the ceiling on the cooperation humans can achieve through trusted social connections (the size of a small tribe). In that mode, we "distributed" the data about each other's history and preferences across people that knew us. We used that data to coordinate our activities as a group: hunting, foraging, searching for a mate. Creating digital identities and storing data and preferences removes the Dunbar ceiling. It introduces cooperation with machines, guided by machine intelligence.

How close are we to that vision?

The blockchain is one key enabler. It lets us set up our own "digital me" identity. It also allows us to gather up our idle data storage and computing power into a sort of universally available, decentralized computer. We can use it as a vehicle for storing our digital expression and executing smart contract code (i.e. about our preferences). All of it can be configured to protect our privacy from central authorities, to put us in control of data sharing.

Today's blockchain technology and encryption provide us with the basic components. Still, I have not answered the question. While the tech exists today, the user experience is still too crude. It asks the user to jump through hoops. It will get better with time and repeated experimentation. There is nothing unusual in that. Most new technology waves that that course.

In my view, this is a bit like the Internet in 2001. Even while we can see its usefulness, its real potential lies five or six years out. The trick is to figure out how to drive and monetize early-adopters before then. Of the visible early use cases, finance and supply chain seem, to me, to have jumped to the head of the line.

Also, that vision I laid out can sound to some like a scary episode of Black Mirror. The show serves up weekly versions of tech dystopias. That data can get into the wrong hands. The AI can veer off in the wrong direction and take control.

That is all possible. We have three choices. We can forego decentralized cooperation, but the fact is we badly need it. So many of our big, intractable, so-called "wicked" problems, like spiraling healthcare costs, require us to cooperate. We can continue with the current centralized data architecture, in which case dystopia seems a closer shore. Or we can test and experiment with this new set of technologies. We can try out the new concept of self-sovereign identity and the sharing of data and preferences attached to it. We can figure out how to guard privacy and yet still flow data to its best use. To me, at least, the choice is clear.

My own course took me away from healthcare. First it seemed a slight pivot, and then, as can happen, the divergence widened.

Along the way, I came to believe that to really influence the flow of data in healthcare requires us to avoid directly influencing the flow of data in healthcare.

I'll explain. I had an important realization about the nature of our data during 2017. Setting up a "digital me" on a blockchain turned out to be not that difficult. It is challenging to maintain that identity's privacy, but not impossible. All that was good news.

But the best news is that our digital expression is actually easy to come by. If you measure it as the amount of our lifetime data, I would say 90% is easy to grab and store through API's that either already exist or are easy to code.

That 90% includes our browsing, social, mobility, financial and purchase data. We perform all those activities either in the digital world or with a digital interface in the physical world (i.e. a credit card at a store). Facebook itself has access to much of it. Surprisingly, we can readily download it from the company's central database. It's not too hard to set up automated downloads (through those API's) from countless other apps. It can take some partnership development, some coding, but this is not rocket science. Most apps, I believe, already make the data available. The rest will not resist societal and regulatory pressure for long. In my view, "digital me" is only waiting for blockchain technology to mature a bit more, to a better level of UX. At that point, it won't take long for the dam to burst, and the river of our data to stream our way. What will take longer is to figure out how to attract partners and users, and how to open up value propositions for all that data. It all requires an ecosystem of apps and protocols. Some of them are in place now, and some we have not even imagined.

What about the other 10% of data? It will be very hard to come by. The inertia is too big. The vested interests that control it won't change easily. I'm referring to our EHR data. It will be the last piece of "digital me" to fall into place. I'm confident it will happen. When it does, though, I hope we won't end up caring all that much.

The reason is that much of the data in EHR's does not inform an alogrithmic model of our future well-being.

Hospital stays, for instance, create much more data relevant to billing than to our future health. I've put the question directly to both doctors and data scientists. They put the number at around 10-20%. That is, only that fraction of data would go into a predictive model. This is not to say the other data is useless. It's just not particularly useful for avoiding illness. A CHF patient generates an ocean of data. What data to we need for that patient to avoid landing in intensive care with heart failure? Their metabolic syndrome, nutrition, stress and activity data would be useful. Perhaps even data on their social connections, driving patterns and mobile phone use. With the help of machine learning, AI, and a heap of cooperation between stakeholders, we can make that data actually matter. By aligning incentives and using tech to coach, and by bringing one's social network to the fore in wellness.

What happens in the doctor's office or hospital bed simply cannot be what maximizes our lifetime health. The minutes and hours of time we spend there are too little and mostly too late. Technology and cooperation both open the door to making those minutes and hours less and less important. This is not only desirable. It is critical if we are going to find a solution to healthcare cost and access.

My tech journey took me down the road of attaching non-EHR data to the "digital me".

I pivoted Healthcoin to become Linnia, an open-source protocol for collecting and sharing one's digital expression from/to apps. My goal was to get the easily downloadable data onto the blockchain and into a user's control. Actually, Linnia was just to be the enabler. The point of open source projects is that developers would do the heavy lifting in connecting their data to the blockchain.

In short, that was the best way to create the thunderstorm off the coast of Africa.

The other part, though, the more important one, is to get enterprises to bring their users to data sharing projects. Insurers, pharma companies, employers — they all stand to benefit from a freer flow of data, and they already have trusted relationships with users. Many of them are looking to launch blockchain POC's.

To them, I propose the following process based on my experience in the space. Many will already familiar be with it. It is my adaptation of design thinking to solve network, rather than user, problems.

1) Don't even think about blockchain initially. That is putting the cart before the horse. Before you decide you need a blockchain, determine if you want some form of decentralized cooperation.

2) Instead, Observe how silos are blocking value creation that could benefit you. What is the "network pain point" that cooperation could cure? How is it keeping you (and the network) from reaping a benefit?

3) Ideate on how could the network behave differently if data — the "source of truth" flowed more freely. How much "network value" would it create if the network changed its behavior? What would that new behavior look like? How much value would you capture, while still maintaining incentives for others?

4) Prototype the set of infrastructure and incentives that would lead to that new type of cooperative network behavior. This is where blockchain may come in. Is the technology a key enabler of that new behavior? What mix of central databases and decentralization makes the most sense? Pick and choose centralization where necessary. The more centralization, the less cooperation. But sometimes, without centralization the solution won't work. There is a trade-off, and it's best made consciously. Lastly, design a path to adoption by the network, or what I call a "network path". What is the thunderstorm, and how does it become a hurricane? Who are the early users? How does the incentive to participate grow with the number of users?

5) Translate that network path into milestones. Track those milestones as you test the prototype. That takes the process out of the theoretical realm and into something you can execute. The key is to hold teams accountable. At the same time, realize that these are experiments, and that learning is more important than results.

Grass roots and enterprise data sharing projects will grow big enough to exert a gravitational pull on the healthcare system. Once we get used to the idea that we should own our data; once we demonstrate the value of sharing it freely and privately; then the healthcare system will find it harder and harder to resist participating. There will be easy pick-offs along the way. We should be able to access blood lab results, scans, biometrics like blood pressure and medications. Plus, genome and microbiome data, which come from outside the formal healthcare system. Once all of that is in our control, along with our other digital expression, the rest will come. It will also be less relevant.

Because we will be healthier.

Chapter 7:
Block Chain in Clinical Trials

Robert Learney

Editor's Note:

Over time the cost and complexity of clinical trials has become a limiting factor in bringing drugs to market. This problem grows as we embrace precision medicine and specialized trials. In this chapter, Rob Learney explains how blockchain holds the promise to reduce costs, increase transparency, and facilitate clinical trials and the process of bringing drugs to market.

Introduction

Clinical Trials are becoming ever more complex, distributed and dynamic. The demand for precision medicine is bringing an unprecedented challenge for containing the costs of biomedical research and maintaining appropriate regulatory oversight.

Contract Research Organisations (CROs) are playing an increasingly important role in clinical trials, and are experts in providing the necessary back-office infrastructure, site management, and human resources to undertake trial activities. CROs are now becoming involved in all aspects of clinical trials from design, conduct, reporting, and final submissions to regulatory authorities. Recent estimates project that up to 70% of all trials will be managed by CROs by 2020. But despite this expenditure and expertise, the vast majority of trials still fail for avoidable reasons.

Blockchain and other Distributed Ledger Technologies (DLT) present the opportunity to transform the management of clinical trials. The role of CROs could be substituted by a technological platform that is more transparent and accountable to all relevant parties including trial sponsors, regulatory agencies, trial sites (hospitals, clinics), and patients themselves. Such a platform could prove far more cost-effective at managing safe and effective clinical trials, improving data availability for review and meta-analysis, as well as preventing non-publication and a posteriori analysis.

Blockchain also holds promise for managing the next generation of clinical trials, which will be vastly more data-rich, individualised, and distributed over a global collection of sites to reach the right patient populations. One can imagine a future trial aided by wearable devices providing real-time data over high bandwidth networks to feed machine intelligences for live statistical analysis. But the management, monitoring, and auditing of such a trial is beyond the capabilities of any traditional regulator and oversight committee. Hence, we need to think beyond current management and reporting methods towards automated systems capable of continuous risk assessment and individualised monitoring and reporting.

All of these goals can be achieved by an improved data architecture based upon the capabilities of blockchain technology to maintain tamper-proof and time-sequenced datasets amassed from the contributions of disparate and unaligned parties engaged in a common enterprise. Totum maior summa partum – the whole is greater than the sum of its parts. In this case, improved global healthcare outcomes through better medicine is more than just the alignment of pharmaceutical companies, clinicians, regulators, hospitals, and patients.

However, whether a blockchain-based platform can truly replace CROs, and whether it can bring greater transparency and efficiency to clinical trials and the rest of biomedical research remains unclear. We need to see groups of trialists and blockchain companies collaborating to take bold first steps, alongside a forward thinking regulator.

The History of Clinical Trials

Clinical trials are the cornerstone of advancement in medical science. They are the only way in which the global community of researchers, doctors, and patients can fairly assess the benefits of new therapies developed for some of the most devastating diseases.

Prior to the 20th Century, the development and assessment of new medicines and treatments was generally an unguided process, involving pooled social knowledge of observations from clinicians reporting what seemed to work and what didn't for different ailments.

This method led to the extremely successful discovery of aspirin, when longstanding folk remedy met modern chemistry in 1899, and the first chemotherapy drugs for leukaemia when young soldiers suffering the effects of mustard gases from the trenches of World War 1 displayed unexpected drops in their white blood cell counts.

Serendipitous discovery quickly gave way to the more structured process of drug development through the 1940s and 1950s, with the blockbuster releases of the first antibiotics (penicillin in 1940, followed by streptomycin and isoniazid for tuberculosis in 1944 and 1953 respectively).

In less than 80 years, drug development had evolved from folk wisdom, to chance discovery, to the highly structured development of novel therapies.

Unfortunately, the disaster of Thalidomide in 1957 showed that medicines could have a dark side. The 'wonder drug' which helped pregnant women overcome morning sickness, and was safe at all doses in animal studies, actually had unpredicted and catastrophic effects on foetal development. The previous perception that all drugs were beneficial was shattered. From the early 1960s, there now had to be a robust process for validating the safety of therapies in a suitable trial population, accompanied by observation and reporting of unwanted side-effects before companies could be allowed to offer their new drugs to the public.

Thus was born the modern regulatory environment establishing the process and governance of clinical trials. These regulations have undergone many decades of rational amendment since, always placing public health and safety before the need to release new medicines. The balance of this approach has been questioned in recent years, particularly in cases where terminal patients have exhausted all other treatment options and wish to take unapproved or unlicensed medicines which may only offer marginal to no benefits. The US FDA has traditionally granted access to medications in this way following applications for 'compassionate use', with 99% of applicants being granted permission.

In May of 2018, the US President signed into law the 'Right to Try' bill which formally gives terminally ill patients the right to access experimental and as-yet-unapproved medications and therapies. The long-term effects of this unstructured experimentation on drug approvals and the traditional clinical trial process remains to be seen.

The Current Clinical Trial Process

Novel therapeutic agents leaving the lab currently progress along an established 3-phase pipeline of clinical trials before they can be offered for sale. These phases seek to:

- document the safety profile of the new drug,

- prove that we understand the underlying disease mechanism,

- confirm the drug has efficacy in treating the target disease

Following these three trial phases in small, controlled, and defined population groups, the drug is then made available to all sufferers of the target disease. This is where a drug meets actual clinical practice for the first time, with all its imperfections.

Because of this, there is now a newer 'fourth phase' of post-marketing observation which feeds side effect data back to regulators and allows them to withdraw dangerous agents or to amend and narrow the scope of prescription if certain populations haven't responded as initially thought.

In essence, every drug in use today is in a global 'phase four' trial, from aspirin to the latest anti-cancer antibodies. It's how we know that the then-breakthrough arthritis drug rofecoxib (Vioxx) could trigger heart attacks and strokes in high doses, and why it was voluntarily withdrawn from the market by the manufacturer in 2004.

Setting aside Phase 4 trials (post-marketing observations) for now, Phases 1 through 3 see a sequential increase in complexity, cost, and failure rates, but for largely different reasons. A successful new drug will proceed through trial as follows:

Phase I Clinical Trial

A drug has been singled out from 5,000-10,000 others in the lab, using molecular, cell, computer, and animal modelling, to show that it is likely to be safe and useful in combatting a certain human disease.

The goal of this phase is to demonstrate basic safety in humans, by testing the drug in a small number (20-100) of healthy adult volunteers well below the dose used in animal trials. There are specific cases (cancer drugs, anti-HIV medications) where sufferers of the disease in question may volunteer to take part in Phase I trials because the drug is likely to be dangerous for healthy volunteers. Otherwise, the participants are drawn from the general population, and the trial is conducted in a regulated and approved location, typically a hospital or clinic environment.

The drug company will typically pay a 'Contract Research Organisation' (CRO) to undertake this trial. The CRO will design the trial protocol, seek regulatory approval, ethical approval, and input from a patient body. It will register the trial on a public database, and then begin to recruit patients, run the trial clinic, administer the drug according to the trial protocol, collect and analyse data, and report back to the drug company and regulator.

- Participants are usually compensated a small amount for taking part in the study
- This phase runs for an average 1.5 years and costs roughly US$169m
- 30% of drugs fail at this stage

Phase II Clinical Trial

This phase takes the drug, now shown to be safe at certain doses, and tests it on volunteer patients rather than healthy individuals to look for desired biological activity. The numbers involved are larger (100-500 patients), and they may have to undergo genetic testing for some newer drugs or immunotherapies, or when differences in metabolism are shown in Phase I.

The design of a Phase II trial is more complex than that of Phase I, and requires careful statistical planning to ensure the desired effect is likely to be observable. Again this phase is usually contracted out to a CRO.

Phase II trials are often designed as randomised controlled trials, beginning with small numbers of patients to keep costs down, or more observational case series. For example, a new cancer drug may have to be useful in 20% of patients at the maximum safe dose in order to progress to a Phase III trial. The CRO will design and recruit patients for a small, perhaps 30-patient, pilot group to demonstrate that at least 6 have shown positive benefit, before expanding to a larger group to see whether this effect persists.

- This phase can last up to 3 years, costing on average US$402m
- 70% of drugs in Phase II fail to progress to Phase III

Phase III Clinical Trial

After a drug has successfully passed a Phase II trial, it now needs to demonstrate benefit in clinical practice. This means a large multi-centre trial on 500-3000 patients, depending on the disease in question.

This phase aims to demonstrate definitive benefit over the current 'gold-standard' treatment, usually in a form of direct comparison study. This requires careful design to ensure the selection is randomised and that both the doctor and patient are blinded to the treatment in use, with patients crossing over between groups to 'double-check' apparent results.

With the larger and more diverse range of patients taking the drug in question, this phase is also used to monitor for adverse reactions which only appear in certain sub-populations or after a longer time of taking the drug.

Again, this work is usually contracted out to a CRO, but perhaps a different one from Phase I and 2 trials as this requires a more global reach to be able to recruit patients across multiple centres over a longer period of time.

- This phase can last up to 4 years (average 2.5), costing an average US$536m

- 50% of drugs in Phase III fail to progress to marketing

Other Costs

A drug must undergo final regulatory review, registration, and approval prior to marketing. This can only occur after the drug has been shown to be safe and effective through the first 3 phases of clinical trials. Here, the regulator gathers reports and reviews all evidence collected during the trial phases over a number of months to a year, before guiding the drug company on writing its prescribing information (drug labelling) in accordance with findings.

This phase of review, registration, and approval can take 1.3 years and cost US$11m

Overall, the process of drug development through various clinical trials can amount to some US$1.7bn of expenditure over 10-11 years.

Health economists are now adding in the cost of capital, and the opportunity costs represented by the study spend over other business activities, to raise the cost of bringing a single drug molecule to market to some US$2.9bn.

Problems facing Clinical Trials

Clinical science is currently stuck in a difficult situation – formal trials are widely accepted as the only way to demonstrate the safety and effectiveness of new treatments beyond any doubt, yet the problems of administering trials are severely limiting the ability for drug companies of all sizes to get new products to market.

The Biotechnology Innovation Organization studied 7,455 drug development programmes across 1,103 companies from 2006-2015 and reported that only 9.6% of drug candidates which made it to Phase I were likely to achieve regulatory approval.

One might think that this perhaps represents an over-cautious approach by the regulator, or maybe that useless drugs are progressing beyond the earliest trial phases.

The most troubling failures are those in Phase III trials. At this stage, one would imagine that the safety and efficacy of the drug have been essentially proven and all that remains is to confirm the results in a larger, more diverse patient population.

Unfortunately, failure at this stage is all too common, and occurs in up to half of all Phase III trials. Around 70% of these failures are due to issues of safety and/or efficacy. The remaining 30% are for commercial reasons (insolvency, corporate strategy, mergers & acquisitions, etc.).

A 2016 publication by the Clinical Research Organisation PAREXEL summarised the five leading drivers of failure of Phase III trials based on presentations at the 2014 summit of the European Center for Pharmaceutical Medicine (ECPM):

- Basic science — Animal models that do not translate or are not entirely related to human disease, poor understanding of target disease biology, or drugs that are simply ineffective

- Clinical study design — Changes in patient definitions (inclusion criteria and exclusion criteria) from Phase II to Phase III, insensitive outcomes measures or Phase II surrogate endpoints that are not confirmed by Phase III endpoints. Inappropriate study design can undermine the ability to show efficacy or the sample size may be too small

- Dose selection — Inadequate dose finding in Phase II. Inadequate therapeutic indices may also lead to suboptimal dosing

- Data collection and analysis — Missing data, attrition bias, rater bias, errors in measurement methods, or inappropriate statistical methods

- Operational execution — Data integrity issues or good clinical practice (GCP) violations. In addition, unexpected variations in recruitment or dropouts can affect results, as can protocol variations, missing data, or unintentional unblinding of subjects

These five major drivers can be grouped into two major categories – 'scientific' failures vs. 'process' failures. These will be explored separately, with discussions of the role blockchain can play to mitigate these modes of trial failure.

'Scientific' Failures

The first key to a successful clinical trial is to ensure that the science is correct. This means that the target is appropriate and well understood, the drug has passed all pre-clinical tests in the lab with molecular modelling, cell modelling, and animal modelling, and that it is likely to be safe and effective in humans.

After ensuring the science of the drug is likely sound, the science of the trial has to be equally sound. This means consulting with experienced clinical trialists, statisticians, ethicists, regulatory bodies, and patient advocacy groups to ensure that the design of the study is likely to meet with approval, and to produce statistically robust results.

Part of this design process is the selection of the right patient numbers for statistical significance, and the selection of good trial 'endpoints' – the measurements to be taken which are believed to reflect the activity of the drug under investigation. Good endpoints have to be clinically relevant, reflect the disease process, be reliable, detectable, and practical. Once selected, a trial must adhere to its endpoints throughout, or else questions will be raised about changing the hypothesis to match the results. Selection of the wrong endpoints may lead to trial failure even if the drug is effective.

Finally, the quality of design and scientific inquiry must be maintained throughout the trial process. It is no good to rush through the confirmatory Phase I to reach the more investigatory Phase II, without fully exploring all relevant dosing schedules and regimes which are likely to be used later in Phase III.

Blockchain's Impact on 'Scientific' Failures

Not all types of 'scientific' trial failures lend themselves to improvement by digital technologies. For example, the selection of clinically relevant endpoints requires a combination of medical knowledge and clinical experience, and statistical design requires engagement with mathematicians and public health specialists.

However, blockchain does have the potential to reduce some forms of 'scientific' failure. Take the example of modelling drug-target interactions during pre-trial scientific research. This currently requires skilled scientists with deep knowledge of chemistry and molecular biology, carefully designed software packages, and hours of trial and error.

There is a strong move to involve aspects of 'artificial intelligence' in these processes to be able to create more realistic simulations and learn from existing datasets. But these efforts are hindered by a paucity of data. Pharmaceutical companies can only currently draw upon their own datasets and historical models, when instead all parties could benefit from sharing models and knowledge of targets so that they can be tested against those of other companies, and vice versa.

Here is where the strength of blockchain to facilitate trustless data sharing between unaligned or unknowing parties comes into play.

With a blockchain-enabled platform, pharmaceutical companies and other holders of IP on molecules or targets could create common pools of these digital resources and manage and track when other parties access them. By using blockchain to manage the platform's access controls and remuneration mechanisms, no single IP holder can censor or exert undue influence over other IP holding parties to the system, to enable the common goal of increasing the amount of data available to the scientific community. In addition to opening up data for improved oversight and review so as to reduce the risks of 'scientific' trial failures, such a common platform would also enable IP holders to also realise new sources of revenue from their existing libraries.

These blockchain-based access control and remuneration methods can be combined with new federated machine learning methods whereby training can be amassed from a number of sources and computed remotely without ever revealing the underlying raw data. Such a system could be immensely transformative across the biopharma sector, allowing unknowing parties to automatically test molecules against targets, and notifying IP holders in the case of a match so that they can pursue future business engagements.

Federated learning and blockchain are both in their infancy, but already companies such as OpenMined and Ocean Protocol are building these 'platforms of the future'. Whether the scientific community is ready to accept the radical transformation that they promise is yet to be seen.

Finally there is a more basic use of blockchain as a technology for building multi-party audit trails of item revisions linked to user identifiers which could improve the timeliness and quality of applications to review bodies and ethics committees. This simple facilitation, relying on the basic functionalities of blockchain, could improve the application and review process for all parties involved.

'Process' Failures

This category is by far the more important of the two, for the simple fact that it shouldn't exist at all. All failures of clinical trials should be solely on scientific grounds – that the hypothesis was incorrect, the understanding of the disease and its target was wrong, or that the study should have used different endpoints (biomarkers, tumour volumes on scans, blood pressure, etc.) which would have more suitably reflected the disease process and therefore the efficacy of the drug.

Given the immense sums of money and human capital invested, drug trials should run perfectly from start to finish, never hesitating in their quest to identify and confirm new cures to devastating diseases. Unfortunately, as the PAREXEL study shows4, there are many non-scientific drivers for trial failure.

If however we assume the 'science' of the trial is correct, we can then focus more clearly on the diverse array of avoidable process issues which should be otherwise predictable and manageable from the outset. The three major problem areas here are:

- Patient Management
- Trial Management
- Data Management

It is here in the avoidance of process failures that blockchain is a very appropriate technological solution to a collection of human-level problems, by ensuring that all parties partaking in the common enterprise of a clinical trial are correctly engaged, guided, monitored, and perhaps even incentivised.

Patient Management

Patients are the core of every clinical intervention. It sounds trivial, but without patient involvement there can be no trial. The process of recruiting, retaining, and informing patients is therefore crucial to the successful execution of a clinical trial.

Unfortunately, adequate patient recruitment is probably the greatest challenge that any clinical trial faces. A 2007 study of 114 multicentre trials funded by the UK's Medical Research Council and Health Technology Assessment programme found that only a third kept up with their planned recruitment schedule. The failure to recruit patients can lead to trials failing to commence, inadequate population sampling leading to safety or efficacy failures (particularly in ethnic minorities), statistical failures, and longer trial durations with cost overruns.

There have been various studies into the issue of engaging the public in clinical trials, with the finding that the public has a poor and generally negative perception of clinical research. But even following the successful initial engagement of a patient who is considering enrolling in a trial, perhaps due to the encouragement of a loved one who had read a recent advert, or a clinical encounter with one of the doctors directly involved in the trial, there are a number of other problems which can arise.

Recording a patient's consent is known to be a difficult issue. The gold standard in much of the world is to obtain 'informed consent'. This simple term carries a lot of weight. It indicates that the patient has been presented with the relevant objective facts, has the capacity to weigh and consider them, and to make a free choice without repercussions. Once given, this consent can be withdrawn at any time of the patient's choosing. Medicine in the world of informed consent has moved from its historic paternalism into a more assistive role.

As such, the documentation presented to the patient must be clear, concise, and unbiased. The manner of recording the subsequent consent, if granted, and its withdrawal, must be simple and maintained for documentation and regulatory purposes. Rather disconcertingly, a 2011 study in the BMJ demonstrated that 31% of trials failed to report patient consent, raising the question of whether it was ever obtained in the first place. The same study found that 26% of trials also failed to report any ethical review.

And once within the trial, there is an unfortunate tendency for patients to fail to comply with the trial protocol, or to drop out entirely. Meta-analyses of trials using pill counting to demonstrate compliance rates find in excess of 90% adhering to the protocol, but when patients are followed with blood markers of medication compliance, these rates fall to 70%. Compliance is a major issue which can lead to apparent trial failures despite true drug efficacy, and is particularly crippling to smaller companies capitalised for 'one shot on goal'. As a calibration point, the rate of real-world non-compliance to prescribed medications is estimated to reach 50%.

Trial Management

This failure category is concerned with organising and executing the events that must occur in order to guarantee the successful running of a trial on a daily, monthly, and longer basis. It is a human-intensive project management task, involving tens to hundreds of skilled individuals of various backgrounds from professional trial managers, to statisticians, clinicians, ward nurses, pharmacists, and primary care physicians.

The project management process begins before the trial has even begun, and includes seeking the approval of the ethics committee, confirming the content of consent forms, the selection of trial sites, human resourcing, and arranging logistics for the movement of drugs and samples between multiple stakeholders.

Coordinating and implementing hundreds of complex and interconnected process requirements as a drug progresses through its trial, ensuring all documentation is correctly maintained for presentation to the regulator, and that the results end up in a database for analysis is extremely costly and burdensome.

Failures of trial management can have serious negative impacts on drug approval, and the types of failure vary from the mundane – late filing of forms, failing to respond to regulators questions on time, cost overruns – to the more serious.

Serious failures generally involve violations of Good Clinical Practice (GCP) – 'a set of internationally recognised ethical and scientific quality requirements that must be followed when designing, conducting, recording and reporting clinical trials that involve people'.

The top five reported GCP violations which can lead to trial failure are:

- Deviation from the approved trial protocol
- Accounting for trial drugs and specimens
- Poor clinical record keeping
- Issues around informed consent, including loss of forms
- Failure to report adverse events

We will cover the first two points here, and the remaining three come under the topic of 'Data Management' to be covered in the following section.

Protocol Deviations

Deviation from the trial protocol can occur in many forms, but the most likely causes of error are human in nature. A protocol may be extremely complex, with an unclear timeline, and difficult for any one person to remember precisely. When the protocol is deployed across multiple sites in parallel, the intercommunication and coordination between all partners can simply fail. The sequencing of myriad events centred around the patient, including clinic booking, results gathering (including blood sampling), and face-to-face discussions, can also be delayed or forgotten leading to cascade failures, loss of data, and patient disengagement.

Other human-centric issues leading to protocol failure include the inadequate training and/or verification of individuals involved in the day-to-day running of the trial, and excessive bureaucracy involved in contract negotiation, review and documentation, leading to the loss of enjoyment and interest from senior staff who once undertook trials out of scientific curiosity. These problems are more pronounced in trials involving community research or primary care physicians, who often have full workloads and booked-out clinics into which they cannot fit the requisite trial activities. In for-profit health systems, primary care physicians even see a financial disincentive for referring patients away from their care into that of a hospital running a clinical trial.

The final serious protocol deviation to consider is that of patient unblinding. Most Phase II and III trials involve some degree of blinding – either the patient doesn't know whether they're taking a drug or a placebo ('single-blind'), or neither the patient nor their physician know ('double-blind'). This is because the placebo effect is incredibly powerful – it can cause patients to manifest the effects of alcohol intoxication, antidepressants, painkillers, and even diarrhoeal infections. Having a patient know which arm of the study they are on can result in statistically significant loss of placebo effects. Similarly, if their doctor is unblinded, they may interact differently with the patient, leading to the same outcome.

Accounting for Drugs and Specimens

Logistical failures should never happen in trials. The number of samples required for endpoint monitoring in each patient are not sufficiently excessive to excuse any loss between the clinic and the lab. Similarly, costly and precious trial drugs should be fully tracked from production through to delivery and discard. Unfortunately, both of these logistical failures are seen in clinical trials. Phase II and III trials are now international businesses, with drugs manufactured in one country shipped to a trial site in another. The supply chain needs to be dynamic and responsive to sporadic patient recruitment rates, with evidence of correct storage and patient delivery conditions to satisfy both clinical staff and the regulators. In response, there are now recognised standards for the manufacture and distribution of investigatory medicinal products, known as GMP and GDP respectively. Adhering to these is just as important as adhering to GCP.

International Trials

Many clinical trials are now attracted to emerging markets across Asia, Latin America, and the Middle East. This is due to a combination of lower trial management costs, and larger population sizes providing more patients with rare conditions or specific genetics. Access to these populations can pose a number of significant regulatory problems. In addition to the international standards of GCP, GMP, and GDP (GxP collectively), each nation has its own changing clinical trial regulations. Additionally, each nation has leeway to interpret the international standards as it sees fit – for example, the UK's regulatory authority interprets GDP more stringently than other EU nations. Navigating trial regulations must often be undertaken on a per-nation basis, which can have serious cost and time repercussions, leading to failure.

Adaptive Trials

One form of clinical trial which has emerged in the past two decades is the 'adaptive' or 'flexible' clinical trial. The FDA defines an adaptive design as "a study that includes a prospectively planned opportunity for modification of one or more specified aspects of the study design and hypotheses based on analysis of (usually interim) data from subjects in the study."

Adaptive trials are becoming increasingly attractive because they allow trials to change according to the accumulating evidence, so that as one hypothesis appears to have more evidence than another, the trial can prevent patients from being exposed to ineffective therapies and focus on those with greater efficacy. This can confirm efficacy sooner, and therefore save time and costs for the trial sponsor, in addition to being more ethically sound. The important part to note here and in the definition by the FDA is that these changes must be pre-planned and in accordance with accumulating evidence. It does not allow a trial to pivot and pursue a completely new hypothesis if the original one fails mid-trial, or to pursue serendipitous findings.

Unfortunately, it is difficult to pre-specify every possible eventuality, and therefore management is more complex than that of a classical clinical trial. Furthermore, statistical analysis may be fraught by early unblinding and false positives, and exposing analyses to trial managers may prematurely influence a decision to adapt.

The FDA and EMA however believe that the potential benefits outweigh these theoretical drawbacks, and thus the number of adaptive trials are likely to increase over time.

Data Management

Data equals money. None of the aforementioned problems – patient recruitment and retention, adherence to GxP and trial protocols, logistics, navigating costly international regulations – are of any value if the resultant data is worthless.

Final marketing approval for a drug hinges upon the quality of the data presented to the regulator. As a result, good data collection practices and clinical record keeping are of critical importance to the success or failure of a costly clinical trial.

Data can include everything from a patient's medical history, to samples and scans obtained to monitor trial endpoints, patient questionnaires, trial ethics approval, patient consent forms, and data regarding GMP and GDP for the drug itself. As mentioned previously, failures to capture these data are often considered as failures to adhere to GCP and are taken very seriously by regulatory authorities.

Errors in data collection itself include delayed or absent data entry, inconsistencies in the dataset, and poor data quality. Examples include:

- Delayed entry – blood metabolites measured 6 hours after drug administration may not be acceptable if the approved protocol required collection at 4 hours. These can be reduced with training and personal interest from those responsible for data entry

- Data inconsistencies – the use of different questionnaires between or within different trial sites, different interpretations of the same subjective scoring system by different trialists, or different measurement methods for the volumes of solid tumours on CT scans. These can be controlled for during the design phase of a trial, by the selection of the correct methodologies, and with rater training to ensure consistent application of recording scales

- Data quality – ranging from simple manual errors in data entry, to using data from the wrong patient, or the wrong scale or data collection tool for the measurement in question

No trial is entirely error free, but even the accepted practice of Source Data Verification (SDV) does not reduce errors to 0%. The lower bound on errors prior to verification is 0.45%, falling to 0.27% after 100% SDV. This is an extremely important finding, as SDV practices are estimated to account for an average 25% of an entire clinical trial budget. Moving to a risk-based SDV may reduce costs and maintain high data quality.

Further data errors arise from biases, either introduced by the raters themselves, or for other reasons such as patient attrition. Humans are inherently subjective creatures, and knowledge of a patient's course of treatment can lead physicians who want a breakthrough cancer drug to succeed, to knowingly or unknowingly influence their interpretation of outcomes. This is part of the reasoning behind double-blind trials, but even blinding doesn't prevent all rater bias.

Attrition bias is more subtle and arises from the unequal loss of participants from the different trial groups. This includes patients who withdraw, fail to comply, or even die. There are a number of statistical techniques that can be applied to overcome attrition bias, but it is better to ensure that good monitoring takes place, and that recruitment numbers into each arm are above the minimum required for significance.

The final data errors can occur during the analysis phase of the trial. Statistical analysis of clinical trials is a specialty in itself, with numerous tests and methods for interpreting the trial data. Unfortunately, errors during analysis can falsely elevate or suppress the significance of results, both of which lead to the failure of the trial.

Non-Reporting

In 2012, the European Medicines Agency mandated that results of trials must be posted on the EU Clinical Trials Register within a year of the end of the trial, and within six months of completion for trials involving children. There is a similar regulation in the USA in the FDA Amendments Act 2007 (FDAAA) which requires sponsors to post the results of certain categories of trial directly onto the public website ClinicalTrials.gov within a year of completion.

Yet a 2018 study published in the British Medical Journal discovered that only around half of EU trials (49.5%) had complied with these regulations, although with pharmaceutical groups faring better than non-commercial trialists such as universities. The results from analyses of ClinicalTrials.gov appear even worse, with fewer than 20% reporting outcomes.

Sadly, non-reporting of outcomes has been a longstanding feature of the clinical trial industry. The reasons can vary from the mundane (delayed paperwork, change of staff and responsibilities) to the malicious (hiding bad results to maintain funding), but there is nevertheless a legal and ethical requirement for trials to report their outcomes and adverse events so that the public may have faith in the trials process, and that the scientific community may learn from mistakes. A website has even been built by a team at Oxford University's Evidence-Based Medicine Data Lab specifically to track reporting compliance by all sponsors active within the EU, with Dr Ben Goldacre, Director of the Lab and lead author on the 2018 BMJ paper summarising the problem as follows:

"This problem strikes to the heart of evidence based medicine. We cannot make informed choices about which treatments work best, as doctors and patients, unless all results are reported.

The European Medicines Agency will gain legal powers to extract substantial fines from sponsors who fail to comply with reporting requirements from 2020 when EU Clinical Trials Regulation No 536/2014 comes into force. Perhaps this will finally close this loophole in the trial data collection process.

Role of the CRO

Given the increasing complexity and specialisation required to design, initiate, and administer the logistics of clinical trials, it is unsurprising that an entire industry has arisen to service these needs in the form of Contract Research Organisations (CROs). As a result of seeking cost-savings through outsourcing, approximately 20% of all R&D expenditure across the pharmaceutical industry is on purchasing services from CROs, an amount estimated to reach US$51.3bn by 2024.

CROs initially appeared in the 1970s as small private statistical or scientific consultancies, and while there are over 1,000 CROs in existence today, many have grown to provide all functionality required for implementing a clinical trial from end-to-end. Large multinational CROs such as Covance, IQVIA, Syneos Health, PAREXEL, PRA, and PPD now control over 50% of the CRO market. While the majority of activity undertaken by CROs encompass the three traditional trial phases, approximately one third are now 'full service' CROs, providing drug discovery in addition to trial services, blurring the lines between the divisions of labour in the industry. Smaller CROs try to differentiate themselves by providing access to highly specialised knowledge and technologies, and deep expertise in regulations, animal trials, or specific GxP.

Unfortunately, CROs have their own range of internal troubles. The increasingly competitive market for CRO services has led pharmaceutical companies to enter shorter contracts with multiple providers simultaneously, rather than building longstanding relationships with single CROs. This naturally forces CROs to compete against each other on time, price, and services.

As a result, CROs can require single monitors to take responsibility for a number of trials across multiple sites. These young professionals often have little specialist technical training and have to learn on the job, all for less pay than their peers in permanent roles at pharmaceutical companies. There are often quotas to fill and deadlines to meet, which has led to their reputation as 'bureaucratic bullies'.

And despite their specialisation and sizeable resources, CROs still fail to meet monitoring requirements set down by regulatory bodies. For example, the FDA's 2016 Bioresearch Monitoring (BIMO) Metrics report uncovered regulatory violations in 35% of trial inspections. These failures fell into all the categories previously discussed – failure to follow the investigatory plan, protocol deviations, inadequate record keeping, poor GxP, and inadequate communications with the review board.

Blockchain's Impact on 'Process' Failures

There are already moves within the industry to overcome 'process' failures through the adoption of better digital technologies. For example, TransCelerate BioPharma, a non-profit formed by multiple pharmaceutical industry members, has released the Common Protocol Template (CPT) in an attempt to harmonise clinical trial protocols.

There is a further recognition that the most burdensome part of the current trial process is the amalgamation and monitoring of documentation. CROs and others are investing in better digital tools for document management, workflow automation, and paper minimisation, called 'Clinical Trial Management Systems' (CTMS). There is a vision across the industry that automated analytic tools will be able to drill down into these electronic records to detect risks and issues such as adverse events, poor compliance, or pending statistical failures before they become too dangerous or costly to manage, or force a regulator to halt a trial.

Examples of current CTMS include Intrinsic, Castor EDC, OpenClinica, Clinical Studio, and ClinPlus. Open Source alternatives include Phoenix and Captivate. Most of these are cloud-based SaaS, and therefore require trust in the cloud provider.

Blockchain-based systems could provide a revolutionary new style of clinical trial management based upon time sequenced data, message standardisation, integrated auditing, process automation, data verification, and collaborative security enforced by all parties engaged in the common enterprise of a clinical trial. The benefits that such a system provides over existing paper-based trial management and monolithic cloud SaaS platforms will be explored for each aspect of 'process' failure.

Impact on Patient Management

While patient recruitment is a serious issue for clinical trials, and one of the reasons why CROs maintain large lists of individuals who have expressed prior interest in trial involvement, it is unlikely that blockchain technology alone can solve these issues. However, blockchain-based systems do have the potential to improve other elements of patient management such as consenting and trial adherence.

Briefly on the point of initial recruitment, patients need to become empowered to become their own advocates for trial recruitment, with the ability to ask their physicians directly about trials, and receive a suitable 'menu' for their personal consumption. The present methods for publishing information about active trials are inadequate and not designed around the potential users of such a system. But ultimately there are too few trials to begin with, particularly for rare conditions or ones requiring multi-site recruitment. Improvements to trial management and the reduction of process failures through blockchain technology could ultimately aid recruitment by increasing the number of active trials and ease with which patients can consent to and progress along a trial.

With respect to patient consent, the process of digitally signing documents and version tracking are solved problems in the realm of blockchain and computer science. But naturally, the technology is not where the problems lie. There are many ways to imagine capturing and tracking patient consent in the digital realm with varying levels of sophistication and security, from scanning a signed paper document, to recording a short video confirmation of consent with an 'app' (a method used by some banks), to using a highly-secure public-private signing mechanism. Different jurisdictions will undoubtedly pursue different technological solutions to confirming digital consent (e.g. the Estonian ID card contains a personal signing key). The blockchain community is also improving the technologies for storing, remembering, and recovering (or reconstructing) cryptographic signing keys.

Once consent has been successfully recorded in digital format, it can be passed into a distributed ledger solution for versioning, time-stamping, and visibility by all parties engaged in the common enterprise. Alternatively, this consent could be shielded using sophisticated cryptographic techniques (e.g. zero knowledge proofs) to hide certain patient details or permissions, but to expose others as needed. In fact, this initial consenting could trigger an entire cascade of trial-related events through smart contracts such as patient randomisation and automated scheduling of drug ordering from the factory or outpatient scans.

Ensuring regulatory compliance is as straightforward as sharing the live status of all recorded consent on the ledger, either directly because the regulator is party to the ledger, or as a collection of mathematical proofs that such data exists and has not been tampered with due to the intrinsic nature of blockchain. Should the trial protocol change, patients could be automatically contacted and asked to digitally affirm their consent to the new protocol. This simple application of version control, blockchain, digital identities and smart contracts would greatly reduce trial failures, wasted time, manpower, and regulatory concerns for all clinical trials.

Improving trial adherence is also within the remit of blockchain technology, though here by using behavioural economics to reward good behaviours and discourage the bad. Blockchain-based event tracking, smart contracting and peer-to-peer transfer of economic value could enable trial sponsors to automatically reward participants of all types (doctors, patients, monitors) for each trial activity they complete, thereby 'gamifying' the trial experience. The correct design and application of such mechanisms are known to motivate participation and productivity.

Beyond the direct reward of patient participation to improve adherence and reduce costs (e.g. directly paying a patient $5 when the system detects they have had their planned blood test within the allotted time period is much cheaper than paying the CRO for implementing the same), simplifying the overall process of engaging with the trial would greatly improve adherence. This can be as simple as using the patient's scheduled participation in a follow-up clinic to allow them to book a taxi on the company's time. Or providing them with a live tracker of their trial progress. Or anonymised statistics of the current numbers of patient enrolled so they feel part of something important that will help others – after all, this is one reason often cited by patients as the motivating factor for enrolling in clinical trials. All of these can be achieved by the application of blockchain technology to enact smart contracts, track identities, and aggregate structured time-sequenced data.

Impact on Trial Management

In order to accomplish true transformation of clinical trials by blockchain technology, we must first consider the process of a clinical trial. Clinical trials are all algorithms. Complex algorithms with many inputs, conditionals, and outputs, but algorithms all the same. And unlike legal or business contracts, clinical trial protocols are far more imperative in their language and terminology, with hard endpoints and conditionals. This makes them naturally more amenable to conversion into 'smart contracts' for execution on a blockchain.

Take for example the trial protocol for PAMELA, a Phase 2, non-randomized, open label, multi-centric translational research study into a specific type of breast cancer which ran from 2013-2017. The protocol describes in exquisite detail the trial design, intent, patient inclusion and exclusion criteria, statistical plan, endpoints, patient pathway, and data to be collected. The document then leads into detailed descriptions of almost every eventuality that has been considered for side effects, dose modifications, concomitant medication warnings, patient identification, adverse event reporting, responsibilities of investigators, when to contact sponsors, ethical standards, etc. The document is nothing if not comprehensive. And it is precisely these types of verbose documents which blockchain can potentially replace, to automate away large parts of the mechanics of a trial, thereby reducing the burdens on clinicians and trialists to give them space to think about the larger picture.

One page in the document presents a basic illustration of the study protocol, described in greater detail in the bulk text, with almost daily breakdowns of patient activity:

The immediate feature of interest is the timeliness of each event. On day 14 these blood tests will happen, in week 6 you will have an ultrasound, every day you will take drug X and in week 9 you will be given drug Y.

It is immediately apparent that beyond the problems of clinician education and engagement about the existence of this trial, thus patient recruitment, there a huge organisational burden of managing the calendars and booking the follow-ups for each patient to match this sequence of events, then monitoring the successful adherence across multiple sites to obtain 150 datasets.

Fortunately this trial used licensed medications. If this was instead a phase 2 trial of an unlicensed drug, the additional logistical complexities and human resources required would greatly inflate the costs and duration involved.

Imagine instead if the time sequenced, highly structured, algorithmic nature of the PAMELA trial was re-created as smart contracts to be executed on a blockchain between the parties to the trial, dramatically reducing the human resources requirement and therefore the costs as well as the chances of failing due to management errors or protocol deviations. Executing the functionality of the trial on the distributed system proves to all parties that the computation has been carried out correctly, and that each party (with the correct permissions) can track the outcomes of that execution. No cloud-based or standalone CTMS can provide these same assurances due to the centralisation of control in the hands of the system administrator. This is particularly problematic when imagining novel behavioural economic mechanisms to improve patient engagement, or the directly disbursement of payments to trial participants and staff for particular activities.

In the emerging world of adaptive trials, the pre-specified decision tree could also be hard-coded into the trial's smart contracts, and fed by live statistical analysis accumulated from the data entered into the blockchain by the trialists. Such a system would greatly simplify the human resource requirement and statistical interventions to undertake an adaptive trial, and if correctly and comprehensively specified, the trial may even manage itself.

While trial protocol paperwork will remain in use for the foreseeable future, this will initially serve as a canonical backup to the automated execution system operating on the blockchain until such time as these have matured and been proven safe and correct. It is already possible to audit the code of smart contracts to ensure proper execution, and such assurances would be essential to build an automated trial management blockchain.

As mentioned previously, the moment a patient consents to take part (potentially from the comfort of their home after watching a brief webinar and then selecting a local specialist physician to track their progress during the trial), the work of the trial manager is done automatically. Drug doses are ordered from the pharmaceutical company and pass through their logistics blockchain to be delivered to the trial site, with this data also logged in the trial report. All appointments, investigations, and operations are scheduled according to the trial's algorithm. Access to pre-paid taxis is enabled for the days when travel is required, and these could even arrive at the patient's doorstep with just a confirmatory text message the night before. Changes in the patient's plans, adverse events, or broken MRI scanners will trigger the automatic rescheduling of the necessary elements of the trial protocol, while also flagging the reasons to the trial monitor and appending this in the final report to the regulator. Furthermore, adherence to multi-jurisdictional regulations can be hard-coded into the system.

Blockchain-based clinical trial management using smart contracts can ensure protocol deviations, record keeping, logistics, and poor adverse event recording are no longer reasons for trial failure, and improve the introduction of adaptive trial designs.

Impact on Data Management

Finally, blockchain has the improvement of data management and trust as its native features by time-stamping each and every data entry (and with certain designs, each request for data from the system), attaching identifiers to each party engaged with the system, and ensuring no user can tamper with data.

This is not to say the old adage of 'garbage in, garbage out' (GIGO) no longer applies – instead blockchain ensures that liability for behaviour is tracked and attached to the correct party. With the regulator as one of the parties to the blockchain, this could improve the route to final approval, enable live reporting and feedback, and ensure that no trial data goes unreported.

One final item to note is that the blockchain also serves as the infrastructure layer of a more elaborate and holistic trial data system. By enforcing universal and transparent standards on data formatting and management, underpinned by secure cryptography so that knowing how to add and read data doesn't automatically grant the ability to do so, other developers and companies can add new features on the layers above.

This extensibility could include tailored data entry software for each role in the trial, or dashboards customised to different groups (e.g. the regulator), all accessed through an 'app store' of sorts. In this way, the users are not bound to the decisions of the software company that provided the blockchain infrastructure, in much the same way that developers are free to build multiple services atop the same internet. This can create a free market of ideas for additional functionality, all using the same data layer enforced by the clinical trial's blockchain.

Clinical trials employing the uniform and incorruptible data infrastructure of blockchain could also benefit from automated analytics, so that trialists can observe live warnings about poor recruitment from certain locations, the need to add more patients matching certain criteria to prevent trial deviation through patient attrition, or warn of the emergence of biases. The software performing the analysis could also be published beforehand to reassure all participants and reviewers that the outcomes were not altered.

With a blockchain-enabled trial, there is also the possibility of 'gamification' to improve data entry, in a manner similar to that used to improve patient adherence, with financial incentives designed to balance desirable and undesirable behaviours. For example, independent cross-checking of data entry could release direct rewards for those who find errors, and equally who have entered correct data. Such a system would necessarily have to be designed to prevent collusion and corruption.

Blockchain technology presents the clinical trial community with the possibility of achieving perfect data management, and even more collaboration and data sharing between regulators, research bodies, pharmaceutical companies, trial sites, and trial managers (including CROs).

Conclusion

We have seen that classical clinical trials are expensive, lengthy processes, involving the coordination of multiple unaligned parties around a common goal. The role of coordination and management has largely been given over to CROs who provide outsourcing services for large pharmaceutical companies, the largest 10 of which control half of the drug trial market.

Despite this growing expenditure, and ultra-specialisation of trial management by CROs, there are still many failure modes which shouldn't exist. These range from failures of the basic science which underpins the trial, to procedural failures of patient, trial, and data management.

If the future treatments for cancer, autoimmune diseases, hypertension, kidney failure, or heart disease are going to be highly individualised therapies based on 'omics',, how do we ever hope to prove these therapies beyond a basic Phase I safety assessment using a classical clinical trial design? Even adaptive trial designs face concerns of ad hoc adaptation and statistical problems.

If we wish to see a future landscape of globally-distributed, highly-tailored, micro-scale clinical trials, we need to improve patient self-enrolment, automaticity, reliability, and data transparency.

While Existing Clinical Trial Management Systems (CTMS) hold some promise for improving aspects of patient recruitment, data entry & collection, trial monitoring, logistics, remuneration and reporting, these systems are monolithic silos, often deployed as cloud-based SaaS without the redundancy, availability, and transparency guarantees of blockchain.

Blockchain presents us with the opportunity to realise the low-cost, highly personalised therapies of the future through secure, distributed, automated, clinical trials.

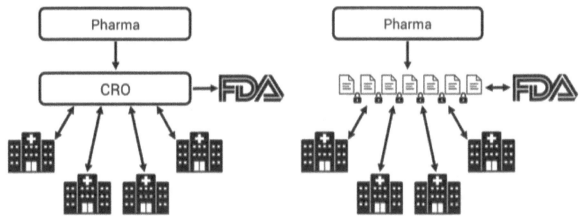

Left: Current clinical trial coordination. Right: Clinical trial coordination through a blockchain platform.

Chapter 8:
Utilizing Blockchain Technology to Improve Clinical Trials

Karin Beckstrom

ERT

Editor's Note:

In the second of our two part conversation on clinical trials, ER's Karin Beckstrom explores how trust and transparency issues between clinical trials stakeholders can affect our ability to speed drugs to market. She highlights how industry groups are coming together to advance new ideas and early stage blockchain and distributed ledger projects.

ABSTRACT

The pharmaceutical industry is in the midst of transformation as a result of confounding demands to accelerate time to market, increase patient centricity and reduce the development and validation costs for new drugs. This chapter explores how the mistrust that exists between clinical trial stakeholders can affect this transformation and identifies areas where distributed ledger technology, aka blockchain, could help. We present how pharmaceutical and other industry consortiums such as PhUSE and iEEE, as well as individual companies, are advancing the concept of blockchain from thought exercises and white papers to pilots, prototypes and beyond. In conclusion, we review our lessons learned from early stage blockchain projects, identify where blockchain can provide the most value and provide a roadmap for standard clinical trial use.

UTILIZING BLOCKCHAIN TECHNOLOGY TO IMPROVE CLINICAL TRIALS

Blockchain provides opportunities to improve three distinct clinical trial areas; data control, data access, and auditing. Note that the use of blockchain for authenticating supply chains, including the drug distribution chain is covered elsewhere in the book. Here we focus on the multiple use cases and potential of blockchain related to clinical trial data.

Before we consider the value and barriers to using blockchain technology in clinical research, we first need to understand the challenges in how clinical trials are conducted today. Matching the lessons learned from current blockchain projects against these challenges' points to a case for how blockchain can help improve clinical trials.

CLINICAL TRIALS UNDER PRESSURE

"While clinical trials have evolved and improved over time—producing impressive advances in diagnosis, treatment, and prevention—there are still major challenges. Therefore, fundamental changes are needed to reflect science and society's movement to increase efficiency, accountability, and transparency in clinical research."

Toward a New Era of Trust and Transparency in Clinical Trials
K. Hudson, M.Lauer, F.Collins [1]

Clinical trials have evolved over the decades and have now reached a unique point, as pharmaceutical companies face multiple, simultaneous pressures to reduce development costs, accelerate time to market, and to share data. These pressures are not isolated but rather behave like billiard balls, play off of one another and amplify the pressure. Luckily, technology advances such as artificial intelligence (AI), translational health data mining, nanotechnology and sensors are disrupting the way clinical trials are conducted. But in order for a true transformation to occur, we must reach a higher degree of trust among clinical trial stakeholders, including patients, clinicians, sponsors, and regulators.

We have seen in the financial sector that the leading blockchain use case is to establish trust between unknown parties. In clinical trials, the first, and most important problem that blockchain could potentially solve is to enable trust among all clinical trial stakeholders. If honesty and truthfulness are bedrock principles of scientific research, then trust is the foundational principle in clinical trials:

- Patients need to trust that participating in a clinical trial won't cause them harm, and that it may help themselves or the greater good

- Sponsors need to trust that clinicians will conduct the study according to the protocol requirements

- Governments need to trust that regulations are met during the trials

- All stakeholders need to trust that the clinical trial data collected are accurate and true and that the data will be maintained should future concerns arise

Today these relationships are easily broken and rely on multiple systems and expensive processes such as source data verification and site monitoring to maintain a minimum level of trust.

Patient Trust

When Rebecca Skloot [2] wrote about Henrietta Lacks' cells being taken and used in clinical research for years, without consent or even her knowledge, she touched upon a growing topic among patients and their advocates — that patients need control of their data because historically, pharmaceutical companies and health institutions haven't always behaved responsibly. Patients being made into unwitting study subjects and their data being distributed without consent are acknowledged, historical problems in the industry.

Clinical trial sponsors have evolved their procedures to address this lack of trust but have not fully succeeded. For example, while government regulations and Institutional Review Boards require clinical trial participants to go through an informed consent process, we find problems still exist today. [3] In 2016 there was a prominent case in France where participants were not reconsented after serious adverse events occurred with other participants. [4] Today's informed consent process, when done correctly, provides patients the knowledge of what data will be collected and the procedure to collect it but does not extend to where the data is stored nor disclose everyone who will access it in the future. More importantly, there is no means for patients to track who ultimately used their data and for what purpose. Most people are altruistic when it comes to sharing health data for the greater good but that does not mean they want their data shared forever without their knowledge or agreement. [5]

"Some people are afraid of their health data being misused, and we cannot ignore these worries. However, there are good, practical solutions to such concerns. For example, we believe block chain technologies will play a key role. They offer an inherently secure way to ensure that large amounts of data can be shared without risk of unauthorized modification or alteration."

Sandoz, a Novartis Division

Protocol Execution Trust

Sponsors wholly depend on the Principal Investigator and the clinical site staff to accurately follow the protocol and document the data correctly. This includes:

- Enrolling only those patients who match the inclusion criteria
- Collecting patient informed consent and reconsent when needed
- Accurately preforming tests
- Collecting data.

While it is difficult to gauge how prevalent protocol violations and fraud occur, a survey of research coordinators found that 19% of respondents had first-hand knowledge of clinical research misconduct in the previous year. [6]

The public must also trust the sponsors' ability to assess effectiveness; with regulators, payers and patients having their say in how effectiveness is defined. Recently the industry has made inroads to include patient's input while the protocol is being written and throughout the trial process, but, in general the public continues to have a degree of uncertainty about how accurately drug manufacturers portray successful medicines and if they are identifying all of their potential harms.

Government Trust

The complexities of phase III clinical trials are exponentially increased by their global reach, as clinical trial sponsors are responsible for adhering to all country, regional and local regulations. Building in mechanisms for monitoring and auditing is expensive and time consuming, two of the critical problems the industry is trying to resolve.

In the area of patient safety, these same regulatory agencies often review clinical trial data retrospectively which can result in risks to patients' health and to the validity of the trial data. An example is a recent case where after a trial concluded, it was found that certain geographic regions did not give the participants the study drug.7 Not only were the patients prevented from receiving medicine with a potential positive health effect, but the data had to be thrown out. By providing real-time access to audit trails through blockchains — including those tracking the medicine from creation through to the patient — clinical trial sponsors can prevent wasted data collection and help improve patient safety.

Trust in accuracy of results

Misconducted research does occur, although thankfully not frequently. Today we rely on a culture which encourages patients, health care providers and other stakeholders to question whether codes of conduct are being adhered to and to investigate suspicious results, so they can trust in the data results. [8]

Record Keeping Trust

It is impossible to know how an approved drug will work for every patient, in every condition over time and, as a result, problems sometimes occur in the field. In some cases, those problems are broad-based, and regulators will call for a review of the trial data to understand more. In the United States trial data must be kept for a minimum of two – three years depending on the type of data. Today, the only way to verify the data is being maintained as required is through manual inspection.

Beyond Trust

As clinical trials and general healthcare move closer together, we continue to see systemic struggles with extracting and moving data between systems. The use of disparate EMR/EHR systems to search for patients and place data into or pull data from adds complexity, cost and time delays. While there are many organizations working on standards —some of which are gaining ground, such as the Fast Health Interoperability Resources (FHIR) — a fully adopted, global standard does not currently exist. Solving or minimizing this struggle will lead to more efficient trials.

One final area of concern is the real possibility for anonymized data to be re-identified. Advanced computers, machine learning techniques, large publicly-available data sets and social media, including online patient support groups are already enabling the re-identification of anonymized data. In particular, patients with less common diseases are at a high risk.9 This real possibility can undermine a patient's trust that their data will stay anonymized while it is used in research.

"Just because something is anonymized, it is still possible to identify who that is when you merge that record with other records that are available. Harnessing [de-identified patient] data for research purposes and targeted therapies is all great unless it falls into the wrong hands."

Sam Hanna, Director Health Informatics Program, George Washington University [10]

Lessons Learned

Pharmaceutical company Pfizer has been very active in developing prototypes and pilots for blockchain. Notably they have collaborated on blockchain with Deloitte regarding the opportunity that patient data donations can have toward improving clinical research. Munther Baara, Head of New Clinical Paradigm and Sascha Mundstein, Senior Technologist from Pfizer are actively involved with blockchain across several fronts, including prototyping how blockchain could enhance the informed consent process.[11] [12]

In order for blockchain to work effectively, it takes a community of participants working together on the same platform. Recently Amgen, Sanofi and Pfizer have collaborated on using blockchain to speed up clinical trials.[13] [14] They are exploring ways to instill patient confidence in data security and potentially incentivizing patients to share their data with researchers — something that regulators have frowned upon due to the risk of influencing research results — but with more control and better anonymization, this risk can be reduced. According to The Center for Information & Study on Clinical Research Participation (CISCRP), 57% of patients consider potential costs and reimbursements an important influencer on their decision to participate in clinical studies.[15]

"Blockchain is really about industrializing trust."
Milind Kamkolkar, Sanofi's Chief Data Officer [14]

ERT conducted a blockchain learning experiment which encompassed tracking protocol updates and the connected patient re-consenting process. One of our key lessons learned in building the code and the infrastructure to run a blockchain solution is that it requires significant technological effort on the part of all validating nodes. Once up and running, costs are reduced but still require engineering or IT support on an on-going basis. The following were identified network/technology considerations that all companies considering creating a chain or becoming a validating node should consider:

- Support for private blockchains (roles, permissions, etc.)

- Parallel transaction processing

- Selecting an economical consensus algorithm versus the Proof of Work method typically used in crypto-currency solutions, as it requires considerable amount of CPU/GPU horsepower

- Is there a user-friendly command-line interface (CLI)?

- How much effort is required to roll out and manage validators (nodes)?

- Are the SDKs offered in the most popular programming languages?

- Is there an active technical support group (online all day)?

By identifying solutions that meet those needs, you will narrow down the list that your proposed blockchain community should consider.

Other organizations have used the informed consent process to test the capability of blockchain. One of the first published examples, entitled "Blockchain protocols in clinical trials: Transparency and traceability of consent" was conducted by three researchers: Mehdi Benchoufi andRaphael Porcher, Département d'Epidémiologie Clinique, APHP, Paris, France and Philippe Ravaud, Centre de recherche Inserm Epidémiologie et Statistique Paris Sorbonne Cité (U1153), Université Paris Descartes, Paris, France.16, 17 Their pilot assigned the patient a private key to use and maintain, something that more recent patient prototypes have tried to work around. The major concerns this first prototype identified included the scalability of blockchain technology and the lack of a network standard.

Scalability is a known concern for all potential blockchain uses. Even when all data except the transactional audit record is stored elsewhere, the time to validate a block of data for the chain increases as blocks are added, eventually causing significant delays if the blockchain grows for a long enough time. Recently there have been distributed ledger alternatives proposed, such as those that provide linear scalability and break up across multiple nodes similar to the peer-to- peer network BitTorrent, but with full consensus security and auditability. It is fully expected that as the industry matures better options will become available. Additionally, standards work, such as that being done by IEEE, will also improve the experience by providing a guide to follow.

Considerations for blockchain use

Today, there are clinical trials so burdensome to patients that they become an "option of last resort." It is critical that this doesn't occur across the board or the current struggle to enroll enough patients and keep them in trials will further slowdown the entry of effective drugs into the market and increase the costs of doing so. It is imperative for the industry to find solutions which make clinical trials more appealing to patients and less burdensome.

With that in mind, any blockchain solution must minimize patient and site effort as well as data risks. Building solutions where the "cost" in terms of training, complexity, or risk is too high will become a wasted effort as adoption rates will not meet expectations. Relying on clinical trial experience, such as knowing that patients will lose passwords or cryptography keys given to them and applying human-centered design principles that elevate known issues and account for typical human behavior will enable blockchain-based solutions to fit into the patient's life and site personnel workflow.

One of the reasons that pharmaceutical companies are banding together to identify blockchain solutions, like the PhUSE consortium on emerging technologies18 is that blockchain only works when there are numerous participants sharing the ledger and the larger the number of validating nodes, the more secure the chain. The consensus-building effect of the research and prototype projects helps to ensure there will be enough participants to make an effective chain. One school of thought is that the pharmaceutical industry will append to general healthcare blockchains as a means of ensuring enough participants.

In the virtual currency world, if users lose their digital wallet or key to access the blockchain, they lose their currency. In the world of clinical trials, you can't allow data loss merely because participants lose their keys. Blockchain solutions must include a mechanism for the retrieval of a security code or alternatively provide management of the security code on behalf of patients and sites. One risk to providing this service is that managing the keys or even providing a key retrieval solution reduces the decentralized nature of blockchain by giving one entity control of access. Providing these safeguards against data loss is crucial and more user-friendly, with only a small reduction in the overall security of the blockchain.

Clinical trials revolve around diverse sets of data. The collection, validation, and analysis of data are the reasons trials exist at all. A study may collect vital information, laboratory data, electrocardiograms, central imaging, respiratory data, patient reported outcomes, clinician reported outcomes and more recently, large amounts of data collected directly from patient-worn sensors. An activity meter worn 24/7 for several weeks can generate gigabytes of data. This data helps assess a drug's impact on the patient's everyday life instead of sporadically during a clinic visit.

Additionally, trial sponsors are starting leverage at-home lab kits or the use of visiting nurses to collect data from patients at their home or office. Currently blockchain solutions are not able to effectively store all this data and any solution will need to identify how the remote data —from multiple devices and sources — is automatically accounted for by creating a transactional record of the data at regular collection intervals. There is an active iEEE project looking at potential standards for tracking health-related Internet-of-Things (IoT) data from the device to blockchain. [19] The important elements data transactional records should contain are: who's data, what device, type of data, the time period covered, when it was captured and where it is stored.

None of these considerations should dissuade the use of distributed ledger technology and the promise of immutable, accessible audit trails but they should be discussed and addressed prior to embarking on a solution.

The Roadmap Ahead

Let's look to the future and identify where, if applied, distributed ledger technology can improve clinical trials: data control, data access and audit trail, and finally how the technology is evolving.

Data Control and Access

Patient Advocate Jack Whelan was diagnosed with Waldenström macroglobulinemia, a rare type of non-Hodgkin lymphoma, in 2007 and metastatic prostate cancer in 2016, when there were no treatment options available. As part of his treatment plan, Whelan took part in several clinical trials and during the trials would manually pull all his data together in a spreadsheet to monitor his progress. He spent this effort and time for two reasons: to be his own health champion and to share the data with his healthcare team and other researchers.

Jack passed away before a systematic method to track and share personal health data became available but distributed ledger technology now provides an option. Tracking clinical trial data and participant-generated data on a blockchain provides a record of what data can potentially be reused by other researchers.

With a complete, immutable record of clinical trial data, potentially combined with general health and wellbeing information is compiled, the next step is allowing others to find that data and request access to it. There are new companies looking at how to allow searching of this metadata without physically sharing it. Enhancing a blockchain with smart contracts can provide access to the data, with search capabilities approved by the participant. [20]

Using blockchain to share clinical trial data in a secure, controlled manner can also help pharmaceutical companies meet regulation requirements. In late 2016 the EU mandated the sharing of health data in order to push this reuse capability and enable faster scientific research, but it stressed the importance of having explicit consent to do so and the rights to withdraw that consent in the future. Blockchain embedded with smart contracts provides a mechanism to meet those mandates.21 While recent US guidelines direct that sharing de-identified clinical trial data does not require separate consent from trial participants, putting patients in control of their data enables them to know when it is shared, and serves as a positive engagement tool. Additionally, the tools and means to re-identify previously de-identified data are common place today and safeguarding even de-identified data becomes a necessary security measure.

Audit Trail

Probably the most immediate advantage of using distributed ledger technology is the audit record that is created as metadata is validated and added to the chain. Once a record of data collection is validated and added to the chain, it becomes a permanent record of a clinical trial action. In the example of tracking patient informed consent, anyone granted access to the data stored on the blockchain — such as a regulator or monitor — can see the history by protocol version, by patient or by site. Additionally, you can layer in smart contract technology that could prevent additional data capture within clinical trial systems if the patient was not properly consented on the latest protocol version.

Example of a readable audit record stored via blockchain technology

Study Name: ENDO7250-002   CURRENT VERSION IS **1.3**
History:

Version	Date
1.0 (Accept)	Aug 13, 2018, 6:44:19 AM
1.2 (Accept)	Aug 13, 2018, 3:40:21 PM
1.3 (Accept)	Aug 16, 2018, 12:40:44 PM

PATIENT **S003-0101** FOR STUDY **ENDO7250-002** IS UP TO DATE, NO ADDITIONAL SIGNATURES NEEDED

Example of encrypted transaction records within blocks on the chain

	Number		
See all transactions	or 17	:	Back Next

Txid	Block	From
0dc93b6774bbd481ea5fd05b2...	61	0218cd555765ecc03aa40d7cb...
469b625465494ce769d69db34...	60	0218cd555765ecc03aa40d7cb...
bc8d7645e9255939f5e89ca43...	59	02af42df72fc8fff6c2917785...
41bb4b979a96328b70c7ff993...	58	02af42df72fc8fff6c2917785...
9697495ee5e4a847bdda8e5c2...	57	03afd214b2f087eea91dd7294...
c9bec4411a756266d9297fa7e...	56	03afd214b2f087eea91dd7294...
5905334df8fe51d9d19aa8272...	55	02af42df72fc8fff6c2917785...
d578bc1bd7163da248093567a...	54	03afd214b2f087eea91dd7294...
8b4b0eb4204ab1f41f507bb02...	53	03afd214b2f087eea91dd7294...
c39dac3e0137dbf0e58d76ac9...	52	02af42df72fc8fff6c2917785...
9673cf934061fcd5fa4484882...	51	02af42df72fc8fff6c2917785...
e0a240f337cb7fcb8aa17eb43...	50	03f3e10239bc88308011bcee2...
f3d618ab216d79e59a8d68947...	49	03f3e10239bc88308011bcee2...
56ec31cc6e43c711f8f0c2a26...	48	03904b9d0a14f05ec40540a68...
f25e090374fcdcc1a08ce37c1...	47	03904b9d0a14f05ec40540a68...
3a95f878068f72bf9d6a3ee8b...	46	027cf65719732bf8e7bad3eb3...
743678c1a2350e398cfe5b979...	45	027cf65719732bf8e7bad3eb3...

This essential audit trail allows you to track the origins of data, just like you track a medicine through the supply chain; you have the ability to know when the data was created, who it was captured for, and where it has been shared.

Decentralized audit record and data

As clinical trials embrace patient centricity, giving patients control of their own data and the ability to further share that data becomes a cornerstone of the movement. The fact that all clinical trial records and related health records are currently not standardized shouldn't get in the way of patients controlling their own data. Even with data generated solely by the patient, it can quickly expand to some lab data and some medical test results as entities join a chain.

There is a movement called DWeb which, like blockchain, has decentralization as a goal, but this movement is focused on allowing individuals to create their own personal online datastore or "POD"22 in which they use blockchain technology to control access and sharing of the data. Clinical trials can leverage this concept by creating distributed individual clinical trial data stores and layer on a pharmaceutical industry blockchain to allow the person auditing, access, and control of their data.

As writers Michael J. Casey and Paul Vigna called out in their article "In Blockchain we Trust,"23 double entry ledgers elevated the entire accounting industry by instilling trust. In a similar fashion, blockchain invokes deep trust through the use of mathematical rules and cryptography which can in turn elevate clinical trials. Creating an immediate, immutable audit trail for all data within a clinical trial, which includes whose data it is, the data collection time period, how the data was generated (device, questionnaire etc.) and where the data are located can enable the trust needed for critical trials to run efficiently. Using this mechanism to put the participant in control of their data addresses historical concerns and current regulatory hurdles.

Going a step beyond the creation of a transactional metadata record on a blockchain is the concept of extending it to personal online datastores as proposed by Sir Timothy Berners-Lee, commonly known for inventing the World Wide Web.24 Offering clinical trial participants a personal data store which itself is maintained in a distributed, secure, immutable manner can enable and encourage participation in research and extend the value of the data by sharing it with other researchers.

In conclusion

While blockchain and distributed ledger software are immature technologies, the data trust it would inherently provide to all clinical trial participants warrants the investment in time and resources to continue moving the early community projects forward. The real goal is to deploy one or more global, phase III trials with blockchain securing the patient data. This goal is really just a starting point for more patient control of their data and more trusted, approved data sharing.

References

1. https://www.ncbi.nlm.nih.gov/pmc/articles/PMC5101947/

2. https://www.shmoop.com/the-immortal-life-of-henrietta-lacks/summary. html and https://www.litcharts.com/lit/the-immortal-life-of-henrietta-lacks/summary

3. https://www.forbes.com/sites/larryhusten/2011/11/20/more-details-emerge-about-the-dutch-research-scandal/#62c7e7543af4

4. https://www.liberation.fr/france/2016/02/04/drame-de-l-essai-clinique-a-rennes-le-deces-reste-inexplique_1431074

5. https://www.ciscrp.org/education-center/charts-and-statistics/ and https://www.ciscrp.org/wp-content/uploads/2018/05/Willingness-and-Knowledge-Clinical-Research-1280x720.png

6. Habermann B, Broome M, Pryor ER, Ziner KW. Research coordinators' experiences with scientific misconduct and research integrity. Nurs Res. 2010;59(1):51–57. [PMC free article] [PubMed

7. https://blogs.sciencemag.org/pipeline/archives/2017/04/27/a-clinical-trial-torpedoed-by-fraud-and-incompetence

8. http://www.appliedclinicaltrialsonline.com/what-can-you-do-prevent-clinical-trial-fraud

9. https://www.georgetownlawtechreview.org/re-identification-of-anonymized-data/GLTR-04-2017/

10. https://www.modernhealthcare.com/article/20180407/NEWS/180409938

11. https://www2.deloitte.com/content/dam/Deloitte/us/Documents/process-and-operations/us-cons-blockchain-opportunities-patient-data-donation-clinical-research.pdf

12. http://theconferenceforum.org/conferences/disruptive-innovations-us/overview/ 2017 conference

13. https://www.technologyreview.com/the-download/609927/drugmakers-think-blockchains-could-improve-clinical-trials/

14. https://www.sanofi.com/en/science-and-innovation/blockchain-technology-the-next-digital-platform-in-healthcare

15. https://www.ciscrp.org/wp-content/uploads/2018/05/Information-Influencing-Participation-1280x720.jpg

16. https://www.ncbi.nlm.nih.gov/pmc/articles/PMC5676196.5/

17. https://f1000research.com/articles/6-66/v1

18. https://www.phuse.eu/emerging-trends

19. https://blockchain.ieee.org/ https://innovationatwork.ieee.org/can-

blockchain-rescue-the-stalled-iot/

20. https://www.technologyreview.com/s/610221/this-new-company-wants-to-sequence-your-genome-and-let-you-share-it-on-a-blockchain/

21. Official Journal of the European Union. 50 Regulation (EU) No 536/2014 of the European Parliament and of the Council of 16 April 2014 on clinical trials on medicinal products for human use. 2014. https://ec.europa.eu/health/sites/health/files/files/eudralex/vol-1/reg_2014_536/reg_2014_536_en.pdf

22. https://www.computing.co.uk/ctg/news/3036546/decentralising-the-web-the-key-takeaways

23. https://www.technologyreview.com/s/610781/in-blockchain-we-trust/

24. https://www.inrupt.com/blog/one-small-step-for-the-web

Chapter 9:
Blockchain Technologies: the View from a Healthcare Incumbent

Kyle Culver

Editor's Note:

In Chapter nine, Humana's Kyle Culver explains the role of the incumbent enterprise in the rapid innovation happening in the healthcare blockchain space. Culver provides visibility in to how enterprise innovation teams approach this new technology, find meaning in the early work, and think through how to collaborate (even with one's competitors).

Only a few years ago, Blockchain was little more than a background detail in the Bitcoin narrative, and certainly not on the healthcare technology agenda. However, that has changed quickly, revealing ample opportunity for innovation across industries. This chapter will look at the emergence of Blockchain, share why it's important for firms to pay attention to disruptive technologies and discuss how firms might approach capitalizing on the Blockchain opportunity in the healthcare space.

In 2013, four years after Satoshi Nakamoto released the Bitcoin whitepaper, a novel idea began to gain credibility: Blockchain is bigger than Bitcoin. In 2014, the notion of Blockchain as significant opportunity continued to gain momentum, expanding across industries from the starting point of financial technology (FinTech). By 2015, the notable enterprise blockchain software firm R3 had formed a consortium that grew to include most of the big-name banks. The Ethereum whitepaper released August 2016 further positioned Blockchain as a viable technology. From the vantage point of healthcare industry participants, it was clear that FinTech was committing to these emerging technologies, investing heavily in startup ventures to compete this new space. Healthcare technology players, commonly known as followers of FinTech trends, were taking notice. The hype surrounding Blockchain technologies continued to grow, but very little collateral had been created to define the opportunity for Blockchain in the healthcare space. That changed in 2016 when, in attempt to add some needed clarity, the Office of the National Coordinator for Health Information Technology (ONC), an entity within the U.S. Department of Health & Human Services (HHS), announced a Blockchain whitepaper challenge. The challenge attracted over 70 whitepaper entries espousing a diversity of ideas for Blockchain applications in healthcare. With this event, the focal points for healthcare became much clearer.

For Humana and many other large firms in the healthcare space, the ONC/HHS Blockchain whitepaper challenge was an opportunity for firms to take a position and showcase ideas that had been forming around emerging Blockchain technologies. Curious thought leaders shared and discussed the whitepaper entries broadly, helping stakeholders across the industry to inform and develop their individual perspectives. By this time, startups like Hashed Health were already emerging as leaders in Blockchain healthcare solutions, knocking on doors of healthcare incumbents, educating leaders on the technology and discussing potential opportunities. Incumbent firms like Humana needed to formulate a point of view.

Incumbents in most any industry must innovate in order to win. They must dedicate resources to paying attention to technology trends and skillfully delivering findings to leadership for consideration in strategic planning. One needs only to recall the fate of firms like Blockbuster, Borders, Blackberry and Nokia, all of which fell from dominance as their incumbent business models were rapidly disrupted by emerging technologies. As an incumbent, it is all too clear how much attention technology trends demand. Failing to seek out and continuously think about opportunities for innovation presented by new technologies – or existing technologies used in new ways – can be disastrous. Furthermore, those charged with thinking about innovation must discern the hype from the real opportunities, for the education they provide to senior leaders will guide where the enterprise will place its bets. During the initial stages of the leader education process, the focus should be on creating a clear, easy-to-understand and compelling narrative. Over time, depth and breadth of detail must be conveyed to decision makers, but to begin the conversation, it's beneficial to speak in simple terms and use analogies.

Because of the breadth of potential implications and the complexity of the technology, developing a point of view for the enterprise takes a blend of business and technology experience and expertise. After its initial fleshing out by a cross-functional group, the point of view must be socialized among senior leaders for the purpose of raising awareness about the technology, discussing implications and sharing context of the evolving landscape. Particularly important to note is that, for a rapidly evolving technology like Blockchain, the process of fleshing out and leadership socialization is not a one-time proposition; it must be ongoing. Actively working to mature and maintain that point of view is critical when working with a potentially disruptive technology to innovate.

The analogy of the internet can help start the Blockchain education conversation. It allows leaders to think about the possibilities Blockchain technologies offer without requiring them to learn everything about how Blockchain works. Today, when asked "What is the internet?" business leaders may not be able to explain its physical technology, but can certainly describe the its value proposition, the business value it creates and the business models it enables. Their answers are informed by the experiences they've had over decades since the internet rose to awareness. At the internet's inception, we simply had no experiences with it, in which case the same question would likely result in a technical description for an answer. Likewise, with Blockchain experiences not yet abundant or well understood, rather than answering the question, "What is Blockchain?" with experiential descriptions, we often end up answering the question "How does Blockchain work?" by responding with a technical description. However, the latter is less useful to the nontechnical audience.

Three other points from the internet analogy are useful when explaining blockchain technologies. First, with the value proposition driven by network effect, Adoption is King. In other words, delivering value to many is better than delivering a lot of value to a few. This is because those making up a narrow participant audience are more likely to leave their smaller network to join a larger network when it becomes available for the same use case in the future as the larger network is more valuable. Explaining the implications of network effect helps enterprise leaders understand how the external relationships should be formed and that they should avoid decisions that hinder adoption. The second point to make is that the term "Blockchain" does not refer to just one thing; rather, it's a collection of technologies that provide a set of common capabilities. The final point is that the power of Blockchain is diminished if limited to the inside of the company, as with an intranet. It's more valuable when used to connect a wide range of external companies.

Ensuring leaders are aware of the above points and the key capabilities of Blockchain technologies enables decision makers to position test-and-learn activities that help mature the enterprise point of view. Understanding these points not only helps facilitate conversations about potential new opportunities, but also helps in understanding which existing revenue streams may be at risk from potential cannibalization or change that comes with wide Blockchain adoption. These conversations are best informed by domain experts who can imagine how these new capabilities can create new opportunities. A cross-functional working group of innovation-minded business and technology subject matter experts can drive these conversations to inform a firm's point of view.

Answering the question: "Why Blockchain?"

To advance the Blockchain discussion in the enterprise setting, it's important to be able to answer the question "Why Blockchain?" Most senior leaders who will ask this question care little about the hype stemming from mass media stories about cryptocurrencies. The first step is separating Blockchain from cryptocurrencies, and helping leaders to understand the difference between them. Misunderstandings are common and can confuse stakeholders, so the point must be made explicitly to dispel incorrect views. Given the lacking maturity of the technology, adding it to the technical stack of a solution adds risk. Risk must be justified, especially when a solution using another technology could be successful. Also, stakeholders need a compelling reason to adopt, since new technologies in and of themselves don't always drive adoption. Consider the facsimile (fax) machine. The fax is, by most standards, a long outdated communication device, yet it remains a prevalent communication channel in our healthcare system even with a variety of more contemporary channels with greater utility available. Will Blockchain be left on the shelf while older technologies with limitations remain as popular as the fax machine? The answer to this question will depend in part on the use case and the friction point being addressed. That said, your educational narrative should include some key points to help leaders prepare for evaluating the ways in which Blockchain technologies might provide the capabilities healthcare needs. When leaders who are experts in a given domain are equipped with information that enables them to understand when blockchain technologies are well suited to address the needs of a given use case, they're prepared to create novel disruptive concepts in that domain.

When creating the "Why Blockchain?" section of the narrative you'll share, you must include the related concepts of transparency and network effect. Transparency is driven by the fact that Blockchain technologies indiscriminately share information with a network of participants. This level of sharing is fundamentally different from the way in which traditional centralized systems exchange information. Consider the real-world example of retailer Walmart requiring suppliers of the leafy green food products they stock to share information about the products on the firm's Blockchain network. This information allows Walmart and the network's participants to understand where leafy green products originate, providing traceability should they need to enact a product recall. The Walmart example helps demonstrate both transparency and network. The platform is shared, with all participants in the network having equal access to read and write information, making it quite different from a traditional black-box centralized solution. Today, many retailers selling leafy greens maintain individual traceability systems, but if they were to participate in the Blockchain network and use the shared capabilities, their common suppliers would no longer need to interact with multiple traceability systems removing duplicated efforts acorss the ecosystem. The example of the Blockchain-enabled unified traceability function helps to answer "Why Blockchain?" by showing the relationship between transparency and network effect, and its overall impact on Blockchain value.

Your narrative should also discuss the advantage of utility. Blockchain technologies are well suited to create "utility" platforms, as in the Walmart example. Utility platforms enable efficient information sharing and collaboration at a foundational level, freeing resources from time-consuming lower level processing so they can work at higher levels where firms can differentiate to compete and deliver real value to stakeholders. An example of a utility platform that doesn't use Blockchain is the marketplace provided by Amazon. Amazon allows sellers to compete at the higher level, where they differentiate based on price, quality or service, while Amazon's underlying capabilities provide utility for those buyers and sellers. NASDAQ is another example. NASDAQ provides capabilities enabling the exchange of securities. NASDAQ's exchange capabilities serve as a foundation for the many trading systems competing in the space. The difference Blockchain-powered utilities offer is that the ownership of the foundational platform is shared – or decentralized – among the group of participants as compared to being owned by a single entity, as with Amazon or NASDAQ.

To help answer the question "Why Blockchain?" your narrative should explain how leaders can determine the capabilities best suited for Blockchain. This will allow them to better assess the value of a Blockchain solution. What criteria should be used to determine the capabilities that are ripe for a shift to the utility platform? Capabilities that do not provide a competitive advantage, especially those seen as sources of shared friction, are ideal candidates for inclusion in Blockchain-powered utility platforms. Consider the healthcare space example of managing clinical provider data in provider directories. Historically, each firm has managed provider data independent of its competitors, even though they are maintaining the same data for providers they have in common. Some firms have competed in this space by marketing "accurate" data, while others have viewed provider data management solely as an operating expense. When viewed as a cost, provider data management is a candidate for collaboration; working together, competitors can reduce duplicated effort. A Blockchain-powered solution is well suited for collaboration among competitors because the ownership of the solution can be shared (decentralized). This is very different from depending on a single company to enable that collaboration in a centralized manner. Additionally, equally shared ownership alleviates disputes about who owns the solution. Think of Bitcoin. For years since its inception, Bitcoin has functioned autonomously – meaning, without centralized ownership. While shared ownership comes with its own set of challenges, it allows participants to avoid questions typical with a centralized solution such as "Who owns the solution and are they influencing its direction to create competitive advantage for only them?" Decentralization distributes the power across the participants, with each participant given the same level of authority and access. This accessibility and transparency allows all participants to compete on the same playing field, much like the internet. In this way, Blockchain technologies help create value for the entire group instead of a few well positioned participants, which means more firms are able to truly innovate and compete

Realizing the full potential of decentralized solutions requires a low barrier of entry to encourage innovation, competition and specialization. Imagine that large incumbent retailers Target, Walmart or others had decided to build a utility web platform on which customers could shop across all participating retailers using one cart! This would shift competition up a level, and instead of users being forced to different websites for each retailer they instead would compete with their offerings via the "shared" utility website. If this had happened prior to Amazon gaining traction these retailers would be much better positioned to compete against Amazon.

One other thing to consider is that Blockchain is typically only one part of a larger technical solution. This is helpful for leaders to know when thinking about the question "Why Blockchain?" Blockchain capabilities can make a solution better or can help overcome a key barrier, like ownership, as mentioned above. However, it's important for leaders to keep in mind that often the majority of the software development needed to enable such solutions occurs outside of Blockchain, so the cost/benefit analysis should be considered on the overall development of a given solution – not just the Blockchain portion. Because Blockchain plays a small role, expectations should be set that advancing a use case requires a more focused effort on governance and the business concept than the shiny emerging technology.

Establishing the philosophical difference

When discussing Blockchain and its implications within a large organization, you must help leaders understand the philosophical differences between Blockchain technologies and traditional centralized architectures and business models. Leaders must grasp that Blockchain is an inherently collaborative platform, thus best suited to address friction points owned by no single organization. As with the internet, no one firm owns it—and like the internet, while it's dependent on centralized systems, its capabilities provide utility for all involved, effectively leveling the playing field to a degree. Before agreeing to build capabilities on this new Blockchain-powered surface, decision makers must see the potential value they can derive from the utility they will gain through collaboration with competitors. Leaders, and eventually everyone involved, will need to not only understand the philosophical change, they will need to think differently during strategic planning activities. Today, when leaders think about where to compete, they focus on how their proprietary offerings can create a competitive advantage. With Blockchain, this thinking needs to shift: Leaders will now have two separate areas to consider when thinking about competing. First, they will need to consider where they can collaborate with competitors, and how they will define and create "utility" capabilities to be shared. In this first area of thought, they should begin by considering the many duplicative activities performed across the healthcare industry, for which the quality and efficiencies gained through Blockchain-powered crowd sourced solution could create value for stakeholders. The second area of thought would include assessing their firm's truly unique competitive advantages in a much more focused way.

Of course, other firms must make this philosophical shift as well, lest there will be no competitors with which to collaborate. Aligning multiple companies on a vision and approach to collaborate via a shared platform is no doubt a challenge. Furthermore, the task of engaging them to invest in the creation of a utility platform focused on solving systemic industry problems is a significant one, yet, by sharing a clear and compelling story, it's possible. It helps to begin by accepting that, historically, leaders of successful companies are accustomed to developing strategies that benefit their own firms and increase their own unique competitive advantages. Asking them to focus on collaboration with competitors requires that both one's own internal decision makers and competitors' decision makers see the value in the adage "a rising tide lifts all boats." The path toward embracing this mindset brings many questions for competitors to answer – for example, "Why now?" "Why us?" "What are the risks?" and "What is the expected return on investment?" – each of which requires time invested in thought. Furthermore, the value for such a collaborative effort is difficult to calculate compared to the value of internal investments. Consider again the analogy of the rising tide. The individual boat builders (competitors) have a lot to gain from that rising tide, but may not at first realize just how much since, up until this point, they have been hard at work building unique boats to set them apart from one another. They must now understand the ways in which collaboration could impact the competitive landscape; some boat builders may be better prepared to capitalize on that "rising tide" than others. A collaborative mindset is achieved when competitors accept with favor the fact that their shared solution will benefit multiple stakeholders, and what they create in the future may look little like the proverbial boats they have built in the past.

In the healthcare space in particular, interoperability issues and friction in data exchange activities remain at the top of the list of systemic problems. While Blockchain technologies are not the silver bullet for solving interoperability issues, they could potentially assist in overcoming some existing hurdles. Assuming this to be true, the implications could erode some of a Blockchain solution's participants' current competitive advantages. In particular, a shared utility enabling smoother and more efficient data exchange could reduce some competitive advantages for vertically-integrated companies and firms that control large data silos. At the same time, with a shared utility to facilitate data exchange, innovation and competition would be accelerated because easy access to data across the healthcare ecosystem is currently a significant barrier to creating innovative digital solutions. Opening up the opportunity for innovation may be seen as a positive or negative, based on how well a firm is positioned to take advantage of it. Depending on the strategic initiatives of a given firm, collaboration on data exchange could be viewed as a significant risk. Such fears of risk can be somewhat allayed when competitors believe the value of the shared solution would offset their estimated losses. Additionally, this risk of not innovating in a rapidly changing environment may be far greater. It's better to start early and be the disruptor as opposed to being disrupted. Think again of Nokia, a once-leading incumbent firm whose leaders were aware of disruption, but thought they had enough market share to delay responding. Their failure to aggressively face competitive innovation resulted in paying a steep price.

Most leaders of large firms understand they are under constant threat of disruption by smaller, more nimble new entrants, in particular. They are beginning to see that the way to win is to invest in a discipline to support actively recognizing innovation opportunities and placing bets by choosing where to invest, accepting that the risk of such investment is worth the reward. It is not feasible for any firm to bet on all opportunities, nor is it prudent to invest in none. They know that without a process for innovation, they risk losing an industry-leading position. The innovation process requires time and resources for rigorous thought to discern which opportunities deserve their bets. Furthermore, investment is required for maturing innovative capabilities once those bets are placed. Many firms understand this, yet interestingly, informal review of budgeting procedures among peer organizations has revealed that organizational incentives are not always aligned to support proactive innovation. Commonly, leaders are incentivized for favorable annual results, which tend to focus investments on lower-risk, well-defined efforts required to run – and sometimes grow – today's business. However, the mindset needs to shift so that a portion of a budget committed to funding innovation and transformation – tomorrow's business – and incentives should be realigned accordingly. Blockchain efforts fall into this "transformation" investment category. Successful transformation initiatives require firms to have a process and discipline for maturing innovation from back-of-a-napkin concepts to execution. This discipline is useful for many innovation efforts but is crucial for those leveraging Blockchain-powered concepts because the technologies are nascent as are the governance processes and business models.

Focusing on meaningful progress

Moving your idea for a Blockchain-powered solution to action takes a financial investment. Because investment decision makers in any organization can be skeptical of funding projects that are dependent on nascent technologies, the path toward securing funding must be navigated thoughtfully. With Blockchain, widespread media coverage was initially a door opener for conversations with innovative-minded investment decision makers, but it brought with it some problems. It left confusion about the relationship between Blockchain technologies and cryptocurrencies, such as Bitcoin. The separation between the two must be established in the minds of decision makers through explanation that's technical in nature, yet understood by the non-technologist. Perhaps more importantly, the media hype far preceded any real proven value that could be cited in conversations, adding to the uphill nature of pitching a Blockchain concept within an organization. Attempting to build a case by "proving" value when examples are scarce can leave you with a poor foundation for your pitch, and perhaps damage your credibility. One approach that seems to resonate with decision makers is to acknowledge the current lack of proof and share a story of an aspirational vision, asking for a minor investment that would enable taking a small but meaningful step toward demonstrating value.

Creating the narrative of your aspirational vision can help advance your organization's Blockchain journey in many important ways, even well before the investment conversation. At Humana, the vision narrative initially took the form of a whitepaper about an aspirational industry solution for medical claims processing. The process of writing that paper required several leaders to provide associates with input and guidance, and grant them time to explore concepts, knowing there would be no immediate return. The permission space provided by those leaders represented a relatively minor but important commitment that set the process in motion. The claims whitepaper was selected as one of fifteen winning entries in the Blockchain whitepaper challenge sponsored by the Office of the National Coordinator for Health Information Technology (ONC), a division of the U.S. Department of Health and Human Services (HSS). In addition to the win leaving the author feeling optimistic about the future of Blockchain at Humana, the whitepaper – along with the other winning submissions from major firms – led to additional learning at the firm and motivated continuing discussions with leaders.

Raising awareness and facilitating discussion around the potential implications of Blockchain technologies in itself is meaningful progress that will eventually strengthen your investment request. A goal of early discussions should be the formation of a point of view. Ideally, the point of view should outline use cases and explain the ways in which those potential opportunities could align with both internal company strategy and the current external landscape of vendors, startups and competitors. The point of view should include perspectives on the likelihood and key drivers of adoption for specific use cases. Since Blockchain is inherently a collaborative endeavor, make sure your point of view describes potential strategic partnership opportunities. Participation of partners and entities across the ecosystem is critical. The Blockchain value proposition is in fact driven by network effect, making adoption by many entities one of the most important indicators of success for Blockchain-related efforts. Including all of these elements in your organization's documented point of view is a valuable step forward.

The point of view serves as a guide for associates across your enterprise on opportunities in the Blockchain space and how the organization should engage. It should address the question, "In what areas of does it make sense to lead / join / watch / ignore?" Industry-leading incumbents must take great care in addressing these questions to successfully maintain their marketplace presence. Facilitating discussions around the point of view not only raises awareness, but also enables making informed decisions about which opportunities to pursue. No organization is able to bet on every opportunity; fleshing out the point of view helps establish guidance for which bets to place. Additionally, the documented point of view should never be considered "final," but rather treated as a living document to be updated as new ideas and information emerge and as the landscape evolves. Humana's first whitepaper was focused on medical claims processing. The claims use case project has not been developed at this point, but the whitepaper's notoriety led to series of steps that positioned Humana to become a founding member of Synaptic Health Alliance joining several other healthcare leaders, working on a provider directory use case. Such is the path of charting new waters, thus the point of view should be fluid. The organization's point of view, as it evolves, should be made available to its innovation leaders, to be used as a lens through which they can evaluate opportunities. These leaders are likely hearing numerous product and service pitches from external parties making claims about Blockchain's ability to easily reduce friction points across the industry, yet the feasibility of any given offering is dependent on its alignment with the organization's unique point of view.

Does developing technology represent meaningful progress? Many organizations wonder whether developing software may be helpful in proving an idea's viability and seeking funding. While this step may prove fruitful later in the process, it is not required to formalize the point of view. In fact, a great deal of effort can be wasted by building Blockchain solutions that are not used for testing assumptions associated with an actual business use case. Likewise, with the wide variety of Blockchain and distributed ledger technologies available today, attempting to find the "best" one can waste precious resources. It's better to find one "good enough" to enable you to move forward. The organization's resources are likely better spent trying to understand how to create value using the Blockchain technologies. This is not to say there is no value in getting hands-on experience with the technology and proving assumptions; quite the opposite is true. However, for optimal efficiency, both those things should be done in the context of testing assumptions around a use case. Furthermore, when testing, the assumptions to test should include business model specifics in addition to the technical requirements. This helps set realistic expectations that development of any Blockchain solution will require engagement from both business and technology teams. Gaining an understanding of Blockchain technologies is only a small part of the overall effort needed to deliver a successful Blockchain-powered solution. More time will be needed on the non-technical aspects of defining and testing the governance and business model for the solution.

Finally, when seeking resource investment and support for a project, consider the organization's many competing priorities. When resources are limited, investment decisions are tradeoffs. To invest in a Blockchain concept means forgoing another project that could provide a quicker or more certain return. This makes defining an approach of meaningful small steps all the more important. The media hype that helped open conversations early on will need to be replaced with demonstrations of meaningful progress to replenish the reservoir of support. Keep in mind that the definition of meaningful may be subjective, with each area of the organization having a different perspective of what counts as progress. It's crucial to set stakeholders' expectations around success criteria. Remember that solutions need also to demonstrate success for your external partners who would be collaborating with you. Each of these participants may have a different way of defining success. A well-thought out plan will address these issues.

Thinking in terms of patient capital

Change of significant magnitude typically takes time. Several Blockchain concepts for which work began in 2015 and 2016 aren't planning to go live until 2020 and 2021 – five or more years later. Accordingly, healthcare industry participants should expect that any Blockchain solution they initiate will take several years to roll out and achieve adoption. Organizational culture – and specifically, risk tolerance within a culture – accounts for some of time it takes. Many firms tend to feel more comfortable with investments that have well-defined ROIs and relatively short payback periods. Blockchain investments, however, don't fit this profile. Therefore, firms must take time to understand and accept this new type of risk and build a process for managing that risk.

If past efforts are an indicator, industry-wide moves to Blockchain-powered solutions take years. Walmart began implementing a Blockchain-powered solution to assist with food safety in 2016, with go live targets in 2020 (source, source). The Australian Stock Exchange (ASX) began working with partner Digital Asset in 2015 to replace a legacy system; their Blockchain project is anticipated to go live late 2020 or 2021 (source). Healthcare industry participants should factor in these examples and relative complexity of their own solutions when considering a reasonable target date for new solution. Projects in this emerging space require patient capital—also known as long term capital. With patient capital, the investor is willing to make a financial investment with no expectation of turning a quick profit; instead, the investor forgoes an immediate return in anticipation of more substantial returns down the road. In the healthcare industry in particular, reaching the scale needed for a Blockchain solution to deliver national value is a significant challenge. Expectations for results and the timeline must be established based not only on similar Blockchain efforts across other industries but also the healthcare system's high level of complexity.

Complexity in healthcare is driven by many current-day factors such as interoperability barriers, the need for personalized healthcare and the scale of adoption required for a solution to be useful for both participating firms and patients. The scale of adoption is grand, as participants would need to include all of the entities with which patients could interact when receiving care: urgent care centers, hospitals, primary care physicians, specialists, pharmacists and more. Although adding a nascent set of Blockchain technologies to the equation can enable new capabilities to facilitate data exchange, it requires additional effort to understand, secure, scale and operationalize these solutions. Before a healthcare firm's decision makers feel comfortable with Blockchain technologies, they ideally would like to witness an example of a solution that's actually in production within the healthcare industry and successfully demonstrating the key tenets of Blockchain – including consensus algorithms, decentralized governance, the handling of privacy in a transparent distributed data structure and, potentially, new types of security protocols such as zero knowledge proofs. Lacking such examples, decision makers may tend to judge an investment in a Blockchain project as being too risky. Even if they understand the value of patient capital, often senior leaders are incentivized and rewarded for shorter-term successes. Advocates of Blockchain must not only be technically astute; they must also be thoughtful in acknowledging and addressing such cultural drivers within an organization.

Industry incumbents should not only take emerging disruption seriously and strive to adapt to remain relevant, but they must also actively look for emerging disruption as a way to inform their strategy. Adapting to disruption can often require an investment of patient capital. Decision makers need to understand that patient capital projects should not be thought of the same way as shorter term, less risky projects. A patient capital project's ROI is not going to stand a chance when evaluated against another potential initiative that can demonstrate a return in 18 months. For perspective on how an organization is "placing bets," it's helpful to use the lens of risk versus reward, focusing on how the budget is divided between the two.

When ROIs are nebulous and proven examples are scarce – as with Blockchain – how does a firm manage the risk? Firms must establish a different way of dealing with patient capital projects. Investments should be made in incremental steps. Each step should be managed closely with a focus on testing assumptions that will inform subsequent, potentially larger investments. An investment in a small first step may result only in knowledge gained, but could be a necessary step toward investing in other projects with a future financial payoff. For example, the Synaptic Health Alliance is working on a Blockchain-powered solution that aims to improve provider directory accuracy. Learnings from the initiative will help inform future Blockchain efforts that will focus on more complex and valuable opportunities. Walmart has taken this approach with their investment in their Blockchain-powered solution focused initially on food safety and the leafy green products supply chain. Pending success with leafy greens, Walmart will likely expand the project to include additional products and value-added services.

Gaining support for investments in Blockchain projects requires acknowledgement and acceptance of these projects as patient capital projects for which a new risk management process must be established. Building this acceptance begins by setting clear expectations for a project's anticipated timeframe for completion and its ROI. Lacking similar patient capital examples from one's own industry, the conversation should be informed by similar patient capital examples from other industries. Additionally, it should be driven in part by leaders' agreement on the need to combat emerging disruption by stepping in early to be a disruptor. Failing to set the right expectations for Blockchain efforts could shut down not only the opportunity at hand, but similar opportunities for future projects. Finally, as daunting as it sounds, consider that Blockchain solutions normally involve other companies, which means all prospective participating firms must understand and accept on these expectations.

Achieving such alignment is no doubt challenging, but it can be done with a thoughtful approach.

Determining where to place bets

Over the next several years, Blockchain technologies will present a wide range of potential implications. Among these is the evolution of firms' revenue sources. Firms need to understand that while some of their existing revenue streams are at risk of being eroded by Blockchain initiatives, new revenue stream opportunities may emerge. To optimize opportunities as the landscape matures, a firm's leaders must consider where to lead, where to lean in and where simply to watch. Developing these viewpoints requires understanding one's own long-term strategy, the industry landscape, technology innovations and the early Blockchain efforts of other consortiums and startups.

When considering where to place bets in the Blockchain technologies space, leaders should consider questions about strategy, partnership opportunities, potential for meaningful progress, long-term implications and market landscape. Depending on the use case, they may need to consider other questions as well. Some basic questions leaders might consider are discussed in this chapter. While simple "yes" or "no" answers are not likely for any potential use case, the context gained by discussing each of these questions should help inform investment decisions as the organization reviews possible opportunities.

Does this use case align with our strategy?

As Blockchain use cases require long-term investment, they must be well aligned with a firm's strategy. A misaligned project will typically face challenges in securing leadership's support and may be seen simply as a distraction. In positioning your Blockchain project, ask "Is it clear in the minds of leaders that this project provides value in terms of realizing the enterprise strategy?" Considering that Blockchain efforts require patient capital, is the connection between the project and your firm's strategy strong enough for others to advocate for project's continuation, even if the initial project sponsor would happen to leave the firm? In 2016 Morgan Stanley published a report that indicated industry incumbents are best positioned to advance Blockchain efforts, arguing that such firms are much more likely than their newer competitors to have the capabilities needed to advance a use case and the experience to play a leadership role. This claim likely hinges on the value a use case provides to the incumbent's core strategy.

Will we be collaborating or competing?

Viewed through another strategic lens, does the firm consider a proposed Blockchain use case an opportunity for collaboration or competition? For example, many health plan firms view a Blockchain solution for provider directory data management as an opportunity for collaboration that will ease administrative burden across the healthcare industry, while not providing any one payor a competitive advantage. However, other types of firms that earn revenue from provider directory data management services may feel differently. Discussing such strategic issues and arriving at a consensus up front among leaders at your firm will help avoid future issues and inform future discussions about both the business model and the incentives needed to support the solution.

Will we be able to secure the right partnerships and sufficient participant base for this use case to enable its success?

Firms must think strategically about the network of participants they are looking to build. Success relies not only execution, but on attracting sufficient participation in the Blockchain-powered solution. You must have both a strategy for identifying prospective participants and an approach for recruiting them to join. Because Blockchain's value proposition is driven by network effect, the value of the solution grows as adoption increases. Similar to the concept of minimum viable product, a Blockchain-powered solution has some degree of minimum viable network. As alluded to earlier, most strikingly for some as they try to wrap their heads around the concept, is that this minimum viable network needs to include one's competitors to demonstrate its utility value and maximize the opportunity for the overall solution. The digital marketplace is a helpful analogy. As the pool of goods being sold in the digital marketplace grows in diversity and more sellers compete, value is created for buyers. As a result, more buyers visit the marketplace, which provides more opportunity for sellers and, in turn, more sellers are attracted to participate. In this way, a healthy market fosters competition, with the features offered to the market buyers and sellers enabling the desired market interactions. Because Blockchain solutions are shared digital platforms that can be similar to a digital marketplace, this analogy is helpful when trying to determine incentives to use to motivate participants to join and engage as you create the minimum viable network. Just as a digital marketplace needs both buyers and sellers who have mutual interest in improving the overall utility of the shared solution, so too does a Blockchain solution. Before you can build your minimum viable network, you must understand prospective partners' roles in the network – as either producers or consumers of value – and determine how to motivate them to participate. For example, Quest Diagnostics has a significant logistical operation engaged in picking up lab samples from physician practice offices across the country. The data that Quest collects each night during this logistical operation is valuable to health plans. It aids health plans in verifying the quality of the provider office location address data in the provider directories each health plan publishes. The fact that many health plans possess data about a given physician address enriches Quest's data, which helps Quest to recover accounts receivable payments that are stalled due to incorrect addresses or missing data elements.

In fact, timing can be used as an incentive to garner participants. When striving to reach critical mass, earlier engagement may be better. It's much easier to entice a prospective participant to use the solution if they feel they had an opportunity to participate in formulating it versus being asked to participate later in the process and simply being told how the product is going to work. Transportation conglomerate Maersk lacked participation in their TradeLens effort, likely due in part to failing to attract them early on. A full ten months after launching, Maersk was struggling to achieve adoption among their competitors when Marvin Erdly, head of TradeLens at IBM Blockchain commented, "I won't mince words here – we do need to get the other carriers on the platform. Without that network, we don't have a product" (source). However, firms should understand the tradeoff with getting others involved early: Speed to market is potentially sacrificed. Getting firms to align on direction is time consuming. Consider this tradeoff when evaluating the best approach for your use case, and think through whether your perspective participants will be willing to join later without having had much input, or if they will need to be brought on early to assist with the solution's creation and planning. Take note, however, that guidance and feedback from future participants in early stages can not only help drive adoption, but perhaps more importantly, it can help mitigate the risk of building the wrong solution, business model or governance structure.

How long will it take to make meaningful progress on this effort?

The estimated time it takes to make meaningful progress on Blockchain-powered solutions differs drastically based on the type of solution. As with any major project, a firm's leaders must understand just how long it may take to derive value, then decide if they're OK with that timeframe. While it may be impossible to estimate an exact timeline, thinking about a couple of factors can help. These include, first, the amount of time needed to overcome anticipated issues related to a specific use case and, second, the overall maturation timeline for Blockchain technologies overall.

The time it takes to make meaningful progress on a Blockchain-powered solution can in part be estimated by identifying the issues it will face. For example, a popular focal point among Blockchain projects in the healthcare space is the consumer-mediated electronic health record (EHR). A consumer-facing EHR-focused Blockchain solution would need to address a number of barriers before making meaningful process. Barriers may include technical issues, such as privacy, security and scalability, as well as business issues, such as business model development, adoption and user engagement. Given these barriers, advancing an EHR use case will likely take longer than achieving meaningful progress on uses cases with fewer issues to address – like those focused on the business-to-business exchange of public data.

Examples of data exchange use cases include those that focus on shared audit trails, supply chain scenarios and the crowd sourcing of public data.

On a more macro level, the maturity of Blockchain technologies will play a role in your progress timeline. Much like the earliest days of the internet, when email worked well but streaming video had not yet become a viable option, some use cases will prove too advanced for the current technology or require too great of a culture shift to be palatable. Although maturity can make an occasional leap forward, more often it results from a series of many small steps with each contributing incremental progress. Collaborative initiatives outside of the Blockchain space – including FHIR 3, Carin Alliance and the Da Vinci project – are making notable progress. Such progress will help accelerate Blockchain efforts targeting similar friction points. Astute leaders will keep tabs on these related initiatives and on overall technology and cultural evolution in the Blockchain space, in an effort to assess when their own use case ideas are ready for development.

If our target use case is successful, what are the long-term implications?

No one can accurately forecast all the long-term implications of a disruptive technology like Blockchain. Far too many unknowns exist. One major unknown risk is based in the notion of collaborating with competitors on a shared solution – and doing so with such magnitude. Some firms will extract value and create a competitive advantage, while others will see existing competitive advantages diminished by the capabilities these technologies offer. Countless other unknowns may exist, making it virtually impossible to anticipate the outcome. That said, getting involved in these efforts early can help your firm establish a better vantage point for understanding implications. Furthermore, early entrants are in a good position to help shape the landscape and guide overall direction in a way that aligns with their strategies. No firm can prevent Blockchain from making progress, as any one firm's decision whether to participate will have little long-term effect. This means that, regardless of your position, the changes are coming sooner or later, so making the effort to understand the implications is a key to being prepared for when they arrive.

How does this use case align with or disrupt the current market landscape?

Friction points in today's healthcare system have been created by a complex web of issues. Some of these include misaligned incentives, negative behaviors, social issues, greed, the regulatory environment and gaps in information sharing. No technology, alone, can solve these issues. In fact, the technical role of Blockchain will likely be relatively minor in the grand scheme; Blockchain will be merely a part of the overall technology stack. Still, we should expect that the stakeholders benefiting from the current state of affairs will fight against new solutions that will bring change.

That said, incumbents make formidable competitors when they are able to bring creative solutions in the face of disruptors. Hulu is a great example of incumbent firms The Walt Disney Company, 21st Century Fox, Comcast and AT&T coming together to compete against the threats posed by Netflix and Amazon. When video content streaming services provided by Netflix and Amazon impacted incumbents' television revenue streams, they collaborated to create a competitive offering. Competition will continue to be fierce and, in fact, early progress will not always guarantee future success. Remember the time between 2005 and 2009 when MySpace seemed to have carved out an insurmountable lead in the social media space? Established market share failed to protect their position in the face of innovative efforts of others. Relative to Blockchain, while incumbents are certainly well positioned to understand how solutions align with or disrupt the current landscape, it remains to be seen whether they will collaborate and execute to combat disruption before startup disruptors force them to.

The most challenging barriers will not be the technical ones

Blockchain technologies are nascent. From a firm's perspective, they provide the opportunity for emergence of new capabilities – but also guarantee new challenges. These challenges include developing appropriate governance, scaling to handle the load a healthcare use case could demand, design of new business models, lobbying to change outdated regulations and, finally, proving the Blockchain technical solution's quality. Of these, the technical problems will likely be the easier ones to sort out. A firm must ensure that the team they appoint to researching Blockchain use cases includes innovative leaders from both technology and business. Due to the hype surrounding Blockchain as a technology proposition, many organizations are focusing on getting hands-on technological experience. However, while technical experimentation is valuable, organizations must dedicate time and energy to addressing business issues. Before technical solutions can advance from the pilot stage, firms must work to develop governance and design a business model that will enable the solution to scale.

Asking a firm to lead in the Blockchain space is, in effect, asking its employees to make a cultural shift from a mindset of competing to one of competing AND collaborating. Such a change is certainly a sharp divergence from status quo. While collaboration does occur today in some ways across the healthcare industry, Blockchain adoption brings a shift of control. Certain activities will no longer be under the control of your firm, but rather controlled by the shared solution. If the collaborative solution is to be successful, a firm's associates will be forced to give up some of their authority. For a variety of reasons, they may not be receptive to this ceding of control and, given negative misconceptions about Bitcoin and Blockchain, it may be difficult to justify this type of innovative solution. Therefore, Blockchain advocates within a firm must take time to engage in conversations for the purpose of raising awareness among their colleagues about the rationale and potential rewards for giving up control, and to establish expectations for the behaviors required to enact this new cultural mindset.

As discussed earlier, the culture shift toward collaboration must also take root among your competitors, and any Blockchain initiative must be supported by governance. To say that aligning a large group of Blockchain participants on a direction is difficult is an understatement. One need only to consider the current state of public Blockchain implementations Bitcoin and Ethereum to understand the importance of establishing governance for the purpose of ensuring participants are aligned on the path forward. Both implementations have had significant disagreements that led to a "fork," meaning that a portion of the network community exited to create a new divergent, competing solution. In any Blockchain initiative, changes to implementation plans can impact some stakeholders negatively, leaving them motivated to lobby for a different direction and putting the project at risk of a fork. Most of these divisive changes are related to the ways in which the participants running the technical infrastructure (miners) are rewarded. For example, should technical changes reduce the reward paid out for infrastructure but improve performance and reduce costs, opinions about the best outcome will differ across community members based on their unique interests.

Public Blockchain networks aren't the only ones susceptible to such problems. The act of JP Morgan leaving R3 (source) demonstrated that this can happen to an industry alliance just as easily as with public Blockchains. For maximum value, all solutions, regardless of industry or purpose would leverage one Blockchain. While that scenario would be ideal, it's likely a utopian aspiration never to be realized. That said, innovators need to bear in mind that the greater the number of separate Blockchain networks emerging, the greater the overhead required to connect these Blockchains will be in the future. With too much separation – meaning, many independent Blockchains – the possibility is very real that the healthcare industry could end up just as disconnected as it is today, despite widespread use of this shiny new technology component. I am optimistic this will not occur, but share this thought to illustrate the motivation for creating innovative business models and governance structures that are appealing enough to the participants to drive continued engagement and collaboration.

As you can see, Blockchain advocates within a firm must be prepared to spend as much or more time thinking through, planning and socializing the non-technical aspects of a use case versus the technical concerns. Considering the emergence of other disruptive technologies, this shouldn't come as a surprise. For example, with analytics taking root in the healthcare space, business leaders are immersed in conversations about how to maximize the value of big data, artificial intelligence and machine learning. These conversations are focused on answering questions about everything from procedures to ethics – much more so than on technical specifics, to be sure. Addressing emerging issues relative to Blockchain requires a balance between business and technology intellects, collaborating to determine the answers as they drive the solution forward.

REALIZATION OF BLOCKCHAIN IN HEALTHCARE

Chapter 10: How will Blockchain Disrupt Health?

Alex Cahana
Dr. David Metcalf

https://hashedhealth.com/blockchain-for-healthcare-book/

Editor's Note:

In a fireside chat, David Metcalf and Alex Cahana discuss projects coming out of their work in Orlando and the convergence of blockchain and the Internet of Things. The following chapter was taken from an interview transcript.

From interview transcript:

David: Greetings. My day job is in academia and my night job is investment, where I try to figure out how to take early early projects and bring them to market.

I sit at the University of Central Florida in Orlando. I'd like to go over some of the things we're seeing in the marketplace.

At UCF we have the highest number of undergraduate students in the nation, and we opened a new medical school. We are in a whole community that is about training and simulation and we are blockchain native. About a billion dollars is invested in medical simulation in Orlando. We are working with the VA fHospital, Nemours Children's Hospital, and many others.

We are looking at the Internet of Things and how it's reshaping wearables, mobility and how we live in the future in intelligent homes like WHIT built by Lake Nona Institute, Cisco, Johnson & Johnson, FL Blue, GE and others. Blockchain is a fundamental technology that can improve all of these. We are looking at how wearables are being used and how data is being organized around them. All of this data has to be managed in some way. Is blockchain one of the ways to manage this?

One of the problems is speed, but we do believe that blockchain will improve. We are looking how to combine blockchain in a simulation, blockchain and IOT. Wearables are not just for the wrist, they also can be shoes, contact lenses and where and how people are going to use them is yet to be seen. Perhaps even embedded inside ourselves for immutable tracking.

In the Mixed Emerging Technology Integration Lab at UCF, we have the opportunity to work with companies like Google, Johnson & Johnson, and others, along with military health, government, and nonprofits for social good.The way we can use the technology and democratize it among the many many nations, as well as with global and population health. I was in a conference with global thought leaders, all thinking how we can implement these technologies on a global scale. The things we can't do in our country because of restrictions will lend itself to medical tourism.

We started projects in blockchain in 2012-2015, We started to work on HealthShares Project with the National Science Foundation I-Corps program, also used by NIH and DoD. Using lean startup principles that have been used in Silicon Valley, we learned how slow-selling the protocols were. We also explored developing an Electronic Healthcare record, and wrote a book called Blockchain Enabled Applications. This is very different than crypto investment. Blockchain is a foundational technology, and is involved in Fintech, Govtech, Regtech, etc., with potential use in real estate and in healthcare.

In our new book [Editor's Note: This section is referencing this book], we're covering all the new actors in the current space. It's a book that we're writing together with HIMSS. We've also been working on a blockchain simulator with multiple testnets and humans in the loop, because the problem is usually not with the algorithm itself but with the humans. We've seen that in the break-in to Japan's Mount Gox. Humans turn out to be the weakest link in the whole process.

We also have Startup Nation Ventures, with our Merging Traffic private equity group. We are investing in Israeli technology.. Bring them to Florida we have a 50% match with the Israeli government to build new projects. And from there to take it to the Caribbean and to Latin America. That is our blockchain global strategy.

We are working with nonprofit organizations like nonprofits, Hashed Health, Health 2.0, IHA, as well as the Distributed Health Conference on a multitude of new projects. Science Distributed is another company that's looking at how to perform science in a new way. Think about the veracity of research projects that we see every day in the news, how many of those studies have been validated, re-validated? Think what the blockchain can do for verifiable information, and this is being done in conjunction with the government that wish for the same validity and reliability of scientific research. It's not an us-versus-them but how do we make this better for the whole world.

We are also looking at early projects, especially electronic health records. See if actually those are have been developed have any impact on the market. And it's interesting to see the big players creating consortia, and that becomes interesting for investors. It'll be interesting to see if in two years some of the big companies will join. They may want to buy smaller companies, projects, ICOs. So those are the things that change the markets in early stages. Similar to the early days of the Internet.

We can also look at the changes with artificial intelligence, Vanderbilt University is looking at FHIR standards, and integrate with blockchain technology. So there are some nice efforts you have to look at in academia. You have to look at the government, as well as some spin-offs and to look for Innovation starts. A lot of innovation is coming from outside the United States in the former Eastern Bloc and Estonia.

We're also looking at new models that are not in the healthcare space and might come into the healthcare space. What if you could pay your patients to be healthier? Steemit is paying for their best posts and people to review it, that's a two-sided economic model. This is a fundamental shift that blockchain can enable. If you can pay for the producer of the knowledge and you can also pay the consumer, This may really drive healthy behaviors and change within the system. There was a conference this summer speaking to gamification of healthcare. They spoke about choice architecture and how do you modify behaviors - same principles applied in another industry segments and in the blockchain space. The use of the data in the electronic health records are changing as well - using AI - allowing benefits for you to use your data - using smart contracts as well. What if we start to apply the principles of smart contracts in the principles in healthcare and put a artificial intelligence on it like a DeepMind or Watson?

I've seen another exciting things from Harvard Business review. On how blockchain is going to reshape the industry. It's like the fundamental change that early Netscape tried to do - using the textual web, combining it with a graphical browser to simplify the workflow, hiding the complexity of the backend from the average user.

It's made it possible for us to distribute things in equal quality as any publisher, push and repeat over and over again.

So what's blockchain? You have the ability to move a thing in space to space with verification not just from one source for from multiple sources. I think that fundamental shift is going to allow all of us to feel better secure about our privacy and to have some democratization and take back ownership and shared ownership of the data with our providers. That's where I think blockchain gives us a new capability.

I hope this inspires you to apply blockchain to either data Healthcare records or payment or insurance.

Fireside chat:

Moderator: From an investor's perspective, I'm interested to see what you think coming from academia cutting edge is relevant for investors? What are your insights that you are gleaning from and that the investors need to look at these startups? How do you think of working with these investors if you are doing your research?

David: Using programs that are structured for innovation has helped frame the ideas and look the same way Silicon Valley looks at startups. What I look at is why these startups cause a fundamental change and what are the patterns of these change. One of the patterns that I'm looking at is what are the change of securitization. STOs versus ICOs. Especially if you're going to be in a highly regulated environment. It's important to look internationally, it's very smart, What's happening where they create for example 3D bio printed body parts or track drug counterfeiting or tracking surgery abroad. Those are really changes when we start looking at blockchain technology.

I might be an investor more hiding in academia then rather being an academic but you find a lot of people that have the same thought process where you take ideas spin them off and make those available out to the market. Those are the things that you might want to look at when you think of startup culture, academic culture, government culture and of course the investment culture.

Moderator: Are there opportunities for investors to work with you on spin offs?

David: Yes they're always projects that start with, and we often partner and co-invest. We have a fund and a fund of funds and we work with a couple of groups in Atlanta as well as our venture fund out of Florida.

So we are open to that to discuss, we're excited about the work we're doing, and move Healthcare but more importantly move wellness. Preventive medicine, Wellness, those are the things that we want to concentrate on, democratizing technology, democratize health. Pull it into an area where you have some control that's going to move the needle forward.

Moderator: As you are talking to the large companies, what are they or arc they ready for this technology how are they dealing with this?

David: Like Alex said, some are angry, some are in denial, some are tech positive and forward-thinking. but I've seen as a trend that companies have a blockchain group that turns into a spin-off and some go rogue and become their own. Because everybody who starts blockchain understand this potential and leave eventually those big companies. Sometimes companies pay them big money to stay or they lock them up and lock clauses, But it's a good virtuous circle because those entrepreneurs will return to the company's and that it might get bought back by 10X by the company with investment opportunities. that's what I watch for, what happens when the Phillips blockchain team goes out? I do a sociogram to see who does what, They already have access to corporate thinking Enterprise level skill that's just one example.

Moderator: I think that is very clever, many of the incumbents have the innovator's dilemma, And they're not going to disrupt the industry and its the spun-off teams that are going to disrupt.

David: I think it's like Clayton Christensen, How do you keep the mother ship from eating their young, Within the organization how to keep it separate? Maybe it's better to let them go? How do they come back?

Moderator: Are there companies that you know that have this strategy, they spin up companies like that?

David: We are working with some companies that were trying to keep their Innovation inside but there are so many that are ready to spin off already spun off, that's how I had my first couple of successes. I worked with NASA and we spun off our lab, And that's my investment thesis that's what I'm looking for.

Moderator: you mentioned the International scene. Have you seen International models some of them are National Healthcare that different systems. I tend to think that it makes it easier to deploy these kind of technologies, is there something we can bring into the US,?

David: We have seen from the NHS From the UK, where they have some centralization of their data. But blockchain is decentralization that's where the decentralisation becomes interesting. But so many of these organizations work internationally if you think about all the ties all the countries throughout Africa, Asia or support they have to have International use of blockchain at a low cost. I'm encouraged by all these countries but I really doubling down on this area like Israel what is Israeli Innovation Authority and they have a grant to come to Florida and launch their innovation. It's a good deal for entrepreneurs has been working one quite well in Israel. and of course you want to come to a state that doesn't have personal income tax, which is advantageous compared to California. those granting strategies, tax advantage Advantage strategies like in Germany. You see these Public Partnerships the government is not the enemy they want to see these Solutions.

Moderator: You talk about public-private Partnerships, are there opportunities for investors to work with your program?

David: Absolutely or Global blockchain Venture fund is open and those are areas where we see some interesting things going on

Moderator: Do you focus on working with companies locally?

David: No we think of bringing the best of Florida to the world and investment from all over the world to Florida and the rest of the u.s. And especially with Israel with our startup Nation fund. Our main principles is former President of Disney Al Weiss, and German conglomerate.

Moderator: And is that specific to healthcare? Or across other Industries?

David: No also in education which is our expertise. We are not doing this alone. We are a $100M with other partners like Stonegate and others, like fund to funds and coinvest.

Moderator: And do you have other use cases in healthcare that you want to go after? Invest or research?

David: My background in healthcare is data science, A lot of things that I'm looking at are pairing up all your data with the internet of things, wearables and when we have the data streams how to use these data streams. So scalability is a huge problem the speed of the networks is important. Blockchain is 1/3 the speed of the VISA network currently for example, and that's just one network. So you don't want to slow down something especially in a life-saving moments in the hospitals those are issues that we need to solve. We think about genetics, genomics, and precision medicine as exciting areas.

We just invested in a company that has great data science behind 3D holograms for Interventional Radiology, which is going to change these new kinds of data sets how to transmit that even in the best of systems you're not ready for this. How would watch and be ready for that change? that's my area this is a team sport doctors investors even the students have a great ideas in small laboratories.

Moderator: I'm always worried about are they ready for it? You mentioned that at least EMRs the data structure is not ready for it.

David: Like Alex said, for me I prefer not be ready and push forward, And help the systems get ready. If you think the investment and ecosystem do you want to be the early adopter if you want to be the early innovator or do you want to be the laggard? We're not going to be the lacquered anytime soon that's why I love seeing some of the things that are coming out like Tim Draper was talking about how the big funds, and Ivy Leagues are doubling down and putting money into the space that's a key signal at least the way I look at things.

Moderator: Absolutely. In Healthcare, are there specific companies or sectors? Do you see people moving ahead? you mentioned the alliance with humana/payers where do you see the early adopters?

David: I wouldn't take any of this as a gospel of a company, where I see things moving is when I see standards like the IEEE start using blockchain and when I see Hyperledger and Ethereum Enterprise Alliance coming together. These are indicators of things to come. I want to see things coming out of that that are driving these collaborations. if you're helping build a standard the chances that you're going to sustain that standard that's going to win the marketplace at scale.

For example, Hyperledger, Etherium Enterprise Alliance, and Bob Metcalfe came up with Ethernet standards and built 3Com. that's how you win a global technology where you can win business on. That's what I'm watching for. I love seeing what Distributed Health is doing and their conferences coming up in a couple of weeks with distributed health, and their standards for medical tourism and also the government, a blockchain standard release of the government NIST 8202 might be worth looking if you're in the technology side of things. Those are bell weathers of what might come in people that are working in this sector like Consensys Health just reformed under Heather Flannery these are all innovators that are driving the ship. Other examples of Blockchain for standards-based integration come from organizations like Dana Zhang at Vanderbilt and Stuart Lackey at Solstar.

Chapter 11:
Enterprise, History, and Change

Emily Vaughn Bailey

Change Healthcare

https://hashedhealth.com/blockchain-for-healthcare-book/

Editor's Note:

Emily Vaughn was one of the early leaders in the blockchain space. In this chapter she reflects on the origins of blockchain and how it arrived in healthcare. This perspective serves to inform her transition in to the healthcare blockchain space first at Gem, then at Change Healthcare. In the latter parts of this chapter, she provides insights in to the earliest proofs of concept by companies like Philips and Tieto. And she goes on to describe how, in her current role at Change Healthcare, she views the various stages of incorporating blockchain in to Change's enterprise strategy.

History | Foundations of Blockchain in Healthcare

Blockchain's Bitcoin Beginnings

The Bitcoin industry emerged from obscurity to mainstream speculation in 2012, garnering interest from Silicon Valley celebrity investors like Sir Richard Branson, Marc Andreessen, Peter Theil, the Winklevoss brothers, and Tim Draper. The interest stemmed from the rising value of bitcoin, a digital currency issued and tracked by a vast network of computers, versus a central service or authority.

There was speculation in the technical community about the use of Bitcoin's public blockchain for applications other than cryptocurrency transactions. But concepts like "proof of ownership" and "chains of provenance" gained a foothold with bitcoin early-adopters and libertarians, who saw this technology as a way to reduce friction created by central administration.

Alt-coins, cryptocurrencies other than bitcoin, gathered a cult following in niche pockets of the community with Dogecoin, a loveable meme-coin, and Litecoin, a proof-of-work cryptocurrency. Investors in 2013 were unaware of the meteoric rise of alt-coin investing that would happen in 2017 with the Initial Coin Offering (ICO) market. For example, Litecoin would eventually rise from a $600M market capitalization in January 2014 to $19.4B in December 2017. In 2013, such a valuation was simply unfathomable for most casual investors, and alt-coins remained obscure and experimental.

In late 2013, Bitcoin experienced a price spike, rising from around $100 in June to over $1200 in November, bringing with it a rush of new investors, hot press, and bitcoin startups. The price teetered into early 2014, but in February, MtGox, a bitcoin exchange accounting for 70% of the trading volume, infamously collapsed, sending the price of bitcoin into decline. The bitcoin industry entered a period of transformation, with startups and investors looking beyond the cryptocurrency to its underlying technology, blockchain.

Enter Ethereum and "Enterprise Blockchain"

In January 2014, a 19-year-old programmer, Vitalik Buterin, shared a new vision with the cryptocurrency community: Ethereum, the world computer. The conference hall at the North American Bitcoin Conference in Miami was brimming with hopeful newcomers, newly wealthy bitcoin investors, and cryptocurrency enthusiasts, unfettered by the calamity of the last few months. Buterin presented his white paper and working model, while the audience sat tense with concentration. Was this Bitcoin 2.0 or another kooky theory about cryptocurrency toppling institutions? The swarm that followed him after his presentation signaled that perhaps it was both.

The following 18 months were a period of technical definition and development for the growing cryptocurrency community. Low Bitcoin prices and bad press kept the hype cycle at bay, while the venture-funded Bitcoin companies and burgeoning Ethereum community grew their user bases and contributed to open-source improvements on the technology.

Many Bitcoin startups turned their focus to blockchain technology. It was a hotly contested trend in the Bitcoin industry but was favored by investors and enterprise companies who had been soured on Bitcoin's reputation as a dark web currency and its lack of technical flexibility.

In July 2015, Ethereum launched its public network, bringing about a major shift in the industry. The promise of private (federated) blockchains and smart contracts, programmable logic powered by Ethereum's blockchain, invigorated supporters of alternative use cases for the technology.

By fall 2015, Visa, Citi and Nasdaq announced their investment of $30M into Chain.com, a blockchain developer platform. The enterprise market for blockchain technology had emerged. By 2018, the percentage of large financial companies exploring blockchain technology would reach 80%, signaling a trend that would spill over into insurance, supply chain, and healthcare in the months and years to follow.

Blockchain Technology Reaches Healthcare

As other industries approached the technology, themes of blockchain applications emerged: digital assets, asset exchange, data provenance/asset tracking, credential management, contract management, and more. These applications brought a new approach to cross-industry networking. San Francisco-based Chronicled was building anti-counterfeiting technology for the high-end sneaker market, while London-based Everledger addressed fraud in the diamond industry with a blockchain solution for tracking and certification.

News of these applications was dispersed among cryptocurrency-focused media, while the emerging market for non-financial use cases lacked a rallying point. The blockchain solution provider Gem noticed enterprise companies had trouble approaching the technology, so they partnered with BTC Media, owner of Bitcoin Magazine and other cryptocurrency publications, to launch an enterprise publication for blockchain technology. The Distributed Ledger, initially an email newsletter service, grew into Distributed.com and a conference series that helped bring blockchain focus to supply chain technology, healthcare, and financial markets.

At the same time in early 2016, healthcare-focused use cases emerged in pockets of the blockchain market. Estonian cybersecurity company Guardtime was putting government health records in a blockchain database. Tierion, a blockchain application programming interface (API) company based in the United States, was cryptographically hashing medical records and had worked with Royal Philips to develop a proof-of-concept. Gem launched a community-building initiative for healthcare called Gem Health, in which they developed proofs-of-concept with Philips and Capital One, sponsored education campaigns around use cases, and collaborated with other companies to engage the healthcare industry.

The Hyperledger® Healthcare Working Group, hosted by The Linux Foundation, was an early effort to bring enterprise companies, blockchain enthusiasts, and healthcare technology to the same table. Announced at the first Distributed Health conference in 2016, the Hyperledger consortium and representatives from Hashed Health, Gem, Kaiser Permanente® and Humana formed the first industry working group with a simple mailing list. This group became 400 members strong over the course of a year, holding regular meetings and education sessions about blockchain technology, the Hyperledger community, and healthcare opportunities.

At the same conference in August 2016, Gartner released its Health IT Hype Cycle report, noting that blockchain and distributed ledger technology were at the forefront of an upward ten-year trend.

From Proof-of-Concept to Production

In the first year, the emerging group of enthusiasts and startups sought to identify and prioritize use cases for healthcare. Several themes materialized around universal patient identity, medical records provenance, insurance claims administration, tokenized payment networks, and supply chain management. The proofs-of-concept (POCs) developed by Philips and Capital One®, in addition to the production release of Estonia's blockchain-based health record solution, proved that the technology worked. The industry seemed to agree that data provenance and distributed computing could solve rampant data reconciliation problems, but to graduate from proofs-of-concepts, companies required a business case with revenue impact–a beachhead.

Challengers against blockchain technology for healthcare questioned its cybersecurity and data privacy implications, a rampant industry problem which ironically created an entry point for the technology. "RegTech" was trending, especially in healthcare and retail/e-commerce, as widespread password security failures, phishing attacks, insider threats, and data integrity attacks caused regulators to increase technical requirements for companies managing consumer data. There is a hard cost for data privacy compliance, and it turns out this industrywide challenge would create the first class of production use cases for blockchain technology.

For example, in 2018, the European Union's General Data Privacy Regulation (GDPR) would go live, setting strict requirements for consent management among companies storing and exchanging personal data. Failure to comply resulted in unprecedented fines. The transparent features of blockchain technology, thought at first to be counterproductive for data privacy, would actually introduce auditing capabilities that could help companies enforce compliance with consent controls. In preparation for this, Tieto, a leading Nordic EHR provider, began developing a person-centric GDPR solution, powered by a blockchain network.

Tieto was early to recognize the cross-industry impact of GDPR compliance and the business value of collaborating across companies to provide this type of service to Northern Europe. They realized that blockchain technology not only improved the economics of data privacy compliance, but it also improved the economics of providing highly personalized applications, powered by automation and artificial intelligence.

Unique geographic circumstances, such as being in socialized healthcare economies, gave companies like Tieto and Guardtime a strong market opportunity to reengineer health information systems with blockchain technology with GDPR as the catalyst. But at the same time, in the United States a different set of business cases emerged, in this case around another industry-wide cost center–health insurance claims management.

The United States, Europe, and other international markets such as China and Australia would all produce slightly nuanced healthcare innovation efforts, each reflecting a desire to reduce cost, increase public safety, and put the patient first. The United States in particular would prove to be a challenging market for startups to organize due to the centralization of healthcare solutions among large technology companies. It would require the leadership of enterprise healthcare companies with significant market share, a role which would be assumed by Change Healthcare, when they produced the industry's first enterprise blockchain network for insurance claims transparency. In just two years, blockchain technology graduated from idea, to experiment, to production at scale in the healthcare industry.

Realization | Enterprise Adoption in Healthcare

Blockchain Technology's Rising Role in Enterprise Strategy

Enterprise Healthcare Companies are Responding to Growing Data Management Challenges.

Harvard Business Review issued a report on How the US Can Reduce Waste in Health Care Spending by $1 Trillion, suggesting that $730 billion of savings could come from innovations to reduce administrative complexity, fraud and abuse, and clinical waste. Enterprise organizations can play a role in making changes to the U.S. healthcare system, and blockchain is one of the technologies that can specifically address these areas of "waste."

Healthcare, like most industries, suffers from the habitual need to reconcile data across parties–providers, payers, healthcare technology companies, and the consumer. Each of these parties are trying to compile the most complete and accurate set of information to serve the patient and empower business decisions.

Today, coordination around shared activities is highly inefficient, with companies often duplicating each other's efforts to verify information, confirm identities, and create a chain of data custody. Blockchain technology introduces a method for keeping systems in sync with each other by establishing a shared historical record that tracks unique digital assets, which might represent money, claims funneling into a revenue cycle, patients moving through an episode of care, or data-access permissions. Companies can use blockchain technology to collaborate more efficiently by using a shared record of events, identity, and data and by distributing the verification process across multiple parties, rather than requiring each company to perform their own verification.

Efforts to improve data quality, interconnectivity, and mobility have launched throughout the industry. Hospital markets have become highly concentrated as more patients receive care via retail health, urgent care, and telemedicine. A landmark 2015 survey by NRC Health found that 43% of consumers had visited a new physician in the prior year; no one owns today's healthcare consumer. Payers are increasingly investing in consumer capabilities. Physicians are more often accepting fees tied to the quality rather than the quantity of care provided, and health plans in the Medicare Advantage program can now earn more in premiums by helping members stay healthy, manage chronic diseases, and get prompt and courteous responses to their questions and needs.

In addition to blockchain, there is an upward trend toward web services, APIs, artificial intelligence, and cloud infrastructure. International Data Corp projects that 60% of enterprises will be implementing a digital transformation platform strategy by 2020 and many of them will incorporate artificial intelligence (AI). McKinsey & Company has calculated that the healthcare system saved $400 billion based solely on early successes in the application of big data analyses. Blockchain is highly compatible with these other advanced technologies that are rapidly being adopted.

The industrywide demand for increased data trust, efficiency, and integrity makes blockchain technology worth exploring for healthcare's cross-industry challenges. As enterprise companies look past the hype and continue to learn the technology, companies are investing in the technology with increased focus and maturity.

Enterprise Influence on Blockchain Adoption

Investment by enterprise healthcare companies has bolstered blockchain adoption across the industry. From the earliest POCs, to the first consortium, to the initial production solutions, enterprise companies have led the disruption. Healthcare startups focused on blockchain are likely to depend on enterprise partners to achieve the scale and exposure necessary to establish network effect behind their solutions. Put another way, enterprise healthcare companies are the key to achieving integrated, scalable blockchain adoption and have taken the lead in unlocking this potential.

There are a few reasons for this. Blockchain solutions require network effect to sustain themselves over a distributed ecosystem. This means that the solution must achieve a self-sustaining balance of user growth and value creation. Enterprise companies are well positioned in healthcare to establish these initial networks, largely because they already have a critical mass of users.

Also, the mix of users on a typical health information system is diverse by design—there are already financiers, service providers, and consumers, or "payers, providers, and patients." Added to this diversity is the reliance on information technology providers for interconnectivity and digital infrastructure. This dynamic is somewhat unique to healthcare versus other industries, because the consumers have not historically been the party paying for services. This diversity plays a large role in why enterprise technology companies have helped establish the blockchain technology trend and will play a critical role in onboarding the rest of the industry.

Incorporating Blockchain In Your Enterprise Strategy in Five Stages

Adopting blockchain technology is no simple task. Blockchain networks introduce new dynamics for creating business value and designing applications. Healthcare organizations should thoughtfully approach their development to affect meaningful change.

What follows are a few of the key considerations pulled from the playbook of Change Healthcare, a leading healthcare technology company that provides data and analytics-driven solutions to help improve clinical, financial and patient engagement outcomes.

In 2018, Change Healthcare launched the industry's first enterprise-scale blockchain solution bringing transparency to the claims management process.

Stage One: Making the Case for Blockchain Innovation

When getting started with blockchain technology, it's important to look at who will be taking the lead on a blockchain initiative to determine the right objectives for the project and set expectations appropriately. An initiative led by an organization's research and development (R&D) team, for example, will generally be looking to show that blockchain can help them do things from an infrastructure or design perspective that cannot be achieved using other types of technology. It won't necessarily be a revenue-generating pursuit. The return on investment (ROI) will be about gaining technical capabilities that may have no immediate business outcomes. The ROI of a business-led initiative, on the other hand, will be about generating revenue and improving an organization's competitive position.

A company might also pursue a blockchain initiative because of customer interest. This type of endeavor is tied to strengthening the customer relationship but is also restricted by the nature of their business dealings with one another.

How a use case gains momentum depends on multiple teams working together and investing in the initiative's success. At Change Healthcare, the initial blockchain use case was conceived by an R&D team and implemented by a product team. Getting to production required the buy-in and investment of both groups.

Stage Two: Identifying a Use Case

When selecting a use case, consider the role your company can play in bringing that solution to market. While early blockchain POCs were intended to test the technology, rather than being designed for commercial adoption, today's large enterprise systems are focusing their investment on use cases that align with their core business competencies.

For the first production blockchain solution at Change Healthcare, the company chose a use case tied directly to its business goals of improving revenue cycle management and claims management. It gave provider customers of Change Healthcare a way to accurately track, in real time, the status of claims submission and remittance across the complete claim lifecycle.

The pervasiveness of Change Healthcare's Intelligent Healthcare Network™ made it well positioned to quickly deploy blockchain at scale in addressing a highly administrative process. The network processes clinical, administrative, and financial transactions for hundreds of thousands of healthcare industry stakeholders.

Other large enterprises have similarly invested in use cases directly related to their business needs and interests. Optum, UnitedHealthcare and Humana, for instance, formed an alliance focused on blockchain's potential to improve the accuracy of healthcare provider directories. Pharmaceutical companies Roche Group's Genentech unit, Pfizer Inc., AmerisourceBergen Corporation and McKesson Corporation teamed up to explore a track-and-trace solution for prescription medicines.

Stage Three: Deciding What Will Be Shared and With Whom

Blockchains are networks, which means data transparency and multi-party participation are fundamental. Multiple design considerations will need to be made around what data to share on the network and the network participants.

Why Enterprises Choose Permissioned Blockchains

Many enterprises end up building their applications on permissioned infrastructure that enables them to regulate who participates and can see their transactions. Many blockchain use cases in healthcare deal with highly regulated information and processes, so being able to identify who did what is important. Relative to a public blockchain, a permissioned blockchain places greater reliance on user identity versus pseudo-anonymity. This allows network operators to identify bad actors, while allowing users to selectively reveal their identity to other network participants with relative credibility.

Transaction performance is another reason companies may choose a permissioned network. Blockchain nodes stay in-sync with each other through a process called "consensus." The consensus model for a blockchain network determines how nodes agree on the validity of a transaction. On a public network, consensus mechanisms like Proof-of-Work eliminate the need for trust between nodes in order to add transactions to the blockchain; they rely purely on mathematical computation contributed by network participants. It creates a dynamic in which it is too computationally intensive, therefore infeasible, to collude on the network. As a result, Proof-of-Work blockchains run much slower and limit the overall function of the blockchain to a basic set of rules the nodes can agree on. Every transaction on a permissionless network is public and can take several minutes to be confirmed. By relying on a less complex consensus mechanism than public networks, permissioned blockchains can achieve better transaction throughput.

The tradeoff for permissioned networks is that they can run faster and are more technically flexible, but participants must trust the node operators. Permissioned blockchains use a variety of consensus mechanisms to maintain synchronization, but most of them rely on a delegated party, usually a consortium, to maintain certain functions in the agreement process, such as ordering the transactions for the other nodes to validate. The difference between the two types of networks is like night-and-day, but performance can make all the difference to your use case.

Additionally, healthcare enterprises will need to make a decision on which protocol and community will best fit their permissioned network needs. Ethereum and Hyperledger are some open-source platform examples.

For example, Change Healthcare chose the Hyperledger Fabric protocol for its permissioned blockchain, with a basic Kafka consensus mechanism. Change Healthcare's permissioned network is able to achieve up to 550 transactions per second, whereas the public Bitcoin network processes around seven transactions per second. For Change Healthcare's claims transparency application, Hyperledger Fabric had the necessary features for production, such as private transaction channels, swappable consensus mechanisms, and the ability to maintain stable, high volume throughput. Hyperledger also had a large community of enterprise contributors and its Healthcare Working Group. Today, the company maintains an open approach to blockchain development, exploring many protocols and platforms for its needs.

What Data to Put on the Blockchain

One of the most critical factors of blockchain solution design for enterprises concerns what data to include in a blockchain transaction. Blockchain technology has several characteristics that can help an organization decide what data is appropriate to put on the network:

- Blockchains are a shared utility. Since multiple entities could be storing a copy of the blockchain and have a full record of every transaction and its contents, it's not advisable to put personal health information or any other type of private, sensitive information in the transaction.

- Blockchain transactions are small. They are limited to 200 to 300 bytes—roughly the size of a text message. They are not designed to store and replicate images, files, or other large packages of data. The blockchain's ledger is an event log, a copy of which gets replicated across every computer that is running a full node on the network. Large transactions slow down the performance of the network and computers' ability to stay in sync with each other.

- Blockchain transactions are permanent. They cannot be deleted once created. Transactions can always be appended if mistakes are made or permissions need to be updated. Applications will take users to the most recent transaction associated with their key. But there is a cost to storing data, so measures need to be taken to make sure the right data is recorded to the blockchain. Edge computing with artificial intelligence and machine learning can help prevent bad transactions at the application level, before it is recorded to the blockchain.

Due to being permanent, shared, and limited in size, the blockchain is essentially a reference system, versus being a storage system. Virtually any type of data can be referenced, with the blockchain serving as an index of what information exists, who has access to it, where it can be found, and when it was created. Reference to a medical record, for example, might include the signature (hash) of the data, a link to its location, and cryptographic keys giving the patient and certain physicians access to the information.

In Change Healthcare's claims management transparency solution, a blockchain transaction contains a timestamp, a transaction ID, a cryptographic hash of the 30 claims lifecycle events stored in the company's database, and some meta-data that describes the type of event that occurred, such as "claim received." There is no PHI or sensitive claim information recorded in the blockchain transaction itself.

How Companies Will Participate and Partner

For inter-enterprise blockchain initiatives, the collaborating companies that finance the network and contribute node infrastructure are usually determined at the time a use-case is being chosen and defined. This is the core group that establishes code-level agreements about how the network will run, including the allowable size of transactions, and a business agreement about how identities on the network will be validated and other network collaborators will be added. Usually, this group considers various options to govern the network, such as, forming a consortium or partnering with other companies, or forming a joint-venture.

There is a difference between the founding partners or operators of the network, and simply being a participant on the network. Often, to get a use case started, operators may make up the entire network of participants, but as the solution grows, application end-users will need to be able to interact with the network without having to store a full copy of the blockchain on their device.

The use case will dictate who these participants will be; for example, physicians and office administrators in a provider data management solution. End-users don't have to validate the blockchain transactions, but their applications will need access to it (usually via API) in order to create transactions on the blockchain, sign their digital signatures, and reference data stored on their device or cloud.

Stage Four: Gauging Value and Success

An organization must create metrics for measuring the value and success of their blockchain investment, but the purpose of the investment differs between departments. Business-led initiatives will want to assess the potential revenue impact of a blockchain solution, taking into consideration the total addressable market size and impact to existing revenue streams. Technology-driven initiatives will instead focus on measuring the efficiency or performance capabilities of the solution, such as how quickly a transaction propagates.

If the technology improves capabilities, the organization must consider its cost relative to existing methods. How much will the organization have to spend to run this solution compared to the cost of running a competitive or alternative solution that does the same thing? How do the features and capabilities of the solution compare to what already exists? Consortiums and other multi-enterprise groups developing a blockchain solution will need to reach agreement on the goals and metrics for evaluating success.

Stage Five: Planning for the Future

Once an organization establishes some basic metrics for the cost and value of a blockchain solution, they will be able to better understand how to prioritize it after the proof-of-concept. If the solution can be proven valuable, organizations will need to provision resources for continued development or post-production maintenance.

Since most POCs are focused on testing a business case, it makes sense to create a model for how the solution will scale if it is successful. What will it take to make improvements and add more data and transactions? How much and how fast will transactional volume grow and how will that affect cloud support and database storage requirements over time? If the innovation team developed the concept, who in the business is going to be responsible for maintaining it moving forward?

Enterprises with use cases that begin as a private blockchain project may want to think ahead about transitioning to a permissioned network, where customers can run and distribute node infrastructure. Blockchains are not designed for a single entity to independently maintain and expand, both in terms of cost and function.

At this stage in the industry's maturity, it is recommended to keep an open mind when exploring new blockchain projects. If it's open source, consider the size of the community, the consensus mechanisms it supports, and the features that support your application's needs. If it's closed-source or proprietary, consider the company's domain expertise and funding, the role of the software in establishing trust on your network, and the integration capabilities it supports.

Whatever path you choose, remember that blockchains are a network – and there's no value in being a network of one. You should pick a platform that is suitable for scale, operationalization, and participation with multiple companies, which may approach the network with a different value proposition than your own.

Change Healthcare's Blockchain Approach to Claims Transactions

Change Healthcare has been intentional about using its interconnected position at the center of the healthcare ecosystem to promote collaboration around the goals of value-based healthcare. When the fiscal year ended March 31, 2018, its Intelligent Healthcare Network facilitated nearly 14 billion healthcare-related transactions covering over $1 trillion in annual healthcare claims and touching one out of every five patient records.

Blockchain at Change Healthcare was of initial interest to the technologists. Through its innovation processes, Change Healthcare began pilots and started pursuing proofs of concepts. Once the value of the technology became more clear, senior management also became interested in the capabilities and opportunities with blockchain technology and aligned with the technologists on the value. In 2017, the company joined the board of Hyperledger and hired a Blockchain Product Director to advance its product strategy.

Change Healthcare made the decision in 2017 to build an enterprise-scale blockchain network for claims administration. The network's first application enables real-time tracking of claims status and makes it available at no charge to its provider customers. Neither the company's customers nor its vendor partners had to develop new code, interfaces, or data formats. The application was purposefully built to be compatible with the company's blockchain-enhanced Intelligent Healthcare Network connecting multiple payers and providers to its healthcare transaction-processing network.

In the current claims management process, there are multiple parties involved—payer, provider, processor and patient—each with its own understanding of the claims process, status and information. They perform many of the same activities to reconcile the information, and therefore, no one party has the full picture of what's happening with the claim. Providers carry the uncertainty of wondering if or when they will receive payment. Payers carry the uncertainty around the validity of the claims submitted. Patients need to determine what they owe and to whom.

Change Healthcare's claims management transparency blockchain solution expands the capability and value of the company's revenue cycle management products. By leveraging blockchain technology, customers can accurately track, in real time, the status of claims submission and remittance across the complete claim lifecycle. The incorporation of blockchain technology in the Intelligent Healthcare Network enables greater auditability, traceability, and trust.

Production-Ready Within Two Months

Reimagining claims administration on the blockchain takes multiple approaches. Change Healthcare felt the best initial use case was one suited for blockchain technology's core record-keeping capabilities—claims lifecycle transparency. This would allow the company to build an enterprise-grade blockchain foundation close to their core business.

A team of six software engineers and architects interviewed the blockchain vendors and came up with a roadmap for quickly getting the enterprise-scale blockchain network into production by January 2018. The company was looking for a system that could sustain 300 transactions per second with a lot of excess capacity to accommodate higher point-to-point transactional volumes expected in the future. They also needed to be able to integrate it with legacy technologies.

With a use case, a blockchain platform, a participant model, and basic performance requirements identified, Change Healthcare began development. The goal was to create a notary system for the large volume of healthcare claims it was processing each year. The function was dissected into more than 30 discrete lifecycle events (e.g., creation of a claim, adjudication of a claim), which were expressed in the chain-code and written to the ledger. The company developed an API for querying the status of a claim or its history of interactions, giving providers a window into the blockchain. This API query feature would be called Claims Management Transparency.

The company announced its intention to launch the network in September 2017 at the Distributed:Health blockchain conference in Nashville, and the team had the infrastructure production-ready within two months.

Two key decisions had to be made during this brief development period—how many nodes the network would need to reach its transaction capacity, and which consensus mechanism would be utilized to keep all the distributed systems in sync with one another—within the confines of Hyperledger Fabric's capabilities.

The required integration work was relatively straightforward. This was both because Hyperledger Fabric is highly modular, allowing for easy plug-in of data sources and transactions, and because Change Healthcare was already caching transactions in an Apache Kafka queue, Fabric's consensus mechanism.

Claims Management Reimagined

The Assurance Reimbursement Management™ application, which provider billing administrators use to submit claims, was the first healthcare application connected to the blockchain network. The claims lifecycle transparency use case helped demonstrate the fundamental security and scalability of blockchain technology to the demands of a typical revenue cycle ecosystem.

Leveraging blockchain technology, organizations can now use the Intelligent Healthcare Network blockchain technology to accurately track, in real time, the status of claims submission and remittance across the complete claim lifecycle. This is improving transparency and efficiency, while enabling greater auditability, traceability, and trust. The single source of truth created by the blockchain is intended to support a new model for sharing health information that is more streamlined and user-centric.

The Intelligent Healthcare Network has the potential to processes more than 50 million claims events daily and up to 550 transactions per second through its blockchain. This capacity and speed significantly exceed the daily national transaction load and throughput requirements of the network, providing headroom for additional scale as blockchain technology adoption grows. A significant increase in this performance baseline is expected as the solution is further optimized and scaled to address demand.

Creating a Stable Strategy for an Evolving Technology

Since the launch of claims management transparency using blockchain, Change Healthcare has been focusing on expanding its blockchain solutions on three areas—financial, clinical, and patient engagement ecosystems. The strategy includes using the technology to create continuity between the three primary contexts for the payer-provider-patient relationship: financing, fulfilling, and optimizing healthcare services.

Product teams across the enterprise have been empowered to develop blockchain solutions with consulting and oversight from a group operating under Chief Technology Officer Aaron Symanski in the R&D department. Since launching its first solution, Change Healthcare has devised a holistic enterprise strategy for adopting blockchain technology across its network and solutions.

The effort began with a companywide educational campaign around the technology, sharing a method for mapping proposed solutions to the company's blockchain product definition and its intended market. The education served to provide a cohesive definition, value proposition, and stable guidelines for approaching the technology with Change Healthcare products. It also served to mitigate conflicting information circulating about the technology as trends come and go. For example, early in 2018, ICOs and digital tokens had captured consumer interest, making its way into everyday conversation, so Change Healthcare employees needed to be able to guide customer questions, or even questions that came up over the dinner table.

The CTO's team became the trusted source of information about blockchain and how it fit into the larger enterprise strategy of Change Healthcare. If product teams wanted to collaborate with a partner or customer on an initiative, this was also where they turned for guidance on vendor selection and the right stakeholders to pull together so decisions could be made quickly. The collaboration also helped product teams put their project in perspective. For example, a POC will have a different resourcing and development plan than a production initiative.

To more quickly develop and test new services for its customers, Change Healthcare is extending connectivity of its Intelligent Healthcare Network to the cloud via Amazon Web Services. Cloud-enablement will provide the next-generation clearinghouse with more data storage and processing capabilities, and the company hopes it will be able to further expand its blockchain capabilities.

At the 2018 Distributed:Health conference, one year from the company's strategic debut, Change Healthcare announced a collaboration to build the first smart contract system for healthcare. It will use the Change Healthcare Intelligent Healthcare Network blockchain technology along with TIBCO's smart contract developer project, Project Dovetail™. The goal is to enable health plans and their financial partners to easily develop and deploy smart contract-based processes that automate events across the healthcare transaction processing lifecycle. The collaboration will leverage TIBCO's Project Dovetail, which provides a development framework to allow payers and financial institutions to build smart contracts governing healthcare transaction processing. With Dovetail, users will gain access to a model-driven environment that promotes the creation of smart contracts that can run on any blockchain or cloud platform, and thus increases agility, flexibility, and time to market.

In pursuit of inspiring a better healthcare system in the U.S., Change Healthcare plans to create application development tools that its customers can use to build their own blockchain applications and workflows, made interoperable by the underlying blockchain network. These tools will include common identity frameworks, for example, for provider identity, or a set of rules for how claims events should be structured, or basic notification frameworks for sending and receiving messages between applications. These tools will also enable healthcare companies to customize their solutions and ensure interoperability with each other over the blockchain. This will bring transparency, accuracy, and speed to not only payers and providers, but most importantly, patients. Change Healthcare recognizes that, in order to be a key catalyst of a value-based healthcare system, it needs to work alongside its customers and partners and innovate with technologies, such as blockchain, to accelerate the journey toward improved lives and healthier communities. As more partners join the Change Healthcare network or create their own networks, blockchain will become ever more effective in connecting the healthcare system, realizing countless synergies.

Chapter 12:
Thought Leader Perspectives: An Interview with David Houlding on Blockchain, Enterprise, and Health

David Houlding

(Interview Transcript)

David Houlding

https://hashedhealth.com/blockchain-for-healthcare-book/

Editor's Note:

Chapter twelve represents a conversation between two of our authors, John Bass and David Metcalf, with Microsoft's David Houlding. In this interview Bass, Metcalf and Houlding discuss a variety of topics including the convergence of technologies around blockchain, how the enterprise blockchain space is maturing, and what the future holds for blockchain in healthcare.

David Metcalf (DM): You've had quite some history in the space. Could you tell us about your background and history in the blockchain and healthcare space?

David Holding (DH): Healthcare background: over 24 years in healthcare spent in the different segments provider, payer, pharmaceutical, life sciences. Worked for over a decade with the Intel Life Sciences team as director of healthcare privacy and security, also covered compliance and blockchain – that's where I first got into blockchain. Initially asserted as a panacea for security, which we all know it isn't. It's got some strengths but also some things you need to take care of, so part of my early work was to clarify what blockchain brings, what you need to take care of, and then got deeply into it from that standpoint. Just under 6 months ago got a great opportunity with Microsoft with the Azure team, the industry experiences team at Microsoft, leading healthcare initiatives for that team and continuing to work 100% on healthcare, very much on the cloud side of healthcare IT, and blockchain is one of many very exciting workloads along with AI machine learning. Still covering cybersecurity, privacy compliance and IoT and all that exciting stuff, but blockchain has a key role to play and it's also very synergistic with a lot of those other technologies.

DM: Great background, too, and coming from your past work I think there's a lot of synergy there. In terms of what you're currently working on and what you're excited about, maybe you could tell us a little about what you're doing now.

DH: I currently also serve as chair of the HIMSS blockchain and healthcare task force. It's an honor and a privilege, working with almost 100 leaders across healthcare segments worldwide to advance the application of blockchain and healthcare. The things that really get me excited is, on the applications side of blockchain, so the different use cases that it's being applied to in healthcare for healthcare benefit. So not talking about the cryptocurrency, Bitcoin side of blockchain, not really talking much about the ICO fundraising side of blockchain, those are exciting in their own right. My focus and what gets me excited is the enterprise use cases for applying blockchain in healthcare and what are the business values that can be gleaned. So reducing healthcare costs is a leading one. Blockchain use cases that promise helping to reduce costs are getting early traction. Some other use cases promise improving patient outcomes, improving engagement of patients, experiences of patients, even experiences of healthcare professionals. It's those use cases ranging from drug supply chain, medical device track-and-trace, even the food supply chain has some relevance to healthcare. If there's a food poisoning of some kind, being able to identify quickly and pull those off shelves can save patient lives. Of course provider credentialing, super exciting things going on with Hashed Health and ProCredEx. Provider directory, antifraud, just a few of the exciting use cases that we're seeing blockchain being applied to in healthcare for those business benefits I mentioned.

John Bass (JB}: David, you have a background in a lot of different areas, not just blockchain but you've done a lot of work on IoT. Back when you were at Intel we talked a lot about things like secure enclaves, but you've also done a lot of work on

AI and machine learning. We think a lot about this convergence of technologies, even some healthcare specific things around genomics and precision medicine. Just put that in context for us. How important and what relationship does blockchain have to those other areas that are abuzz right now?

DH: One of the ways I try to explain is sort of a layered view of it. Today we have the healthcare data mostly in silos across organizations locked up, a lot of latent potential to share that in a targeted secure way for those business benefits I mentioned. Blockchain of course can be the platform to enable that targeted secure sharing, but on top of blockchain of course you can have smart contracts to automate the execution on the blockchain, you've got cryptocurrencies that can incent collaboration on the blockchain and reward engagement, so patient engagement could be rewarded, patient compliance etc., sharing of data, collaboration on blockchain can be rewarded with cryptocurrencies. But then AI machine learning on top of that. I've done a lot of work at the intersection of AI and blockchain. The thing with AI and machine learning is they're super data hungry, right, and almost all AI effort are constrained in how good an inference they can get by the data that they have to train the model. Usually that's because the data that they're pulling is from one silo within one organization. Blockchain gives us the opportunity to collaborate across a consortium of healthcare organizations to source data from across the consortium, so vastly increases the data available to train models. Even much more specialized models, where you need a specific type of data to train a specific model, because you're sourcing it from a consortium, you can get a critical mass of data to get a reasonable inference or a reasonably low error rate. But any task really that you can accomplish better as a team, as a consortium, blockchain is an opportunity to catalyze and incent that with cryptocurrencies. So not just sourcing training data but actually collaborating on training models. You can imagine a model being passed around like a football between different healthcare organizations in a consortium, and incrementally trains, so those organizations wouldn't even have to share the raw data. Say there were constraints, they could share the models within each organization, pass it around and share the models. They could also collaborate on the results that come from those models and validation of those results. How do you trust a new model? Well, you could learn to trust it yourself by trying it on lots and lots of data and figuring out was it right or not. That's going to take a certain amount of time for one organization going it alone, but if you have a consortium of organizations collaborating they can learn to trust the model much faster as a group and establish that trust. Pretty much any task again that can be accomplished better as a team, as a consortium of healthcare organizations, blockchain has an opportunity to enable that with a targeted secure sharing and incent with crytopcurrencies and tokens. You mentioned IoT as well. IoT has some super interesting intersects with both blockchain and AI machine learning. On the blockchain intersect side, you look at use cases like drug supply chain where you're tracking medications from the point of manufacturing to distribution to dispensing or retail like at a pharmacy and being able to verify the provenance, the authenticity, the safety of the medication – it's not a counterfeit, it's safe to consume. Especially if it comes over a channel like the Internet you want to make sure it's the real thing, it's safe to consume. But just tracking the drug is one thing, but what if you could track, especially for drugs that are sensitive to environmental parameters like temperature, what if you could track what were the temperature parameters of this vaccine as it made its way through the supply chain, and that's where IoT like temperature sensors could track the environmental conditions throughout the supply chain, and so when you do your verification check at the point of dispensing or use, you're checking not just is this the real thing and is it safe, but has it been kept within safe bounds of humidity, temperature, or whatever the constraints are to make sure it hasn't gone off or something like that. So you can actually record that kind of information on the blockchain, the IoT sensors can record that on the blockchain. Intersect with AI machine learning, of course, again, super data hungry, and that data – AI machinery gives us the opportunity to process vast quantities of data in near real-time and get near real-time, actionable insights to improve healthcare – reduce costs, improve outcomes, etc. I think of IoT as the eyes and ears of AI machine learning. You can have sensors in patients, implantables, on patients, the wearables, around patients, whether it's in a patient home like remote patient monitoring, whether it's in a clinical setting, in your car even, these different IoT sensors monitoring the patient, being able to detect in near real-time, hey this patient's vitals are trending outside of safe bounds, we need to intervene, we need to intercept, we need to course correct so that the patient doesn't have an episode. An episode is not just a huge cost event – like a heart attack, a patient going to the hospital is very costly but it actually degrades the patient's quality of life, so if you can intercept that before it happens and get that patient onto a safe path where they don't have that episode, that's some of the amazing, proactive preventative healthcare potential around IoT, again the eyes and ears and sourcing AI machine learning to give us those near-real-time insights to intercept and proactively prevent episodes and improve healthcare.

JB: IoT's not new, right. It seems like we've been struggling with a lot of issues around security and scalability for quite some time for IoT platforms, IoT initiatives. Can you comment on the key ability for blockchain and distributed ledgers to provide the trust and secure platforms so that these IoT products can scale up in a meaningful way?

DH: Some of the work I did at Intel was around their Sawtooth Lake or what became Hyperledger Sawtooth blockchain platform. It uses a different consensus algorithm called POET, or Proof-of-Elapsed Time. POET I think of like a deli counter. You go there, you take a ticket and that's your place in line. With Sawtooth Lake, instead each blockchain node running on top of Intel SGX or software guard extensions hardware, each blockchain node can reach down and get a ticket, and that's what we call a guaranteed wait time, and the one with the lowest wait time can be essentially elected as the leader and the validation of the next block to go on the blockchain. The reason why that's so interesting is we all know proof-of-work type consensus algorithms can require massive amounts of hardware and electric power, and this gives it a much more democratic, over time all the nodes would participate as leaders in validating blocks going onto the blockchain vs. in the bitcoin world, you only really participate if you've got monstrous amounts of hardware and electric power to throw at mining blocks or solving the crypto puzzles to become the one that commits the block. These kinds of technologies, these hardware security technologies like SGX, give you the opportunity to implement new hardware roots of trust which can underpin consensus algorithms, which can greatly increase the decentralization of blockchain and nodes and participation and consensus and things like that. Although blockchain is asserted as decentralized, if you have a consensus algorithm like proof-of-work where you effectively only have about 10 mining operations worldwide that are competitively mining Bitcoins, is it really decentralized if you only have 10 that are really doing it? So you can have this perception of decentralization vs. the reality. To have true decentralization, you really want to have almost random, white noise selection of nodes, that over time every node could participate, and then you've got true decentralization and of course decentralization underpins the whole availability value of searching the blockchain, where you don't just want to have a single or a few points that could compromise the whole blockchain network. So, I know I went very deep there, but IoT obviously, you can have hardware security in IoT devices and they can underpin blockchain nodes and enable those devices to participate as actual nodes in a blockchain with new types of consensus algorithms and decentralization.

JB: What does blockchain bring to the table that hasn't been there in the past that will allow IoT to reach its full potential? I think that layer of trusted data around the security and scalability of IoT needs that foundation to sit on, same with AI machine learning. If you can provide a platform of information for these things to run, it really allows it to scale. Following up, some of your comments started to talk about decentralization. I've said in a lot of my talks in 2018 that decentralization to me feels like a beautiful dream that's just yet to be realized in really anything other than Bitcoin. Can you provide some of your thoughts from your perspective on that topic?

DH: Full disclosure, I tend to take a very practical, sort of pragmatic approach to blockchain. I steer clear of what I call the blockchain religion, where we can get caught up with the concept of decentralization, and when something isn't on a public blockchain it's not blockchain. In the near-term, the vast majority of healthcare blockchain use cases and pilots and production usages are going to be on private consortium blockchains which are not public. They're going to have a very well-defined set of healthcare organizations participating that are highly trusted and that are well-known to each other. So I think in terms of decentralization, you have to take a practical approach, and rather than grounding it in blockchain religion, I think it makes sense to ground it in what are the healthcare use cases and what are the healthcare values. Again, is it reducing healthcare costs, is it reducing adverse events like improving patient outcomes, is it improving patient engagement, improving patient experience or healthcare professional experience? That's what you've got to ground it on. The healthcare values, the business values that healthcare is seeking, not any technical concept like decentralization. That said, the concept of decentralization obviously is important for the reliability value assertion of blockchain. If you reduce it to one blockchain node then you essentially have a single point of failure again and the argument comes up why use blockchain. So you need some level of decentralization just to get that availability benefit and also a lot of people miss the anti-fraud value prop of blockchain and the immutability to prevent fraudulent modification or deletion and improve transparency to detect new fraudulent transactions, but to really realize that anti-fraud benefit, you need to have enough decentralization so that collusion is not practical. If you have two nodes, or three nodes, if two of the nodes collude, you could essentially corrupt the blockchain or introduce fraudulent type transactions. So you want to have enough nodes that you get the availability benefit, you get the anti-fraud risk mitigation benefit, and there are other benefits. I see it as more of a gray-scale, not you're either fully decentralized or you're not. It's somewhere in between and where you set the slider to me should depend on balancing the technical objectives like availability and anti-fraud with the business objectives, the business values you seek, and making sure those are realized. At the end of the day what's going to get blockchain traction in healthcare is the realization of those business values by real healthcare organizations and the publication of those pilot results in case studies where those organization attest to the business values. That's a critical step that we're trending towards as an industry, and we really need to see those case studies in the next six months or so. That'll be a sort of watershed moment I think for blockchain in healthcare. Once you get a sort of critical mass of healthcare organizations standing up and saying we're not just talking, we've done, we've done this blockchain use case, these are results, this is the business value we sought, the ROI, this is what worked well, this is what could be improved. I think that is going to be a beachhead on which blockchain will grow. Right now, there's all these private consortium blockchains which I think of as blockchain islands in an archipelago. Some will get there and some won't. The ones that don't will die off, they'll get selected out. The ones that do get there will rapidly acquire new healthcare organizations on their island, they'll grow in terms of the size of the consortium, as well as being able to layer on additional use cases. If they start with provider credentialing, they could layer on provider directory or the various supply chain use cases or healthcare information exchange. The technology is the easy part. Building the consortium and the trust and getting buy-in, getting organizations to actually connect their enterprise systems and transact on blockchain is the hard part, layering on additional use cases is relatively easy once you've done that for the first one.

DM: I want to build on that. Where do you see some of that synergy and some of that realism right now in where we're at in the space?

DH: I think there's definitely five or so leading use cases that have very strong healthcare value props. In particular, any use case that has a strong value prop of cost reduction seems to be getting early traction in healthcare. I think some of the ones that are asserting empowering the patient and better patient outcomes are coming but may not be the first ones, the killer use cases to get the first traction. Almost all of the five that we're tracking – those being drug supply chain, medical device track-and-trace, health information exchange, provider credentialing, provider directory – they, almost all of them, have a very strong cost reduction value prop.

DM: How about the trust between distributed payers and the providers, whether that's in a hospital setting or the individual doctors and healthcare workers in particular? Any thoughts there on what's going to change over the next couple of years?

DH: It demands a mindset shift and just the concept of sharing, even with another organization that you've traditionally considered to be a competitor and in short, I think it has to be a case of the benefits outweigh the risks, and everything you're sharing has to be very intentional from realizing those business values standpoints. Building the consortium again is the hard part. Anyone out there that's thinking about blockchain,thinking about a use case, thinking about technologies, you need to start from square one thinking about who is your consortium, what are the organizations with an s, multiple, blockchain is not a single organization thing in general, and getting them engaged and getting them bought into the concept right from the get-go and building the blockchain and designing the blockchain with their participation, I think is really key. As the saying goes, trust is won in drips and lost in buckets. You've got to get people bought in and connected and transacting around a simple use case that's relatively benign, if you have one that minimizes PII or personally identifiable information and protected healthcare information (PHI), security privacy, compliance risk is greater with PII and PHI. A lot of the early use cases actually avoid or minimize the presence of PII or PHI on the actual blockchain, but getting people to buy into the use case, the business value assertions, and what data do you actually share on the blockchain should be minimum but sufficient for the actual use case. You're only sharing what is absolutely critical to go on the blockchain. The rest of the data can remain in the secure access controlled enterprise systems where it lives today, whether it's EHR on the provider side, whether for membership eligibility, claims adjudication or the pharmacy system, pharmaceutical system. The data can live in its current silos unless there's a compelling need for it to live elsewhere. Blockchain can serve this role as a sort of catalyst to enable the collaboration and secure sharing of data but the sharing doesn't actually have to happen all through the blockchain. Blockchain could facilitate this publication of metadata or transactions, the discovery of that information by other members of the consortium and once they find something of interest, they can initiate a direct peer-to-peer request to the source organization and facilitate that secure exchange on an as-needed basis, and that direct peer-to-peer exchange doesn't have to happen through blockchain. Again blockchain, minimum but sufficient, avoid PII, PHI if you can, avoid anything heavyweight, images, genomics, don't try to put that on blockchain. There's real performance reasons you don't want to do that as well.

DM: Or the portable electronic healthcare of a person we keep talking about – not a good idea.

DH: It's the blockchain religion asserts let's put all our data on blockchain and figure out later how to make use of it. As we all know, that's not a recipe for success. There's huge privacy, security compliance, competitive and performance scalability reasons why you don't want to do that.

DM: It's blockchain + whatever else is going to be effective for your use case and your business case outcome that you're looking for, or health outcome that you're looking for.

DM: That's a great way to look at it. It's almost like a machine. We have this machine today which is all these cogs which are inside each organization in enterprise systems in the organizations, and what's been missing is this central cog which sort of allows all those organizations to collaborate. And that's the blockchain central cog, but it's just one cog in the overall machine. A lot of the blockchain religion asserts hey, blockchain's going to replace all the enterprise systems. We don't see that at all. It's this back end middleware that takes this minimum but sufficient role to facilitate collaboration and coordination, but the enterprise systems live on. Blockchain has no user interface. Where are the user interfaces? It's the user interfaces of the enterprise systems or maybe new user interfaces you add – web interfaces, mobile app interfaces, but they're not really talking to the blockchain directly. Typically there's a sort of mid-tier that's integrating with the blockchain on the back end.

DM: The next question maybe you can think about which direction you'd like to take it, but what are the things that you are most concerned about in the future of blockchain, or which things are you most hopeful for in the future of blockchain?

DH: I'll take that in the direction of cybersecurity because we haven't talked about that a whole lot and I think it needs a little bit more attention. In healthcare, we've seen the risk that comes from covered entities or data controllers working with business associates or data processors, and a breach can occur at a business associate or data processor, and it impacts the covered entity or data controller. Blockchain really introduces this concept of consortiums on a whole nother level, right, and when you start putting data on blockchain and collaborating with a network of other healthcare organizations, there are risks associated with that. You want to try to contain those risks or mitigate them from a security standpoint, so you're going to use a multi-layer defense in-depth approach. First, minimum but sufficient information on the blockchain. That's the biggest lever you have to pull. The second one is limit who can connect to that blockchain. Again private consortium, 99% of the use cases we're seeing in blockchain and healthcare are private consortium, and they know exactly what are the organizations connecting, why are they connecting, what's their business need, do you trust them, etc. They're all well-known and highly trusted. And then of course Encryption and not just one encryption key but key rotation functions, key derivation functions, so that if the key is ever broken it doesn't expose the entire blockchain, etc. You've got all these layers of defense to put in any blockchain initiative to mitigate what we call residual risk. There's this concept of adequacy where wherever you have a network of organizations collaborating and sharing data, and you don't even need to put the PII or PHi on the blockchain. If the blockchain facilitates the discovery and sharing of the PII or PHI and a breach subsequently occurs, that's going to backfire on the organization where the breach happened plus the blockchain network and the source organization. There's the concept of if you are going to join a blockchain, make sure you trust everybody that's connecting to that and how they're using the data. You actually want to proactively get a measure of the adequacy of their security and privacy compliance, because if you have a consortium of 10 organizations joining and one of them is kind of a weak link if you will in terms of they're connecting to the blockchain and they're pulling information off the blockchain or in interactions that are enabled by the blockchain and putting information in their own enterprise systems which are insecure and then a breach occurs, it impacts everybody. This is something not a lot of people are talking about, but if we have a breach event that happens in a blockchain network and taints that blockchain, it could really stall or impede the adoption of blockchain in healthcare. I think we need to think about these kinds of risks. Healthcare has struggled to secure their own healthcare organizations adequately from a privacy, security, and achieving compliance standpoint. When it comes to a blockchain network, that takes it up to a whole nother level where you're not just worried about securing your own organization, you've got to make sure that everybody connecting to that blockchain is adequately secure. The good news is there's techniques like risk assessment and compliance audits and so forth that can be done proactively, which you might say as an organization, if I'm joining this blockchain network, have all the other organizations that are connecting to it had their risk assessment done, can they share that at least under NDA, have they achieved compliance, whatever the jurisdiction they're in. If it's Europe, it's going to have certain data protection laws, if it's the US it's going to have HIPAA, maybe high-trust. This sort of proactive benchmarking or measurement of security and privacy compliance, and identification of weak links and mitigation of those weak links proactively so that we don't have these breach events that derail or impede the adoption of blockchain.

JB: I think as we have been in the space for several years now, I think we're all seeing this concept of enterprise reputation coming forward, especially as some of the business models behind some of these use cases look more and more like marketplaces. A lot has to do with the reputation of the buyer or seller on the marketplace. I've been thinking about that concept from a data standpoint. So everything you just said around security also goes for the quality of the data that an enterprise is bringing to a marketplace business model. The quality of the credentials or the quality of the master data file that we're turning into a utility model, utility marketplace for a market. I think that's a really interesting connection that what you just said connects to lots of different use cases that are out there.

DH: John's comment on the integrity and the quality of the data is super interesting. In security, as professionals we're tasked with protecting the confidentiality, the integrity and the availability of data. But too often we equate security with protecting just confidentiality, but to John's point you've really got to protect the integrity and that's making sure the Data is accurate, up-to-date and complete. Blockchain can only protect what arrives at blockchain. From an immutability standpoint, a transparency standpoint, if the data is compromised or of poor quality before it reaches the blockchain, essentially, you end up with a garbage in and garbage out where you're protecting garbage on the blockchain. Super important that the data has the integrity and the quality that's needed, otherwise blockchain's not going to realize its potential.

DM: Idea that Microsoft and really your span with HIMSS and others is global. As a global enterprise, I'm sure you're looking at the different jurisdictions. You mentioned HIPAA of course, which we all know. What happens when we get over to GDPR and Safe Harbor and other areas of the world too, like Europe in particular? Any thoughts there on how the blockchain may change when we get over there?

DH: Safe Harbor's an interesting thing you brought up because it also had this concept of adequacy that if European citizen data is going to be shared in the US, they wanted to make sure you had adequate security, privacy, etc. And the US regulations and the Patriot Act and things were deemed to be not adequate security, so Safe Harbor introduced additional bars organizations have to meet to get adequate in the eyes of European law. In terms of compliance with regulations, one of the tie-ins as well is what regulations or data protection laws you're held ot are going to depend on two key things – the type of data you're putting on the blockchain, especially if it's PII or personally identifiable information of any king, it can be used to locate, contact, or identify an individual, then you need to be careful. What citizens is that PII coming from? If it's coming from European citizens, then GDPR could be applicable. The other thing that's important is the actual physical location of the blockchain nodes, because the data that is in the shared ledger is essentially replicated to wherever the blockchain nodes are. If you start off with your blockchain in Europe and that's subject to some jurisdiction like GDPR but then at some point you stand up a node in the US, then the data in the shared ledger is going to be replicated over to that new blockchain node in the US and you can end up with something called data sovereignty concerns or transport of data flow concerns, and you need to be careful based on the jurisdictions and the compliance frameworks you're held to, are there any restrictions on data sovereignty transfer, data flow, and it's not an easy question because blockchain startups don't always know the directions the blockchain could grow in the future. They might start local but aspire to go global, but the thing is with blockchain is any data you've put on the blockchain from day one is going to be replicated wherever you put those nodes. It maybe is a good idea to be conservative again, minimum but sufficient data on the blockchain. Avoid PII, PHI if you can. One of the other wrinkles with data protection laws like GDPR is this right to be forgotten. If a patient comes along and says, hey I want you to delete my data to the data controller, the healthcare organization, then they essentially have to delete that data to comply with GDPR. If you put their PII on the blockchain, as we know, it's immutable, so you can't delete it off the blockchain without compromising that blockchain's immutability. So, another reason to keep the PII and PHI off the blockchain, so if you get that kind of request you can delete it in a secure access controlled enterprise database. Essentially de-identify whatever's on the blockchain. You could still have an identifier on blockchain, but it's going to be a benign identifier not like a social security number, just something that's unique within that blockchain, so if it's compromised very limited usefulness outside that blockchain.

JB: GDPR and blockchain, these concepts around self-sovereign identity are very much aligned philosophically, but it's an example of where in practicality, they very much do not agree with each other in terms of how you'd make that happen.

DM: Great point. So, David, just as we start to wrap up, is there anything else you'd like to say about the future or anything we didn't cover today that you'd like to tell us about?

DH: Some of the thoughts on my mind just from the Distributed: Health conference, which John and Hashed Health team great job on that, really great event from the sessions and the networking there, and the discussions I've had there and in other forums. I think one of the things we can use as a tool to help people understand the potential of blockchain is to take a data-centric view and if anybody's ever changed a phone number or changed an address recently, we know the pain of having to go to hundreds of accounts and update that information. In healthcare we have a similar problem, we have the same redundant information all over the place. Even if it was possible to maintain it accurately in all of the locations, which it's not, and data gets out of date and inaccuracies. That causes a lot of friction in the healthcare system and friction means mis-identification of patients, duplicate records, claims bouncing, etc. What we really have to get to looking at a data-centric view is data that is common by nature needs to be maintained in a shared ledger in a way that eliminates that redundant effort, eliminates or mitigates the opportunity for inconsistencies that cause friction, and that in and of itself will greatly improve healthcare in terms of cost reduction, in making it less friction to share information, to render great healthcare, and so forth. So I think there's a ton of opportunity. I'm confident blockchain will take hold, but we need to have early use cases get piloted with real consortiums of healthcare organizations, have those case studies, have those attestations, what worked well, what can we improve, and then build from there, and concurrently just make sure that we don't step on some of the obvious mines from a cybersecurity privacy compliance standpoint with breaches. One can never be one hundred percent mitigated but do what we can with eyes wide open to mitigate risk of breaches or other adverse events that could taint, derail, or impede blockchain initiatives.

Chapter 13:
Pharmacy, Pharma, and Blockchain: Healthcare Financials, Pharmaceutical Supply Chain, Clinical Trials, and Social Good

Kevin A. Clauson, PharmD

Elizabeth A. Breeden, DPh, MS

Editor's Note:

This chapter provides an overview of the pharmaceutical world, and the various opportunities for the application of blockchain towards supply chain management, clinical trials and financial records. Kevin and Elizabeth present a history of the pharma industry to show specific use cases where a need for distributed ledger technology has emerged. Additionally, they delve into medical devices, the opioid crisis and a focus on social good that can be enabled by implementation of next-generation blockchain technology.

Introduction to Pharmacy and Pharma

The practice of pharmacy has evolved considerably from its "weeds and seeds" origins in tomes of materia medica, through the establishment of the first pharmacies in modern-day Iraq, and as an independent profession developed in the 19th century, but its core of pharmacologic knowledge, societal service, and patient care has largely been preserved during its changes over time (Zebroski 2016).

Pharmacy in the United States

The first pharmacy in Colonial America opened in Philadelphia in 1729, preceding the foundation of the United States (US); that location of Marshall's Apothecary later served as a supply depot during the American Revolution (Griffenhagen 2002). Going forward, there and elsewhere in the nascent country, pharmacists diagnosed diseases, compounded medications, and dispensed them without a physician order. However, in 1938, this changed as the Food Drug and Cosmetic Act (FD&C Act) was enacted, followed by an amendment in 1951 that restricted pharmacists from dispensing medications without a prescription (Zebroski 2016). The last 50 years have seen significant advances in the growth and role of pharmacy. The number of community pharmacies has grown to nearly 70,000 (Qato 2017) and the Bureau of Labor Statistics estimates there are 309,330 pharmacists in the US (Bureau of Labor Statistics 2017) as of 2017 (Figure 12.1), with the majority practicing in the community setting (e.g., CVS, Walgreens, Walmart, Medicine Shoppe, etc.). Additionally, over a quarter of all pharmacists practice in the hospital setting, followed by other settings including pharmaceutical companies, wholesalers, academia, and professional organizations. Reflecting the movement to a more clinically focused path, starting in 2000, the entry level degree for graduating pharmacists has required a doctoral degree (i.e., Doctor of Pharmacy; PharmD degree).

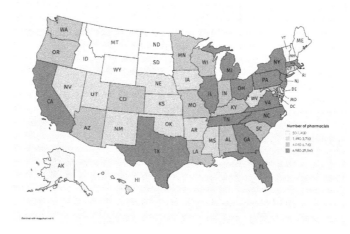

Figure 12.1. Employment of pharmacists, by state in 2017.
Adapted from US Bureau of Labor Statistics data using mapchart.net

The pharmacist's scope of practice varies by state and continues to expand, with all 50 states enabling pharmacists to provide immunizations (Healthmart 2018). In certain states, pharmacists that participate in collaborative practice agreements with physicians, are able to prescribe medications and receive reimbursement for their professional services. The goal is for pharmacists to achieve full provider status to assist as the healthcare needs of the US population continues to grow, healthcare costs continue to rise, and the shortage of physicians in primary care continues (Healthmart 2018). Pharmacists remain the most accessible healthcare professional, with 90% of the US population living within two miles of a pharmacy (PharmacistsForHealthierLIves 2018) and remains one of the most trusted and ethical professions (Morotta 2018). The ubiquity of internet-connected mobile devices also ensures that a pharmacist consultation can be accessible for patients irrespective of location, whether residing in urban or rural areas, needing specialized services, as well as in response to a changing patient paradigm.

The Role of Pharma

The move to production on a wholesale level by apothecaries, and the parallel move to establish research labs for drug discovery by chemical and dye companies, were the genesis of the current pharmaceutical industry (Daemmrich 2005). Merck is one example of an apothecary that operated for nearly 200 years before "beginning wholesale production in the 1840s". Several companies started soon thereafter and include Schering in Germany, Hoffman-La Roche in Switzerland, Burroughs Wellcome in England, and Smith Kline, Abbott, Parke-Davis, Eli Lilly, and Upjohn in the US. Their focus was development of synthetic drugs and the evaluation of their impact on pathological conditions and disease treatment (Daemmrich 2005).

The regulatory landscape changed in response to drug issues and mishaps and, in 1930, the US Department of Agriculture's Food, Drug, and Insecticide Administration was renamed and re-tasked as the modern Food and Drug Administration (FDA) (Rahalkar 2012). Additional regulatory elements soon followed with the passage of the FD&C Act to ensure the safety of medicines (Rahalkar 2012). This law mandated that pre-marketing approval of medications was required along with proof of scientific safety and the provision of directions for safe use. After experiencing incremental advances during this period of time, following the war efforts, pharmaceutical companies had attained capabilities (e.g., technological, organizational), funding, and opportunities that were unprecedented (Garavaglia 2013). Following the 1940s, the roles of both sales and science became more prominent in the pharmaceutical industry.

The research and development (R&D)-sales ratio increased from 3.7% in 1951 to estimates of 25% of spend and higher, due to an increased focus on marketing, including legally permissible direct-to-consumer (DTC) marketing in the US (Gagnon 2008). However, sources including the US General Accounting Office (GAO), via IMS data, as well as the Pharmaceutical Research and Manufacturers of America (PhRMA) asserted that spend on R&D continues to eclipse that of "all promotional activities" (Gagnon

2008). Another shift occurred following the stabilization and consolidation in the 1980s, as there was "significant entry" into the industry by biotechnology companies (Cockburn 2004).¬¬¬ And despite the European origins of the industry, by 2016, the US held over 45% of the global pharmaceutical market, representing 446 billion U.S. dollars (Statista 2018).

With a parallel emphasis on science, a golden age of discovery resulted in the development of many new critical drugs, as well as an accompanying desire for clinical objectivity. These efforts laid the foundation for pharmaceutical industry support of the modern clinical trial model for the assessment of new treatments and therapies. Clinical trials have continued to evolve over the years and recent developments suggest another milestone is approaching. The exploration of virtual clinical trials, sometimes referred to as remote clinical trials, is becoming a reality due to advances in technology, the decrease in cost associated with data storage and transmission, and the ubiquitous nature of mobile devices. It represents a new model to remotely collect safety and efficacy data from study participants using apps, monitoring devices, etc. while decreasing participant burden and costs in the process (Andrews 2017; Donnelly 2018); modeling-based virtual clinical trials and research are also being investigated due to their potential (Lehrach 2015).

Fit-for-Purpose Opportunities in Pharmacy with Blockchain

As with any emerging technology, blockchain proponents risk employing a "solution looking for a problem" approach due to their enthusiasm about the capabilities of this tech. While some excitement about the potential of distributed ledger technology (DLT) is merited, it should be tempered by a methodical approach, inclusive of a framework for assessing "fit-for-purpose" for pharmacy and healthcare (Barkovich 2018; Feig 2018). Key questions developed by Feig and adopted for assessing fit-for-purpose are: 1) who are the users, 2) what data do users input, 3) are any inputs irreversible, 4) who are the peers, 5) how do peers create blocks, 6) what do peers validate, 7) how do peers validate, 8) how do peers reach consensus, 9) is the blockchain immutable, and 10) how are peers incentivized (Feig 2018)? All or a subset of these questions may have applicability in a given instance, but predicated on those determinations, the fit-for-purpose framework recommends mapping core blockchain design elements to the needs of the specific healthcare problem in question. In considering elements like design type (i.e., public, private, hybrid), data sharing needs (e.g., on chain, off chain, permissioned, etc.), and governance (e.g., nodes, users, individuals, consortia, etc.) absence or presence of alignment between the characteristics of the distributed ledger technology and the challenge in pharmacy should become readily apparent.

These design concepts have been applied to varying degrees ranging from proof of concept to production for pharmacy-related challenges. Rather than detailing the theoretical underpinnings of these approaches, this chapter will provide an overview of four of the best fit-for-purpose use cases for blockchain in pharmacy (Figure 2). These sections will be followed by a brief overview of emerging categories and use cases for blockchain in pharmacy. Cases studies and an emerging use case will also be used in this chapter to provide a more detailed look into the intersection of blockchain and pharmacy.

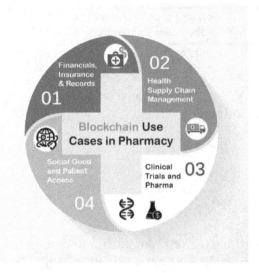

Figure 12.2. Fit-for-purpose blockchain use cases in pharmacy.

Healthcare Financials, Insurance, and Records

The most recognized application of blockchain is Bitcoin, so it is unsurprising that the financial sector's interest in utilization of DLT is significant. According to the National Health Expenditure Accounts (NHEA) estimates, healthcare spending accounts for a 17.9% share of the US Gross Domestic Product (GDP) (CMS NHEA 2018). Specifically, healthcare financials and insurance are areas particularly fertile for development and enhancement, with notable use cases including: 1) enhancing insurance claim processes, 2) improving provider data accuracy, 3) streamlining provider credentialing and 4) automating events in the payment processing life cycle.

Enhancing insurance claim processes

Automating health insurance claims using platforms like Fast Healthcare Interoperability Resources (FHIR) combined with DLT-enabled smart contracts is often pointed to as a goal for managing tasks in healthcare financing as well as management of Medicare beneficiary management – due to their perpetual exit and reentry into the system (Kuo 2017). Table 12.1 outlines the benefits and relevant mechanisms in harnessing blockchain technology in claims processing.

Table 12.1. Benefits of blockchain for enhancing insurance claims processing

Key Benefit	
Decentralized Management	Claim processing in real-time can be achieved via disintermediation of potentially nebulous health plan intermediation and replacement with the transparency of blockchain technologies
Immutable Audit Trail	Superior fraud detection and improvements in claim auditing can be realized due to the immutability of blockchain
Data Provenance	Distributed solutions like blockchain can better provide records for verification to accelerate claims qualification
Accessibility	Leveraging distributed ledger to improve accessibility of patient data for all stakeholder sources from varying silos
Security	Security of health insurance information is more resistant to efforts to comprise it (e.g. hacking) due to blockchain architecture

Adapted from Journal of the American Medical Informatics Association. doi: 10.1093/jamia/ocx068

Improving provider data accuracy

One of the most ambitious uses of blockchain to date in health care finance is being advanced by the Synaptic Healthcare Alliance (SHA White Paper 2018). Its initial collaborators include Humana, Multiplan, Optum, Quest Diagnostics and United Healthcare and their first effort is to improve provider data management, which despite the $2.1 billion spent annually, is beset by challenges with provider directory accuracy, efficiency, and its siloed nature. Alliance members have proposed a "provider data exchange (PDX)" in order to address interoperability challenges to allow sharing of data to demonstrate cost savings while improving data quality and user experience (SHA White Paper 2018). Proposed cost savings can be realized via: 1) reduction of high error rates, with consequential daily fines of up to $25,000 per Medicare Advantage beneficiary, 2) opportunity cost of consumers unable to correctly identify providers accepting new patients or accepting their health insurance plan, and 3) improving reimbursement rates tied to core business functions. The provider data management use case was prioritized as it allowed fostering of the alliance endeavor since it is dependent upon the "non-proprietary, non-competitive nature of provider demographics" to better allow more frictionless data sharing across separate entities (SHA White Paper 2018).

Streamlining provider credentialing

Provider credentialing is another use case that has drawn considerable attention due to its thematically similar challenges around efficiency, sharing, and cost; during the four to eight month time period and $500 to $3,600 it can take to credential a single physician, estimates suggest that hospitals can concurrently miss out on revenues of up to $7,500 per day of specialty-dependent physician revenue (Merritt Hawkins 2016, Salzman 2018).

While the initial interest has been in credentialing of physicians due to its highest associated costs, the same approach integrating blockchain technology can be applied to pharmacist credentialing and other health care professionals to gain efficiencies as well. The credentialing process can take months because there are still many manual processes and an entire constellation of degrees, certifications, attestations, employment verifications, etc. that must be collected from disparate sources. As concurrent credential-related efforts advance, blockchain could help shorten the time to access or harmonize those individual artifacts, streamline the entire credentialing process for health care professionals, and most importantly serve as the voice of truth for the credentials.

One such example for an individual artifact category is the partnership between Hashed Health and Lipscomb University College of Pharmacy, in which the Ethereum platform was used to allow for verification of student pharmacist graduation status (Chaudoin 2018). This degree data could be combined with licensure information from the National Association of Boards of Pharmacy (NABP), state boards of pharmacy licensure status, and accredited pharmacy residency completion from the American-Society of Health-System Pharmacists (ASHP) using a blockchain-enabled credentialing platform such as Professional Credentials Exchange (https://www.procredex.com/). Notably, ProCredEx, as part of "blockchain hub Hashed Health", recently announced a partnership including Accenture, National Government Services, the Spectrum Health System, and WellCare (Hartnet 2018). The aim of this partnership is for its network of collaborators to provide and share substantial verified credential datasets; a go-live for existing participants is slated for 2019, with the intent to expand to include other entities in 2020.

Another effort in the provider credentialing space, Intiva Health (https://intivahealth.com/) has proposed to build using Swirlds Hashgraph DLT and their Intiva (NTVA) token to help launch their service and incentivize participation by licensed health care professionals (Intiva White Paper 2018). Solve.Care (https://solve.care/), which focuses on "global blockchain solution for coordination, administration, and payments of healthcare", has seen its CEO, Pradeep Goel weigh in on the shortcomings of the current provider credentialing system as well. Goel asserts that the only real utility of the current system is to discover if "a physician has done harm before" and "That's not really credentialing – that's just weeding out the egregious." (Salzman 2018). Finally, provider credentialing is not a problem unique to the US, as evidenced at the recent "world's largest" hackathon, overseen by the King Abdulaziz City for Science and Technology (KACST) and held in Saudi Arabia in conjunction with MIT Hacking Medicine (TradeArabia 2018). The second place winner in the Blockchain and Artificial Intelligence for Healthcare and Forensic Science track at the hackathon was Tawthiq, for "Authenticating certificate of healthcare workers on the blockchain, issued direct from their university...". Blockchain platforms for credentialing pharmacists will likely generate additional interest if the profession of pharmacy gains the provider status that they have long been seeking to help address the shortage of primary care providers in the US.

Automating events in the payment processing life cycle

Manual input and intervention, and additional coding are historically the approaches necessary to rectify and reconcile systems created and customized for processing health care transactions (Brett 2018). Smart contracts that can trigger based on predefined transactional criteria offer the potential to auto-reconcile and auto-update (i.e., the system via a shared ledger) to produce a more efficient and cost-effective approach to health care transaction processing. Change Healthcare (https://www.changehealthcare.com) and TIBCO Software (https://www.tibco.com) have partnered to "build a smart contract system for healthcare." The intent is to combine the Change Healthcare Intelligent Healthcare NetworkTM blockchain technology and TIBCO's Project Dovetail, which is comprised of its developer framework and tools for healthcare transaction and governance smart contracts. The goals are to automate events in the payment processing lifecycle, inclusive of transaction processing efficiency (e.g., clams adjudication, payments), performance improvements in revenue cycle of providers, and faster remittance. Depending on ultimate deployment, the scope of this endeavor is likely the largest in all of healthcare and blockchain, since Change Healthcare reports having processed $14 billion in healthcare transactions with value totaling $2 trillion in its most recent fiscal year (Brett 2018).

Internal process management is an expanded blockchain use case, and for pharmaceutical companies, the appeal includes reconciliation of multiple internal systems (Krishnamurthy 2017). Managing inbound sourced materials and navigating across product lifecycle stages require numerous internal systems and development of reconciliation processes. Blockchain technology can reduce this "artificial reconciliation" with a unifying single shared source of transactional truth (i.e., ledger) across their multiple systems.

Pharmaceutical Supply Chain

One of the earliest verticals determined to be a positive fit-for-purpose for pharmacy and blockchain was the pharmaceutical supply chain (Clauson BHTY 2018). This is likely due in part to the magnitude of the problem to be solved (i.e., $200 billion global market for substandard and falsified medicines) and how well aligned that blockchain characteristics are with legal and regulatory efforts intended to enhance supply chain management of pharmaceuticals. In the US, this is the Drug Supply Chain Security Act (DSCSA), which was enacted by Congress and mandates an electronic and interoperable framework that allows for identification of and tracing medicines (US FDA 2014). It was enacted to help strengthen the security of the supply chain, remove dangerous drugs, and reduce substandard and falsified (SF) medicines (e.g., counterfeit, grey market). The implementation timeline for the DSCSA spans a 10-year period from 2013 to 2023, which will then require unit-level traceability. The DSCSA is anchored by its key requirements (e.g., identification, verification, notification, etc.). So the question then becomes: are the capabilities of blockchain technology compatible with those requirements? As seen in Table 12.2, those blockchain capabilities map extremely well to all DSCSA key requirements and allow for innovative means to satisfy those mandates.

Table 12.2. Blockchain applicability for Drug Supply Chain Security Act (DSCSA) key requirements

Key Requirement	Applicability	Compatible
Product identification	Unique product identifier can be required with contributed information validated as a side chain	YES
Product tracing	Allows manufacturers, distributors and dispensers to provide tracing information in shared ledger with automatic verification of important information	YES
Product verification	Creates system and open solution to verify product identifier and other contributed information	YES
Detection and response	Allows public and private actors to report and detect drugs suspected as counterfeit, unapproved, or dangerous	YES
Notification	Creates shared system to notify FDA and other stakeholders if an illegitimate drug is found	YES
Information requirement	Can create shared ledger of product and transaction information including verification of licensure information	YES

Reproduced with permission. Blockchain in Healthcare Today. doi: 10.30953/bhty.v1.20

The entry of SF medicines into the supply chain is not limited to the United States. Efforts in the European Union (EU) to combat these problems include the Falsified Medicines Directive and Council of Europe MEDICRIME Convention (EU 2011; CoE 2018). Similarly, blockchain would help with the Food and Drugs Act (and Amendments) of Health Canada as it applies to its Four Phases – particularly drug manufacturing, drug procurement and distribution and extending to front-line delivery (GoC 2014). While countries in North America and the EU are battling these problems, countries such as Vietnam are especially vulnerable to supply chain disruption as most (i.e., 90%) of their medications are imported – thus increasing the number of vectors of attack (Angelino 2017). Regardless of the locales and the varying nature of the vulnerabilities by region, they are linked by the commonality that superior supply chain practices are possible when facilitated by blockchain or DLT technology (Kuo 2017). In part based on this universality, there are already over a dozen companies that are focusing on or exploring the use of blockchain for the broader health supply chain (Table 12.3).

Table 12.3. Selected companies exploring blockchain for health supply chain management

Company	Features	Website
BlockVerify	Extending anti-counterfeit solutions from luxury valuables to medications	http://www.blockverify.io
Chronicled	Partnered with The LinkLab for a blockchain-supported DSCSA compliance platform	https://www.chronicled.com
FarmaTrust	UK org developing blockchain solution for pharmaceutical supply chain, Initial Coin Offering (ICO)	https://www.farmatrust.com
IBM Blockchain	Early work with supply chain management in food products with multiple partners	https://www.ibm.com/blockchain
iSolve	Advanced Digital Ledger Technology, BlockRx ICO	http://isolve.io
Modum	Blend of blockchain and sensors, MOD token Initial Token Offering (ITO)	http://modum.io
OriginTrail	Recognized by Walmart Food Safety, partnered with Yimishiji; TRAC token	https://origintrail.io
Provenance	UK org starting with chain-of-custody for food; positioned to extend	https://www.provenance.org
RemediChain	Reclaiming high-cost cancer meds and redistributing to underinsured patients	http://remedichain.com
Solaster	Ecosystem focused on interoperability, GO-70 protocol standard; Good Shepherd partner	https://www.solaster.io
TBSX3	Australian-based company; compatible with Fabric, BigchainDB	https://tbsx3.com
The LinkLab	Knowledge resource, development partner, partnered with Chronicled	http://www.thelinklab.com
T-Mining	Belgians partnered with NxtPort for container shipping; adaptable tech	http://t-mining.be
VeChain	Combining blockchain and IoT; food/drug forays in roadmap; VEN/VET token	https://www.vechain.com
Viant	ConsenSys spoke collaborating with GlaxoSmithKline and Microsoft	https://viant.io
Walton	Early phase to use RFID and IoT; goals to scale to business ecosystem; WTC token	https://www.waltonchain.org

Adapted from Blockchain in Healthcare Today. doi.org/10.30953/bhty.v1.20
DSCSA=Drug Supply Chain Security Act, IoT=Internet of Things, RFID=radio frequency identification, UK=United Kingdom

Medical Device Supply Chain

Facing similar vulnerabilities and critical safety risks as the pharmaceutical supply chain, is the medical device supply chain. In addition to quality issues, crucial devices such as medication pumps and implantable cardiac devices are susceptible to compromise, or even control, by bad actors. In one high-profile case in the US, half a million patients had to be located, notified, and scheduled for an in-person visit so that the firmware could be updated for their pacemakers to close a known security vulnerability (Goodin 2017). As with the DSCSA, there are device-related regulatory efforts such as the requisite Unique Device Identifier (UDI) for medical devices by both the US and EU; Health

Canada is still pending final decision via the Medical Devices Bureau of the Therapeutics Products Directorate (Trend Micro 2018). Enhanced supply chain management for medical devices is possible due to this broad adoption of the UDI as well as the creation of the Global Unique Device Identification Database (GUDID). To that end, a partnership including National Health Service (NHS) Scotland, Edinburgh Napier University, and Spiritus is piloting use of blockchain technology to "track medical devices through their lifecycle" (Kamel Boulos 2018). The intent of this pilot includes monitoring the patient care pathway in order to become more timely and responsive with issuing notices and initiating recalls. Greater opportunities and challenges also exist with so-called consumer grade devices related to the Internet of Healthy Things (IoHT) and the ubiquitous sensors funneling patient-generated data to myriad endpoints. Researchers have already uncovered security vulnerabilities in wearables market leader Fitbit, including intercepting messages, flashing malware wirelessly, and extracting "private information from victims without leaving a trace" (Classen 2018).

Emerging Use Case: Cannabis

While all use cases for blockchain and DLT in pharmacy can arguably be considered as emerging, some are closer to the earlier stages of development, involve an application of an existing use case for a novel purpose (e.g., supply chain for medical cannabis), or still firmly reside in the feasibility stage (e.g., drug diversion). Therefore, the purpose of the Emerging Use Case is to give a brief glimpse into pharmacy-related blockchain endeavors that warrant investigation. One example is the case of cannabis (i.e., medical and recreational), which actually spans several use case categories including supply chain (Abelseth 2018, ICA 2018), clinical trials (Blackburn 2018), and opioid-related credentialing and treatment (ICA 2018). There is no shortage of blockchain companies exploring the health supply chain space (Table 3), but the number seeking to tackle blockchain and cannabis – both nascent areas with some controversy – remains relatively small (Table 4). However, with voters in an increasing number of states in the US endorsing the use of medicinal and/or recreational marijuana (Jones 2017), and the recent (i.e., October 2018) legalization of cannabis Canada-wide (Abelseth 2018), this may soon change. Already, companies ranging from startups (e.g., Blockstrain) and subsidiaries (e.g., Greenstream Networks) to industry giants (e.g., IBM) are actively pursuing cannabis-related blockchain opportunities. Not included in this section, nor Table 4, are projects focused primarily on crypto payments or banking for cannabis. While this entire segment operates with a degree of uncertainty in the US due to differences in the legal status at state and federal levels, a cannabis blockchain company has also been the recipient of the first civil penalties levied by the Securities and Exchange Commission (SEC) against an ICO specifically for violating registration procedures (US SEC 2018). Blockchain and DLT remain an area of interest for the burgeoning cannabis and cannatech industries as the technology's characteristics align well with the needs to withstand increased scrutiny and provision of superior transparency relative to conventional pharmaceuticals.

Table 12.4. Selected companies exploring blockchain for cannabis-related efforts

Company	Features	Website
Blockstrain	DNA-based product validation and intellectual property protection; WeedMD partner	https://blockstrain.io
Budbo	Cannatech blockchain and ancillary services via API; partnered with CannLiv	https://budbo.io
Cureall	ICA credentialing and clinical trial effort from pharmacist co-founders	https://cureall.app
Cannablox	Liberty Leaf and Blox Labs partnered for supply chain and smart contracts ledger	https://www.cannablox.ca
Greenstream Networks	Platform for Canada using Hyperledger stack; supply chain, payments, and identity	https://www.greenstream.tech
IBM Blockchain	BlockChain: An Irrefutable Chain of Custody Audit for the Seed to Sale of Cannabis in BC	https://www.ibm.com/blockchain
Medicinal Genomics	StrainSEEK using DASH blockchain for genetic information and patent protection	https://www.medicinalgenomics.com
Nuvus	Supply chain, auditing, data exchange, and related cannabis services; Hyperledger	https://www.nuvus.io
Paragon	Supply chain, identity, and co-working spaces; reached ICO settlement with SEC	https://paragoncoin.com
Parsl	Supply chain for growers, processors, and users; EOS-based airdrop and multiple tokens	https://www.parsl.co

CASE STUDY: Opioid Crisis and the Supply Chain

Across North America, Europe, and Oceania, the rates of opioid use have risen dramatically (Fitch 2018). The countries with the highest rates of opioid use (i.e., buprenorphine, codeine, fentanyl, hydrocodone, hydromorphone, methadone, morphine, oxycodone, pethidine, etc.) as reported by the United Nations International Narcotics Control Board (INCB) are depicted in Figure 3 (INCB 2017). This rise in use has been followed by increased levels of abuse, misuse, and diversion, as well as staggering levels of addiction, death, and societal financial costs (Shafer 2016). The US, in particular, is currently in the grips of an epidemic-level opioid crisis (Kertesz 2018), presenting numerous regulatory and ethical challenges (Stratton 2018). In one of the most concerning indicators, opioid-attributed overdose deaths have risen almost six-fold since tracking in 1999, culminating in 47,600 deaths in the United States in 2017 alone (CDC 2018). These increases parallel the US opioid consumption rate of 46,090, which is 50% greater than the next highest in the INCB global rankings (i.e., Canada at 30,570).

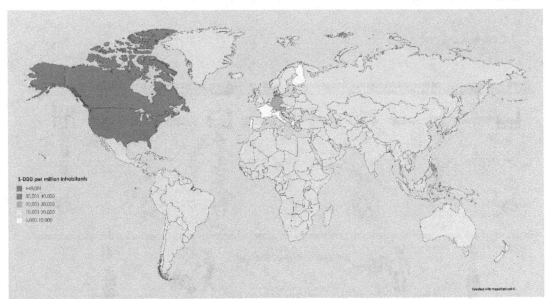

Figure 12.3. Countries with highest levels of opioid consumption in S-DDD, defined daily doses for statistical purposes, per million inhabitants per day
Adapted from International Narcotics Control Board data using mapchart.net

One of the secondary effects of this crisis has resulted in expanded roles for pharmacists to assist with this public health dilemma including: participation in prescription drug monitoring programs, distribution of naloxone (an opioid antagonist), operation of medication-disposal kiosks, recommendations for addiction treatment programs, development of novel agents, and facilitation of destigmatization) (Compton 2017; Shafer 2018). While the opioid crisis has generated a massive number of proposals to help combat its multi-faceted nature, harnessing blockchain technology to do so remains largely unexplored (Skolnick 2018).

One recent effort to align the characteristics of blockchain and digital assets (e.g., crypto bonds) to address challenges with the drug diversion component of the opioid crisis has been proposed (Figure 12.4). This model builds on research including behavioral economics, game theory, loss aversion (i.e., decision theory assertion that individuals take action to avoid loss preferentially over action leading to acquisition), and prospect theory to align incentives for all members of the drug supply chain to maximize good practices, accountability, and vigilance. While the concept of "coopetition" can be traced back to the introduction of Linux, it has also been suggested that blockchain and particularly the Ethereum ecosystem can be leveraged to foster coopetition (SingularDTV 2018). Coopetition (or the coopetition paradox) has also been explored by consultancies like McKinsey (Carson 2018) and specifically for logistics and enhancing supply chain management by Deutche Post DHL Group (Kuckelhaus 2018). As outlined in Figure 12.4, a blockchain protocol (e.g. Ethereum) capable of supporting smart contracts and a native crypto asset could be used to engender an operational philosophy of coopetition across all parties in a supply chain. Such a system allows for construction of a single compelling deterrent to dissuade purposeful negative actions as well as failure to maintain adequate vigilance regarding other members of that supply chain ecosystem.

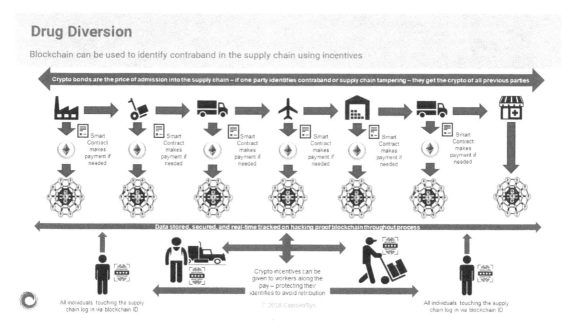

Figure 12.4. Drug Diversion. Blockchain to identify contraband in the supply chain using incentives.
Reproduced with permission. Adams T. Drug diversion. ConsenSys 2018.

Concurrently, with a focus the individual suffering from an opioid addiction, their support system, and the industry that has developed around them, blockchain can be used to align incentives with the recovery process – and the business of recovery (Figure 12.5).

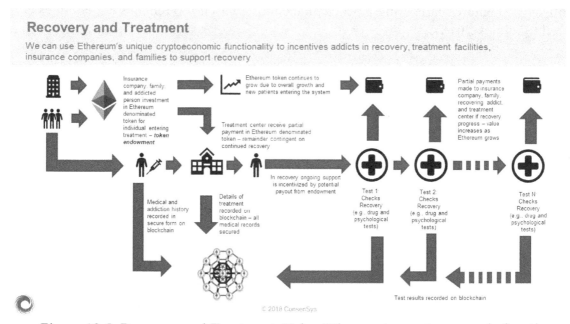

Figure 12.5. Recovery and Treatment. Using Ethereum's cryptoeconomic functionality to incentivize addicts in recovery, treatment facilities, insurance companies, and families to support recovery.
Reproduced with permission. Adams T. Recovery and Treatment. ConsenSys 2018.

Regarding incentivizing the recovery cottage industry, this is not a dissimilar approach to the move towards value-based care in which providers are incentivized (i.e., reimbursed) based on patient outcomes, rather than simply the provision of a health-related service or documentation of a treatment plan (i.e., fee-for-service). Rather than that fee-for-service approach, the proposed structure would focus the economic incentives on ongoing support and, importantly, the progress of recovery and relapse delay or avoidance (e.g.., Test 1, Test 2, Test N). While these approaches remain untested, they offer insight as to how blockchain might help address two of the historically most difficult elements in combatting progression of the opioid crisis.

Clinical Trials and Focus on Pharma

In addition to the peer-reviewed biomedical literature, grey literature, and mainstream news sources, several interviews were also conducted with individuals employed by pharmaceutical companies regarding their work at the nexus of blockchain and the pharmaceutical industry to inform this section of the chapter. Most of the individuals who provided responses are also participants in one or more collaborations or consortia, including the Innovative Medicines Initiative (IMI) Blockchain Enabled Healthcare (IMI 2018) and the Pharmaceutical Users Software Exchange (PhUSE) Blockchain Project (PhUSE 2018). The IMI (https://www.imi.europa.eu/) is an EU "public-private partnership aiming to speed up the development of better and safer medicines for patients" and also funds research and innovation. IMI industry consortium members are from European Federation of Pharmaceutical Industries and Associations (EFPIA) (https://www.efpia. eu/) companies including: Abbvie, AstraZeneca, Bayer, Johnson & Johnson, Novartis, Novo Nordisk, Pfizer, Sanofi, and UCB. Its members collaborated to produce a proposed blockchain vision of a three-level system (Figure 12.6).

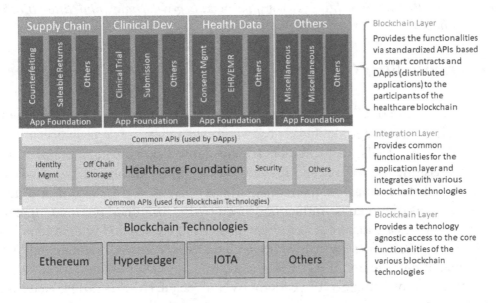

Figure 12.6. High-level architecture of the three-level blockchain-enabled healthcare system. *Adapted from Innovative Medicines Initiative Blockchain Enabled Healthcare (IMI 2018)*

PhUSE (https://www.phuse.eu/) was originally created as a European forum for Pharmaceutical Programmers to share ideas; in its current form it is an independent, not-for-profit, global volunteer organization that works with FDA and European Medicines Agency (EMA). PhUSE is presently the largest pharmaceutical industry-focused blockchain project based on membership (Table 12.5). In addition to efforts by consortia, end-to-end approaches to integrating blockchain into clinical research to improve quality have also been proposed by individuals (Benchoufi 2017).

Table 5. Member organizations of PhUSE Blockchain Project

23Consulting	Drug Dev eConsent	IEEE	ObesityPMM
Astrazeneca	Embleema	Information Technologies Institute	Otsuka
BAH	ERT	Infosys	ParticleHealth
Block Health	FDA	IOTA Foundation	PatienTrials
Biogen	GE Healthcare	Johnson&Johnson	Pharmaceutical Society
Biosolutions Clinical Research Centre	Gilead	Lilly	Proxima Clinical Research
Bowhead Health	GLP Health MedExpress	Longenesis	SAAVHA
CDC	GSK	lyfescience	Savvy Cooperative
Cognizant	Hashed Health	Medicalchain	Shivom
Consilx	Health Unlocked	Medidata Solutions	SimplyVital health
Covance	Highbury Regulatory Science Limited	Mercantis	Sunny Lake
Coverus	HMS Analytical Software	Merck KGaA	Syneoshealth
Curlew Research	Honeycomb health	Nebula	TRPMA
Digital Treasury Corp	IBM	NNIT	UCB
DOCS Global	Icahn Institute	Novartis	ZS

Adapted from PhUSE Wiki https://www.phusewiki.org/wiki/index.php?title=Blockchain_Technology

Clinical Trials – Brief Overview

The umbrella term of clinical studies (i.e., research with human participants designed to add to medical knowledge) includes observational studies (i.e., non-interventional research) and clinical trials. Clinical trials are those in which human participants are prospectively assigned to receive specific intervention(s) based on investigator-designed research protocols to evaluate interventional effects (US NLM CT 2017). For drug development, clinical trials can be further described by FDA-defined phases. Clinical trial registration/registries are also required elements both in the US and internationally (WHO 2012). The framework for these critical research pathways are well-defined, but the total time for translational research (i.e., basic science to potential product to healthcare practice) has remains approximately 17 years for over a decade (Morris 2011). Determining which of the steps in translational research are most conducive to acceleration by leveraging blockchain and DLT is a mainstay in the search for "Faster Miracles" (Manion 2018).

Accelerating Recruitment and Improving Engagement and Retention

Recruitment and retention are routinely cited as two of the biggest challenges in clinical trial research, with recruitment capable of lasting one-third of total trial duration and up to 20% of sites unsuccessful in recruiting any patients (PhUSE 2018). One way proposed to speed the process by a factor of 3-5 years is to leverage a blockchain-enabled patient data platform (reliant on FHIR standards) to source EHR data that could be made available to researchers, and integrate an e-consent process that could abbreviate the recruitment process to a single day (PhUSE 2018). Components of the research process including blockchain for Institutional Review Board (IRB) protocols (i.e., inclusive of recruitment) and smart contracts (Choudhury 2018), as well as consent management (Genestier 2017) with an eye towards privacy and security, have also been explored in-depth. For participant engagement and retention in clinical trials, a variety of block-chain-facilitated efforts have been conceptually suggested including partnering with participants to allow them to monetize or donate their data (Gammon 2018) as well as to-kenizing behavior change (Hanna 2017). Of note, these challenges with clinical trials are not limited to the US or EU. For example, the first prize winner in the Riyadh hackathon held by KACST and MIT Hacking Medicine in the blockchain track was Med Chain for "… blockchain and artificial intelligence systems to match patients with applicable clini-cal trials." (TradeArabia 2018).

Focus on Pharma Insights

Responses for the Focus on Pharma insights were primarily provided by: Munther Baara, Head of New Clinical Paradigm, Pfizer (https://www.pfizer.com/); Disa Lee Choun, Head of Innovation, Global Clinical Services & Operations, Development and Medical (Patient Value) Practices, UCB (https://www.ucb.com/); and Stan Swigoda, Director, IT Business Process Partner, Commercial Operations, GlaxoSmithKline (https://www.gsk.com/). While they each drew upon their experiences in their roles at pharma-ceutical companies, their responses and opinions may not necessarily reflect those held by their employers. Responses often appear in aggregate; when an individual or varying response is provided, a specific source may be indicated.

Genesis of company interest in blockchain

The earliest exploration of the technology among respondents occurred in 2015-2016, with most official inquiry and resource allocation occurring in 2017. Collaborative mem-berships also began at this time, including the largest (i.e., by number of member organi-zations represented), PhUSE.

Most mature blockchain projects

Respondents had a degree of consensus individually as well as in alignment with their respective collaborative bodies (i.e., IMI, PhUSE) regarding the most mature project(s) at their companies including: blockchain-enhanced supply chain management. This project type was in varying stages of maturity among the companies and some reported multiple ongoing efforts for that purpose. One partnership that was not part of the interview, but deserves attention, is an announced partnership including GlaxoSmithKline (GSK), Viant, and Microsoft for supply chain tracking, as well as "helping GSK license its technologies to researchers around the world while ensuring that they're using that IP properly" (Newman 2018).

Another notable project mentioned was value-based contracting; in general there was enthusiasm at the prospect of leveraging blockchain to enable internal systems to reconcile as well as multi-party data and transactional adjudication and reconciliation (as discussed in the Healthcare Financials section of the chapter). This also reflects the desire to use blockchain to conquer "data obstruction syndrome" defined as the "inability of multiple parties to share real-time clinical information in the health care environment in an easy and useful manner" in order to fully realize value-based healthcare (Klein 2018). Consistent with the disintermediation potential of the technology, it was further asserted that, "No longer would pharma companies, payers, and delivery systems looking to execute VBCs be held hostage to health information intermediaries." (Klein 2018). There was also a non-explicit belief voiced in the potential of "Moneyball Medicine" (Glorikian 2018) and that blockchain would more fully allow for harnessing data analytics for optimizing healthcare processes and outcomes.

Additional use cases of particular interest to respondents included: accelerating recruitment and increasing participant engagement in clinical trials, incentivizing patients and enabling access of patient data for clinical research, increasing patient access (globally) to medications, combatting the increasing risk of threats tied to centralized storage, and advancing drug discovery via artificial intelligence (AI) and recurrent neural networks (Mamoshina 2018).

Most common challenges

While those unfamiliar with blockchain may be surprised, technical challenges did not rank at the top of any respondent's list. Change management, governance, consensus within consortia, and resource allocations were commonly reported challenges with blockchain; coding resources was an unsurprising inclusion as well. Interestingly, in the PhUSE guide to pre-requisites for adoption document, the need for an "exit strategy" was included – suggesting that a series of contingency plans be developed to prepare for the need to make changes post-smart contract deployment, what to do if one party in a collaborative effort returns to a centralized system, etc. (PhUSE 2018). Alternately, one respondent reported that with their recent change of CEO, that a renewed and almost unprecedented spirit of innovation was encouraged throughout the company. One way this manifested was a recognition that blockchain pilots could be beneficial by helping highlight challenges in a low risk environment, creating an opportunity to "eke value" along the path to a more substantial return on investment (ROI), and empower employees to explore leadership and tech expertise.

The next horizon and future developments

Much of the conversations were about near- or intermediate-term goals, but looking forward there was considerable optimism about more ambitious goals with blockchain and DLT. Rather than just use cases, the potential included broad solutions for challenges around interoperability and creation of vibrant health data marketplaces. This is also reflected in the IMI statement that it, "envisions a future state where application of blockchain technology extends beyond use cases in scope as an enabler for digital transformation of the industry." (IMI 2018). Improvements in patient care through multiple paths in accelerated and more frictionless drug discovery, heightened patent control of their data, disposition, and decisions, and data sharing across blockchain protocols were also foreseen in this timeframe.

Facilitating Social Good via Patient Access

One of the most appealing promises of blockchain is that of social good; it has been described for access and inclusion for finance, protection for vulnerable populations like refugees and migrant workers, and proxies for empowerment like transparent land registries (Bartoletti 2018). One example in pharmacy that weaves together many of those social good threads is blockchain to enhance patient access to crucial medications.

CASE STUDY: Reclamation of Cancer Medications

Almost all community (i.e., retail) pharmacies in the US operate as for-profit endeavors. However, there are rare cases of non-profit or "charity" pharmacies like Good Shepherd (https://www.goodsheprx.com/), that work exclusively to serve uninsured and underinsured patient populations. Good Shepherd employs a membership model to enable their 1000 patients to obtain all of their medications for free or at minimal cost. Those medications are often, but not always, donated to nonprofit pharmacies at no charge by pharmaceutical companies. However, opportunities for individuals to donate their unused medications for redistribution to eligible patients are considerably more limited. Less than half of the states in the US have an "operational program" in which medications can be legally collected and redistributed – and that is inclusive of hospitals, clinics and pharmacies (Figure 7) (NCSL 2018). Hence, the number of states where collection of donated medications by individuals is legally allowed and has an operational program specifically by a pharmacy is likely smaller.

Figure 12.7. Legal and operational status for medication reclamation and redistribution, by state.

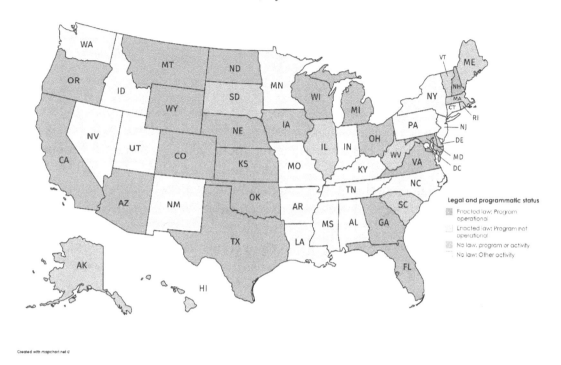

Created with mapchart.net ©

Adapted from National Conference of State Legislatures data using mapchart.net
Note: The most recent states enacting laws were NY and TN; both in 2017.

Specialty Pharmaceuticals and Cancer

The specialty pharmaceuticals category employs expensive medications to treat complex and chronic conditions like cancer, as well as HIV/AIDS, multiple sclerosis, and rheumatoid arthritis (Patel 2014). Specialty pharmaceuticals account for a disproportionate amount of expenditures as this category equates to approximately one-third of all spend on medicines. In oncology, the cost for a month's supply of the most commonly used oral chemotherapy ranges from $30,000-$45,000. Despite this massive cost burden and the related "financial toxicity" observed with cancer treatment (NCI 2018), only 13 states have enacted laws to permit cancer-specific collection and redistribution programs (Figure 12.8) (NCSL 2018; Chaudoin 2018).

Figure 12.8. Legal status for cancer-specific programs allowing medication collection and redistribution, by state.

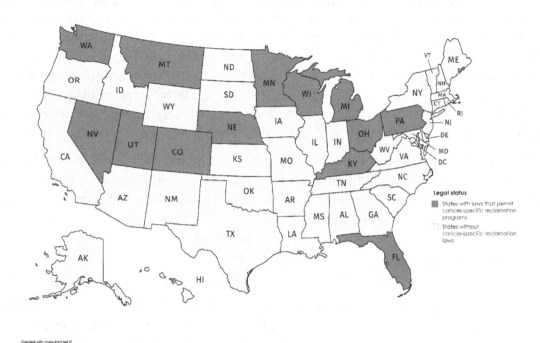

Adapted from National Conference of State Legislatures data using mapchart.net

RemediChain: Blockchain + Pharmacy

So when Good Shepherd CEO Phil Baker, PharmD led the charge to change the law in TN to permit pharmacies to reclaim medications for redistribution, he and the supporting legislators, Department of Health, and Board of Pharmacy made certain it was authored to be inclusive enough to allow for rescue of the staggering amount of unit-dose, oral cancer medications being lost to waste (Corbet 2018). "I would have people come in with a bag of medicine and say, 'My grandpa was on hospice. Now, I have all this medicine'." Dr. Baker recalled. (Corbet 2018). After passage of the law in TN, he could finally tell his patients that he could get their donated cancer medicine to economically disadvantaged members of the community, rather than just having to dispose of it for them.

Given the logistics involved with medication intake and redistribution to qualified (i.e., income-based) individuals, the elevated interest among many stakeholders due to the extremely high value of these oral chemotherapeutic agents, and the desire to create a digital platform to expand to a national network of pharmacies dedicated to this mission, Dr. Baker also created a separate entity, RemediChain (https://www.remedichain.com). RemediChain will use blockchain to enable end-to-end traceability and visibility from a medication's point of (donation) origin, throughout the remainder of its newly generated supply chain, as well as allowing for auditability and transparency via a shared ledger. Because the DSCSA effectively ceases mandating medication tracking at the point of the dispensing pharmacy, that need for a blockchain-verified reestablishment of chain of custody for this emerging category of reclaimed medications is even more pronounced. RemediChain's initial reclamation efforts with cancer medications could allow it to prioritize the indicated states with cancer programs in Figure 8 for expansion on a blockchain-facilitated national network of such pharmacies; those states could serve as beachheads for a literal and figurative map of strategic growth and expansion. Similarly, smart contracts could be used to ensure compliance with the variations of state laws that may stipulate different requirements tied to medication reclamation and redistribution.

Overall, Good Shepherd is positioned to be the first blockchain pharmacy in which every patient is provided with their own DLT-facilitated health record – including the capability to control and monetize their own data. The entry point for that blockchain pharmacy ecosystem would be RemediChain.

Partnership with Solaster and Interoperability

Common themes identified in this chapter across nearly all use cases and categories with blockchain and pharmacy are the needs for collaboration, efficiency, interoperability, and improved transparency. Good Shepherd's status as a membership, non-profit pharmacy with radical price transparency and aspirations to connect with broader ecosystems made them an ideal partner for Solaster (https://solaster.io/). Solaster is perhaps best known for its introduction of the GO-70 interoperability healthcare data standard, which represented a first for DApps. The two companies have a shared mission of leveraging DLT to lower healthcare costs, improve efficiencies and enhance connectivity and community. Solaster's blockchain development platform is built on the GoChain network and its GO-70 standard is patterned after the Health Level Seven (HL7) FHIR framework. In both approaches, the aim is to allow for a modular approach while providing a means of exchanging health information. Additionally, the Solaster Smart Tokens (SST) could serve to facilitate a transactional layer, a mechanism for incentivization, or another tool to help create more frictionless interoperability. In a joint announcement, it was outlined that "Good Shepherd will join Solaster's decentralized health marketplace and build an updated solution" in order to bring their approach to community pharmacy to a broader market (Solaster 2018).

Conclusion

Overall, the impact of blockchain on pharmacy, pharma, and life sciences is still likely too early to measure (Chavali 2018). However, progress has been made by self-organized blockchain-focused consortia led by pharmaceutical companies and related stakeholders. Additionally, a handful of use cases have developed meaningful traction, highlighted by enhancing supply chain management, streamlining clinical trials, improving provider data accuracy, and reconciling multiple internal and external systems and transactional data sources. Blockchain technology is also being explored to combat the opioid crisis, improve the burgeoning medical cannabis industry, and connect economically disadvantaged patients with high-cost cancer medications. While blockchain is an emerging technology, multiple sources – including experts from the pharmaceutical industry – indicate that the most daunting implementation challenges are non-technical in nature. However, the spirit of coopetition that blockchain promotes may lend weight to the old adage, "if you want to go fast, go alone; if you want to go far, go together."

References

Abelseth B. Blockchain tracking and cannabis regulation: Developing a permissioned blockchain network to track Canada's cannabis supply chain. Dalhousie Journal of Interdisciplinary Management. 2018;14. https://ojs.library.dal.ca/djim/article/view/7869/7249

Andrews L, Kostelecky K, Spritz S, Franco A. Virtual clinical trials: One step forward, two steps back. Journal of Health Care Law and Policy. 2017;19(2):2. https://digitalcommons.law.umaryland.edu/cgi/viewcontent.cgi?article=1346&context=jhclp

Angelino A, Khanh DT, An Ha N, Pham T. Int J Environ Res Public Health. 2017 Aug 29;14(9). pii: E976. doi: 10.3390/ijerph14090976.Zehrung 2017 28364941

Barkovich R, Mackey TK. Fit-for-Purpose: Blockchain Design. Blockchain Healthcare Workshop. May 24-25, 2018. University of San Diego Extension. IEEE. https://extension.ucsd.edu/UCSDExtension/media/UCSDExtensionsMedia/landing/blockchain/Blockchain-UCSD-4-24-18.pdf

Bartoletti M, Pompianu L, Cimoli T, Serusi S. Blockchain for social good: A quantitative analysis. ArXiv. https://arxiv.org/pdf/1811.03424.pdf

Benchoufi M, Ravaud P. Blockchain technology for improving clinical research quality. Trials. 2017;18: 335. doi:10.1186/s13063-017-2035-z.

Blackburn H. Blockchain in Clinical Trials for Cannabis with Steven Malen. Talk To Your Pharmacist. 2018. https://player.fm/series/talk-to-your-pharmacist/blockchain-in-clinical-trials-for-cannabis-with-steven-malen

Brett C. Change Healthcare + TIBCO bring smart contracts to healthcare. Enterprise Times. 2018. https://www.enterprisetimes.co.uk/2018/11/07/change-healthcare-tibco-bring-smart-contracts-to-healthcare/

Carson B, Romanelli G, Walsh P, Zhumaev A. Blockchain beyond the hype: What is the strategic business value? McKinsey & Company. https://www.mckinsey.com/business-functions/digital-mckinsey/our-insights/blockchain-beyond-the-hype-what-is-the-strategic-business-value

Centers for Disease Control and Prevention (CDC). Data Brief 329. Drug Overdose Deaths in the United States, 1999-2017. 2018. https://www.cdc.gov/nchs/data/databriefs/db329_tables-508.pdf

Centers for Medicare & Medicaid Services. National Health Expenditure Data. Historical. https://www.cms.gov/Research-Statistics-Data-and-Systems/Statistics-Trends-and-Reports/NationalHealthExpendData/NationalHealthAccountsHistorical.html

Choudhury O, Sarker H, Rudolph N, Foreman M, Fay N, Dhuliawala M, Sylla I, Fairoza N, Das A. Enforcing human subject regulations using blockchain and smart contracts. Blockchain in Healthcare Today. 2018;1. doi.org/10.30953/bhty.v1.10.

Chaudoin K. New collaboration to use blockchain technology to improve prescription care for underinsured patients. Lipscomb University. 2018. https://www.lipscomb.edu/news/archive/detail/101/34095

Chaudoin K. College of Pharmacy & Health Sciences, Hashed Health partner to develop innovative system to verify graduation credentials using blockchain technology. Lipscomb University. 2017. https://www.lipscomb.edu/news/filter/item/0/32178.

Chavali LN, Prashanti NL, Sujatha K, Rajasheker G, Kava Kishor PB. The emergence of blockchain technology and its impact in biotechnology, pharmacy, and life sciences. Current Trends in Biotechnology and Pharmacy. 2018;12(3):304-310.

Daemmrich A, Bowden ME. A rising drug industry: The pharmaceutical industry since 1870 has become gargantuan, but consumers cling to a love-hate relationship with drugs for health. Emergence of pharmaceutical science and industry: 1870-1930. Chemical and Engineering News. 2005;83(25):28-42. doi: 10.1021/cen-v083n025.p028

Classen J, Wegemer D, Patras P, Spink T, Hollick M. Anatomy of a vulnerable fitness tracking system: Dissecting the fitbit cloud, app, and firmware. Proceedings of the ACM on Interactive, Mobile, Wearable and Ubiquitous Technologies. 2018;1(1):42. https://doi.org/0000001.0000001.

Clauson KA, Breeden EA, Davidson C, Mackey TK. Leveraging blockchain technology to enhance supply chain management in healthcare: An exploration of the challenges and opportunities in the health supply chain. Blockchain in Healthcare Today. 2018:1. doi: 10.30953/bhty.v1.20.

Cockburn IM. The changing structure of the pharmaceutical industry. Health Affairs. 2004;23(1):10-22.

Compton WM, Jones CM, Stein JB, Wargo EM. Promising roles for pharmacists in addressing the U.S. opioid crisis. Res Social Adm Pharm. 2017. pii: S1551-7411(17)30977-4. doi: 10.1016/j.sapharm.2017.12.009.

Corbet M. Local pharmacist changes state law to put high-dollar chemo drugs in the hands of low-income Tennesseans. Daily Memphian. 2018. https://dailymemphian.com/article/694/Local-pharmacist-changes-state-law-to-put-high-dollar-chemo-drugs-in-the-hands-of-low-income-Tennesseans

Council on Credentialing in Pharmacy. A white paper prepared by the Council on Credentialing in Pharmacy (www.pharmacycredentialing.org), 2215 Constitution Avenue, NW, Washington, DC 20037, September 2000. https://www.medscape.com/viewarticle/406934_4

Council of Europe. The MEDICRIME Convention. 2018. https://www.coe.int/en/web/medicrime/the-medicrime-convention

Donnelly S, Reginatto B, Kearns O, Mc Carthy M, Byrom B, Muehlhausen W, Caulfield B. The burden of a remote trial in a nursing home setting: Qualitative study. J Med Internet Res. 2018;20(6):e220. doi: 10.2196/jmir.9638.

European Union. Directive 2011/62/EU of the European Parliament and of the Council of 8 June 2011 amending Directive 2001/83/EC on the Community code relating to medicinal products for human use, as regards the prevention of the entry into the legal supply chain of falsified medicinal products. 2011 https://ec.europa.eu/health/sites/health/files/files/eudralex/vol-1/dir_2011_62/dir_2011_62_en.pdf

Feig E. A framework for blockchain-based applications. ArXiv. https://arxiv.org/pdf/1803.00892.pdf

Fitch P. The Canadian opioid crisis: CSHP's commitment. Canadian Journal of Hospital Pharmacy. 2018;71(3):220. doi: http://dx.doi.org/10.4212/cjhp.v71i3.2592

Gagnon M-A, Lexchin J. The cost of pushing pills: A new estimate of pharmaceutical promotion expenditures in the United States. PLoS Med 2018;5(1): e1. https://doi.org/10.1371/journal.pmed.0050001

Gammon K. Experimenting with blockchain: Can one technology boost both data integrity and patients' pocketbooks? Nature Medicine. 2018;24(4):378-381. doi: 10.1038/nm0418-378.

Garavaglia C, Malerba F, Orsenigo L, Pezzoni. A simulation model of the evolution of the pharmaceutical industry: A history friendly model. Journal of Artificial Societies and Social Simulation. 2013; 16(4):5. doi: 10.18564/jasss.2314

Genestier P, Zouarhi S, Limeux P, Excoffier D, Prola A, Sandon S, Temerson J-M.

Blockchain for consent management in the eHealth environment: A nugget for privacy and security challenges. Journal of the International Society for Telemedicine and eHealth. 2017;5(GKR):e24: (1-4). https://journals.ukzn.ac.za/index.php/JISfTeH/article/view/269

Glorikian H, Branca MA. MoneyBall Medicine: Thriving in the New Data-Driven Healthcare Market. 1st ed. Boca Raton: Taylor & Francis; 2018. 272 p.

Goodin D. 465k patients told to visit doctor to patch critical pacemaker vulnerability. A year after calling advisory "false and misleading," maker warns patients to patch. August 2017. Available at: https://arstechnica.com/information-technology/2017/08/465k-patients-need-a-firmware-update-to-prevent-serious-pacemaker-hacks/

Government of Canada. Canada's Drug Supply Chain. 2014. https://www.canada.ca/en/health-canada/services/drugs-health-products/drug-products/drug-shortages/canada-drug-supply-chain.html

Griffenhagen GB. Great moments in pharmacy: development of the Robert Thom series depicting pharmacy's history. J Am Pharm Assoc. 2002;42(2):170-82.

Hanna E, Remuzat C, Auquier P, Dussart C, Toumi M. Could Healthcoin be a revolution in healthcare? Value in Health. 2017;A399-A811:PHP115.

Hartnet K. Credentialing startup partnering with big names. Blockchain-based Pro-CredEx plans to go live in mid-2019. Nashville Post. 2018. https://www.nashvillepost.com/business/health-care/information-technology/article/21029948/credentialing-start-up-partnering-with-big-names

Healthmart. Pharmacist as provider: A view of the future. 2018. https://join.healthmart.com/business-and-operations/pharmacist-provider-view-future/

Innovative Medicines Initiative (IMI). Blockchain Enabled Healthcare. 2018. https://www.imi.europa.eu/sites/default/files/uploads/documents/apply-for-funding/future-topics/Blockchain_vJune2018.pdf

Integrative Care Alliance (ICA). The Blockchain Solution to the Opioid Epidemic. 2018. https://www.integrativecarealliance.com/

International Narcotics Control Board. Narcotic Drugs 2017. Estimated World Requirements for 2018. United Nations International Narcotics Control Board. https://www.incb.org/documents/Narcotic-Drugs/Technical-Publications/2017/Narcotic_drugs_technical_publication_2017.pdf

Intiva Health. Empowering Licensed Medical Professionals with Intiva Token And A Decentralized Credentialing Platform. Intiva Health White Paper. 2018. https://token.intivahealth.com/wp-content/uploads/2018/04/Intiva_Whitepaper_040318.pdf

Jones M. 'Seed to sale': Canada weighs up blockchain to track legal sales of cannabis. The Block. Blockchain Technology News. 2018. https://www.blockchaintechnology-news.com/2018/07/27/seed-to-sale-canada-weighs-up-blockchain-to-track-legal-sales-of-cannabis/

Kamel Boulos MN, Wilson JT, Clauson KA. Geospatial blockchain: promises, challenges, and scenarios in health and healthcare. International Journal of Health Geographics. 2018 Jul 5;17(1):25. doi: 10.1186/s12942-018-0144-x.

Kertesz SG, Gordon AJ. A crisis of opioids and the limits of prescription control: United States. Addiction. 2018. doi: 10.1111/add.14394

Klein I. Blockchain, data obstruction, and the promise of information sharing for a value-based health care world. J Clin Pathways. 2018;4(7):27-30. doi:10.25270/jcp.2018.09.00035

Krishnamurthy R, Chowdhury C, Ranganathan V. Blockchain: A Catalyst for the Next Wave of Progress in Life Sciences. Cognizant. 2017. https://www.cognizant.com/white-papers/blockchain-a-catalyst-for-the-next-wave-of-progress-in-the-life-sciences-industry-codex2749.pdf

Kuckelhaus M, Chung G. Blockchain in Logistics: Perspectives on the upcoming impact of blockchain technology and use cases for the logistics industry. DHL. Accenture. https://www.logistics.dhl/content/dam/dhl/global/core/documents/pdf/glo-core-blockchain-trend-report.pdf

Kuo TT, Kim HE, Ohno-Machado L. Blockchain distributed ledger technologies for biomedical and health care applications. J Am Med Inform Assoc. 2017;24(6):1211-1220. doi: 10.1093/jamia/ocx068.

Lehrach H. Virtual clinical trials, an essential step in increasing the effectiveness of the drug development process. Public Health Genomics. 2015;18:366-371. doi.org/10.1159/000441553

Mamoshina P, Ojomoko L, Yanovich Y, Ostrovski A, Botezatu A, Prikhodko P, Izumchenko E, Aliper A, Romantsov K, Zhebrak A, Ogu IO, Zhavoronkov A. Converging blockchain and next-generation artificial intelligence technologies to decentralize and accelerate biomedical research and healthcare. Oncotarget. 2017;9(5):5665-5690. doi:

10.18632/oncotarget.22345

Manion S. Distributed: The Way to Faster Miracles - A Blockchain Book Preview. LinkedIn. 2018. https://www.linkedin.com/pulse/distributed-way-faster-miracles-block-chain-book-preview-sean-manion/

Merritt Hawkins. 2016 Physician Inpatient/Outpatient Revenue Survey. A survey showing net annual inpatient and outpatient revenue generated by physicians in various specialties on behalf of their affiliated hospitals. 2016. https://www.merritthawkins.com/uploadedFiles/MerrittHawkins/Content/Pdf/Merritt_Hawkins-2016_RevSurvey.pdf

Morotta R. Pharmacists Remain Among Most Trusted and Ethical Professions. Pharmacy Times. 2018. https://www.pharmacytimes.com/news/pharmacists-remain-among-most-trusted-and-ethical-professionals

Morris ZS, Wooding S, Grant J. The answer is 17 years, what is the question: understanding time lags in translational research. J R Soc Med. 2011;104(12):510-20. doi: 10.1258/jrsm.2011.110180.

National Conference of State Legislatures. State Prescription Drug Return, Reuse and Recycling Laws. 10/1/2018. http://www.ncsl.org/research/health/state-prescription-drug-return-reuse-and-recycling.aspx

National Cancer Institute. Financial Toxicity and Cancer Treatment (PDQ®)–Health Professional Version. National Cancer Institute. 2018. https://www.cancer.gov/about-cancer/managing-care/track-care-costs/financial-toxicity-hp-pdq

Newman P, Aouad A. DIGITAL HEALTH BRIEFING: Viant, GSK partner for blockchain in pharmaceuticals — CMS moves to increase the use of digital health solutions — Hospitals to save big from teleservices. Business Insider. 2018. https://www.businessinsider.com/digital-health-briefing-viant-gsk-partner-for-blockchain-in-pharmaceuticals-cms-moves-to-increase-the-use-of-digital-health-solutions-hospitals-to-save-big-from-teleservices-2018-1

Patel BN, Audet PR. A review of approaches for the management of specialty pharmaceuticals in the United States. PharmacoEconomics 2014; 32(11):1105. https://doi.org/10.1007/s40273-014-0196-0

Pharmaceutical Users Software Exchange (PhUSE). How Blockchain Can Transform The Pharmaceutical And Healthcare Industries. PhUSE-WP005. 2018. https://www.phuse.eu/documents/working-groups/deliverables/phuse-blockchain-white-paper-final-version-1-18843.pdf

Pharmacists for Healthier Lives. https://pharmacistsforhealthierlives.org/home/#accessible

Qato DM, Zenk S, Wilder J, Harrington R, Gaskin D, Alexander GC. The availability of pharmacies in the United States: 2007–2015. PLoS ONE 2017;12(8): e0183172. doi: 10.1371/journal.pone.0183172

Rahalkar H. Historical overview of pharmaceutical industry and drug regulatory affairs. Pharmaceut Reg Affairs 2012;S11:002. doi: 10.4172/2167-7689.S11-002

Salzman S. Vetting Physician Credentials: Tech to the Rescue? Blockchain touted as ensuring that docs are who they say they are. Medpage Today. 2018. https://www.medpagetoday.com/practicemanagement/practicemanagement/74651

Shafer E, Bergeron N, Smith-Ray R, Robson C, O'Koren R. A nationwide pharmacy chain responds to the opioid epidemic. J Am Pharm Assoc. 2017;57(2S):S123-S129. doi: 10.1016/j.japh.2016.12.075

SingularDTV. Blockchain, Coopetition, and Aligning Incentives in the Emerging Economy. SingularDTV. https://medium.com/singulardtv/blockchain-coopetition-and-aligning-incentives-in-the-emerging-economy-86c7ab25abe6

Skolnick P. The opioid epidemic: Crisis and solutions. Annu Rev Pharmacol Toxicol. 2018 Jan 6;58:143-159. doi: 10.1146/annurev-pharmtox-010617-052534.

Solaster. Solaster Health Officially Partners with Good Shepherd Pharmacy. 2018. https://medium.com/solaster/solaster-health-officially-partners-with-good-shepherd-pharmacy-965f65428605

Statista. US Pharmaceutical Industry – Statistics and Facts. https://www.statista.com/topics/1719/pharmaceutical-industry/. Accessed Dec 2, 2018.

Stratton TP, Palombi L, Blue H, Schneiderhan ME. Ethical dimensions of the prescription opioid abuse crisis. Am J Health Syst Pharm. 2018;75(15):1145-1150. doi: 10.2146/ajhp170704.

Synaptic Health Alliance. Improving Provider Data Accuracy: A Collaborative Approach Using a Permissioned Blockchain. Synaptic Health Alliance White Paper. 2018. https://cdn2.hubspot.net/hubfs/4801399/18-SYN-001-Synaptic-Website/downloads/Synaptic_Health_Alliance_Blockchain_White_Paper.pdf

TradeArabia. Over 1,000 take part in Saudi health hackathon. 2018. http://www.

tradearabia.com/news/HEAL_348259.html

Trend Micro. Securing Connected Hospitals: A Research on Exposed Medical Systems and Supply Chain Risks. April 2018. Postmarket Management of Cybersecurity in Medical Devices https://bit.ly/2pSyQwJ

United States Department of Labor, Bureau of Labor Statistics. Pharmacists Occupational Employment Statistics. 2017. https://www.bls.gov/oes/current/oes291051.htm#(1)

United States Food and Drug Administration. Title II of the Drug Quality and Security Act. US Department of Health and Human Services. 2014. https://www.fda.gov/Drugs/DrugSafety/DrugIntegrityandSupplyChainSecurity/DrugSupplyChainSecurityAct/ucm376829.htm

United States National Library of Medicine. ClinicalTrials.gov. Learn About Clinical Studies. 2017. https://clinicaltrials.gov/ct2/about-studies/learn

United States Securities and Exchange Commission. Two ICO Issuers Settle SEC Registration Charges, Agree to Register Tokens as Securities. 2018. https://www.sec.gov/news/press-release/2018-264

World Health Organization. International Standards for Clinical Trial Registries. World Health Organization. 2012. http://apps.who.int/iris/bitstream/handle/10665/76705/9789241504294_eng.pdf;jsessionid=60EC14A7C9B393C8EDC7B-7F8839EBC12?sequence=1

Zebroski B. A Brief History of Pharmacy: Humanity's Search for Wellness. 1st ed. New York: Routledge; 2016. 206 p.

Chapter 14:
Improving Provider Data Accuracy

Collaborative Approach Using a Permissioned Blockchain

Synaptic Health Alliance

Editor's Note:

This chapter provides an overview of the Synaptic Health Alliance, a collaborative effort between Humana, MultiPlan, Optum, Quest Diagnostics and United Healthcare to use the blockchain for secure and reliable data exchange. A permissioned blockchain based on Quorum is being used by the Alliance in a proposed pilot program. Additionally, the Alliance discusses the opportunities that arise from using blockchain technology and the realistic challenges they face in creating a provider data exchange.

Billions of dollars are spent annually on provider data management, yet highly accurate provider directories remain a challenge. The Centers for Medicare & Medicaid Services (CMS) reported that 52 percent of the provider of ce locations listed in the online provider directories reviewed between September 2016 and August 2017 contained at least one error.[1] Accurate provider data is critical for connecting patients with appropriate network care providers.

Now, Humana, MultiPlan, Optum, Quest Diagnostics and UnitedHealthcare have formed the Synaptic Health Alliance to explore the use of blockchain technology in tackling the challenge of accurate and ef cient provider data management and sharing. This new healthcare alliance is unique in its member composition and among the rst to have a national footprint.

The Alliance views blockchain technology as a means to a critical end: ensuring that data is accurate and sharable for reliable use across the healthcare ecosystem. Thanks to the members' large collective data volume and national footprint, this collaboration could prove the business value of cross-company data sharing in healthcare and, ultimately, help facilitate a signi cant positive impact in the healthcare market space. Blockchain is a logical choice for technological disruption because it features built-in transparency and veri ability of transactions without an intermediary, so control will be decentralized and all participating organizations will be peers. These are important prerequisites if diverse stakeholders are to collaborate productively in service to healthcare consumers.

The Alliance plans to hit the ground running with a pilot project that explores how blockchain technology can be used to help ensure that provider directories contain the most current and accurate information possible. Through what it is calling the "provider data exchange" (PDX), Alliance members would be able to actively share data with the aim of showing potential administrative cost savings for payers and providers while demonstrably improving provider demographic data quality and the experience of care for healthcare consumers.

> "Everyone in this industry has been dreaming of interoperability for a long time. Blockchain is a key to that. Better quality data leads to better decision-making, better patient care and experiences – that's the promise of what this alliance hopes to deliver."
>
> *-Lidia Fonseca, Chief Information Officer, Quest Diagnostics*

Ultimately, the Alliance intends to expand beyond the original ve founding members to include other sakeholders in the healthcare ecosystem. According to Lidia Fonseca, chief information of cer, Quest Diagnostics, "Everyone in this industry has been dreaming of interoperability for a long time. Blockchain is a key to that. Better quality data leads to better decision-making, better patient care and experiences – that's the promise of what this alliance hopes to deliver."

Provider Data Management: A Costly Investment

Provider data is a key building block of the U.S. healthcare system. It's essential for connecting patients with providers and supporting consumers in making decisions related to their care. Across the U.S. healthcare ecosystem, more than $2.1B is spent annually by hospitals, doctors and health insurers to maintain provider data, according to conservative estimates.[2] Despite this staggering investment, the system is still inef cient and reliant on manual processes.

State and federal laws, regulations and guidance require health plans to regularly update provider directories, such as monthly with some requirements being even tighter. Additionally, many of those same laws require insurers to contact every provider in their directories, sometimes as often as every three months, and make updates to those directories much faster than has been done in the past. The present model encourages potentially duplicative outreach and maintenance costs while creating silos of data.

This large-scale duplication of effort also means redundant expenses. On average, providers are af liated with 20 health plans [3] and often have to make updates with each health plan individually. Yet health plans typically maintain their own provider data sets and rarely collaborate on the daunting task of provider data management, while bearing the high administrative costs.

> **The U.S. healthcare industry spends more than $2.1B annually to maintain provider databases.**

Inaccurate, outdated provider data can negatively impact payers, providers, and consumers. Maintaining vast amounts of ever- uctuating data, and ensuring its accuracy, is critical for health plans when performing essential business functions. [4] In fact, health plans participating in the Medicare Advantage program may face penalties of up to $25,000 per day per bene ciary or be banned from new enrollment and marketing if their directories have high error rates. [5]

Data errors also make it harder for providers who are incorrectly listed as being out-of-network or not accepting new patients to maintain full panels, and the wrong contact information can prevent prospective or current patients from getting in touch and impact certain business functions including reimbursement. In addition, multiple recurring requests from multiple health plans for the same data attestation are a distraction that add to a provider's administrative burden.

Perhaps most concerning, however, is the impact on consumers, who routinely search provider directories to check whether a provider is accepting new patients, to nd doctors who meet speci c criteria, such as plan participation, location or of ce hours, or to nd a provider's contact information. Discovering that the information is inaccurate is frustrating and can undermine con dence in health plans.

Why Blockchain Technology?

Managed care organizations, health systems, physicians, diagnostic information service providers and other healthcare stakeholders typically maintain separate copies of provider data. Changes to the data les affect only the copy in which they are made. When discrepancies are found, efforts to reconcile them are time-intensive, costly and sometimes ineffective. Moreover, having many siloed copies of overlapping provider data scattered throughout the healthcare system makes it impossible to compare, validate and reconcile them.

Blockchain technology enables the ef cient creation of a synchronized, shared source of high-quality provider data through a decentralized, distributed ledger across a peer-to-peer network. Transactions are recorded chronologically in a cooperative and tamper-resistant manner, and updates entered by any party on their record are replicated almost immediately across all the other parties' copies. When updates to a transaction are entered and accepted, those updates amend, rather than alter, those transactions. All transactions and updates remain visible and unchanged, providing a real-time audit trail and ensuring data integrity.

A permissioned blockchain solution, such as the one being pursued by the Synaptic Health Alliance, could enable participants to share some of the administrative burden and cost of data maintenance and reconciliation, improving data quality while substantially reducing the time and expense. Effiencies also might be achieved by automating certain manual and redundant processes, such as address cleansing and federal sanctions monitoring.

|Provider Data Management: A Logical Starting Point

There are many promising use cases for blockchain technology in healthcare. The main considerations that led the Synaptic Health Alliance to choose provider data management as the focus of its initial pilot include:

- • The dependency of the healthcare system on accurate provider data.

- The pervasiveness of inaccurate provider data.

- The negative impact of widespread provider data errors on consumers.

- The inef ciency of current provider data management processes.

- The non-proprietary, non-competitive nature of provider demographics and, therefore, the low barrier to sharing and comparing this data across companies.

In a 2018 white paper, non-profit organization The Council for Affordable Quality Healthcare (CAQH) issued an industrywide call to action to develop an industry roadmap for improving provider data quality, standardize de nitions and requirements, de ne and maintain high-quality data and centralize data resources. [6] The Synaptic Health Alliance's rst pilot is an effort to address the noted challenges.

David Murtagh, vice president of operations, MultiPlan explained, "Throughout healthcare, there are so many reasons to share data. With increasing state and federal requirements relating to provider data maintenance and quality, tackling the high cost and redundancy in this space is a logical starting point. We're looking forward to exploring how blockchain technology can make the process more ef cient while reducing costs, ideally to build investments that can enhance the provider and patient experiences."

> **"We're looking forward to exploring how blockchain technology can make the process more ef cient while reducing costs, ideally to build investments that can enhance the provider and patient experiences."**
>
> *-David Murtagh, Vice President of Operations, MultiPlan*

Why the Alliance?

The Synaptic Health Alliance is a unique collaboration bringing together large, industry-leading companies with national footprints and varying business relationships (vendor/ client, provider/network, competitors) all drawing on their complementary perspectives and shared desire to improve the healthcare ecosystem.

The Alliance members' collective focus on working together for the greater good – for the benefit of all healthcare stakeholders in this country, rather than just their own constituents – is unique in its use of blockchain technology. This is demonstrated by the Alliance members' commitment to create a new shared source of high-quality provider data. Ultimately, the founding members are attempting to build the framework and technology for sharing provider demographic data that could be leveraged for other use cases, such as patient-consented sharing of clinical data between plans and providers to enable faster and better care decisions.

"Blockchain is the trigger that brought us together," said Mike Jacobs, senior distinguished engineer, Optum, "but the collaboration to solve widespread healthcare problems is our real goal. We envision the possibility of effecting change at scale – helping to make the health system work better for everyone."

The Synaptic Health Alliance plans to build a permissioned blockchain that would let members view, input, validate, update and audit non-proprietary provider data within the network, with the goal of improving data accuracy and lowering the associated administrative burden and costs.

Following the pilot phase, the founding members envision creating an industry market that would enable further collaboration on the data and connect the current data silos to improve provider data management for the overall healthcare system.

The pilot is examining whether sharing the administrative efforts related to provider data management lowers the individual share of that burden for health plans and care providers. It is also testing whether incentives could also be built in to motivate data sharing with everyone in the blockchain network, which would improve data quality and decrease data maintenance costs.

Technology

A blockchain is a distributed system for synchronizing transactions or information among many computers in a network. A permissioned blockchain is a private network in which only computers that are authorized to participate – referred to as nodes in that network – can synchronize information throughout the network.

Blockchain is made up of four parts...

1. A distributed database
2. An append-only structure
3. Smart contracts
4. Incentives

...that enable

 Improved resiliency, security, and integrity

 A shared source of provider data with immutable records that eliminates variations and versions

 Reduced costs of reconciliation and manual processing steps

 Participant incentive alignment, value transfer and bootstrap funding of a network or development

Blockchain was originally developed as a public, permission-less network to enable direct transactions of virtual money without a central authority, bank or middleman. Although the intent is for the transactions of the parties to be anonymous, participants in this type of blockchain network are identi ed using publicly viewable strings of numbers and letters, called addresses, which serve as pseudonyms, just as some authors write under a pen name to protect their true identities for privacy reasons. If someone discovers the identity of the person associated with a blockchain participant's address, his or her transactions are no longer anonymous.

For this reason, enterprise blockchains typically are permissioned, with participation by invitation only. A permissioned blockchain enables approved participants to blur industry lines to share and exchange information in a cooperatively-owned, synchronized, distributed ledger, addressing administrative cost and data quality issues that impact all stakeholders. Permissioned blockchains are used by consortia in industries such as nance to manage industry value chain opportunities.[7]

Blockchain Technology

The Synaptic Health Alliance technology team invested considerable thought into the selection of the blockchain technology. The selection criteria focused on features – what can be done with the technology – and suitability for enterprise/consortium use, including deployment options, technology maturity, number of enterprises and consortiums using it, licensing and level/availability of professional support.

The technology team prototyped two blockchain technology stacks for the pilot. Based on lessons learned from that experimentation, the alliance ultimately chose Quorum, an enterprise-focused version of Ethereum whose key attributes include:

- Close association with the largest open source community for blockchain (Ethereum)
- Open-source license
  - GPL/LGPL open source license ensures the Quorum platform will be free to use in perpetuity. This also makes it an attractive choice for experimentation, e.g., pilot programs.
- Mature Technology
  - Ethereum is one of the fastest growing public blockchains. Because the Quorum version is designed to develop and evolve alongside Ethereum and in- cludes only minimal modi cations to Ethereum's core technology, Quorum can incorporate most Ethereum updates quickly and seamlessly.
- • Enterprise-ready capabilities: privacy, security and zero-knowledge proofs
  - On public blockchains, participants are anonymous (pseudonymous) and

transactions are completely transparent. Healthcare, however, requires private transactions between known participants. The Quorum version of Ethereum, designed for enterprise and consortium use, supports both transaction-level privacy and network-wide transparency to enable veri ability and trust.

▫ One of Quorum's key security features is zero-knowledge cryptography. Zero-knowledge proofs allow the system to authenticate a single data element in an encrypted le without revealing any of the other data in that le. Authentication is binary (yes/no). Even the system doing the check does not decrypt the data. This entirely automated authentication process also minimizes the possibility of human error and can allow sensitive information to be distributed across the network without being viewable by potential bad actors. And if human error does occur, the system can identify the source of the breach and remedy it.

Although zero-knowledge proofs are not needed for non-con dential information such as basic provider data, they are a powerful tool in the healthcare setting, positioning the Alliance for potential future blockchain use cases involving sensitive, con dential information, such as protected health information (PHI). For example, a node on the blockchain with suf cient privacy protections and protocols could query a personal health record to nd out (verify) whether a patient is prediabetic (yes/no) without revealing or exposing any of the information that health record contains (including prediabetes risk factors).

The Synaptic Health Alliance Blockchain

The Alliance is deploying a multi-company, multi-site, permissioned blockchain. Unlike a public anonymous blockchain, the alliance consciously chose to deploy a permissioned blockchain. This is a more effective approach, consistent with enterprise blockchains. Each Alliance member has the exibility to deploy its nodes based on its enterprise requirements. Some members have elected to deploy their nodes within their own data centers, while others are using secured public cloud services such as AWS and Azure. This level of exibility is key to growing the Alliance blockchain network.

Each node runs the Ethereum-based Quorum technology. The Alliance's technology team has created a repeatable, automated approach to deploy nodes consistently across the Alliance. Quorum nodes use the go-ethereum client to maintain transaction data that is visible to all network participants as well as private data that is visible only to parties of private transactions. Private transactions are enabled through the Constellation extension of Quorum.

Multi, Cross-Cloud Structure

The Alliance envisions three approaches to implementing applications on its blockchain. Legacy applications would be able to interact with the blockchain network through custom integration bridges. New applications and distributed applications are other possible approaches to adding more value to the blockchain.

|Potential Benefits of Blockchain Technology

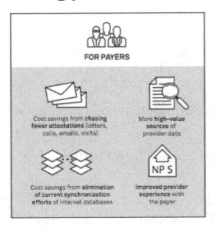

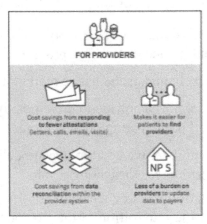

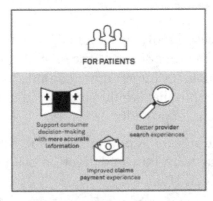

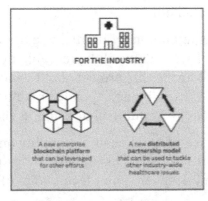

Pilot Scope

Many blockchain pilots run all their blockchain nodes, and the entire network, on a single computer or in a single data center. From an architecture perspective, those pilots aren't providing a valid proof of concept. The nodes in the Synaptic Health Alliance blockchain network communicate over the internet, and the Alliance hopes the pilot will demonstrate the viability of a permissioned blockchain whose nodes are distributed within different companies and in the public cloud.

The public cloud provides a convenient infrastructure capability, and the Alliance technology team has created best-practice cybersecurity controls designed to protect even sensitive healthcare information using infrastructure-as-code (IAC), a new approach that completely automates the configuration to circumvent errors that can occur when human intervention is required.

> **"The promise of blockchain is exciting and it's about putting consumers at the center of their healthcare. This alliance helps us learn how to deliver on that promise."**
>
> *-Ramu Kannan, Chief Technology Offier, Humana*

The scope of the initial pilot is expected to include the development of the following:

- • A permissioned, cooperatively-owned blockchain "utility" with nodes for contributing and consuming provider demographic data.

- • A blockchain data exchange marketplace and application.

- • A model for incentives to drive positive contribution and consumption behaviors across all participating organizations.

- • An administrative cost savings model to be used by all participating organizations for measuring results.

The expectation is that each Synaptic Health Alliance member in this pilot will be responsible for the integration of their respective systems and databases to contribute data to the blockchain.

The pilot is intentionally limited to a use case involving simple data elements and development of work that will be reusable by the founding Alliance members. The work achieved during this project could complement future, more complex payer- or network-speci c work by an expanded membership that would be required to achieve many of the bene ts of publishing a highly accurate provider directory.

"The promise of blockchain is exciting and it's about putting consumers at the center of theirhealthcare. This alliance helps us learn how to deliver on that promise," explained Ramu Kannan, chief technology of cer, Humana.

References

1. "Online Provider Directory Review Report," US, Department of Health & Human Services, Centers for Medicare & Medicaid Services (January 2018). Retrieved April 10, 2018, from https://www.cms.gov/Medicare/Health-Plans/ManagedCareMarketing/Downloads/Provider_Directory_Review_Industry_Report_Round_2_Updated_1-31-18.pdf

2. "Streamlining Provider Data Management Could Save Billions...but Is It Possible?", Health Plan Week, Vol 27, No. 4 (January 2017). Retrieved April 10, 2018, from https://www.availity.com/-/media/ les/ availity/ resource-library/articles/health-plan-week-january-2017.pdf

3. EY, Humana. (2018). A Marketplace for Provider Data – Using Blockchain to Reimagine How Health Plans Manage Physician Identity Information. https://www.slideshare.net/ernstandyoung/a-marketplace- for-provider-data-using-blockchain-to-reimagine-how-health-plans-manage-physician-identity- information

4. "Streamlining Provider Data Management Could Save Billions...but Is It Possible?", Health Plan Week, Vol 27, No. 4 (January 2017). Retrieved April 10, 2018, from https://www.availity.com/-/media/ les/ availity/ resource-library/articles/health-plan-week-january-2017.pdf

5. Susan Jaffe, "Obamacare, Private Medicare Plans Must Keep Updated Doctor Directories In 2016," Kaiser Health News (March 2015). Retrieved April 10, 2018, from https://khn.org/news/health-exchange- medicare-advantage-plans-must-keep-updated-doctor-directories-in-2016/

6. "De ning the Provider Data Dilemma: Challenges, Opportunities and Call for Industry Collaboration," CAQH (September 2016). Retrieved April 10, 2018, from https://www.caqh.org/sites/default/ les/ explorations/de ning-provider-data-white-paper.pdf

7. "Blockchain: How this technology could impact the CFO," EY (no date). Retrieved April 12, 2018, from

8. http://www.ey.com/gl/en/industries/technology/ey-how-blockchain-technology-could-impact-the-cfo

Chapter 15:
HHS Accelerate: A Synopsis

Jose Arrieta

Editor's Note:

In this chapter, Jose Arrieta introduces the Human and Health Services (HHS) Accelerate technology stack aimed at enabling modernization of legacy systems. He presents about a brief history of HHS, it's role in the public health economics, and the recent Accelerate initiatives. In combination with the blockchain, the Accelerate program can immensely reduce costs for it's providers and contracted small businesses that rely on HHS services.

Background

The Department of Health and Human Services (HHS) is the U.S. Government's principal agency for protecting the health of Americans and providing essential human services. HHS is responsible for almost a quarter of all Federal outlays and administers more grant dollars than all other Federal agencies combined. HHS is made up of eleven operating divisions, plus staff divisions, and also engages globally to fulfill its mission.

The 2018/22 strategic plan of the Department of Health and Human Services (HHS) laid out a framework for approaching specific health and human services challenges, such as the high cost of health care, and the epidemic of opioid addiction and overdose. HHS embarked on a process called ReImagine HHS, to identify and implement transformation initiatives to address those health and human services challenges. With an annual spend on goods and services of over $24 billion across 100,000 contracts, acquisition (the procurement of goods and services) is one of the focus areas for ReImagine, and HHS Accelerate is the cornerstone of the acquisition transformation effort.

HHS Accelerate

HHS Accelerate was conceptualized as a business network, based on HHS and external acquisition data, which enabled the agency to better fulfill its core mission. It would augment the capabilities of the workforce, provide real time information from across the agency for effective decision making, free program staff to focus on their core mission activities, improve process efficiency, and enable dramatic savings on HHS' $24 B in acquisition spend.

One of the early proofs of concept was automating the analysis of spend data to identify savings opportunities across products. Preliminary analysis showed price variances up to several hundred percent across items such as software licenses and medical supplies, pointing to hundreds of millions of dollars in potential point of purchase savings.

The HHS acquisition technology and data environment consists of over 45 systems, including five core contract writing systems and over a million pages of unstructured contract data spread across the operating divisions. HHS Accelerate was architected not as an application but as a technology stack which enables modernization and enhancement of capabilities off legacy systems. It collects data from dispersed, siloed systems, indexes this data and rebuilds business processes and capabilities off that layer. It in effect distributes authority to individuals on the business network and empowers them with the information to do their jobs. In this architecture, there is also centralized governance and understanding of user behavior to guide continuous improvement. This capability can be used in a wide range of mission environments, from managing Sepsis research data to facilitating the efficient procurement of goods and services.

HHS Accelerate uses a combination of emerging technologies to create this layer and build intuition into the system. A standard taxonomy was applied to the data, and a blockchain infrastructure established. Blockchain was an appropriate foundation for this solution due to its distributed structure, cryptographic processes and immutability. Value enhancement comes from the use of small programs, microservices, against this blockchain layer. The microservices, based on artificial intelligence, robotic process automation and machine learning provide the value multiplication effect of HHS Accelerate.

This combination of blockchain and other emerging technologies allows decision making to be pushed to the end user at very low cost and provides system wide transparency. For example, an HHS contracting professional is now able to access in real time, historical prices paid and appropriate terms and conditions at the point of placing an order. Similarly, process automation now eliminates the drudgery of acquiring and manually entering the same bit of information four different times, using cut and paste from a range of systems and applications, in order to conduct routine business activities. HHS' industry partners, in particular small businesses, will also experience a welcome reduction in the administrative and financial cost of doing business with the agency.

The HHS researcher or non-acquisition professional is similarly freed to focus on the core business of cancer research or responding to an epidemic, due to the system wide insight and automated processes afforded by HHS Accelerate.

HHS Accelerate was launched as a series of micro initiatives, to establish the technological feasibility and user acceptance. A proof of concept was successfully conducted and moved to a government approved cloud environment within 3 months, and a working application was ready for the Authority to Operate (ATO) process within seven months. This work was performed without shutting off existing systems or creating business disruption. The HHS Accelerate team also utilized a combination of Human Centered Design and Agile development principles to ensure that capability built reflected actual business processes and challenges, and was rapidly delivered to and verified by the end users across the agency.

Conservative estimates show HHS Accelerate having a measurable return on investment of over 800%.

What's Next

HHS Accelerate is expected to receive its ATO in December 2018. This will be a first in government and will enable users to tap into this transformational capability. Users will be empowered and have the data to do effective business planning, negotiate large scale contracts, and interact more efficiently with HHS. Processes which took 5 months of data analysis will be able to be done in a matter of seconds. Some of the initial uses and value sources will be prices paid analysis, savings realization at the point of purchase, market research and reduction of the cycle time for contracting. Additionally, the HHS Accelerate ecosystem will be utilized as a low risk mechanism for transforming operations and performing controlled business disruption. Individual operating divisions intend to build capability off the technology stack to address business needs unique to their divisional missions. These include emergency response, identity management, grants administration and scientific research.   HHS will also be able to sunset several of its legacy acquisition support systems as a result of HHS Accelerate.

Chapter 16: Standards

Heather Flannery

https://hashedhealth.com/blockchain-for-healthcare-book/

Editor's Note:

In this chapter, Heather Flannery from ConsenSys talks to Vikram about her experiences with development of standards and protocols. Heather's unique background puts her in an interesting position to discuss the entire ecosystem around blockchain deployment. Her special focus has been on creating standards that promote creativity and remove barriers, while focusing on the ethical implications of the work and how it impacts society. Moreover, she talks about the crucial need for interoperability to be baked into standards, and the fear of creating even more silos with new technology.

This section is an interview with Heather Flannery, who talks about her unique experience contributing to the blockchain.

Introduction: I'm Heather Flannery, Health Circle Global Lead at ConsenSys responsible for ConsenSys Health. I'm also the chair of the standards developing working group p24 18.6 at IEEE developing blockchain healthcare and life-science standards. I'm the co-founder and board chair for Blockchain and Healthcare Global under IEEE, ISTO. Finally, I'm the co-chair for blockchain task force at HIMSS.

Editor: Can you talk a bit about your background and how that has brought you into the blockchain space?

Heather: It's an amazing thing to have twice in one lifetime, an opportunity to participate in a wholesale paradigm shift. My career got started at the dawn of commercial internet. As a very young and precocious person, I was able to participate in a really revolutionary and extraordinary transformation. Through the course of my career, I've always been a technologist and I've carried that forward. Eventually, because of my own experience as a patient, I became very passionate about healthcare and lifesciences. That part of my career started in about 2005-2006, and the areas that I was most passionate about focusing on was creating integrated care delivery models - Clinical interfaces between the specialties that treated complex chronic diseases and manifesting a model where precision medicine and individualization of care would be possible.

As I went into the field, as an entrepreneur, working on those kinds of structural systemic challenges and bringing with me, my technology background that I had always had - Naturally, I gravitated toward using innovative technology in order to drive new business models. Thinking about care delivery from a systemic perspective that spans organizational boundaries and crosses jurisdictions had me focusing intently on the kinds of challenges that blockchain can address, and the kind of misaligned incentives and distorted incentives that characterized the relationships between these adversarial groups of stakeholders.

So, prior to blockchain I was working to solve the same kinds of problems that are at the heart of this community, and the potential of this technology, but without this technology. I was doing things the very very hard way, and in a sense being stymied by what theoretically is possible at an engineering level, but we all know has not actually worked at scale. For example we do exchange data, we do trade information, people do sell data and patients do receive care but all this information moves but it moves exceedingly slowly and very expensively. The legal and compliance environment, the rapidly increasing cyber security threat vectors, attack frequency and severity that our industry has been subject to all affect this dynamic where the current state is untenable.

Now we have new technology that opens up new doors and new possibilities. While I had not been particularly engaged in the crypto space, I wish I had been. It would have been a much better call on my part, but I became really interested in in blockchain when Etherium was released and I'd had my eye on it just as a curiosity prior to that but hadn't really focused in.

For me it was all about how do I apply this new technology to accomplish precisely what my business objective happens to be. In that process of attempting to implement ecosystem level mutualized federated infrastructure, I learned all of the very concrete reasons why we have real problems to solve before we can get this technology adopted at scale. Scalability is only just one of many challenges, most of these barriers live in non technical categories and standards features significantly among them. Governance, capital formation, the mutualization of risk, for example no one knows how to write an insurance instrument to protect the interests of a consortium of actors in a blockchain ecosystem today. That's just one example many, many challenges.

In my process of attempting to do this, often we learn we learned so much through failure and striving, so I ended up with what I think is a pretty crystal in view of what doesn't work and what what needs to be fixed. That's carried me forward now into working to contribute to the industry to the best of my ability - Broad-based sectoral level attempts collectivized attempts at addressing these these these challenges.

It's a great honor to be part of part of ConsenSys and leading ConsenSys health who has so much to offer from a technology perspective, an infrastructure perspective, capital formation, and all these other categories. So a lot of my work is in that category and a lot of my work is purely volunteer. so Everything that I do for IEEE and for HIMSS is not compensated. It is it is done for the best interests of the industry of the whole as a whole and for the best interests of the patient which represents every single human being on earth so to speak.

Editor: Speaking on contributing and having things to offer, looking at this opportunity for the book - Can you speak a little bit about what you're contributing to the book and why it's important to you to bring that topic to discussion?

Heather: So this I think this book is going to represent a very important contribution to the lexicon, at a point in time when it is most needed, and using a distribution model that will make it particularly accessible and consumable to the parties that are that are seeking to adopt this technology. My particular contribution to what I think is gonna be a remarkable piece of work is at the area or at the intersection of standards and blockchain. So I find myself in an interesting position where I am at a nexus of a number of different organizations that are driving and contributing substantially to the advancement of this technology.

One thing that bears mentioning is that there are two philosophies for standards development and one giant risk. The biggest risk is that standards are developed in such a way that squashes innovation, that they slows the process of solving major problems. Perhaps standards could be drafted around a technology that it really doesn't meet the needs of the end state or the end state vision, and if you look back through the history of how these things have happened there are successful attempts at creating standards that added a tremendous amount of value and enabled commercial success. There are also examples of standards and stories of failed attempts that created problems, inhibited industries and slowed things down. So the people that have been close to standards development usually have representative examples of where it's worked well and where it's worked very poorly.

The most fundamental principle is to enable but not inhibit innovation. Then, the two philosophies are either de facto standards development, where effectively something is already in place and then it is later codified, blessed, instantiated and formalized. But that's a backward or rearward looking standards development activity. The other philosophy or model is a forward-looking "shine the light" to what could be possible and use the standards development process to remove barriers to being able to adopt this technology. One thing that is particularly characteristic of this technology is that it involves ecosystems of actors using this new utility, or this new service layer. So the requirements for semantic and ontological structure of data for potentially hundreds of micro use-cases that extend far beyond where the data standards models have gotten to today - That is a defining characteristic of what we're looking at here.

A lot of the standards that have been developed at the data layer are more static and less transactional. They're less about data in motion and more about data at rest. There's also metadata components that that aren't really present or aren't working well in other standards that we need to articulate. The P-2418 body of standards is anchored in the IEEE standards Association and that's their that's their blockchain family and each of the dots P-2418 such as P-2418.1, P-2418.2, P-2418.3, etc build a particular layer of the architecture, or add a certain verticalization of structure. The working group that I chair is P-2418.6, that's healthcare and life sciences. So it's adding that verticalization on top of horizontal infrastructure layer standards that are P2418.1 and P-2418.2 and others. Also, cross-sectionally IEEE has an extraordinary legacy of collaboration with other international standards development organizations such that there is harmonization and we also have already embedded de facto standards or other standards that parties have created within hours. So we're not seeking to compete with standards, we want to accelerate the good work that's already been done. An example of that is the decentralized identity foundation, the DID standard - We have embedded that within a blockchain related standard that pertains to identity management.

Aside from my role my volunteer role with IEEE, I also am a member of the healthcare working group at the Enterprise Ethereum Alliance, where Ethereum specifications and reference architectures are being developed. These specifications also work with standards that are coming out of the Ethereum foundation for different kinds of crypto assets like ERC20 and ERC721 for non fungible crypto assets and many many others. So those very rapidly and efficiently emerging de facto standards that are not being put forward by an official standards development body, but instead where we are working through the Ethereum foundation, harmonizing with IEEE and the Enterprise Ethereum Alliance in order to create unity. In addition to that, one thing that's incredibly important important for healthcare and life sciences is that blockchain architectures don't become the new data blockers, they don't become the silos. So one of the reasons that early standardization is essential is not to quash innovation but to ensure interoperability and liquidity.

For example: We need portability of smart contracts, we need portability of crypto assets, we need cross chain data flow at scale and we need it sooner than later. In fact the whole industry is nervous about the ability of the competing blockchain platforms to actually demonstrate what we say is a shared value. Everybody says we're gonna live in a multi-chain future, there's not going to be one winner, and the basis of competition between the platforms can't be blocking the flow of transactions. I think everyone is in alignment with, I know leadership from the Hyperledger project within the Linux Foundation is in alignment with that. The Enterprise Ethereum Alliance has just had the Hyperledger project join them. The two healthcare working groups are aware of one another's existence and are now coming together around a shared mission. Those things are taking shape right now, and by the time of the publication of this book there will be more that we can share about that kind unity and common cause that can bring us together and clarity. There will be competing platforms, competition isn't bad or immoral, it's only if we use things as the basis of competition that are inappropriate. So driving that interoperability message, and for the benefit of the patient for the things that we are all accountable for doing in this space is really important and top priority work.

Editor: What do you see being some other real pressing issues as far as blockchain coming into the healthcare field

Heather: So we have a we have a real significant challenge in the area of identity and that intersects with with privacy, cybersecurity, policy and patient or the citizen sovereignty. There's a lot of dialogue in the blockchain healthcare community that tends to orient around de-identification of absolutely everything and focusing on use cases that don't deal with any identified data.

What I would call to all of our attention is that while they're there there is incremental value for us to gain down the path of those use cases and I'm a huge advocate for that, but the actual structural revolution that is possible for us ultimately involves getting the patient in the center or the research participant in the center. We cannot move around that party like the current state data brokerage industry does. They are selling anonymized data and it has some value, but because you can't re-identify it, and move it back to mainstream medicine for example to deliver an intervention, or to deliver precision medicine to activate someone into a trial to be on, etc, there is value but it is capped. So we have to solve the patient matching problem, which is a long-standing incredibly difficult issue that many brilliant people have spent entire careers trying to solve.

We should not be trite and oversimplifying about what that really means, but we have a possibility of solving it now. The the policy and ethical questions about the role of biometrics, how we want to use that about our genetic data, how that is going to be protected and its role in identity - These are these are very challenging questions. We have the technological means to to deliver confirmed identity to a level of certitude that meets the needs of healthcare. There are a number of ways of accomplishing that but a decentralized identity potentially a paired with a biometric attestation is one way. There's also identity by consensus which is a way of effectively crowdsourcing attestations of a claim that something is a certain thing or a certain person. As we think about identity, it's very easy to think that we only mean a person but places and things also require identification. They require that same level of certitude, particularly in life-and-death situations, for instance a certain prosthetic actually goes at us on a certain leg of a certain person at a certain time, not a different person, not a different leg and not a different device, etc. I think that's going to be a very significant challenge, it's going to require a lot of experimentation and it's hard to experiment with things that can impact life-and-death situations. We have to manage risk very carefully, and we have to be very ethnically intentional about as we go about it. I mentioned biometrics and identity, but there's also implants, chips, there's a merger of man and machine, or a human being and and other things that are also introduced into this picture - All are happening on approximately the same event horizon and we're going to need to make decisions and act.

We won't have the option of inaction, it will be impossible not to act because these changes are coming at us. So how can we be ethically intentional, how can we be patient-centered, mission focused, collaborative, and facilitate a healthy transformation of our industry, rather than wall everything off with the intent of maintaining and impossible stasis. That will never happen, so myself and many other leaders in the field are thinking of it in those terms. Let's facilitate a positive ethically intentional transformation, but it has to happen soon. It has to happen now, the change is happening all around us and we can't hold on to the present state.

Editor: When you look at blockchain as both the technology and as its implementation into the healthcare industry, where do you see it in terms of maturity?

Heather: As a technology, the blockchain is a composite - A composite use of a lot of technologies that arc actually in the legacy category. There's many things that we're using from a tech perspective that aren't new in any way. They're not particularly novel, but we do have an unusual first-ever intrinsically longitudinal data structure with directed acyclic graphs (DAGs) and DLT tech and blockchain as a data structure. But what we're using to cryptographically verify each transaction is not intrinsically new. Distributed systems architectures aren't intrinsically new. Cloud computing is a legacy at this point. So what we have is an assemblage of previously existed proven technology put together in a brilliant innovative way, and then at where we have game theory and behavioral economics layered on top of it. So we're talking about something that's not just a technology, it's also brand-new disciplines being brought to bear in a way that we don't yet know how these behavioral economic experiments will actually work. What we have are really compelling hypotheses: We have our known distorted incentive structures. We know what those are, and we have great ideas about things that might work. If we ran them as experiments, they might produce the result. In terms of where we are I believe we should be approaching all this very empirically. We should be thinking of these as experiments that we need to run, things that we need to learn and discover about what does and doesn't actually produce the desired results. Those are partially technical experiments, but I would say there the majority of what is involved with it is not technical its clinical, its social, its economic, its legal, its governance, its ethics, its its its new structures, and systems that we need to run them and we need to observe them very carefully and and see what's actually happening.

That means we should be approaching these projects and initiatives as studies and executing them under research protocols. I think more of us should be talking about. It's a it's a real priority of mine, to see that work getting done in the construct of studies, which i think is one of the only ethically viable ways that you could move to the point of experimenting with this technology - Doing things like this under a research protocol. It's a walled garden from the perspective of technology infrastructure, from protocol ethical oversight, funding structure, it's a microcosm that I think of as a walled garden. In that model, we can we can do work and see what happens. That's the point - To learn what happens. We would not be able to approach doing in mainstream medicine, and I think that's the stage that we are moving into now. The other thing that has happened finally is that there has been a tipping point in the understanding that the question for an organization to be asking is not how do I use blockchain technology, Finally the tipping point has come that it's how do we use blockchain technology. Who is the "we" - Sometimes it might be my competitors, and others it might be my trading partners, and many a times, it might be my constituents my patients, the actual human beings involved and not in an ecosystem

So when you when you start thinking about it as "How do we do this", defining who are the parties, what are their needs, how can their incentives be aligned and how can you use crypto economic models to experiment with those hypothetical incentives because we must remember we don't know how it will work. What we have is a good idea, we have we have reason to believe that it's worth doing the experiment and then whatever we learn will be valuable including null findings. So that's where we are right now. We're moving to formalizing ecosystems and consortium where we are maturing governance models. We're recognizing the need for governing entities in the picture. We're recognizing the need for ethical intentionality and structure from a methodological perspective that the ethical design phase needs to be formalized and incorporated. I hope to see our industry recognizing the need to do this work under studies, and use the walled gardens of research protocols as how we're able to advance ahead of knowing the answers conclusively, such that they could be scaled out in in mainstream medicine.

Editor: so looking forward them into you know 2019 and beyond that what excites you about blockchain healthcare where some things that you are eager to see happen

Heather: I have a great passion for seeing the entire wide arc of research, development and innovation all the way through to commercialization. "From bench to bedside" as they say takes about 17 to 25 years on average. From the time that a discovery is made in a laboratory to the point that it is treating someone's disease or reversing their cancer or preventing their diabetes for example.

There are so many points in that long wide process where we can strip time, costs, risk, and efficiency. We can strip all those things, we can bring the timelines in, we can bring the cost down and what that means is something that my good friend and colleague Dr. Sean Mannion calls "faster miracles" for each of us who are living beings that are subject to the common human experience and preventable suffering. We also have the opportunity to democratize and equalize disparities and access to care using these models. Some of the reasons that those disparities exist are because of distorted incentives, because we don't have models where we can create the motivational systems. The reasons that people can't get access to care aren't because there isn't enough health information technology in the world. So we have the possibility to do great good.

That's why I keep talking about ethical intentionality, because it's the deliberate focus on knowing that those opportunities are there and doing the hard work of discovering them, then validating them experimentally and scaling them out so faster miracles through the entire wide arc of clinical research to translational medicine back to guidelines back to validation, we can speed that process. We can save a huge amounts of financial resources that then can be fed back into that virtuous cycle to speed that process. I think that we can design a future where where we don't leave behind our most vulnerable members of our population. I'm very excited about those things I'm moved by those things do you talk a little bit just kind of pivoting off of that point

Editor: You talked a little bit about what you look forward to working on yourself going forward and how you see yourself making change?

Heather: I have a number of ways that I feel that I can personally contribute and I hope to personally contribute. One of those ways is through through my role at ConsenSys health. We are uniquely positioned to influence the development of viable crypto economic systems that can affect these distorted incentive models on the Ethereum platform using the technology that we're building, and developing an ecosystem of partners and collaborators and allies that we're that we're working with. In the hats that I wear with IEEE I have an opportunity to coalesce stakeholders around a common vision, and engage individuals and the broadest possible group of stakeholders to give a voice to their priorities. One of the most important elements about applying ethics as an active process is doing the work to make sure that you're making your really best effort at getting those stakeholders at the table. This process is inconvenient and difficult, and if it were easy, it would already have been the way that we approach it. So I'm really passionate about doing that hard work and seeing the benefits of that come to pass. So it's a great honor to be a part of the IEEE. I'm very proud of them and honored to be a part of what they're doing.

I think that the HIMSS organization also has a tremendous amount of value to add globally. They are another global institution that's a terrific vehicle for education and a trusted resource for health information technology professionals globally, who are you know the tip of the spear of needing to evaluate and utilize this technology. So I think it's a wonderful opportunity to be part of these different organizations that play very different roles but they're complementary and they're all they all align in a vision that I carry in my mind as I'm moving between moving between these roles.

Editor: In conclusion, thinking about the readers and the viewers who are gonna be in taking this content, do you have any thoughts or comments that you would like to leave them with or give to them to lead them into reading this book

Heather: In conclusion, as as a new practitioner beginning to learn about this technology and its potential the most important thing I would remind you is that blockchain isn't only technology it's also behavioral economics and game theory. It's an opportunity to apply those new disciplines to to our field and we've never had any tools that we could use to apply that thinking, and now we do. So it's all the technology and it's more so much more than that.

Another really important idea is that blockchain doesn't exist in isolation. It is hitting commercial viability, and industrial viability at around the same time as many other equally revolutionary commit innovations. So there's there's a great convergence happening with this technology. It's also thinking about the whole family of artificial intelligence technologies, just the combination of putting natural language processing and robotic process automation together with smart contracts and blockchain, and you didn't even enter the internet of medical things into that picture. How about 3d printing drugs or organs and and so on.

So we have we have this great convergence of totally revolutionary technologies all hitting at the same time, and we also are required to rethink the way that we secure information. The increasing attack frequency, severity, from a cyber security perspective is just as all of this exponential value is potentially being created, so too does it represent new threat vectors and risk. We also need to think of blockchain as an entirely new architectural paradigm for how it is that we secure our information and that's equivalently important to focus on both the benefits and the risks in parallel and to think bigger than just blockchain as a tech plus behavioral economics and game theory plus the convergence of everything that it's had that's happening in concert. So think big.

Chapter 17:
Financing Healthcare with Blockchain: From ICOs to STOs and Beyond

https://hashedhealth.com/blockchain-for-healthcare-book/

Editor's Note:

This fascinating chapter connects the two very different themes of blockchain technology and crypto (short for crypto-currencies). It reviews in detail the use of crypto-currencies (like tokens) in healthcare, either as a method to incentive patients and stakeholders to access their digital platform through an Initial Coin Offering (ICO) or as an alternative method for start ups, to raise capital through a security token offering (STO). Both Robert Miller, CEO of Honeycomb and Dr. Alex Cahana, head of CryptoOracle Health, share their research on the ICO landscape in healthcare in 2018, while John McCorvey, CEO of Blockchain Financial Group and Devin Carty, CEO at Martin Ventures and Co Founder of Trilliant Health complete the chapter by explaining security tokenization (STOs), Digital Security Offerings (DSOs), and the investment perspective on these new exciting financial instruments, while developing new decentralized economies in Healthcare.

Initial Coin Offerings

Robert Miller and Dr. Alex Cahana

The past two years has seen the dizzying ascendancy and ensuing fall of the Initial Coin Offering, or ICO (pronounced I-C-O). An ICO is a new type of fundraising mechanism using cryptocurrencies. A new cryptocurrency is generated and a portion of the total supply of this cryptocurrency is sold in advance of the cryptocurrency's future functional utility being created. Casual speculators, professional investors, future users of this coin, and people who support the project in question are the usual participants in ICOs.

The vast majority of ICOs are ERC20 "tokens." These are a specific type of cryptocurrency called "tokens" which adhere to a specific set of technical standards called "ERC20." The "E" in ERC20 stands for Ethereum, and all ERC20 tokens are deployed on top of the Ethereum network. Moreover, for our purposes, you can think of token and cryptocurrency to be analogous.

Divergent Narratives

There are two dominant narratives around ICOs: one idealistic narrative that highlights their promise and one that characterizes ICOs as everything wrong with cryptocurrencies. The first narrative characterizes ICOs as "the future of fundraising – not only for cryptocurrency projects but for all startups, and finally, perhaps years in the future, for nearly all organizations whatsoever." This narrative holds that ICOs are an emergent global capital market that is democratizing access to investing in high growth opportunities and enabling more equitable businesses. To speak to the latter, a driver for Uber in 2008 benefited from the wages they received, but although those drivers were instrumental in Uber's success, they ultimately didn't benefit from Uber's meteoric rise to a $120bn market valuation and ensuing IPO. The same story is true of countless technology companies today. In contrast, if you were an early user of Bitcoin you both were instrumental in Bitcoin's success, and you benefited handsomely from Bitcoin's appreciation in the coming years. Cryptocurrencies create a more equitable and symbiotic system, allowing users to benefit from the networks they helped create. That trend is applicable beyond just money, like Bitcoin, but to any decentralized network, such as a decentralized personal health record.

Moreover, in stark contrast to the control that a small group of big tech platforms have over our economy, ICOs are often held as a way to align the incentives of diverse parties and create open ecosystems. This narrative began to coalesce in 2016 and its intellectual roots can be gleaned by reading Chris Dixon's "Crypto Tokens: A Breakthrough in Open Network Design", "Why Decentralization Matters", or Joel Monegro's "Fat Protocol Hypothesis."

The second narrative focuses on the unsavory aspects of ICOs. First and foremost, they highlight the immaturity of the space manifested in its lack of accountability, high profile scandals, sky-high risk, mind-boggling valuations, and pump and dump schemes, where groups coordinate to unnaturally "pump" a cryptocurrency's price as high as they can before "dumping" it, oftentimes on retail investors. Second, they question the motives of ICOs. Does this use case really need their own cryptocurrency? Or are they opportunists trying to raise money from unsophisticated retail investors? I suspect that the latter is true more often than the former. Lastly, there is uncertainty about the ability for ICOs to create and sustain value for their stakeholders in the long term. There are long-standing and clear ways to value traditional financial instruments like a bond or a share in a company, but we have yet to figure out the proper way to value a cryptocurrency. There are concerns that outside of a small range of use cases, like digital gold, the vast majority of cryptocurrencies have no fundamental value.

There is truth to both narratives. The cryptocurrency space has undoubtedly been rife with charlatans and scammers, but on the other hand, there are incredibly driven, mission-oriented, and talented people working on potentially world-changing ideas.

A Brief History of ICOs

The first ICO was conducted by Mastercoin in July 2013. Ethereum followed a year later, raising $18 million dollars, a jaw dropping amount at the time. Ethereum released an experimental version in July 2015 and the ERC20 technical standard, was released shortly thereafter. The ERC20 technical standard allowed anyone to easily deploy a cryptocurrency on top of Ethereum, drastically reduced the cost to create your own cryptocurrency. In turn, this lead to a proliferation of new tokens. Augur, a decentralized prediction market, launched the first major ICO raising on top of Ethereum a month later, and the flood gates for ICOs were officially opened.

An early ICO, the Decentralized Autonomous Organization, or DAO, raised $150 million dollars in April of 2016, surpassing all expectations and offering a glimpse into what was to come. The first months of 2017 saw explosive growth in ICOs. Quickly, far more money was being raised by ICOs than by traditional venture capital. Several high profile ICOs with lofty missions raised eye watering amounts in minutes of beginning to fundraise, and that garnered the attention of traditional media and retail investors. With this attention, even more money began to flow into the space with very little oversight. From day one this has been an inherently global phenomenon touching nearly every country on the planet, and with much higher interest from retail investors in Asia than in the West.

Teams with little track record and no product were able to raise tens of millions of dollars in months. Several mega projects were spawned. Below is a table of some of the largest ICOs available to the public:

Name	Amount Raised	ICO Dates	Project
EOS	$4.1 billion	6/26/17 - 6/18/18	Smart Contracts
Telegram	$1.7 billion	01/18-02/18	Encrypted Messaging & Blockchain Ecosystem
Dragon	$320 million	02/15/18 - 03/15/2018	Decentralized Currency for Casinos
Huobi	$300 million	01/24/18 - 02/28/18	Cryptocurrency Exchange
Hdac	$258 million	11/27/17 - 12/22/17	IoT Contract & Payment Platform
Filecoin	$257 million	08/10/17 - 09/10/17	Decentralized Cloud Storage
Tezos	$232 million	07/01/17 - 07/14/17	Self-Amending Distributed Ledger
Sirin Labs	$158 million	12/16/17 - 12/26/17	Open-Source Blockchain Smartphone
Bancor	$153 million	12/6/17	Prediction Markets
The DAO	$152 million	05/01/17 - 05/28/17	Decentralized investment fund

Decentralized investment fund

To date, there have been thousands of ICOs. Autonomous Research, an independent research provider focused on finance, found that ICOs raised over $7 billion in 2017 and are slated to raise $12 billion in 2018. The overall ICO market peaked in December 2017, raised in aggregation $2.6 billion that month alone. Since then, ICO funding consolidated. Most of the money in the space was going to a giant smart contract platform ICOs, and the amount that was being raised significantly declined. In September of 2018, approximately $300 million was raised, a 90% draw down from the peak in 2017. The decline in ICO funding strongly correlates to the decline of the overall cryptocurrency market, which peaked in December of 2018 and has been descending since then.

Over time there has been evolution in the standards and norms of ICOs. They began highly unstructured, often declining to do basic background checks on their participants, and without any cap on how much money was being raising. Famously, Tezos, one of the most anticipated and largest ICOs of 2017, initially let people anonymously contribute to its ICO. Much to the chagrin of the community, after nearly a year Tezos demanded that investors produce their identity documents in order to comply with requisite anti-money laundering and know your customer laws. Slowly, some norms emerged: preset caps on how much money a team was raising, vesting periods on teams' tokens, and both anti-money laundering as well as know your customer checks became regular. Moreover, there has been some discussion of milestone based ICOs, such as in Vitalik Buterin's article "Explanation of DAICOs", where funds would slowly be released to projects as they meet key objectives and requirements. These discussions have yet to materialize into action.

Much of the buzz around ICOs has shifted to a different class of cryptocurrency offering called a security token offering or an STO. These are cryptocurrencies that are 1 to 1 equivalent to shares except ownership of these shares is recorded on a blockchain and trade similarly to other cryptocurrencies. The argument for an STO is that they lower transaction costs compared to traditional trading, offer liquidity, and there are is more regulatory certainty around STOs. Despite the buzz, there has been far less investor demand for STOs than there was for ICOs.

Healthcare Example Use Cases

Healthcare ICOs overview

What about healthcare specific ICOs? Over the past year Vince Kuraitis has curated and crowdsourced a public list of 138 healthcare ICOs. [LINK] The Center for Biomedical Blockchain Research ("the CBB") independently created and crowdsourced a remarkably similar list. [LINK] I collated both of these resources to form one list of 148 healthcare ICOs. The CBB categorized each project through two lenses: an industry focus representing the area of healthcare that a project focuses on, and the functional focus, representing how a project is using a blockchain. For the purpose of this analysis, data was narrowed to only healthcare specific projects and only ICOs.

Healthcare ICOs funding

An integral part of ICOs is the funds they raise. There are no clear data sources and few standards for tracking who has raised how much funds. Oftentimes this number is simply self-reported by the ICOs themselves, with little ability for outside parties to verify the integrity of a claim. Alternatively, an ICO may simply declare their ICO to be over at the end of their fundraising period, with no specificity over how much money they actually raised. Moreover, due to the regulatory uncertainty of ICOs, projects may prefer to not disclose how much money they have raised in order to not draw future scrutiny from regulators. Lastly, although the data for exact start dates of many of these projects is not clear, almost all raised their funds in 2017 and early 2018.

Out of 148 healthcare ICOs, data on the amount of funds raised was available for 41 ICOs. Those 41 projects have raised $496,508,000 in total, raising an average of $12,000,000 per ICO with a median raise of $7,000,000. To help put these numbers in context, RockHealth reported that in 2017 $5.8 billion in venture funding was invested in digital health companies across all stages of companies, including several mega-financing rounds that raised more than $100 million dollars. Of the $5.8 billion, we can extrapolate from further data RockHealth provided that around $350 million was invested in seed stage digital health companies in 2017 and 2018 and these companies are on track for reaching similar numbers. The average size of these rounds was $4m$4,000,000 in 2017 and $5m$5,000,000 in 2018.

Considering the fact that almost all healthcare ICOs were pre-product while they raised funds it is generous to compare them to seed stage companies, as it is doubtful that these companies would have been able to raise an average seed stage round. Despite this, the average healthcare ICO raised millions more than the average seed stage company and gave up no board seats or equity to do so. Moreover, while many of these projects promised to decentralize data, disintermediate processes, and provide altogether better solutions, there was an extreme dearth of go-to-market strategies and a lack of thoughtfulness around business models. With these things in mind, and given how new blockchain technology and cryptocurrencies are, it is remarkable that $500,000,000 was invested in healthcare ICOs.

Healthcare ICOs categorization

Below is a table summarizing the breakdown of healthcare ICOs' industry focus:

Industry Focus	Count	Funds Raised
Healthcare Operations	46	$ 196,081,000.00
Digital Medicine / Care Delivery	31	$ 6,212,000.00
Personal Health Record	27	$ 77,207,000.00
Fitness / Wellness	12	$ 39,500,000.00
Research & Clinical Trials	10	$ 20,458,000.00
Pharmaceutical	7	$ 83,350,000.00
Healthcare - unspecified	7	$ -
Genomics	5	$ 38,200,000.00
Blockchain Infrastructure	3	$ 5,500,000.00

Healthcare operations was the most popular with 46 projects representing 31% of all healthcare ICOs. These ICOs raised just under $200,000,000 dollars, or 42% of the total funds raised. Broadly healthcare operations included projects that improve system management, such as hospital managed medical records as well as payment and billing management.

Second was digital medicine / care delivery, which captured projects supplying digital medicines and clinical care. Two examples would be incentive systems for medication adherence or blockchain enabled telemedicine. These were popular projects to start, but not popular with investors, representing 21% of all healthcare ICOs, but raising only 1% of the funds.

Personal health records came in third. Most of these projects envision one decentralized electronic health record system, perhaps even reaching across national borders, that would simultaneously empower patients to control their health information and solve problems of interoperability. This lofty dream is one of the most talked about use cases for blockchain in healthcare, and it has raised a corresponding $77,207,000 dollars. The difference between this category and healthcare operations is that these electronic health records are designed specifically to be used by patients.

Fourth was a class of fitness or wellness projects, most of which center around cryptocurrency driven gamification or giving users control over their fitness data. Use cases include monetization of wearables data, gamification to nudge users towards better behavior, consumer health products verification, and ecosystems for fitness or wellness.

Research & clinical trials took the fifth spot. These included projects using blockchain in some way to improve or augment research. Oftentimes, these projects are focused on AI, analytics, and data science.

Projects categorized as pharmaceutical all have some application to pharmaceutical supply chain use cases. With the exception of one significant outlier, these projects fell short of the average amount a healthcare ICO would raise.

A number of projects did not have a primary focus and were classified as "unspecified." Not surprisingly, these projects were not successful in raising money.

Genomics projects aimed to give patients control of their genomic data and allow them to monetize it as well. These projects raised a formidable $38,200,000.

Lastly, blockchain infrastructure projects are healthcare focused and are creating infrastructure for other projects to build on top of. Common examples are blockchain based identity management or data management platforms.

Below is a table summarizing healthcare ICOs by their functional role:

Function	Count	Funds Raised
Data & Asset Management	60	$ 162,107,000.00
Marketplace	40	$ 69,808,000.00
Data Science & Analytics	19	$ 47,408,000.00
Payments & Claims	18	$ 102,635,000.00
Supply Chain Management	11	$ 84,550,000.00

The most popular project focus was data and asset management, which aims to manage data and digital assets, such as identity, patient data, health system operations data, credentialing, and more. A similar, but distinct, category was marketplaces, which consists of projects that seek to facilitate the exchange of data between agents in healthcare. More than that, a number of them focus on the monetization of patient data and creating pipelines to researchers who can use that data. These two categories make up nearly 70% of healthcare ICOs and raised 50% of total funds allocated to healthcare ICOs. They are part of a broader trend of using blockchain technology as a way of owning your own data and disrupting the proprietary data networks that dominate our economy today.

Data science and analytics projects use blockchain technology as a tool for access management, and on top of that focus on adding value by providing advanced analytics, often leveraging some form of artificial intelligence. Only 3 of 19 of these projects were successful in fundraising, with the bulk of the money disproportionately going to a single project focused on genomics.

Payments and claims focus on creating digital infrastructure for healthcare payment systems built with blockchain technology and leveraging smart contracts. Despite only having 12% of the projects, payment and claims projects have raised 22% of total funds.

Supply chain management projects use blockchains to create more auditable, efficient, and transparent supply chains. Generally these are focused on pharmaceutical supply chains, although other use cases, like a supply chain to track breast milk, have emerged. Pharma supply chains are a use case that seems to naturally resonate with people, and their funding reflects that. Supply chain management projects reflect 7% of total projects but raised 18% of total funding.

A Distributed Community

An interesting nuance about healthcare ICOs is that their investor base and communities are much more global than traditional early stage healthcare businesses are. Blockchains and cryptocurrencies have always been a global phenomenon and the networks they have created transcend national borders. For example, Earn.com's Bitnodes, a service being developed to estimate the size of the Bitcoin network, lists Bitcoin nodes in 100 different countries, including Iran and Venezuela. The burgeoning ICO fundraising landscape also reflects that global nature. Cryptocurrencies made it significantly easier to send money across the globe and the global nature meant that there were ample opportunities for people to invest their cash. Enterprising investors were constantly hunting for the next big project, regardless of its location. It was common for ICOs to have their website and whitepaper translated into several languages to try to attract foreign investors. The pseudonymity that cryptocurrencies brought, as well as the new nature of these assets, led many people to feel that they did not need to comply with existing regulatory frameworks. In some cases, governments passed legislation or regulatory guidance that explicitly permitted their citizens to invest in ICOs as well. As a result, money flowed mostly freely across borders and the cryptocurrency community has retained its global roots.

It remains to be seen how this global nature will affect blockchain in healthcare businesses in the future. However, it is not a mistake that there are several projects which have explicitly international ambitions. These ICOs invoke rhetoric of "open," "global," or "borderless" healthcare, proselytize for electronic health records that move seamlessly across national boundaries, and proposing global networks of digital care, like cross border telemedicine or second opinions services. These ambitions have yet to be realized, but the world would be a better place if they were successful. I hope they are.

Geographical Breakdown

Country	Count
US	55
Russia	14
UK	9
Switzerland	8
Singapore	6
Australia	5
Hong Kong	5
Germany	4
Estonia	3
Canada	2
France	2
India	2
Netherlands	2
Austria	1
Belarus	1
Bulgaria	1
China	1
Czech Republic	1
Gibraltar	1
Guernsey	1
Hungary	1
Indonesia	1
Israel	1
Jamaica	1
Latvia	1
Lithuania	1
Malta	1
Mexico	1
Nigeria	1
Poland	1
Slovenia	1
South Korea	1
Spain	1
Turkey	1
Ukraine	1

It bears restating that the data for this analysis was collected by Americans, and although it was crowdsourced and anyone could contribute, this data is likely biased towards Western countries. Location was recorded for 148 projects. Of those 148 the US was by far the leader with 55 projects. This dominance was surprising to find, as the regulatory environment in the US, for better or for worse, is more difficult for ICOs than other countries and the industry consensus is that it is generally a bad idea to run an ICO in the US.

What was equally surprising was that there were not more Chinese, Japanese, and South Korean ICOs. Interest in blockchain and cryptocurrencies is much higher in these countries than it is in the US or Europe. A report by Dalia Research found awareness and knowledge of cryptocurrencies was highest in South Korea (87 percent, 60 percent) and Japan (83 percent, 61 percent). Moreover, Chinese President Xi Jinping himself called blockchain a 'breakthrough' technology, indicating the level of national interest and recognition of the technology's importance by major political figures. Despite this, Chinese and South Korean ICOs make up a fraction of the list and there were no recorded Japanese healthcare ICOs.

The rest of the table is relatively unsurprising. There were a plethora of Russian ICOs and healthcare was no exception. Moreover, in London, United Kingdom, Zug, Switzerland (also known as Crypto Valley), and Singapore are all burgeoning blockchain hubs. It makes sense that these hubs of activity and capital would attract healthcare ICOs.

State	Count
California	12
Texas	6
Georgia	5
Florida	4
New Jersey	3
Tennessee	3
Colorado	2
New York	2
Connecticut	1
Illinois	1
Kentucky	1
Massachusetts	1
Pennsylvania	1
Virginia	1
Washington	1
Wyoming	1

Within the US the largest cluster of healthcare ICOs is in California, which makes sense given the high concentration of business and technology talent in California. Similarly, several projects are headquartered in Atlanta, Georgia, Austin, Texas and Dallas, Texas, taking advantage of the existing healthcare communities close by. It is moderately surprising that given the size of the blockchain communities in New York that there are not more healthcare ICOs based there.

Platform	Count	Funds raised
Ethereum	96	$ 398,600,000.00
Hyperledger	8	$ 24,467,000.00
Waves	3	$1,008,000.00
Stellar	3	N/A
NEO	3	N/A
EOS	2	N/A
Grapevine	2	N/A

Ethereum was by far the most dominant platform; at least 64% of healthcare ICOs chose to build on Ethereum. These ICOs raised an incredible $398,600,000 dollars, outraising any other platform by a massive margin.

It's important to note that several projects have a dual blockchain structure. In 6 instances this was using both Ethereum and Hyperledger. The idea behind this architecture is to create your token on top of a public blockchain, but combine that with a private and permissioned blockchain that manages sensitive data or operations. That provides more flexibility, privacy, and makes it easier to comply with healthcare privacy laws.

Ethereum has built up a considerable ecosystem to date but three factors might erode this lead. First, there are drastically fewer ICOs taking place. Ethereum was by far the most popular platform for ICOs in the past and that drove significant interest in adding it into a technology stack. Second, a new wave of platforms are emerging to compete with Ethereum. EOS, Dfinity, Tezos, Hashgraph, Solana, Algorand… the list goes on. The point is that each of these new platforms differentiates itself in some way from Ethereum, offering higher levels of transactions per second, a different consensus algorithm, a better way of upgrading, lack of transaction fees, and so forth. These new platforms might convert some projects to build on them or capture new entrants into the space. Lastly, Ethereum will need to scale to retain projects. CryptoKitties, a cat game made on Ethereum, famously went viral and caused transactions to slow to a crawl on Ethereum for several days. If that remains the status quo then projects will not hesitate to switch one of the aforementioned new platforms offering a more scalable blockchain.

Healthcare ICOs Return Methodology

A few words on methodology: for this section we began with the list of 152 healthcare ICOs that the CBB has put together. We cross-referenced this with Vince Kuraitis' list of 138 healthcare ICOs to ensure all projects were covered and created a total list of 148 healthcare ICOs. These were then cross-checked against CoinMarketCap on 10/31/2018. CoinMarketCap has created a list of cryptocurrencies, what exchanges these coins are listed on, and historical price and volume data about these cryptocurrencies. It is the most comprehensive source available for this kidn of data.

However, CoinMarketCap will only add those cryptocurrencies that were listed on cryptocurrencies exchanges for active trading, or a rare few cryptocurrencies that have large followings and are very likely to be listed in the future. In total there were 16 healthcare ICOs that were on CoinMarketCap. More on the importance of this metric later.

Historical price and volume data for these 16 healthcare ICOs was downloaded from CoinMarketCap. Generally, this data begins when a cryptocurrency is first listed on CoinMarketCap, but it is possible that in select cases a coin was trading for a period prior to CoinMarketCap listing it, and, as a result, there is not data available for that period. Regardless, the date that data "starts" is recorded as the "listing date." This should not be confused with the date that a project was conceived or formally started. Many of these projects were underway for several months before their cryptocurrencies became listed.

Market capitalization data was also collected on each of these healthcare ICOs. Market capitalization for cryptocurrencies seeks to capture the total value of a cryptocurrency network and is found by taking the price of a cryptocurrency multiplied by the total supply.

$$market\_capitalization = price*total\_supply$$

Market capitalization for cryptocurrencies has a nearly identical equation to that of stocks, but they are two distinct concepts and comparing them is like comparing apples to oranges. A market capitalization of a billion dollars doesn't mean a billion dollars has been invested into a cryptocurrency. A dollar invested in a cryptocurrency can generate increases in market capitalization multiple times higher than a single dollar. Chris Burniske estimated that the increase in market capitalization was between 2x – 25x during 2017. A Citibank analyst estimated this increase to be 50x.

Price, market capitalization, and volume was augmented with how much money each ICO raised. There is no single data source for this information. Instead, a range of sources was drawn upon, including project blogs, press releases, project social media pages, community chats, and ICO review websites. Unfortunately, this is an imperfect process with imperfect data. Oftentimes, there was conflicting information or no official number put out by the team leading the process. In three cases there was no public information available at all.

Regardless, every effort has been made to ensure the data collected is as accurate and as robust as possible. We strongly believe this data to be highly representative of the overall market. Moreover, the goal in this analysis is not to analyze or highlight any one specific ICO, but instead to analyze broad market trends.

Healthcare ICO White Paper Evaluation

We created an ICO evaluation matrix with emphasis on team quality (i.e. domain expertise, presence on LinkedIn), token design and incentives, expected market volume and revenue model. We were particularly curious how many projects remained active (live) vs. abandoned (dead) vs. unknown (zombie).

Among the 143 projects we reviewed 69% of them were still active, whereas 20% and 11% were dead or zombie, respectively. This number is similar to the 72% survival rate in 2017 of all ICOs as described in the Autonomous Next 2018 report.

Interestingly we found that although many, if not most companies, DID NOT have their team members on LinkedIn or specified a business plan. However when they did, the projects were significantly more likely to be alive than zombie or dead ($p < 0.0001$, $p < 0.0014$, respectively).

Project	Listing date	Raised	Listing price	Price 10/31/2018	Return to date	Return in 2018
Modum	10/23/17	$13,400,000.00	$0.49	$0.80	64%	-88%
Farmatrust	8/14/18	$7,000,000.00	$0.01	$0.01	29%	29%
Encrypgen	11/20/17	$1,000,000.00	$0.05	$0.05	-1%	-93%
Lympo	3/1/18	$14,000,000.00	$0.02	$0.02	-2%	-2%
Ambrosus	10/23/17	$32,000,000.00	$0.20	$0.17	-12%	-73%
Dentacoin	8/11/17	$3,000,000.00	$0.00	$0.00	-29%	-61%
Docademic	10/1/18	$1,100,000.00	$0.05	$0.03	-32%	-32%
Timicoin	8/30/18	$20,000,000.00	$0.06	$0.03	-45%	-45%
Medishares	12/13/17	N/A	$0.03	$0.02	-50%	-66%
Medibloc	12/22/17	$6,000,000.00	$0.02	$0.01	-70%	-86%
Nam-coin	8/4/18	N/A	$0.00	$0.00	-73%	-73%
Curecoin	5/26/14	$6,800,000.00	$0.80	$0.07	-91%	-91%
Shivom	6/7/18	$35,000,000.00	$0.05	$0.00	-92%	-92%
Medicalchain	2/6/18	$24,000,000.00	$0.32	$0.02	-93%	-93%
Patientory	6/6/17	$23,000,000.00	$0.65	$0.04	-94%	-94%
Aldoc	1/10/18	N/A	$0.23	$0.01	-96%	-96%

Key findings:

- Only 16 of 148 healthcare ICOs were listed on exchanges where they can be actively bought and sold

- Of those 16 listed ICOs, 2 have positive returns to date.

- In 2018 only one healthcare ICO has been profitable.

Healthcare ICOs have had very poor performance to date. Despite the substantial amount of activity in the space, only 16 of 148 healthcare ICOs were listed on exchanges. Of those 16, only two have given investors positive returns since their listing, and if we narrow our focus to 1/1/2018 and onward then only a single healthcare ICO generated positive returns. The average healthcare ICO had -43% return to date, the highest return was 64% and the lowest was -96%. Moreover, these 16 ICOs raised an estimated $186,300,000 dollars, with data unavailable for 3 projects.

Market capitalization data on exchange listed healthcare ICOs was collected. The market capitalization was relatively low for years, entering 2017 at around $1,000,000 dollars. As new healthcare ICOs came online this figure exponentially increased before reaching a peak of $2.78 billion, a 3000x increase from a year prior. Since that peak the total healthcare ICO market capitalization has been in a overall decline, resting at around $200 million dollars at the time of writing.

These numbers are inflated because of the inclusion of an outlier healthcare ICO, Dentacoin, which ballooned to an unreasonable valuation in January of 2018 before deflating to a slightly less unreleased valuation today. Data for the total healthcare ICO market capitalization is presented with and without Dentacoin. Without Dentacoin the peak market capitalization of healthcare ICOs was $1.1 billion in January 2018, and has similarly been declining. As of October 31st it is $133 million.

Another observation is that the healthcare ICO market capitalization is heavily correlated with Bitcoin's market capitalization. Healthcare ICOs rocketed up following Bitcoin's ascendancy in late 2017, early 2018, and fell to earth along with Bitcoin. This suggests an inefficient market driven more by hype and sentiment than fundamental valuation. An interesting trend is that these Bitcoin and healthcare ICOs seem to have diverged slightly over time. In late 2018 several upticks in Bitcoin's price had no discernible effect on healthcare ICOs, and although Bitcoin has been relatively stable in value for a few weeks, healthcare ICOs have remained in decline. Should this trend continue it could be an indication that the market is becoming more efficient and is providing a condemnation of healthcare ICOs.

Commentary on Healthcare ICOs Returns

The overall cryptocurrency market has been in a severe decline for months. Bitcoin plunged from nearly $20,000 to $6,500 and has been sitting near that mark for several weeks now. Ethereum's decline was even more acute, plummeting from a summit of $1,400 to under $200 at the time of writing. Comparing fresh faced healthcare ICOs to cryptocurrency juggernauts is a bit unfair, healthcare ICOs are performing similar to the overall ICO market. EY reported that of the 141 largest ICOs in 2017, 86% are trading below their listing price and 30% have lost almost all their value. Similarly, 87.5% healthcare ICOs are trading below their listing price, and 31.25% have lost almost all their value. So, while healthcare ICOs have performed abysmally, this is largely in line with the overall ICO market.

Those are just the ICOs that have gotten listed. There are 132 other ICOs which have not. A potential explanation for this is that exchanges do not see healthcare ICOs as a market enticing enough to drive retail demand, and thus bring the exchange profits from trading. Ethereum's "world computer," Dfinity's "decentralized cloud," or Decred's "autonomous digital currency" are probably more exciting to the average person than a cryptocurrency designed to "revolutionize FHIR based interoperability" or "drive value based payments." As such, although the latter two cryptocurrencies might catch the interest of any healthcare professional raise their eyes, exchanges might simply shrug and move on.

In the long run, and with current technologies, not being listed on an exchange an extreme liability for ICOs because exchanges are the central place where users or investors would buy and sell tokens. That liquidity is vital to a sustainable and functioning product powered by cryptocurrency. It provides an onboarding ramp for new users to get their hands on what's necessary to use an ICO's product or serve.

Equally as important, it provides an exit ramp for investors in ICOs to exit or hedge their positions. At the earliest stages of an ICO an investor would have their capital locked up for months in a high risk, high return venture. The ultimate goal in this endeavor is for the ICO to have an exchange listing promptly after the ICO ends, bringing in a swarm of new users who suddenly have access to this new asset, and fully capitalizing on the hype that usually accompanies an ICO. If there is not a listing it becomes much more difficult, but not impossible, for an investor to sell the cryptocurrency they have bought. Investors can still sell to others in private, peer to peer or over the counter markets, but these have minimal liquidity and carry with them other risks. There are some reasons for which a legitimate project might seek to not be listed or delay their listing. In particular, teams could be waiting for additional regulatory clarity or trying to wait out the current market conditions. But, in the long term, as the regulatory environment becomes more certain and the market stabilizes, almost all legitimate ICOs will seek listing.

How market conditions affect healthcare ICOs

Healthcare ICOs benefitted significantly from the ever-rising prices and market euphoria of the past year.

- These conditions gave them easy access to non-dilutive capital.
- Generated interest in their industry.
- Provided opportunities for free press.
- Attract third party developers looking to build on top of platforms that will make them money.
- Drove consumers to their products.
- Made it easier to hire top talent,
- Kept their investors happy.

If the market rebounds someday most of these qualities will resurface in some form. On the other hand, a sharply falling market has brought extreme pain to healthcare ICOs.

- The bar for raising money through an ICO has become much harder.
- Users may stop using a product given depressed prices.
- Projects don't benefit from the organic user growth that comes with appreciating prices ("What's this token that's up 5% in a day? Oh it's a health record? Let me try it out…").
- Exchanges tighten their listings.
- Employee salaries, which are usually in part paid in tokens, suffer.
- Overall team morale suffers.
- Brings more pressure and scrutiny from the community, investors, and press.
- Investors become unhappy. If they are not long term investors or subjected to a lock up period they will exit their investment if possible.

Similar to the above, but most of these will be ameliorated if prices stabilize or march back upwards.

Moreover, due to the nascent state of cryptocurrency regulation as well the crypto space's unsavory public image, ICOs oftentimes have difficulty establishing banking relationships. That means that when they raise millions of dollars in cryptocurrency, they may be unable to convert their funds into dollars. Furthermore, teams might not have wanted to, after all, rising prices meant that their treasuries were also growing in nominal value. The music had to stop someday, and there was a near universal recognition that the market would inevitably correct, but it hadn't just yet, so why not ride out the bumps and reach for a little bit more? Nonetheless, cryptocurrency prices eventually fell back down to earth. When these prices fell treasuries, project runaways also fell with them. Budgets suddenly were much tighter than expected. For example, Forbes estimated that one ICO in 2017 (unrelated to healthcare) only had $18,000,000 left after originally raising $42,000,000.

Changing token models and misaligned incentives

Nominally many of these ICOs stated they were creating their own cryptocurrency to serve as the method of payment within an ecosystem. The implication in this statement was that their cryptocurrency would serve as the only method of payment within their ecosystem. There are some more nuanced reasons why you would do this, but in general the thinking is that by limiting method of payment to a project's own cryptocurrency, you would be forcing users to buy it in order to access the ecosystems goods and services. More users translates into more demand, and in turn this should cause a cryptocurrency to appreciate in value.

But, ICOs that have shipped a product are now struggling to grapple with the realities of consumer adoption today. By limiting payment for services to your own cryptocurrency, you drastically reduce your potential customer base. Only a sliver of society owns any cryptocurrency, and even fewer people still are able to navigate the dizzying array of steps it takes to buy an esoteric cryptocurrency on an obscure exchange. Moreover, assuming a user achieves this step, the interfaces we have today to use these cryptocurrencies are arcane to the average person. They would much prefer to use their credit card or PayPal.

And some projects are accommodating those users by allowing for payments using credit cards or other cryptocurrencies. That would be fine except their tokens were sold on the idea, explicitly said or implicitly agreed upon, that it would be the sole method of payment. Communities are rightfully asking "Why does this token even exist then?" and have not been kind to projects that take other payments.

At the core of this trend also lies a problem with the economic incentives of projects seeking to build products with their own cryptocurrencies. Companies naturally try to maximize shareholder value, but that doesn't necessarily translate to maximizing token value. What's good for shareholders isn't always good for token holders. The decision to accept other methods of payment makes sense for a business trying to maximize its profits and generate shareholder value, although it might shatter the value of a token.

Lastly, a key difference between traditional startups and those with ICOs is that employees are usually unable to sell shares of their company for several years. The median time to IPO for a startup was 7.7 years in 2017. That gives early employees a strong incentive to increase the value of the company, stick with a company, and think long term. Similar to equity, early employees at an ICO typically get a % of the total supply vested over time, and the founders often take a significant portion. It is not uncommon for employees to have their salary paid in tokens as well. However, in contrast to traditional startups, the time from company creation to token listing is significantly shorter. It was entirely reasonable for projects to have liquid markets for their tokens within a year of creation. That means employees have less incentive to stay long term, are less long term focused, and have the ability to sell their tokens and exit with some cash, albeit without their full vesting, at any point.

The Shifting Landscape:

Most Healthcare ICO's have built a redemptive ecosystem (like BitMed or MedRec) with a utility token to incentivize providers to encourage and patients to engage, in healthy behaviors. The hope is that a well-informed, activated patient will reduce the morbidity associated with chronic diseases like hypertension, diabetes, obesity, alcohol and substance abuse and consequently lower healthcare costs.

However benefits from behavior modification through rewards is complex, incentivizing health may actually result in increases in healthcare utilization and most wellness programs have struggled with ROI. For example a Rand Corporation report found that among 600,000 employees 87% who participated in wellness programs generated only 13% of healthcare cost savings, whereas inversely, 13% of employees who were in disease management programs were responsible for 87% of the savings (below).

Not surprisingly savings from disease management programs were $136 per member per month (pm/pm) and significantly higher than the $6 pm/pm generated from wellness programs (Source)

Security tokens on the other hand are digitized financial instruments that represent ownership in an asset (like stocks and bonds) and can be exchanged securely and instantaneously using blockchain technology.

Their advantage, beyond embedding legal and regulatory compliance into the token, is that a security token brings fractional ownership that can be traded 24/7 without intermediaries on a secondary platform (e.g. Open Finance Network, Templum). In addition, these tokens are trustless (no need for third party verification) and liquid.

Therefore security tokens add an unrecognized incentive where patients also own the very same health solution they engage with, in order to stay healthy. Thus they become committed to the success of their company with their community of other patient-investors ('skin in the game').

Most Investors have not yet recognized the impact of an engaged community on Crypto-companies. (For an excellent review on the value of security tokens please read Lou Kerner: Prepare Yourself! The Security Token Tsunami Is About To Hit)

Looking Forward

Healthcare ICOs were in a bubble these past two years. The question is if in retrospect this bubble is more akin to the dot.com bubble or tulip mania. In the case of tulip mania, the masses' hysteria drove prices skyward in a speculative bubble with nothing to show for it. In contrast, the dot.com bubble, like the railroad bubble centuries prior, was ignited by a fundamental technological revolution leading to an overflow of money scrambling to get into new business schemes. Markets inevitably overheated and crashed, but because of these bubbles money was invested in crucial infrastructure that created a foundation for the future.

So if Healthcare ICOs boomed and busted, what can the next generation of healthcare ICOs do better?

First, there needs to be more accountability. ICOs across the board have been able to raise millions of dollars, oftentimes with significant portions from retail investors, and were able to do so with very little consumer protection for those retail investors. They then operate with relatively little oversight and, as described earlier, may take self-interested actions that are against token holder's interests with near impunity. This has to change.

A step towards this change could be simple disclosure forms. Teams should each fill out a standard document clearly disclosing the total token supply, if and how that supply can be inflated, how many tokens were sold in a pre-sale, to whom, and at what discount, how many tokens they own, how many tokens their advisors will be paid, how many aren't being sold but are controlled by the company, and the vesting schedules for that.

Furthermore, teams should release audits of their treasury, both the funds raised and the potential tokens a team is sitting on. How teams deploy these funds has a material impact on the value of their token, and disclosures would help keep teams accountable. To my knowledge, no healthcare ICO has done this. Aragon is a great example of a project being open and transparent. Decred, a self-described "autonomous digital currency," has gone a step beyond just transperency and decided to let their token holders control just over $20,000,000 worth of their cryptocurrency that their treasury control. It remains to be seen whether this experiment in collective decision making at scale is good for the value of a network.

Second, projects need to be more thoughtful about governance. There has been a rush to launch decentralized networks in every healthcare vertical, but few stop to consider what happens after these networks are brought to life. What stakeholders do I need on a network to make it work? Will they actually use this network? How will changes to the network be made? What happens if there are bad actors? In the case of a permissioned ledger, who has what permissions? Will you have enough computers on this network to ensure its security? These are some of the questions projects will be asking themselves when they seek to implement their solutions in real life, and I suspect these questions might render projects commercially unsuccessful as well.

Third, the next generation of healthcare ICOs will need to create innovative and new token designs. The popular model of using a token as payment for goods and services within a closed ecosystem has not been successful at creating value or driving consumer adoption. No one, in any industry, has cracked the code of how to create long term sustainable value for their token. But in order to compete today with traditional solutions, or blockchain solutions without their won cryptocurrency, ICOs will need the extra edge that theoretically comes with a token that creates network effects and drives users' engagement.

Lastly, healthcare ICOs need to be realistic about the nascent state of blockchain technology and the change they will be able to affect. Tackling the biggest problems in healthcare all at once is admirable, but not the best way to build a successful product. Nor is blockchain technology or cryptocurrency a solution to all of those problems. The next generation of healthcare ICOs needs to think critically about whether an ICO is prudent, if blockchain technology should be used, how they can demonstrate value, and how their project can scale.

Security Tokenization & the Decentralization of Healthcare

John McCorvey

Security Token Offerings (STOs) and Digital Security Offerings (DSOs) represent a transformative shift in the healthcare industry in terms of capital markets transactions, investment opportunities and incentives, regulatory compliance, health plans, healthcare costs, patient incentives, and patient control over their own healthcare records and data.

STOs are beginning to have a material impact on various enterprises and components within the healthcare supply chain, including hospitals, third party administrators, physician practices, pharmacies, pharmacy benefit managers, to labs, health plans and insurance companies. Gross conflicts of interests have been created through mergers between pharmacy benefit managers and insurance companies, hospitals and TPAs, physician staffing companies and health systems. In each of these more-centralized situations, patients are increasingly at a disadvantage in terms of quality of healthcare service, increased costs, reduction of healthcare service options, as well as control over their own healthcare data.

Decentralization of the healthcare industry is essential for reducing healthcare costs and improving the lives of patients. Blockchain technology deployed through digital security offerings, coupled with smart contracts and embedded patient incentive programs, is beginning to break the monopolistic control of healthcare industry by these market participants. The deployment of STOs in healthcare allows for the removal of gross conflicts of interests, the removal of which would serve to drive healthcare costs significantly lower.

There exists a unique opportunity in healthcare to benefit from blockchain technology and digital securitization. This confluence of technology and economic incentives helps providers, patients and intermediaries with transparency, cost management and data sharing. However, a healthcare data standard protocol needs to be established as this is critical to these processes. The further development of the Healthcare Information eXchange (HIX) protocal into blockchain systems, similar to the Financial Information eXchange (FIX) protocol in securities transactions, is key in providing a uniform standard and protocol for the healthcare data across blockchains and institutions utilizing blockchain technology and digital securities.

For the first time, patients can be in control of their own healthcare data, their own health, and can be rewarded for medication adherence, as well as for good diet and exercise, all through Health Insurance Portability and Accountability Act (HIPAA) compliant healthcare platforms. Patients can now decide to share their healthcare data with researchers, hospitals, drug companies, and other market participants in order to assist with and support clinical trials and other medical studies.

Creating a sense of community and openness in terms of healthcare data is key to reducing growing healthcare costs. This system will allow healthcare data to be securely shared in real time and various applications can be automated. This aspect alone would have a tremendous impact on healthcare costs by improving communication, research, data analytics, and ultimately diagnosis, patient care and treatment.

In the United States, the Department of Health & Human Services (HHS) laid out a goal of converting 30 percent of all fee-for-service Medicare payments to value-based payment models by the end of 2016, and the agency anticipates 50 percent of traditional payments to make the transition by the end of 2018. Value-based care is a reimbursement system that ties payments for care delivery to the quality of care provided. It also rewards providers for efficiency and effectiveness. VBC has emerged as an alternative and potential replacement for fee-for-service (FFS) reimbursement model, which pays providers for services delivered based on bill charges or annual fee schedules.

The VBC model is groundbreaking, as never before have various healthcare market participants and supply chain members been required to coordinate care in such a manner and follow their patients outside of the clinic. The VBC model holds organizations accountable for cost control and the quality of the healthcare service provided.

Clearly a superior model versus FFS, the VBC reimbursement model can be easily integrated into a blockchain-based solution via smart contracts and a tokenized system of rewards for all stakeholders, including patients, physicians, healthcare providers, hospitals, insurance companies and others. This system relies on trust, accessibility, immutability of shared data, and transparency, which speaks directly to the need for utilizing blockchain technology. Blockchain technology, through STOs/DSOs, are now having a major impact on insurance underwriting and costs as patient care improves, patients recover quicker, and as patients as a whole become healthier in general.

STOs/DSOs are a catalyst for the decentralization of the healthcare industry, and they are revolutionizing the definition of patient care and control.

-John McCorvey, CEO Blockchain Financial Group & Blockchain Venture Studios

Blockchain Financial Group is a diversified blockchain technology and financial services company. Blockchain Venture Studios provides structuring and deployment of Security Token Offerings (STOs), Digital Security Offerings (DSOs) and Tokenized Investment Funds (TIFs).

View on Investing in Blockchain

Devin Carty

The first decision we had to make around investing in blockchain is three-fold…

- Do we believe in the technology?

- Do we believe the technology is going to be around for an elongated period of time?

- Do we believe the technology will make a positive impact on the healthcare ecosystem (i.e., are there tangible use cases)?

Our answer for all three is, yes. We believe a technology is real. We believe that the technology will be around for a while. And, we believe there are plenty of tangible use cases where the blockchain technology and the distributed ledger can make meaningful improvements to the healthcare ecosystem.

To answer these questions, we did a great deal of diligence – white papers, articles, etc. One interview that I particularly enjoyed was the with Ben Horowitz at Disrupt SF 2018. In summary, he articulated that there is a massive amount of developer activity targeted at blockchain. There hasn't been this much developer activity since the launch of the internet. A new computing platform comes around ever decade or two (mainframes, PCs, smart phones, etc.), but most importantly, each new computing platform needs to bring something that has never existed before; something that makes it better. For the blockchain technology it's, trust. The idea that you don't need to trust another company, person or people on the network is unique. You just have to trust math, which is what differentiates this computing platform. It allows developers to build things that they could never built before – money, ledgers with contracts, etc. Each of which has the potential to both solve major issues in the current healthcare system and remove waste from middlemen (transfer of data, claims, money, etc.). There is a lack of transparency and trust in the healthcare ecosystem, which creates waste. The blockchain technology and distributed ledger has the opportunity to bring solutions.

Once we answered those more philosophical questions and completed our diligence, the next logical question as an investor is, are we a subject matter expert to make these investment decisions? If so, great, plow forward. If not, how do we find the subject matter expertise to help influence the investment decisions. For each investment, we look at this as an analysis of strengths and weaknesses. For Martin Ventures, we don't pretend to be blockchain experts, but we are experts on healthcare and healthcare operations. We needed to fill our "weakness gap" of subject matter expertise in the blockchain technology to complement our firms' strengths as being subject matter experts in healthcare. The power is in the combination – healthcare expertise and blockchain expertise. We made the decision to partner to build the company Hashed Health.

Hashed Health is the perfect balance of blockchain expertise and healthcare expertise. We invest in Hashed Health, allowing them to make decisions to build, buy or partner around tangible use cases to impact the healthcare ecosystem. I like to think of Hashed Health as the healthcare blockchain venture arm of Martin Ventures; we fund them, and they make the healthcare blockchain investments.

All that said, we don't for a second think this is going to be easy. It's hard to make any startup successful. Blockchain startups have the same headwinds that every other startup has – TAM, unit economics, staying focused, product market fit, finding top talent, competition, revenue, growth, etc., but they also have one more massive headwind, a new technology that most don't understand. That's big hurdle to overcome. Healthcare organizations by their nature are conservative. They are rarely on the forefront of adopting new technology. Each company must prove the value of the blockchain technology far supersedes traditional technology platforms. Then, they need to convince healthcare companies to give up something they hold so dearly, their data. Most healthcare companies believe their intellectual property is in their data, and they are very unwilling to allow anyone to have it. The reality is the data belongs to the consumer. It should be up to the consumer to share their data with whomever they wish to share it with, but that's a completely different topic.

Chapter 18:
My Personal Journey with Blockchain, Healthcare and Estonia

Ruth Amos

https://hashedhealth.com/blockchain-for-healthcare-book/

Editor's Note:

In this chapter, Ruth Amos accounts her journey towards blockchain from a critical care nursing perspective. She has an incredible background coming from Estonia, a country that's trying to go completely digital and using the blockchain technology as a smart government. In the near future, Estonia's health data may be connected to a blockchain implementation on the scale of a country.

I am often asked how I became so obsessed with blockchain and what it can do to vastly improve healthcare. My story is a mix of curiosity, frustration and Divine Providence. It also includes ancestry; I come from a long line of Estonians who have produced, according to WIRED and others, the most advanced digital society in the world- and it runs on blockchain.

Curiosity

My story in healthcare began as a Registered Nurse in Critical Care. I enjoyed helping patients return to health and was always interested in finding ways to optimize the latest treatments. A large part of that curiosity was with the new (at that time) ways of monitoring and tracking vital signs and other parameters, such as Intercranial and Left Ventricular pressures. In my experience, continuous access to this additional data was instrumental in being able to bring a patient from a critical state to a stable one.

Frustration

As I progressed in nursing, I noticed the healthcare market heading in a direction that directly impacted patient care and treatment decisions. With the advent of HMOs and DRGs, there was a noticeable shift in how patients were admitted, treated and discharged. Physicians seemed more stressed and hospital administrators appeared several times daily to check unit status, crunch numbers and dictate next steps for us. I found myself keeping a journal to vent my frustrations with this new and uncertain system and vowed to somehow make a difference one day.

The vow and frustration manifested themselves in my next career move: law. I was determined to find ways to master current laws and regulations and seek changes that would restore healthcare delivery to a more civilized profession. I continued working in Critical Care as a Nurse and attended law school at night on the four- year plan. It was grueling, but I was young and didn't pay attention to the crazy schedule much- I was on a mission.

After law school, I attempted the traditional legal path as a duly licensed attorney, which was really the only viable option at that time. My frustrations grew when I discovered that the changes I sought were hard won and afar off. It seemed the US was not ready to embrace the changes that I knew in my soul were necessary to mend what was breaking in healthcare before my eyes. My frustration with the healthcare system was soon outweighed by my frustration with the legal and legislative systems. My total frustration level was significant and unsustainable- I had to find another way to tackle these issues.

Divine Providence

The answer, ironically, was that I chose to return to the hospital and work at the bedside caring for patients. Since I have no children of my own, I decided to work in Neonatal ICU (NICU), which satisfied my maternal instincts while giving me the opportunity to help heal the most fragile population in healthcare. It felt good to be back doing good, but I still had the nagging feeling I was meant to do more. Nursing documentation was an interesting combination of digital and paper workflows that in no way coordinated care, nor protected patient identity. Physician orders and labs were on paper and faxing was the way of communicating between departments. It was a common practice at the time and required constant diligence to prevent errors.

One fateful day, I was working in the NICU alongside a nurse who had similar frustrations. She had been a Chief Nursing Officer at several major hospitals and found herself working beside me, voicing the same concerns. We had fun venting and coming up with new ideas of how healthcare needed to be. After a long morning, I excused myself to take a break and walked toward the Nurses Lounge. When I arrived at the door, it was open with yellow caution tape blocking the entrance. The place was a disaster area with sewer water spewing from the ceiling- like a tsunami, only from above.

I stood frozen at the doorway of the Lounge like I was in a trance, watching two brave men from the Engineering Department attempt to tackle this mess. One man held a large bucket to catch the smelly liquid avalanche; he then dumped it in a nearby sink where we usually washed our dishes and hands. This process was repeated over and over in a futile attempt to stem the flooding on the floor which was already about 3 inches deep. The second man was wearing a HAZMAT (Hazardous Materials) suit and stood on a ladder, trying to locate the leaks in the plumbing system and repair them. Once he had managed to find a few of the broken areas of pipe and stem the flow, the scene improved immediately. There was still a long way to go to create a clean environment, where turning on the sink faucet would deliver clean water and flushing the adjoining bathroom toilets would sweep away unwanted waste.

After watching the scene at the Lounge doorway for several minutes, I walked away with what I consider to this day to be a Divine Epiphany that changed the direction of my life in amazing ways. In my mind, I saw the tsunami of sewer water coming from the ceiling as healthcare data. It's coming at us at lightning speed with no way of detecting what is good and useful information from what is unnecessary. The result is that healthcare providers and clinicians are left with the job of the guy with the bucket. We take whatever is poured into our view and dump it into the nearest convenient portal to get on with our next task of caring for sick patients. There is no time to filter out what is useful from what is not, and the result is a continuation of the disaster with perhaps a temporary band aid to stem the flooding. I knew as long as I stayed at the bedside working as a nurse, I would be the bucket guy.

In my healthcare data vision, the second man on the ladder was who I needed to be. He was, in my mind, performing the critical work of finding ways to securely direct data to its proper place in the ecosystem to provide the desired outcomes. This understanding was pivotal in my next decision to become intimately involved in health informatics and EHR deployment. Within a month of this epiphany, I had packed my belongings and moved 400 miles away to begin my next adventure- a large EHR deployment at a major Children's Hospital. A year later, I was privileged to be a leader on an amazingly talented team in Kaiser Permanente's massive deployment of EPIC- the largest civilian database in history. Fortunately, I remembered to pack my virtual HAZMAT suit- it was a wild ride!

The Estonia Blockchain Connection

One day in 2013, I was bored and decided to enter a silly quiz I found on Facebook. A relative of mine from Estonia had posted it- the Estonian Foreign Ministry Department decided it would be great to offer a free trip to Estonia for one lucky winner who could answer some trivia questions about the country. All the online entries would be placed in a big bin, each on a small piece of paper- ironic for a totally digital country, but the visual effect helped with publicity. The Foreign Minister would spin the bin and select one entry to win the grand prize. It was a global contest so all countries were able to participate. I entered online, then promptly forgot and told no one.

A few months later, I was casually clearing out my spam email box when I spotted the following message:

> For this year the Estonia Quiz is over and according to the results of the draw taken place on May 29th in the Ministry of Foreign Affairs of Estonia I am very pleased to inform you that you have won the main prize of the quiz http://quiz.mfa.ee/2013.
>
> Congratulations!
>
> Once more congratulations for your win and we hope to see you in Estonia this summer!
>
> Best regards
>
> Department of Public Diplomacy
>
> Estonian Ministry of Foreign Affairs

At first I was confused- was this some kind of email scam? Then I remembered that I actually did enter this particular contest! I quickly confirmed that it was real by calling the Embassy and the Foreign Affairs Department. Out of 16,000 entries from 126 countries I was the single grand prize winner selected- I took it as a sign. After a flurry of emails and calls to get time off work (by this time I was working on a huge IT project for EY), I jetted off to meet my Estonian relatives in person- most of them for the first time. Although I was raised by my Estonian grandmother in the US, this was the first time I was able to actually visit the country. It was a red carpet fantastic event, and I'm forever grateful to the Estonian Foreign Ministry for hosting my first trip there.

For those not familiar with Estonia, it is a curious little country that was occupied by Hitler and Stalin for many years. The regaining of its independence in the early '90's was no small feat, and the Estonian people have been fiercely defending that independence by creating the most advanced digital society known to mankind. Estonia leads cybersecurity for NATO, and its government records were placed online almost 20 years ago. The New Yorker said it well in an article describing how data is configured there: "Data aren't centrally held, reducing the chance of Equifax-level breaches. Instead, the government's data platform, the X-Road, links individual servers through end-to-end encrypted pathways, letting information live locally. Your dentist's practice holds its own data; so does your high school and your bank. When a user requests a piece of information, it is delivered like a boat crossing a canal via locks."

Blockchain and the Way Forward

After years of EHR optimization attempts, we are still afar off in the US from interoperability and useful data- I've been feeling my old frustrations beginning to resurface. We are inching ahead, but there is still much to do.

Since 2013, I've returned to Estonia numerous times to visit family and to learn more about how the country set up this fantastic way of handling data. I have been extremely fortunate through influential relatives there to have seen intimate one on one demonstrations of how this was accomplished. They literally have it wired! In 2015 through a series of new laws, I became a citizen of Estonia with a passport and digitalized ID card. As a dual citizen of the US and Estonia, I'm told by my attorney this is allowed unless I run for government office in either country.

As of 2014, those not qualifying for citizenship can become an "e-resident" under a program that allows anyone who passes required background checks, etc. from across the globe to do business from Estonia remotely- building a true borderless society. Soon Estonia may be launching its own version of cryptocurrency, dubbed the "ESTCOIN"- stay tuned!

An interesting article that explains how and why Estonia became a global leader in blockchain technology looks at it from a survival perspective, which rings true, considering its history:

"One of the key events behind Estonia's current position as a leader in blockchain was their being the target of a cyber attack in 2007. In retrospect, this attack was somewhat inevitable. In the 1990s, Estonia rushed to join NATO and the EU, to some extent pitting itself against former Russian leadership. Following a controversial decision to remove a Soviet Statue from a Tallinn park, the Estonian parliament and several public services suddenly went offline in one of the biggest-ever DOS attacks. Most concluded the attack came from Russia. This was a wakeup call for a country already heavily invested in building/using digital infrastructure, and it made them consider more carefully the security implications of the technology they were

implementing."

As I learned more about Estonia's path forward, I began to explore how the US healthcare system could benefit from blockchain. Estonia has successfully incorporated blockchain on government systems since 2012, and on health records specifically since 2015. If this tiny country can do it, why can't we do something great here in the US?

The year 2018 has been instrumental in paving blockchain use in healthcare into almost every aspect of my life and career. The following are some examples of my current associations and activities in this space. I strongly encourage anyone interested in making healthcare better to become involved:

- **HIMSS:** As a long-time member of HIMSS on their Legal Task Force, I saw the need to connect with the new HIMSS Blockchain Task Force to collaborate on a regular basis. We are now starting monthly calls together that I believe are critical to the future of how blockchain will be implemented in the US.

- **BiHG:** I am a co-founder and Board Member of Blockchain in Healthcare Global ("BiHG"), a new trade association launching soon, formed under the IEEE ISTO (see https://ieee-isto.org/) by a multidisciplinary team of industry leaders in blockchain and healthcare. Our mission is to mitigate risks and barriers to adoption of blockchain and converging innovations (AI, IoMT, etc.) in healthcare and the life and social sciences while advancing progress in scientific replicability, medical ethics, human rights, and global inclusion.

- **GBA:** The Government Blockchain Association (GBA) has several verticals including healthcare and is launching some interesting pilots in various parts of the world. A current ongoing pilot is using blockchain to match blood and organ donors to appropriate recipients.

- **Private projects:** I am fortunate to be involved in several private blockchain projects with consortia across the globe that I believe are extremely valuable in advancing healthcare and improving lives.

The road ahead is long and filled with much promise. I plan to be very active in seeking ways to promote industry self-regulation and legislative action to help pave the way for blockchain to fulfill its vast potential in healthcare. Please join me!

Chapter 19:
Three Public Health Use Cases the Blockchain Can Solve

Patricia Buendia[1],
Amin El-Gazzar[1],
Lorenzo Delzoppo[1],
Giri Narasimhan[1,2]

https://hashedhealth.com/blockchain-for-healthcare-book/

Editor's Note:

In this chapter, Patricia Buendia, Amin El-Gazzar, Lorenzo Delzoppo, and Giri Narasimhan present three compelling use cases related to CDC Disease Surveilance, opiod risk, and tracking of connected health technologies for cancer survivors. The use cases present system architecture, user-interface, and blockchain data structures that are part of a solution set using the Cygned token. Like the Estonia examples from the previous chapter, there is strong potential for blockchain to help US government health organizations like the CDC as well.

1   **Cygned, Inc.**

2   Florida International University

Introduction

The potential effectiveness of blockchain-based HIPAA-compliant protected health information storage presents crucial opportunities for public health, especially in the areas of disease surveillance and prevention. In July 2017, the American Research and Policy Institute published a review article arguing that public health programs such as the U.S. Medicaid program could benefit from the use of a Blockchain based distributed ledger and smart contracts [1]. A year later, the first US federal project announcements are coming in. In late 2018 it was announced that IBM and the US Centers for Disease Control (CDC) were teaming up to build a blockchain and cloud-based data system that could track public health issues including opioid addiction [2]. Also in 2018, it was announced that US Congressman David Schweikert and Majority Leader Kevin McCarthy introduced legislation to support Valley Fever infection research using multiparty encryption computing and blockchain technology [3]. Other governments started public health initiatives earlier, as is the case with Estonia which in 2016 partnered up with Estonian-founded, Amsterdam-based software security company Guardtime to implement a blockchain-based management system of patient healthcare records on the national level [4]. In a 2018 partnership with the same company, the British National Health Service is offering 30 million patients instant access to their primary care information [5]. In 2017, trade giant Alibaba announced the collaboration with Chinese authorities from the government of Changzhou city in East China's Jiangsu province to launch a pilot program securing and sharing healthcare data in the blockchain [6].

In this chapter, we will take a deeper look at three blockchain-based public health care use cases that Cygned, Inc designed for the CDC, the National Institute on Drug Abuse (NIDA), and the National Cancer Institute (NCI) respectively. The solutions are based on a blockchain for healthcare business model that focuses on personalized medicine and involves empowering people to take ownership of their health data by securely storing and managing it in the blockchain. Personalized medicine is a medical model that considers people to be unique individuals deserving of medical decisions, practices, interventions or products being tailored to them based on their predicted response or risk of disease. The prediction is possible with new technologies such as artificial intelligence (AI) that will study a person's unique lifetime medical data to train the prediction models. An enduring challenge in making personalized medicine become a reality is the lack of access to the complete medical records of a person. Presently, health data is stored in isolated silos, i.e. databases or electronic health records (EHR) systems from the different doctors and hospitals that a person has visited over a lifetime, or in databases from the wearable technologies, sensors and genetic testing services the person uses. In particular, the genome sequence data of a person, which is stored and owned by the company that provided the service, is currently being used to make millions of Dollars in profit by selling it for research without any profit sharing with the individuals who paid to have their genome sequenced [7]. By law, people have access to all their health data while others need to ask for permission to access it. The blockchain for healthcare model can solve the limitations of the current isolated health information infrastructure by handing over the keys of the health data records to the patients and individuals described by the data. In this model, different stakeholders can access the data for different uses with the individuals' authorization through a blockchain health information exchange (BHIE) system, with the original health care providers keeping a copy of the data they produced. The most common use cases are listed below and involve two-directional data sharing in which stakeholders access data but also store data or predictions in the blockchain. For cases when additional data is generated from a patient or individual, the data gets deposited in the person's secure, private and anonymized blockchain space. An individual's data can be accessed by any stakeholder with the individual's permission through the BHIE system in exchange for cryptocurrency compensation in the form of tokens, or in exchange of additional health data, health guidelines, or predictions stored into the blockchain space of that person:

- In disease surveillance, public health agencies with a subscription to the BHIE access lab tests and self-surveys uploaded periodically to the blockchain to monitor, and prevent new outbreaks. In exchange, individuals get tokens or health advisories.

- Research Institutes or pharmaceutical companies with a subscription to the BHIE train or generate personalized medicine prediction models using a privacy-aware artificial intelligence platform without direct access to the data. In exchange, individuals get tokens, or access to the models for health self-monitoring.

- A doctor, hospital or caregiver with a subscription to the BHIE accesses the medical history of a patient, or accesses predictions from a trained machine learning model for a better diagnosis and personalized treatment plan. In exchange, patients get tokens, and get the diagnosis or treatment plan stored in their personal blockchain data repository.

- Pharmacies access drug abuse predictions for a person with a subscription to the BHIE. In exchange, individuals get tokens, and get the history of prescriptions from the pharmacy stored in their personal blockchain data repository.

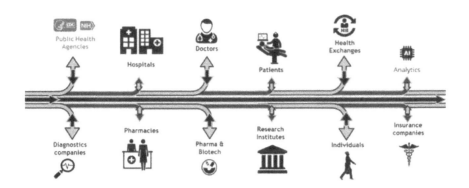

Figure 19.1: Health Ecosystem with a health information exchange that serves different stakeholders in which public health agencies can be an active driving force of innovation

The blockchain for healthcare business model has sprouted many startups in the last four years. The early adopters of this business model focused on developing a product that is an alternative to Electronic Health's record (EHR) systems. Patientory was founded in 2015 in Georgia, USA, and is building an EHR exchange system with patient participation in which storage and exchange of EHR data occurs between patients and physicians [8]. Similar companies with a focus on EHR exchange systems are Medical Chain, a London startup, founded in 2017 [9], Medcredits, a Michigan startup founded in 2016 and renamed to MedX [10], and Coral Health, a Canadian company founded in 2017 [11]. Although Coral Health has not announced any definite collaborations, it is promoting public health solutions in its web site to "improve disease surveillance and monitoring with real-time alerts on potential disease trends and outbreaks". Other companies, such as Gem Health and PokitDok, which were founded in 2016 and 2017 respectively, focus on developing and marketing "middleware" technologies that can be used for blockchain-based EHR exchange systems [12, 13]. Other companies such as Medibloc [14], MedChain [15], AI Crypto [16], focus on building a health-AI ecosystem allowing software engineers to access their API and SDK to exchange data with the platform and drive innovations though new health applications such as data-intensive AI and deep learning. In the next sections we will discuss how the products and technologies developed by these companies can be molded to serve public healthcare needs. A fourth group of blockchain for healthcare startups, Nebula Genomics [17], Luna DNA [18], Zenome [19], Encrypgen [20], and doc.ai [21] are looking into the far future of medicine in which individuals get their genome and possibly also their microbiome or metagenome sequenced, or get metabolomics and other omics screening tests done through home lab solutions for system biology prediction analysis. As the omics science is still new and quality standards for the data are still being explored [22–25], these solutions do not have immediate application for current public healthcare use cases. Other health-related applications, such as monitoring and keeping falsified and counterfeit drugs out of the drug market, processing insurance claims, among several others, are relevant to public health, but do not directly apply to the three use cases presented here.

In the next sections we will present three public health use cases and the technology that will support the implementation of a solution for all three use cases. Several public health use cases have been proposed recently with an implementation that relies on a DApp prototype that emulates a minimal version of a personal EHR system [26]. The use cases presented here are different in their scope and implementation. The implementation centers on a blockchain health data repository that is managed by the patient or individual who owns the data. Next, we will introduce the three use cases, the requirements of the system that addresses them, the high-level design of the blockchain architecture, the design of all the needed technological components, of the user interfaces, the description of the roles of the different stakeholders and their interactions with the system, and the business and collaboration models that fund the transactions in the system. The objective in developing these new health care technologies is to accelerate innovation and collaboration and to provide a complete solution in which multiple stakeholders look after the well-being of patients, prevent relapse for people with chronic conditions, and prevent disease in healthy individuals. The blockchain technology can enhance current health care efforts and medical practices for public health agencies, the pharma industry, insurances, pharmacies, hospitals, and physicians, and it can also guide individuals in taking charge of their health and get better results with a personalized approach. Both of these objectives go hand in hand and are the guiding force in transforming health care through the use of the blockchain technology.

Three Public Health Care Use Cases

CDC Disease Surveillance

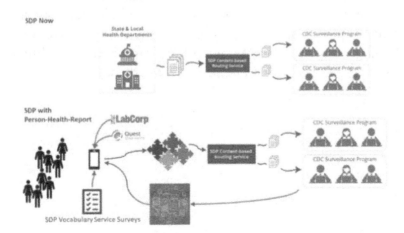

Figure 19.2: Flowcharts showing (1) SDP health data transfer now, and (2) a blockchainbased method using Person Health Self-Reports

Predicting Risk for Opioid Use Disorder

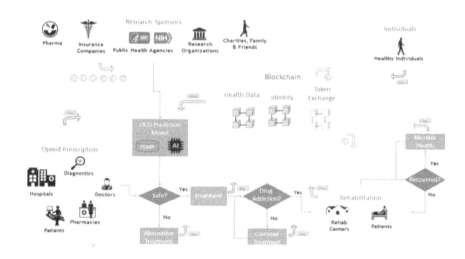

Figure 19.3: Flowchart showing a collaborative complete solution that focuses on the well-being of individuals affected by the opioid crisis and on protecting healthy individuals from succumbing to the epidemic

The flowchart in Figure 19.3 shows a collaborative complete solution that focuses on the well-being of individuals affected by the opioid crisis and on protecting healthy individuals from succumbing to the epidemic shows a collaborative complete solution that will be best accomplished in parts. These parts intersect with the disease surveillance use case and the health monitoring of cancer survivors use case in that the technology can be reused and adapted to opioid addiction. In this solution, individuals and patients store health data in the blockchain in exchange for tokens or treatment. Research sponsors pay tokens for evidence-based treatments in exchange for data to augment the PDMP database and train predictive models. Evidence of success is assessed based on patient's data (e.g. lab results) and psychological screeners. The blockchain can then support safe and appropriate treatment prescriptions using evidence-based technologies as a key component of a comprehensive public health approach to the crisis of opioid misuse, addiction, and overdose.

Connected Health Technologies for Cancer Survivors

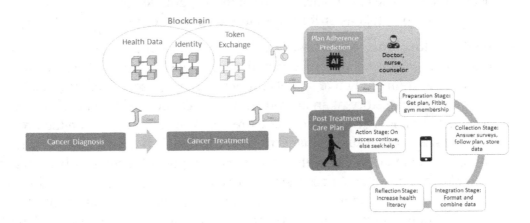

Figure 19.4: Flowchart showing activation of cancer survivors to follow a survivorship care plan

System Requirements

The use cases presented here use the blockchain-based personalized model of healthcare to solve urgent public health needs. The design of the system needs to support the following requirements in order to address the needs of all stakeholders:

- **Secure and Standarized Safe Data Storage:** The validated medical data is stored either "on-chain" in a blockchain environment or "off-chain" in the cloud and managed through a database engine. The reason for splitting up the data this way is the complexity and size of the medical records, especially medical images, genome sequence data, and unstructured data like physician notes or reports. Data integration is a particular problem when merging data from different providers, even in the case of structured data such as pharmacy prescriptions and laboratory test results. Such data is downloaded in a spreadsheet/table format from a patient portal system, but the codes used by each provider often link to different vocabulary systems and are not easily standardized.

- **Secure Data Sharing with Identity Management:** In a public health data exchange model, the security of the data and of the transaction is more imperative than in the case of sharing of data between patient and a physician which is a common process. Validated medical data for an individual can be deposited by the owner, usually the individual himself or herself, into an anonymized health data repository within a blockchain environment to allow for data sharing in exchange of receiving a personal health benefit or compensation. Such a blockchain health exchange needs to offer a well-tested paradigm for ensuring security, privacy and anonymity in a trustless environment. A decentralized identity management approach is a critical component of the underlying blockchain and cryptography technologies necessary to support the vision of self-sovereign identity. Through access to this identity management system, the data owner will be able to confidently decide with whom to share what component of his/her anonymized health record. The data owner will be able to negotiate anonymously for compensation in tokens or for access to the benefits of the analysis/diagnosis.

- **High-Performance Analytics:** The validated medical data once stored in a blockchain environment can be shared anonymously with healthcare analytics software to train predictive models for developing personalized treatments based on the medical history of an individual. Graphics processing unit (GPU) devices are most commonly used for cryptocurrency mining which rely on the Proof of Work (PoW) consensus mechanism. GPUs have also become a hot commodity for the AI and machine learning space. The analytics strategy involves creating a blockchain-powered AI ecosystem where the "mining" participants share their hardware-based computing power and other resources in exchange for rewards provided in the form of tokens. AI researchers will then be able to use these high-performance GPU resources to come up with innovative research models.

- **Rewards:** Individuals will have the incentive of free access to their own blockchain repository of health data allowing them to compile a complete medical history that they have the ability to review or share with their physicians. Moreover, when individuals share data with an AI engine to build predictive machine learning models or share metadata used in aggregate statistics with public health agencies or researchers at academia or the pharma industry, they will be rewarded in one of two ways:

  □ with cryptocurrency tokens

  □ with access to a free app that is used to either self-monitor one's health or monitor the public health landscape through health advisories

System Architecture

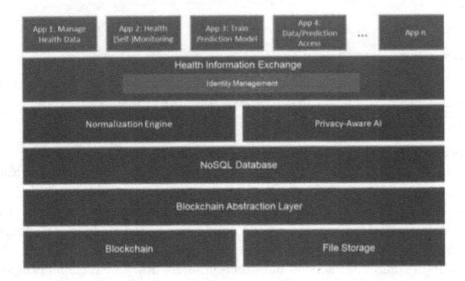

Figure 19.5: Generic system architecture serving the requirements for current public health needs

A proposed system architecture is shown in Figure 19.5 for a platform which addresses current public health needs and makes personalized predictions from medical history records stored in a securely encrypted form in a publicly accessible blockchain. The components of the system are designed with a focus on security of health data in which each component interfaces with another in such a way that privacy of data is preserved. Most of the functionality in the blockchain will be related to securing the record of a transaction, maintaining the immutability of the smart contracts, gather data for health management, monitor health for predictive treatments, and for the use of machine learning/ AI. The architecture shown in Figure 5 is comprised of five layers:

1. A blockchain-based data repository with a cloud-based file storage securely stores all patient's health information as well as immutable records of any third-party access to the data.

2. A blockchain abstraction layer allows for seamless access of the data in the blockchain, independent of the implementation of the blockchain, which in this case is a hybrid public/private blockchain.

3. A database engine stores and retrieves data from the blockchain as if it were a traditional database.

4. A normalization and a privacy-aware analytics layer serves the user interfaces.

5. A health information exchange with an identity management system provides access to the system

6. A user interface layer with several components serve different types of users.

Three classes of end-user roles are expected to interact with the system in the public health use cases:

1. Individuals, including patients

2. Researchers training the models

3. All others: Healthcare providers, insurance companies, pharmacies, or public health agencies, which can be research sponsors or treatment sponsors

The proposed implementation uses a hybrid Ethereum and Hyperledger architecture. The Enterprise Ethereum Alliance and Hyperledger group announced a new collaborative framework which will bring together permissioned blockchains and open/public blockchains facilitating the type of hybrid architecture proposed here with improved standardization among the open source projects [54]. The encrypted identity of all the stakeholders is stored in the Ethereum blockchain. Tokens are created through smart contracts on the Ethereum network. The metadata is stored on the Hyperledger blockchain whereas the actual individual's health data is stored in a cloud-based data storage, using cloud-based encryption.

Identity Management

A blockchain identity verification technology has to be integrated into the system architecture to allow individuals to take control of their digital identity and to secure and protect personal information transfer. Identity management is built on top of an identity & trust management framework usually provided by a biometric identity management system like Civic [38] or similar which records a set of biometric identifiers to establish a person's digital identity. The goal is to allow anyone to establish a unique and powerful digital identity within a global blockchain ecosystem to shift the power and control over that identity to the person rather than a centralized organization. With such a system, the individuals truly own, control and manage their personal data and control who they will grant access to that data. This is especially true for health records. No third party has the key needed to decrypt any portion of the identity. Beyond the digital identifiers, the system also manages claims about a person. Claims are assigned to 3 different levels of confidence: (1) Claims made by trusted third parties (eg. physicians), (2) Claims made by untrusted claimants, (3) claims persons make about themselves. The confidence level for (2) and (3) is naturally low, but can be boosted by the person requesting trusted third parties to warrant their claim according to a compensation scheme. In such a decentralized identification system, verification of claims is carried out collectively by the network.

In a healthcare setting, every efficient identity management system must fulfill three requirements. First it must provide an irrefutable way to confirm one's identity, second it must allow an immutable and secure way of storing personal information including health records, and third it must provide an efficient way for an individual to grant access to that personal data as needed. A public blockchain like Ethereum is used for identity management. All three requirements need to be fulfilled in the public health uses cases proposed here through a self-sovereign identity-management system that streamlines the collection of personal health & lifestyle information by individuals who own the data and have financial, research-oriented or health-oriented objectives.

Health Information Exchange

A Blockchain Health Information Exchange (BHIE) is implemented as a data exchange API that uses cryptography algorithms to enable secure and protected information flow between different apps and the blockchain decentralized layer. A cryptography protocol manages and protects data access. The BHIE enables collection and exchange of data by merely providing the network infrastructure without owning or controlling access to the data. Only individuals who own the data can assign rights to access that data. It is thus tightly integrated with the identity management system that allows individuals to securely share their health data for various health-care oriented objectives, among them health research, health monitoring, screening algorithms, disease diagnosis, predictions or aggregate information shared with public health agencies or other healthcare providers.

In the proposed system any patient data is stored in a securely encrypted form in different types of databases, on-chain, or off-chain. Data is under the exclusive control of the owner of the data, who is the individual. In order for the different stakeholders and apps to be able to access the data and run analytics on the data, a data exchange layer is necessary. The BHIE is best implemented as an object-oriented API that accesses the information that is stored in the underlying datastores. One of the common challenges of a health-related data storage and exchange solution is, on the one hand, the amount of data that is accumulated over time for each patient, and on the other hand, the complexity of the data. A proposed data modeling approach therefore uses classical object-oriented principles for the data, whereas the patient is the main object that is defined through a complex set of data and data relationships.

The BHIE provides the interface between the blockchain based datastore and the interfaces to the different stakeholders. One implementation of the BHIE API runs it as a dApps on top of the Hyperledger blockchain using the native rest API provided for Hyperledger Fiber [39]. The API is implemented using a JSON/JSONB internal datatype modelled after the XQuery v1 and XPath v3 standards.

On the smart contract front, Hyperledger supports the use of existing programming languages and new smart contract specific languages such as Go, Javascript and Java. The transaction processors are pluggable objects that allow to query and modify the blockchain state. They connect to a validator using REST API. The blockchain is supplemented by Intel Software Guard Extensions (SGX) [40] to boost the blockchain's privacy, security and scalability. The system can be described in terms of the assets, participants and transactions that are to be shared in the blockchain network. Assets are patient health data that can be shared or transacted. Transactions describe what can be done to the assets within the network and are effectively stored procedure calls that are run in the network and whose outputs are agreed upon by the different stakeholders as specified by the BHIE. To query the data in the Hyperledger blockchain, the Block Explorer is used to provide a list of assets of interests. The platform is permission based and the control is always with the individual. The individual is in charge of sharing granular health assets with other BHIE participants, in the public health use cases, it is the CDC, physicians, rehab clinics, and a machine learning engine.

Block Explorer

An indexing tool called the "Block Explorer" queries the blockchain to locate blocks with specific search parameters. Data is accessed by pointers directly, and the granular access control that the individual can exert is thereby limited to the granularity of the pointers. These pointers can be stored in the blockchain for security and quick access. Each new dataset has exactly one pointer, and each pointer is stored in the blockchain. The block explorer is used to find and aggregate the pointers for any given query. If more refined granularity is needed a new dataset is broken up into separate and distinct sets of data that then can be accessed individually. The block explorer API runs as a dApp on Hyperledger and Ethereum blockchains, but in addition it provides a web based interface that allows to run queries and retrieve result metadata without accessing the actual results. This can be useful in answering statistical questions about the available dataset for a given research topic.

Stakeholders

The patient or individual who has data to share is the main user of the system. Each use case has different stakeholders accessing the BHIE:

1. In the CDC use case, the CDC accesses the Person-Health-Reports, self-reported health information answers from surveys designed by the CDC. Lab test results can also be exchanged via the BHIE. The CDC stores public health advisories in the blockchain which are shown to the individuals through a mobile app.

2. In the opioid use disorder (OUD) case, there are multiple stakeholders interested in accessing different types of data. Two machine learning engines will access the patients' data to train the models, one will predict OUD, and the other will predict relapse into addiction. Prescribing physicians and pharmacists will access the OUD prediction and the answers to drug screeners to make an informed decision on the prescriptions. Rehabilitation centers will access the relapse prediction, the self-tracking information and answers to the drug screeners in order to offer guidance and personalized treatment.

3. For the successful self-monitoring of adherence to a cancer survivorship care plan, the survivors may grant access to their physicians to the data and

predictions. A machine learning engine will access the data to train the model. Cancer survivors will use a mobile app to access the predictions if the option is selected. Predictions will be used to personalize reminders and guidance to help users follow the care plan.

Normalization Engine

Medication information is an important facet of a person's medical history, especially for patients being prescribed pain medication in the opioid use case. In the disease surveillance use case, a sudden increase in the prescription of a certain type of medication might be indication of a possible disease outbreak or epidemic. It is also relevant for the cancer survivors' use case. A feature importance analysis will determine the importance of the different types of information for training the survivorship care plan adherence machine learning models. Medication data can be obtained by patients through their EHRs or pharmacy patient portals. Often the history of medications is stored in several pharmacy providers and the codes of the drugs do not align. Data integration processes need to be designed to match drugs to an internal code system which uses RxNorm codes. When codes don't match to RxNorm, the drug name is treated as unstructured free text medication information, and converted into computable drug data, applying a pipeline described previously [41]. As shown in Figure 19.6: Overview of drug mapping from free text information to drug classes., a good choice is to employ the National Library of Medicine's (NLM) RxNorm API to match drug names extracted from

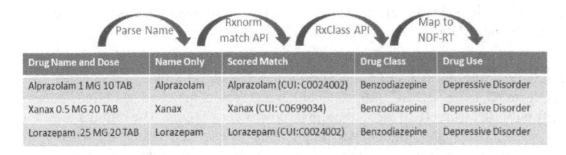

Drug Name and Dose	Name Only	Scored Match	Drug Class	Drug Use
Alprazolam 1 MG 10 TAB	Alprazolam	Alprazolam (CUI: C0024002)	Benzodiazepine	Depressive Disorder
Xanax 0.5 MG 20 TAB	Xanax	Xanax (CUI: C0699034)	Benzodiazepine	Depressive Disorder
Lorazepam .25 MG 20 TAB	Lorazepam	Lorazepam (CUI:C0024002)	Benzodiazepine	Depressive Disorder

Figure 19.6: Overview of drug mapping from free text information to drug classes.

In addition to EHR data, some use cases will require collecting mood, diet, and fitness data, and other kinds of data from sensors or wearables or genome sequencing service providers. The data from mood states, diet and wearables are easier to integrate as they use standard units, such as "number of steps", "miles walked", "calories", and in the case of mood, a mobile app will do self-tracking of mood through standard color-encodings as described in the user interface section.

Privacy-Aware Machine Learning

The design of the machine learning methods, because of the sensitivity of the data, focuses on models that do not require storing the data in a single location in order to train the model. Instead, models will be sequentially and conditionally trained and tested on clusters of data from different sites. Sites are defined by their training data which is clustered by geography, or by storage date, or by type of blockchain, or blockchain database service provider, or through association with a hospital, a rehabilitation center, or other organization. In health research it is imperative to develop a model for data analysis and machine learning that adheres to privacy constraints. The design of the privacy-aware AI engine is based on work done on distributed privacy-preserving machine learning algorithms like EXPLORER [43], and the Distributed Autonomous Online Learning [44] which are "online" machine learning algorithms, and on a blockchain-specific algorithm called ModelChain [45]. Thus, the privacy-aware characteristics of this method rely on predictive modeling by communicating partially-trained machine learned models from one site, without any exchange of patient data from that site. A proof-of-information algorithm is designed on top of the original proof-of-work consensus protocol, to determine the order of the online machine learning on sites, aiming at increasing efficiency and accuracy. The basic idea is similar to the concept of boosting where the site which contains data that cannot be predicted accurately using current partial model probably contains more information to improve the model than other sites, and thus that site is assigned a higher priority to be chosen as the next model-updating site. In the case any site adds new data, for example, a hospital or rehabilitation facility has all its patients join the network, there is no need to re-train the whole model. Instead, the proof-of information is defined again to determine whether the model needs to be updated using the new data.

For this privacy-aware model a standard recurrent neural network (RNN) is trained on different types of medical information such as drug codes matched to RxNorm CUIs or NDF-RT [46, 47] and lab test results matched to LOINC codes [48] with its results (e.g. high, abnormal, positive) as inputs. The outputs used for the supervised training are the known assignments for each individual at each site. In the case of binary classification, the assignment is often a case/control classification. The proof-of information algorithm determines whether the model needs to be updated by running it on number of sites that contain ground truth data, i.e. the known output classification. The efficacy of machine learning algorithms, such as Recurrent Neural Network (RNN) in modeling longitudinal healthcare data has been shown through many state-of-the-art models: RETAIN [49] adopts a temporal attention generation mechanism to learn both visit level and code level weights; GRAM [50] is a graph-based attention model, which uses medical ontologies to handle data insufficiency and combines with an RNN to learn robust representations. Recently, RNNs were used to predict heart failure of patients based on clinical events in their records [51]. The aforementioned models are RNN-based frameworks which use medical codes as inputs to make a binary prediction to decide whether the diagnosis or treatment will recur on a future visit. The privacy-aware RNN model satisfies the requirement that the resulting model reveals no information about the raw data. The supported models will be implemented with Keras [52] and TensorFlow [53] and trained on the high-performance GPU resources provided by miners or trained on an Amazon AWS P2 instance type running multiple GPUs and then ported to the blockchain for predictions or to let the proof-of-information determine whether the models need updating. Pretrained models with trained weights in HDF5 format are deployed to worker nodes using standard Keras and TensorFlow libraries for use on selected sites.

Blockchain Database

Blockchain layers

An initial implementation uses a hybrid Ethereum and Hyperledger architecture. The Ethereum blockchain is used for identity management. The metadata is stored on the Hyperledger blockchain and the health data is stored encrypted in a cloud-based data storage. Future implementations will expand the different blockchain varieties supported by the system, using an interoperability layer that houses the business logic of different blockchains and will connect the major blockchain platforms Ethereum, Hyperledger Fabric, and Quorum.

Off-Chain/On-Chain Solution

The system uses two databases, an on-chain solution for granular transaction data, and an off-chain database where files are stored in a file storage and indexed in a NoSQL database. The off-chain storage includes file storage of raw files with medical history data from a specific time interval from an online EHR portal, and the process of adding a file to the off-chain is recorded as an on-chain transaction to the blockchain. In the initial implementation, especially for the CDC disease surveillance and opioid addiction use cases, the focus is on historic drug prescription data and laboratory test results such as blood and urine screening tests. In order to develop a secure and scalable platform for the healthcare blockchain solution Hyperledger Fabric [39] is chosen as the foundation for the secured distributed blockchain database. For the NoSQL solution a MongoDB database is implemented. A number of databases were considered but MongoDB was the obvious choice as a document database that supports JSON. As described in Figure 19.7: Example showing off-chain and on-chain storage of health data, raw files are stored in a file storage and the contents of the file stored in the NoSQL database as a blob. Next, specific items in the files, the assets, are parsed and normalized, and stored in a hash in the blockchain (on-chain) and also in the NoSQL database. The normalization engine breaks the data apart into individual information items for granularity, then each item is standardized by using the same code system. Each recording of such a granular item in the blockchain, the metadata, such as a lab test code, is called a transaction. Metadata are standardized data fields containing summary information in text form (lab test code, lab test flag) and will be stored off-chain and on-chain, but can only be accessed on-chain. The off-chain database can be accessed through Hyperledger through a hash reference (index) that is stored in the chain in order to add more assets to the Hyperledger blockchain. Users of the system can only access the blockchain through the BHIE, never the off-chain database. The on-chain database is used to create a simple, secure, easily adaptable record that can be accessed by physicians or a machine learning engine through the blockchain. Hyperledger is therefore used as an index to the off-chain database to access and control access rights to information off-chain. Smart contracts are then used for data sharing and for access control.

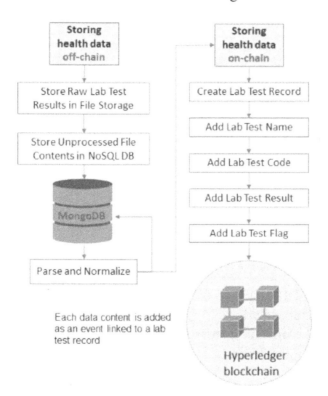

Figure 19.7: Example showing off-chain and on-chain storage of health data

User Interfaces

The user interface layer in the system architecture shown in Figure 19.5 includes mobile and browser interfaces and implements different functionality for the different use cases, as well as common functionality shared among all use cases.

Mobile App for Data Storage, Management, Review, and Sharing

Applicable to all use cases, a mobile app will empower individuals to store and manage their health data in a health portfolio in the blockchain and share it with their physicians, or share metadata with researchers or public health agencies in return for timely health guidance, public advisories and/or tokens. The patient-centric app allows individuals to collect, securely store and manage their health data, including genome sequencing data, data from EHR patient portals, from wearable devices and other sensors, from self-tracking surveys that focus on fitness, diet, mood, and other health topics. The app will also manage third party access permissions at a granular level by accessing the BHIE API.

Mobile App and Online Portal for Physicians and Caregivers

Physicians, therapists and other caregivers who have joined the BHIE exchange will have an online portal and an app at their disposition to access the records of their patients and to communicate with the patient through the app and sending SMS-notifications and advice.

User Interface for AI Model Training

Researchers and developers of machine learning models use this interface to register with a researcher account. They publish new models or access existing models. They publish their Keras or TensorFlow batches that include neural network architecture serialization to JSON format (supported by Keras and TensorFlow). The models are pretrained on external data with trained weights in HDF5 format. Researchers can choose to share their models by listing them on the AI tracker, a dashboard describing all available models. They will receive Cygned tokens as a compensation when other researchers use their models. The proof-of information algorithm described earlier is accessible through the UI and determines whether the model needs to be updated by running it on a list of sites that contain ground truth data.

Use Case 1: CDC Disease Surveillance

The user interfaces serve two types of stakeholders, the CDC officials, and individuals from the general population, which includes healthy people, people with undiagnosed diseases, people with chronic diseases, and patients under medical care. CDC officials access the aggregate health information compiled from the individuals' data. The CDC has access to the blockchain-based SDP-interoperable APIs for survey collection. Only the API is supplied to the CDC, not a user interface, as these are developed in-house with confidential single sign-on authentication protocols. This use case does not involve AI model training nor predictions.

Mobile App for CDC's Person-Health-Reports

A mobile app-based UI for patients/individuals will include a reporting interface that pushes information into the CDC's Surveillance Data Platform (SDP). The reporting engine allows submissions to the CDC SDP contingent on the data owner's permissions.

As shown in Figure 19.2, a person downloads and uses the app to store lab results downloaded from the online portals of lab test providers (Labcorp, Quest) or pharmacy prescription information downloaded from the online portals of pharmacies such as Walgreens and CVS. A Health Portfolio will aid the individuals in securing the data in the blockchain in exchange for public health advisory information and guidelines. Lab test results and health agency information are presented in attractive charts with health guidelines. For infection data the app ensures confidential sharing with health agencies with promise of up-to-date health advisories. A person may provide data through an SDP-V survey following a doctor's visit after doctor verification through the Identity Management system. Once the person answers the survey, the answers are stored on the blockchain and from there, they are accessible to CDC via the SDP. In return, the individual receives the most recent data on local infection epidemiology and health advisories. Figure 19.8 shows two mobile user interfaces, one to log into the person's health portfolio, and the second to request information about antibiotic resistance from the CDC. The surveys will be built using the SDP-V features. Each filled survey can receive compensation in Cygned tokens (shown as coins at the bottom of the screen). Number of tokens depends on the significance and content of the survey. Up-to-date health advisories are received from the CDC in return.

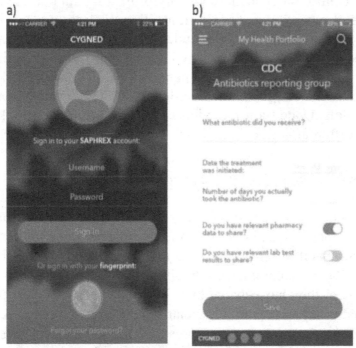

Figure 8: Mobile App user interfaces: (a) Sign up page, (b) An SDP-V survey

Figure 19.8: Mobile App user interfaces: (a) Sign up page, (b) An SDP-V survey

Use Case 2: Opioid Use Disorder

An extension to the mobile app which allows people to manage their health data in the blockchain will be added for users who need pain medication prescription after a surgery, a cancer treatment, or another health-related issue that requires treatment for pain. Their data will be sent to the privacy-aware machine learning model for a prediction of opioid use disorder. Predictions are sent to physicians and pharmacists who have joined the BHIE exchange and are prescribing opioid medications.

Rehab Alumni Mobile App

A mobile app for individuals who have completed rehabilitation will allow them to participate in an alumni network of their rehab clinic to continue to monitor their health. This is ideal for rehabilitated individuals seeking structure and support in their current environment, as they will continue to receive medical and psychiatric guidelines through the app, and establish the healthy coping strategies learned during treatment. The guidelines are presented as information material and will be defined by the rehabilitation centers participating in the project. In order to monitor their health, users of the app will participate in questionnaires that have been shortened from their original versions, such as the shortened SOAPP-R screener [55, 56]. The app allows users to store their health data and answers to screening questionnaires in the secure person-centric blockchain repository of health data that the users manage with the objective of receiving personalized health guidelines or sharing the data with therapists or physicians. The app includes a reward system for sharing of data or predictions. Users are rewarded either by joining their rehab alumni network, by receiving cryptocurrency tokens, or by personalized health guidelines. The app connects to the BHIE exchange to send health data to the machine learning engine for training of the models. Once trained models exist, they are used to make predictions that are used in a different app for physician and pharmacists, described below.

User Interface for Physician, Pharmacists and Therapists

This app allows access to the AI model predictions for users who have set up a unique blockchain identity and given permission to access the prediction. In collaboration with rehabilitations centers, their therapists will access the predictions when individuals who have completed rehabilitation are going back to their home environment and after they have shared their health data with the AI engine to receive a personalized post-rehab care plan. Physicians and pharmacies will get a prediction of opioid misuse for users who are being prescribed opioid medication for the first time. The app uses the BHIE to connect to a prediction for a user who has authorized access to it. A future version of the app will display a set of additional functions that allows physicians and therapists to more fully monitor a patients' progress after rehabilitation and predict different treatments depending on a patient's medical health history.

Use Case 3: Cancer Survivorship

An app for cancer survivors is developed with the objective of offering cancer survivorship care plans and health monitoring. It can send information to a physician, who uses the standard app described earlier.

Cancer Survivorship Mobile App

This app learns to predict adherence to a care plan over time. Initially, during pilot testing, the self-reported answers to surveys are used to identify the non-adherence to a plan, i.e. a break in the commitment to follow a recovery plan. The answers represent the binary outcome, adherence or non-adherence, and the individuals' health data is used to train the prediction models. Once the models are trained, adherence to a plan can be predicted before the care plan is developed and the prediction can inform on the best approach to help the individual stay committed to a health plan. A stage-based model of personal informatics systems - systems that help users collect, reflect on, and gain knowledge on their personal data is used to develop this app [57]. This model is a widely-adopted conceptual framework that can be used to develop the different stages of the self-tracking process. The personal informatics model describes five stages:

- the Preparation stage consists of planning that occurs before users start collecting personal data,

- the Collection stage refers to when users record their data,

- the Integration stage includes formatting and combining data,

- the Reflection stage involves making sense of and learning from their personal data, and

- the Action stage, when users act based on the insights gained through reflection.

During the **preparation stage** the user will design or obtain from a health provider a follow-up care plan with a long-term strategy for monitoring their health. The user can use the app to design a post-cancer treatment health plan by using the recommendations offered by the app, or recommendations by a physician, or by importing a physician ordered plan. The objective of the plan is to stay physically and emotionally healthy. Guidelines implemented in the app to guide in the design of the plan are taken from the LIVESTRONG Surveys [58]. During the **collection stage**, the app will require users to store their medical history records in a secure space in the blockchain that they can manage. Diet, mood and fitness will be tracked using journals, while also supporting importing of data from other apps, including data from wearable devices such as Fitbit. Mood is collected by letting the user chose a color from a spectrum of colors where each color is labeled with a mood description and each mood color-coded for easy data integration (red is linked to angry, pink to anxious, and so on). During the **integration stage**, the different data types are integrated and sent anonymized to the deep learning models to monitor the cancer survivors' health and fitness. The **reflection stage** presents the user with information about the best practices for cancer survivorship including charts and graphs of their own data. The goal is to increase the health literacy level of the user as that has been shown to activate the person to seek to better manage their health. The **action stage** offers different options based on the users' predefined guidelines: (1) seeking physician advice by sending an alert signal to the physician, (2) accessing online resources, and (3) accessing personal reminders encoded by the users themselves. The user can also select to automatically send updates to a physician who monitors their health instead of receiving a suggested action from the app. In this way, the mobile app will offer positive encouragement through personalized recommendations of best practices for recovery and health maintenance based on person-centric machine learning predictions.

Evaluations

Evaluations of the prediction models used in two of the use cases are described below. They involve a learning period in which the BHIE requests data from users to train the machine learning engine with the incentive of Cygned token rewards, physician communication, or personalized health guidelines. During a later stage evaluation period, the app is tested with data that has not been used for training. The area under the curve (AUC) will be computed to determine the ability of the app to discriminate between two binary outcomes. System Usability Scale evaluations of user interfaces will also be performed.

- For the Cancer Survivorship use case, a verified cancer diagnosis will categorize individuals as cancer survivors. During the learning period, positive outcome of adherence to a care plan will be assessed by the app through the cancer survivor's own self-reports and survey answers and used as the binary outcome for the training of the models. During the evaluation period, the health data of new users will be used to get a prediction from the trained models. Evaluation is performed by comparing the app user's survey or self-reported answers to the predictions of the models which are generated once all the health history data is available.

- For the Opioid use case, individuals who have completed therapy or detoxification at a rehabilitation center will be classified as cases. Individuals with no history of opioid prescriptions will be categorized as controls. All individuals have their health data stored in the blockchain. The SOAPP-R predictions will be used as the Gold standard for comparison with the predictions in order to compute the AUC.

Conclusion

We are in the early days of the blockchain technology, and public health agencies and the US government have the opportunity to be a bridge between the healthcare industry and federal/local agencies to foster collaboration, ensure competitiveness and address urgent health problems. The future of personalized medicine and timely disease surveillance is within our reach, but it has been delayed by the current challenges of fragmented data in incompatible medical record databases and a healthcare industry entangled in a web of competitive paradigms of the past. The blockchain technology is changing this. A recent collaboration between major health insurance companies has shown that a partnership focused on innovation and problem solving can allow them to stay competitive while improving health care services for their customers. The unique alliance of Humana, MultiPlan, Optum, Quest Diagnostics and UnitedHealthcare uses the blockchain technology to improve inaccurate doctor directories [59] motivated by a Centers for Medicare & Medicaid Services ruling that penalizes insurers for inaccurate medical care provider directories. Through federal legislation, through grants and contracts, new collaborations can pave the way to healthcare innovation that relies on the coming together of the different stakeholders that participate in the health services and medicine ecosystem. The Blockchain Caucus, formed in 2018 in the US congress [60], sees the blockchain's potential to reshape the health care industry and has introduced, in an effort to participate in this health care industry overhaul, a legislation that supports basic research for Valley Fever and other fungal diseases through a blockchain pilot program. This is only the beginning of efforts to building a modern health ecosystem around the blockchain technology and providing access to the medical history and health data of individuals for research and better health care outcomes. Innovations and collaborations advancing healthcare should not look only at financial gains but at the human suffering caused by disease, and put emphasis in alleviating and eliminating it. Ensuring that the patient becomes an active player in these collaborations will help remind everyone that compassion for people affected by disease is a key ingredient in any collaboration. In the use cases proposed in this chapter, it is the individual who manages his data and grants access to it, ensuring that his voice is heard. The blockchain is the foundation of this collaborative solution by keeping immutable records of data belonging to people, organizations or machines in a secure, but accessible manner, allowing trusted, transparent transactions that benefit all participants in the health ecosystem. Public health agencies, individuals, and healthcare-oriented business are the collaborators in this ecosystem with a common goal to cure and prevent diseases, to provide relief from the suffering that comes with sickness, and to help people lead healthier lives.

References

1. Randall D, Goel P, Abujamra R. Blockchain Applications and Use Cases in Health Information Technology. Journal of Health & Medical Informatics. 2017;8:1–4.

2. IBM and CDC blockchain project uses records stored on cloud. Cloud computing news. 2018. https://www.ibm.com/blogs/cloud-computing/2018/09/07/ibm-cdc-blockchain-cloud/. Accessed 29 Oct 2018.

3. McCarthy and Schweikert Introduce Historic Valley Fever Legislation. Congressman David Schweikert. 2018. https://schweikert.house.gov/media-center/press-releases/mccarthy-and-schweikert-introduce-historic-valley-fever-legislation. Accessed 3 Nov 2018.

4. UK OW-G Business Insider. Estonia is using the technology behind bitcoin to secure 1 million health records. Business Insider. https://www.businessinsider.com/guardtime-estonian-health-records-industrial-blockchain-bitcoin-2016-3. Accessed 31 Oct 2018.

5. Estonian Guardtime launches a personal care record platform for the UK NHS patients. Estonian World. 2018. http://estonianworld.com/technology/estonian-guardtime-launches-a-personal-care-record-platform-for-the-uk-nhs-patients/. Accessed 31 Oct 2018.

6. Alibaba (BABA) Thinks Blockchain Will Change The World. NASDAQ.com. 2018. https://www.nasdaq.com/article/alibaba-baba-thinks-blockchain-will-change-the-world-cm1018125. Accessed 31 Oct 2018.

7. Surprise! With $60 Million Genentech Deal, 23andMe Has A Business Plan. https://www.forbes.com/sites/matthewherper/2015/01/06/surprise-with-60-million-genentech-deal-23andme-has-a-business-plan/#6f05d01c2be9. Accessed 26 Oct 2018.

8. Patientory. Patientory. https://patientory.com/. Accessed 30 Oct 2018.

9. Medicalchain - Blockchain for electronic health records. https://medicalchain.com/en/. Accessed 30 Oct 2018.

10. MedX Protocol. https://medxprotocol.com/. Accessed 30 Oct 2018.

11. Coral Health - Building a more connected future in healthcare. https://mycoralhealth.com/. Accessed 30 Oct 2018.

12. Gem Health. Gem. 2016. https://enterprise.gem.co/health/. Accessed 30 Oct 2018.

13. Healthcare API Platform | PokitDok. https://pokitdok.com/. Accessed 30 Oct 2018.

14. MediBloc - Reinventing Your Healthcare Experience. MediBloc. https://medibloc.org. Accessed 1 Nov 2018.

15. MedChain - Control Your Health Records. https://medchain.global/. Accessed 1 Nov 2018.

16. AI Crypto - AI BlockChain for Decentralized Economy. https://aicrypto.ai/?lang=en. Accessed 1 Nov 2018.

17. Nebula Genomics. https://www.nebula.org/. Accessed 31 Oct 2018.

18. LunaDNA -- The first people-powered platform where you share health data, advance science and take part in the value created. https://lunadna.com/. Accessed 31 Oct 2018.

19. Zenome - Home. https://zenome.io/. Accessed 31 Oct 2018.

20. Encrypgen - Security Privacy Trust. https://encrypgen.com/. Accessed 31 Oct 2018.

21. doc.ai. https://doc.ai/. Accessed 31 Oct 2018.

22. Bouhifd M, Beger R, Flynn T, Guo L, Harris G, Hogberg H, et al. Quality assurance of metabolomics. ALTEX. 2015;32:319–26.

23. Sinha R, Abnet CC, White O, Knight R, Huttenhower C. The microbiome quality control project: baseline study design and future directions. Genome Biol. 2015;16. doi:10.1186/s13059-015-0841-8.

24. Chervitz SA, Deutsch EW, Field D, Parkinson H, Quackenbush J, Rocca-Serra P, et al. Data Standards for Omics Data: The Basis of Data Sharing and Reuse. Methods Mol Biol. 2011;719:31–69.

25. Kauffmann H-M, Kamp H, Fuchs R, Chorley BN, Deferme L, Ebbels T, et al. Framework for the quality assurance of 'omics technologies considering GLP requirements. Regul Toxicol Pharmacol. 2017;91 Suppl 1:S27–35.

26. Zhang P, Schmidt DC, White J, Lenz G. Blockchain Technology Use Cases in Healthcare. In: Advances in Computers. Elsevier; 2018. p. 1–41. doi:10.1016/bs.adcom.2018.03.006.

27. Revere D, Hills RH, Dixon BE, Gibson PJ, Grannis SJ. Notifiable condition reporting practices: implications for public health agency participation in a health information exchange. BMC Public Health. 2017;17. doi:10.1186/s12889-017-4156-4.

28. Revere D, Calhoun R, Baseman J, Oberle M. Exploring bi-directional and SMS messaging for communications between Public Health Agencies and their stakeholders: a qualitative study. BMC Public Health. 2015;15:621.

29. Kish LJ, Topol EJ. Unpatients—why patients should own their medical data. Nature Biotechnology. 2015. doi:10.1038/nbt.3340.

30. Terry SF, Terry PF. Power to the People: Participant Ownership of Clinical Trial Data. Science Translational Medicine. 2011;3:69cm3-69cm3.

31. Kostkova P, Brewer H, de Lusignan S, Fottrell E, Goldacre B, Hart G, et al.

32. Who Owns the Data? Open Data for Healthcare. Front Public Health. 2016;4. doi:10.3389/fpubh.2016.00007.

33. Public Workshop: Strategies for Promoting the Safe Use and Appropriate Prescribing of Prescription Opioids | Margolis Center for Health Policy. https://healthpolicy.duke.edu/events/public-workshop-strategies-promoting-safe-use-and-appropriate-prescribing-prescription. Accessed 19 Sep 2018.

34. Lutz J, Gross R, Long D, Cox S. Predicting Risk for Opioid Misuse in Chronic Pain with a Single-Item Measure of Catastrophic Thinking. J Am Board Fam Med. 2017;30:828–31.

35. National Cancer Institute. Cancer Statistics. National Cancer Institute. 2015. https://www.cancer.gov/about-cancer/understanding/statistics. Accessed 13 Oct 2018.

36. Levit L, Balogh E, Nass S, Ganz PA, Population C on I the Q of CCA the C of an A, Services B on HC, et al. Delivering High-Quality Cancer Care: Charting a New Course for a System in Crisis. In: Introduction. National Academies Press (US); 2013. https://www.ncbi.nlm.nih.gov/books/NBK202150/. Accessed 13 Oct 2018.

37. Mayer DK, Terrin NC, Menon U, Kreps GL, McCance K, Parsons SK, et al. Health behaviors in cancer survivors. Oncol Nurs Forum. 2007;34:643–51.

38. Williams K, Steptoe A, Wardle J. Is a cancer diagnosis a trigger for health behaviour change? Findings from a prospective, population-based study. Br J Cancer. 2013;108:2407–12.

39. Civic Secure Identity Ecosystem - Decentralized Identity & Reusable KYC. Civic Technologies, Inc. https://www.civic.com/. Accessed 2 Nov 2018.

40. Introduction — hyperledger-fabric. https://hyperledger-fabric.readthedocs.io/en/release-1.3/whatis.html#hyperledger-fabric. Accessed 11 Nov 2018.

41. Intel SGX Homepage | Intel® Software. 00:00:00 UTC. https://software.intel.com/en-us/sgx. Accessed 22 Oct 2018.

42. Blach C, Del Fiol G, Dundee C, Frund J, Richesson R, Smerek M, et al. Use of RxNorm and NDF-RT to normalize and characterize participant-reported medications in an i2b2-based research repository. AMIA Jt Summits Transl Sci Proc. 2014;2014:35–40.

43. Raebel MA, Haynes K, Woodworth TS, Saylor G, Cavagnaro E, Coughlin KO, et al. Electronic clinical laboratory test results data tables: lessons from Mini-Sentinel. Pharmacoepidemiol Drug Saf. 2014;23:609–18.

44. Wang S, Jiang X, Wu Y, Cui L, Cheng S, Ohno-Machado L. EXpectation Propagation LOgistic REgRession (EXPLORER): distributed privacy-preserving online model learning. J Biomed Inform. 2013;46:480–96.

45. Yan F, Sundaram S, Vishwanathan SVN, Qi Y. Distributed Autonomous Online Learning: Regrets and Intrinsic Privacy-Preserving Properties. IEEE Transactions on Knowledge and Data Engineering. 2013;25:2483–93.

46. Kuo, T-T, Ohno-Machado L. ModelChain: Decentralized Privacy-Preserving Healthcare Predictive Modeling Framework on Private Blockchain Networks. arXiv.org. 2018. https://arxiv.org/abs/1802.01746.

47. RxNorm. https://www.nlm.nih.gov/research/umls/rxnorm/. Accessed 7 Oct 2018.

48. NDF-RT API. https://rxnav.nlm.nih.gov/NdfrtAPIs.html#. Accessed 7 Oct 2018.

49. UMLS - LOINC. https://www.nlm.nih.gov/research/umls/loinc_main.html. Accessed 7 Oct 2018.

50. Choi E, Bahadori MT, Kulas JA, Schuetz A, Stewart WF, Sun J. RETAIN: An Interpretable Predictive Model for Healthcare using Reverse Time Attention Mechanism. arXiv:160805745 [cs]. 2016. http://arxiv.org/abs/1608.05745. Accessed 2 Oct 2018.

51. Choi E, Bahadori MT, Song L, Stewart WF, Sun J. GRAM: Graph-based Attention Model for Healthcare Representation Learning. arXiv:161107012 [cs, stat]. 2016. http://arxiv.org/abs/1611.07012. Accessed 2 Oct 2018.

52. Choi E, Schuetz A, Stewart WF, Sun J. Using recurrent neural network models for early detection of heart failure onset. J Am Med Inform Assoc. 2017;24:361–70.

53. Keras Documentation. https://keras.io/. Accessed 15 Oct 2018.

54. TensorFlow. https://www.tensorflow.org/. Accessed 15 Oct 2018.

55. Stanley A. Hyperledger And Enterprise Ethereum Alliance Join Forces In Enterprise Blockchain Boost. Forbes. https://www.forbes.com/sites/astanley/2018/10/01/hyperledger-and-enterprise-ethereum-alliance-join-forces-in-enterprise-blockchain-boost/. Accessed 12 Nov 2018.

56. Butler SF, Fernandez K, Benoit C, Budman SH, Jamison RN. Validation of the revised Screener and Opioid Assessment for Patients with Pain (SOAPP-R). J Pain. 2008;9:360–72.

57. Finkelman MD, Jamison RN, Kulich RJ, Butler SF, Jackson WC, Smits N, et al. Cross-validation of short forms of the Screener and Opioid Assessment for Patients with Pain-Revised (SOAPP-R). Drug Alcohol Depend. 2017;178:94–100.

58. Li I, Dey A, Forlizzi J. A Stage-based Model of Personal Informatics Systems. In: Proceedings of the SIGCHI Conference on Human Factors in Computing Systems. New York, NY, USA: ACM; 2010. p. 557–566. doi:10.1145/1753326.1753409.

59. LIVESTRONG Research Library. LIVESTRONG. 2016. https://www.
    livestrong.org/what-we-do/our-research. Accessed 26 Sep 2018.

60. Optum, Quest And Humana In Blockchain Deal To Improve Doctor
    Directories. https://www.forbes.com/sites/brucejapsen/2018/04/02/
    unitedhealths-optum-and-humana-in-blockchain-deal-to-improve-doctor-
    directories/#2be4e3173998. Accessed 10 Nov 2018.

61. Blockchain Caucus. blockchaincaucus. https://www.
    congressionalblockchaincaucus.com. Accessed 12 Nov 2018.

FUTURE OF BLOCKCHAIN IN HEALTHCARE

Chapter 20:
Looking Ahead at Blockchain in Healthcare

Rick Krohn
HealthSense Inc.

https://hashedhealth.com/blockchain-for-healthcare-book/

Editor's Note:

Rick Krohn, CEO of HealthSense, starts the third part of our book, "the future of blockchain Healthcare" with a riveting overview of how Blockchain will team up with other emerging technologies like IOT (internet of things) to create IOHT (the internet of health things). Rick's expertise in digital innovation, technology-enabled transformation, new products and new ventures, brings to light how future "connected Health" looks like and where blockchain technology fits in. The chapter goes over how blockchain technology will impact data sharing, electronic health records, the pharmaceutical industry, healthcare finance and even peer-to-peer insurance. Rick speaks not only to the promise of how transparency, immutability and security of distributed ledgers can help us better manage the ocean of data in healthcare, but also what are the current obstacles needed to overcome to effectuate that change.

Blockchain, like other young and disruptive technologies, offers wide opportunities to impact healthcare - an industry that is primed for disruption. Despite being the largest sector of the U.S. economy, healthcare has been plagued by slow systems, wasteful financing, and resource utilization, and operational inefficiencies. To address these issues, innovative solutions like Blockchain contribute to many of the industry's goals: clinical coordination; data security and patient privacy; operating efficiency; trust and scalability. The solution set is wide ranging: Blockchain can secure sensitive research and clinical data while ensuring its' responsible access among a broader range of involved stakeholders. It promotes a true linear patient record and the Internet of Healthy Things ("IoHT") – which includes wearables, nearables, invisibles and sensors. It creates an efficient framework of asset and supply chain management and establishes the security and authenticity of medications. It is a rich field for innovation - companies like IBM, Oracle, Microsoft and Change Healthcare are developing Blockchain solutions to augment patient health records, asset management, licensing and credentialing, data sharing, revenue cycle and more. This essay opens Section 3 and examines the applications – now and in the near future – of blockchain technologies in healthcare.

Healthcare is a highly transactional industry. Each interaction among patients, providers, payers, pharmacies, pharmaceutical companies and other healthcare professionals generates yet another in a massive amount of data that is often channeled between separate, isolated systems. The transactional nature of Healthcare, however, lends itself well to Blockchain, which can dramatically reduce the complexity and cost of transactions while improving transparency. The vision for blockchain in healthcare, then is to create a trusted, efficient, common database of health information that payers, providers and patients can securely (and seamlessly) share across information platforms. It's a paradigm shift in access: anyone can build on top of an open Blockchain network, in contrast to prevailing network architectures that limit access to a limited number of stakeholders who control large amounts of data. Blockchain can tie together complex healthcare relationships with frictionless connectivity, strengthened by smart contracts and authorization. Its' transaction layer enables access to anonymous and non-patient identifiable information. With blockchain solutions, there will be no need for a central administrator, and research and clinical data can be shared in a streamlined but secure way. And with that preamble, let's look at where Blockchain is going to impact healthcare.

A Linear Health Record

Healthcare offers a host of potential Blockchain deployments, foremost among them the potential to establish a true linear electronic medical record. A longitudinal patient record capturing encounters, registries, lab results, medications and treatments can be achieved through blockchain, including inpatient, ambulatory and wearable data. A Blockchain-enabled EMR model can empower trusted parties across the spectrum of healthcare venues - hospitals, practices, clinics, payers and patients to view and populate records from multiple databases on a shared ledger. The potential benefits of a truly comprehensive patient record extend to care coordination, clinical research, wellness and patient engagement. The flow of data, though securely encrypted, can be shared among an unlimited number of non- integrated, approved stakeholders. Below is a simple representation of this "closed loop" data sharing model.

Some early deployments demonstrate Blockchain's value in establishing a data sharing framework across healthcare verticals, and within a circle of stakeholders. MedRec, a decentralized record management system to manage authentication, confidentiality, accountability and data sharing using blockchains, is intended to improve electronical medical records and allow patients' records to be accessed securely by any approved provider. MedRec gives patients and doctors an immutable log of healthcare records. The Company uses Smart Contracts to map patient-provider relationships where the contract shows a list of references detailing the relationships between nodes on the Blockchain. It also puts control of these relationships in the hands of the patient, giving them the ability to accept, reject, or modify access with healthcare providers such as hospitals, insurers, and clinics. The goal of MedRec is to give patients and their providers one-stop access to their entire medical history across all providers and encounters.

Guardtime has launched what it's calling the world's first comprehensive blockchain-supported Personal Care Record Platform, MyPCR. The system uses Healthcare Gateway's Medical Interoperability Gateway and will provide instant access to primary care information for up to 30 million patients in the UK. The system will focus heavily on patient adherence to a personalized treatment plan, continuous monitoring and verification. It has been estimated that implementing these Blockchain-enabled patient record models could deliver significant savings based on compliance alone, in the range of $100-290 billion annually.

Asset Management

Medical device tracking represents another near-term opportunity for Blockchain to disrupt healthcare. From deployment to decommissioning, persistent tracking allows the efficient utilization of devices, prevention of unnecessary shrinkage and repurchasing, and fraud analytics. In concert with RFID/RTLS location tracking solutions, a "smart contracts" blockchain approach to asset tracking offers several benefits. The immutability and tamper-proof qualities of Blockchain prevent a malicious user from changing the location history of a device or deleting it from the record. In addition to medical device theft and shrinkage (a multi-million-dollar problem), a Blockchain solution will also prevent devices being lost and reordered, poorly maintained or underutilized. [The insertion of Blockchain to the medical device industry is given an added urgency with the rise in connected devices and mobile health (mHealth) applications].

In a related application, Blockchain can mitigate the risks of a compromised supply chain - risks that can directly impact patient safety and health outcomes. These risks include the threat of failing to secure and distribute medical commodities, adverse events associated with supply chain breaches, and increased morbidity and mortality to the medical consumer. And the challenge: globalization, increased adoption of non – integrated information systems and a sector populated with many stakeholders has given rise to a complex health supply chain A decentralized asset management system could create a "single source of truth" surrounding the movement of goods and ensure that all transactions between supply chain partners are accurately recorded and easily shared. With a Blockchain-enabled supply chain, every time a product changes hands, the transaction is documented, creating a permanent history of a product from manufacture to sale. With enhanced transparency, better security and limitless scalability, Blockchain can dramatically reduce the layers of complexity, added costs, and errors that plague healthcare transactions today. A number of large data management companies including Microsoft, IBM, SAP, and Oracle have made investments in Blockchain and supply chain management.

Pharma

Within the pharmaceutical industry, Blockchain can help address the growing risk, particularly in Global South, associated with counterfeit, unapproved and fake drugs. Fake medicines can occur as a result of importing substandard drugs without institutional controls, poor manufacturing practices or improper storage, theft and diversion of drugs, and the infiltration of poor quality or fake products into grey markets (outside of legitimate pharmaceutical distribution channels). Today, the global market for fake, substandard, counterfeit, and grey market medicines accounts for up to $200 billion per year.

In the U.S. With the opioid epidemic raging and some Pharma's coming under fire for insufficient monitoring of distribution to vulnerable communities, Blockchain could offer an innovative way to ensure that abuse-prone medications are better controlled. Blockchain-enabled drug tracking leverages the immutability of the blockchain to develop tracking and chain of custody from manufacturer to patient. With a Blockchain-enabled drug provenance model it is possible to define smart contracts for drugs and then identify pill containers with integrated GPS and chain-of-custody logging. AmeriSource Bergen and Merck are collaborating on a Blockchain-enabled chain of custody model showing where the drug was manufactured, where it has been since, and when it has been disbursed to patients. Using this model, the provenance of the product is guaranteed, ensuring it hasn't been tampered with all the way through the chain to the patient. It's estimated that the pharmaceutical industry could achieve savings of $200 billion in defining a chain-of-custody for the supply chain.

Within clinical trials, integrating blockchain technology can address issues ranging from the tracking and sharing of data to the need for transparency and privacy for patients. Blockchain technology can directly increase the quantity and quality of patients recruited for clinical trials - the distributed ledger could allow individual patients to store their medical data by anonymous methods, making it visible to trial recruiters. It can create a layer of de-identified data that researchers can tap to recruit patients. Blockchain smart contracts can ensure transparency and traceability over clinical trial sequences and provide financial incentives for a patient's participation and sharing of their data. It can overcome the problems of fraudulent results and removal of data and streamline communication between doctors and patients. MIT's Project Enigma provides an early example of Blockchain's unique characteristics applied to data sharing and security-layered programs like clinical trials.

Healthcare Finance

Health insurance processes like claims processing, client onboarding and underwriting could also benefit from a blockchain approach. Smart contracts could automate these processes and decrease the time and resources needed to execute the terms and conditions of value-based contracting. Administrative processes could be streamlined to accelerate the validity of a claim, manage pre-authorizations, and ensure that providers are meeting the criteria laid out in their contracts. The result is a process that eliminates the traditional claims clearinghouse and reconciliation layers and lowers administrative costs.

Both payers and providers may be able to use blockchain as the basis for more stable, predictable, revenue cycle. Blockchain's ability to create validated identities and accurately record tamper-proof transactions makes it easier to conduct payer–provider transactions, and to collect patient payments. Early developers include Gem, Pokitdok, and Change Healthcare.

Medicare fraud caused more than $30 million in losses in the United States in 2016, and Blockchain-based systems could help minimize it with validated identities. It could reduce administrative costs for billing by eliminating the need for intermediaries with automated and efficient processing.

From a population health perspective, by connecting payers and providers with more timely, complete patient data, health plans could develop more sensitive risk stratification protocols that identify patients likely to incur high costs. These Blockchain-enabled insights could aid payers in planning for chronic disease spending, incentivizing patients to adopt healthy behaviors, and intervening earlier with at-risk patients.

Data Sharing

Data sharing represents another great opportunity but also one of the largest privacy challenges. Blockchain could enable a new model for health information exchange ("HIE") by making electronic medical records more efficient, disintermediated, and secure. With a centralized ledger and "clean" data repositories, medical research, clinical trials, treatment protocols and personalized medicine can all become vastly more effective. But currently, with non-standardized and disconnected systems in play, the value to be gleaned from this wealth of information is not being optimized. Blockchain could solve this riddle. The challenge - data must pass between healthcare providers to insurers and patients while adhering to data and patient privacy standards. It's a growing issue - Between 2015-2016, 140 million patient records were breached according to a Protenus Breach Barometer report. And with the growth of connected devices and the Internet of Medical Things (IoMT), securing health IT infrastructures is increasingly problematic. Blockchain can create a data sharing environment that keeps health data private and secure while embracing the ever-expanding nodes of data and catalog of connected medical devices. Blockchain offers an opportunity for interoperability in healthcare systems via a decentralized ledger where the user interfaces may be different, the central ledger will be identical across all providers. Blockchain -driven interoperability can be achieved by the use of sophisticated APIs to make medical record interoperability and data storage a reliable process while eliminating the cost and resource consumption of data reconciliation.

Other Blockchain Applications in Healthcare

Beyond those applications already described, the range of possible Blockchain applications in healthcare continues to evolve – in some unexpected ways. A few examples:

Medical Research - doc.ai is a platform that collects and manages health data securely in one place and helps accelerates medical research with the power of artificial intelligence. doc.ai's blockchain-based infrastructure enables aggregating all imported data on edge devices (e.g. cell phone). It is decentralized, anonymized and encrypted, protecting shared data in a fully anonymous and HIPAA compliant way.

Gaming -. XAYA is true Blockchain gaming, using cutting edge technology to provide new genres, decentralized virtual worlds, and no central servers. The platform enables real-time, costless, and infinitely scalable gameplay in a decentralized fashion.

Medical Tourism - Medipedia.io is a blockchain-based project that seeks to develop a digital healthcare delivery system that links medical tourism patients to healthcare organizations and institutions Through the utilization of blockchain, unauthorized third parties cannot access personal medical information as its encrypted and access is only granted to medical service providers who want to offer the desired medical service.

AI - BotChain is a decentralized bot registration, identification, and audit platform, a Blockchain-based platform for ensuring certainty and security in A.I. Autonomous Agents for business.

Peer-to-Peer Insurance

A game changing concept in insurance, the concept: policyholders pool themselves together. If there is a claim, they all contribute financially to that claim. If there are no claims, then premiums are reduced. Blockchain technology maintains the ledger of claims and premiums paid. This entire concept and technology take the traditional insurer out of the picture. Dynamis provides an early example of this Ethereum -based platform.

Obstacles

And now for the reality check. Today, electronic health records reside within a spaghetti soup of legacy systems, non- standardized data sets, and unaffiliated stakeholders. Integration with existing systems will be very challenging. Regulatory concerns alone will likely slow implementation. And because of the nature of healthcare transactions, patient record management requires large amounts of digital storage and frequent data transactions, which are each rate-limiting steps of Blockchain systems. To counteract the inevitable data duplication, the blockchain will require anonymized identifiers to identify patients across all systems and inputs. Further, a blockchain technology solution requires participants being able to communicate via disparate data sources. This will require some form of data standardization.

The sheer volume of data generated in healthcare environments is only set to increase further (as a reference, Kaiser Permanente maintained between 26 and 44 petabytes of data on its 9 million members from EHRs and other medical data in 2014), and the volume of data logged and referenced to will add to this scalability problem. Although speed and data storage capacity are constantly evolving, any Blockchain solution that handles large amounts of patient data in real time likely will need to be faster than is currently found in enterprise environments.

Incentivizing people to join the blockchain network will be another hurdle. Scalability and human centered design will be key to driving adoption, and the more people who join the network, the more robust the entire blockchain solution becomes. But there is a wrinkle- the incentives of stakeholders – the payer, the provider, the healthcare consumer are not always aligned.

Equally challenging is the need to address privacy and data protection considerations unique to the healthcare industry as illustrated by the need to comply with policy frameworks in the USA such as Health Insurance Portability and Accountability Act (HIPAA), the HITECH Act, and numerous benchmarks established by the Centers for Medicare and Medicaid. Finally, Blockchain is a new technology whose proof points are still in the development stage, and as an industry, Healthcare is notoriously reluctant to adopt disruptive technologies.

A Blockchain Model For Health Care

Blockchain has the potential to propel innovation across the spectrum of healthcare verticals. The central feature of this capacity - the distributed ledger, guarantees data integrity while creating a secure data sharing environment that is both scalable and adaptive to healthcare's trends towards collaboration and personalization. Blockchain provides frictionless connectivity, strengthened by smart contracts and authorization to access all electronic health data. Blockchain can facilitate faster and easier interoperability between systems and can efficiently scale to handle larger volumes of data and more users. Its transaction layer can enable instantaneous access to a diverse set of standardized, anonymous and non-patient identifiable information. Blockchain can tie together complex clinical and finance processes. Conceptually, a Blockchain model for healthcare would incorporate the following characteristics:

Additionally, any blockchain for healthcare would need to be public and would need to include solutions for three key elements: scalability, access security and data privacy.

- Scalability: A distributed blockchain ledger that contains health records, documents or images would have data storage implications and data throughput limitations. For health care to realize benefits from blockchain, the blockchain will need to function as an access-control manager for health records and data.

- Access Security: Blockchain can establish a secure way to electronically share and manage health data and allow a person to control who sees it and who doesn't. The increasing numbers and capability of connected medical devices present additional risks for access security.

- Privacy: Security and Privacy (in compliance with regs. like HITECH and HIPAA) must be baked into any Blockchain solution. A weak encryption protocol or code will subject the data to potential liability. That risk can be mitigated if Blockchain is employed to store data pointers, rather than the data itself (this would also relieve the strain of data volume transacted through the Blockchain).

Final Assessment

The healthcare industry is drowning in data—clinical trials, patient medical records, complex billing, medical research, retail devices, and more. Data integration, data sharing, and data standardization solutions like Blockchain, can mitigate – though not eliminate the challenge of exponential growths in recorded health data. That said, the benefits of blockchain technology include: 1) reducing or eliminating fraud, errors and malicious activity, 2) establishing a foundation of trust, data integrity and secure data sharing, 3) improving asset management and supply chain, 4) enabling complex clinical and financial transactions, and boosting information systems interoperability, and 5) streamlining care processes with measurable improvements to patient outcomes.

But Blockchain's ability to impact healthcare will depend in the industry's willingness to invest in technical infrastructure – and to surpass an industry culture that is insular and reluctant to adopt new technologies. Blockchain is costly, there are some concerns regarding its integration with the existing technology. Most likely, aadoption and implementation of blockchain in healthcare will be incremental and evolutionary, as business models gravitate towards clinical collaboration and data normalization. And a fundamental principle of technology adoption applies – focus on the problem, not the platform.

About the Author:

Rick Krohn is an expert in Connected Health corporate strategy and business development, strategic marketing and multi-channel communications, technology-enabled transformation, alliances, new products and new ventures, digital innovation, project management and thought leadership, whose consulting experience spans the healthcare, telecommunications, education and technology fields. He is the author of more than 100 articles on a wide range of health technology topics and 2 HIMSS books detailing Connected Health Innovation. His latest Book titled Connected Health: Improving Care, Safety, and Efficiency with Wearables and IoT solutions, is available from CRC Press. He can be reached at 912.220.6563 and rkrohn@healthsen.com

Chapter 21:
A Universal Patient-Centric Electronic Health Record System:
The Ethical Implications

Amanda Stanhaus

Editor's Note:

Amanda Stanhaus, now completing her PhD in Health Management and Policy from the University of Michigan has written one of the most scholarly and well-referenced chapters in our book. She skillfully not only speaks to the shortcomings of the current state of electronic health records (EHRs) in the US Healthcare system, but systematically reviews the benefits of creating a self-sovereign EHR using blockchain technology. Amanda speaks specifically to the advantages of MIT's MedRec EHR and how by using distributed ledger technology it has successfully tackled the challenges of authentication, confidentiality, accountability, data sharing and inter-operability. The chapter deftly speaks to the use of the EHR data as a tool to improve personal health, but also the challenges of creating an up-to-date knowledge repository necessary in maintaining and promoting population health.

While patients legally own their health record information, patients are not currently privy to nor in control of their health records. With the advent of Blockchain technology, the elusive goal of a universal patient-centric Electronic Health Record (EHR) system can soon be a reality. Blockchain, the technology underpinning the cryptocurrency Bitcoin, enables multiple stakeholders to securely share data on a distributed ledger in real-time. The ethical impacts of Blockchain technology applications are an emerging area of research. The ethical implications of this technological advancement are analyzed using a patient-centric EHR prototype, MIT's MedRec, and traditional bioethical principles, found in UNESCO's Universal Declaration on Bioethics and Human Rights, as well as the latest Blockchain research and health IT ethical analysis. The design of a universal patient-centric EHR system is an ethical solution that strikes a fine balance between collective principles (solidarity, sharing of benefits, etc.) and individualistic principles (human dignity, autonomy, consent, etc.). Patient inclusion in the design process, stakeholder collaboration, and consistent deference to ethical solutions will be essential as patient-centric EHRs go from prototype to production.

The ability to share a patient's health records across multiple healthcare providers has been an elusive goal. Currently, technology's inability to share data while preserving privacy in accordance with law limits the design of Electronic Health Records (EHRs)[1], forcing EHRs to be institution-centric. Siloed health records do not do justice to the interconnected physical, psychological, and social dimensions of health.[2] Simultaneous data privacy and sharing are made possible with the invention of Blockchain technology. Blockchain is equivalent to how the collaboration tool Google Docs solved the frustrating email exchange of conflicting versions of Microsoft Word documents. But there is one crucial difference with Blockchain. Data ownership is retained and not given to a third party like Google. Blockchain has the potential to allow the multi-stakeholder healthcare industry to implement a universal patient-centric EHR system. Assessing the ethical implications of a technological advancement is an essential step on the path to adoption. Given that universal patient-centric EHRs will impact healthcare delivery systems, the analysis must take on a bioethical[3] dimension.[4] Universal patient-centric EHRs have global bioethical implications because they have the potential to impact the world and the human species in a unified and comprehensive manner.[5] Using MIT's MedRec prototype, the

1   Electronic Health Record (EHR) is the chosen term for this paper because the proposed design discussed reflects the multi- dimensional, interconnected definition of health. EHR is sometimes used interchangeably with Electronic Medical Record (EMR). But EMR is not as relevant for this paper because an EMR is traditionally considered solely a record of one's medical episodes. For more information: D.A. Ludwick and John Doucette, "Adopting electronic medical records in primary care: Lessons learned from health information systems implementation experience in seven countries," International journal of medical informatics 78 (2009): 23-4.
2   Allen Keller, "Global Bioethics," (Presentation, NYU's Global Bioethics Class, New York, NY, Spring 2017).
3   Allen Keller defines Bioethics as, "the discussion and application of moral values and responsibilities in the biomedical sciences including clinical practice, healthcare delivery systems, and research." For more information: Keller, "Global Bioethics."
4   Keller, "Global Bioethics."
5   Henk A. M. J. ten Have and Bert Gordijn, "Global Bioethics," in Handbook of Global Bioethics, eds.

ethical implications of a universal patient- centric EHR system will be analyzed using the principles outlined in UNESCO's Universal Declaration on Bioethics and Human Rights. A universal patient-centric Electronic Health Records system that leverages Blockchain technology is a promising ethical solution due to its ability to balance patient autonomy, privacy, and data ownership with unprecedented research access to population health data that can expedite the creation of cures for humanity's ailments.

Electronic Health Records (EHRs) signal a broader innovation than just the transfer of a doctor's handwritten notes to a computer. Medical encounters and the resulting payments are the design inspiration for current EHRs, instead of a patient's care and health outcomes.[6] Current EHR solutions are vertically integrated and meet the required privacy and security standards by utilizing siloed walled-data- gardens that inhibit collaborative industry-wide sharing of medical data.[7] EHRs are inspired by the previous paper-based system, limiting their ability to be innovative and create solutions that could improve health outcomes.[8] The current state of institution-centric EHRs is a product of limited technological capabilities and restrictive policies intended to preserve a patient's right to privacy. Currently, the patient experience is inefficient due to siloed information; patients lack a comprehensive record of their health history, and when they go to a new healthcare provider it is inconvenient to repeat their health status over their lifetime let alone reconcile the fragmented information.[9] Fragmented, inefficient design of institution-centric EHRs makes evident that ease of payment, not patient experience, is a top design priority.[10] Current EHRs systems serve institutions more than patients.

Robert Greenes, a leader in the Biomedical Informatics field, thinks that the healthcare industry is in the midst of philosophical shifts, from institution to patient-centric design, from competition to collaboration, and from decision-making based on incomplete information to comprehensive data, which are well timed with technological advancement to re-design EHRs.[11] Greenes predicts "there will be an expanding effort to develop standards for interoperability, integration, and management of the data, and business models for providing these capabilities on a broad basis to the public. Concomitant with that will be the evolution of methods to integrate such data with providers as needed."[12]Regarding security and privacy protection, Greenes foresees "using role-based authentication and

---

Henk A. M. J. ten Have and Bert Gordijn (New York: Springer, 2014), 10.

6   Thomas Payne, "Snapshot at Mid-stride: Current State of EHRs and Their Use by Clinicians from a CMIO's Perspective," in Healthcare Information Management Systems: Cases, Strategies, and Solutions, eds. Charlotte A. Weaver, Marion J. Ball, George R. Kim, and Joan M. Kiel (New York: Springer, 2016), 62.

7   Chris Burniske et al., How Blockchain Technology can Enhance EHR operability (Gem, 2016), 3; Robert Greenes, "Health Information Systems 2025," in Healthcare Information Management Systems: Cases, Strategies, and Solutions, eds. Charlotte A. Weaver, Marion J. Ball, George R. Kim, and Joan M. Kiel (New York: Springer, 2016), 580.

8   8 Payne, 61.

9   Burniske et al.

10   Payne, 62.

11   Greenes, 579-600.

12   Ibid, 587. 13 Ibid.

authorization controlled by the user (consumer or patient)."13 [13]Greenes views data management as key to the shift of power from institutions to patients, "these future data management capabilities will clearly be one of the more impactful trends if and when it occurs, since it will change the primacy of data for health and healthcare from the enterprise-focused EHR to the patient-centric continuous (and greatly enhanced) lifetime record."[14] With the shift to patient owned data, so will the patient's role in informed decision making about their care shift, correcting for the previously lopsided exchange with physicians.[15] Greenes concludes with his prediction that, "the shifts, e.g., in locus of control from provider to patient-centric, degree of integration of data from multiple sources, and the power of innovation, unleashed through apps and interoperable infrastructure, will be far-reaching – eventually – and the system that results will be quite different. Actually, I do think that 10 years may be a conservative estimate, because the trends are well underway. The future is ours to shape."[16] O'Brien and Mattison summarize, "we have finally arrived at the perfect storm for fundamental changes, many of which will be driven by consumers and technology."[17] O'Brien and Mattison describe the ideal outcome, "Seamless and secure availability of interoperable longitudinal health data, reliable automation of identity management, and robust health information exchange will ensure that individuals' decisions are grounded in a comprehensive understanding of their health over time."[18] The next iteration of EHRs will reflect the industry's focus on patient-centric, collaboration, and data-driven care.

The U.S.'s Office of the National Coordinator for Health IT (ONC) is attuned to industry trends and is leading industry-wide efforts to advance EHRs technology. This office serves as the government's Health IT innovation hub, facilitating public-private partnerships to adopt new technology.[19] In 2016, the ONC issued a "Use of Blockchain in Health IT and Health-Related Research" Ideation Challenge, requesting white papers regarding the ability of Blockchain technology to address privacy, security, and scalability challenges of managing EHRs.[20] Blockchain's unique properties are well suited to meet the challenges associated with EHRs.[21]

13   Ibid

14   Ibid

15   Ibid

16   Ibid, 598.

17   Ann O'Brien and John E. Mattison, "Emerging Roles in Health and Healthcare," in Healthcare Information Management Systems: Cases, Strategies, and Solutions, eds. Charlotte A. Weaver, Marion J. Ball, George R. Kim, and Joan M. Kiel (New York: Springer, 2016), 200.

18   Ibid, 203

19   Margo Edmunds, Douglas Peddicord, and Mark E. Frisse, "The Evolution of Health Information Technology Policy in the United States," in Healthcare Information Management Systems: Cases, Strategies, and Solutions, eds. Charlotte A. Weaver, Marion J. Ball, George R. Kim, and Joan M. Kiel (New York: Springer, 2016), 152.

20   "Announcing the Blockchain Challenge," HealthIT.gov, https://www.healthit.gov/newsroom/blockchain-challenge.

21   Ariel Ekblaw et al. on page 3 illustrate Blockchain's unique properties, "The blockchain uses public key cryptography to create an append-only, immutable, timestamped chain of content. Copies of the blockchain are distributed on each participating node in the network. The Proof of Work algorithm used to secure the content from tampering depends on a 'trustless' model, where individual nodes must compete to solve computationally-intensive 'puzzles' (hashing exercises) before

Information privacy takes on a whole new meaning, Accenture's Brodersen et al. explain, "a blockchain environment protects information at the data element level rather than in aggregate, and appropriate parties can only access data using appropriate permissions."[22] Once data is added to the ledger, it can only be appended, not edited, and all parties have access to the version history.[23] Burniske et al. describe the influence of this infrastructure technology, "because each stakeholder has the same view of the complete ledger, blockchains could become the basis of trust that underpins information exchange between related and unrelated parties."[24] The ONC selected 15 winners from 70 white paper submissions.[25] The question is not if Blockchain will be used for EHRs, but how and when.

One of the most promising papers submitted to the ONC's challenge was MIT's MedRec Blockchain EHR prototype because it dualistically addressed data privacy and data sharing. Ekblaw et al. cited the current landscape and industry trends as the impetus for their design, "a long-standing focus on compliance has traditionally constrained development of fundamental design changes for Electronic Health Records (EHRs). We now face a critical need for such innovation, as personalization and data science prompt patients to engage in the details of their healthcare and restore agency over their medical data."[26] Ekblaw et al. summarize their MedRec prototype:

A novel, decentralized record management system to handle EHRs, using blockchain technology. Our system gives patients a comprehensive, immutable log and easy access to their medical information across providers and treatment sites. Leveraging unique blockchain properties, MedRec manages authentication, confidentiality, accountability and data sharing—crucial considerations when handling sensitive information. A modular design integrates with providers' existing, local data storage solutions, facilitating interoperability and making our system convenient and adaptable. We incentivize medical stakeholders (researchers, public health authorities, etc.) to participate in the network as blockchain "miners." This provides them with access to aggregate, anonymized data as mining rewards, in return for sustaining and securing the network via Proof of Work. MedRec thus enables the emergence of data economics, supplying big data to empower researchers while engaging patients and providers in the choice to release metadata.[27]

---

the next block of content can be appended to the chain. These worker nodes are known as 'miners,' and the work required of miners to append blocks ensures that it is difficult to rewrite history on the blockchain." The implications of Blockchain technology, not its technical underpinnings, are the focus of this paper. For more information on technical details, please read the following papers in full: Ekblaw et al. Brodersen et al., Burniske et al., Ekblaw and Azaria, and Peterson et al.

22   C Brodersen et al., A. Blockchain: Securing a New Health Interoperability Experience (Accenture, 2016), 5. 23 Burniske et al., 1.

23   Burniske et al., 1.

24   Ibid, 1.

25   Mary Pratt, "Healthcare, retail industries give blockchain a try," Computerworld, November 2016, http://www.computerworld.com/article/3137490/enterprise-applications/article.html.

26   Ariel Ekblaw et al., A Case Study for Blockchain in Healthcare: "MedRec" prototype for electronic health records and medical research data (MIT, 2016), 2.

27   Ibid

MedRec is an innovative solution addressing many of the current EHR issues with its design and utilization of Blockchain. MedRec's design fulfills the future state goal of Mayo Clinic's Peterson et al., "We believe that a patient's record should be consistent and available across institutional boundaries, and the terms of its access strictly dictated by the patient. As a secondary goal, this data should not only be shared, but shared in such a way that all interested parties can understand the structure and meaning, ultimately leading to improved data utility and patient care."[28] While MedRec is a promising path forward, assessing the ethical implications of such a technological innovation is a prerequisite to industry adoption.

The bioethical principles outlined in UNESCO's Universal Declaration on Bioethics and Human Rights[29] provide a framework to analyze the ethical merits of MedRec, as a case study for universal patient-centric EHRs more generally. While each UNESCO bioethical principle is independently important, the principles combine to create synergies as well as complex dynamics regarding the role of the individual and society. An ethical solution strikes a balance between the collective principles (solidarity and cooperation, social responsibility and health, sharing of benefits) and the individualistic principles (human dignity and human rights, autonomy and individual responsibility, consent and persons without the capacity to consent, respect for human vulnerability and personal integrity, and privacy and confidentiality). MedRec's altruistic ethical design aligns with the principles analyzed below; an ethical implementation will be the real challenge for a universal patient-centric EHR solution, like MedRec.

MedRec gives patients, the rightful owners of their health data, control of who accesses their information; MedRec's patient-centric design appropriately addresses the principles of human dignity, human rights, autonomy, and individual responsibility. MedRec author Andrew Lippman summarized the implications of the patient-centric design in an interview, "Medrec is designed to give people control of the distribution of their medical records...the tip of an iceberg that changes the notion of ownership of those records."[30] MedRec authors Ekblaw and Azaria summarize the patient experience, "MedRec restores patient agency by empowering users with a focal point for access and review of their medical history, and an easy mechanism for sharing their data across medical jurisdictions. Patients can authorize a new doctor to review their record and obtain a second opinion, or grant viewership rights to a guardian they trust."[31] MedRec's patient access controls preserve human

28   Kevin Peterson et al., A Blockchain-Based Approach to Health Information Exchange Networks (Mayo Clinic, 2016), 2.

29   UNESCO's Universal Declaration on Bioethics and Human Rights Principles are as follows: human dignity and human rights, benefit and harm, autonomy and individual responsibility, consent, persons without the capacity to consent, respect for human vulnerability and personal integrity, privacy and confidentiality, equality, justice and equity, non-discrimination and non- stigmatization, respect for cultural diversity and pluralism, solidarity and cooperation, social responsibility and health, sharing of benefits, protecting future generations, protection of the environment, the biosphere and biodiversity.

30   Andrew B. Lippman, e-mail message to author, April 18, 2017.

31   Ariel Ekblaw and Asaf Azaria, "MedRec: Medical Data Management on the Blockchain," September 2016, https://www.pubpub.org/pub/medrec?version=f6785304b51890cc47492d-

dignity and human rights, prioritizing the interests and welfare of the individual over the sole interest of science or society, and the institutions that currently control access to patient's EHRs.[32] The patient-data-ownership model present in MedRec aspires to implement the intent of HIPAA, the U.S.'s Health Insurance Portability and Accountability Act; Kiel, Ciamacco, and Steines explain, "the physical medical record belongs to the provider, but what is not known by many, is that the information contained within belongs to the individual."[33] By having the EHR be digitally native, eliminating its physical form, the patient can truly own and control access to his or her information. Ekblaw et al. describe patient access controls, "the MedRec model restores comprehensive patient agency over healthcare information—across providers and treatment sites, empowering citizens with the data they need to make informed decisions around their care."[34] With access to their own information, patients can become true partners with their providers.[35] Now that patients can access their health information, they will need proper education to interpret the information, as Duqenoy, Mekawie, and Springett note, "medical terminology and patients understanding of it can also raise challenges for the patient."[36] Yet, on certain sensitive topics, patients should not have access to all of their own health record information. Ekblaw et al. cite psychotherapy notes and physician intellectual property, acknowledging that "MedRec does not presume to be an automatic content-management system for all of a Physician's output."[37] Specifically, Kiel, Ciamacco, and Steines outline the HIPAA exceptions to patient access to their heath records: "psychotherapy notes, information to be used in legal proceedings or for forensic matters, information that could cause harm to oneself or another especially when inmates are involved, research information when a patient is in the sample, and if the requestor is judged that they may be further harmed by having seen the information."[38] There is some health information that could harm patients if they had access to it, so the design should be shaped accordingly. While MedRec does not address the patient's ability to share information selectively, there could be negative ethical implications if this functionality existed. For example, it would be unethical for a patient who is taking opioids to hide their prescription list from a new doctor, while seeking another prescription.[39] The ability for patients to have access and control access to their health records is a great achievement, but must be responsibly implemented.

8bae173f1dbbe105a5.

32   UDBHR, article 3.
33   Joan M. Kiel, Frances A. Ciamacco, and Bradley T. Steines, "Privacy and Data Security: HIPAA and HITECH," in Healthcare Information Management Systems: Cases, Strategies, and Solutions, eds. Charlotte A. Weaver, Marion J. Ball, George R. Kim, and Joan M. Kiel (New York: Springer, 2016), 444.
34   Ekblaw et al., 10.
35   Penny Duqenoy, Nermeen Magdi Mekawie, and Mark Springett, "Patients, Trust and Ethics in Information Privacy in eHealth," in eHealth: Legal, Ethical and Governance Challenges, eds. Carlisle George, Diane Whitehouse and Penny Duquenoy (Berlin: Springer, 2013), 285.
36   Ibid
37   Ekblaw and Azaria.
38   Kiel, Ciamacco, and Steines, 444.
39   William Yasnoff, "The Health Record Banking Model for Health Information Infrastructure," in Healthcare Information Management Systems: Cases, Strategies, and Solutions, eds. Charlotte A. Weaver, Marion J. Ball, George R. Kim, and Joan M. Kiel (New York: Springer, 2016), 347.

It is imperative to create an alternative method for those who are unable to exercise their autonomy and manage their health records. There is an obvious limitation for children, those who either do not have online access and those who don't possess the skills required to manage access controls of their EHR.[40] An alternative solution will need to be provided for them to preserve individual choice.[41] Perhaps a service or a designated confidant can manage their EHRs for patients in need.[42] Yasnoff concludes, While there are legitimate concerns that some patients may not be sufficiently informed to make such decisions and could make access choices that may be harmful, delegating this decision-making to anyone other than the patient will likely have a much larger (and more certain) negative impact. As an analogy, we as a society agree that individuals should retain the right to decide how their financial resources are allocated, even though this clearly leads to negative consequences when consumers act unwisely.[43]

Ideally, outsourcing of patient EHR management will be kept to a minimum, perhaps following the norms around personal finance. Overall, a patient is ethically the best person to handle their health record information; an ethical EHR solution would include an alternative approach for a patient who is unable to fulfill the responsibility of managing his or her EHR.

With patients owning and controlling access to their EHR comes a newfound management responsibility. MedRec author Andrew Lippman admitted in an interview that this new responsibility creates more work for the patient, or those who manage EHRs for those unable to manage their own records, "The main downside we worry about is that people don't want to do this. It may involve work, like balancing your checkbook."[44] The scope of patient time and effort in managing their EHR is unclear, if one is healthy and not switching doctors frequently, the upkeep will hopefully be minimal. Patients controlling access to their EHRs is a positive ethical development, but with a monumental shift in responsibility from institutions to individuals; education will be needed, so individuals fully understand what their new responsibility entails and its implications. Yasnoff describes the scenario, "In a system where patients control access to their own medical information, education and assistance related to decisions about sharing that information would clearly be needed. Managing access to personal information is a new concept for most people, so some confusion about this new responsibility is inevitable."[45] Patient education regarding the short and long-term implications of sharing their EHR can prevent oversharing of health data. Also, patients must be trained to use the technology properly and be protected from phishing and the EHR equivalent of an accidental reply-all email. Blockchain is a nascent technology that has not solved the usability issue of key management and proper use of wallets that hold the keys to accessing information

40   Duqenoy, Mekawie, and Springett, 285.
41   Yasnoff, 337.
42   Duqenoy, Mekawie, and Springett, 285.
43   Yasnoff, 337.
44   Lippman, e-mail.
45   Yasnoff, 337.

locked with those keys.[46]Mismanaged keys increase the likelihood of stolen or lost data.[47] Proper key management is a Blockchain-wide issue and therefore the brightest minds in the space are researching a solution; it will be solved as the technology matures. A user-friendly key management solution is a prerequisite to adoption of a universal patient-centric EHR system. Patients must understand the implications of their new responsibility and be trained to use the proper tools to protect their own health data in their EHRs.

MedRec's prioritization of privacy stems from the need to preserve the principle of respect for human vulnerability and personal integrity. MedRec's designers understand their system handles sensitive information, and if this was inappropriately shared or leaked this could put the patient in a vulnerable position. The patient could be stigmatized or taken advantage of because of data housed in their EHR.[48] To minimize patient vulnerability, the ability to consistently keep the information associated with the correct person will be key; universal identity management solution is another Blockchain-wide area of development and a prerequisite for adoption that will be addressed as the technology matures.[49] With patients responsible for access controls, the fate of their information is in their hands, minimizing patient vulnerability is yet another reason patients must be set up for success through education and user-friendly tools to manage their EHR.

MedRec's use of patient access control and Blockchain's innovative security paradigm addresses the principles of privacy and confidentiality. Privacy and confidentiality are commonly used interchangeably, yet the proper term to use is usually confidentiality; Yasnoff explains the distinction, "'privacy' strictly refers to prevention of information release while confidentiality covers the appropriate use of sensitive information after it is released."[50] With MedRec's patient access controls, patients are in control of their confidential information and release it by choosing to share it with relevant stakeholders in their healthcare. Generally, MedRec's security model is an improvement on current standards and is designed to withstand a current-day cyberattack on centralized systems given the distributed nature of the system, Ekblaw et al. explain, "our system does not create a central target for content attack—a crucial consideration in an age of cyberattacks and data leaks."[51] Yet, MedRec is not immune from security threats. An important vulnerability is patient key management, discussed above; patient access control holds the patient responsible for sharing information with only those providers who will keep their information confidential. Ekblaw et al. note another vulnerability, "MedRec does not claim to address the security of individual provider databases—this must still be managed properly by the local IT system admin."[52] Again, the nascent status of Blockchain technology leaves room for improvement, this time regarding the pseudonymous – not

---

46   Tierion, Blockchain Healthcare 2016: Promise & Pitfalls, (2016), 7. 47 Ibid.
47   Ibid.
48   Yasnoff, 336.
49   IBM, Healthcare rallies for blockchains: keeping patients at the center (2017), 8 and 10.
50   Yasnoff, 335.
51   Ekblaw et al., 9.
52   Ibid.

anonymous -- status of information as this moves through the system.

Ekblaw et al. acknowledge that the pseudonymous property currently allows for inferences to be made if network traffic is analyzed, even if no identifying information is shared.[53] Anonymity is a pivotal area of Blockchain development; promising privacy solutions are beginning to emerge and continued innovation will solve this Blockchain-wide problem.[54] Trusting that one's information will be kept confidential is essential to the flow of information that is critical to maximizing benefit and minimizing harm, Duqenoy, Mekawie, and Springett explain, "If patients do not feel that the information that they give to a doctor is protected, in the sense of considering all such things to be private, and that their privacy is at risk, they might choose to be more selective about the information they provide to the doctor in the future. This can undermine the patient/doctor relationship and impede diagnosis and appropriate treatment."[55] As with all Blockchain solutions, data is secured at the element, not aggregate level; MedRec's security integrated model is an improvement on the perimeter defenses of institution-centric EHRs.[56] MedRec's combination of patient access control and robust security solution will bring much-needed improvement to the healthcare industry's data security.

MedRec properly addresses the principle of consent because each time a patient shares their EHR with a health care provider they are giving consent. MedRec's ability to track who has access to patient EHRs acts as a record of consent. While not discussed directly by MedRec's authors, there will need to be a consent alternative for emergencies when patients are unable to provide consent. Yasnoff suggests a solution, a preemptive consent functionality so patients could grant access in advance for emergency situations for a limited amount of time, yet this backdoor option does pose a security threat.[57] Another principle is preserving the rights of persons without the capacity to consent, which is related to the discussion above about preserving the autonomy of those who cannot manage their own EHRs. As with patients who are unable to bear the responsibility of access controls and the consent that entails, patients could deem a family member or confidant to provide consent on their behalf.[58] Today, there are a few cases where the need for society to know one's health status overrides one's ability to consent, and a MedRec-like solution would need to preserve those procedures. Yasnoff cites exceptions of communicable diseases and controlled substance prescription information, concluding, "with medical information access controlled by patients, it seems likely that a limited number of additional public policies, such as access control policies for minors, will be needed to ensure that, when it is appropriate, essential community interests supersede individual rights."[59] The individual will be in control of who can access their EHR, yet the rights of the

53   Ibid.
54   Disclosure: the author works for J.P. Morgan, who has open-sourced Quorum, a leading Blockchain data privacy solution.
55   Duqenoy, Mekawie, and Springett, 281.
56   Brodersen et al., 5.
57   Yasnoff, 348; Tierion, 7.
58   Duqenoy, Mekawie, and Springett, 285.
59   Yasnoff, 347.

individual need to be balanced with the rights of society.

Ekblaw et al.'s mechanism of population-level data sharing is MedRec's novel feat and appropriately addresses the principles of solidarity, cooperation, social responsibility and health, and sharing of benefits. Preserving individual autonomy, MedRec gives patients a choice in how much metadata to share with researchers who earn census level data as they work to sustain the network.[60] Researchers could include academics, pharmaceutical companies, the CDC, regulated healthcare NGOs, insurance companies; since the network would be closed, patients and providers would govern which researchers could join.[61] An ethical conflict of interest could arise if a patient is providing data that facilitates a research breakthrough resulting in a new medication, which a pharmaceutical company could then sell for a profit. While it may not be ethical to have patients sell their data, similar to how it considered unethical to sell organs, this will be a murky unexplored bioethical territory.[62] Compensating research participants for their time and effort is a norm, so why could we not expand that norm to include their data? Anonymized longitudinal research data allows for ethical data sharing that will benefit society. Ekblaw et al. note, "By leveraging a data orchestration system like MedRec where the records would already be gathered, organized and available for analysis, this type of research can be achieved with significantly less overhead than traditional research trials, which often require expensive recruitment procedures and in-person access to patients."[63] Blockchain technology lowers the cost of secure information sharing; research will no doubt benefit from the unprecedented data access. The possibilities of medical research will improve thanks to increased access to population health data, aiding society's fight against the threats to the survival of humanity.

Ekblaw et al.'s design appropriately addresses the principle of benefit and harm for both the individual and society. By allowing patients to share their complete health history with any healthcare provider they deem needs access, health outcomes will improve from the added context of a patient's longitudinal EHR. In addition to traditional health record information, MedRec can incorporate health data, like sleep patterns and heart rates, from fitness trackers to add further context to a patient's health history.[64] Mayo Clinic's Peterson et al. concludes, "Ultimately, better and more available data leads to better care for the patient."[65] Duqenoy, Mekawie, and Springett describe the importance of trust and sharing of complete information, "On the patient's side, this involves trust that the doctor will act in the best interests of the patient and, from the doctor's side, trust that patients are transparent with regard to offering details about the precise status of their health condition."[66] Preserving privacy and confidentiality is foundational to form a trusted

60   Ekblaw and Azaria. 61
61   Ibid.
62   Lippman, e-mail.
63   Ekblaw et al.
64   Ekblaw et al., 10.; IBM, Healthcare rallies for blockchains: keeping patients at the center, 9-10.
65   Kevin Peterson et al., 8.
66   Duqenoy, Mekawie, and Springett, 292.

patient-physician relationship Yasnoff notes, "perhaps more importantly, failing to assure the privacy of medical records will make patients much less willing to divulge critical personal details to their providers – and perhaps even avoid seeking medical care at all."[67] With MedRec, there will no longer be data silos that segment information, impeding doctors from having a patient's longitudinal health data to use for decision making.[68] Society will benefit from population health tracking features, such as tracking communicable disease in real time to limit their spread.[69]MedRec allows for more than just access to a comprehensive log of a patient's health history; the design could be expanded to include automated suggestions based on analysis of the information. Ekblaw et al. explain that on an individual level, "MedRec data can also feed into emerging technologies for predictive analytics, allowing patients to learn from their family histories, past care and conditions to better prepare for healthcare needs in the future."[70] On a collective level, Ekblaw et al. elaborate, "due to the linked interoperability between provider databases in a MedRec network, better-unified access to data could facilitate a wide range of trend discovery. MedRec's modularity could support an additional analytics layer for disease surveillance and epidemiological monitoring, physician alerts if patients repeatedly fill and abuse prescription access."[71] Sharing anonymized data on an unprecedented scale has unquestionable benefits for research, but potentially harmful outcomes await if research results are not used in an ethical manner. Kohli and Tan note that research outcomes should not be applied as cure-alls for the whole population in a purely utilitarian manner, but instead multiple solutions should coexist, "At the aggregate-level, patients are concerned that consolidation of EHRs may lead to changes in medication or therapy that works for them if national authorities found such medicines and therapies to be generally less effective for other patients."[72] Stanton-Jean et al. note the importance of preserving the balance of needs between the individual and society; if the balance is too weighted to the individual, it would lead to the displacement of health system costs. [73] MedRec appropriately addresses the need to maximize beneficence and minimize maleficence on both the individual and societal level with its anonymized data sharing that requires patient consent.

Data sharing is made possible by MedRec's interoperable design. Ekblaw et al. explain, "we have developed MedRec not as a proprietary system, but as a set of open APIs to facilitate EHR review and exchange. MedRec is a layer that can be added to existing provider [systems]."[74] MedRec is committed to being open source

67   Yasnoff, 336.

68   IBM, Blockchain: The Chain of Trust and its Potential to Transform Healthcare – Our Point of View (2016), 2.

69   Ibid, 5.

70   Ekblaw et al., 10.

71   Ibid.

72   Rajiv Kohli and Sharon Swee-Lin Tan, "Electronic Health Records: How can IS researchers contribute to transforming healthcare?" MIS Quarterly 40, no. 3 (2016): 557.

73   Michele Stanton-Jean, Hubert Doucet, Therese Leroux, and Julie Cousineau, "Canada," in Handbook of Global Bioethics, eds. Henk A. M. J. ten Have and Bert Gordijn (New York: Springer, 2014), 977.

74   Ekblaw et al., 9.

software, Ekblaw and Azaria state their goal as, "use of MedRec will not entail system ownership of the data. We believe this policy is key, especially for a medical record system that emphasizes patient agency."[75] Given the open source nature of MedRec, which allows for transparent review and improvement, the maleficent opaqueness of current proprietary institution-centric EHRs will be eliminated. Vendor contacts currently have "hold harmless" and "non-disclosure" clauses to ensure they are not responsible for faults in their software.[76] If a vendor's software glitch negatively impacts the provision of healthcare, the vendor is 'held harmless,' and users cannot publicly communicate the error due to 'non-disclosure' clauses.[77] With an open source solution like MedRec, but there will be a transparent process to report and fix errors. MedRec's open source nature would eliminate this issue because of its transparent design, plus its ability to publicly report errors and transparently apply fixes.

The implementation of MedRec will address the remaining principles outlined by UNESCO. Regarding equality, justice, and equity, an ethical implementation of MedRec would comprehensively provide system access to all patients and their healthcare stakeholders, as well as benefits from the research that results from MedRec's data sharing. Regarding the principles of non-discrimination, non-stigmatization, respect for cultural diversity and pluralism, the research conclusions using MedRec's data should strive to be non-discriminatory while preserving diversity. The ability for family members to share health history with each other addresses the principle of protecting future generations.[78] Patients would be much better informed of their genetic health risks. Plus, all of the research stemming from MedRec's data sharing would improve health outcomes going forward; conclusions of population-level data analysis could then inform patients regarding their likelihood of disease based on a variety of factors including family histories.[79] MedRec's elimination of paper records would have an obvious environmental impact, preserving the principle of protection of the environment, the biosphere and biodiversity. Yet, the current design is highly reliant on computer power to sustain the system; this is a Blockchain-wide problem, a scalable, sustainable solution will be found as this technology matures. If inspired by MedRec's ethical design, it is a reasonable goal that implementation of a universal patient-centric EHR system will be ethical.

The altruistic ethical design of MedRec is impressive; the real test will be for healthcare's many stakeholders to ensure ethical use once implemented. To uphold its status of a global bioethical solution that properly balances both the individualistic and collective principles, an implementation of a MedRec- like solution must allow for unified and comprehensive healthcare solutions that benefit all of humanity. MedRec could even enjoy expedited adoption, Ekblaw et al. note MedRec's interoperable design "will ease adoption, lower integration costs and aid compliance

75 Ekblaw and Azaria.
76 Ross Koppel, "Great Promises of Healthcare Information Technology Deliver Less," in Healthcare Information Management Systems: Cases, Strategies, and Solutions, eds. Charlotte A. Weaver, Marion J. Ball, George R. Kim, and Joan M. Kiel (New York: Springer, 2016), 110-111.
77 Ibid, 110.
78 Ekblaw et al., 10.
79 Ibid.

with HIPAA regulations."[80] As MedRec, or a similar universal patient-centric EHR system, continues on a path to adoption co-current efforts from technology researchers, healthcare industry leaders, policymakers, and patients will remove the remaining roadblocks to production. These efforts will need to consistently analyze the ethical implications of their actions and adapt as needed. Blockchain technology must continue to mature, solving for key management, identity management, privacy, and sustainability features that are essential to wide-spread adoption. Academia will hopefully play a leading role in developing this nascent technology, Halamka, Lippman, and Ekblaw conclude, "One outcome we can all hope for is that Blockchain continues to be developed at a disinterested, nonprofit university so that the idea can mature before it's optimized for commercial purposes."[81] Industry coordination and policymaker support will be key to support a MedRec- type solution from prototype to production. Areas for future study include how to align incentives among industry competitors to coordinate implementation of a universal EHR Solution. Blockchain is an industry infrastructure technology that will re-architect the competitive landscape; any industry adopting this innovative technology will need to solve the coordination problem, so all can benefit.[82] The benefit to the healthcare industry would be substantial, IBM cites the Premier healthcare alliance, "sharing data across organizations could save hospitals USD 93 billion over five years in the U.S. alone."[83] In addition to cost savings, competitive dynamics will evolve. Once all stakeholders have access to the same information, healthcare providers can compete by providing the best care, and no longer will information hoarding equate to a competitive advantage in retaining patients.[84] A universal patient-centric EHR system ideally avoids commoditizing care, but instead, improves patient choice of doctors and provides a solid foundation as new relationships begin. Some believe a Blockchain-based EHR system is a non-starter due to regulation.[85] That is short-sighted. Instead, innovation must shape regulation, regulation must not stifle innovation. A universal EHR system will necessitate updates to HIPAA given the paradigm shift, as data ownership and control shifts from institutions to patients, proper patient protections will need to be updated accordingly. No longer elusive, as patients gain ownership and control of their health data, patients must be active, influential participants on the path to adoption of universal patient-centric EHRs.

---

80   Ekblaw and Azaria.

81   John D. Halamka, Andrew Lippman, and Ariel Ekblaw, "The Potential for Blockchain to Transform Electronic Health Records," Harvard Business Review, March 03, 2017, https://hbr.org/2017/03/the-potential-for-blockchain-to-transform-electronic-health- records.

82   Brodersen et al., 3.

83   IBM, Healthcare rallies for blockchains: keeping patients at the center, 8.

84   Peterson et al., 8.

85   Mike Miliard, "Blockchain and healthcare privacy laws just don't mix," Healthcare IT News, May 3, 2017, http://www.healthcareitnews.com/news/blockchain-and-healthcare-privacy-laws-just-dont-mix.

References

"Announcing the Blockchain Challenge." HealthIT.gov. https://www.healthit.gov/news-room/blockchain- challenge.

Brodersen, C, Kalis, B, Leong, C, Mitchell, E, Pupo, E, and Truscott, A. Blockchain: Securing a New Health Interoperability Experience. Accenture, 2016.

Burniske, Chris, Emily Vaughn, Jeff Shelton and Alex Cahana. How Blockchain Technology can Enhance EHR operability. 2016.

Duqenoy, Penny, Nermeen Magdi Mekawie, and Mark Springett. "Patients, Trust and Ethics in Information Privacy in eHealth." In eHealth: Legal, Ethical and Governance Challenges, edited by Carlisle George, Diane Whitehouse and Penny Duquenoy, 275-295. Berlin: Springer, 2013.

Edmunds, Margo, Douglas Peddicord, and Mark E. Frisse. "The Evolution of Health Information Technology Policy in the United States." In Healthcare Information Management Systems: Cases, Strategies, and Solutions, edited by Charlotte A. Weaver, Marion J. Ball, George R. Kim, and Joan M. Kiel, 139 - 162. New York: Springer, 2016.

Ekblaw, Ariel, Asaph Azaria, John D. Halamka, MD, and Andrew Lippman. A Case Study for Blockchain in Healthcare: "MedRec" prototype for electronic health records and medical research data. MIT, 2016.

Ekblaw, Ariel and Asaf Azaria. "MedRec: Medical Data Management on the Block-chain." 2016. https://www.pubpub.org/pub/medrec?version=f6785304b51890cc47492d-8bae173f1dbbe105a.

Greenes, Robert. "Health Information Systems 2025." In Healthcare Information Management Systems: Cases, Strategies, and Solutions, edited by Charlotte A. Weaver, Marion J. Ball, George R. Kim, and Joan M. Kiel, 579-600. New York: Springer, 2016.

Halamka, John D., Andrew Lippman, and Ariel Ekblaw. "The Potential for Blockchain to Transform Electronic Health Records." Harvard Business Review. March 03, 2017. https://hbr.org/2017/03/the-potential-for-blockchain-to-transform-electronic-health-records.

Have, Henk A. M. J. ten, and Bert Gordijn. "Global Bioethics." In Handbook of Global Bioethics, edited by Henk A. M. J. ten Have and Bert Gordijn, 3-18. New York: Springer, 2014.

IBM. Blockchain: The Chain of Trust and its Potential to Transform Healthcare – Our Point of View. 2016.

IBM. Healthcare rallies for blockchains: keeping patients at the center. 2017.

Keller, Allen. "Global Bioethics." Presentation at NYU's Global Bioethics Class, New York, NY, Spring 2017.

Kiel, Joan M., Frances A. Ciamacco, and Bradley T. Steines. "Privacy and Data Security: HIPAA and HITECH." In Healthcare Information Management Systems: Cases, Strategies, and Solutions, edited by Charlotte A. Weaver, Marion J. Ball, George R. Kim, and Joan M. Kiel, 437-449. New York: Springer, 2016.

Kohli, Rajiv and Sharon Swee-Lin Tan. "Electronic Health Records: How can IS researchers contribute to transforming healthcare?" MIS Quarterly 40, no. 3 (2016): 553-573.

Koppel, Ross. "Great Promises of Healthcare Information Technology Deliver Less." In Healthcare Information Management Systems: Cases, Strategies, and Solutions, edited by Charlotte A. Weaver, Marion J. Ball, George R. Kim, and Joan M. Kiel, 101-125. New York: Springer, 2016.

Lippman, Andrew B. E-mail message to author. April 18, 2017.

Ludwick, D.A. and John Doucette. "Adopting electronic medical records in primary care: Lessons learned from health information systems implementation experience in seven countries." International journal of medical informatics 78 (2009): 22–31.

Miliard, Mike. "Blockchain and healthcare privacy laws just don't mix." Healthcare IT News. May 3, 2017. http://www.healthcareitnews.com/news/blockchain-and-healthcare-privacy-laws-just-dont-mix.

O'Brien, Ann and John E. Mattison. "Emerging Roles in Health and Healthcare." In Healthcare Information Management Systems: Cases, Strategies, and Solutions, edited by Charlotte A. Weaver, Marion J. Ball, George R. Kim, and Joan M. Kiel, 199-217. New York: Springer, 2016.

Payne, Thomas. "Snapshot at Mid-stride: Current State of EHRs and Their Use by Clinicians from a CMIO's Perspective." In Healthcare Information Management Systems: Cases, Strategies, and Solutions, edited by Charlotte A. Weaver, Marion J. Ball, George R. Kim, and Joan M. Kiel, 59-72. New York: Springer, 2016.

Peterson, Kevin, Rammohan Deeduvanu, Pradip Kanjamala, and Kelly Boles. A Blockchain-Based Approach to Health Information Exchange Networks. Mayo Clinic, 2016.

Pratt, Mary. "Healthcare, retail industries give blockchain a try." Computerworld. November 2016. http://www.computerworld.com/article/3137490/enterprise-applications/article.html.

Stanton-Jean, Michele, Hubert Doucet, Therese Leroux, and Julie Cousineau. "Canada." In Handbook of Global Bioethics, edited by Henk A. M. J. ten Have and Bert Gordijn, 959-992. New York: Springer, 2014.

Tierion. Blockchain Healthcare 2016: Promise & Pitfalls. 2016.

UNESCO. Universal Declaration on Bioethics and Human Rights. 2005.

Yasnoff, William. "The Health Record Banking Model for Health Information Infrastructure." In Healthcare Information Management Systems: Cases, Strategies, and Solutions, edited by Charlotte A. Weaver, Marion J. Ball, George R. Kim, and Joan M. Kiel, 331- 354. New York: Springer, 2016.

Chapter 22:
Genomics

Ofer Lidsky

Tal Sines

Digital DNAtix Ltd

Editor's Note:

The chapter Blockchain and Genomics, written by Ofer Lidsky and Dr. Tal Sines, co founders of DNAtix combines two of the most exciting disruptive technologies in Healthcare. Since the completion of human genome sequencing almost 20 years ago, the field of genomics, metabolomics and proteomics has exploded. Both the medical and direct to consumer (DTC) uses of genetic testing have become ubiquitous, creating new challenges in the veracity, security, privacy and ownership of genetic data. In this chapter Ofer and Tal explain both the healthcare, wellness and forensic use of genetic testing, as well as their compression algorithm that allows the use of genomic data on distributed ledgers. The chapter describes in detail the decentralized ecosystem around genomic information and how patients and families, healthcare professionals and researchers can benefit from secure, accurate and private storage, transfer and update of genetic data.

DNAtix, the genetic ecosystem, is bringing new possibilities in preventive and personalized medicine by applying advanced genetic services.

The genetic ecosystem will enable all players operating in the field to collaborate and create new solutions for the genetic world and exciting possibilities for medical research. The use of blockchain technology provide users with the ability to use their genetic information in an anonymous manner, making genetics more accessible for all.

DNAtix is developing a cutting-edge genetics blockchain-based platform, providing anonymous and encrypted genetic services including: analysis, storage, and transfer of digitized DNA sequences direct-to-consumer.

Genetics

About DNA

DNA (short for Deoxyribonucleic acid) is the molecule that carries the genetic instructions for growth, development, functioning and reproduction of almost all known living organisms. Most DNA molecules consist of two biopolymer strands coiled around each other to form a double helix. The double helix is composed of long chains of four nucleotides: (cytosine [C], guanine [G], adenine [A] or thymine [T]). DNA is arranged in structures called chromosomes and humans carry 23 pairs of chromosomes. DNA is composed of coding and noncoding regions with the coding sequences storing biological information in genes that code for proteins - the building blocks of living organisms. Human DNA consists of about 3 billion bases, of which approximately 99 percent are the same in all people. The order, or sequence, of these bases determines the information available for building and maintaining an organism, similar to the way in which letters of the alphabet appear in a certain order to form words and sentences.

DNA Sequencing

DNA sequencing is the process of determining the precise order of the four bases—adenine, guanine, cytosine, and thymine within a DNA molecule. The rapid process attained with modern DNA sequencing technologies has made sequencing of the DNA genome inexpensive, fast and accurate.

Determination of the exact sequence of a human can assist in identification of genetic risks and subsequently be used in preventive medicine for the inhibition and sometimes complete prevention of the development of those genetic conditions. Since the completion of the Human Genome Project in 2003, resulting in the first full draft of a human DNA genome, sequencing speeds have increased and costs significantly reduced. Today individual genes can be sequenced routinely, and some labs can sequence well over 100,000 billion bases per year. Today an entire genome can be sequenced for just a few thousand dollars and it's predicted that within the next two years, human sequencing intends to cost as low as $100USD [2].

Personalized Medicine and Genetics

Personalized medicine is referred to as the medical doctrine for treating patients that belong to different groups and aims to tailor medical decisions, practices, interventions and pharmaceutical treatment to

the individual patient. Personalized medicine today, is based on the development of several fields that include diagnostic, (Bio)informatics, big data analysis and genetic/genomics approaches that offer understanding of the molecular basis of disease and genetic conditions.

Every person has his own unique genomic sequence with minor differences between individuals. While most of the variations between individuals has little or no effect on their phenotypes (the composite of an organism's observable characteristics or traits) there are cases where such minor differences (e.g. mutations) could lead to significant variances between two people. In some cases, these variations can have a major impact on

an individual's health. Personalized medicine relies on technologies which analyze the DNA, RNA, protein, microbiom and epigenetics make-up of a person, which eventually leads to tailoring specific medical solutions to a disease or condition. One of the tools frequently being used in personalized medicine is DNA sequencing which covers parts or the complete human genome. By revealing alterations such as mutations, deletions, repetitions and etc... in DNA that influence the diseases outbreak and progression, such diseases as sickle cell anemia, cystic fibrosis and cancer can be properly and effectively treated.

Personalized medicine that is genetics based is the basis of the shift from reactive (treatment) medicine to preventive medicine. Using predictive tools to assess health risks, one can design personalized health plans to help patients mitigate risks, prevent disease, treating it more precisely when it occurs.

Genetic Testing Past and Future

Genetic testing is the process through which DNA is examined and the relation between a specific part of the DNA (single nucleotide, DNA sequence, chromosome etc) and a genetic condition are determined. Genetic testing can assist in risk identification of genetic conditions or diseases that could later be translated into predictive and/or pro-active medical treatment.

The world of genetic testing is undergoing a revolution as reflected in the following areas:

1. Transition from repeated "wet genetic tests" (based on biological sample such as saliva, blood or stool) to digital tests based on a digital sequence depended on one-time DNA sequencing).

2. Transition from genetic tests conducted in hospitals or health care centers to tests that are marketed direct-to-consumer.

3. Expansion of the scope of genetic testing from medical genetic test to tests in areas such as lifestyle and wellbeing, genealogy and forensics.

Genetic tests available today cover diverse fields:

• Health: 'Personalized medicine' includes the identification of the risk for developing a genetic condition or disease and subsequently receiving a tailored medical treatment, as it becomes available.

• Lifestyle: Administration of various aspect of a person's daily life including for example determination of personalized dietary needs (referred to 'Nutrigenetic and nutrigenomics'), management of hair loss, improved sports performance and more.

• Crime: Tests that supports CSI: Crime Scene Investigation.

• Ancestry: Tests to support Genealogical analysis and related tests such as paternity.

We are witnessing a constant increase in the number and types of genetic tests being offered and performed each year.

Direct-to-Consumer Genetic Testing

Traditional genetic testing involves a health practitioner that retrieves a DNA sample (by collecting blood, saliva or buccal swabbing) that is sent to the genetic lab for analysis. The next step, is usually the meeting with the practitioner who could be a physician or a genetic counsel, to obtain the results and understand their meaning. In recent years a slightly different approach towards genetic testing has evolved in which the clients perform the sample collection at home usually via saliva or buccal swabbing kits. The sample is then delivered to the genetic service provider via courier and the results are sent back electronically to the client. On-line counseling services or genetic counseling services over the phone replaces the traditional face to face meeting with the genetic counsel.

The regulations for performing DTC genetic testing varies from country to country so in some countries the DTC process is mediated by a physician that orders the test for a patient. For several years it was not clear whether or not DTC services could be offered in the US however in November 2013, the US Food and Drug Administration (FDA) sent a warning letter to 23andMe, Inc. ordering the company to discontinue marketing the 23andMe Personal Genome Service (PGS). On April 2017, 23andMe services were re-approved by the FDA now covering 10 genetic conditions including Alzheimer's disease, Celiac and more. It is clear that as more people have their full genomes available at hand, so the demand for DTC genetic tests intends to increase.

The DNA Sequencing Market

The Genomic market covers several services including:

- DNA Microarray: In these arrays single nucleotides polymorphisms (SNPs) also referred to as mutations are analyzed. Different Arrays may cover varying numbers of SNPs ranging between hundreds to over 2 Million. A DNA array intends to typically cost between $100-500. There are three basic types of microarrays: (A) Spotted arrays on glass, (B) self-assembled arrays and (C) in-situ synthesized arrays.

- Genes Panels (Such as Amplicon-SEQ or Targeted Hybridization Method): These panels are pre-designed to focus on targeted gene sets and are ideal for analyzing specific mutations or genes that have suspected associations with disease. Typically, the cost of gene panels would range between: $200-2000. Pathway Genomics is an example of a service provider offering Gene panels.

- Exome Sequencing (ES):Exome sequencing or whole exome sequencing is sequencing genomic analysis of the protein-coding genes in a genome (known as the exome). The human genome has roughly 20,000 genes and the cost for analyzing these genes by Exome sequencing, costs between: $200-2500. BGI (Beijing Genomics Institute) is one of the leaders in the field.

The Genetic Testing Market

Human DNA stores immense amounts of data that define who we are. Through our DNA analysis we can learn about our physical traits, mental aptitudes, our ancestry as well as our genetic risks for developing genetic diseases. The personalized medicine market is estimated to reach $149+ billion by 2020 and Covering Companion Genome data sets can be used to identify associations between genetic variants and diseases. This increase in Genetic testing intends to enable a tailored approach to drug matching that intends to modify selected genes and produce more precise therapies.

"Big data" platforms applying Genomic data intends to enable personalized medical drugs to be tailored for patients with a particular genetic makeup. These opportunities are advancing the growth of the genomic market to become a multi-billion-dollar one. Several Biotech companies including for example "deCODE

Genetics" have launched initiatives for privately held genome projects. DeCode, based in Reykjavík, Iceland was founded in 1996 by Kári Stefánsson[13] to identify human genes associated with common diseases using population studies. deCODE's approach was to identify genes combining genetic analysis with patients' data found in the Health Sector Database (HSD) holding medical records of all Icelanders.

In December 2012, deCODE genetics was purchased by Amgen for $415 million [14] which in October 2013 spun off deCODE genetics' systems and database to a new company called NextCODE Health [15]. The constitution of large collections of whole genomes or exomes held by private companies appears to be on the rise. AstraZeneca announced a 10-year partnership with J. Craig Venter's Human Longevity Inc., a StartUp Health company, to sequence 500,000 genomes, WuXi NextCODE announced an alliance with Abbvie and Genomics Medicine Ireland to sequence the genomes of 45,000 participants from across Ireland. [16]

DNATix

DNAtix intends to create the future ecosystem for Genetics where consumers, researchers, laboratories and clinics meet to use and make Genetics in a more transparent, accessible, applicable and secured manner.

DNAtix is a cutting-edge Genetics and Blockchain company that intends to provide anonymous and encrypted genetic services including: analysis, storage and transfer of digitized DNA sequences through a Direct-to Consumer platform (D2C). DNAtix intends to create a crypto Token – the DNAtix token, that intends to be integrated into the use of its DNAtix genetic platform. The DNAtix platform enables users to upload genomic sequences in an easy and manner that upon integration with the blockchain technologies intends to be also anonymous. It allows genetic tests to be performed and offers clients the opportunity to get referrals to an appropriate solution provider for the identified genetic condition. DNAtix enables its users to take ownership of their genetic data, encouraging them to manage their health today, moving from reactive to preventative medicine.

The Story

Friends since 1985, Ofer A. Lidsky and Dr. Tal Sines relationship begun at Elementary School, where they both shared a love and curiosity for technologies and science-related subjects. Through this interest, and eventual knowledge and experience, they launched a breakthrough scientific and technological venture - DNAtix. Their joint vision was to create a future ecosystem for Genetics where consumers, researchers, laboratories and clinics meet to use and make Genetics better. In 2008 when Tal finished his Ph.D. in Molecular Genetics at the world renown Weizmann Institute of Science, he and Ofer set up the first phase DNAtix, a direct-to-consumer genetic services company. An agreement was signed with a US company named HairDX that led to the distribution of genetic testing for diagnosis of, the risk of developing hereditary hair loss, "Androgenetic Alopecia". Parallel partnerships followed with companies in the field of personalized medicine in the context of nutrition and genetic diagnosis of diseases.

The second phase of DNAtix begun in 2015, Ofer and Tal recognized that the world of genetics was undergoing the revolution of going digital. The genetic testing world was shifting from repeatedly taking samples (blood and saliva) and analyzing them in the laboratory, to a technology where DNA is sampled and extracted once and is then sequenced becoming a digital code that could be stored on the computer. Subsequently a prototype of the DNAtix genetic platform was developed and a genetic algorithmic language was created to enables users to upload and test DNA sequences.

Phase 3 of DNAtix occurred in August 2017 when Digital DNAtix decided to implement blockchain technologies into genetics, thus creating the new DNAtix ecosystem idea. Genetic data is extremely sensitive and contains information about the person's identity, origin, family ties and of course the risk for developing genetic conditions or diseases such as Alzheimer's, cancer, diabetes and more. The fear that this information would reach the wrong hands prevented many people from using advanced genetic services and performing genetic tests. Blockchain technologies intends to solve once and for all the lack of anonymity issues and the fear of depositing the user's personal genetic information in the hands of the service providers. By developing a distributed and secure genetic ledger system based on encrypted blocks of information and based on a peer-to- peer communications network it is possible to separate the identity of the paying consumer from his genetic information. With that in mind DNAtix is developing a dedicated crypto token for genetics.

DNATix Genetic Ecosystem

DNAtix intend to build the genetic ecosystem of the future that will eventually bring to the world new possibilities in genetic preventive and personalized medicine. The ecosystem that will emerge will support different players participating in it. It will form new and exciting grounds for genetic research. DNAtix believes that by merging genetics and blockchain the next phase of genetics where people can stay anonymous but still have access to the important knowledge of genetics. Among potential participants making use of the DNAtix genetic ecosystem are genetic labs, genetic research institutes, genetic researchers, hospitals, companies that provide full genome sequencing, crypto-miners and etc..

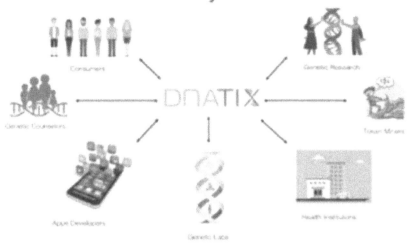

- Paying for Genetic Services

- Transferring DNA/RNA Sequences – The possibility of giving rights to a third party to access a certain DNA/RNA sequences on the

- DNAtix Blockchain.

- Storing DNA Sequences – The possibility of storing a DNA sequence on the DNAtix Blockchain. Full genome and partial sequences.

- Participating in Genetic Research. Giving limited access to your DNA sequence.

- Performing Genetic Counseling and providing advisory services. - Developing GDAPPS to earn Tokens.

Our Values

Our values are part of our DNA. They guide the way we work with each other and the way we treat our customers. We believe that through integrity, accountability, passion, simplicity and a focus on success, we are creating a revolution in the direct-to-consumer genetic services market, being a part of an evolutionary paradigm shift, providing people with an opportunity to discover more about themselves and take better care.

Case Study: DNATix Technology

The DNATix Platform

The process of partial or full genome sequencing results in a digital DNA sequence that is provided to the user. This sequence has hardly any meaning for the private end-user as it is just an endless string of letters made of the four building blocks of the DNA - Cytosine [C], Guanine [G], Adenine [A] or Thymine [T]. Once fully developed, the DNAtix platform will enable users to upload genomic sequences in an easy manner. It will then enable the user to run genetic tests and will offer clients the opportunity to get referrals to an appropriate solution provider for many identified genetic conditions. DNAtix intend to enable its users to take ownership of their genetic data encouraging them to manage their health today, moving from reactive to preventative medicine.

Genetic tests will be offered through the DNAtix platform in areas such as: lifestyle and wellbeing, genealogy, forensics and of course medical genetic tests.

Technology of Blockchain Token Background

Native tokens, like Bitcoin or Ethereum, are part of the incentive scheme to encourage a diverse group of people who don't know or trust each other to organize themselves around the purpose of a specific Blockchain. The native token of the Bitcoin network also referred to as Bitcoin, has token governance rules based on a crypto economic incentive mechanisms that determines under which circumstances Bitcoin transactions are validated and new blocks are created (Consensus mechanisms). The concept of decentralized ledger trustless systems which disrupts classic top down governances [5].

There are different types of tokens (Crypto Economics is so new, that we are still in the early stages of exploring different roles and types of tokens) [5].

Usage Tokens

A token that is required to use a service. Bitcoin and Ether are the best examples of usage tokens — token ownership does not give you any specialized rights within the network, but does give you access to the service (the Bitcoin payment network and the Ethereum Virtual Machine in the case of BTC and ETH). Scarce tokens combined with a useful service can create massive value for token holders and entrepreneurs.

Work Tokens

A token that gives users the right to contribute work to a decentralized network or DAO (whether on blockchain level or smart contract level) and earn in exchange for their work. That work can be serving as an oracle (in the case of Augur), being the backstop in a collateralized debt system (in the case of Maker), or securing the network (in the case of Ethereum when it switches to proof of stake).

Application Tokens

With Ethereum, tokens can now easily be sold on the application layer through smart contracts on the Ethereum Blockchain as so-called complex dApp tokens or complex DAO tokens.

Asset-Backed Tokens

Sold by a party onto a Blockchain for redemption later. They are the digital equivalent to physical assets, (like the gold), that you need to claim from a specific person (the goldsmith). The transactions as tokens get passed between people and are recorded on the blockchain. [5]

The DNATix Virtual Machine

Background

In a similar concept to the Ethereum Virtual Machine ("EVM") - Ethereum is a programmable blockchain. The concept that differentiates Ethereum from Blockchain is that instead of providing users with a set of pre-defined operations Ethereum supports creation of any complex operation users wish to design. Ethereum can be envisioned as platform that can serve various types of decentralized Blockchain applications such as cryptocurrencies.

Ethereum includes a set of protocols that define a platform for decentralized applications. At the heart of it is the Ethereum Virtual Machine ("EVM"), which can execute code of arbitrary, algorithmic complexity. Developers can create applications that run on the EVM using friendly programming languages modelled on existing languages like JavaScript and Python [11].

DNATix Virtual Machine

DNAtixVM – The DNAtix Virtual Machine runs as a node on the DNAtix Blockchain.

DNAtix is developing its own Virtual Machine DNAtixVM – that operates as a node on the DNAtix Blockchain. The DNAtixVM will be distributed and deployed by the different players (service providers) in the Genetic Ecosystem – These are genetic labs, genetic research institutes, genetic researchers, hospitals, companies that provide full genome sequencing, crypto-miners and etc.

What Do Genetic Service Providers Gain?

A branded genetic portal that runs on the Virtual Machine that can provide their clients with genetic services that are anonymous and secured via the Blockchain.

What do the Crypto-Miners Gain?

Crypto-miners would be rewarded for devoting their computer power to the network.

What Does DNATix Gain?

- Deployment of nodes that intends to support the DNAtix genetic blockchain.
- Increase in the use of the DNAtix token as new GDAPP's are developed and distributed.

What Do Developers Gain?

The ability to develop and assimilate new GDAPPS (Genetic Distributed Applications) that could be offered to their clients.

DNATix POC (Proof of Concept)

DNAtix has completed the first proof of concept test by uploading the sequence of the Enterobacteria phage phiX174 sensu lato, complete genome and transferring data through an Ethereum Blockchain using Transactions. The Enterobacteria phage phiX174 sensu lato is a single-stranded DNA (ssDNA) virus and the first DNA-based genome to be sequenced. This work was completed by Fred Sanger and his team in 1977.[6] Nobel prize winner Arthur Kornberg used ΦX174 as a model to first prove that DNA synthesized in a test tube by purified enzymes could produce all the features of a natural virus, ushering in the age of synthetic biology.[8][9][10]

The DNAtix development team conducted an internal test in order to perform a proof of concept and technical research on transferring DNA sequences on a Blockchain. The trial test was conducted during December 2017 using the Ethereum Blockchain infrastructure to store a full DNA sequence of a virus. As part of the research and development being done by the innovative development team at DNAtix, new technologies and solutions are being developed that will form part of the DNAtix Blockchain ecosystem.

Since the beginning of time, people have traded valuables for exchange of money or other valuables. Since the invention of credit cards, people have found a way to store large amounts of money. New technologies have been developed and improved to store and spend money however so have the tools and techniques to hack those technologies.

In some cases, people have been fired, companies have gone into bankruptcy, and money has been taken from hard working people by hackers. Because of these incidents, people know exactly who to blame – the organization that wasn't cautious enough to fix the vulnerabilities the hackers exploited, and this logic is understandable. One company which holds all the passwords of all users as well as personal information regarding those users, on one or more servers, held on another server that coordinates their operations, has a potential attack path for hackers to obtain access and control over the servers.

To fix the centralized issue, blockchain was invented. To fix the issue, Ethereum has a Blockchain, which is basically a distributed ledger. The Blockchain logs all transactions of Ether and can provide the current balance of an Ethereum wallet based on its transactions history. A surprise with this Blockchain is the location on which it's stored – everywhere. Every Ethereum user must store a copy of the ledger on the Blockchain (as of December 2017 – more than 470GB of data).

Forcing users to be part of the network will ensure that every user donates to the integrity of the ledger. With no specific address or target to attack, it is almost impossible to alter the Blockchain. With every transaction made and logged, the user can optionally add data to it. Imagine receiving money with a letter embedded in it. With an Ethereum transaction, money and data can change hands therefore theoretically we can send data through the Ethereum network and it will be decentralized, broken into pieces and stored on many computers to ensure greater security. It sounds great but there are some limitations on moving data through that network:

- Maximum data length is limited and varies on every new block created

- A fee is paid for every Byte of data transferred through the Blockchain

Ethereum is a network, also known as a Blockchain. Ether (ETH) is the fuel for that network. When you send tokens, interact with a contract, send ETH, or do anything else on the Blockchain, you must pay for that computation.

That payment is calculated in Gas and Gas is paid in ETH. Miners must validate the transaction. Whether the transaction succeeds or fails, you pay for the opportunity to transact. Gas is typically referred to Gas Limit or Gas Price and is measured in Wei, which is one quintillionth of ETH (1 Wei = 10-18 ETH). The total cost of a transaction (the "TX fee") is the Gas Limit * Gas Price.

You must include enough Gas to cover the computational resources you use, or your transaction intends to fail due to an Out of Gas Error. If you want to spend less on a transaction, you can do so by lowering the amount you pay per unit of Gas. The price you pay for each unit increases or decreases depending on how quickly your transaction is mined.

The data (hex representation of bytes) changes the total TX fee as well.

(21000+68*LENGTH_OF_DATA_IN_BYTES)*GAS_PRICE =TX_COST

For our experiment, we had to find a way to send a 5390 Nucleotides long DNA sequence using a transaction while minimizing its TX fee. First, we found a way to compress and encrypt the DNA to a quarter of its length and then implement that to a Python script.

Using this script, we expressed the nucleotides as hex representing binary and attached it to the transaction.

Since the Blockchain is too large for a consumer to download (and very time consuming), an alternative that allowed us to perform actions on the Blockchain, was to connect a wallet endpoint. We used Etherscan.io to make the transaction. Using the easy-to-use UI and UX of MyEtherWallet. com, we imported a Keystore of an account with about 0.2 ETH. We created another Ethereum wallet to receive the money and data.

The Website uses Etherscan's API first to check balances, then to connect to a wallet, calculate the amount, estimate the Gas required to successfully pull off the transaction, then queue the request to the Blockchain.

We estimated the Gas limit using the function above and added more Gas to have a leeway and prevent the Out of Gas Error. We sent most of the account's balance with the data of the virus.

When the transaction was performed, we waited and received a TX Hash on the Blockchain. Once the TX Hash is generated, EVERYONE has access to the data we sent.

An important note regarding posting data on the Blockchain: the data is public and can be seen by everyone. It's crucial to encrypt your data before sending it through the Blockchain.

The DNATix DNA Compression Algorithm

DNAtix has developed a dedicated compression algorithm for digital Partial or Full Genome Sequences. The idea is based on the conversion of 4 Genetic Code letters into a 2-bit code, which can then represent any of the 4 letters; C,G,T,A. The current working algorithm can compress any sequence to approximately 25% of its size.

All the DNA sequences that are being uploaded into the system intends to be converted to the compressed form in order to save space and make processing faster.

DNATix Intellectual Property

DNAtix has filed a provisional patent application US 62/637,499 DNAtix is in the process for preparation and filing an additional provisional patent application. DNAtix has filed for a US trademark US Serial Nos. 87/850,695 & 87/850,702.

DNATix Tokenomics

The Initial DNATix Token

The initial DNAtix Token is an Ethereum based token which will be used in the DNAtix Genetic Ecosystem.

The initial DNAtix Token is created on the basis of the ETH standard ERC- 20. This standard guarantees that the token will work in the ETHEREUM blockchain in a predictable manner. Based on this standard, more than 8,000 tokens have been released. For more information please look at this: https://etherscan.io/tokens

Our smart contract for token release will be available soon at: www.github.com/dnatix

The DNATix Genetic Wallet

DNAtix intends to develop the most innovative Genetic crypto-wallet that is intended to enable different kinds of users of the ecosystem to perform and pay for different Genetic services.

The DNAtix Genetic Wallet is intended to connect between the two worlds of Genetics and Blockchain. Through the wallet users can upload DNA sequences to the DNAtix Blockchain.

DNATix Token Usability Storing DNA Sequence

Storing DNA sequences on the DNAtix blockchain will be easy and secured. The task is performed by a specially designed Smart Contract embedded in the DNAtix token using the DNAtix Wallet allowing users to encrypt their DNA. As part of the proposed process the next step will use sophisticated compression and encryption algorithms designed by DNAtix team. Once compressed the data is then stored on the secure DNAtix Blockchain.

Transfer DNA Sequence

Transferring a DNA sequence on the DNAtix blockchain simply means giving a third party specific and defined access rights to access certain DNA sequences that are stored on the DNAtix blockchain.

This ground-breaking concept was designed to allow high level Genetic research to be conducted within the DNAtix eco-system.

Utilizing a large database of DNA sequences, Genetic specialists will be able to study, perform tests, and find solutions to some of the most difficult-to-solve mysteries in the world of genetics, while simultaneously providing those who have volunteered their data worthwhile returns for their contributions. The transfer allows third parties to access the DNA sequence code based on the following options:

- Partial Sequence Access (PSA) Onetime Access
- Quanta Access – 5,10,20...N times. Lifetime Access.

Once access is granted by the user (the owner of the DNA Sequence), he will be rewarded with DNAtix tokens. Reward mechanism will be based on type of access that was granted (E.g. giving limited access to only certain chromosomes).

Testing DNA Sequences

Each user in the system can perform analysis on the DNA sequences that he owns in a user-friendly manner. That means the users can run different genetic tests (GDAPPS) on their sequences and analyze them.

Computations on sequences will run on different nodes of the network run by miners and genetic service providers. The blockchain consensus mechanism ensures that the genetic data is maintained in high integrity which is crucial due to sensitivity of this type of data. The party who initiated the computation will be required to pay a transaction fee which will be proportional to the complexity of the computation initiated. This fee will be given to the miners who ran the computation as a mining fee.

The results from the different analysis that will be performed will be saved in the users DNAtix wallet for future use.

Inherit DNA Sequence

The DNAtix Token Smart Contracts will also have a useful and important feature that will allow users to choose who they wish to inherit their DNA sequences to. This smart contract will enable your heir to access the inherited DNA sequence.

Introducing: GDAPPS - Genetic Distributed Apps

DNAtix is going to develop the infrastructure for developing and deploying genetic applications on the DNAtix Blockchain, thereby enabling any participant in the DNAtix ecosystem to develop their own Genetic Applications such as:

- Genetic Tests
- Genetic Comparison
- Genetic Big Data Algorithms And more... Some examples of GDAPPS:

- Androgenetic Alopecia Genetic Test – A GDAPPS that scans your DNA for a point mutation (SNP) that has to do with hair growth and getting bald.

- VR GDAPP – a Virtual Reality Distributed Genetic Application

- Compare App – a GDAPP for comparing different DNA sequences. - Dating

- Diet

- Fitness

- Learning

- Entertainment

- Self help

The business model behind the GDAPPS is that for every work that will be carried out in the network running the GDAPP code and performing DNA analysis, tokens will be distributed to the miner that used his computer power and the developer of the GDAPP. The DNAtix genetic ecosystem incentivizes developers to develop new and innovative GDAPPS and introduce them into the system.

The DNATix Token - Smart Contracts

The DNAtix Token will incorporate specialized Smart Contracts for deployment of different Genetic services. Based on the ERC-20 Ethereum Token standard which includes the basic smart contracts for transactions, DNAtix intends to develope its own Genetic smart contracts. This will be enable to:

- Store DNA

- Transfer DNA

- Test DNA

- Inherit DNA

- Other DNA functions

- Revoke Access

- Update Access

References

1. https://www.fda.gov/NewsEvents/Newsroom/PressAnnouncements/ucm551185.htm

2. https://www.statnews.com/2017/01/09/illumina-ushering-in-the-100-genome/

3. https://ark-invest.com/research/genome-sequencing

4. From integrative disease modeling to predictive, preventive, personalized and participatory (P4) medicine - Scientific Figure on ResearchGate. Available from: https://www.researchgate.net/The- rise-of-genome-based-diagnostic-applications-The-number-of-genetic- tests-for_fig1_258334953 [accessed 16 Mar, 2018]

5. https://blockchainhub.net/tokens/

6. Sanger, F.; Air, G. M.; Barrell, B. G.; Brown, N. L.; Coulson, A. R.; Fiddes, J. C.; Hutchison, C. A.; Slocombe, P. M.; Smith, M. (1977). "Nucleotide sequence of bacteriophage ΦX174 DNA". Nature. 265 (5596): 687– 95. Bibcode:1977Natur.265..687S. doi:10.1038/265687a0. PMID 870828.

7. Fiers, Walter; Sinsheimer, Robert L. (1962). "The structure of the DNA of bacteriophage ΦX174". Journal of Molecular Biology. 5 (4): 424. doi:10.1016/S0022-2836(62)80031-X.

8. National Library of Medicine Profiles in Science. The Arthur Kornberg Papers. "Creating Life in the Test Tube," 1959-1970. link[non-primary source needed]

9. Goulian, Mehran; Kornberg, Arthur; Sinsheimer, Robert L. (1967). "Enzymatic Synthesis of DNA, XXIV. Synthesis of Infectious PhageΦX174 DNA". Proceedings of the National Academy of Sciences. 58 (6): 2321–2328. Bibcode:1967PNAS...58.2321G. doi:10.1073/pnas.58.6.2321. JSTOR 58720. PMC 223838 Freely accessible. PMID 4873588.

10. https://en.wikipedia.org/wiki/Phi_X_174#cite_note-4

11. http://ethdocs.org/en/latest/introduction/what-is-ethereum.

12. html#ethereum-virtual-machine

13. https://www.washingtonpost.com/news/wonk/ wp/2018/03/06/23andme-gets-fda-approval-to-report-breast-cancer- risk-without-a-doctor/?utm_term=.c52b492f4403

14. Herper,Matthew(6March2001)DeCode-ingSchizophreniaForbes, Retrieved 28 January 2015

15. Newswire, PR. "Amgen to Acquire deCODE Genetics, a Global Leader in Human Genetics". amgen.com. Amgen. Retrieved 3 May 2013.

16. Proffit, Allison (24 October 2013) NextCODE Health Launches deCODE's Clinical Genomics Platform Bio IT World, Retrieved 28 January 2015.

17. https://healthtransformer.co/the-rise-of-the-private-genome- databases-42a14d5988f5

Chapter 23:
DAO Concept
How Self Sovereign Identities will Fix the Healthcare Industry

Leah Houston

https://hashedhealth.com/blockchain-for-healthcare-book/

Editor's Note:

Dr. Leah Houston, an Emergency Department physician and CEO of HPEC has created a DAO for doctors. Based on her own experience, Dr. Houston goes over the shortcoming of the current healthcare system from a provider perspective and explains how physicians have lost control over the medical profession to insurance companies, hospital administrators and to less qualified medical personnel. The chapter offers practical blockchain-based solutions to overcome the current lack of mobility that providers have in their credentialing process, limiting their ability to overcome the extreme shortage of physicians in the US. Dr. Houston explains how by creating a decentralized ecosystem by doctors and for doctors, providers can regain control over the patient-physician visits and solve problems like administrative inefficiencies, physician burn-out due to EHR use and even how to combat the high prices of medications through transparent marketplaces.

Blockchain is about decentralization, disintermediation and removing the need for a third party in any transaction. Blockchain has the potential to eliminating the mal aligned incentives that have been created by consolidation regulation and exploitation of markets. Healthcare is one industry that has experienced increasing consolidation and centralization over the years and it has a heavy regulatory burden. As a result, has become radically inefficient, and in many cases borders on a monopoly. There are single health systems dominating entire geographic areas, leaving little to no choice for patients. Third party administrators are gaining market share and driving up the cost of healthcare through consolidation deals and price obscuring practices.

Examples:

Pharmacy benefit managers are merging with insurance companies, as with the recent CVS – Aetna and Express scripts and Cigna mergers. This creates a situation where the one controlling the supply of the medication will be negotiating the payment and pricing for those medications. Furthermore with the invention of in pharmacy minute clinics they can then also hire prescribers of those medications and give them protocols to follow.

Physician staffing companies are merging with health systems

Envision healthcare and HCA plan to merge which will put them in control the supply chain of physicians into their hospitals. Often in order to work for one of these systems you must sign a non-compete which leads to physicians being trapped in these systems, unable to move and fearful of retaliation if they don't comply with practice guidelines enforced upon them.

Physician practices are being bought up –and at times the physicians are being replaced by less qualified personal to save money- example Children's Health in Texas where the group was purchased and the physicians were replaced by non-physician practioners in order to save money.

Health systems also merge.

Hospitals also own other third-party administrators (TPA's) around the pharmaceutical supply chain such as the group purchasing organization (GPO) Intalere owned by Intermountain Healthcare. Intalere is one of the 4 GPO's in the country that control the in-hospital supply chain of prescription drugs (Interlare was formerly Amerinet- one of the tactics of these organizations is to frequently change names in order to obscure cronyism) Intermountain health claims to be "fixing the problem" by making their own medications- because they own the TPA's that controls it they are profiting on both ends at the expense of the patient.

Mergers like this not only leave patients with little choice, but drives up the cost of healthcare because it creates lack of competition in the markets. It is for reasons outlined through the examples above that decentralization enthusiasts are turning to blockchain in hopes that this technology will disrupt this trend. The lack of a need for a trusted third party to broker a deal is especially interesting for healthcare considering the mal-aligned incentives and back door deals that plague our healthcare system. Blockchain has the potential to revolutionize how healthcare is delivered and paid for, but only if it is implemented properly.

The question is how can we create an optimal and truly decentralized healthcare system for the benefit of the majority? First, we must let go of the idea that we must work within the current system, and integrate with current legacy systems. Those systems are the very systems that need to be decentralized. Every aspect of the system is inefficient and fraught with mal-aligned incentives.

One blockchain solution that is frequently discussed is the concept of the self-sovereign medical record. The health records and data industry are currently also centralized, siloed- and in need of reform. Electronic health records are inefficient, non-interoperable and an intrusion on the doctor patient relationship. Patients who need copies find it expensive and difficult to obtain the right information, and when they do they are often unable to interpret that information themselves. Health systems and insurance companies that own these records also continue to consolidate and gain market share as mentioned above. The minority stakeholders who have worked so hard to build this inefficient system do not have an incentive to change it, as they are the ones benefiting from control and centralization- so they would prefer to keep it that way. We must not be discouraged because all of these entities are just made up of people, and those same people want the best for themselves and the ones they care about- so if the solution is a true solution the solution will prevail.

The only true solution is to completely reorganized and decentralize power away from the consolidated third parity minority stakeholders; the health systems, pharmaceutical companies and insurance companies and other third parties and towards the individual people who consume create and utilize healthcare. To simplify who these people are; it is the caregivers, and those receiving care. In other words, the individual people who utilize, consume and created the current healthcare system will now collectively build the new decentralized system. At this point the only true barrier is the people- they must be willing to take that step, to make a change and consider themselves part of the solution. Right now, those individuals are extremely frustrated with the current system, so it makes sense that the solution lie with them, and it may be the optimal time for them to take that initiative.

Do a simple google search and find out why patients are frustrated and you will quickly learn there are many reasons. The cost of healthcare is rising and the user experience for the patient is not getting any better. The leading cause of bankruptcy is due to medical expenses, so they have every right to be angry. They know the cost is high so they avoid getting medical care, and this leads many to wait too long- which worsens their outcome. That is only one reason that patients in the US also have on average overall worse outcomes than other countries. The US also spends almost double per capita as other industrialized nations who have much better outcomes. The wealthiest sometimes also get too much care, which can be just as harmful as too little. Over care can also lead to harm, as there are risks and benefits to everything we do. Incidental findings and over testing can lead to incidental findings that then end up being over tested and obver analyzed as well. If complications arise from some of this care the patient may end up worse off than they started. Over consumption of care, is incentivized when insurance pays well in the current fee for service model. The very poor have Medicaid, but often cannot get the care they need due to limited resources, or limited number of qualified providers. Unfortunately when that happens the poorest populations are the most vulnerable because they have no other choice but to see non-physician practioners who often also order more tests than necessary over-refer, and inappropriately treat- further exposing these vulnerable populations to unnecessary harm, while also driving up the cost of care.

Physicians are also frustrated and many are leaving medicine. They are increasingly becoming employed, and therefore have lost autonomy in how they practice. Much of this has to do with regulation of the practice of medicine. Employed physicians have metrics placed on them and time limits on the ability to provide care. If a highly intelligent competent person is disincentivized to dig into a problem because they have restrictions on the time they are allowed to spend with a patient, yet they are not disincentivized to refer or order more testes they will naturally order more tests to try to get to the answer quicker. As we mentioned those tests cost the system more than their time may have, and may also lead to worse outcomes in the end. Over testing is also encouraged due to mal aligned incentives in the malpractice environment. Physicians are also incentivized to order more tests to prove what they often knew already in order to document proof of their decision making. Also despite what people think, physicians in the US do not get paid overall the most of all industrialized nations. Other countries provide better security in old age, less expensive education and better healthcare overall than than the US for the same cost in taxes. Other industrialized nations also often subsidize the cost of medical education and the US education system is not subsidized.

The system is expensive, and inefficient and the physicians and the patients- those who are on the front lines- are unhappy, Unfortunately the bureaurocracy that lead to these costs and disappointments are the result of layers of regulations that have been stacked on top of one another over the years.

Here is a summary:

1965　　CMS- Center for Medicare and Medicaid – the United States Taxpayer sponsored healthcare coverage for the elderly disabled and the poor created from the amendments to the Social Security Act of 1965.

1971-1972 More social security's acts amendments widened enrolment in CMS

1973　　HMO's Health Maintenance Organization act of 1973- incentivized the privatization of insurance

1981　　ACGME created to fund advanced medical education

1982　　EFRA Equity and Fiscal Responsibility Act of 1982 - created more government incentives to utilize the for-profit HMO's

1986　　EMTALA Emergency Medical Treatment and Labor Act -requires every patient to be screened for an emergency regardless of ability or willingness to pay.

1991　　OIG HSS safe harbor law that protects PBM's and GPO's &18

1992　　Current Procedural Terminologies (CPT'S) Diagnostic Related Groups (DRG's) and Relative Value Units (RVU's) and International Classification of Diseases (ICD's) all created in an attempt to control costs by monitoring and controlling how physicians spend healthcare dollars – all controlled by the AMA (American Medical Association)

1996　　HIPPA was created - The Health Insurance Portability and Accountability Act of 1996 which created standards for the electronic exchange, privacy and security of health information. Final privacy rule published in 2000

1997　　SGR- sustainable growth rate created. A freeze on graduate medical education was created which has contributed to the current physician shortage

2009　　The Health Information Technology for Economic and Clinical Health (HITECH) Act, enacted as part of the American Recovery and Reinvestment Act of 2009 to attempt to address the privacy and security concerns associated with the electronic transmission of health information, in part, through several provisions that strengthen the civil and criminal enforcement of the HIPAA rules

2010　　ACA "Affordable Care Act" incentivized everyone to have insurance coverage by penalizing those that do not.

2014/2015 MACRA The Medicare Access and CHIP Reauthorization Act of 2015 and MIPS Merit Based Incentives Payment System- attempts to tie payments to "outcomes"

2016　　PQRS- Physician Quality Reporting System – ended 2016 and became MIPS

Despite efforts by the government to regulate and control the healthcare system it continues to get more expensive and less efficient. Considering our laborious legislative process, the likelihood for major change is low when attempting to go through the traditional legislative process. Also, special interests who have a lot to lose spend money on lobbying to keep their interests in favor. Furthermore, many of the above policies took years to create, and with the acceleration and advancements we are making in technology it is becoming impossible to create policies in a timely enough fashion in order to keep up.

One piece of legislation that aimed to improve the medical records industry was the HITECH act. It created more problems by forcing electronic health records on a system that was not yet ready for it. It was a well-intentioned piece of legislation that attempted to foresee the future, but because the policy was guided by the enterprise systems that sought to gain from its implementation it only led to more mal-aligned incentives. The lack of data standards within these records has led to the creation of siloed records filled with dirty data that also lack interoperability. The result has been a very expensive inefficient system that does not help patients or the physicians who care for them., 9 Health systems however do now have the ability to extrapolate that data and commoditize on it as they choose for their personal gain. Insurance companies and pharmacies also hoard the data of patient and sell it.

The arugement is that this data will be used for the benefit of all, but there has been increasing evidence to the contrary. It is also becoming an increasing concern that the de-idenificaiton methods are not always secure. Since the cambrage anylitica scandal with facebook, society is becoming increasingly aware of the value of their personal information. When it comes to healthcare most agree that any healthcare data should belong to the patient not the health system.

So it is clear that the minority stakeholders in the system are not necessarily looking out for the patients best intersts. Mal aligned incentives are amplified through over-regulation consolidation. In order to create a new, optimized system we need to think about what the people want not the minority stakeholders. People who truly understand blockchain know that the true solutions that implement it will be community driven. Therefore in order to truly decentralize healthare you need to put the power directly into the hands of the community- and the individual people that matter in the healthcare system- and that is the patients who are receiving the care and those caring for them.

So we must identify these individuals, and first understand who these patients are, and what they truly want. Identity is a more difficult topic than one would think, and the data generated from it is valuable. For the purpose of this discussion we will talk about identity as it relates to the healthcare industry, and the individuals interacting with the healthcare industry, and first we will discuss the patients. Who are the patients? The dictionary will define it as "a person who is under medical care or treatment" The likelihood is that all of us have been or will fall under that definition at some point, so I will argue that the definition of patient applies to all humans. What do patients want? A person undergoing medical care wants to feel safe, secure to know the care they are receiving is the right kind of care- Patients prefer a physician to be the one who makes decisions with them, not a hospital or insurance company deciding for them. Patients want to be able to choose their physician. They want time with their physician and want to feel heard.

The good news is that physicians and patients want the same thing. Physicians also want more time with their patients than they currently have. Physicians have been increasingly employed, and their employer often determines how much time they are allowed, so unfortunately the time they spend when they are employed is out of their control. Despite what industry may say, the increasing consolidation of physician practices and employment is also driving up the cost of healthcare. There is no incentive to improve the quality of the physician patient interaction when physicians are being controlled and squeezed by their employer to meet metrics rather than provide high quality care to their patients. Therefore, the result of health system consolidation and physician employment is that people are dissatisfied with the time, quality and increase in cost. The good news is that the people that actually matter in this system want that to end.- better quality care, less intrusion on the doctor patient relationship and more time with the patients.

It should come as a relief that physicians and patients are on the same team in this healthcare system quagmire. It makes it clear that the solution lies in their collective efforts. In order to create a truly decentralized healthcare system the patients and physicians first need to be organized and identified. In order to do this in this new digital era they mush each have a self sovereign identity. Self sovereign identity allows for the individual to have ownership and control over the data that creates the digital version of themselves – a culmination of the sense of self in a digital space. It also provides an ability to store all of the data associated with the self in a digital wallet which becomes your digital identity.

There are blockchain solutions attempting to fix the user experience for the patients in the form of a self-sovereign healthcare record. A self sovereign health record medical record that is part of ones own self sovereign digital identity. An identity and record that only the patient controls. In order for it to be self sovereign the record would need to be portable, so the patient could move freely throughout the healthcare system. Patients would also need to be able to choose where they get care and would need that record to be able to be interoperable wherever they go.

A persons digital health identity can be intrinsic, extrinsic, and malliable or fixed. Other parts of your health identity may be innate and important for non health issues they can also be implied, and subjective

- Intrinsic: no need to interact with the healthcare system to be generated, an example being your age . You can have fixed or mailable versions- intrinsic and fixed as with your DNA, intrinsic and mailable such as your weight, or how many steps you take In a week.

- Extrinsic: a diagnosis or treatment given to you by the healthcare industry or physician

In the sense of your healthcare identity It can also be extrinsic and mailable as in the form of a diagnosis of "obesity," "bi-polar disorder with manic episode" or "Hypertension" and it can be extrinsic and fixed such as a diagnosis related to your DNA like "Huntington's chorea." An external part of your digital health identity could be measured in the form of a blood pressure reading or other biometric test. Innate parts of your identity are fixed and can be in the form of your birth date that gives you an age. Implied health identity characteristics could be in the form of healthy or unhealthy, safe or unsafe etc. These are only some ecamples of characteristics make up your digital health profile – which is part of your digital identity.

We are not of course a bundle of data – we are humans who in general don't want to think much about our digital health or identity or data, and want to live a healthy and peaceful life. In other words in general people don't want to have to think about their healthcare much, and certainly don't want to think of their healthcare data much. That data however is valuable, and with the US healthcare system approaching a 3.9 trillion dollar price point that digital health data that makes up a persons digital identity is very valuable, currently nearly a 40 billion dollar industry, and will continue to increase at a projected rate of 26% annually through 2025. That is why, in order to create a truly decentralized blockchain solution the value of that digital health data needs to be retained and controlled by the end user, but who creates the data, and how will the extrinsic data points generated and stored in a decentralized way?

It is clear that the current record systems either lack the infrastructure or have no interest in creating a self-sovereign record for patients, because they currently work within health systems. The electronic records companies are also increasingly consolidated and centralized. Cerner and epic control nearly 50% of the market. They have created contractual arrangements where they secure the data, and many of these agreements were based on HIPPA and created for the centralized world that currently exists so they are also stuck as well. The current record systems are also not interoperable which wouldn't work for a truly self-sovereign system, because in a self-sovereign system patient need to be able to move and choose, and lack of interoperability limits mobility and therefore choice.

According to US law patients "own" their data- so even the law favors this concept.30 Furthermore, records that are owned and controlled by the end user that are truly self-sovereign and truly decentralized will make heavily bureaucratic laws like HPPPA easier to follow, because they will no longer be stored on in house servers that are the target of digital health attacks due to the value of these records. If the medical record is truly self-sovereign the user must have full agency over the record, and it must be fully interoperable with other identity platforms. The patient must be able to choose who they will share the record with.

In the interest of true decentralization and removal for the need for a trusted third party it only makes sense for the individual patient to then be able to choose who creates that record as well. If a patient is interreacting with a truly self-sovereign medical record platform then they will not be interacting with a health system or insurance company or government- but with the person they have chosen to care for them. Therefore, the person that patient chooses must also have a self-sovereign identity, and they too must have agency over that identity and it must also be portable for them as well, therefore physicians and other non-physician providers will also need identity as well.

We will use the example of why physicians as caregivers in order to demonstrate the need a self-sovereign identity. Claiming ownership of ones personal identity, data and professional brand in a digital space will free the physician patient relationship from the current health system. When physician talent is no longer tied to the health systems they work for, both patients and physicians have more choice, and more mobility- and options are always good. Physicians will be able to recommend what they know is right, without fear of retaliation for advocating for their patients. Many do not know that when a physician contracts with a health system they must sometimes choose between recommending the right thing for their patients, and risk retaliation or termination, or recommending what the hospital protocol allows and putting their patients at risk. This is an obvious conflict of interest, but is the result of health system consolidation. When patients and physicians can freely choose who to work with, rather than a third party deciding than physician-patient relationship will be restored. Physicians will again provide care for patients untethered from the healthcare system, hospital, or insurance company. Patients will feel safe, knowing that their physician is making decisions for them based on what is right- not based on policies that save hospitals and insurance companies money. Physicians will be free to tell patients the truth about their healthcare without fear of retaliation from the companies they work for. When documenting they will document what actually happened during the visit, and no longer waste time clicking meaningless boxes for meaningless metrics.

There are many other pain points physicians deal with in the currently healthcare system, that could be addressed with this model. Credentialing is one of them. It can take 2-4 months, and sometimes more to credential for a hospital or insurance company. The physician often has to fill out stacks of redundant forms, filling out the same hand written information costing them 10-30 hours of uncompensated time every time they must go through the process. It is a process filled with antiquated and laborious ways of validating and authenticating facts that are a part of a physician's immutable record. For example, Physicians needed to graduate from medical school in order to take the last exam. This only happened once, but needs to be reported on and recorded on every time the physician credentials. The same thing goes for residency and many other occurrences.

But why blockchain? Why cant we just find a more efficient way of credentialing? Why cant the government or state licencing boards find a way to make this more efficient? Why must credentialing be decentralized and self-sovereign? The physician is the one who finished medical school, and the rigorous testing and licensing exams, residency, and board certifications. This is already part of the physician's immutable piece of truth, something they created for themselves through their hard work and effort, so because they are the creators of that data it only makes sense that they should have authority and oversight of that data.

Some point out that the board of medical specialties already does this, however they are centralized and there is growing evidence that they don't do it inefficiently or ethically. Physicians are becoming increasingly more aware as the licensing boards slowly increase the testing requirements to maintain certification while not improving physician knowledge or abilities. Furthermore, there is growing consensus by the physician community in regards to the futility of the maintenance of board certification. The certification is not required to practice medicine and was once a completely voluntary extra step a physician would take to go above and beyond what was necessary in order to practice medicine. Over the years however many of those that govern the board certification exams have made it increasingly more onerous and expensive for physicians to maintain their certification. There is evidence for example that the American Board of Internal Medicine has spent physician testing fees on luxurious properties and have been used to build shadow foundations to hide how they promote their agenda. Potential conflicts of interests have also been uncovered to the point that there is now a class action law suit being filed by a physician lead organization. This is another example of the end result of increasing consolidation of any system so it should not be a surprise, and only provides further support for the need of a decentralized model.

Physicians train each other, and validate each other anyway in the current model. Medical students and residents are taught by physicians who will eventually become their peers. The USMLE is also standardized already, and changes are also ultimately made by individual physicians. There is no need for a third party if standards are agreed upon by cryptography. The current academic medical system has become diluted by the monetization model. When CPT codes and RVU's were introduced into how physicians should be compensated it not only created another way to obscure the trie cost of healthcare but created a disincentive to spend time with patients because those activities are not rewarded with RVU's. This not only leads to a worse experience for patients, but disincentivizes academic physicians from teaching which is bad for the future of care. The measurement of physician performance at this arbitrary level of payment incentives will not be needed when physicians and patients are independent from these requirements once again.

Those who are credentialed on an open decentralized database will have their abilities and skills in plain view for all to see. Physicians can then work directly with patient and there will be no question as to their skills or years in practice. A decentralized physician database will eliminate much of the administrative waste in the current model that is used to update this information. Portable credentials attached to the self-sovereign identity will become part of the physician's personal data. Physicians cold easily move throughout the healthcare system creating employment mobility much quicker than the current 2-4 month process. If a physician is allowed to work for more than one system at a time, it will also improve patient choice in who they see. Physician digital identities and portable credentials will also create a way for insurance reconciliation to be streamlined. If the identity of a physician is validated on a decentralized ledger one of the longer steps of the reconciliation process will be eliminated. Physicians can be paid immediately at the time of service for non-emergency services which may eliminate the need for insurance reconciliation all together. When payment is immediate at the time of service it will also create price transparency and lead to healthy and fair market competition, something patients want. Most individual physicians could easily place a price on their service if they weren't employed by hospitals who deploy obscuring price practices.

In the current model there are 10 administrators for every physician. Those administrators spend the majority of their time working to improve inefficiencies in the system rather than improve the system itself. Time is spent dealing with bureaucracy and red tape rather than finding ways to improve patient care. Although many hospitals are "non-profit" the executive administrators take home large bonuses and salaries. In order to keep things this way in the fee for service model administrators encourage employees to increase services not improve services, squeezing the employed physicians and patients for as much as they can. This is why patients are afraid to get care and are sometimes going bankrupt when they do. This is why physicians who are being abused in this way are leaving medicine. A self-sovereign identity platform for physicians and patients could eliminate these mal-aligned incentives created and could change all of this. We will no longer waste 30% of healthcare dollars on unnecessary care, and much of the administrative waste will also be removed. Physicians will have more time with patients because the physician and patient will be in charge of healthcare again, and most importantly care will improve.

The new decentralized system will still have a need for hospitals, so they will also need identities in order to interact with the patients and caregivers. If the patients continue to demand the services of insurance companies or other third parties each entity will also need a digital identity. The difference is that insurance and health systems will no longer be the ones making decision on patient care. They will no longer be needed to broker the deal between the patient and caregiver. When interacting with enterprise patients will choose when to give permissioned access to this data and how much they want to share. Despite the fact that enterprise or government may have an identity in this scenario the cryptography must preserve rights of the individual over the needs of industry or enterprise identity. In a true self-sovereign and decentralized healthcare system the cryptography must preserve the rights of the individuals over enterprise. If Healthcare systems are providing a service they will get rewarded by the individuals. If they are not, they won't. The identities must attempt to be blockchain agnostic when it comes to interoperability, and they must be free from censorship. The W3C consortium is a working group that creates standards for self-sovereign identity authentication and verification, certificate validation, and reputation assessment. Currently many of the blockchain identity platforms are working together to create interoperable standards for purposes such as this.

Medical records were historically created for communication from physician to physician in order to best coordinate care for the patient. It later became a form of evidence for malpractice attorneys, and slowly the way things were documented began to change. The government HITECH mandate imposed electronic health records on the physician community, and penalties were applied if they were not implemented. The records are timed and dated and create a picture of the patient. Having an immutable ledger of this information has obvious benefits from a medical-legal perspective, so the objectives made sense. Electronic health records are not able to be altered after they are signed. In a court of law, the time the physician signed the chart is an important piece of data, because it shows the record is the true unaltered snapshot of what was observed to be happening at the time. Unfortunately, this has also created a way to measure how quickly a physician sees a patient, and a way to punish those who are not fast enough. Therefore, the HIPPA and HITECH laws were applied primarily to create a mechanism for EHRs to be for the industry- no longer for patients and no longer for the physicians who care for them. The result is that medical records are no longer just a way to coordinate and document medical decision making, but a way to document in order to bill and collect bills, and to reward and punish those in the system.

What the HITECH act also did was allow all electronic records to be owned by the health systems or the health records companies. Despite the fact that the law says patients need access to these records there was no regulations or standards to make that so. When a physician contracts with health systems, they do not own the record, nor does the patient. The law states that the patient has rights to the record, but the process to obtaining them are expensive and obstructive. Even when a physician is in private practice they record is often still owned by the electronic health record company often times the physician only pays for the ability to use software, to create the record. Physicians then have had to pay tens of thousands of dollars to obtain access to their own patient records that they created if they change practices or want to migrate to a new system.

The patient's information is trapped, and often times the records companies have retained the rights to sell any data attached to those records as long as it is de-identified. When it comes to patient care the majority of information in the current EHR systems is junk according to most physicians.8 It is impossible to document everything, and physicians are generally not compensated for documenting so often times it is not a complete record, which makes true interpretation difficult Very small portions of valuable data are recorded, and unfortunately due to the time restrictions employed physicians have combined with, fear of litigation and the lack of HER interoperability. Often the only way to truly know what happened to a patient during the stay is to call up the physician who wrote the note and ask- defeating the whole purpose of the original medical record all together. This creates a huge problem for the future of the digital health industry, and has set an unfortunate precedent with the industry that that is the way it should be. That data and information should belong to the patient to whom that record belongs, and the physician that created that record, not the record company, or health system.

The current documentation model is not good for patients or physicians. It is important to realize however as that the people who still currently create the records are the physicians. Every operating room note, radiological study, and office visit is documented by a physician. Therefore, in order to create a truly decentralized and self-sovereign medical record for patients the owner of that record cannot be with an electronic health record company like Cerner, or Epic, or with the health system that the patient receives care, but must be with the self-sovereign physician who deliverers the care. If a physician has a self-sovereign identity, and can once again document what is necessary for care coordination and continuity the electronic health record will once again be a documentation of the patient encounter, not a billing and coding ledger.

The law says that patients own their records. If you have ever been a patient however you will know that it is very difficult and at times impossible to get those records. Furthermore once the records are obtained it is even more difficult for the patient to differentiate and interpret which records are important and which are not. Relevant and clean data is rarely found within health records in their current state.

Although patients own their records by law they lack access to them because they are trapped in siloed health systems. At times it can cost a patient up to $500 to obtain copies of their records, and it is never in a timely fashion. The bottle neck exists with the health systems themselves. Hospitals contract with record companies, who create record keeping software to their likening and then the health system harvests the data on their servers. Two of the largest health records companies: Cerner and Epic control nearly 50% of the hospital marketplace. If Cerner and epic decided to create a blockchain healthcare record solution and allow patients to have access to those records it would still not be truly decentralized, because Cerner and epic would still be the central point of control, as would the health system who contracts with them, So how can this be resolved?

When blockchain is appropriately applied it has the potential solve the problems of dirty or incomplete data, as well as security and interoperability. When patients and their chosen physicians control the records in a decentralized way it will also decrease potential security risks. In the current centralized system these breaches occur 2x as much in our current systems than other industries largely because data siloes create a central point of attack. With HL7 standards now open we can work together to create interoperable ways to securely transfer data in these records, while protecting patients and preserving their rights to their data, and there is increasing efforts towards preserving prominence – which is important for research and development. When the patient owns the data, they can permission applications for Data capture, analysis, encryption, federated learning, sharing and de-identified data creation, and can be incentivized to share their data when they want to.

Some of the most important parts of the medical record are created by physicians. It includes the history of the patient illness from the perspective of the patient, observations made by the physician, what happened during the course of treatment and what the physician did in response. The records are timed and dated and create a picture of the patient. The records haver always beggun with the physician patient encounter, and therefore it makes sense for it to continue to do so on this platform. No longer will the data be stored on a centralized database but it can now be duplicated and shared between the physician and patient. Later if desired it can interface and be shared only with keyed permissioned access as governed by the code. Having an immutable ledger of this information has obvious benefits. The HITECH act of 2009 created an opportunity for this, now electronic health records are not able to be altered after they are signed. In a court of law the time the physician signed the chart is an important piece, because it shows the record is the true unaltered snapshot of what was observed to be happening at the time. It is impossible to document everything, and physicians are generally not compensated for documenting so often times it is not a complete record, which makes true interpretation difficult

What the HITECH act also lead to was electronic records that are owned by the health systems or the health records companies not the patient. When a physician contracts with these systems, they do not own the record, nor does the patient. The law states that the patient has rights to the record, but the process to obtaining them are expensive and obstructive. Even when a physician is in private practice they are forced to pay the electronic health record company for that record, even after they purchased the software, and created the record. The patients information is trapped there and often times the records companies have retained the rights to sell any data attached to those records as long as it is de-identified. This creates a huge problem for the future of the digital health industry. That data and information should belong to the patient to whom that record belongs, and the physician that created that record, not the record company, or health system. .

Our current medical record system is one example of how patient data is siloed and hoarded. The law says that patients own their records. If you have ever been a patient however you will know that it is very difficult and at times impossible to get those records. Furthermore once the records are obtained it is even more difficult for the patient to differentiate and interpret which records are important and which are not. Relevant and clean data is rarely found within health records in their current state.

Although patients own their records by law they lack access to them because they are trapped in siloed health systems. At times it can cost a patient up to $500 to obtain copies of their records, and it is never in a timely fashion. The bottle neck exists with the health systems themselves. Hospitals contract with record companies, who create record keeping software to their liking and then the health system harvests the data on their servers. Two of the largest health records companies: Cerner and Epic control nearly 50% of the hospital marketplace. If Cerner and epic decided to create a blockchain healthcare record solution and allow patients to have access to those records it would still not be truly decentralized, because Cerner and epic would still be the central point of control, as would the health system who contracts with them, So how can this be resolved?

In order to recommend a solution we must return again to one's identity. Because your digital health identity should be self-sovereign meaning only yours you must also be the one who owns and controls your records, which creates the digital health portion of your identity. The problem is- if your centralized health system hoards the data how can the record be truly self sovereign? The answer is that it cant! The only way the record can be truly self sovercign and decentralized is if the end user chooses who creates the records on their own and only shares it with those that they choose.

For the next step It is important to realize that the people who currently create the records are the physicians who care for patients. Every operating room note, radiological study, and office visit is documented by a physician, and since the

HITECH act of 2009- a government mandate imposing electronic health records on the physician community, this has been increasingly been done electronically. Therefore, in order to create a truly decentralized and self-sovereign medical record for patients the owner of that record cannot be with an electronic health record company like Cerner, or Epic, or with the health system that the patient receives care, but must be with the self-sovereign physician who deliverers the care and in turn creates the record that documents that patient encounter.

More importantly the record that the physician creates is usually the most important and relevant information that a patient needs and wants. Laboratory results

So how can we create records that are relevant accessible and truly self-sovereign? In order to do so you must acknowledge that the most important and relevant records are created by physicians, therefore in order to allow patients to have access to the highly relevant self-sovereign records the individual physician creating the document must also have a self-sovereign digital identity (SS-DI) to create the SSR

How this can fix the various problems in Heallthcare:

Global economy

1) cost of prescription drugs:

Problem:

Both the pharmacutical and insurance industry artificially inflates prices through kickbacks between insurance companies and health systems and the only people that lose are the patients. Group Purchasing Organizations (figure 1) and Pharmacy Benefit Managers (figure 2) are third party administrators that provide no value but only control the supply chain and drive up costs.

Lets take the simple example of a dose of aspirin in the hospital. We all know that we can get a bottle of 500 generic aspirin for $3.75 retail that is $0.0075 per dose. Now go to the hospital and get a dose and you could receive an itemized bill with the price of $52 for only that one pill. How does this happen? Some has to do with third party administrators that control the supply chain and receive legal kickbacks which they call "rebates" others It is not only the cost of pharmaceuticals but all costs are driven up by mal-aligned incentives created by third parties such as this. The above is only one example of how third parties drive up the cost of healthcare.

Solution:

Give each entity a self sovereing digital identity so when any product passes through, you can easily see what they are getting in return for the exchange. (will fix figures for final)

Chapter 24:
The Convergence of AI and Blockchain in Healthcare

Ken B. Farrington

Editor's Note:

In this chapter Ken B. Farrington provides a well needed and detailed explanation of the different technologies in AI, including machine learning, supervised and unsupervised learning, artificial neural networks, and their applications in Healthcare. Ken successfully explains why combing blockchain and AI both improve each other and allow a trustworthy control over large data sets. This not only enhances analytics and predictability, but translates into better decision making. An example of these enhanced features are demonstrated in the NIH "All of us" program, that collects data from surveys, Electronic Health Records (EHRs), physical measurements, blood and urine samples as well as mobile, wearable technologies, and geospatial, environmental data. This vast amount of information generates vital personal as well as population health information. Dr. Walter De Brouwer ends the chapter with a case study, explaining the limits of our knowledge, even in this era of Big Data.

From SIRI to self-driving cars, artificial intelligence (AI) is a technology that is progressing rapidly. While science fiction often portrays AI as robots who are going to take over the world, in actuality AI can encompass anything from Google's search algorithms to Facebook's automatic image tagging to autonomous weapons.

When it comes to our health, especially in matters of life and death, the promise of artificial intelligence (AI) to improve outcomes is very intriguing. While there is still much to overcome to achieve AI-dependent health care, most notably data privacy concerns and fears of mismanaged care due to machine error and lack of human oversight, there is sufficient potential that governments, technology companies, and healthcare providers are willing to invest and test AI-powered tools and solutions. In order to really understand how Blockchain and AI may be combined to benefit the healthcare industry in the future, we really need to first understand the current and future role of AI in its own right.

Artificial Intelligence

Artificial intelligence today is properly known as narrow AI (or weak AI), in that it is designed to perform a narrow task (e.g. only facial recognition or only internet searches or recommending titles to watch on Netflix). However, the long-term goal of many researchers is to create general AI (AGI or strong AI). While narrow AI may outperform humans at whatever its specific task is, like playing chess or solving equations, AGI would outperform humans at nearly every cognitive task.

Narrow AI is quite a broad field. It covers everything from Machine Learning to Natural Language Processing, Computer Vision and even Robotics. The graphic on the left shows some of what is encompassed in Narrow AI. Rather than go into all of these technologies in the context of this book, we will highlight a few major topics as they are relevant to Healthcare.

Machine Learning

At the core of current narrow AI is machine learning (ML), which is a subfield of AI that is devoted to algorithms that learn from data. ML is generally the technique that is used for most modern day AI applications. Arthur Samuel, a computer scientist, first coined the term "machine learning" in 1959. He defined it as the field of study that gives computers the ability to learn without being explicitly programmed. He advanced the field by creating a program that allowed a computer to play chess. At first he gave the program simple rules to follow and then eventually the program played thousands of games against itself. This is essentially machine learning – learning from large amounts of data. AI is where the program was following a simple set of rules that allowed it to play chess.

Within the field of machine learning, there are two main types of tasks: supervised, and unsupervised. The main difference between the two types is that supervised learning is done using a ground truth, or in other words, we have prior knowledge of what the output values for our samples should be.

Supervised Learning

The most straightforward tasks fall under the umbrella of supervised learning. In supervised learning, we have access to examples of correct input-output pairs that we can show to the machine during the training phase. The common example of handwriting recognition is typically approached as a supervised learning task. We show the computer a number of images of handwritten digits along with the correct labels for those digits, and the computer learns the patterns that relate images to their labels. In the supervised learning example below we are given a dataset of labeled dog images and the algorithm is trained to recognize which images are dogs and which ones are not dogs.

Unsupervised Learning

Unsupervised learning, on the other hand, does not have labeled outputs, so its goal is to infer the natural structure present within a set of data points. Supervised learning tasks find patterns where we have a dataset of "right answers" to learn from. Unsupervised learning tasks find patterns where we don't. This may be because the "right answers" are unobservable, or infeasible to obtain, or maybe for a given problem, there isn't even a "right answer" per se.

A large subclass of unsupervised tasks is the problem of clustering. Clustering refers to grouping observations together in such a way that members of a common group are similar to each other, and different from members of other groups. A common application here is in marketing, where we wish to identify segments of customers or prospects with similar preferences or buying habits. A major challenge in clustering is that it is often difficult or impossible to know how many clusters should exist, or how the clusters should look.

In the unsupervised learning example to the right we are given a dataset of unlabeled images and the algorithm divides data into like groups.

Artificial Neural Networks (ANNs)

Throughout the course of comprehensive healthcare, many patients develop problems with their minds and bodies that can lead to severe discomfort, costly treatment, disabilities, and more. Predicting those escalations in advance offers healthcare providers the opportunity to apply preventative measure that might improve patient safety, and quality of care, while lowering medical costs. In simple terms, prediction using networks of big data used to evaluate specific people, and specific risk factors in certain illnesses could save lives, and avoid medical complications.

Today, many prognostics methods turn to Artificial Neural Networks when attempting to find new insights into the future of patient healthcare. ANNs (Artificial Neural Networks) are just one of the many models being introduced into the field of healthcare by innovations like AI and big data. Their purpose is to transform huge amounts of raw data into useful decisions for treatment and care.

What is a Neural Network?

Neural networks really help take the machine learning techniques we previously discussed to new heights and scale. Understanding Neural Networks can be very difficult. After all, to many people, these examples of Artificial Intelligence in the medical industry are a futuristic concept.

According to Wikipedia (the source of all truth) : "Neural Networks are a computational approach which is based on a large collection of neural units loosely modeling the way the brain solves problems with large clusters of biological neurons connected by axons. Each neural unit is connected with many others…These systems are self-learning and trained rather than explicitly programmed…"

One way to think of it is this: Imagine that a doctor wants to make a prediction regarding a patient's health – for instance, whether she or he is at risk of suffering from a certain disease. How would a doctor be able to ascertain that information? In most cases, it would involve using blood tests, taking tests of the patient's vitals, and more to identify features that have proven to be good predictors of patient health. However, what if doctors only know a handful of risk-factors for a specific disease – or worse, they don't know the risk factors at all? It would be impossible to make predictions.

ANNs help to provide the predictions in healthcare that doctors and surgeons simply couldn't address alone. They work in moments wherein we can collect data, but we don't understand which pieces of that data are vitally important yet. These abstractions can therefore capture complex relationships that might not be initially obvious – leading to better prediction for public health.

What are the Possibilities for Neural Networks in Healthcare?

Though they may seem like a futuristic concept, ANNs have been used in healthcare for several decades. In fact, the book "Neural Networks in Healthcare" covers the various uses of this system prior to 2006. Before 2006, the main successes of ANNs were found in areas like speech processing and image processing. Today, as new technologies emerge, capable of changing the way that we approach neural networks in the first place – it's worth noting that there may be numerous new options for changing the industry. Today, the possibilities for Neural Networks in Healthcare include:

- Diagnostic systems – ANNs can be used to detect heart and cancer problems, as well as various other diseases informed by big data.

- Biochemical analysis – ANNs are used to analyze urine and blood samples, as well as tracking glucose levels in diabetics, determining ion levels in fluids, and detecting various pathological conditions.

- Image analysis – ANNs are frequently used to analyze medical images from various areas of healthcare, including tumor detection, x-ray classifications, and MRIs.

- Drug development – Finally, ANNs are used in the development of drugs for various conditions – working by using large amounts of data to come to conclusions about treatment options.

Current Healthcare Examples of Neural Networks

Neural networks can be seen in most places where AI has made steps within the healthcare industry. For instance, in the world of drug discovery, Data Collective and Khosla Ventures are currently backing the company "Atomwise", which uses the power of machine learning and neural networks to help medical professionals discover safer and more effective medicines fast. The company published its first findings of Ebola treatment drugs last year, and the tools that Atomwise uses can tell the difference between toxic drug candidates and safer options.

Similarly, options are being found that could insert neural networks into the realm of diagnostic. For instance, in 2014, Butterfly Networks, which are transforming the diagnostic realm with deep learning, devices, and the cloud, raised $100M for their cause. This organization currently works at the heart of the medicine and engineering sectors by bringing together world-class skills in everything from electrical engineering, to mechanical engineering, and medicine. At the same time, iCarbonX is developing artificial intelligence platforms to facilitate research relating to the treatment of various diseases and preventative care. The company believes that soon they will be able to help enable the future of truly personalized medicine.

The Future of ANNs in Healthcare

Perhaps the most significant problem with ANNs is that the learned features involved when it comes to assessing huge amounts of data can sometimes be difficult to interpret. This is potentially why ANNs are more commonly used during situations wherein we have a lot of data to ensure that the observed data doesn't contain too many "flukes". Think of it this way – if you toss a coin three times and receive "tails" every time, this doesn't mean that a coin only has a "tails" side. It just means that you need further evaluation and more testing to get a proper reading of probability.

ANNs are going to need some tweaking if they're going to become the change that the healthcare industry needs. However, alongside new AI developments, it seems that neural networks could have a very important part to play in the future of healthcare.

AI Applied in Healthcare

Aid clinical judgment or diagnosis

Admittedly, using Machine Learning to diagnose patients is undoubtedly in its infancy, but there have been some exciting use cases. A Stanford University study tested an AI algorithm to detect skin cancers against dermatologists, and it performed at the level of the humans.

A Danish AI software company tested its deep-learning program by having a computer eavesdrop while human dispatchers took emergency calls. The algorithm analyzed what a person says, the tone of voice and background noise and detected cardiac arrests with a 93% success rate compared to 73% for humans. Baidu Research recently announced that the results of early tests on its deep learning algorithm indicate that it can outperform humans when identifying breast cancer metastasis.

Prime Minister Theresa May announced an AI revolution would help the National Health Service (NHS), the UK's healthcare system, predict those in an early stage of cancer to ultimately prevent thousands of cancer-related deaths by 2033. The algorithms will examine medical records, habits and genetic information pooled from health charities, the NHS and AI.

AI-Assisted robotic surgery

With an estimated value of $40 billion to healthcare, robots can analyze data from pre-op medical records to guide a surgeon's instrument during surgery, which can lead to a 21% reduction in a patient's hospital stay. Robot-assisted surgery is considered "minimally invasive" so patients won't need to heal from large incisions. Via artificial intelligence, robots can use data from past operations to inform new surgical techniques. The positive results are indeed promising. One study that involved 379 orthopedic patients found that AI-assisted robotic procedure resulted in five times fewer complications compared to surgeons operating alone. A robot was used on an eye surgery for the first time, and the most advanced surgical robot, the Da Vinci allows doctors to perform complex procedures with greater control than conventional approaches. Heart surgeons are assisted by Heartlander, a miniature robot, that enters a small incision on the chest to perform mapping and therapy over the surface of the heart.

Virtual nursing assistants

From interacting with patients to directing patients to the most effective care setting, virtual nursing assistants could save the healthcare industry $20 billion annually. Since virtual nurses are available 24/7, they can answer questions, monitor patients and provide quick answers. Most applications of virtual nursing assistants today allow for more regular communication between patients and care providers between office visits to prevent hospital readmission or unnecessary hospital visits. Care Angel's virtual nurse assistant can even provide wellness checks through voice and AI.

Workflow and administrative tasks

Another way AI can impact healthcare is to automate administrative tasks. It is expected that this could result in $18 billion in savings for the healthcare industry as machines can help doctors, nurses and other providers save time on tasks. Technology such as voice-to-text transcriptions could help order tests, prescribe medications and write chart notes. One example of using AI to support administrative tasks is a partnership between the Cleveland Clinic and IBM that uses IBM's Watson to mine big data and help physicians provide a personalized and more efficient treatment experience. One way Watson supports physicians is being able to analyze thousands of medical papers using natural language processing to inform treatment plans.

Machine Learning and Healthcare Bias

AI has the potential to revolutionize healthcare, ushering in an age of personalized, accessible, and lower-cost medicine for all. But there's also a very real risk that those same technologies will perpetuate existing healthcare inequalities. A large part of this risk comes from existing biases in healthcare data.

Machine Learning algorithms are built using data that is trained to inherently make assumptions. When given new input data, a machine learning model generates values based on a trained machine learning model. This means the data are wholly dependent on the set of training data it's given for scoring. Scoring is also called prediction. Without proper attention, cognitive biases that are common in society will inevitably bleed into the results. Training data that doesn't account for variances in race, sexual orientation or identity, or age, can have outcomes that very negatively affect people's lives.

Joy Buolamwini, a PhD student at the MIT Media Lab completed a research study in early 2018, called the Gender Shades Project, on facial recognition software at three major companies, IBM, Microsoft, and Face++ and found that they all demonstrate both skin-type and gender biases. Across all three, the error rates for gender classification were consistently higher for females than they were for males, and for darker-skinned subjects than for lighter-skinned subjects.

Another example of ML bias is a product currently in courtrooms across the nation called Correctional Offender Management Profiling for Alternative Sanctions, or COMPAS, which utilizes machine learning algorithms to determine whether or not a criminal is at risk of repeating their crime. This information is then used to determine who can be set free at every stage of the criminal justice system, from assigning bond amounts to fundamental decisions about defendants' freedom. In 2016 ProPublica did a study because bias was suspected in the output of this program. They found two disturbing things about the output. The first was that the formula was particularly likely to falsely flag black defendants as future criminals, mislabeling them this way at almost twice the rate as white defendants. Secondly, white defendants were labeled as low risk more often than black defendants.

The result of all this negative press in regard to modern machine learning shortcomings is that the general public is increasingly more uncomfortable with being the subject of the outcomes. Many are calling for stricter legislation to ensure that their rights are not infringed upon by biases in machine learning algorithms.

This bias is even more detrimental in a healthcare scenario. AI's transformative potential comes from its ability to interrogate, parse, and analyze vast amounts of data. From this information, AI systems can find patterns and links that would have previously required great levels of expertise or time from human doctors. For this reason, AI is particularly useful in diagnostics, creating personalized treatment plans, and even helping doctors keep up to date with the latest medical research. If we want to use AI to facilitate a more personalized medicine for all, it would help if we could first provide medicine that works for half the population.

But this use of data risks exacerbating existing inequalities. Data coming from randomized control trials are often riddled with bias. The highly selective nature of trials systemically disfavor women, the elderly, and those with additional medical conditions to the ones being studied; pregnant women are often excluded entirely. AIs are trained to make decisions using this skewed data, and their results will therefore favor the biases contained within. This is especially concerning when it comes to medical data, which weighs heavily in the favor of white men.

AI and Blockchain Merger

The marriage of AI and Blockchain may help to mitigate some of the shortcomings of both technologies. What would this merger of two technologies look like though?

At its core a blockchain is a data structure that makes it possible to create a digital ledger of transactions and share it among a decentrralized, peer-to-peer network of computers. It uses cryptography to allow each participant on the network to make additions to the ledger (transact) in a secure way without the need for a central authority. Additions and changes must be validated and agreed upon by a majority of participants, as adhering to the rules of the blockchain protocol. Additionally, the incorporation of custom logic programs on the blockchain, known commonly as smart contracts, allow for the automation and enforcement of agreements and conditional logic (if something, then do something, else do something else), which further expands the capabilities of blockchains beyond traditional party to party payments and simple value exchange.

AI aids decision making through the assessment, analysis, and understanding of certain patterns and datasets, with the end goal of ultimately engendering autonomous interaction.

AI and blockchain share several characteristics which promote seamless interactions in the near future, and the potential for a highly synergistic relationship. Three key features are listed below.

- AI and Blockchain Require Data Sharing – Blockchain, essentially a decentralized, append only data structure, supports the prospect of sharing data between multiple clients on a single peer-to-peer, shared governance network in a trust minimizing way. Similarly, AI relies heavily on Big Data, specifically, data sharing to support algorithm development and advancement in support of better modeling, predictions, and actions taken in response. A probabilistic system, with more open data to analyze, predictions and assessments of AI have a higher probability of correctness, and the algorithms generated are more reliable.

- Security – Security is paramount to the success of blockchain systems as tamper-resistant data structures. The decentralized nature of the network and nodes provides great security guarantees as no single point of failure exists, while cryptography provides the means to prove the authenticity of transactions as well as the underpinnings for the consensus mechanisms that governs transaction validity and enforces the protocol's rules. For Artificial Intelligence, the autonomous nature of the machines also requires a high-level of security in order to reduce the probability of a catastrophic occurrence.

- Trust Is a Requirement -- There is no greater threat to the advancement of any widely-accepted technology than lack of trust and neither AI nor blockchain are excluded. To facilitate machine-to-machine communication, there is an expected level of trust that the systems operate and act as expected. Blockchains provide trust in the system by minimizing trust in the process. Middle men are eliminated in favor of coded rules, and all activity can be verified since genesis, or the first block.

AI and Blockchain Future Technology Enablers

Open Market for Data

As stated earlier, the advancement of AI technology hinges on the availability of data from a myriad of trustworthy sources. Even though companies like Google, Facebook, Amazon, etc. have access to large sources of data which can prove useful for lots of AI processes, this data is generally not accessible on the market, and if any is made available it is heavily altered and limited, making it of little use. Blockchain partially aims to tackle the issue of data availability by introducing the concept of peer-to-peer, transaction-based networks with a shared or decentralized governance component that enable tightly coupled incentives for actions and outcomes.

Blockchain enables unique incentives for data sharing that haven't really existed in centrally managed data stores mainly due to the lack of trust placed in the third parties managing those stores. The lack of transparency in data ownership or custody, how that data is used or exchanged after the fact, the complicated state and federal laws governing the proper use and handling of that information, and the all-too-frequent headlines highlighting the inability of the systems that exist today to secure and protect personal information all create an atmosphere of distrust and unwillingness to participate or share.

We now live in a world where large data maintainers and brokers can extract additional value from individuals or patients by selling and profiting off of the very data the maintainers or brokers have collected from them. It becomes a business model where quantity is prized over quality and accuracy, and as a result low quality, unverified data is frequently obtained from sources like wearables, anonymous surveys, and subjective lifestyle analysis and sold to organizations whose own AIs and algorithms make determinations over coverage, access to care, and even treatment paths despite the low quality of data received and assessed. Through a blockchain based open data system it becomes possible to add additional incentives for individuals, patients, or research subjects to share their personal data in a secure way while adding the ability to monetize that data in open data marketplaces and exchanges, and ultimately putting it to work for them. This incentivizes individuals or patients to not only take ownership of their personal data, verifying it for accuracy and controlling the flow, but also to sell directly to data consumers with the added benefit of the information coming unaltered and verified by the source versus the present-day data brokers and middle men who cannot provide the same level of assurance over key pieces of data.

AI (or multiple AIs) with access to the pools of information backed by a blockchain data layer can greatly benefit from the increased participation and higher quality data that blockchain-specific incentives and a greater level of trust can lead to. The widespread availability of the data and the tearing down of walls built around it by large data hoarders like Google and Facebook, will usher in not only improved accessibility, but also improved AI functionality, decision making, sourcing, and learning capabilities that should result in far greater benefit for the people and organizations relying on AI based technology in support of business missions.

Large-Scale Data Management Mechanism

Even after the data has been made available, managing it is another hurdle to scale. The amount of data currently available is estimated to be 1.3 Zettabytes. There is a subfield of AI known as Artificial General Intelligence which can be modeled as a feedback control system. This feature helps autonomous agents interact with the physical environment better.

With large volumes of data stored and transmitted in a decentralized system, there are several advantages enjoyed compared to the conventional central storage hub. In the event of a crisis and natural disasters, the data is not stored in a single physical location, hence it is preserved. Also, strong cryptographic security guarantees and the distributed nature of the governance (enforced by a network of multi-party managed nodes) means the risk of unauthorized write operations or successful attacks against the blockchain are less likely versus a single point of failure or single source of truth such as a central database, and thus protects the data stored and transmitted by the blockchain from unauthorized manipulation or alteration.

Blockchains are extremely resilient and secure data structures due to their peer-to-peer networks and decentralized governance models. All nodes store and process all transactions while enforcing the coded rules for validation and verification. This means that, depending on the rules of the blockchain over half of the nodes must be compromised to force changes to the blockchain. This includes changes to the consensus rules for what transactions are valid, the blockchain state, and the history of transactions. Because of this security, resiliency and high availability, blockchains are well suited to serve as the base data management layer in support of large scale, data driven systems, providing a more trustworthy, always available source for the AI driven applications and managed services built atop it.

More Trustworthy AI Modeling and Predictions

One underlying principle of computer systems is GIGO. Garbage In, Garbage Out. The field of Artificial Intelligence is heavily dependent on large streams of data. Some individuals or corporations intentionally tamper with the data provided to alter the results. Garbage data might also result from unplanned malfunction of sensors and other data sources.

By creating segments of verified databases, models can be successfully built and implemented upon only datasets which have been verified. This will detect any faults or irregularity in the data supply chain. It also helps to reduce the stress of troubleshooting and finding abnormal datasets since the data stream is available in segments. Leveraging the tamper-resistant, secure, and resilient nature of a blockchain (as discussed previously) a strong data source can emerge in support of modeling and predictions. This is, however, a two way street where AI can also support blockchain in becoming that viable, trustworthy data source to begin with.

While blockchain provides secure, traceable transactions and the ability to store and transmit data in a trustworthy, tamper-resistant way, the blockchain provides no guarantees that the data itself has been verified and is valid and high quality. Blockchain still suffers from the Garbage In, Garbage Out problem in that low quality, bad, or incomplete data must be prevented from entering the blockchain, otherwise bad data in may become bad data forever. This can have a marked effect on the ability to create accurate models and for AI to leverage the blockchain as a trustworthy data source. Many processes in Healthcare suffer from the bad data problem, from grants management and research data sharing, to provider credentialing and claims processing. When data coming in is untrustworthy additional back end processes must be implemented to ensure the data does not impact outcomes, such as the processing of an improper claim, the award of a grant to the wrong entity, or hang-ups in the credentialing process due to data inconsistencies.

How can this problem be addressed before the data enters the blockchain? Through AI and machine learning. Using these technologies to pre-populate from available sources, validate against additional authoritative databases, and cleanse and normalize data to prevent low quality data from entering the blockchain and corrupting the dataset. By leveraging artificial intelligence and machine learning at the point of entry, system owners can eliminate some of the manual burden that is necessary for data validation, review, and normalization. Current manual processes can be supplemented or augmented by artificial intelligence to increase efficiency by decreasing time spent pre-validating data, and increase quality by utilizing algorithm driven tools for data interrogation and verification that don't suffer from the exhaustion or apathy present in many manually driven processes. With AI we can't completely solve the bad data problem, but it can absolutely decrease the likelihood of bad, low quality data from entering the blockchain and threatening its position as a trustworthy data source for highly automated processes or additional modeling activities.

Control Over the Usage of Data and Models

Ownership and custody of personal data is a polarizing subject, with most believing that the patient or individual should retain ownership rights and custody over their data. This has major implications for many healthcare related processes, as well as for the integration of blockchain technology and Artificial intelligence.

When you log into Facebook and Twitter, you relinquish the rights to any content you upload onto their platform based on the terms identified in their users agreements. The same thing happens when a singer signs a record deal and are subject to the ownership rights defined in the terms of the contract. The same concept can be applied to AI data and models. Ownership of data as it stands today, resides with those large data collectors and maintainers, like Google and Facebook, who can pick and choose how to disseminate and use your data in support of modeling and predictions. Insurers routinely obtain data on individuals seeking coverage or who are currently covered by buying their data from these brokers. They then use this to make determinations on coverage, acceptable care, and premiums. All the while the covered individual or patient is unaware.

Blockchain can be used to not only incentivize participation and data sharing, but also in a way that gives the participants individual ownership rights to the data they own and choose to share. By tokenizing data and using smart contracts to define terms and conditions (T&Cs) to granularly control how that personal data is accessed (such as the information contained in their personal health history or EHR) and by whom, the power is given back to the individual. Not only does the blockchain allow individuals to set terms and conditions for access and uses, but also provides the ability to verify that only data they have expressly granted access to is transmitted to the authorized counterparty. This has the added effect of building trust in the system. That trust serves as a strong incentive for greater participation and has the ability to create a more conducive environment for data sharing, one that is open and gives the data owner greater control. AI driven modeling and predictions that are dependent on available data and free flow of information should greatly benefit from the increased availability and access this provides by removing the middle men and brokers, and tearing down the walls that companies like Google, Facebook, and Amazon have built around the data they collect. Data can be obtained through agreements directly with its rightful owners, or through marketplaces, exchanges, and commons as made available by the owner, under the smart contract enforced T&Cs.

Promoting enhanced analytics and decision making

In addition to providing increased availability of higher quality data by building trust and allowing individuals to own and potentially monetize their data, blockchain can aid AI simply by the very nature of the technology's openness and transparency to onlookers. While some may shy away from the transparency of such an open ledger in many cases the transparent nature of a blockchain is a boon rather than a bane.

Taking a step back and a look at public infrastructure blockchains like Ethereum, one major knock against them is that for any sort of proprietary or personal data sharing, some yet-to-be-determined transaction privacy mechanism, be it zero knowledge proofs or ring signatures, must be incorporated to preserve privacy in the transaction lifecycle. They've shown they're just not quite there yet and ready to handle applications requiring privacy such as those that may be subject to the requirements of HIPAA, for example. However, what they do show, is that the open availability of information is valuable, especially for data analysis in support off-chain decision making for the users and stakeholders of the blockchains.

Even with a basic block explorer like one provided by service providers like www.blockchain.info or www.etherscan.io, or one created for a private, permissioned blockchain, a wealth of information is available to inform deep chain analytics, trending, and reporting. Metrics like daily active application (smart contract) users, individual address interactions and metrics, unique address activity, smart contract daily transaction volume, average and median transaction value, median transaction fee, average transaction lifecycle time, and more technically relevant diagnostic focused metrics like verifying average block creation time, average block size, orphaned block rates, active nodes, etc. are easily discernible and highly useful for stakeholders and maintainers. This data can be used for identifying areas requiring technical process improvement, identifying bottlenecks in the transaction lifecycle, identifying potential issues of security or attacks in progress (e.g. DoS attacks or spam attacks), or identifying who your most active participants are and how they're using the system and who they're interacting with on a transaction by transaction basis. Combining this level of openness and transparency with AI in the form of intelligent monitoring and analysis tools and learning algorithms, can provide organizations with useful heuristics and actionable reporting in near-real-time in support of strong business and operational modeling and decision making.

For example, due to the open nature of blockchains, AIs can use the data directly obtained from them to support the reduction of inefficiencies over time. As the AI monitors transactions and the transaction data end-to-end, via something akin to the block explorer mentioned previously, it can identify choke points, or unoptimized logic that can be used to improve processing and execution of the code embedded in that contract. The AI can then use that information to form recommendations for improving the smart contract code, and developers can deploy updated contracts to the blockchain to implement the optimizations recommended. Perhaps the most ambitious projects will grant the AI the ability to deploy updated contracts to the blockchain itself.

AI and Blockchain in the Future of Healthcare

While it is clear that blockchain and AI can be leveraged to enable each other's greater potential and value propostion, it is time to examine how they can leverage that synergy to tackle a few complex areas in the Healthcare space: Provider Credentialing, and large scale research programs like that NIH's 'All of Us' program.

AI and Blockchain use in Provider Credentialing

Provider credentialing is a complex, costly, and time-consuming process mandated throughout the healthcare industry to ensure that a practitioner can competently deliver (and be compensated for) patient care within a specific clinical setting. Today, the process largely consists of organizations independently collecting, verifying, and analyzing information pertaining to an individual's background and experience. These artifacts include education, employment, and clinical assignment histories, licensure and certification histories, on-going training, insurance coverages, and the like.

AI can help to automate the credentialing process by learning from historical data and using doctors' qualifications and career history including their education, training, residency and licenses, as well as any specialty certificates to provide an automated risk score to regulatory and accreditation organizations. Blockchain could help facilitate the collection of these key data points for the machine learning algorithms. A blockchain-based utility would record and confirm, on the first requested verification, the provenance (source) of the information, the information contained within the verification itself, the result of the verification, and a formulaic key confirming that the information has never changed from its initial issuance. Similar processes could be employed for both publically available sources (e.g., licenses, certifications, OIG sanctions) of information and private enterprises. In time, the vast majority of historically verified transactions could be disseminated to requesting organizations and substantially reduce the level of costly repetitive reverification that pervades the industry today.

AI and Blockchain in the 'All of Us' Program

Data Sharing and Availability

The National Institutes of Health (NIH) All of Us Program (include footnote for https://allofus.nih.gov) is a cornerstone of the national Precision Medicine Initiative (PMI). The precision medicine initiative was launched by President Obama in February of 2016 with the objective of enhancing innovation in biomedical research to understand how a person's genetics, environment, and lifestyle can help determine the best approach to prevent or treat disease. As a part of the All of Us Program, NIH is in the process of establishing a group (cohort) of over one million volunteers from across the United States. The volunteers will represent the diversity of the US population and will have the opportunity to provide various types of data on an ongoing basis. The goal is to provide researchers the largest, richest biomedical dataset ever that is easy, safe, and free to access. The volunteers will be treated as partners in the research study and will be involved in what data is collected, what laboratory analyses is performed, what research is conducted, and how the data gets returned. Data sharing as well as privacy and security are a priority for the program.

The program will start by collecting data from a limited set of sources that include: participant surveys, Electronic Health Records (EHRs), physical measurements, biosamples (blood and urine samples), mobile/wearable technologies, and geospatial/ environmental data. Data types and sources will expand over time as will the science and technology.

There are various stakeholders that are key to the All of Us Program and are all a part of the research network required to ensure an effective study. Stakeholders include: the volunteers; the research community; the data and research center (DRC) – responsible for big data capture, cleaning, curation, & sharing in a secure environment; the Biobank - repository for processing, storing, & sharing biosamples; Participant Center – responsible for direct volunteer participant enrollment, digital engagement innovation, & consumer health technologies; Participant Technology Systems Center - web & phone-based platforms for participant; Health Care Provider Orgs (HPOs) - clinical & scientific expertise network, enrollment & retention of participants (includes 30+ regional med centers, Federally Qualified Health Centers (FQHCs), the Department of Veterans Affairs (VA) .. this network will continue to grow over time.

As noted above, through the 'All of Us' program, NIH will collect massive amounts of data from participants and healthcare providers. Hidden within this data there exists patterns and trends that will lead biomedical researchers to the next big breakthrough in medicine. This data has incredible value and can contribute to tailoring medical treatment to the individual. NIH has the opportunity to set a bold new standard in the way that data is shared within the research community. The intersection of blockchain technology with artificial intelligence offer a platform for researchers to collaborate effectively, efficiently and securely using shared assets like data resources and machine learning models. A blockchain established around the biomedical data collected by the 'All of Us' program will create a protected marketplace where patients, healthcare providers, and biomedical researchers can all come to extract valuable insight to create shared knowledge.

Blockchain facilitates a safe way to share data and creates a symbiotic relationship between medical institutions where sharing data is mutually beneficial. Incentives for data sharing and active participation on the development of new diagnostic models can be managed on the blockchain through the release of digital tokens, which may simply be reputation tokens in support of a reputation system, or redeemable for research grant awards; some of the most impactful applications of machine learning have come out of public competitions, especially on sites like kaggle.com.

As we discussed earlier, artificial neural networks are the powerful machine learning technique that has enabled the realization of amazing technology like driverless cars and real-time language translation, but these systems needed to be trained on large quantities of data to achieve reliable results. The more examples that an artificial neural network processes, the better the results generated by the model in future predictions. Especially within the medical community, data sharing is in the best interest of all parties in order to realize the best outcomes for patients.

To take full advantage of the growing community of data scientists the NIH can make their stores of medical data available by request over the blockchain. The blockchain can be used to publish metadata about available data resources, which can include instructions on how to gain permissions to access the data. The peer-to-peer transaction is conducted on the blockchain and is fully auditable and tamper-resistant as a source of record. Furthermore cryptographic techniques can be used to generate a hash code that uniquely identifies a dataset, which can subsequently be used to verify that the data has not been altered in any way by a malicious user or otherwise.

The blockchain enables collaborative machine learning model development throughout the building, validation, and production lifecycles. Access to digital assets like training data or machine learning models can be distributed and managed over the blockchain. Any changes to the registered digital assets by developers will be recorded. This blockchain is its own audit trail. The trail becomes useful as iterative changes are made to the model, and new data is incorporated. This function also mitigates a central problem in machine learning – avoiding bias in the development of predictive models. For example, parameter tuning has a significant impact on the performance of artificial neural networks; the audit trail of model development can be used by independent medical researcher to validate the model results. Validation teams would be comprised of experts in both the specific medical discipline that the model addressed and the discipline of machine learning techniques that were used to generate the model. These experts would find incentive in tokenized reward offered on the blockchain for completing valuable work that drives the AI systems forward. Additionally, an organization that provides medical data and buys into the program would gain access to use the model to make predictions on new patient data.

For healthcare organizations that are precluded from explicitly sharing sensitive medical data, the blockchain allows that data to still be used in training diagnostic models in an anonymized way. Neural networks can be trained incrementally, so organizations can each take turns improving the model performance by exposing it to more and more data. The organization can "check out" the model as a digital asset and train the model on the data themselves. Once they are done they can return the model to the community along with the audit record of and changes made to the model, which preclude any specific data used to improve the model. In this way the blockchain is able to derive value from data while still respecting institutional boundaries and data protection best practices.

Patient as a Partner Owning Their Data

As previously discussed blockchains are an effective tool for managing ownership and property rights to assets. If treated as a digital asset similar to a single unit of a cryptocurrency in a public blockchain, or a digital property record in a property records management blockchain, or a tokenized digital representation of a physical asset in a blockchain based supply chain, data can be managed in a similar way on the blockchain. That is, custody and ownership rights of individual data can be enforced by the blockchain with smart contracts serving as conditional logic programs enforcing predefined terms and conditions.

The enforcement of ownership rights and custody, and the ability to track, trace, and revoke those rights allows blockchains to be used to empower data owners to define the terms and conditions that govern the usage of the data they choose to share. Whether it is the amount of time the requestor has access to specific pieces of data using a 'self-destruct after' condition in a smart contract to revoke access after time has expired, or using non-fungible tokens to transfer subsets or information to only those pre-authorized addresses belonging to authorized individuals or parties, the blockchain changes the way data is obtained and the way it is controlled, giving the power back to the patient.

One of the goals of the NIH's 'All of Us' program is to empower the patient, and to make them a partner in the program, not outside it looking in. Yet currently, the process for data collection, and the transparency in data use are subpar. Individuals are expected to turn over required subsets of personal health data, and will only be informed of the study results and their final comprehensive data set. Usage specifications, data storage and handling, and sharing is all left to the program, rather than the patient.

There is no better way to empower a patient and make them feel like a true partner than by granting them ownership of their data, giving them the ability to choose how much or how little they share, and how that data is used. If partnership is to be achieved, a blockchain that supports granting ownership rights and custody of patient data to the patients can go a long way toward building that partnership. In return this will create rich, diverse data sets as patients share under their conditions and no central controller can limit access to or exploit the data. These diverse data sets will allow the development of diverse AI algorithms that can be used to model and predict in ways they never could with central data managers limiting accessibility and providing only narrow, controlled data sets. NIH's 'All of Us' program would certainly benefit from this approach, versus the current path for data collection, management, and sharing.

A Consent Registry

In lieu of granting patient partners the ability to control their data sets and define the T&Cs around usage and access, why not look to blockchain and AI to register, enforce, and monitor consent/eConsent for program participation. By leveraging a blockchain based registry for consent, the auditability, tamper-resistance, and transparency of such a system allows all stakeholders to agree beyond a doubt that consent was provided, or it wasn't.

Not only can the blockchain reinforce verification of such informed consent (by verifying the patient's unique digital signature on the transaction committing the consent to the blockchain), but when combined with smart contracts, microservices, and AI, consent committed to the blockchain can be further validated for completeness and errors, protecting the patient from incomplete documentation serving as evidence of informed consent.

Further, through more advanced smart contracts with additional logic conditions applied, more granular consent can be captured, and automatically enforced by the smart contract. For example, the consent form could allow the patient to check boxes for specific pieces of data they consent to providing for certain types of research studies. Those selections get incorporated into another smart contract responsible for managing requests for information and data from other participants, and can apply the coded logic to determine which requests are authorized to obtain which pieces of information the patient has consented to providing.

Case Study: Are we the Last Generation to Know So Little about our Health?

Walter De Brouwer, PhD

It would appear so.

One of the problems of the Second Artificial Intelligence (AI) Winter (1987-1993) was that there was not enough data going around. We did not yet understand the value of "Big Data," and academia was working on models fueled by "Small Data." However, now we have entered the era of "Bigger Data Than We Ever Imagined." We are producing data on the order of exabytes (1018) and it is predicted that in 2020 we will use zettabytes (1021) and by 2024 yottabytes (1024) is in sight. Hyperscalars are frantically expanding their clouds to meet the demands of the 21st century and the whole planet will become one giant hard disk attached to, hopefully, a capable calculator. Exascalars, on the other hand, are obsessed with "Fast Data", the application of big data analytics to smaller data sets in near-real-time and are racing beyond the petaflop (1015) to reach exaflop speed (1018), by 2021.

Both Big Data and Fast Data have already drastically reconfigured the landscape of the Financial Times Global companies by market cap. In 2009 there were no information technology companies in the FT Global 500 top 5, but a mere nine years later, all companies in the FT Global were information technology companies (see table below) which took over from big energy. Importantly all of these companies are in the process of rewriting themselves in AI. One of them is Tencent, the first Chinese information technology company that entered the top 5 (admittedly only for Q1, then lost its position after their earnings call in Q2).

2009

PetroChina

Exxon Mobile

Wal-Mart

ICBC

China Mobile

2018

Apple (AAPL)

Alphabet (GOOG and GOOGL)

Microsoft (MSFT)

Amazon (AMZN)

Tencent (TCEHY)

However, a new data inflection point is coming driven and influenced by the pressing need in healthcare. The 2018 quintuple has undoubtedly been pondering two questions in 2018: which industries provides the most data and which ones need the most speed? They all arrived at the same conclusion: Medical and Life Science. Why? Because in medicine and life sciences there are power laws at work that dwarf Moore's law. In the USA every 73 days health data is doubling estimated to arrive at hefty 2.3 zettabytes (ZB) by 2020. This is a hockey stick scenario that the technology companies cannot afford to miss. The 3 Super-A's (Amazon, Alphabet, and Apple) all announced a ground-breaking restructuring of their divisions and far-reaching collaborations (ABC-Amazon, Berkshire, Chase) to jump on the "big and fast data" bandwagon. This could produce surprising ripples in the top quintuple or n-tuple of the near future.

By 2020 some of the information technology companies won't be information technology anymore but Life Technology companies, pointing their search and intelligence engines towards healthcare and life science, thereby posing a legitimate challenge to the current biopharmaceutical and healthcare companies with their dwindling intellectual property assets and lackluster efficiency of discovery. Interestingly, by Q3 of 2018, Facebook lost its spot to Berkshire Hathaway, a well-known investment company focused on reinsurance of the healthcare and life insurance industry. It is entirely possible that by 2025 most of these companies merge technology and healthcare it is entirely possible that by 2025 most of these could be mandated by anti-trust laws to break up into Information Technology and Life Technology corporations.

Imagine the following forward-looking scenarios:

2020

Apple (AAPL)

Prime Health (PHAM)

Google Health (GOOGL)

Alphabet (GOOG)

Amazon (AMZN)

2025

Alphabet (GOOG)

Prime Life (PHAM)

Google Life (GOOGL)

Apple Life (APLL)

Baba Life (BABL)

However, the confluence of big and fast will also turn the tables and disrupt who owns what. Today, big and fast data lies in the hands of the privileged few, many in the top 5 or top 10 of the FT Global. However, in 2025, the world we will be living in will be drastically different from the one today and individuals will own their own information, health or otherwise. The first generation that will thoroughly enjoy their personal privileges of Life Data will be Generation Beta (2025 to 2039). This generation will be the children of Generation Z (with Z we exhausted the Latin alphabet and returned to the Greek).

All information, coupled with accessible calculators, will belong to its rightful owner and they will be free to do with it whatever they want: move it, sell it, share it, donate it, add to it, maintain it, remix it, delete it and create it again. New personal devices will be designed to collect, store, encrypt, and manage personal and structured medical data on an opt-in basis encrypted on their edge device. They will have become "the edge" and consider themselves nodes. All of their medical information (all medical data will be sequenced by then) will be encrypted and governed by a smart. All of their medical information will be governed by a "smart contract" – contracts as computer code -- that will stipulate a priori who and when can access it.

New economies will be born, and medical information will have become an alternative financial asset, with individuals receiving dividends on their data and due monetary benefit for participation in massive clinical trials and prospective health studies. For the first time, individuals will not be passive donors of their information, but will be incented to be more an engaged consumer and producer of research, potentially a planetary medical data project.

Medicine will finally break out of its silos. Individuals will have the choice between "portfolio managers" researching on rare diseases, hereditary diseases (including both genetic diseases and non-genetic hereditary diseases) and non-communicable diseases (NCD), based on their personal data store of health information, selling their data into their client's trial coordinator's data lake. They will get real-time dividends on their health data because medical information will have become an alternative financial asset.

Individuals will be kept up to date in real time with research on their condition. Algorithms -- fast data -- will continuously be monitoring new and upcoming trials tailored for the individual consisting of cohorts with common diagnostics, genetics, environment, family history, and predicted clinical trajectories. We claim the confluence of these data will finally make research understandable to individuals and elusive etiologies less obtuse and accessible.

GenB will be born in an always-on world with quantum computing algorithms and their own AIs that harnesse the advances of big and fast data. Everything around them will be autonomous and smart. They will have edited genomes, which will make them no longer our descendants, but ancestors in their own right who are ready to become the first space-faring civilization.

Chapter 25:
Medical Tourism, Innovation and Blockchain

Dr. Max Hooper

https://hashedhealth.com/blockchain-for-healthcare-book/

Editor's Note:

Artificial Intelligence, machine learning, and artificial neural networks were discussed in the previous chapter along with AI and Blockchain future technology enablers. This chapter goes into Medical Tourism, Innovation, and Blockchain and illustrates the continued future ways that healthcare can be impacted by blockchain applications.

Introduction

Definitions

Medical Tourism, Innovation, and Blockchain are being used in many new and unique ways in healthcare around the world. Originating from a universal definition of Medical Tourism, a unified understanding is illustrated, "Medical Tourism refers to people traveling to a country other than their own to obtain medical treatment. In the past this usually referred to those who traveled from less-developed countries to major medical centers in highly developed countries for treatment unavailable at home." [1] "Medical Tourism, also called health tourism, surgical tourism or medical travel, international travel for the purpose of receiving medical care. Many patients engage in medical tourism because the procedures they seek can be performed in other countries at relatively low cost and without delay and inconvenience of being placed on a waiting list. In addition, some patients travel to specific destinations to undergo procedures that are not available in their home country." [2]

History

Medical Tourism is an old concept that has evolved over time with an interesting history. "Throughout history people have traveled long distances for healthcare. In ancient Greece, for example, worshippers of Asclepius, the Greco-Roman god of medicine, would make pilgrimage to the temple of Epicurus, where they would undergo healing through "incubation rituals," which were rooted in prayer, fasting, and ceremony. Likewise, spas and public baths have long been destinations for those seeking medical cures. In the 17th century the emergence of spa towns in appealing settings like the Pyrenees attracted wealthy people from all over Europe. In later centuries, as travel and tourism increased, spas and health resorts in countries world-wide often attracted clientele from overseas. In addition, the establishment of facilities such as the non-profit Mayo Clinic in Rochester, Minnesota, provided new opportunities for patients in need of treatment and surgical procedures not available elsewhere." [3]

Social and Ethical Issues

As Medical Tourism evolves much research is needed to maintain social and ethical standards. "Several social and ethical issues area found in medical tourism application and practice. Inconsistency in the quality of care is a major source of criticism for the medical tourism industry. One of the primary mechanisms implemented for the standard of international healthcare is accreditation. Accreditation attempts to ensure that medical tourism facilities meet basic safety standards, are staffed with trained personnel, and have appropriate medical equipment to perform the procedures offered. Among the major accredited organizations for international hospitals are the Joint Commission International (JCI), a branch of the U.S. based Joint Commission Resources: Accreditation Canada International; and the Australian Council on Healthcare Standards International. Those organizations charge fees to clients who want to have their facilities surveyed for accreditation, and each organization maintains a list of accredited hospitals to help persons wishing to travel internationally for healthcare select a facility that will need their needs.

Another issue in medical tourism concerns the illegal trafficking of organs. Countries with indigent or vulnerable populations frequently have a greater availability of organs for medical use, since members of these populations are often tempted to risk their health and give up an organ with the promise of monetary compensation. Combined with the lack of adequate resources for donor care, the practices surrounding organ obtainment have been targeted as an aspect of medical tourism in need of greater regulation and oversight. Likewise, the exploitation of medical procedures for which efficacy is unproven or for which safety is unknown is a point of discussion for standardization and regulation.

In addition, in all countries, medical tourism could polarize national healthcare policy, creating or furthering discrepancies in healthcare services made available to citizens versus foreigners. Because the latter brings money into countries and hence bolster national economies they often enjoy greater access to doctors and medical resources than do the actual citizens of the country." [4]

Medical

A Game Changer in Medical Tourism

Medical Tourism is in a unique position to impact many people, systems, and technologies globally. The speed of innovations and growth must be closely monitored and reviewed to not compromise patient safety. Unique innovation using Blockchain technology is considered a 'game changer' in various areas of healthcare and medical tourism. Renee'-Marie Stephano authored an article in Medical Tourism Magazine titled, "Blockchain Technology: A Game Changer in Medical Tourism."

"The medical tourism industry is experiencing a rapid revolution as healthcare becomes more patient-centric. Blockchain technology, although a novel concept, is one of the catalysts of the evolving paradigm shift in healthcare delivery. Stakeholders are starting to make huge investments in this innovative technology to achieve its vast potential.

Blockchain is a decentralized digital ledger made of chronologically arranged immutable, distributive data between connected devices in a blockchain system. Records and transactions are stored in the blockchain system as blocks of data connected to previous records in the system to form a blockchain.

The advantages of blockchain are its decentralized system of data control, as well as its validity, authenticity, transparency, and security. The records and transactions in a blockchain system are encrypted with cryptographic keys with each user having a shareable key and a private key. This secures the data and ensures it cannot be accessed or used by unauthorized persons. This stored data is shared with each participant's identity undisclosed." [5]

Ms. Stephano goes on to detail how Blockchain has the potential to help Medical Tourism. "Blockchain technology is permeating healthcare rapidly, bringing healthcare solutions to promote better patient experience for medical travelers. Blockchain technology offers solutions to several barriers in medical tourism and health tourism, such as poor pre-travel logistics, record exchange between healthcare providers, and loss of patient visibility in a tourist destination country.

These problems often lead to a waste of money and potential health risks for the patient, as well as reduced destination attractiveness for the medical tourist destination." Ibid

Turning next to Healthcare Mobility and interoperability of Healthcare Systems, Ms. Stephano makes the case for healthcare globally. "Healthcare has gone global. Today for example, patients who live in the United States can travel to Singapore for cosmetic treatment. One important factor that drives and promoted health tourism is the mobility of a patients' health data.

A lack of access to a patient's health records can slow down the care process, lead to healthcare mishaps, and ultimately, ruin the reputation and attractiveness of a hospital or health travel destination. With blockchain, a patient's health data are made accessible to providers (and anyone) to whom the patient grants authorization. This ensures a free-flow of health information between local and international healthcare providers.

Geographical barriers are a major limitation in health travel and often impede the continuum of care. Because of the interoperability of systems blockchain offers, patients are able to access their health history and records through the decentralized record system. Similarly, healthcare providers can share details concerning a patient to maintain the continuum of care. Patients can also make smart contracts, allowing them to access quality healthcare providers anywhere in the world." Ibid

Finally, Ms. Stephano points out the strength of security regarding the authenticity of medical research data, as well as, Claims and Billing Management. "The quality of healthcare services is a key driver of health tourism, often tied to the volume and quality of medical research and clinical trials conducted in the destination country. Blockchain technology can help reduce the incidence of errors and fraud in clinical trial records by providing verifiable records of clinical trials and results.

Also, blockchain-enabled technology can address outcome switching and selective reporting in clinical trials. A recent study by researchers in Cambridge University showed that modified or incorrect clinical trial data can be detected by using a unique code generated by the blockchain system.

Modifying data stored in a blockchain system generated a 'hash' which can be identified by other users. This action prevents data theft and with the help of cryptographic keys which help to secure data, blockchain also helps to prevent data spying.

Health insurance and billings are plagued by fraud and scams, which accounts for 5-10% of healthcare costs every year. In 2016, Medicare lost $30 million to fraud and scams. Examples of these scams plaguing medical insurance programs include patient billing scams, phantom billing scams, and upcoding schemes. Billing errors also cost insurance programs a lot of money.

Patient billing scams involve both patients and providers. In this case, patients provide their insurance number to the provider who bills the insurer for a treatment the patient did not receive. This is often done with the patient receiving kickbacks from the provider at the end of the transaction.

Phantom billing scams are somewhat similar but do not involve the patient participating in the scam. In a phantom billing scam, the provider bills the insurer for unnecessary procedures of medical tests, procedures or tests that were never done, as well as the cost of unnecessary equipment.

In an upcoding scheme, the provider inflated bills made to the insurer by using a billing code that suggests that the patient requires more (often unnecessary and expensive) procedures.

Blockchain technology can automate many claim payments and adjudications, eliminating middlemen who may manipulate the process. In addition, its decentralized control of data provides transparency and ease of tracking billing and payment records, allowing auditors to detect any discrepancies and billing errors.

Blockchain can also provide an advantageous environment for smart contracts in healthcare between patients and providers and providers and payers. In an overall system where contracting and payments necessarily requires a financial transaction, the security of the transaction and the elimination of the costly intermediary presents a very attractive proposition. Some governments are requiring healthcare organizations to implement Blockchain technology. With this technology changing all of the time, it should be very interesting to consider the financial impact for healthcare systems to keep up to date and for these systems to integrate with existing healthcare information systems.

Blockchain technology is still in its developing stages and rapidly revolutionizing many industries, particularly the healthcare industry. As more research is being done to establish a sustainable mechanism for wider application of this technology in health tourism, there is no doubt healthcare will become more simplified, secure, and patient-centric in the future." Ibid

The Dubai International Health Forum advances Medical Tourism through events and a platform for exchange of knowledge and expertise. At the 2018 Dubai International Health Tourism Forum, Brian de Francesca, CEO of the telemedicine company VER2 talked about how telemedicine could support medical tourism. "Dubai is aiming high when it comes to medical tourism. The targeted number of medical tourists by 2020 is 500,000. On the other hand, the authorities wish to decrease the number of Emirati nationals that travel overseas for their care.

In his address, de Francesca stressed the importance of pre and post-travel consultations, as well as the use of cloud-based health records.

Several problems occur in medical tourism, causing risk to patients, waste of money, potential comprise of medical institutions due to:

- **Limited 'pre-travel' preparations** (Some patients come in with a wrong diagnosis or lack of tests that should have been done before their travel).

- **Loss of patient visibility gone abroad.**

- **Limited follow-up upon return.**

- **Reluctance of home-based doctors to pick up care,** as patients treated elsewhere are perceived risk patients if the doctor is unfamiliar with treatments and procedures that were administered abroad.

- **Prescriptions from abroad are not on local formulary or devices are not locally supported.**

40% of outbound patients travel abroad due to lack of confidence in local diagnosis or treatment plan. In Brian's experience, telemedical 2nd opinion by a trusted specialist could reduce overseas travel by 40%.

Telemedicine can improve the experience of patients and caregivers, increase the efficiency of medical institutions. The technology is available; the challenge is changes in workflows and processes, scheduling, communication, planning and coordination.

As de Francesca stressed a "blockchain foundation" to health records and health monitoring devices will significantly improve safety, effectiveness, and profitability of medical tourism. Blockchain can enhance the degree of trust in the continuum of care, which is essential for thriving medical tourism." 6

Transforming Healthcare

A recent article, "Blockchain and Medical Tourism Reinforce Each Other", illustrates how Blockchain and Medical Tourism expand one another. "A growing number of people travel outside of their home country to obtain medical treatment that is cheaper and at least as high quality. Whether for cosmetic surgery, dental implants, a joint replacement, or other medical services, this trend signals a new normal in the globalization of healthcare. A coming phase of this trend is "Blockchain-Centric Medical Tourism." [7]

Currently, most hospitals, no matter where they're located, don't have shared access to patient records. This poses an inconvenience to the patient and a time-consuming hurdle for physicians and other clinical practitioners, Instant access could be a game changer.

Blockchain and Medical Tourism Empower Patients

The blockchain facilitates access to a patient's history. It's a record of which doctor performed what. It also documents who has access to the records.

With blockchain technology in place, patients could

- Consult any doctor in the system with ease and efficiency,
- Self-designate the type of care they want, and
- Even include advance directives and do-not-resuscitate orders

When patients have access to their own data, they can self-manage their health conditions. Of course, they'd continue to receive support from clinicians and others in healthcare. But clients could reduce their healthcare costs.

Blockchain and Medical Tourism Empower Doctors

Without access to records during an emergency, health clinicians are placed in a compromising situation. That may result in subpar care or even harm. With a flow of health information, healthcare professionals could resolve the situation and save lives.

Further, when a person has a very rare condition, you could locate the right doctor or the right are at the right time in another country. That expert would have access to the patient's data remotely. Healthcare would go global. With data analytics and other measurement tools, blockchain would also assist in managing a health crisis like a disease outbreak.

Blockchain and Medical Tourism Get Started

Blockchain is being tested for improved data integrity, security, and patient trust in electronic sharing among health providers of health records. Ibid

Author, Renee'-Marie Stephano in another of her articles, "How Blockchain Technology Can Transform Healthcare" illustrates unique ways of innovation using Blockchain technology. These include the following areas:

- Healthcare Data Exchange

- Drug Traceability and Clinical Trials

- Cybersecurity

Zion Market Research recently released a report on the global medical tourism market. "According to the report, global medical tourism market was valued at approximately USD 15.5 billion in 2017 and is expected to generate revenue of around USD 28.0 billion by the end of 2024, growing at a CAGR of around 8.8% between 2018 and 2024.

Modern healthcare at affordable prices is offered to medical tourists in various countries at the different level of economic development. Western population travel to other countries for their medical treatment. Long waiting lists, increasing healthcare costs, and limitations on the availability of treatment options, coupled with the ease of travel, medical tourism is gaining popularity. Medical tourism offers growth opportunities for healthcare providers. The medical tourism industry is evolving quickly and also increasing awareness levels among individuals across the world. Emerging market economies with medical expertise and medical facilities at low cost, coupled with attractive tourism sites, are expected to drive medical tourism market over the forecast period."[9]

Barriers to Growth in Medical Tourism

"A Solution on Storage: How Blockchain Breaks Down the Biggest Barriers to Medical Tourism" makes the case for the potential growth in medical tourism. "Few markets have more potential than medical tourism. From improving healthcare affordability to opening up a wider range of services to allowing people to seek better care, medical tourism benefits patients and providers all over the globe. This explains why the industry has grown so rapidly in recent years, and is projected to keep growing at a brisk pace. As healthcare prices rise and quality concerns increase, more and more patients are seeing the benefits of seeking care abroad.

Unfortunately, for all the potential of medical tourism, this industry creates some serious challenges. Getting care in another country is risky, both because it's harder to judge provider quality and because each nation has its own epidemiological issues. Medical tourism also creates problems with payments, advertising, and a host of other elements, which can negatively affect both patients and providers. But thanks to blockchain technology, it may soon be possible to eliminate these problems and create a secure, transparent, and efficient medical tourism market." [10]

Patient Risk

The single greatest problem by far with medical tourism is the risk it presents to patients. "Even under the best of circumstances, different countries have different epidemiological issues, meaning different diseases abound. In addition to these epidemiological issues are a host of other problems with potential harm to both providers and patients, these include:

- Low Transparency
- Marketing Limitations
- Payment Problems
- Data Security Shortcomings

Due to these issues, many patients hesitate to seek healthcare abroad and in addition physicians have difficulty in attracting patients. As long as these problems persist, medical tourism will not reach its full potential." Ibid

Storage Solutions

Despite these very real problems, blockchain offers the technology that can solve them. "A method of storage that involves tying pieces of data together into immutable chains, blockchain creates record that are virtually impossible to tamper with. This makes it possible to develop a number of resources that directly address the problems of the medical tourism market, including:

- Secure Databases
- Physician & Patient Matching
- Cryptocurrency Payments
- Smart Contracts
- Security Features [Ibid]

Use Cases

Grey Reh, Deloitte Consulting, LLP, Vice Chairman and U.S. and Global Life Sciences Leader states, " Early blockchain adopters may fear other organizations will not fully embrace the technology, reducing ROI for those who currently invest in it. However, given the potential, it may be time for healthcare stakeholders to move beyond the hype of blockchain and begin to explore current and likely blockchain applications." [11]

Deloitte's article "Beyond Bitcoin: 5 Uses for Blockchain in Healthcare" discusses blockchain benefits and opportunities. He noted that while, "… the health care industry could benefit from varied applications of blockchain technology, including, for example, improved ability to capture and maintain patient records and claims data, people tend to have one of two views of blockchain. They see it either as synonymous with bitcoin and other digital currencies, or as an overhyped technology. Though blockchain isn't likely to turn healthcare on its head—and we might still be five or ten years away from realizing its potential—the technology could help life sciences and health care organizations streamline process and improve patient experiences.

Blockchain is essentially a living list of linked digital records. Each transaction is verified and stored by each network participant based on a set of previously agreed-upon rules and without a governing central authority. Information can be added but not copied or deleted. As a result, multiple groups—healthcare plans, physicians, hospital systems, and even patients—can share information through a secure system." [Ibid]

The following are five areas where blockchain might be useful in health care:

- Supply chains
- Clinical trials
- Provider directory management
- Patient records
- Insurance coverage, preauthorization, and claims adjudication [12]

Use Cases

Digital Patient-Ordered Networks

The Robomed Network is a unique use case as described in an article in the International Medical Travel Journal titled, "Blockchain Comes to Medical Tourism". "Robomed Network is promoting a decentralized, cross-border ecosystem of healthcare providers based on an open smart contract and crypto currency. A patient-ordered medical network is where patients can manage and control their healthcare data through a mobile electronic medical record (EMR) and allow doctors access to when requested.

A global digital platform known as Robomed Network (https://robomed.io) has introduced a solution that allows the medical industry to replace the old, prevailing ways of managing healthcare process with new ones designed to boost efficiency, effectiveness and transparency. This is achieved through the elimination of non-value-added processes and clinical errors." [13]

Additionally, "Robomed Network means that patients around the globe have access to bureaucracy-free, affordable and quality medical care targeted to their specific needs. What drives all of this is a medical network managed by a blockchain token, designed to provide the most effective medical care. Robomed serves as the linkage point between health service providers and patients, all tied to a smart contract built on top of the Ethereum platform." [Ibid]

Philipp Mironovich, Robomed Network co-founder states, "Robomed's blockchain is designed to constantly expand available capacity for record-keeping, transactions tracking and accumulation of a diverse database of medical knowledge and clinical pathways applied to treating a numerous range of medical cases. We believe that the scope of medical services rendered to patients is bound to grow with the process for obtaining these services streamlined." [Ibid]

Process-automation system

The International Medical Travel Journal article goes on to highlight the Robomed Network's process-automation system created for participating in-network clinics.

"Participating clinics use Robomed EHR, a process-automation system, which includes unified medical data storage and health management tools. Its primary purpose is to integrate all participating clinics into a single information space, allowing various service providers to quickly interact without bureaucratic, financial or legal barriers. This bridge between the patients seeking quality medical care and access to it is a smart contact. This interactive digital mechanism allows patients to obtain access to a chain of healthcare providers committed to delivering the best medical care consistent with the digital clinical guidelines registered in Robomed Network.

These clinical guidelines are adopted via a constantly upgraded, competitive and transparent voting process involving the medical and patient community. The goal is to use a diverse set of healthcare treatments and high standards to fulfill patient expectations." [Ibid]

Tokens

Robomed Network issues its own tokens to drive the smart contract engagement between healthcare providers and patients. This elevates service value by granting token owners full accomplishment of clinical guidelines for cases.

Ethereum Blockchain Platform

Patients engage with the Robomed Network via Robomed Mobile or Robomed Web. The proprietary smart contract technology creates a single system of coordinates with clinical outcomes as a reference point. This is one of the first healthcare uses of the Ethereum blockchain platform. The Robomed Network is promoting this decentralized, cross-border ecosystem of healthcare providers based on an open smart contract and crypto currency. Robomed is based in Moscow and launched with $30 million from investors. The logic is that blockchain is potentially a tool to help deliver better and less expensive health care without patients or doctors needing to know the first thing about the technology.

Smart Technology

Blockchain technology is used to create smart contracts and payment systems between patients and doctors. The system helps set a market-based price between doctor and patient. The smart contract lays out milestones for diagnosis and treatment, with various metrics and checkpoints along the way. A patient puts money into the Robomed system using cash or a credit card, and it's held there in a virtual currency wallet. As the doctor proceeds through the contract, some money is released along the way. The system also allows patients to list symptoms, suggest possible medical issues, and then get matched with doctors who have expertise in those areas. Twenty-three clinics around the world have signed on to use the Robomed platform, and now the company is looking to accelerate its growth. Clinics accept tokens as payment backed by Robomed Network guarantee to buy them out at a fixed price. Patients do not have to purchase RBM tokens as they can pay in a local currency converted to the price of RBM token in Ether. Smart contracts are computer protocols intended to facilitate, verify, or enforce the negotiation or performance of a contract. Proponents of smart contracts claim that many kinds of contractual clauses may be made partially or fully self-executing, self-enforcing, or both. The aim of smart contracts is to provide security that is superior to traditional contract law and to reduce other transaction costs associated with contracting." Ibid

Blockchain-Based Software – Use Case

Michael Yuz, MD, MBA, and a group of individuals have started a unique company, Medical Diagnostic Web (MDW) recently described by AuntMinnie.com.

Medical Diagnostic Web is a blockchain-based software application designed to connect all players in the diagnostic digital imaging space.

With its open, decentralized communications infrastructure, encrypted data transmission, and immutable audit trails, MDW's blockchain marketplace enables individual radiologists and radiology groups to create new business relationships and get compensated immediately for services rendered." [14]

MDW's executive summary describes the company as follows. "MDW is a decentralized platform that will bring together global players in the field of image-rich medical diagnostic specialties and subspecialties, such as radiology, cardiology, dermatology, pathology ophthalmology, and neurology to create an efficient, open and fair marketplace for infrastructure by delivering cost efficiencies, reducing fees paid for interpretations of diagnostic reports, improving report detail and quality, reducing medical diagnostic errors, and improving turn-around-time (TAT) of interpretations. The platform also enables participants to derive additional revenue streams by monetizing the data they own and making it available to artificial intelligence (AI) companies that need data to train deep learning algorithms, as well as serving as clearinghouse of algorithms that AI companies can sell to customers using the platform.

The platform will utilize blockchain technology and smart contracts to provide physicians, healthcare facilities, and associated stakeholders (including patients, healthcare facilities, and physicians) with a secure, cost-effective, and straightforward way to conduct and pay for medical diagnostic transactions. The decentralized nature of MDW will promote egalitarian principles among participants and make it more difficult for dominant players, or a centralized private interest to control the flow of data and money.

The platform will collect fees from participants and distribute portion of proceeds to the holders of security tokens. The fees will be coming from four main revenue sources: marketplace interpretation fees, In-house payment processing fees, image sales and AI algorithm sales. MDW's founding team has many years of experience and domain expertise within various areas of the medical diagnostic field, including teleradiology, telemedicine, diagnostics, business technical infrastructure, and complex IT development. The team is uniquely positioned to execute on the plan to create a global leader in medical diagnostics field." Ibid

Conclusions

Many challenges are to be overcome as we move toward the total acceptance and usage of blockchain technology coupled with Medical Tourism. Many groups must collaborate and come together to benefit all participants in the healthcare and medical tourism ecosystems. The many players include governments, public and private agencies, hospitals, practitioners, medical record databases, health insurance companies, research organizations, healthcare business, and many others. The remarkable innovation and speed of acceptance are drivers to the healthcare industry. The focus should always be that the patient plays an active role in these endeavors. The common goals should be to cure and prevent disease and have the patient involved so that the patient can live a healthy and productive life.

References

1. https://en.wikipedia.org/wiki/Medical_Tourism

2. https://www.britannica.com/science/medical-tourism

3. https://britannica.com/science/medical-tourism

4. https://britannica.com/science/medical-tourism299316

5. https://www.medicaltourismmag.com/blockchain-technology-game-changer-medical-tourism/

6. https://medium.com/iryo-network-/medical-tourism-will-benefit-from-telemedicine-and-blockchain-fod15a82fc18

7. https://www.medicaldental-tourism.net/blog/blockchain-and-medical-tourism/

8. https://medicaltourismmag.com/blockchain-technology-can-transform-healthcare/

9. https://globalnewswire.com/news-release/2018/06/25/1528923/0/en/Global-medical-tourism-market-expected-to-reach-USD-28-0-Billion-by-2024-Zion-Market-Research.html

10. https://medium.com/@medipedia/a-solution-in-storage-how-blockchain-breaks-down-the-biggest-barriers-to-medical-tourism-ef92b626111a

11. https://deloitte.wsj/cio/2018/04/26/beyond-bitcoin-5-uses-for-blockchain-in-health-care/

12. https://deloitte.wsj/cio/2018/04/26/beyond-bitcoin-5-uses-for-blockchain-in-health-care/

13. https://www.imtj.com/news/blockchain-comes-medical-tourism/

14. https://www.auntminnie.com/index.aspx?sec=nws&sub=thd&pag=dis&itemid=123484

Chapter 26:
Smart City Initiatives in the Healthcare Sector

Dr. Mohammed Shael al Saadi

Editor's Note:

Global healthcare impact for the "overall good of the community" is illustrated in this chapter in the various global Smart City initiatives in the healthcare sector using blockchain models. The previous chapter discussed Medical Tourism and this chapter discussed how world class healthcare systems are models for the future. Global healthcare impact for the "overall good of the community" is illustrated in this chapter in the various global Smart City initiatives in the healthcare sector using blockchain models. The previous chapter discussed Medical Tourism and this chapter discussed how world class healthcare systems are models for the future.

Introduction

Dubai has been consistently at the forefront, taking a proactive approach to adopt emerging digital technologies suited for the progress of the Emirate and the United Arab Emirates nation as a whole. On October 2013, H. H. Sheikh Mohammed bin Rashid Al Maktoum, Vice-President and Prime Minister of the UAE and Ruler of Dubai announced a project to turn Dubai into the smartest and happiest city. The project aspires to facilitate a citywide transformation "to empower, deliver and promote an efficient, seamless, safe and impactful city experience for residents and visitors." It has presently evolved into over 1000 initiatives across the fields of communication, education, healthcare, utilities, environment and vehicular traffic, government services, etc led by the Smart Dubai Office, the government entity formed to lead this transition.

An extension of the Smart city formation, the 'Dubai Blockchain Strategy 2020' was introduced to integrate the technology into all government establishments by 2020. This will allow the government to tap into the new economic opportunities that blockchain offers and enhance the city's global competitiveness. The key use of the technology will be to develop digital records and settle financial dealings using computer algorithms that don't need third-party verification. Despite the unique nature of blockchain technologies, Dubai Health Authority has capitalized on and innovated blockchain technology to improve the healthcare sector.

Dubai's has significantly improved its health infrastructure over the years. The city's past efforts to enhance its position as a healthcare destination in the region include building an entire city centered on world-class healthcare, introducing mandatory health insurance for all citizens and expatriates, supporting private sector investment and implementing an Emirates-wide electronic health record (EHR) system. Now, empowered by blockchain technology, programs are already being piloted to create an efficient health economy and reform the current healthcare system. Furthermore, this has the potential to control medical costs, improve quality of care, and enhance the overall happiness of Dubai's population.

Purposing Blockchain for Healthcare

Blockchain is generally defined as a distributed system which records and stores transaction records. More specifically, it is defined as a shared, immutable record of peer-to-peer transactions built from linked transaction blocks and stored in a digital ledger. Interactions with the blockchain become known to all participants and require verification by the network before information is added, enabling trustless collaboration between network participants while recording an immutable audit trail of all interactions.

Each participant (or node) connected to the blockchain network has a secret private key and a public key that acts as an openly visible identifier. The pair is cryptographically linked such that identification is possible in only one direction using the private key. As such, one must have the private key in order to unlock a participant's identity to uncover what information on the blockchain is relevant to their profile. Imagine a database which stores all the information but this data can now be accessed by all who have the permission, it is no longer controlled by a central authority. Thus, it is identified that there are distributed, permissioned, and secured properties to blockchain's utility in healthcare.

In healthcare, this distributed model would enable each patient's medical record to be on a blockchain specific to the patient. Providers and payers may maintain their own nodes. Implications of distributed ledgers may include:

- Reducing reserves: The speed at which the blockchain processes information can reduce the average lag time from the date a service is incurred until it is paid, effectively adjudicating claims in near real time.

- Timely care management: Care management programs can query the blockchain and scan for new patients to enroll based on a set of pre-defined eligibility requirements. This prevents cases from escalating without proper care management. It results in more efficient overall care and may help disease management programs more carefully track enrollment and patient health status.

- Real-time decision support: Having a concise and comprehensive summary of the patient's most recent health history readily available may help doctors quickly understand a patient's unique background. It should help providers reduce medical errors and streamline a new patient's onboarding process.

- Increasing resilience to security breaches: It is nearly impossible to completely shut down a blockchain. If any single node is compromised, blockchain medical records are still accessible because the system will still operate as long as one node is available, ensuring there is still access to information.

- Lowering administration cost: A distributed ledger ensures safer and faster data exchanges among payers, providers, and members. Removing reliance on paperwork, third parties, and data security will reduce administrative expenses.

- Near real-time adjudication: Claims adjudication will no longer rely on bills submitted electronically. Insurers may adjudicate claims as they are appended to the blockchain. This will allow members to settle their out-of-pocket cost sharing as claims are incurred.

Implications of the permissioned feature of a blockchain may include:

- Empowering patients: Patients have full access to their medical records. They may query their records at any time; this may lead to an increased awareness of their own health status and recognition of the cost of medical services, empowering them to take control over their health and comply with medication requirements and medical professionals' instructions.

- Differentiating access in the value chain: Blockchain permissions can provide appropriate stakeholders in the healthcare value chain with secure access to the information they need. This secure transfer of data improves consumer safety by granting stakeholders access to only the specific information they need and nothing more.

- Integrating with other sources: A blockchain is interoperable, so it can integrate data from multiple sources. A medical blockchain may incorporate data from non-traditional sources, such as fitness trackers and food journals. This data would provide a more holistic perspective of the patient's health.

Implications of the additional security blockchain provides may include:

- Securing data transfer: Any actions taken to the blockchain, including data viewing and downloading, are recorded. A user's awareness that others are able to see exact actions taken may lead the user to behave with higher integrity (i.e., the sentinel effect).

- Protecting patient identity: The public and private key eliminate the need to use a patient's resident identity number. A consumer's public key will unlock access to the individual's blockchain, but the public key cannot derive the private key. This maintains the confidentiality of the patient's resident identity number and private key, which reduces the chances that an individual's identity could be stolen.

- Reducing incorrect coding: Patients should corroborate medical records before they are appended to the blockchain. This sort of double-checking involves patients more with their health and can reduce incorrect coding and fraud as it adds an additional layer of scrutiny to ensure data accuracy.

- Streamlining claim audits: A new record on the blockchain should be thoroughly vetted because nothing can be modified. This scrutiny serves as an algorithmic audit of each block in the chain. Immediate validation should eliminate duplicate claims and simplify data cleaning. Additionally, all claims records will leave auditable trails.

Current Initiatives for Blockchain in Dubai

The Dubai Health Authority is the leading government authority undertaking the initiative to implement the regional Health Information Exchange (HIE). Among the KPI's set for adoption of technologies, the greatest positive impact is aimed to tackle – prevalence of diabetes in the region and the Healthcare Quality Index with the sub-measure of healthcare infrastructure. The Dubai health authority is working on adopting blockchain technology to create digital medical records and store patients' information that could be shared between public and private health institutions.

SALAMA Program

The Electronic health record project spanning across public hospitals is called 'Salama'. A unified electronic medical record that doctors can have access to patients' medical information across multiple public healthcare facilities. However, it is necessary that patients allow the disclosure of their medical information. This will help the doctor follow a treatment protocol in the event of a hospital transfer and to ensure homogenous treatment.

A smart contract gives the patient the control to share his information with a doctor. The smart contract is an online version of a contract that is kept and maintained through the blockchain technology and could be accessed by any party or person upon the request of any of the involved entities or persons. Aside from blockchain being used to help the authority access patients' medical records, it can be further leveraged to provide e-prescriptions upon request.

The Salama project will bolster effective doctor-patient communication, and will facilitate the establishment of a comprehensive database that economises time and effort, all the while providing sufficient medical information about patients. To ensure it is effective, 11,000 DHA employees will be trained to use Salama. While the 60 employees who have worked on implementing Salama have been trained in the UAE and in the US. This strengthens the overall infrastructure of the health sector in Dubai and will eventually lead to ensuring customer satisfaction and achieving sustainable development.

NABIDH Program

The Network & Analysis Backbone for Integrated Dubai Health (NABIDH) extends Salama to Dubai private hospitals and integrate e-records. The ultimate target for NABIDH is the health and wellbeing of all individuals living or working in or visiting the Emirate of Dubai. Like Salama, the key objectives of NABIDH include :

- Improvement of individual's health
- Increased patient safety
- Accessibility of Healthcare includes the deployment of telemedicine applications for elder populations to access virtual care
- Affordability of healthcare for expats which is reducing the cost to health insurance payers for better quality at lower unit cost
- Overall Efficiency of the Healthcare in Dubai

As NABIDH has progressed through its initial design and strategy development phase, the next step is to establish strong communication among facilities and gather technical information to evaluate existing infrastructure and capabilities across healthcare facilities in Dubai to analyse and build the backbone accordingly.

Other future supporting DHA initiatives on medical informatics and technology include - revising and updating interoperability standards at the Dubai level, establishing smart solutions for non-clinical services, establishing a consumer centric online data platform and finally establishing smart solutions for clinical services.

Future Benefits of Blockchain to Dubai's healthcare system

For the UAE and Dubai in particular, blockchain will vastly improve healthcare industry practices, addressing some shortcomings while improving other processes:

- Enabling value-based provider reimbursement: Providers are predominantly compensated on a fee-for-service basis by the type of service provided. The blockchain enables reimbursement by value-added and quality of care. Value can be calculated using patient health outcomes, avoided costs, patient satisfaction, resources consumed, and timeliness of provided care. Providers with consistently poor performance may have lower reimbursements and vice versa for higher-performing providers.

- Enabling value-based member cost sharing: Patient cost sharing based on metrics other than service category is possible. Payers may incentivize behaviour by reducing cost sharing for patients who stay in compliance with medications and other timely check-ups. It can also discourage avoidable utilization by increasing cost sharing for those who develop patterns of unnecessary office visits or whose lab results consistently prove no illness present.

- Facilitating population health analysis: With easy access to more demographic information, actuaries could spot more trends in the underlying population, and recommend care programs to implement in anticipation of the population's needs. Furthermore, it can help in the form of precision medication finding ways to recommend cost-effective long-term treatment for individuals.

- Refining premium calculation: New predictive methods and tools for projecting claims may be possible. This would circumvent the conventional approach of applying a broad trend factor to historical period claims, and adjusting the underlying experience to match characteristics of the projection period. Ultimately, incorporating non-traditional and real-time data from the blockchain can provide actuaries with a more precise estimate of future experience.

- Improving quality metrics: The blockchain offers a trustable way of measuring provider quality. It contains standardized information that can be used to identify providers with lower efficiency, higher readmission rates, and higher avoidable conditions. Standardized data through the blockchain can enable provider networks to identify and help underperforming physicians, and could ultimately improve the overall quality of hospitals and all healthcare facilities.

- Improving risk adjustment accuracy: Currently risk adjustment methods can quantify the risk relativity among individuals but with limited predictive ability. They mostly rely on provider coding accuracy and the individual's past claims experience. With access to the information stored on blockchains, actuaries may develop better algorithms and predictive models to improve accuracy in risk adjustment programs. This could enable more accurate, more confident provider risk-sharing calculations.

- Introducing new group quotes approach: Longitudinal patient history may enable insurers to incorporate the prior experience of each individual when issuing quotes for new groups. This provides much more accurate initial pricing than would be developed through traditional manual rating. Insurers could query the blockchain for each individual's claims and provide a quote based on actual claims experience.

Conclusion

Dubai's digital drive and aim to develop a 'world class healthcare system' has led to the adoption of blockchain technology which further enables the emirate's ability to achieve both goals. The nature of healthcare is reforming and continues.

In line with the Dubai Smart city initiative and Blockchain strategy 2020, the first steps began with changing the format of traditional medical records to electronic health records. The introduction of programs like SALAMA and NABIDH has enabled the improvement of health and well-being of individuals receiving their treatments through the public and private healthcare institutions. By enabling patients to access their medical health records through blockchain there has been a transfer of responsibility back to the patient to securely distribute their records with doctors. This has improved doctor-patient communication and provides patients a holistic approach to their medical experience. For medical staff, blockchain has provided reduced costs for patients and insurance providers, allowed doctors to provide more efficient treatments and improved the local healthcare system overall.

In efforts to upkeep these initiatives, Dubai Health Authority will continue to promote programs in line with the goals to forming a world class healthcare system. These include advancing an innovative care model, promoting an innovation culture and reinforcing the use of patient engagement tools offered through HER systems.

References

1. Dubai health Authority (2018). Dubai Health Strategy 2016 - 2022 : Towards a Healthier and Happier Community. [online] Dubai: Dubai health Authority. Available at: https://www.dha.gov.ae/Documents/Dubai_Health_Strategy_2016-2021_En.pdf .

2. Dubai Health Authority (2018). Sub. Intergrated Dubai Health (NABIDH) - Dubai. Circular 127. [online] Dubai: Dubai Health Authority. Available at: https://www.dha.gov.ae/Documents/تعميم%20رقم%20127%20بأشن%20 مشروع%20ان-%20-20%نابض%20 Copy.pdf .

3. IBM Global Business Services Public Sector Team (2018). Blockchain: The Chain of Trust and its Potential to Transform Healthcare – Our Point of View. [online] IBM. Available at: https://www.healthit.gov/sites/default/files/8-31-blockchain-ibm_ideation-challenge_aug8.pdf .

4. IBM Global Business Services Public Sector Team (2018). Blockchain: The Chain of Trust and its Potential to Transform Healthcare – Our Point of View. [online] IBM. Available at: https://www.healthit.gov/sites/default/files/8-31-blockchain-ibm_ideation-challenge_aug8.pdf .

5. Kong, J. (2018). Blockchain UAE: Global healthcare implications. [online] Milliman. Available at: http://ae.milliman.com/insight/2018/Blockchain-UAE-Global-healthcare-implications/ .

6. Ponce de Leon, J. (2018). Shaikh Mohammad announces Smart City project to transform Dubai. [online] GulfNews. Available at: https://gulfnews.com/news/uae/general/shaikh-mohammad-announces-smart-city-project-to-transform-dubai-1.1244658 .

7. Saleh, Y. (2018). Patient privacy the main challenge facing blockchain in health sector - Dubai official. [online] Zawya.com. Available at: https://www.zawya.com/uae/en/story/Patient_privacy_the_main_challenge_facing_blockchain_in_health_sector__Dubai_official-ZAWYA20180111081700/ .

8. Smartdubai.ae. (2018). Smart Dubai Blockchain Initiatives. [online] Available at: https://smartdubai.ae/initiatives/blockchain .

9. Smartdubai.ae. (2018). Smart Dubai Website. [online] Available at: https://smartdubai.ae/about-us .

Chapter 27:
Global Smart Cities: Using Blockchain to Catalyze Advancement in Citizen Experiences and Technology Adoption

AJ Ripin

https://hashedhealth.com/blockchain-for-healthcare-book/

Editor's Note:

New viewpoints on what constitutes the characteristics of Smart Cities continues to redefine how blockchain can offer disruptive technologies and innovation. Additional information is covered on advancement of the human experience and reaching blockchain adoption.

Introduction

The viewpoints of what constitutes the characteristics of Smart Cities continues to be redefined as new disruptive technologies and innovations are advanced throughout marketplaces and future thinking of what's possible are being envisioned and pursued by thought-leaders. As an initial concept, "Smart Cities can upgrade the efficiency of city services by eliminating redundancies and finding ways to save money, as well as provide higher-quality services at a lower cost. A smart city's goal is to enrich the lives of its residents and the environment." [1] As this is evaluated further, city services can be considered infrastructure matters "involving functions like: Networks, Electricity, Communication, Water, Gas, Sewer, Storm, Transportation, and Tourism." [2] The "smart" component is often viewed as the ability to collect, analyze, and utilize electronic data obtained from these infrastructure systems in parallel with other public or private systems where transactions are conducted by its citizens resulting in "smart (or connected) communities"—the integration of "information and communication technology (ICT), and various physical devices connected to the network (the Internet of things or IoT) to optimize the efficiency of city operations and services and connect to citizens."[3]

What city wouldn't want to become a Smart City? It's becoming commonplace for cities to describe themselves as being (or transforming) into Smart Cities producing intense intra-city competitiveness to position themselves as being a "Smarter" City or staking claim as the "Smartest" City, being significantly transformative (or first) in specific aspects within its smart community. The variable of competition, coupled with the: (1) abilities of Cities in leapfrogging (e.g. disruptive innovation allowing new entrants to 'leapfrog' existing participants in the marketplace); and (2) the multitude in areas of pursuit throughout a Smart Community, is truly creating the right environment for the optimization of cities—supporting the ultimate goals of cities—enriching the lives of its citizens. Therein lies the transformative potential of Blockchain Technology—to accelerate the advancement of these habitats' capabilities to impact these habitats in domains like Healthcare, Education and Agriculture.

"A smart city needs the capacity to sense a current condition, interpret the resulting data to find patterns, and react – or create the capacity for city managers to react – appropriately." Dietman Offenhuber, Professor at Northeastern University, Boston [4]

Why Blockchain?

"Incorporating new technologies into the development of smart cities means rethinking the way different services are provided. From this perspective, Blockchain might represent the future of both smart cities and smart communities as it offers new alternatives for individuals and institutions. Through its persistent and at the same time private storage of data, Blockchain enables the development of a large number of new models of interaction that could not even be conceived of before the advent of the technology." [5] A Blockchain is a digital, distributed ledger of transactions, using consensus algorithms to facilitate trust throughout the network. [6] Blockchain is a subsection of distributed ledger technology (DLT), a class of decentralized database spanning over many different users, geographic areas, sites, etc. According to Michael Rauchs and others, DLT is: 'A system of electronic records that: (i) enables a network of independent participants to establish a consensus around (ii) the authoritative ordering of cryptographically validated ('signed') transactions. These records are made (iii) persistent by replicating the data across multiple nodes, and (iv) tamper evident by linking them by cryptographic hashes. (v) The shared result of the reconciliation/consensus process—the 'ledger'—serves as the authoritative version for these records.' [7]

It is anticipated that Blockchain Technology will impact securing transactions like what the Internet did for access to information.

Many in Leadership of Smart City initiatives, such as the Governments of Estonia and Dubai are evaluating though implementation approaches in using Blockchain as a replacement in centralized ledgers to 'create a trusted, tamper-proof repository of information on an individual, which spans multiple facets of their identity' [8] in a decentralized process. Since blockchain technology is not dependent on a single resource of storage or computing, 'each user of the blockchain uses his or her computing resources, on a peer-to-peer basis.' [9] Here is a look into some of these initiatives.

e-Estonia

Estonians celebrated its 100 years of independence in 2018. The country has seen quite a transformation over the past century. It has been focused the past two decades in IT solutions and has continued to place significant investment in information technology. Estonian has often been referred as 'e-Estonia' due to the pervasive implementation and adoption of digital solutions throughout the country. It has been designated by Wired as 'the most advanced digital society in the world. Almost 100% of public services are available as 'e-solutions,' and, in most cases, there isn't even a need to for a citizen to physically visit the government agency fulfilling the service. The digitization has proliferated through its tax, roads, and other services, including digital identification, which grants access to all the country's e-services like voting. Its 'i-Voting' has been reported to only take up to 3 minutes and captures citizen votes from across the globe. The authentication into these systems is through a 'national universal public key infrastructure' (PKI) the allows for citizens to securely authenticate and authorize transactions. This chart describes Estonia's journey of digitization over the last twenty years.

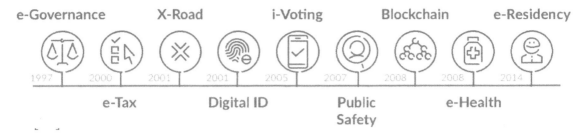

Estonia KSI Blockchain Technology

Estonia is the first Nation State in the world to deploy blockchain technology in production systems. The country has been using the blockchain technology in these systems since 2012 (testing since 2008). The catalyst in using the blockchain technology originated from the intent to strengthen data integrity from its government and related data systems. The country established an internal division, Estonian Information Systems Authority (RIA) as its centralized body to monitor and administer access to the blockchain ecosystem. It's equipped and empowered other state agencies with the ability to design and deploy it own managed solutions through turnkey starter solutions like integration packages. Estonia continues to expand its use of the blockchain technology referred as, 'Keyless Signature Infrastructure' (KSI) Blockchain technology, which is currently being used for several of its systems: National Health (e-Health Record); Security and Commercial Regulations (e-Business Register, e-Land Registry); Legislative and Judicial (e-Law and e-Court production systems); Embassy (Data Embassy), Medicine (e-Prescription database) with expectations to expand adoption in areas like cybersecurity. It has even demonstrated use in official state communications. The Estonian Government selected Guardtime as its technology partner to secure its public and private records with blockchain. 'The same KSI Blockchain technology is used by the NATO Cooperative Cyber Defense Centre of Excellence, European Union IT Agency, US Defense Department and also by Lockheed Martin, Ericsson and others.' [11]

A Model for Implementation with Healthcare

The country has focused in positioning itself as a blueprint for implementation of blockchain technology and applications, including its approach of blockchain applied to its healthcare. It is often viewed as the first country to implement blockchain technology for its healthcare technology at a national scale with more than 1.3 million citizens. "We are using blockchain as an additional layer of security to help us ensure the integrity of health records. Privacy and integrity of healthcare information are a top priority for the government and we are happy to work with innovative technologies like the blockchain to make sure our records are kept safe," said Artur Novek, the foundation's Implementation Manager and Architect. [12] The focus of the security is not the health records itself but on the transactions associated with these records by using the blockchain technology in securing the log files of these transactions. An example of the digital healthcare solutions on live production systems in Estonia is the e-Health solution. In Estonian, every citizen that has visited a physician has access and ownership of his or her own online e-Health record and that of their children. Additionally, the individual can determine who has access or doesn't have visibility into the data with various access controls. More than 95% of the information produced by physicians and hospitals are digitized. Since its inception, this represents more than three hundred million (300,000,000) events and greater than twenty million (20,000,000) health documents in its e-Health system! Using blockchain technology, The National Health Information System (ENHIS) integrates information from every different healthcare providers resulting in a unique data record for every patient. This digitization provides physicians with real-time access to the visitor's e-records like doctor notes, assigned prescriptions, scanned images, testing data, etc. The blockchain technology assures the data integrity of the digitized medical records for each patient. Every inquiry into the patient is traceable and logged. Access is directed by the patient allowing visibility to other family members, services providers, and more. "A more extensive and systematic implementation of e-health solutions will allow us to make the service more flexible, improve the health of people by exercising more efficient preventive measures, increase the awareness of patients and also save billions of euros." Toomas Hendrik Ilves, former President of Estonia. [13] Patients can log into the 'patient portal. A patient's perspective of the e-Health system can be seen in the figure below.

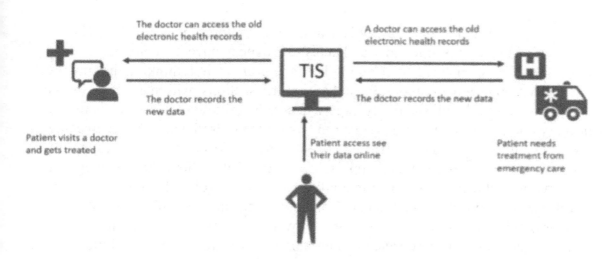

Patients have access to previous events with physicians, active prescriptions, and are provided basic health recommendations. Additionally, doctors can view patient's e-records anywhere, anytime creating opportunities in delivering more efficient and effective treatment consultation. The connectivity of patients and providers including the patients' families (and generational medical histories) as well as healthcare providers produces exponential dividends in producing identities of health and wellbeing. The efficient linkage and interoperability between various production systems and centralized access to time-critical data, real-time notifications, case summaries, prescriptions, health declarations, dental care events, immunization logs, ambulance data, and examination results has proven to generate savings in billions of euros. An adjacent production system in healthcare using blockchain technology in Estonia is the 'e-Prescription' solution. It's close to a 100% digitized system that manages the entire prescription supply chain. The efficiency of the centralization pays dividends to all relevant parties (patients, physicians, hospitals, pharmacies, etc.). This represents a significant downsizing in paperwork and has show reductions in patient visits to the doctor, hospitals, and pharmacy. It's very straightforward. 'Doctors can prescribe medicine electronically, and all a patient needs to do at the pharmacy is present their ID card. The pharmacist then retrieves the patient's information from the system and prepares the prescription.' [15] Additionally, patients can grant additional authority to other family members. This allows for a citizen to pick up prescriptions for children, parents, and friends as allowable under the system records.

As Estonia advances the proliferation of blockchain technology across additional production systems, the country's efforts will continue to serve as a model for implementation and also benchmarks in lessons learned. Additionally, the integration of the various systems within it's smart city infrastructure lays the groundwork for connectivity in other connected systems and applications throughout the community like mobile prescription fulfillment stations and other solutions to provide real-time care.

Dubai Blockchain Strategy

The Dubai Blockchain Strategy is heading into its fourth year in 2019. The program's objective is to identify and analyze the most current technologies and innovations in Blockchain perceived to hold the promise in rethinking the future of connectivity through 'simple, safe, and secure transactions' within a 'seamless, safe, efficient, and impactful' smart city experiences. The initiative encompasses three primary components: (1) Improvement in Government Proficiency; (2) Increasing Overall Commerce; and (3) Advancing Identity as World-Leaders in Blockchain Transactions. Several sectors are represented in the Dubai Blockchain Strategy, such as: 'Living (smart liveable & resilient city), Governance (digital, connected, lean government), Environment (clean environment by cutting-edge ICT innovations); Economy (globally competitive economy powered by disruptive technologies); Mobility (smooth transport driven by autonomous & shared mobility solutions); and People (interconnected society with easily accessible social services). [16]

Improvement in Government Proficiency

The Dubai Blockchain Strategy calls for 100% utilization in Blockchain Technology by the Dubai Government for all its transactions. At the time of this report, close to three dozen (30+) distinct government divisions encompass its consortium to create comprehensive governance, identify, evaluate, and establish blockchain technology platforms, and assess how blockchain technology can support its various transactions. These divisions identified uses cases across several Smart City sectors including Energy & Water, Transport & Logistics, Economic Development, Tourism, Safety & Justice, Municipality & Land, Health, Social Services, and Smart Districts. At the time of this report, there are have been more than thirty Government and Private Blockchain Technology Use Cases. These use cases were identified through a series of technical expertise scoping, proof of concept development, and implementation. For example, the Dubai Health Authority is redesigning its Health Regulation Department's Licensing and Inspection System for Health Facilities and Medical Professional (Sheryan). "The new Sheryan programme is another initiative that will further advance Dubai Health Authority's digital reinvention journey to provide citizen-centric experiences in the healthcare sector that are infused with innovation and powered by emerging technologies," said Amani Al Jassmi, Director of Information Technology at Dubai Health Authority. "To enable healthcare professionals and facilities operating in Dubai to better meet the health and wellness needs of a growing population with higher patient outcomes and delivery of care." "We are building a UAE level Healthcare Professional Registry (enabled on blockchain), which will help the country create a distributed network of healthcare professionals shared by UAE health authorities as a single source to seamlessly issue part-time and temporary medical licenses to professionals and enable them to care for the need of Expo 2020's exhibitors and visitors." [17] The government forecasts that using the Blockchain Technology in this use case will save the United Arab Emirates approximately $1.45B USD annually in reduction of document processing costs. It is anticipated the blockchain technology will allow health facilities administrators the capabilities to identify, apply, obtain, manage, modify, and renew all required healthcare licenses and expand to more than 100+ services spanning various facilities-related matters. The Dubai Health Authority is also implementing the use of blockchain technology as a connect point between public and private sectors. "As part of its healthcare transformation journey, DHA is planning on extending its platform to allow private facilities to share patient's health related information as per each patient's consent in a more secured and efficient manner," explained Amani. Dubai is encouraged and strongly believes The Dubai Blockchain Strategy will help the country match the pace of its burgeoning population growth without jeopardizing the access to care and desired outcomes. The intrinsic benefit of improved healthcare and quality of life is serving as the backbone of Smart Cities' use of blockchain technology—a true link between public and private sectors and citizens—the realization of Smart Communities.

Increasing Overall Commerce

The need of powerful capabilities is necessary to support the call for 100% utilization in Blockchain Technology in Dubai, such as developing a pipeline talent, cultivating the advancement of innovation, and supporting its scale and growth. Part of The Dubai Blockchain Strategy focuses on increasing overall commerce centralized in Dubai in blockchain technology. The country is developing programs and activities to support the development of blockchain-based businesses. Dubai is gleaming from successful models in establishing technology innovation clusters like Silicon Valley and Israel by concentrating in developing policies to support research, development and commercialization and models to support early-stage venture development. For example, in the summer of 2017, the country's smart city initiative, Smart Dubai, implemented an accelerator, Dubai Smart City Accelerator. The campaign had worldwide reach with participation from almost 20 cities from across the globe through representation of more than 20 companies. Focusing on industry advancement in the domain of Smart Cities, is 'Smart.' Smart Cities include so many sectors like Healthcare, Education, Agriculture, Tourism, Cybersecurity, and City Infrastructure, etc. It holds the opportunity to serve as a catalyst for the advancement across so many areas. The only other comparable sectors I can think of would be Space Exploration or perhaps, Deep Sea.

Advancing Identity as World-Leaders in Blockchain Transactions

The Dubai Blockchain Strategy includes positioning Dubai's identity as world-leaders in the design, development, and execution in blockchain technology networks and supporting the highest volume of related transactions. The country as established international conferences, meetings, and events in blockchain regularly with a concentration in Smart Cities.

A focus on outcomes, not technology

One underlining components of The Dubai Blockchain Strategy is a concentration in opportunities of positive social outcomes of people. "The adoption of this technology will reflect on the quality of life in the UAE and will enhance happiness levels for citizens," said Sheikh Mohammed at the launch. He said blockchain technology will "save time, effort and resources" and enable individuals to conduct most of their transactions in a timely manner that suits their lifestyle and work. [18] The figure below displays the Smart Dubai Model of Strategic Focus on Happiness [19].

In fact, the ability to measure the comfort, health, or happiness of those who interact with Dubai's Smart City is the center-point in its design and execution. Smart Dubai's mission is to 'create happiness, by embracing technology innovation-making Dubai the most efficient, seamless, safe and Impactful experience for residents & visitors.' [19] If it isn't measurable, then it isn't worth doing. The Smart City initiative operates around a set of transformational y key performance indicators (KPIs) to measure the outcomes of the various programs in production across the country, including:

- 'The Happiness Meter: one of Dubai's first strategic "smart city" initiatives. It aims to collect citizens' experience and feedback, through a centralized data dashboard'

- The Dubai Data initiative: led by the Dubai Data Establishment and decreed by the Dubai Data Law of 2015, is the most comprehensive citywide data initiative guiding the opening and sharing of city data across the public and private sector; and

- Smart Dubai Index: an impact assessment tool to be developed by Dubai to measure how initiatives and services in Dubai contribute to the vision of Smart Dubai, based on ITU's KPIs for SSC. It also incorporates additional KPIs pertinent to Dubai's smart city strategy.

Following this model, Smart Cities, under direction from its administrators and guidance to its third-party partners (public or private) will be driven by data and analytics—positive outcome-focused actions for the betterment of their citizens. The competition is to fierce and the opportunity costs are too high to miss out on the economic impact. The worldwide blockchain adoption trend that saw $1.1 billion invested by the private sector in blockchain technology in 2016.

Smart City, Smarter Choices

Smart Cities present significant opportunities in advancing the adoption of blockchain technology. Smart City models cast a wide-reaching net in systems and applications touch points including the Internet of Things (IoT). It has the capacity of becoming the standard practice in securing all transactions throughout a Connected Smart Community. In a people-first, citizen-centric model, positive outcomes will drive behaviors. The ability to capture, access, analyze and use data to guide decisions to achieve optimal results relates to every aspect within a community—from efficiencies in waste pick-up to optimization in healthcare. The community-driven incentivization of improving efficiencies and effectiveness are nearly boundless towards improving the quality of life of citizens and of their cities. As cultures of optimization proliferates throughout smart cities so do opportunities to advance healthcare. Blockchain Technology, as demonstrated in a few of these case studies, offers abilities to leapfrog into overall enhancements. Citizen empowerment lies as a focal point of Smarter Cities as people have the potential to directly influence their health and wellness through ownership. Direct control. Direct impact. A culture in responsibility. As the saturation of adoption into mobile societies expands so do opportunities in healthcare to leverage blockchain technology in mobile, point-of-care technologies—empowering citizens to take action in health interventions themselves.

References

1. Len Calderone for | RoboticsTomorrow (11/8/2018)

2. The smart city infrastructure development & monitoring (Mahmoud Al-Hader) - Article in Theoretical and Empirical Researches in Urban Management · January 2009 (Source: RePEc)

3. https://en.wikipedia.org/wiki/Smart_city

4. https://www.theguardian.com/media-network/2015/oct/14/manchester-barcelona-smart-cities-open-data

5. Using Blockchain as a Platform for Smart Cities, Christian Nãsulea, Stelian-Mihai Mic, University of Bucharest, Bucharest, Romania

6. Blockchain (Deepak Agarwal), Presenter, ICMA Conference, September 2018

7. Distributed Ledger Technology Systems: A Conceptual Framework," Cambridge Centre for Alternative Finance, August 2018

8. A Blockchain Enabled KYC Solution: New Horizon or False Dawn? (Thomas Reuters, 2018)

9. A Blockchain Enabled KYC Solution: New Horizon or False Dawn? (Thomas Reuters, 2018)

10. https://micropreneur.life/what-your-country-could-learn-from-estonia/

11. Frequently Asked Questions Estonian Blockchain Technology, e-Estonia.com (2018)

12. https://nortal.com/us/blog/blockchain-healthcare-estonia/

13. https://www.researchgate.net/publication/44668701_Patient_opportunities_in_the_Estonian_Electronic_Health_ Record_System

14. https://www.sm.ee/sites/default/files/content-editors/final_inglk_etervise_uuring.pdf

15. https://e-estonia.com/wp-content/uploads/facts-a4-v02-e-health-2.pdf

16. SMART DUBAI INSPIRING NEW REALITIES, H.E DR.AISHA BINT BUTTI BIN BISHR, DIRECTOR GENERAL, SMART DUBAI (2018)

17. https://www.dha.gov.ae/en/BetterHealth/Betterhealth2018Jan22-71.pdf

18. https://www.arabianbusiness.com/technology/394073-sheikh-mohammed-launches-the-uae-blockchain- strategy-2021

19. Happiness Impact (Palladium & Smart Dubai 2017)

Chapter 28:
Block Chain in Global Health

Melek Somai[1]
Behrooz Behbod[2]
Georgina Kyriakoudes[2]
Soulla Louca[2]

Editor's Note:

Blockchain and global healthcare solutions that can be advanced with new technologies are discussed in this chapter. This overview ties into the continued theme of new ways to advance healthcare techniques for the world.

1 Centre for Cryptocurrency Research and Engineering, Imperial College London, London, United Kingdom.
2 Blockchain Initiative, University of Nicosia, Nicosia, CYPRUS.

Global health Initiative across the world are facing an increasing complexity around disease management, surveillance, and healthcare provision. Countries around the globe are required today to address a range of complex and often intertwined actions matters to prevent disease and reduce cost, whilst effectively improving healthcare pathways to improve clinical and cost effectiveness and population health. To tackle those challenges in a systematic and evidence-based manner, stakeholders in global health are increasingly supporting the deployment of technological tools to support decision-making, risk management, data science, and innovation. These approaches, whilst increasing the capabilities of data collection, analysis, and decision making globally, have produced new challenges that hinder their effectiveness. One challenge is the limitation to share, coordinate, curate, and use the data being generated at an unprecedented scale by public health surveillance and sensors (e.g. Internet of Things).

To coordinate global health crisis and epidemics, data sharing is of utmost importance where coordination of different actors and the timely sharing of data is critical and the primum movens of any potential coordinated intervention. This is inherent to the current architecture of information exchange built atop the current information systems and the internet.

A new solution, coined by some as the fourth industrial revolution, might provide the remedy to the challenge of data-driven global health intervention: An innovative technology that is promising to add value to multiple sectors is blockchain.

We highlight the potential benefits and current applications of blockchain technology across the main pillars of global and public health; health protection, health promotion, healthcare public health and academic public health. We also discuss its limitations and implications for real-world implementation in the healthcare and public health sector.

So, is this all hype? Or are we now at the same phase in the development of blockchain technology as we were with the Internet in the 1990s? The potential opportunities are remarkable, many of which have not yet been considered. We have the chance to bring together all stakeholders to study, pilot and implement new models of evidence-based public health practice. In combination with other technologies such as artificial intelligence and machine learning, blockchain may optimise the use of knowledge and intelligence for action in the promotion of health and wellbeing.

Shift of global strategy from vertical programmes to health system strengthening.

Introduction

Our National Health Service (NHS) turned 70 this year, having been seen as one of the best health systems in the world, with care available free-at-the-point of use. However, as we all know too well, the NHS is not without its problems. Challenges include supply being outweighed by demand, caused by factors such as an ageing population and an increasing prevalence of chronic non-communicable diseases. Public health teams across the country are addressing a range of actions in collaboration with clinical and other multidisciplinary partners to prevent disease and reduce the burden on the NHS. Public health also helps contribute to the strategic design of healthcare pathways to improve clinical and cost effectiveness and population health.

Public health teams' activities are supported by technological tools such as databases, geographic and other information systems, and software to support decision-making, risk management, or statistical analyses. [1] To be equitable and effective, there is a need for timely knowledge and intelligence.[2] At best, health records are currently either paper-based or electronic, with public health data usually kept in silos, limiting their usefulness, timeliness, and impact. Moreover, lack of access to patient health records can cause clinical harm through delayed or inappropriate treatment, and increased costs from unnecessary duplication of clinical consultations and investigations. [3]

An innovative technology that is promising to add value to multiple sectors is blockchain. In the healthcare sector, for example, there is increasing attention on its potential role in electronic health records[4] [5], tackling counterfeit drugs5, and improving the efficiency of human resource management. [6] However, population health and wellbeing are only partially determined by healthcare services, requiring attention across all policy sectors. [7]

To enable public health action, knowledge and intelligence are required that:

Are multi-sectoral, including healthcare, housing, transport, business, agriculture, economy, energy, engineering, media, and law;

Cover the full pathway of a person's journey through healthcare, from prevention to primary, secondary, tertiary, social and palliative care;

Cover the life-course, including preconception, perinatal, early-life, adult and elderly years.

A Very Basic Primer on Blockchain

Blockchain has been defined as "an open, distributed ledger that can record transactions between two parties efficiently and in a verifiable and permanent way". [8] Consider a single centralised database consisting of data from multiple sources. While this exists today, limitations include timely accessibility by all stakeholders, data security, the need for data cleaning and de-duplication, and reliance on central parties to responsibly protect and manage highly sensitive data.

Now imagine identical copies of the same database being saved in multiple locations, accessible and modifiable by all stakeholders, updated in all copies at the same time, with a log of all edits to ensure auditability and security. However, the data would have no central controller, rather all stakeholders would have equal influence in ensuring only verified information is entered in the system, with ultimate agency over individual records being held by the patient themselves. Meanwhile, access to data may either be open, or limited to permitted users to ensure confidentiality (a feature that may often be required in the health sector).

These are some of the basic principles underlying blockchain technology. Introduced in 2008 as the technology underlying Bitcoin [9], blockchain represents one of the most disruptive technological innovations in the last twenty years, impacting all sectors.

So what are the potential applications of this technology in safeguarding the public's health?

Problems Blockchain can Potentially Solve

Health Protection

Preparedness against infectious, environmental and other hazards to health includes surveillance systems that track multiple sources of data. [10] A US healthcare innovation firm, Hashed Health, is designing a blockchain prototype to serve as a platform for reportable disease surveillance with three functions: 1) a real-time audit log of the transfer of data from the source to the centralized repository; 2) a registry compiling clusters of connected data, associating multiple, disparate data sources; and 3) coordinate and track inventory and location of vaccines, pharmaceuticals and medical supplies in the preparedness against epidemics and other major incidents. [11] [12]

The potential role of blockchain technology in preparedness and response initiatives against the growing threat of climate change and natural disasters has been recognised in the Encyclopedia of Environmental Health [1]. For example, a challenge faced during response efforts is the timely delivery of resources and aid to the right place. By facilitating transparent and rapid transfers of financial aid, without exchange or transaction fees, blockchain can save both time and money. Moreover, blockchain may be highly valuable in solving many of the problems associated with the establishment of registers of individuals exposed to the incident, such as data not being available in real-time by all stakeholders, limited interoperability between multiple databases collected by various stakeholders, and most importantly delayed public health actions due to the time required to clean and merge data, run analyses and communicate findings and recommendations. Blockchain would enable a database linking data from multiple stakeholders, with an identical copy in all relevant locations (i.e., decentralized), with data that is updated in all copies at the same time. Combined with artificial intelligence (AI) and machine learning (ML), public health messages can be tailored, automated and sent to at-risk individuals.

The US Centers for Disease Control and Prevention (CDC) is exploring the use of blockchain to store and share personally identifiable information at speed during a public health crisis, while complying with security and privacy laws. [13] In disaster relief efforts, blockchain may support a rapid, real-time, and reliable collection of data from and viewable by multiple stakeholders (e.g., local and national public health agencies, hospitals, pharmacies). [14] IBM has proposed a blockchain-based disaster management system that allows displaced residents find the nearest shelter with space available and if needed, equipped to deal with certain medical conditions (Figure 1). Meanwhile, the system supports the delivery of food, transport, medical care and other resources. [15]

IBM has also teamed with leading retailers and food companies to use blockchain to enhance access to information and traceability across the global food supply chain, facilitating the fast identification of contaminated sources causing outbreaks. This is particularly important given that each year, 1 in 10 people fall ill due to contaminated food, killing 420,000 people globally, a third of whom are children under 5. [16]

A recent report by Sanofi and The International Longevity Centre – UK explored how technology is beginning to influence the delivery and uptake of vaccination. [17] The report suggested that blockchain could: a) ensure electronic patient records include up-to-date and accurate vaccination histories [18]; b) develop tools to provide people with greater confidence in online information and counter 'fake news' [19]; and c) increase efficiency, maintain quality and reduce costs in the delivery of vaccinations [20]. The report also highlighted two blockchain applications: a) ImmunoTracker (https://www.proofofpurpose.org/immunotracker) is a UAE-based solution to make vaccination records secure, accessible and reliable, with an app to keep citizens informed and up-to-date on their vaccinations, and real-time immunisation data shared with health professionals and authorities; and b) StaTwig (https://statwig.com/), based in India, aims to improve vaccine supply chain management through a combination of sensors and blockchain technology. [17]

Moving beyond infectious diseases and environmental incidents to the troubling rate of mass shootings in the USA, blockchain technology may improve background checks and gun registration, particularly considering the barriers to changing gun control laws21.

Health Improvement

The surveillance of chronic exposures and diseases, and the wider determinants of health is gaining momentum [22-24]. Blockchain may enable the interoperability and security of data from a range of sources at the individual (e.g., wearables measuring physical activity, nutritional intake, sleep, mental health and personal environmental and occupational exposures), home (e.g., monitoring indoor air pollution, radon, lead, and asbestos levels), community (e.g., noise, crime), and population level (e.g., outdoor air pollution, deprivation). Blockchain may also target the confidentiality concerns associated with surveillance systems aimed at assessing mental health and suicide prevention. [25]

Moreover, intelligence can inform blockchain-based public health interventions. For example, one system uses the blockchain and bicycle-powered sensors to allow cyclists to receive financial compensation from local authorities interested in promoting physical activity, sustainable transportation, and reducing traffic-related air pollution. [26] This data can then be fed back to health insurance companies, thereby reducing individual premiums. [27]

Further, blockchain may address poverty and inequalities through the increased financial inclusion it offers with cryptocurrencies for the unbanked and underbanked. [12]

Healthcare Public Health

In addition to the management of disease at the individual level, healthcare systems may improve population health through blockchain technology increasing the efficiency, equity, quality and value of services. Opportunities include trusted longitudinal healthcare records spanning the life-course, automated adjudication of insurance or reimbursement claims using smart contracts, data interoperability, verifying and recording patient consent, as well as patient-centred care with electronic health records owned by the patient, selectively and securely granting access to providers. [28-30]

In 2008, Google Health attempted to develop a centralized personal health records service to improve people's access to their personal health and wellness information. This was unsuccessful due to limited widespread adoption. [31] Blockchain technology's inherent characteristics may address the public's security concerns that led to the retirement of Google Health in 2011. [31]

Drug safety and pharmaceutical clinical trials may be enhanced by improving data transparency using smart contract[32], securing pharmacovigilance records33 and patient consent forms34, and minimizing the risk of counterfeit medicine by confirming their authenticity, expiration date and patient-administration record. [12]

Combined with AI and ML, blockchain may optimise disease prediction models and the interpretation of diagnostic investigations such that healthcare providers can make better and faster patient management decisions. [35] Meanwhile, the decentralized nature of blockchain facilitates the real-time distribution of knowledge gained through ML.

Academic Public Health

The bedrock of public health and healthcare practice is solid evidence. Longitudinal health records, linked with multi-sectoral data is of tremendous help to epidemiological research to identify determinants of disease and effective health interventions. Blockchain may minimise risk from recall bias and errors related to historical exposure assessment for diseases with long latency periods (e.g., cancer). In exchange for access to this high-resolution data, researchers could serve as 'miners' verifying transactions.

Workforce training and development may also be enhanced by blockchain technology, by tracking the lifespan of a clinician's education, certifying their licensure, and verifying their credentials in an immutable, transparent, global and verifiable record. [36]

Limitations

Blockchain, as a power-intensive technology, has caused many to question its carbon footprint. [38] To run Bitcoin alone, the energy consumption has been compared to the electricity usage of Ireland. [39] Conversely it may mitigate the carbon footprint by introducing more transparent and efficient supply chain processes, ensuring ethical production of goods with full information on the materials, chemicals and fair-trade standards that have been used.

Scalability has proven to be a problem with current solutions not yet being optimized for high volume data due to the energy requirements as blockchains grow larger. [38] The storage of data formats other than just text, such as video and images, may aggravate the problem as networking and computing requirements would be increased. [38]

We must be clear that blockchain is still in its infancy, with many projects in the proof-of-concept or early piloting phase. Culturally, the healthcare industry has a natural trend towards avoiding change and is often slow to introduce new technologies. [37] Without tangible examples and agreed standards, its adoption may be hindered. As reported in the recent BMJ feature, "What matters to the people in the NHS is not the tech you use but what problem do you solve…With blockchain it's still a very tech led conversation. What we need to see this year is one clear demonstration of how blockchain has solved a small problem—there are lots of trials but the NHS is on its knees, so it needs evidence that the blockchain can do a better, cheaper job". [5]

Implications

Given the need for pilot studies to demonstrate the real-world benefits and challenges to blockchain technology, one company has initiated the UK's first trial of blockchain-based electronic health records, in partnership with four GP practices consisting of over 30,000 registered patients. [40]

Such pilots are also required in public health teams in local authorities and regional and national levels of organisations such as Public Health England. This must be led by public health specialists and clinicians to identify the problems, but in close collaboration with computer scientists that can design appropriate blockchain-based solutions. Evaluations of these pilots will provide essential results on the clinical- and cost-effectiveness, feasibility, acceptability, safety and limitations of blockchain technology in healthcare and public health settings.

In addition to pilots, the successful implementation of blockchain technology will require education of all relevant stakeholders, including patients, carers, and the general public, as well as the development of laws to regulate the technology, provide standardisation and protect users.

Conclusion

So, is this all hype? Or are we now at the same phase in the development of blockchain technology as we were with the Internet in the 1990s? The Internet gave way to the open exchange of knowledge and information, leading to the dawn of health apps, telemedicine and digital health. Blockchain technology is now paving the way for the open exchange of value and trust.

The potential opportunities are remarkable, many of which have not yet been considered. When the Internet first launched, who would have thought of social media such as Facebook and Twitter, which are now being studied for their role in outbreak response and public health interventions, amongst their other benefits.

We have the chance to bring together all stakeholders to study, pilot and implement new models of evidence-based public health practice. In combination with AI and ML, blockchain may optimise the use of knowledge and intelligence for action in the promotion of health and wellbeing.

References

1. Lauriola P, Leonardi G, Righi E, et al. Natural disasters - environmental health preparedness. Encyclopedia of Environmental Health. 2nd edition (in press).

2. Behbod B, Lauriola P, Leonardi G, et al. Environmental and public health tracking to advance knowledge for planetary health. Eur J Public Health 2016;26(6):900.

3. Southey S. Blockchain – the future of healthcare? Available at: http://www. doctorpreneurs.com/blockchain-future-healthcare/; accessed 22 August 2018.

4. Ekblaw A, Azaria A, Halamka JD, et al. A Case Study for Blockchain in Healthcare: "MedRec" prototype for electronic health records and medical research data. IEEE. Available at: http://dci.mit.edu/assets/papers/eckblaw. pdf; accessed 22 August 2018.

5. Armstrong S. Bitcoin technology could take a bite out of NHS data problem. BMJ 2018;361:k1996.

6. TechUK. How Can Blockchain Help Solve the NHS Crisis? Available at: http://www.techuk.org/insights/opinions/item/12334-how-can-blockchain-help-solve-the-nhs-crisis; accessed 22 August 2018.

7. Leppo K, Ollila E. Health in All Policies: Seizing Opportunities, implementing policies. Ministry of Social Affairs and Health, Finland: Helsinki 2013.

8. Iansiti M, Lakhana KR. The Truth About Blockchain. Harvard Business Review. January 2017. Available at: https://hbr.org/2017/01/the-truth-about-blockchain; accessed 22 August 2018.

9. Nakamoto S. 2998. Bitcoin: A peer-to-peer electronic cash system. Available at: http://bitcoin.org/bitcoin.pdf; accessed 22 August 2018.

10. Nsubuga P, White ME, Thacker SB, et al. Public Health Surveillance: A Tool for Targeting and Monitoring Interventions. In: Jamison DT, Breman JG, Measham AR, et al., editors. Disease Control Priorities in Developing Countries. 2nd edition. Washington (DC): The International Bank for Reconstruction and Development / The World Bank; 2006. Chapter 53. Available from: https://www.ncbi.nlm.nih.gov/books/NBK11770/ Co-published by Oxford University Press, New York.

11. Hashed Health. Blockchain Public Health Surveillance. Available at: https://hashedhealth.com/blockchain-public-health-surveillance/; accessed 22 August 2018.

12. Thomason J. Blockchain: an accelerator for women and children's health? Global Health Journal 2017;1(1):3-10. Available at: http://www.

abtassociates.com/AbtAssociates/files/42/42940e74-d80f-465e-8c39-ca684b55208a.pdf; accessed 22 August 2018.

13. Orcutt M. Why the CDC Wants in on Blockchain. MIT Technology Review, October 2017. Available at: https://www.technologyreview.com/s/608959/why-the-cdc-wants-in-on-blockchain/?utm_source=MIT+Technology+Review&utm_campaign=5e937b6947-The_Download&utm_medium=email&utm_term=0_997ed6f472-5e937b6947-153825697; accessed 22 August 2018.

14. Stanley A. Centers for Disease Control to Launch First Blockchain Test on Disaster Relief. Coindesk, September 2017. Available at: https://www.coindesk.com/us-centers-disease-control-launch-first-blockchain-test-disaster-relief/; accessed 22 August 2018.

15. Mohan P. Disaster Management Solution – Part 1: Cloud, IoT, Blockchain. IBM Blockchain Dev Center, December 2017. Available at: https://developer.ibm.com/blockchain/2017/12/09/disaster-management-using-blockchain-iot/; accessed 22 August 2018.

16. WHO. WHO estimates of the global burden of foodborne diseases. 2015. Available at: http://www.who.int/foodsafety/publications/foodborne_disease/fergreport/en/; accessed 22 August 2018.

17. Sinclair D. The future of adult immunisation. The International Longevity Centre – UK & Sanofi. June 2018. Available at: http://www.ilcuk.org.uk/images/uploads/publication-pdfs/The_Future_of_Adult_Immunisation.pdf; accessed 22 August 2018.

18. Crypt Bytes Tech. Medicalchain—A blockchain for electronic health records. Medium. November 2017. Available at: https://medium.com/crypt-bytes-tech/medicalchain-a-blockchain-for-electronic-health-records-eef181ed14c2; accessed 22 August 2018.

19. González PJ. Could Blockchain help solve the fake news crisis? Good Rebels. April 2018. Available at: https://www.goodrebels.com/could-blockchain-help-solve-the-fake-news-crisis/; accessed 22 August 2018.

20. Kucheryavenko O and Dominguez A. How blockchain technology delivers vaccines, saves lives. The World Bank. June 2017. Available at: http://blogs.worldbank.org/health/how-blockchain-technology-delivers-vaccines-saves-lives; accessed 22 August 2018.

21. Heston TF. (2017) A blockchain solution to gun control. PeerJ Preprints 5:e3407v1 Available at: https://doi.org/10.7287/peerj.preprints.3407v1; accessed 22 August 2018.

22. PAHO. Noncommunicable diseases surveillances. Available at: http://www.paho.org/hq/index.php?option=com_content&view=article&id=1512&Itemid=1663; accessed 22 August 2018.

23. CDC. Chronic Disease Prevention and Health Promotion. Available at: https://www.cdc.gov/chronicdisease/stats/index.htm; accessed 22 August 2018.

24. Public Health England. Environmental public health surveillance system (EPHSS). Available at: https://www.gov.uk/government/publications/environmental-public-health-surveillance-system/environmental-public-health-surveillance-system-ephss; accessed 22 August 2018.

25. Morch C. Big Data in Suicide Prevention. Available at: https://www.researchgate.net/profile/Carl_Moerch/publication/308403790_Big_Data_and_Suicide_prevention/links/57e2ebc308aecd0198dd82ac.pdf; accessed 22 August 2018.

26. Jaffe C, Mata C, Kamvar S. Proceedings of the 2017 ACM International Joint Conference on Pervasive and Ubiquitous Computing and Proceedings of the 2017 ACM International Symposium on Wearable Computers. September 2017. DOI: 10.1145/3123024.3123141. Available at: https://dl.acm.org/citation.cfm?id=3123141; accessed 22 August 2018.

27. Southey S. Blockchain – the future of healthcare? Available at: http://www.doctorpreneurs.com/blockchain-future-healthcare/; accessed 22 August 2018.

28. Stagnaro C, Freed Associates. White Paper: Innovative Blockchain Uses in Health Care. Available at: https://www.freedassociates.com/wp-content/uploads/2017/08/Blockchain_White_Paper.pdf; accessed 22 August 2018.

29. Brodersen C, Kalis B, Leong C, et al. Blockchain: Securing a New Health Interoperability Experience. Accenture, 2016. Available at: https://www.healthit.gov/sites/default/files/2-49-accenture_onc_blockchain_challenge_response_august8_final.pdf; accessed 22 August 2018.

30. Heston, Thomas. A case study in blockchain health care innovation. Int J Curr Res 2017;9:60587-60588. Available at: https://www.researchgate.net/publication/321478417_A_case_study_in_blockchain_health_care_innovation; accessed 22 August 2018.

31. Google. An update on Google Health and Google PowerMeter, June, 2011. Available at: https://googleblog.blogspot.com.cy/2011/06/update-on-google-health-and-google.html; accessed 22 August 2018.

32. Nugent T, Upton D, Cimpoesu M. Improving data transparency in clinical trials using blockchain smart contracts. F1000Research. 2016;5:2541.

33. Beninger P, Ibara MA. Pharmacovigilance and Biomedical Informatics: A Model for Future Development. Clinical Therapeutics 2016:38(12);2514–2525.

34. Jelsma S. Consent, Clinical Trials, and the Blockchain. February 2018. Available at: https://hashedhealth.com/consent-clinical-trials-blockchain/;

accessed 22 August 2018.

35. Borad A. Disease Prediction, Machine Learning, and Healthcare. DZone, January 2018. Available at: https://dzone.com/articles/disease-prediction-machine-learning-application-fo; accessed 22 August 2018.

36. Peters A. Can blockchain disrupt health education, licensing, and credentialling? October 2017. The Lancet Global Health blog. Available at: http://globalhealth.thelancet.com/2017/10/31/can-blockchain-disrupt-health-education-licensing-and-credentialling; accessed 22 August 2018.

37. Fairley P. Blockchain world - Feeding the blockchain beast if bitcoin ever does go mainstream, the electricity needed to sustain it will be enormous. IEEE Spectrum 2017;54(10):36-59.

38. Pareras LG. 2011. Innovation and Entrepreneurship in the Healthcare Sector: From Idea to Funding to Launch. 1st edition. Greenbranch Publishing.

39. UK Government Chief Scientific Adviser. 2016. Distributed Ledger Technology: beyond block chain. Government Office for Science. Available at: https://assets.publishing.service.gov.uk/government/uploads/system/uploads/attachment_data/file/492972/gs-16-1-distributed-ledger-technology.pdf; accessed 22 August 2018.

40. Medicalchain. Medicalchain announces a partnership with the Groves. Available at: https://medicalchain.com/en/partnership/; accessed 22 August 2018.

Chapter 29:
Block Chain for Games and Health

Dr. David Metcalf

Director, METIL

UCF Institute for

Simulation & Training

https://hashedhealth.com/blockchain-for-healthcare-book/

Editor's Note:

This chapter offers a new way to understand how blockchain for gaming can impact healthcare. This overview of how learning is impacted and advances through gaming is interesting and provides a look into the future. The final part of this chapter discusses Blockchain Simulation and the innovative models for healthcare impact.

In this chapter, we transcribe a talk from Dr. David Metcalf on the topic of blockchain for gaming. Recall that in the introduction, we talked about how microtransactions and in-game currency have been in use for a long time. The transition to blockchain based cryptocurrencies is not too far fetched for users who are familiar with microtransactions. This chapter will focus on gaming and our efforts at Institute of Simulation and Training. The chapter finishes with a look to the future – The establishment of a blockchain simulator at the University of Central Florida.

This is a really hard session to design, because there is so much going on in the space. Things have changed so much in the past three months, so what I am trying to do is tease you a little bit with some of the information in the space. We will be looking at some things you may want to go back and explore in more detail yourself, because there is no way we can fit everything about blockchain in a 45-50 minute session but do have time for games, and so we are going to begin by looking at how we think about a social group contest, as one of the primary things, and then tie that into, of course, into education, and health, and media. Those are some of the different areas we are looking into recently and are receiving a lot of investments too.

I am David Metcalf, with the University of Central Florida, we have an Institute of Simulation and Training.

I have a few slides that will go over who we are and what we do, but that is more for people who did not get to come to the session. I saw like "triple booking" across a lot of my friends, so I understand that that could not make it and had to listen to the recordings, but with that end, this is what we are going to try to cover in this session today and leave some time for your questions, too:

Blockchain is really changing a lot of industry segments. Let's begin by what blockchain is; it is a distributed trust system where you have multiple people that are doubtedly giving transactions. We might think of transactions as many different things including financial, healthcare, but it is also a matter of convenience if you think about using different networks and validating who you are or things you may have, which we call digital assets.

We are going to look at the short history and some of the liability of blockchain, along with some examples of where we find impact in society.

I am going to go through each for about 5 seconds. With the Institute for Simulation and Training at UCF, we do a lot of work with the military and healthcare space. A lot of the work with blockchain has been part of the Internet of Things and cyber security. I immediately got excited to see that a new discipline is rising, but we have been at this for a while now, yet what I haven't seen in critical mass is gaming.

What we found is that transaction speeds were just too slow for a lot of gamified applications, so that was one of our big "aha-s" too. We look at the things that were successful and the ones that were not. We found this because of some early work with the National Science Foundation (NSF) in a program called "Health Shares"- actually housing some of our students. So you learn about the core technologies, core team, core ideas and visions.

There is a lot more information on specific vertical market segments, such as fintech, healthtech, med tech. And that is part of the reason why we are working across the board in the laboratory.

Some of the things would like to focus on are our social causes; some of things I d like to solve with games while still looking at other areas too.

I think you will benefit from watching this video. The way I look at it in the existing framework is that a lot of what we have done so far is to tie blockchain to something that secures transactions within a connected city or industrial settings. These are some of the areas we have been working on so far, as well.

One of the things we are growing to find is that people are interested in something called Crypto, and so if you think about using these in one game, you can actually use earnings across multiple games.

VIDEO PLAYING

I wanted to show this upfront because it kind of blew my mind in many ways. First of all, people are paying for some of these assets online. I started thinking about Pokemon-Go and the new ability to trade. Trading is not new, but now we have the ability to monetize and democratize, it is global, it is verifiable across gaming networks platforms. This could be very useful when it comes to things you might want to do with learning assets that you might want to translate; that are unique objects or some things that might be collectible and rare, too.

Those are things that have the wheels of possibilities turning. Some of the other things that we have seen recently come from TBS, and I dont think this is a great video, but I'd like to encourage you to watch some parts of it too. I just thought "I got put it in there to give people some context".

While we wait for this for second, some of the things I am encouraged by companies and organizations like NGNI that are starting to look at ways in which you can tie this to things like Unity and game platforms that I have already used. I am now thinking that I can plug this into the things I am already using like a I would with a library. To give you an example of how this is coming into the art segment, here is a little intro so you can see just how many companies are already talking about this, and even crypto. You can see the title "Blockchain Plus Gaming, Dominating GDC". This is starting to happen and it is a trend we should watch in the serious gaming industry, because it is overtaking the gaming initiative. The fact that you have this much money in investment and this many opportunities to have things you did not have before across assets that are verifiable and can be used across multiple different settings.

It looks like even though I tested this before this session, that this is not going to work.

VIDEO PLAYING

So, how many of you have a digital wallet? Good, good.

And how hard was it to set up? Everyone thinks it is easy. Except for me.

I thought "this is a hassle, I got to go all through my customers" and things like that too to tie money to games. So, I think that just like we talked about before, things are being made easier to go into.

When you start looking at what is happening inside blockchain and games, you start to see that this is going to start to take hold, because it becomes much easier and it is going to fall through in time and pick up on these deficiencies of an unclear system, unsatisfying performance. Is there real game play or just trading? Is another example, including hiring professional talent to go and actually build these things. These are some of the things that will need to happen to actually move the needle.

There is also this things about EOS, here is an interesting thing: on November '17 they almost brought Ethereum, one of the main cryptocurrency platforms and blockchain platforms to its knees, because 10-20% of all transactions were of people buying CryptoKitties. So you thought Poke-mon Go was a phenomenon, well this is happening with real money and blockchaing. Here is an example of these CryptoKitties.

On February/March of just this year, the market suddenly changed with the addition of financial games coming to market. You have to think about where this is going in terms of things like handling. We talked about some of the positive gains, these are things that we want to look at.

How many here have heard of the term "smart contract"? Smart Contract is when you are trying to have a trusted transaction that is complex. The example I always use is of a "mortgage" where you have the buyer, the insurer, the bank, the agent, and if you could have a way to automate those things, well that is in essence what a smart contract does in multiple entities. Both in organization that have to agree on that. Think about where that might be useful in gaming, too, or game play. These are some of the things we are starting to see and looking at some of that as an initial transparency of smart contracts is very useful.

How many of you have a Telegram account?

Telegram is the chatbot platform that is most primarily used within developers within blockchain. If you want to go find people who are into this stuff, you might want to make a Telegram account and go look there. Here is what a Telegram platform looks like, and you can see I have a few gaming platforms on there, too- RPG, Arena Battle Game, Battle Park Game.

You can see some of the different games and game play. Here you get to store your cryptocurrency and also get to play some new games online or via the chatbot.

I want to show you something though that I discovered that starts to show some of those social elements I mentioned before. This game is called "Dino Park Game". The way you play is you just start like any other premium game or you can buy a certain balance if you want to get ahead. What it does is teach everyone from kids to adults about cryptocurrency using dinosaurs who get to go mining for gems every day and you get to buy a certain number of dinosaurs. Some of those dinosaurs are really expensive and others are really cheap. I always get the cheap ones, because those are the ones you can get overtime for free. Probably now, I get two of those cheap dinosaurs per day. You can see the number that you have and you can turn those into dollar signs and bitcoins. You can actually see what you sold and you get a purchase dollar balance and about one third goes into a cryptowallet. You have essentially paid your audience to play your game and given them the opportunity to have both digital crypto currency and real money.

Now, there are a couple of things that I don't like: you can do adware video on channels, and then all of the sudden you may have kids having to deter their attention to advertising and all that. But, if you can stomach that, this is what can happen in just three months of play:

- $45 earned while playing for those three months. Now, this might not seem like a lot for your budget, but I actually showed this to a friend of mine in Haiti who is a professor, and he was actually saying that a difference of $0.50 a day in his economy makes a big difference. For them, this is the difference between school kits for their kids, or immunization, or food on the table.

- In the global economy, you will have talked about and learned a bit about mining, and I have also allowed them to earn some money. Some of them can translate this into actual currency faster than we can. There is a company in Africa that is light years ahead of PayPal, and if there is a way that they can actually go into microtransactions and take this to where it is debunked and can accept credit cards, they now have something that contributes substantially to their economy.

- The other thing that is important to know is that I play this game for 20-25 seconds per day. It is not one that I really find fun, to be quite keen with you, and I think that there is a lot of room for improvement in this and the model, but as a start, it is pretty interesting that you have something that you could tell to global citizens and everybody works to monetize and you have a return.

First things first, this is really just a resource management manual teaching you the core principles, too. So that is what it teaches you. I talked to developers who were in Russia and India. I talked about creating a serious game for our team at the University of Central Florida. They said "We never really thought of it teaching something" but it is, so they weren't really aware of the teaching capabilities. I sent them some chats back and forth and reports about what we were doing and they thought that was cool, so they maybe will help us with some development too using the same model that is used for mining to teach another subject. It might be more relevant to something we are doing in healthcare, or something we are doing in the education space, too.

So, I want you to tinker with taking your mind to this idea first, and just think about a simple chatbot game that could be played even from some picture buttons too in these growing economies and inputted into these basic level smartphones, too. We have already started to help; in my case, one of my friends in Haiti who just suffered from yet another hurricane after we just helped rebuild his house. It is one thing after another there too, and these things, while small really does mean something, especially when you are looking at making about $20 a day, that is real money in that economy, too. So probably looking at regular $40 per month income.

[Editor's note: There was an audience comment asking where is the money coming from in this arrangement.]

Dr. David Metcalf: The money is coming from two groups:

- Companies who are paying for marketing. We do joint development on this and that money goes towards the play, so it is a form of digital advertising that goes from their channel immediately into that chat channel. It sounds to me like it's part of the attention economy and so, in a way, advertising.

- You might of seen it in the very beginning, that actually if you want to get into the game, you can cheat by buying to get into the game too, now my friends in developing countries are not going to do that, but a lot of people are to get more and better dinosaurs when looking at all these bonuses too. So a part of that money comes from these premium players, so its a subsidization too.

Those are the two main ways of how these development companies make money and make it sustainable and not a ponzi scheme so that when you try to cash your money, you end up not being able to.

Here are some example of the dinosaurs, and farming… I don't know if you can see it, but it is not that fun of a game. That is the one thing I wish was a bit more fun, but at least it gives you an idea. Here's is a better idea of how it works, where you can get more dinosaurs, what you can purchase with half a bitcoin, etc. and that's where the game starts to show those capabilities.

There are other games too, that are teaching things and allow you to have crypto collectibles, like cookies, combined and mixed with what we just talked about before, too. So if you want to teach someone about geography, why not let them purchase that country in digital cryptocurrencies? I want you to see this, I want to make it big enough so you can see it.

In the early 2008, it took seven days for 45,000 ethereum worth of transactions, exceeding crypto kitties, to go and grow the purchase of different countries. One lucky player wanted to buy China, and sold it to someone for 600 ethereum, so 600 times 800 is $480,000. Someone bought a digital version of the country of China in this one game, maybe China struggled in other games. So think about what that is doing in other markets, too. That one kind of blew me away. We have to think about if some of these things are ponzi schemes, we have to be careful and watch for that; I think that is something we all want to be very mindful of, too.

You asked a great question, the leading question to what might come next. If you are in a resource finding game, would you be willing to let someone use the 20% of your processor that you are not using in exchange for a little bit more rewards or ether in the game. The first one to do is was called EtherYou, this is called a crypto idle game. Your idle resources are used and in exchange for that you can either get rewards in the game, well in this case, the computer rewards the game, but those rewards you make can be cashed out later for real Ethereum. This is a way to monetize in which you are actually processing power. I wish I had something to show you for each one of these games, but I did try to at least put them up in the powerpoints, so you can go and see those in more detail. You can see that this is a resource planning game, too, it lets you go in and define which resources you want to buy, but in the background, it is also using a little bit of your processing power. The question being: are you ok with that? If you are being rewarded for it, both in the game and something from the game that again you are getting paid for your attention to the game and the processing power of the game, and those two things equal out to a real currency transaction.

So when we talk about serious games, that have a serious impact, how could that have an impact on our friends around the world. So, those are things that I keep kind of looking at, too. In a little bit more detail, too.

So there's other things that you can bring into the gaming experience too, that may be important for you. These are not as important to me, but I thought I'd include them in here. You can have ownership of actual game assets, so think if you have imperial sort of notary in one game and you can move that into another company in the network because of blockchain being able to find those transactions and being able to evaluate those transactions across multiple sources that can be multiple game companies, that could become game centers, that could be across all those. Now, they might not let you do that, but there is the potential to do that. And someone will do it, because a big problem for these companies is that they are not in control of those things.

Those assets can be interacted with at any time, and they also be used to reuse other assets in other places. You also have a new way to get new users, too. If thinking about getting into other games too, this will automate that process so it's going to lower the marketing cost for you.

Those things, again, are things that are not as important to me, but if you are a specialty company, marketing may be important to you. So, some of the real challenges we are going to face here are things we have to be aware of, and I am also excited by the fact that some of these things are going to not only get us back to the essence of game play, but you got games that have been lost for 20,30 years and are starting to come back because now we have given importance to it.

There is one called PointMan, which is a like a Pacman but you earn point that you can then cash out for each time you play. So, some of the more popular games now, Ether Warfare, Crypto Celebrities, and then looking at one that I thought I'd show here too, is one of the few that is actually mobile enabled is called Spell of Genesis. This is a resource battle game, and you are likely to see a lot of them out there, but here is something unique about it: when I open the menu, I don't know if you can see this, but there is a pass that links to a blockchain wallet. And this is a pretty easy process to link to a blockchain wallet. You can see here that it says "start collecting blockchain cards" and those are things you can win through the games, but you can also sell to other people, and you can access in both Apple and Android.

I am going to click on this square because I am on an Apple device, connect to the server, and I need your wallet here too, asks for you to confirm my IU address..... It is not working.

However, this shows you some of the routine things you like and can add things to be crypto enabled.

[Editor's note: An audience question about any kind of regulatory storm on the horizon that will completely change the dynamics of gaming + blockchain]

So many regulatory revisements. A lot of the storms have already been brewing and already sent people to jail for about 65 violations. If you are going to do this through an ICO, an Initial Coin Offering, you need to make sure you are compliant with all FCC regulations. If you are going to do this anywhere in the US, this is very important, so keep that in mind. That is item one. And some of the things that may happen, you may want to watch to see if there is somebody there. All that we have talked about is utilities versus securities, in the future though, that could change. I think that some of the companies that are doing some of these things right now, are starting to be more sensitive to that, and especially ones that have a social good component to them and global are not compliant. A lot of these are just allowing you to move assets using blockchain technology. They are not trying to sell through a monetizing cryptocurrency. So, I think some of these are going to be a little bit safer within the space. But that is a good question, it is a question we should all be asking ourselves. I appreciate you bringing that up too.

As far as other storms too, I think there is going to be a lot of things that go by the wayside, too, and there are some things that supersede productivities that are popular, but I think that is just the nature of what we do and how we do it. What I am excited about is when we start using it for more gaming purposes, too. That is what starts to get me kind of excited, too.

A couple of the other things that get me excited too, is when you start to see companies like Microsoft working on projects on blockchain for gaming, and how they want to develop not only for their platform but other platforms, too, tying into virtual and augmented reality platforms- those are things that start to become exciting and this just shows some of that resource management within those games, too.

And then, the other things here too is that I tried to look for places that are already doing some of this and I really came up fairly short, but I thought I'd at least show some of the things I found.

CryptoStake for CryptoFights is one of the things that is starting to show some game play that teaches.

Game Design for Social Change at MIT's Game Night- they actually ran a blockchain simulation last January, that was one of the first things that I saw, and there is the Game for Change series that offer some "playful technologies" where they did a blockchain exercise lego set simulation at MIT also.

Those are a couple of examples where blockchain is being used for serious games and we can go into more detail with later today, but these were some of the things that I found and thought might be of interest.

The other bell leather sign I saw was Pineapple Arcade, this was a coin with two "i"s - C-o-i-i-n. They are allowing you to play Atari like games and monetize that into coiins- the first thing with this is the personnel, Higgins gave Steve Jobs his first internship and is behind this. He has a great video that I really don't have time to show you, to show just a bit just wouldn't do it justice, but you might want to watch it talking about this and you can find it at coiin.io.

I think there is a lot of interesting things going on. With Pineapple Arcade, there is sort of an Alternate Reality, virtual game in there too. You look at what does it mean to "control wellness and freedom" "what is this crypto bank receipt" and I also have to figure out what it means, and decrypt this crypto chain and this give me that next algorithm, kind of like the next step.

The other thing is as simple as building a game like PacMan and earning points.

I know it sounds really simple, like it is not in the essence of what would be a serious game, but think about what you could do with that altered reality game. It has scattered data on any topic that you might have. This idea of scavenger hunt that teaches you how to solve puzzles and where to go to, and those can be taken to be literally anything. The crypto reward for something can go to $5,000 if you're the one to solve it, and there is all of these game discussion boards too. I think that there is another for $10,000 too. So we can play games and have a jackpot.

Now, I am aware of your point about some of the things in gaming that may move like a debt or sus stakes or any type of rewards, especially in states like Florida or California, that are heavily regulated especially for people who don't follow regulations. There are some risks there too that people need to be aware of, most people in academia and industry know those things and will follow the right rules, but some people just getting started or some other companies might not know those rules and can be a little wary on how to follow those rules. Especially when thinking about gaming and e-sports, that was a topic that I thought "we only have 45 minutes, there is no way we can try to cover e-sports too" especially now, when there is not much connection with learning or serious game type of outcomes, but that is a real things and is going to have regulations in the same way that they camp out on games before.

I did put some screens on here too just in case it wasnt working on my phone, but that is just the same thing you saw before, along with a couple of articles. And then there's the Ether Wallet that allows you to travel and connect to your own wallet, and I have noted that process via screen captures, just so you know what I had to go through to do it and how in real life you could do it. What I hope you get out of this is that it is not that hard to get started and see where it takes you.

It also shows you some of the games that are up and coming, and I thought that was really exciting because it wasn't out yet and then it becomes another resource playing game. A lot of the work that we do is resource planning for acquisitions from the government, or hospitals and their work flow, for things like that too. So anytime I see resource planning, I get a little excited. That is my space, or the space that we help people out with too.

So, we have a few things to think about and here is this box that shows you some of the other games too, and then any protocols and the ability to go in and easily apply features or have libraries you can link up, now this is not yet complete, but the idea is that you can easily plug-in is going to be helpful to all of you who don't want to hire your own blockchain developer or have to learn everything yourself. "Hey, let's plug in the library unity" "let's plug in another thing or framework" just like has already been seen by any developer and make that easier for ourselves.

What are some of those next steps that you might want to take, as we start to wrap up? You want to leverage your strengths, look at games for social causes or industries that this might affect, find a good base of developers if you can, that is something or interest here, and I say find because we found a lot inert who found this of value and also were interested in some of the use cases. We then looked at our own shoes and asked how do we do this at the University of Central Florida in some of our cyber security groups, some of our other special industry groups in computer science. Barter wisely and seek out projects you can get grants with social value with something you are involved in. With UCF, I can't really say a lot about the projects we are working on yet, but I did get permission to put all this together too, which was a bit of a mess to do. A lot of the industry focuses on IoT, beacon, and blockchain solutions. Not necessarily gaming, but one of those that we are working on now and have some early examples on is a blockchain simulator. We are the Institute of Simulation and Training, so we are building a blockchain simulator and that is going to be useful for a number of purposes.

We have also been asked to help different number of nonprofit organizations to track their metrics. That might be monetary metrics, but if I can track how many people they help get fresh water, how many they get to educate, or get healthcare, and things like that, we think that there is some greater value to use blockchain to track those. Now we have not gamified that yet, but those are some of the things we have in mind of doing within that context. If anybody has an interest in those areas, too, you have an open invitation. If you want to know more about what we are doing, and in what ways we look to partner, I am open to that too.

We are also looking at some healthcare solutions using blockchain, too, even though our personal health shares didn't perform as well as medical health records, we are working with team who are doing things called "procredits" and you are able to do medical credentials across state lines. It's hard to do that when transitioning from a place like Washington to Tennessee, they don't speak the same language. Blockchain has that redeemable value and multiple sources of trust with multiple entities and the ability to do that. Now at the beginning, on set of that, do we look at game theory and drive the psychology in building those? Absolutely. Those are the things we are interested in working on.

And then you also have to think about what sectors society would benefits most from, too. Military, government, and healthcare for us, but also fintech finance, transportation, insuretech, are all areas that have good, social qualities for using a solution such as this that ties into blockchain and gaming.

So, if we find that being in a neutral zone, we can borrow from one industry segment and help another industry segment that is not as far along. Or pick something that we have done for appropriation, and go and review that with the government to try to lower costs and spending. Or even if you take something you learn at 10x less cost in Haiti or Ghanda and be able to bring that back, and offer it at a lower cost because you have cost innovation. That said is why we tap into all of those areas between industry, government, healthcare, and social and nonprofit settings to.

So, we are always looking to partner in some of the visions shared by both profit and non-profit, universities, and we have a lot of projects in similar spaces, and we are also trying to build a sustainable innovation pipeline for our students to give them interesting things to work on so that when they go out into the workplace, they are better ready to meet the challenges of the new technology like blockchain or augmented reality. Those are a few of the things that might be of interest to you guys.

Do you guys want my contact details? I want to make sure I have time for questions.

[Editor's note: Audience question from the VA: I am your next door neighbor in Florida, there, with the VA, and am very interested if you had more thoughts on healthcare and simulations using blockchain. I am at the National Simulations Center, but it is less of the types of things you do.]

Dr. David Metcalf: If you think about having to track all of your credentials and looking at overall system to track competency down to the actual competency level across various sectors. CEDERS is actually an initiative and group from the ADL developed by Robbie pulling from various APIs to actually move those credentials across the network. Early days. But I wanted to make sure you knew that based on your question. And we are watching that closely to see if we can pull from the xAPI libraries and tie those together with interoperability that blockchain affords us across medical credentials.

The company I mentioned before, too, ProCredits, is in Tampa and are looking for places to implement the technology they already developed. It might be useful to use a pilot rather than try to build something themselves. We talked to other hospitals about how to tie into some of their assets tracking, there is something called RFLS, radiofrequency tracking Location Systems which are like sponges.

Let's follow-up later.

[Editor's note: Audience question on the name of the paypal like coin]

Dr. David Metcalf: Yes- it is called M-P-E-S-A. Definitely look that up, it is a really cool technology. It is almost like trusting your cell phone company to keep track of your money.

Case Study: UCF Blockchain Simulator

A fundamental component for previewing the functionality of blockchain applications are the test nets that can be used to model transactions and evaluate potential problems before they arise on an immutable blockchain. This fundamental tenet of the development process is important and useful, but may not go far enough.

In order to truly test the effectiveness, reliability, and security of a blockchain solution, it is important to evaluate the entire scenario including: both the system and non-system components. As of any technology solution, weak points exist in the handoff between systems and particularly in the vulnerabilities between humans and processes where they touch the systems. These touch points can be evaluated using the traditional tools and techniques of the simulation industry. There are however many nuances to what must be evaluated in blockchain solutions.

The University of Central Florida Institute for Simulation and Training has begun the development of a blockchain simulator that can accommodate multiple test nets and protocols while including additional modeling of human behavior and processes, as part of a more comprehensive evaluation framework that further defines and measures adherence to industry practices, standards, government regulations, and international privacy laws.

Meeting all of these tests will prove particularly important within the healthcare field. Patient privacy and the fines associated with being out of compliance will require solutions that involve blockchain to also meet the test of Personally Identifiable Information (PII) and International Privacy Standards like GDPR and Safeharbor for international solutions; providing a holistic framework for modeling and evaluating the overall solution— not just the blockchain components-- they identify additional vulnerabilities across the threat surface of an associated solution. Scenario generation can be used to provide repeatable scenarios to model out many variables across a number of blockchain use cases and the myriad of protocols that exist now, and those that will be developed in the future.

The UCF blockchain simulator will provide an additional tool to speed development and ensure that cybersecurity best practices are met and hardened solutions are released to meet the rapidly changing market demands.

Chapter 30:
The Next Generation of Distributed Ledger Technology

Dieter Kondek

Editor's Note:

The theme of new innovation in blockchain and the impact of global healthcare innovation continues in this chapter and follows the previous chapter's discussion of innovation; however, in previous chapter the innovation was using gaming with blockchain as innovation. In this chapter a very advanced technology named IOTA is discussed. IOTA is a distributed ledger technology but differentiates itself in that it has no blocks, no chains, and no miners. This model continues the theme of innovation in healthcare and illustrates what the future of healthcare innovation might look like.

In this section of the book, we will explore a next generation technology called IOTA that like blockchain is a distributed ledger technology but differentiates itself in that it has no block, no chain, and no miners. [12] IOTA has the potential to impact the digital health ecosystem as a whole, but for the purpose of this section we are focusing on IOTA's key characteristics and their ability to impact and/or enable patient centric control of data, security and Integrity of data, and the ability to seamlessly transfer data through a unique streaming extension MAM (Masked authenticated messaging).[6]

As participants in the healthcare sector attempt to integrate blockchain technology, specifically in eHealth, they will run into some well-known fundamental difficulties of blockchain which could make its use and integration impractical. [13] In order to practically upgrade healthcare systems to be more efficient and secure, these issues need to be addressed. Some distributed ledger technologies (DLT), such as IOTA, are exploring what they believe to be a solution to offer a framework for healthcare systems to integrate practical solutions with respect to data security and integrity. 6 Data collection and mobility are growing factors in the evolution of medical research and development and IOTA possesses some clear benefits in enabling medical record digitization, data control, data security, and data transfer. [13]

We will start by giving an overview of IOTA, how it functions and differentiates itself from blockchain technology. Afterwards, we take a closer look at the specific uses mentioned earlier including a helpful overview that we received from Dr. Navin Ramachandran eHealth stream lead at the IOTA Foundation to explore how IOTA's unique approach could be integrated.

IOTA

IOTA is an open source distributed ledger that uses a DAG, called the tangle, as its underlying data structure, instead of blockchain, to store its ledger. IOTA aims to become the backbone of the IoT economy by overcoming restrictions of traditional blockchains while maintaining the fundamental benefits of a decentralized system. [19] The focus is on speed and scalability while providing provenance and security of all data to enable seamless data control and transferability.[9] [13]

IOTA utilizes a different data structure from traditional blockchains which allows it to achieve consensus and facilitate transactions without miners. [19] We will explore some of these characteristics and take a closer look at the novel technology behind IOTA to harvest a better understanding of its possible impact on the future of healthcare.

Tangle

The tangle is the name given to IOTA's directed acyclic graph (DAG). IOTA defines a DAG as, "Directed Acyclic Graph (DAG) is a specific data structure based on a graph without any directed cycles. Instead of having a single branch with nodes having only one edge, in a DAG there can be multiple branches." [8]

Just as blockchain is the underlying technology behind bitcoin, the tangle is the underlying technology behind IOTA. Much like a blockchain, the tangle is also a distributed ledger technology that provides the structure to securely collect, house, transfer and track data and value transactions over time. [19] Once again, it differentiates itself from blockchain technology in that is has no block, no chain, and no miners. [12]

According to the IOTA whitepaper the main idea behind the tangle is the following:"to issue a transaction, users must work to approve other transactions. Therefore, users who issue a transaction are contributing to the network's security." [19] This alleviates a huge drawback from traditional blockchain technology in terms of incentives, fees, scalability, and speed that we will discuss in a later section. [13]

Some important IOTA characteristics

Scalability (Transaction Rates)

"IOTA can achieve high transaction throughput thanks to parallelized validation of transactions with no limit as to the number of transactions that can be confirmed in a certain interval." [12]

IOTA's architecture is fundamentally structured to scale proportionately. The process that each sender of a transaction (n) must verify two random previous transactions (n*2) not only increases the security of the system but increases the ability to scale.24 These inherent qualities of the tangle and IOTA enable seamless scalability potential becoming faster and more secure as it grows.

Decentralization

"IOTA has no miners, every participant in the network that is making a transaction, actively participates in the consensus." [12]

This process inherently makes the sender also be the validator. [19] This process of not decoupling consensus instead making it an intrinsic part of the system leads to a completely decentralized and self-regulating network consisting of peers (or nodes) which are connected with each other to perform the necessary functions of the network. [8]

No Transaction Fees & Low Resource Requirements:

Since IOTA does not utilize miners for consensus there are no transaction fees. This makes it possible and even encourages participation with non-monetary , macro- or nano- transactions to store data and utilize the full security and features of the tangle. Additionally, low resource requirements for devices to participate on the tangle allow smaller devices such as sensors to participate. [23] These features allow IOTA to be a true enabler of a machine economy involving billions of IoT driven data transactions.

Quantum- Resistance:

5 Resistance to quantum computations

It is known that a sufficiently large quantum computer could be very efficient for handling problems that rely on trial and error to find a solution. The process of finding a nonce in order to generate a Bitcoin block is a good example of such a problem. As of today, one must check an average of 268 nonces to find a suitable hash that allows a new block to be generated. It is known (see e.g. [15]) that a quantum computer would need $\Theta()$ operations to solve a problem that is analogous to the Bitcoin puzzle stated above. This same problem would need $\Theta()$ operations on a classical computer. Therefore, a quantum computer would be around $= 234 \approx 17$ billion times more efficient at mining the Bitcoin blockchain than a classical computer. Also, it is worth noting that if a blockchain does not increase its difficulty in response to increased hashing power, there would be an increased rate of orphaned blocks. [19]

For the same reason, a "large weight" attack would also be much more efficient on a quantum computer. However, capping the weight from above, as suggested in Section 4, would effectively prevent a quantum computer attack as well. This is evident in iota because the number of nonces that one needs to check in order to find a suitable hash for issuing a transaction is not unreasonably large. On average, it is around 38. The gain of efficiency for an "ideal" quantum computer would therefore be of order $34 = 81$, which is already quite acceptable. More importantly, the algorithm used in the iota implementation is structured such that the time to find a nonce is not much larger than the time needed for other tasks that are necessary to issue a transaction. The latter part is much more resistant against quantum computing, and therefore gives the tangle much more protection against an adversary with a quantum computer when compared to the (Bitcoin) blockchain. [19]

Offline-Transactions (Partitioning)

"The beauty of the tangle is that you can fluidly branch off and back into the network. This partitioning is key in being adaptive to the rigorous requirements of an asynchronous IoT environment. There is no such thing as always-on connectivity, as such you need to be able to make transactions and secure data even in an offline environment." [20]

Clusters of devices can interact in an off-line environment by branching off and utilizing different communication protocols for P2P communication. 20 IOTA enables these clusters to rejoin the network once they come back on-line. [13]

The IOTA Foundation

The IOTA Foundation is a non-profit organisation based in Germany established to drive development and adoption of the IOTA platform. The IOTA Founders designed the foundational layer of IOTA to be open-source, free to use and led by an independent and neutral non-profit entity that could bring together governments and industries to help achieve the IOTA vision. [11]

The IOTA Foundation's vision extends to many different realms which are all dependent on access to a single source of truth. Data is only as valuable as it is valid. Ensuring what is true is precisely what distributed ledger technology enables. Their vision is to enable all connected devices through verification of truth and transactional settlements which incentivize devices to make available its properties and data in real time. This gives birth to entirely new general-purpose applications and value chains. [10]

The IOTA Foundation's goals are to:

- Research and secure the foundational protocol layer, and create new knowledge to benefit the ecosystem behind the economy of things. [11]

- Develop production-ready software for the community, partners and ecosystem to use and expand upon. [11]

- Educate and promote technologies and use cases for new generations to understand and to ensure the Foundation's success. [11]

- Standardize and ensure the maturity and widespread adoption of the economy of things.[11]

IOTA in Healthcare

IOTA's view:

The digitization of the healthcare ecosystem will continue to yield big rewards in terms of information sharing, care coordination and research, but it also requires advances in medical technology. [6] "Big Data" collection in healthcare and its use in machine learning to improve outcomes have been key focus points to enhance diagnostic, preventative, and precision medicine. [15] However, the integrity and security of the data has been in question as it is being used for machine learning and transferred for research and development efforts. [3] Thus, we need to address practical and secure methods of transferring and storing data that can accommodate the data that is being collected at scale. [6]

The IOTA Foundation believes that the next evolution of the digital medical record should bring back the integrity of data, with an immutable record that cannot be maliciously altered. This data will inform management decisions by clinicians, and form the basis of trustable decision support systems. The IOTA protocol supports initiatives to free the data, using novel secure open-source messaging protocols and common healthcare interoperability standards. IOTA researchers are working towards a longer term vision- of decentralized and secure data stores, controlled by the patient, and following them through their journey. Instead of private data access being controlled by institutions, the individual can be given much more control over which of their discrete medical records can be shared. [6]

IOTA's healthcare potential overview

IOTA and its inherent characteristics are poised to impact the healthcare industry in a tremendous way. Dr. Ramachandran from the IOTA Foundation laid out a clear outline for us where he positioned IOTA's impact into three broad but well-defined categories.

- Security and integrity of data

- Mobilizing algorithms and models at scale

- Authenticity and integrity of data generated by wearable and embedded devices

- Quantum Resistance

- Decentralization impact

- Patient centric control of data

- Decentralization of data, ownership to citizens

- Access to data simplified through zero-value, micro-, and nano- transactions
- Greater incentive to trust and share data for research
- Seamless transferring of Data
- Masked authenticated messaging (MAM)
- Simplified process (streaming data)
- Access control granting patients agency over their own data

Security and integrity of Data

"IOTA aims to enable greater data integrity within the health industry. By securely transmitting and storing individual medical records on the IOTA distributed ledger, access to private medical records can be trusted, secure and controlled." [6]

Centralized digital records are prone to corruption and unsecure compared to a decentralized counterpart. "There were 117 disclosed health data breaches in the third quarter of 2018, leading to 4.4 million patient records breached, according to the Q3 Protenus Breach Barometer report."[14] Data should be immutable and verifiable, if the integrity and security of the data used to train models and algorithms cannot be ensured, then these algorithms and data driven models cannot be mobilized at scale. 3 IOTA acknowledges that data goes through a security life-cycle from collection to storage all the way to the process of transferring it. It is important to ensure security and integrity in every step of the life-cycle. [1] IOTA aims to provide a scalable, immutable, and verifiable data storage and transfer solution with future proof quantum-resistant qualities. [13]

Another important factor to consider is the impact of the wearables market on healthcare. Authenticity and integrity of data is the key to utilizing data sets that are constantly being generated by wearable and embedded devices. 3 The problem is these data sets are prone to data manipulation and can even act as gateways for hackers to access larger systems. [24] As IOTA explores the interoperability of devices, systems, and other solutions, the tangle's security characteristics fill a huge gap that has yet to be practically solved in the digital health ecosystem. [3]

Patient centric control of data

"IOTA will enable the transition from an institution-centric model to a citizen-centric model of healthcare." 6

Quoting Dr. Ramachandran, "The aim of my work is to help build systems that do not allow tampering, but maximise usability – because usability is the key to adoption." [1]

IOTA's feeless structure allows it to maximize usability of securely storing and transferring data over time. [20] Fees associated with traditional blockchain protocols are not a feasible solution to secure the amounts of data input and output received from the exponentially increasing number of connected health devices and transactions each day. [13] Micro-, nano-, and even zero-value transactions for trustworthy and immutable information in a medical context becomes possible on the tangle which enables individuals, companies, and even machines to utilize all of the benefits of the tangle to store and transfer data. [6] "We often do not get access to the data that is collected about us," 1 but the benefits of IOTA could allow citizens agency over their own data. Citizens could share this data with machines, doctors, and other institutions on-demand to securely and accurately provide them with health and mental clues that they would otherwise not have access to. [1] [3]

At the moment we are limited to how we can further share and analyze our own data, "Healthcare data has traditionally been siloed in different institutions or even within a single institution. These silos prevent meaningful sharing and reuse of data, and limit the quality of care that can be delivered." [6]

IOTA aims to change this, "IOTA gives an incentive and a mechanism to actually share the resources and at the same time enabling the rightful companies or individuals to make money from those resources." [2]

Everything mentioned above relies heavily on the availability, security, and integrity of the data that is being collected, shared, and used to make decisions. 23 This data integrity comes for free through IOTA's feeless structure and can be controlled and owned by the citizen.[6]

As stated by Dr. Ramachandran, "with proper identity and consent management, the patient may be empowered to control their own data and its use for secondary purposes such as research." [24]

Seamless Data Transfer

"To receive medical treatment, an individual may need to consult with multiple providers for a single incident. When individuals transition from primary care clinics to hospitals to specialists and back again, records are not shared seamlessly, reducing their continuity of care." [6]

It has been no secret that to secure data and information on traditional blockchains a lengthy process must take place due to the nature of how data gets attached/secured. This process becomes more time-consuming when attempting to transfer the bits of data that have been secured on the blockchain to another party, since the new party now has to go through a similarly lengthy process to be able to read/receive the data. 3 IOTA on the other hand is experimenting with an extension to reduce this lengthy process using streaming technology to make the act of transferring data more seamless. The extension is called masked authenticated messaging (MAM) which acts as a second layer data communication protocol. MAM resolves some issues distributed ledgers may run into when attempting to improve privacy while preserving auditability. During the MAM process, transaction addresses get randomly generated by the issuer, thus, eliminating the need for two entities to interact. Additionally, transaction addresses are independent of the parties that have the details needed to fetch the encrypted data. [3]

Below is an excerpt from "Authenticating Health Activity Data Using Distributed Ledger Technologies" in part authored by Dr. Ramachandran, it includes the summary of their findings, but to fully understand the technology behind MAM and how IOTA utilizes this novel technology we advise interested readers to check out the article which can be found in full online.

IOTA is a permissionless distributed ledger protocol that provides the fabric for an immutable audit trail of activity data broadcasted from wearable devices. MAM is an extension module housed in the application layer of the IOTA stack, and has the potential to enable patients to store, retrieve, and share their authenticated, encrypted activity data on-demand via the tangle. This communication protocol empowers patients by giving them agency over their activity data, and allows them to be better informed of their current status and prior trends. The restricted mode of MAM gives patients granular controls over the way their data is exchanged between participants in the digital healthcare ecosystem, while the added layer of integrity from the tangle establishes trust that the data has not been altered. This report explored the emergence of an on-demand digital healthcare ecosystem that algorithmically processes large volumes of data, and addressed the need for this data to be authenticated, distributed, and immutable. We demonstrated how distributed ledger technologies can play a key role in ensuring authenticity of encrypted activity data by using theMAMmodule of the IOTA protocol. This module also enabled patients to define granular access controls that could be updated over time. While the current implementation of MAM proved to be an effective conduit for authenticated activity data, it has room for design and performance improvements. Such a method for secure and effective coordination of interoperable activity data can open the door for remote monitoring, and other on-demand services that catapult healthcare into the digital age. [3]

Use case focus – Remote patient Monitoring

Remote patient monitoring could benefit greatly from the use of distributed ledger technology for both personal and professional use-cases. [6] IOTA has the capabilities to enable sensors and devices to communicate with one another due to its scalability, low computational requirements, and feeless structure. [13] Below is some interesting input from the IOTA website that covers how utilizing IOTA in remote patient monitoring could look in the future,

Health sensors are becoming increasingly prevalent, both consumer grade and medical grade. Data from these sensors may provide greater insight into the patient's health state between clinic visits. This is particularly useful in chronic disease, where deterioration may be identified sooner, or in medical trials where response may be more granularly monitored. However securing and actioning these data streams remains problematic. [6]

The IOTA masked authenticated messaging (MAM) protocol can help to secure these data streams over the tangle, using modern healthcare interoperability standards. The IOTA ledger may also be used as a record of the security of devices, proving that they have been updated to the latest most secure internal software (firmware). [6]

Use case focus – Health Data Exchange

Health data exchanges can be optimized using distributed ledger technology. [3] Healthcare information exchanges, if secured and developed right, have the potential to exponentially impact healthcare research and development. Several problems with traditional technology have halted innovation and have worked against the idea of the exchange of healthcare data. [6] To date, no reasonable method has been perfected to facilitate the control and integrity of the data and to correctly outline and facilitate potential monetary value add for sharing data. Below is additional input from the IOTA website with interesting thoughts on the possibilities of utilizing IOTA and MAM in developing a Health Data Exchange,

The IOTA MAM protocol may be leveraged for transfer of patient data between hospitals. MAM allows for encrypted streams of data that can carry either granular data about a patient or their entire health record. The inbuilt payment system also allows feeless charging for these streams of data, so that institutions can easily recoup the costs of data transfer. [6]

The MAM streaming technology and core IOTA ledger can also be combined to form the basis of a distributed healthcare information exchange. [6]

Use case focus - Research data integrity

Probably the most prevalent use-cases when converging distributed ledger technology and healthcare are research data integrity and digital medical records. [21] In order to advance in innovation, it has become clear that we need to utilize all of the data that is being made available through all of the new technology enabled outlets. We have already covered how distributed ledger technology can play a major role in this, but below is an excerpt from the IOTA website providing additional input on why their technology may be a great fit to develop solutions,

Clinical research is reliant on the integrity of data collection. The IOTA ledger can act as an immutable ledger to prove the integrity of research data. IOTA's scalability and feeless structure means that very granular continuous real world data can be recorded as it is produced, rather than on episodic case report forms. We expect that this approach will herald a new approach to the collection of real world evidence in trials. [6]

Use case spotlight – Untangle Care / Pact.care

Dr. Ramachandran pointed us to an interesting group, Untangle Care, that is being backed by the IOTA Development Fund and is working on tangle-based solutions in healthcare such as pact.care. [5] We are showcasing this project in this book to provide our readers with a view of a real-world project that is progressing in its development stages to revolutionize aspects of eHealth through the tangle technology.

The goal of the "Untangle Care" project is to develop key IOTA-based tools that will allow healthcare data to flow between healthcare institution-based solutions (e.g. Electronic Medical Records) and citizen-based solutions (e.g. Personal Health Records) in a secure, seamless and healthcare-interoperable way (using Fast Healthcare Interoperable Resources - FHIR). [4]

Main project deliverables include an open source MAM FHIR integration code as well as a web interface and a MAM FHIR API. Secondary deliverables will include an open source Xamarin and IOTA based Chat App, IOTA C# Port, and IOTA based logging system. [4]

Pact.care is a new generation of simple and highly secure file transfer. It's one of the first distributed websites running in your browser, meaning you are in complete control of your own data. We neither have access to your encrypted data nor can we prevent you from sharing and receiving this data. By design, it's impossible to alter your data during the transfer process. Additionally, the integrated transfer history allows you to claim the ownership of your data and provides a transparent logging system. [18]

We are using the latest advantages in the field of the distributed ledger technology for our file transfer service. The files are uploaded on a distributed file system named IPFS and uploads, as well as downloads, are logged on an immutable distributed ledger named IOTA. This way files are transferred immutable and distributed on IPFS. IOTA makes sure that nobody can delete or alter the logs. Furthermore, we implemented the Web Crypto API (AES256-GCM) to fully encrypt the files inside your browser before they get even uploaded. The same encryption algorithm is, for example, recommended by the German Medical Association.18

IOTA's potential within GDPR framework

It is important to note IOTA's positive view on a future with the General Data Protection Regulation (GDPR) framework, as well as IOTA's potential to be a leader in the DLT space despite the obvious conflicts with the GDPR. [17] According to an interview with Julie Maupin, Director of Social Impact & Public Regulatory Affairs at The IOTA Foundation,

The IOTA Foundation is a strong supporter of data privacy and end-user-controlled data policies. We are registered in Germany, in the heart of the EU, and we are working closely with European authorities to make sure the GDPR is interpreted and applied in ways that accomplish the regulation's underlying policy goals. Unfortunately, the GDPR was written for a pre-blockchain world. Some of its provisions – in particular its definitions of data controllers and data processors – fit uneasily with the architecture of distributed ledger technologies, where anonymous and distributed nodes all over the world interact in novel ways with different types of encrypted user data. Our approach is to actively partner with leading innovators and regulators to find sensible ways of implementing the GDPR without stifling the exciting innovation that's happening in the DLT and IoT spaces. [17]

IOTA could be complementary to the mission of the GDPR, since the GDPR's and IOTA's goals for data privacy and control ultimately align and some of IOTAs inherent capabilities are effective solutions to many problems the GDPR is trying to solve. [16] IOTA believes solutions must be jointly explored, in order to combat some of the GDPR's obvious conflicts against the fundamental characteristics of DLT. The GDPR was written in a world where personal data would be stored with traditional centralized parties and not spread globally across decentralized nodes. [22] This notion does not translate feasibly to decentralized systems and could negatively impact innovation in DLT. Considering that some of IOTA's features inherently provide the kind of data privacy and control described in the GDPR, it may be wise to find a solution where both can co-exist. Some examples of how IOTA's features answer the GDPR's framework include; future proofing data through quantum-resistance, self-sovereign identity constructs, MAM streaming with revoke access features, and zero-knowledge proofs, which provide useful and effective methods of securing the data from third parties, managing consent, permission, and revocations. Zero-knowledge proofs for instance, may solve the notion of "right to be forgotten." Since, in the case of IOTA, the relevant data that is asked to be protected such as "personal identifiable information" is never "remembered" in the first place. [16] [17]

Although time will ultimately tell, Julie Maupin and the IOTA Foundation are hopeful in their efforts to play a role in the future of data privacy in Europe and beyond. [17] Finding a solution for the GDPR and DLT to co-exist is an extremely important task that IOTA is exploring. The GDPR as it stands could have a negative impact on European business, but collaboration with DLT solutions such as IOTA could alleviate these issues with respect to improved data privacy regulation. 16 Additionally, IOTA's global stance and reach could be beneficial to global organizations affected under the GDPR, since data handlers outside the EU may have collected or processed data with people, entities, or infrastructures within the EU.17 In summary, IOTA's location in the heart of Germany coupled with their collaborative efforts with policymakers and regulators may position them favorably for a future where IOTA and the GDPR not only co-exist but could complement one another. [7] [17]

IOTA in healthcare Summary

IOTA is a distributed ledger that utilizes the tangle (DAG) which differentiates itself from traditional blockchain technology bringing with it a variety of benefits and characteristics that could positively disrupt and spur innovation in the digital healthcare ecosystem and beyond. IOTA has begun its efforts in this space and their vision to increase efficiency, security, and integrity of data whilst promoting patient-centric control of data.6 IOTA is also leveraging novel technology extensions such as MAM as answers to common scalability bottlenecks that can be found when attempting to practically implement other technologies such as blockchain for similar use-cases. 3 The researchers and founders of IOTA are working on a long-term vision and many new exciting projects, announcements, and integration verticals are being explored. The vision is to change the way machines interact with people and each other, including the way data gets stored, moves, and is used personally and professionally.6 & 13 IOTA is involved in so much more than we could cover in this section of the book, some interesting topics and projects that we did not discuss or cover in this section but are worth mentioning will be listed below. We advise any interested readers to dive deeper into the potential of IOTA and to check out the resources below to get a better understanding of IOTA and their vision for the future.

- Qubic – Oracles – Smart Contracts – Interoperability (qubic.iota.org)

- IOTA Data marketplace (https://data.iota.org/#/) (https://blog.iota.org/iota-data-marketplace-cb6be463ac7f)

- IOTA Ecosystem (https://ecosystem.iota.org/)

- IOTA Ecosystem Development Fund (https://fund.iota.org/)

- Other documents and useful information (https://docs.iota.org/)

- Research & Academic papers (https://www.iota.org/research/academic-papers)

- Research & Development roadmap (https://www.iota.org/research/roadmap)

- News (https://blog.iota.org/)

References

1. Alger, Leah. "NHS Doctor Explains Why Healthcare IoT Needs Better Oversight." DevOps NEWS, 18 July 2018, www.devopsonline.co.uk/the-need-for-secure-healthcare-devices/. Accessed 15 Nov. 2018

2. Bjørnstad, Magnus Vitsø, et al. A Study on Blockchain Technology as a Resource for ... Norwegian University of Science and Technology, June 2017, brage.bibsys.no/xmlui/bitstream/handle/11250/2472245/17527_FULLTEXT.pdf?sequence=1.

3. Brogan, James, et al. "Authenticating Health Activity Data Using Distributed Ledger Technologies." Computational and Structural Biotechnology Journal, vol. 16, 17 July 2018, pp. 257–266., doi:10.1016/j.csbj.2018.06.004.

4. Fialho, Andre, et al. "IOTA ECOSYSTEM DEVELOPMENT FUND PROJECT PLAN AND BUDGET UNTANGLE CARE." PACT CARE BV. Accessed 22 Nov. 2018

5. Fialho, Andre, et al. "Untangle Care." IOTA Ecosystem, Untangle Care, ecosystem.iota.org/projects/untangle-care. Accessed 22 Nov. 2018

6. IOTA Foundation. "EHealth." The Next Generation of Distributed Ledger Technology, www.iota.org/verticals/ehealth. Accessed 15 Nov. 2018

7. IOTA FOUNDATION. "For Regulators and Policymakers." The Next Generation of Distributed Ledger Technology, www.iota.org/get-started/for-regulators-and-policymakers. Accessed 25 Nov. 2018

8. IOTA Foundation. "Glossary of Terms." The Next Generation of Distributed Ledger Technology, docs.iota.org/introduction/other-stuff/glossary. Accessed 15 Nov. 2018

9. IOTA Foundation. "Meet the Tangle." The Next Generation of Distributed Ledger Technology, www.iota.org/research/meet-the-tangle. Accessed 15 Nov. 2018

10. IOTA Foundation. "Our Vision." The Next Generation of Distributed Ledger Technology, www.iota.org/the-foundation/our-vision. Accessed 15 Nov. 2018

11. IOTA Foundation. "The IOTA Foundation." The Next Generation of Distributed Ledger Technology, www.iota.org/the-foundation/the-iota-foundation. Accessed 15 Nov. 2018

12. IOTA Foundation. "What Is IOTA." Introduction - IOTA Docs, docs.iota.org/introduction. Accessed 15 Nov. 2018

13. IOTA Foundation. "What Is IOTA?" The Next Generation of Distributed Ledger Technology, www.iota.org/get-started/what-is-iota. Accessed 15 Nov. 2018

14. Leventhal, Rajiv. "4.4M Patient Records Breached in Q3 2018, Protenus Finds." Healthcare Informatics Magazine, 7 Nov. 2018, www.healthcare-informatics.com/news-item/cybersecurity/44m-patient-records-breached-q3-2018-protenus-finds. Accessed 19 Nov. 2018

15. Mandelli, Anthony. "IOTA Partners Healthcare Providers for Blockchain Research in Norway." CCN, CCN, 1 July 2017, www.ccn.com/iota-spearheads-dlt-research-in-norway/. Accessed 15 Nov. 2018

16. Maris, Koen. "Privacy Is Not a Currency – IOTA." IOTA, IOTA, 5 Feb. 2018, blog.iota.org/privacy-is-not-a-currency-63018fc45920. Accessed Nov 25. 2018

17. Michele, Daniel De. "Interview with Julie Maupin." Hello IOTA, HelloIOTA, 2 July 2018, helloiota.com/interview-with-julie-maupin-iota-foundation/. Accessed 25 Nov. 2018

18. Pact Care. "PACT Care – Patient Active." PACT Care, PACT CARE, pact.care/. Accessed 23 Nov. 2018

19. Popov, Serguei. "The Tangle." IOTA, 30 Apr. 2018, iotatoken.com/IOTA_Whitepaper.pdf. Accessed 22 Nov. 2018

20. Schiener, Dominik. "A Primer on IOTA (with Presentation) – IOTA." IOTA, IOTA, 21 May 2017, blog.iota.org/a-primer-on-iota-with-presentation-e0a6eb2cc621. Accessed on 19 Nov. 2018.

21. Stampa, Karsten, and HealthBank. "How Distributed Ledger Technology Will Transform Health Data." Hospitals | Healthcare Global, Staff Writer, 9 Nov. 2018, www.healthcareglobal.com/technology/how-distributed-ledger-technology-will-transform-health-data. Accessed 19 Nov. 2018

22. Steinbeck, Dean. "How New EU Privacy Laws Will Impact Blockchain: Expert Take." Cointelegraph, Cointelegraph, 30 Mar. 2018, cointelegraph.com/news/how-new-eu-privacy-laws-will-impact-blockchain-expert-take.

23. Tsac token. "IOTA & Distributed Ledgers – A Presentation by Dr Navin Ramachandran." Online video clip. YouTube. YouTube, 7 February 2018. https://www.youtube.com/watch?v=2N_jK9TDvxA . Accessed 19 Nov. 2018

24. Unblocked Events. "DLT & EHealth: Interview with Dr Navin Ramachandran, IOTA Foundation." Unblocked Events, 21 July 2017, unblockedevents.com/2017/06/28/ehealth-interview-dr-navin-ramachandran-iota/. Accessed 23 Nov. 2018

Chapter 31:
The Future of Electronic Health Record: Amchart – Creating a Global Sandbox for Innovation

Aman Quadri

https://hashedhealth.com/blockchain-for-healthcare-book/

Editor's Note:

In this late breaking chapter, Aman Quadri from Amchart shares an innovative model for using their international hospital to rapidly evaluate the effectiveness of future ideas for blockchain and electronic health records. From a frank review of the challenges and barriers to entry, to a review of potential clinical, business and technology models— Quadri shares his method of rapid testing of new ideas that could lead us to the future of Blockchain in Healthcare.

"Relationships Matter, Especially in Healthcare"

As the landscape is changing and user ownership of data is starting to be considered a type of property in certain jurisdictions, we must examine the way patients will interact with their own data and how we can enhance provider's ability to diagnose and treat these patients. Amchart development began in early 2018 and we believe that launching a platform outside of the United States will allow for quick deployment, experimentation and revision to then allow for global participation.

The main goal for the Amchart initiative is to test a patient-centric incentive-based platform that combines mobile applications with integrated IoT devices, a personal health record, and a fully functioning EMR with emerging technology tools to providers allowing seamless use of data and continuity of care. Patients can earn incentives through keeping track of health data through connected devices, sharing their data for research, or be involved in clinical trials. We are not the only organization attempting these objectives and want to learn from the successes and failures from these companies as well as providing insight into what we learn.

Some Problems Noted in the Healthcare System

During our conversations with patients, providers, and patients, we discovered major pain points that are different for each stakeholder in the equation. Some of the basic issues can be summarized below:

- Limited access to real time data

- Excessive documentation needs in a healthcare system

- Limited collaboration between patients and providers

- Difficulty obtaining complete medical records

- Lack of incentive programs

- Sick care vs Well care

- No clinical insights for patients

For example, one of the correlations recently made by a few studies showed that for every 2 minutes a provider spends with a patient, 3 minutes are needed for documentation. This can lead to a significant amount of time spent at the end of the day documenting reducing the quality of life metrics for a provider. In the United States, one physician commits suicide on a daily basis.

HYPERLINK "https://www.webmd.com/mental-health/news/20180508/doctors-suicide-rate-highest-of-any-profession#1" https://www.webmd.com/mental-health/news/20180508/doctors-suicide-rate-highest-of-any-profession#1

Although the underlying causes continue to be studied, part of the equation has been related by anecdotal data to decreased satisfaction in the workplace, increased pressures to document quickly, increased documentation time, less time with patients, decreased quality of life measures, etc. Can changes with technology improve these metrics? It is unknown at this time, but trials and experimentation are important to discuss and test.

Patients on the other hand either are inundated with information they do not understand or have difficulty with access to their records in a timely manner. It is common for patients to have limited access to their records, like the NHS in the United Kingdom, or have access, but cannot attain it, like in the United States. There is a growing trend of health technologists who believe that patients should own their healthcare data, but can they manage it? Will they do the research to understand what it means? Or, can we use technology to provide insights into clinical data, trends, and accountability that becomes an extension of the physician?

Payors also have increased pressures to maintain level premiums with an aging population and rising utilization of higher level care. How can technology work to monitor, incentivize, and alert payors, providers, and even family members and decrease the use of emergency room and urgent care facilities? If patients can be monitored through connected IoT devices through mobile apps creating constant feedback loops, then organizations could work to reduce costs and possibly return premiums for those clients willing to be monitored from blood pressure, blood sugar, weight, etc. Only testing these theories would provide answers to see what could be successful in live production.

Example of a linear model of care – patients tend to go down the line with limited feedback and follow-up. Current healthcare models put the responsibility on the patient to follow-up with the provider if the desired interventions are not beneficial.

Example of a feedback model – providing a consistent feedback loop with multiple accountability partners can allow for maintaining progress towards goals. Also, keeping everyone involved in the care continuum focuses on proactive disease management.

Barriers of Entry to Healthcare Blockchain Adoption

Industry Wide Education and Testing Use Cases

Healthcare organizations have had little education or experimentation with emerging technologies, including blockchain and big data initiatives. They have a tendency to equate blockchain with cryptocurrency, and that can stop them from exploring DLT to help improve efficiencies, increase security of information, and have improved assurance of data for Big Data initiatives. By allowing simple proof of concepts for limited to no cost to the organization, companies can improve adoption of new platforms to affect change in healthcare. Upcoming use cases that are being tested in production include: credentialing, marketplace transparency, electronic health records, decentralized insurance, etc. By working on one inefficiency in a healthcare organization, improved adoption of emerging technology can occur.

Developing Industry Standards and Pan-jurisdictional Frameworks

As technologies are tested and adopted, it will be necessary for organizations to collaborate and work on creating rules and standards to allow for integration and interoperability. There must also be good ethical guidelines on how to work within the large data lakes which will develop, improved use of communication standards for integration between disparate organizations, and how to work within geographical boundaries.

Since disease processes do not abide by geographical borders, we must work with any organization who want to share in connectivity standards, understand localization of healthcare information, and work on using data appropriately for clinical decision making tools, etc.

Frameworks in which both HIPAA and GDPR rules are integrated and respected will allow companies to work through the international marketplace and allow for increased utilization of new platforms.

Demonstrating Interoperability at Scale

Interoperability has been an enormous challenge in healthcare. For example, since the United States has had standards and even laws on the books since 2009, healthcare organizations maintain data blocking on a regular basis. Patients have difficulty with access to medical records in a timely manner and providers continue to work with older data, which can limit interventions. There is no need for new technologies to prove interoperability, but more willingness for large, legacy systems to open their tech stack and allow for data to flow freely between other organizations. It is only seen at a small scale, but not within the silos of the healthcare industry.

Resolve Patient Matching and Digital Identity

A major issue in healthcare systems is the lack of a universal patient ID that can go across multiple organizations. In the United States, patients can utilize a social security number and hospitals utilize master-patient indexes, but they differ from one site to another. By creating a universal patient ID with attestation recorded on a blockchain, patients could then have a single identity to utilize through multiple providers. Also, if multiple providers are connected, such as HIEs, EMR's, labs/

diagnostic centers, etc. then an AI platform could engage these data sources and help to identify any matching issues. By combining blockchain and AI strategies, there could unique ways to solve identity issues which can plague hospital and clinic systems.

A Collaborative EMR with Patient Incentives

Current EMRs are designed for billing purposes more than being a collaborative tool. Providers complain about increased documentation time with limited information on symptom change in patients or help with reconciling other data sources or medications. As mentioned earlier, the move needs to be away from linear models of care and more towards feedback loops with incentives.

A model to test would be to see if patients and providers could work towards creating achievements which can be tracked and rewarded. For example, imagine a newly diagnosed diabetic patients. Some of the challenges may include monitoring and taking medications, taking blood sugar regularly, reporting any results out of parameters, and creating a pathway to reduce the impact of diabetes or perhaps eliminating it all together. So with a physician and patient working together:

Patient visits physician.

Physician examines patient.

After testing, patient is identified with diabetes.

Education on diabetes management through exercise and medication.

Goals/Achievements discussed.

Provider sends these goals to patient's mobile app for monitoring.

Patient begins taking medication, monitoring blood sugar, vitals, etc. on mobile app.

If blood sugar is out parameters, goals not met, etc. then alerts are sent to an accountability tree, which could be a combination of family, physician, nursing, payor, etc.

When patient meets goals/expectations, he or she is awarded points in the platform, which can be redeemed for goods/services.

During follow-up visit, patient and provider can review goals and understand what worked and didn't allowing for revision of the next set of goals and increase potential rewards.

There are multiple incentive strategies being tested by various companies, and some do not get past the testing stage, since it can be difficult to find a large group willing to try unique opportunities.

Because healthcare can be a difficult market to penetrate and organizations typically have limited time to engage in platforms that do not provide immediate ROI, it is imperative to test theories before engaging a live patient population. Also, some strategies work differently based on culture, socioeconomic status, and so it makes sense to test and retest until a homogenous strategy can be deployed among varying populations.

Mobile apps have tended to be more about tracking and not about collaboration, so understanding behavioral psychology and motivation tactics will be important in helping both patients and providers to share. Capturing vital signs, goals, steps are easily attainable through the phone or connected IoT devices, but where the biggest challenge will be is to capture data and report back to the provider. When patients ignore or not within guidelines, will positive or negative reinforcement work? If certain achievements are not met, can goals be modified in a way that patients feel successful? What kind of marketplace can be created through a token economy? Will a patient want to redeem tokens?

There are many questions when it comes to engagement models with patients, so it is vital to create the right tokenomics/marketplace model to truly provide value to patient. On the other hand, as good strategies develop to hold patients accountable, can unique strategies be deployed so that other stakeholders in this model, like providers and payors, also be incentivized and work towards collaborative communication?

Building a Sandbox Outside of the United States

Even though Amchart has been theorizing various strategies to deploy, we fall into the same issues of testing and adoption. Healthcare organizations have limited time and resources and are not in the mode of testing with existing populations, they would rather have a product, which is ready to go and be deployed with all the "bugs" worked out and tested. The ideal environment would be then is to create an innovation sandbox with live patients, and that is what Amchart did. We launched Amsys Heart and Diabetes Clinic in Mumbai, India, HYPERLINK "http://www. amsyshd.com" www.amsyshd.com. The goal was create an environment, not only for us, but also for other emerging tech healthcare companies who need a place to work in collaboration and in a live environment.

Clinic Setup

We wanted to design a simple clinic with its focus on diabetes and hypertension as initial chronic diseases to be addressed. Our clinic flow includes the ability for a patient to be seen, have labs performed with results given the same day along with filling the prescription within the in-house pharmacy. This allows any organization to explore workflow pathways, improving inefficiencies, and testing various user experience pathways. Again, this is a new format for a clinic since you only get those services in a hospital, so testing it in the ambulatory care market will be an interesting experiment. This could also be a place to test out efficient clinical trials, research studies, and pharma research with life sciences partners, which will be determined later.

Potential revenue models

In the end, any company is about the generation of revenues to sustain its business model. Having a global sandbox will allow Amchart to test various revenue streams and identify the potential of each. Nearly $14.7 billion dollars was paid for health data in 2017 and expected to rise to $68.5 billion by 2025. There are plans to utilize several models for revenue generation including:

- SaaS based EMR subscriptions
- Clinical monitoring of high risk patients
- Gain share in partnership with payers
- Directed advertising through PHR/Mobile app
- Brokerage of permissioned healthcare data
- Licensed access for marketplace partners

After testing marketplace strategies, exploring partnership, and adoption strategies, we can use this as a template for our own growth strategy, but also as an educational tool for other companies who want to leverage what knowledge we have gathered.

Identifying Results

In the end, what results are we seeking? Healthcare change? Provider – Patient relationship improvement? Revenue generation? Improved collaboration between companies? How about all of the above?

Integrated Amchart Platform with others

Amchart believes that interoperability and integration are going to be key components for success. Part of that success will be first to integrate all pieces of Amchart together allowing data to flow from the EMR to the PHR and straight through to the mobile health companion. From there, we would like to create connectivity with other providers, labs, HIEs, healthcare organizations, other EMRs. This would be able to show integration success and that is a good result for the healthcare marketplace.

Incentive Plans Showing Healthcare Improvement

Creating incentive plans is one thing, working towards behavior change is another. Success in this category is not wholesale change in disease management, but incremental change through incentives. Amchart will experiment with using tokens to improved medication adherence, improve vital sign capture, and to maintain achievements. We believe that different cultures will experience and engage incentives differently, so we will partner with local economists and strategists to experiment with varying economies for success.

Successful Revenue Generation

Once launched and data aggregation begins, success in this area will be creating of databases that can be queried for monetization, organizations wanting to utilize the platform for patient monitoring, and payors wanting to engage with patients to reduce utilization of higher level services. Creating monetary success will also mean validation of incentive programs and partnerships with payors, providers, and patients to impact healthcare.

Summary

In the end, what Amchart is wanting to prove is that through technology, we can impact change. We hope that through our successes and failures, other organizations can learn and build the next iterations that will help to improve healthcare engagement. Healthcare comes through relationships between all stakeholders and that is the key to enact change. Technology can be used as an adjunct to propel that change.

Chapter 32:
Advancing Health Research with Blockchain

Sean T. Manion, PhD

https://hashedhealth.com/blockchain-for-healthcare-book/

Editor's Note:

To cap off the book, Dr. Sean Manion of Science Distributed shares his vision for how blockchain can shape health research and perhaps the scientific method itself. Major sections cover the current state and value of solutions, potential areas of application, areas of consideration, and a road map for redefining the future of scientific and clinical research by leveraging blockchain. The editors and authors wish to thank our readers as we end on this positive and thoughtful chapter on the future of Blockchain in Healthcare.

Overview

Scientific research is the foundation of evidence-based medicine. Health research provides advances in every aspect of healthcare to save money and save lives. Health research consists of a complex array of studies ranging from basic and pre-clinical biomedical science to clinical trials, population health studies, and 'big data' health data analyses. This complex flow of data is combined, analyzed, debated, and replicated until enough support exists for safe new treatments to be implemented to improve patient outcomes and quality of life.

Health research takes on average 17 years to go from bench to bedside, or idea to treatment [1]. The process involves researchers, clinicians, patients, administrators, funders, and regulators across universities, hospitals, industry, government, and non-profits. The health science community serve as gatekeepers for the advancement, consolidation, and synthesis of the information along the way. This takes place in funding agencies, regulatory bodies, professional conferences, peer-reviewed publications, and clinical practice guideline development.

Demand for improved health treatments and outcomes along with growth of the multi-pronged health industry has fueled rapid growth in health research in recent decades. This has resulted in scaling of the traditional research systems in a way that has degraded the research return on investment [2,3] and degraded quality. Of the $150 Billion spent annually on biomedical research in the US each year, at least 20% is not reproducible [4]. This represents not only wasted money and effort, but also produces flawed science that can infect the body of medical knowledge on which future health science research, policy, and healthcare are founded.

Blockchain is a tool that can help improve speed and quality of health research at multiple levels, improving health outcomes. Blockchain tech and process has demonstrated the ability to drastically reduce administrative delay and cost [5,6]. If applied at key points across the research cycle (Figure 1), it could drastically reduce the 17 years from bench to bedside, at an administrative cost savings that could refocus resources on creating new advancements in medicine.

Blockchain for health research is still in an early conceptual phase. Applications at different phases across the research cycle will advance independently and in parallel over the next few years. Early applications over the next 1-3 years will resemble those financial and administrative applications in other industries. More advanced applications in publications and clinical trials will follow in 3-5 years as developing pilots show the most successful approaches. Advanced and integrated implementation will take hold in 5-7 years, with what will likely be a rapid cascade towards adoption as blockchain will provide the same assurance for the evidence portion of evidence-based medicine, as we currently require for the medicine itself.

This chapter will give you a look at the value proposition, areas of application, considerations for adoption, and a road map for how blockchain can transform health research. For simplicity, I am using blockchain in the general sense to include blockchain and associated distributed ledger technologies; including public, permissioned, and hybrid applications. More detail on these distinctions can be found elsewhere in this book and should be part of the requirements/platform discussion with a technical team prior to any potential use case development.

Value Proposition

The value proposition of blockchain for health research is three-fold: improved quality, reduced cost/increased return on investment, and faster medical discovery and adoption into practice. These address key areas of concern of three major stakeholder groups: researchers, funders, and providers and patients, respectively:

1. Improved Quality – Blockchain can improve the quality of research in additional ways. The semantic data standardization required across each scientific discipline will create better quality data overall. This will be especially true for meta-analyses and cross study comparisons. Many scientific studies also suffer from use of incorrect or degraded materials (e.g. antibodies). The application of blockchain to the tracking and supply chain of these materials will increase quality as well.

2. Reduced Cost/Increased Return on Investment – There has been a declining return on investment of research dollars spent in recent years [2,3]. While the reasons behind this are complex, blockchain can offer better research value on several levels. Application of the technology to administrative processes such as vendor proposal review and contract purchasing has already been shown to decrease administrative costs and increased the value of research dollars [5,6]. Advanced applications of smart contracts can automate a great deal of the data management and early analyses. This will reduce data management costs.

3. Faster Medical Discoveries and Adoption into Practice – The greatest impact of blockchain to research will be the acceleration of findings it will bring. The time from "bench to bedside" will shrink, allowing for improvement in treatments and outcomes to move forward faster. Higher quality data and data auditability will result in focused steps forward with fewer backwards steps of irreproducible research and shorter time to correct those that remain. Administrative time, from proposal review and funding distribution, to IRB processing and even peer-review, will shrink compounding the advance in speeding up idea into treatment.

Figure 1. Research Cycle

Major Impacts

Blockchain applied to health research will have two transformative effects that would not just speed up the process but transform it to new levels of scientific quality and advancement of medicine. First, blockchain applied to health research data would bring huge advances in better quality science. By recording standard 'data transaction' variables (e.g. methodological details, patient genotypic & phenotypic information, analytical approaches, etc.) on a blockchain, research would become rapidly auditable, reducing reproducibility issues [7]. This would have the added benefit of identifying clearly where separate data sets are mergeable for increased statistical power and discovery.

Second, this type of tracking of research data would allow for the provenance of data to include patient/clinician/researcher input for future compensation and professional credit. This could underlie a transformation of an antiquated publication authorship system that is limited in its ability to track attribution across the decades long trek from bench to bedside. These limitations in the current system of research have resulted in misaligning the short-term incentives for patient and researcher alike, which has curtailed the impact of research funding on improving health outcomes. A longitudinal, transparent, immutable record of contribution to health science that crosses both organizational and time boundaries could transform health research by incentivizing data sharing and merging at the earliest possible time for maximum impact on health outcomes. Blockchain is a tool that will change health research and give us more rapid and widespread access to cures and treatments.

Beyond blockchain's ability as a new tool to improve and transform science, blockchain applied to health research may also serve as an early testing ground or "sandbox" for future health application of the technology that touch on personal health information (PHI). The regulatory issues surrounding these broader health applications (i.e. The Health Insurance Portability and Accountability Act of 1996 or HIPAA) are challenging for any enterprise system. Research allows for a controlled environment of limited use and patient consent where blockchain approaches may be tried, tested, refined, and developed under the watchful of the HIPAA regulators to allow them to grow comfortable with this new and unknown technology.

The Supply Chain of Health Research Data

Health research can be viewed as a supply chain for collection, identification, consolidation, verification, transferring, and processing data into published findings. These in turn are reviewed, selected, refined, and combined into meta-findings, which are then finished and shipped as knowledge products in the form of formal clinical practice guidelines or informal changes to clinical practice. The process is iterative and requires repeated cycles at different stages. It can vary across disciplines. Data is gathered as a raw material, these are shaped into findings or parts, which are formed into meta-findings or unfinished product, and eventually sent out as finished or unfinished knowledge products to change clinical practice and improve patient outcomes.

In this light, advances in utilizing blockchain for supply chain tracking (e.g. Walmart's mango pilot that it is now expanding to more produce [8,9]) becomes a template for health science and clinical practice. Consider the challenges with auditing and authenticating provenance of data that contributes to the reproducibility crisis. This could be significantly reduced by tagging data with design, demographic, and methodological data markers that are transparently available for review and rapid audit on a blockchain. Changes and analysis steps (including the hypothesis tested with each analytical approach) could be tracked anytime someone touches the data like truck temperature and shipping manifest details can be captured on a blockchain for a physical supply chain.

This system could also put an identifying tag on the tracking of data, findings, and products that would enable identification of patient, clinician, researcher, group, funding agency, and any other desired contribution. These could later be analyzed for compensation, professional credit, organizational input, and funding tracking to assess attribution and return on investment along the way. This could encourage more patient participation in, and compensation for, research. This could advance sharing of research data at earlier stages to accelerate findings. And this could create a whole new level of administrative decision-making at the funding and programmatic levels to optimize research investment and mission success.

Figure 2. Farm to table, bench to bedside

Road Map

The road map to implement blockchain in health research is straightforward and similar to what has advanced the technology in other industries utilizing incremental steps.

4. Administrative and financial use cases (i.e. grant proposal review) are the best way for funding agencies, researchers, and research institutions to learn to use the technology. It will allow for challenges and opportunities to be identified, comfort and capabilities to grow, and value of the technology to be demonstrated with little down-side or risk.

5. Regulatory use cases (i.e. human research protection offices and institutional review boards (IRBs)) are another early pilot area for research and blockchain. The efficiency it will bring to the IRB review process will speed the research cycle up considerably. The ease it can create in the regulatory audit process will be another huge value. An added bonus will be that the benefit it brings the regulators will help make them comfortable with more advanced applications that touch research data when they begin seeing these type of research plans later.

6. Working groups/consortia will need to be developed across scientific disciplines and sub-disciplines in order to begin discussion of semantic standards of the data used in those research areas. These should include individuals from funding agencies, professional societies, along with knowledgeable researchers in the field and be facilitated by those familiar

with the technology.

7. Pilot studies, particularly those that cross institutions and stretch across research networks will be the next stage in development of enterprise wide usage of the technology. This will allow for compartmentalized demonstrations in complex research environments. Early pilots might mirror current standard data processing in order to allow for side by side comparison of effectiveness.

8. Funding agencies can play a pivotal role in the implementation and adoption of these new technologies at an early stage until a critical threshold of use is reached. By encouraging early funded pilots and later promoting the use of the technology where it has shown value, agencies will help to realize a greater impact sooner.

Human Centered Design

Human centered design is a critical approach to successful development and implementation of blockchain solutions across industries. In health research, with complex data and workflows, this is especially so. Researchers are very sensitive to adjustments and changes in their workflow, as each research study requires a meticulously designed research protocol. These are prepared in advance of the study to ensure solid execution of hypothesis testing, reproducible results, regulatory approval, and future communications with the research community for evaluation and critique. A blockchain solution that does not take these aspects into consideration and put the research at the forefront of the design process is less likely to be successfully implemented. Here are the basic steps to the approach:

1. Select use case – Identify the specific use case to be considered for applying the blockchain framework. This will include a preliminary assessment of the business use case to ensure cost, benefit, and other potential solutions are considered.

2. Identify stakeholders and gather input on data and workflow – All relevant stakeholders in the current process should be considered including anyone that is involved in inputting or handling the current data flow for the use case to any end user or other relevant party. This may include different individuals within a current system or representatives across an enterprise collaboration. Information from these individuals will be critical in assessing the current workflow and status of data standards.

3. Select common data elements and consensus to standardize data – Where it does not already exist, standards will have to be defined and determined for the data elements that will be included. These common data elements will need to be input in a standard fashion across users, with any new standards agreed upon through consensus of the stakeholders (for an example for research data elements standardized across specific subdisciplines see:

https://www.commondataelements.ninds.nih.gov/TBI.aspx#tab=Data_ Standards).

4. Develop data governance plan including incorporation of smart contracts – How the data will be handled by the system including any automated processing with smart contracts will need to be agreed upon by the appropriate representation of the stakeholders.

5. Review requirements and select the appropriate platform for design – Technical experts that have been involved in the earlier data discussions and governance design will then be able to select the best blockchain platform and validation system to be used for each use case.

6. Design, code, and build – Based on the input and using the selected blockchain platform, the system can then be designed, coded, a developed with an appropriate user interface by the technical team. This will then be configured across the current legacy systems.

7. Pilot, feedback, and analysis – The system can be piloted in parallel to the existing systems alone in a sandboxed environment or with retrospective data. Feedback from the users and analysis of key metrics (data quality, access, speed, cost) compared to current practice can be done to refine the system. Once ready the system can be put into practice.

It is important to stress that this is still a very early stage of development for blockchain, especially with respect to research. While the potential widespread impact of this technology requires the due diligence of exploration across industries, in research it is important to be asking the right questions at this stage. Does blockchain applied to the current systems provide speed, reliability, and/or cost savings that aren't being realized with just the current legacy systems alone? Is this value worth the cost of implementation including standardization and implementation/training costs? If this same value can be achieved without blockchain, what is keeping this from happening? Could blockchain change the value proposition of achieving increased economy and effectiveness in different phases of research?

Consider each phase of science and what those involved in the execution and management should be asking about what value they may want to have beyond what is currently available:

Questions for Phases of Research

1. Hypothesis development – What hypotheses have already been tested? By whom? When? What happened? What was the approach? What was the result? What is the current status? **Can blockchain improve access to information about research hypotheses?**

2. Research Design – What methods are available? What variations have been developed? Are skilled collaborators available? Where are they? Are other shared resources available? **How could sharing of research methods and resources be improved with blockchain?**

3. Funding – Where are funds available? Does my plan match programmatic need? Have I applied here before? Why am I filling in all this information again? How is the money being tracked? **Can blockchain speed the funding cycle and allow researchers to spend more time on research?**

4. Regulatory – Can parts of this process be automated? Will that be faster and more reliable for researchers and regulator? Can multiple IRBs be aligned? Can parts of IRB review be crowdsourced? Can audits be easier? **Can blockchain speed up regulatory approval and making auditing easier for regulators and researchers?**

5. Data Collection – What are the data standards? Will they be mergeable with other studies? What are the quality assurance steps? Is PHI secure? Is there existing data that can be used? How accessible is the data? What is the ROI for the data? **Does blockchain provide opportunities to enhance data quality and auditability?**

6. Analysis & Interpretation – Are analyses tied to original hypotheses? Are analyses outlined in the protocol? Justification of new analyses? Record of attempted analyses? Statistical power? Lit basis of interpretation? Quality of refs? Replicable? Retractions? **Can blockchain allow for expanded access while improving for analysis tracking and quality control?**

7. Publishing – What are the pre-publication presentations? What is the quality or confidence level? How is feedback captured? Gray lit? What are the comments? Are there objective criteria? Crowd-sourced peer review? **Can blockchain help maintain intellectual property and researcher attribution while speeding and improving the quality of peer-evaluation of research?**

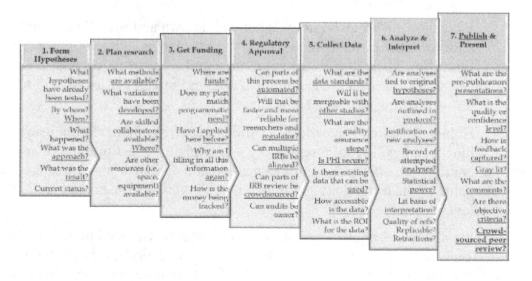

Figure 3. Considerations for blockchain value in each phase of health science

Additional Areas for Consideration

8. Knowledge translation – As research on a particular area or treatment advances, findings are analyzed and compiled to develop new knowledge products such as clinical practice guidelines that inform practice of evidence-based medicine. **Could blockchain be used to advance the translation of research findings into practice?**

9. Return on Investment – The return on health research investment is difficult to tabulate due the long lag time between research investment and subsequent changes in medical practice along with complexities of attribution. **Could the tracking of research dollars across the longitudinal record of blockchain applied to research enable better return on investment calculations?**

10. Setting programmatic priorities (funding) – Major federal and other health research funding organization set programmatic priorities for funding based on mission requirements, clinical gaps, research gaps, and successful administrative portfolio strategies. **Could blockchain enhance information tracking across research portfolios to optimize targeted funding and be a force-multiplier to research funding?**

Challenges

There are challenges to realizing the full value of blockchain applied the health research. These must be approached on both the individual and the enterprise level. Working groups and consortia for different disciplines will be critical in overcoming these. The five top challenges are:

1. Education – This technology is not well known and sometimes poorly understood or misconstrued with cryptocurrency applications alone. Education of the details, differentiation and value of blockchain for health research at the executive, administrator, and researcher levels will be critical before this can advance.

2. Human Research Protections – Clinical research augmentation using blockchain will require regulatory approval at the institutional review board level. This will require education and demonstration of safety and value of the technology to the regulators involved at local and national levels.

3. Standards – Technical and semantics standards will need to be established. Technical standards will need to satisfy organizational requirements for cybersecurity as well as allowing for future scaling and interoperability. Semantic standards will have components common to all areas of health research, but also require differentiated standards for some types of data by each discipline and sub-discipline.

4. Data Governance – Agreement on governance standards will be critical for each application across different phases and disciplines of research. This will determine the consensus at the core of each blockchain application, along with the interoperability with other areas of health research.

5. Access and Compliance – Access for those individuals and institutions that want to be involved, particularly at the early stages of development where the standards will be set, will be important for equity and inclusion as systems go enterprise-wide. Funding for pilots that range across different organizations and health research disciplines will be necessary.

Current Status

There is a growing interest in how blockchain can be beneficial to health research and scientific research more broadly. The interest is still largely conceptual with some pilots in development, but only a few of the most basic projects underway. Blockchain for Science has a list of many of the projects underway across the different phases of scientific research (www.blockchainforscience.com). The majority of these do not seem to differentiate between health/life sciences and other areas of research.

In the health research area, much of the early focus has been on transparency for clinical trials [10] and projects involving publishing [11]. Publishing seems to be the most mature phase of research with respect to blockchain. The peer-reviewed journal Ledger (www.ledgerjournal.org) became the first journal to use the technology in 2016. Other publishers from Springer Nature to Blockchain in Healthcare Today have also begun blockchain pilots applied to publishing. Additional publications such as Journal of the British Blockchain Association and Frontiers in Blockchain have begun publishing peer-reviewed articles on blockchain use cases including health research.

The Future

As the technology continues to mature and become more commonplace, people will understand the tremendous value it can bring across the health research enterprise. Once it is in place for basic financial and administrative tasks and paying dividends, early pilots relating to the more advanced use case will begin to move across enterprise-wide research. When a certain tipping point is reached, the idea of not having your data transactions on a rapidly accessible, instantly auditable, contribution tracking, and data standardizing blockchain will become unacceptable.

When mixed with the parallel advances of other emerging tech: artificial intelligence to assist in everything from hypothesis development to publication writing, automated machine processes to speed and clean up data gathering, and quantum computing to speed complex data analysis; we will truly enter a time of better science, cheaper research, and faster medical miracles.

References

1. Morris ZS, Wooding S, Grant J. The answer is 17 years, what is the question: understanding time lags in translational research. J R Soc Med. 2011;104(12):510-20. (https://www.ncbi.nlm.nih.gov/pmc/articles/PMC3241518/)

2. Bowen A, Casadevall A. Input-outcome disparities in biomedical research. Proceedings of the National Academy of Sciences Sep 2015, 112 (36) 11335-11340. (http://www.pnas.org/content/112/36/11335)

3. Moran N. ROI continues to decline for top pharma firms: Deloitte. Bioworld. 2017. (http://www.bioworld.com/content/roi-continues-decline-top-pharma-firms-deloitte)

4. Freedman LP, Cockburn IM, Simcoe TS (2015) The Economics of Reproducibility in Preclinical Research. PLoS Biol 13(6): e1002165. https://doi.org/10.1371/journal.pbio.1002165

5. Thorton D. GSA experimenting with blockchain to cut contracting time. Federal News Network. Nov 2017. https://federalnewsnetwork.com/it-modernization-2017/2017/11/gsa-experimenting-with-blockchain-to-cut-contracting-time/

6. Thorton D. HHS turns to blockchain for novel acquisition model. Federal News Network. Sep 2018. https://federalnewsnetwork.com/blockchain/2018/09/hhs-turns-to-blockchain-for-novel-acquisition-model/

7. Barnett AG, Zardo P, Graves N (2018) Randomly auditing research labs could be an affordable way to improve research quality: A simulation study. PLoS ONE 13(4): e0195613. https://doi.org/10.1371/journal.pone.0195613

8. Kamath R. Food Traceability on Blockchain: Walmart's Pork and Mango Pilots with IBM. Journal of the British Blockchain Association Vol 1, Issue 1. June 2018. https://jbba.scholasticahq.com/article/3712-food-traceability-on-blockchain-walmart-s-pork-and-mango-pilots-with-ibm

9. Corkery M, Popper N. From Farm to Blockchain: Walmart Tracks Its Lettuce. New York Times. Sep 24, 2018. https://www.nytimes.com/2018/09/24/business/walmart-blockchain-lettuce.html

10. Benchoufi M, Porcher R and Ravaud P. Blockchain protocols in clinical trials: Transparency and traceability of consent [version 5; referees: 1 approved, 2 approved with reservations, 2 not approved]. F1000Research 2018, 6:66 (https://doi.org/10.12688/f1000research.10531.5)

11. Flannery H, Naqvi N, Manion S, Rajendran L, van Rossum J. Scientific Publishing and Replicability, a Multi-Organization Panel. Blockchain in Healthcare Webinar Series. June 28, 2018 https://www.gotostage.com/channel/fbe5c0a47b7d4ed3815b39156dba0ed8/recording/ae0dfa518540482a861eaa2a546f2f2a/watch

Index

Page numbers followed by i, f, and t indicate illustration, figure, and table

E

G

U

V

W